An Introduction to Modern Economics

Fourth Edition

PHILIP HARDWICK
BAHADUR KHAN
JOHN LANGMEAD

Uche Aghaulor

ELBS with Longman

Educational Low-Priced Books Scheme
funded by the British Government

Addison Wesley Longman Limited
Edinburgh Gate, Harlow,
Essex CM20 2JE, England

Associated companies throughout the world

The Educational Low-Priced Books Scheme is funded by the Overseas Development Administration as part of the British Government overseas aid programme. It makes available low-priced, unabridged editions of British publishers' textbooks to students in developing countries.

First published 1982
Reprinted 1982, 1983, 1984, 1985
Second edition 1986
Reprinted 1986, 1987 (twice), 1989
Third edition 1990
Fourth edition 1994
Reprinted 1996

ELBS edition first published 1983
Reprinted 1985
ELBS edition of second edition 1986
Reprinted 1988, 1989
ELBS edition of third edition 1990
Reprinted 1991, 1993
ELBS edition of fourth edition 1994
Reprinted 1994, 1996

ISBN 0 582 30562 4

Set in 10/12 pt Compugraphic English Times
Produced by Longman Singapore Publishers Pte Ltd
Printed in Singapore

CONTENTS

PREFACE

This book has been written with the objective of introducing students to the interesting and important subject of economics. It is intended primarily to be of value as a textbook for students in first-year degree courses in economics, the social sciences, business studies, financial services and other areas of study which include economics among their foundation subjects. The material covered is suitable for many professional courses and should be helpful to 'A' level students in the United Kingdom and to students of similar courses overseas.

As teachers of economics at degree level, we have felt for some time that the efficiency and equity aspects of resource allocation have been inadequately treated in many introductory textbooks (where the analysis is often omitted completely) and in intermediate microeconomics books (where the topic is normally left until the last few chapters). In an attempt to correct this deficiency, we have included at an early stage two chapters entitled 'Resource allocation' (Ch. 7) and 'Introduction to welfare economics' (Ch. 8): these come after chapters on production and demand (which cover isoquant and indifference curve analysis), but before the chapters on the theory of the firm, the public sector and the theory of distribution. This lay-out enables us to compare more rigorously the effiency and equity aspects of different market structures and different policy changes. None the less, much of the material in the chapters on the theory of the firm, the public sector and distribution can be used (with the omission of the welfare sections) by those teachers who prefer the more traditional introductory course. We think, however, that the early introduction of a simple treatment of welfare economics is of great value to beginning students.

An important development in modern economics has been the recognition that economists can make an important contribution to the debate about how to deal with environmental pollution at national and global levels. For this reason, we have included a new chapter in this fourth edition entitled 'Environmental economics' (Ch. 13). This chapter presents an analysis of environmental problems and discusses alternative policy approaches.

A number of other major changes have been made in preparing the fourth edition. As well as bringing all the statistics and examples up to date, many new sections have been added and others completely rewritten. Mathematical appendices have been added to several chapters (Chs 3, 6, 9, 10, 19 and 23). A further appendix has been added to Ch. 12 on the theory of public goods. New sections on the application of game theory to oligopoly and on contestable markets have been added to Ch. 10.

The treatment of the AD–AS model, which enables a more effective analysis of the effects of changes in the economy on real income and the price level to be undertaken, has been considerably expanded in Ch. 23. This model has been applied in the analysis of macroeconomic policy problems in Chs 26, 27, 28 and 29. A new section on open-economy macroeconomics has been added to Ch. 29, and a discussion of the proposals for monetary union in the EC has been included in Ch. 31.

Although not intended to be primarily a book on applied economics, there is throughout an emphasis on economic policy. Chs 11–15 are concerned entirely with the activities of the public sector. Chs 26–32 are concerned with issues of macroeconomic policy. These sections on economic policy draw on examples from the United Kingdom and other member states of the European Community (EC), as well as a selection of other developed and less developed countries. Indeed, one of our main objectives is to include examples and statistical data for the countries of the EC and, where appropriate, to include a discussion of the economic problems and policies of the EC. This is intended to reflect the growing importance of European economic activity to both consumers and producers. Ch. 31 ('The European Community') includes an outline of the historical development of the EC, describes its main institutions and discusses the workings of the Community's agricultural policy and monetary system. Readers who are unfamiliar with the extent and composition of the EC may find it helpful to consult the map and table of populations, geographical areas and population densities, shown on page xv.

Now a brief note on the structure of each chapter. Each one begins with a set of *learning objectives* which highlight the main concepts and principles which we believe that beginning students should aim to learn from the chapter. Each chapter then has a brief *introduction* designed to link the chapter with related ones and to explain the importance of the material to be covered. Throughout, definitions of key terms are highlighted in the margins and all figures have been given explanatory captions. Each chapter ends with a *summary* and a set of *exercises*. The exercises are designed to reinforce the reader's understanding of the chapters and, of course, to help in the preparation for examinations. Nearly all chapters have at least one numerical exercise or data-response question in addition to a number of essay questions.

At the end of the book, we have included twelve further essay questions, all on topics which often feature prominently in economics examinations. Each of these questions has a short suggested outline answer intended to show the student how the question might be tackled. Of course, these suggestions should not be regarded as definitive answers to the questions set as there are often many different ways in which questions may be answered. The outline answers simply aim to help students identify the main points to be included in a good examination answer. Also, at the end of the book, we have included brief outlines of the work of five famous economists (Smith, Ricardo, Marshall, Keynes and Friedman), all of whom have made important contributions to the development of mainstream economics.

We are very grateful to Lars Lund and Damsgaard Hansen at the Copenhagen Business School, and to Keith Gray and Perry Yavash, for many helpful comments. We are particularly grateful to Lars Lund for contributing the Appendix to Ch. 12. We are also considerably indebted to Stuart Wall whose many comments helped us with the first edition of the book. In addition, we have received lots of useful suggestions from readers of earlier editions. (We would welcome further comments and suggestions for improvement from readers of this new edition.) For selflessly typing a large part of the manuscript, our thanks go to Jenny Gibbins and Pauline Lever. Finally, special thanks go to our wives for putting up with our over-long preoccupation with the book. We three, of course, bear full responsibility for all errors and omissions.

Philip Hardwick, Bahadur Khan, John Langmead. Bournemouth University

ACKNOWLEDGEMENTS

We are grateful to the following for permission to reproduce copyright material:

The Bank of England for tables 21.1 and 21.3; European Communities Commission, Statistical Office for a Preface table, and tables 2.1, 18.5, 28.5 and 31.2; Her Majesty's Stationery Office for tables 11.3, 11.4, 11.5, 14.1, 14.2, 15.1, 18.1, 18.2, 18.3, 20.2, 20.3, 20.6, 21.2, 27.3, 28.2, 29.1, 32.1, 32.4, 32.6, 32.9, and tables 27.2, 28.1 and 28.3, Crown copyright. Reproduced with the permission of the Controller of Her Majesty's Stationery Office; Lloyds Bank for table 14.3; OECD for tables 11.1, 11.2, and figure 13.5; Oxford University Press and The World Bank for tables 25.1, 25.2, 25.4, 32.7, and 32.8.

Though every effort has been made to trace the owners of copyright material, in a few cases this has proved impossible and we take this opportunity to apologise to any copyright holders whose rights may have been unwittingly infringed.

THE EUROPEAN COMMUNITY

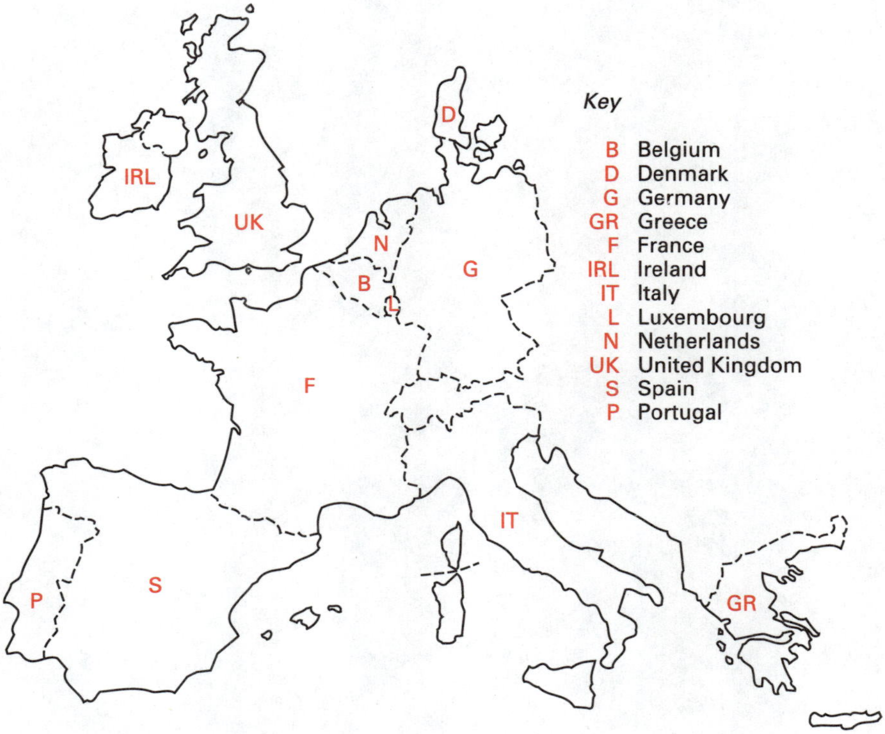

1991	Population (000s)	Area (000 km^2)	Density (per km^2)
Belgium	9,987.0	30.5	327
Denmark	5,146.5	43.1	119
Germany	79,700.5	356.6	223
Greece	10,200.0	132.0	77
France	56,893.2	549.1	103
Ireland	3,518.3	70.3	50
Italy	57,746.2	301.3	192
Luxembourg	384.4	2.6	148
Netherlands	15,010.4	41.8	361
United Kingdom	57,485.8	244.1	235
Spain	38,993.8	504.8	77
Portugal	9,858.6	92.4	107
EC	344,924.7	2,368.6	152

Source: Eurostat, 1992.

INTRODUCTION

THE NATURE AND SCOPE OF ECONOMICS

PRODUCTION

1 THE NATURE AND SCOPE OF ECONOMICS

Learning objectives

After reading this chapter, you should be able to:

- articulate the basic economic problem faced by all human societies
- define and explain the concept of opportunity cost and illustrate this concept graphically using the production possibility frontier
- define the meaning of the terms *efficiency* and *equity*
- define the meaning of the terms *equilibrium* and *disequilibrium* and appreciate their importance in economics
- outline the alternative methodological approaches to the study of economics
- appreciate how different types of diagrams and graphs can be used to illustrate relationships between economic variables

Introduction

Economics is a social science which seeks to explain the economic basis of human societies. The purpose of this introductory chapter is to identify the basic *economic problem* encountered by all societies and to focus attention on the basic concepts which modern economists employ in their attempts to analyse this problem.

Wealth *A country's stock of resources that can be used to produce goods and services*

Welfare *Welfare refers to the level of satisfaction that a person or group of persons derives from the consumption of goods and services*

Human existence has been preoccupied with the production and consumption of wealth, the desire for which seems to arise from man's basic impulse to increase his welfare. The concepts of wealth and welfare, therefore, stand at the heart of economics. A country's wealth consists of its stock of resources that can be used to produce goods and services. Such resources include, for example, machines, buildings and human skills. Welfare, on the other hand, refers to the satisfaction that an individual or a society derives from wealth and can be regarded as being synonymous with that individual's or society's standard of living. If the welfare of one person or group of persons is increasing without at the same time anyone being made worse off, we could say that this is a definite improvement in the welfare of society as a whole. As a criterion for judging welfare changes, though, this is rather too simple because the world we live in is exceedingly complex and most economic changes make some people better off and others worse off. For example, cheap imports of cloth make a lot of people better off as they can buy cloth at lower prices, but many domestic textile workers may lose their jobs and so be made worse off. It is because economic changes generally impose gains and losses on different groups in society that we need criteria of both *efficiency* and *equity* in order to judge policy measures designed to increase social welfare.

In this chapter, we first of all consider the economic problem itself; then we return to the important concepts of efficiency and equity; in the remainder of the chapter, we explain economic concepts like equilibrium and disequilibrium, microeconomics and macroeconomics and we outline the methodology of economic analysis.

The economic problem

The economic problem *Arises because individuals' wants are virtually unlimited, whilst the resources available to satisfy those wants are scarce*

The production of wealth is necessary because it enables individual and collective wants to be satisfied. Unfortunately, wants are virtually limitless whilst the resources to satisfy them are scarce. The most pressing wants are for food, housing, clothing and warmth – these essentials are the first to make a call on a nation's resources. Advances in technology and the development of new means of transport and communications, however, have added new wants and brought about new ways of satisfying existing wants. For example, our wants for cars, television sets, video recorders and home computers were unknown to previous generations and the wants for travel, regarded as difficult in the past, have become capable of being satisfied easily from several modes of transport.

Opportunity cost *The opportunity cost of a decision to produce or to consume more of one good is the next best forgone alternative. A decision to buy a compact disc, for example, might mean giving up the purchase of a ticket for a pop concert*

The scarcity of resources in relation to the call made upon them imposes a choice on society as to the range of wants it wishes to satisfy. A decision to satisfy one set of wants necessarily means sacrificing some other set: this sacrifice is called by economists the opportunity cost of satisfying given wants. In a regime of scarcity and restricted choice, economic welfare is determined to a very large extent by the quantity and quality of goods and services which can be produced. This leads us to the next important point: the constraints on economic production.

The quantity of resources available and the state of technology are the major constraints on production. Many resources, like coal and oil, are non-recoverable – the faster the rate at which they are used up in production the sooner will be the limit to the growth in wealth. New and improved technology open up new ways of doing old things more efficiently and may lead to the discovery of new resources. More modern techniques enable a larger output to be produced, whereas antiquated methods of production act as a barrier to increased wealth and prosperity. Unfortunately, technical changes usually take a long time to come about so that it is the existing technology which determines how efficiently resources can be used at any given time.

To sum up, we can say that the basic economic problem is that of *allocating scarce resources among the competing and virtually limitless wants of consumers in society*. All nations have to decide in some way *what* goods and services to produce, *how* to produce them and *for whom* to produce them. Different economic systems tackle the basic economic problem in different ways.

Economic systems

Market economy *An economy in which resources are allocated through the price mechanism*

Economic systems are concerned with the ownership and control of resources. The two main types are the *market economy* and the *command economy*.

In a market economy, resources are allocated through the price mechanism and the ownership and control of such important resources as land and capital are in the hands of private firms and individuals. Property laws give the owners the right to make decisions concerning access to these resources and to determine the purpose for and manner in which they are to be used. The United States, the countries of the European Community (EC), Japan and those less developed countries (LDCs) where the majority of firms are privately owned and controlled are, to a large extent, market economies.

Command economy *An economy in which resources are allocated by a central planning authority appointed by the state*

In a command economy, resources are allocated by a central planning authority and key industries and resources are owned and controlled by the state. Under this system, the public sector is the main arbitrator of the access to society's resources. China and those LDCs where most economic activities are owned and controlled by the state may be said to be command economies.

These economic systems and the three questions of what, how and for whom are discussed in greater detail in Ch. 7. For now, consider how the economic problem can be illustrated by means of a production possibility frontier and the concept of opportunity cost.

The production possibility frontier and opportunity cost

A production possibility frontier joins together the different combinations of goods and services which a country can produce using all available resources and the most efficient techniques of production. Assume for simplicity that a country produces only two goods, food and cloth. Figure 1.1 shows the different combinations of these two commodities which can be produced. The vertical axis measures the quantity of food in tonnes and the horizontal axis measures the quantity of cloth in metres. The straight line AB is the production possibility frontier. It shows that when all resources are efficiently employed in the production of food, 0A tonnes can be produced and when all resources are employed in the production of cloth, 0B metres can be produced. *All points on the production possibility frontier represent combinations of food and cloth which the country can just produce when all its resources are employed. All points inside the line, such as point* M, *represent combinations which can be produced using less than the available supply of resources or by using the available supply with less than maximum efficiency. Points outside the line, such as* N, *represent combinations which are unattainable.*

Suppose initially that the country is producing at point A. That is, all resources are being used in the production of food. If it now decides to produce cloth, it is obvious from the downward slope of the production possibility frontier that some

Fig. 1.1. A country's production possibility frontier. This straight line production possibility frontier represents constant opportunity costs.

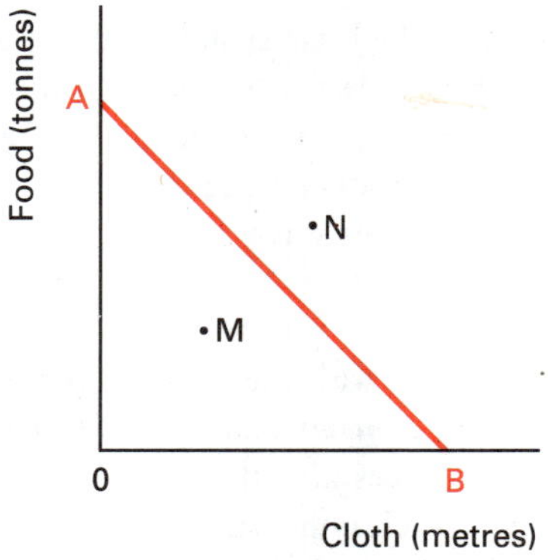

food production must be given up. The quantity of food which has to be forgone is called the opportunity cost of producing cloth. In Fig. 1.1, where the production possibility frontier is drawn as a straight line, the absolute value of the slope of the line, equal to 0A/0B, measures the opportunity cost in terms of food of producing 1 extra metre of cloth. Similarly, the reciprocal of the slope, equal to 0B/0A, measures the opportunity cost in terms of cloth of producing 1 extra tonne of food. All this means is that every additional metre of cloth produced requires that 0A/0B tonnes of food be forgone and that every additional tonne of food produced requires that 0B/0A metres of cloth be forgone.

As well as measuring opportunity cost, the slope of the production possibility frontier can be interpreted as measuring the rate at which food can be 'transformed' into a metre of cloth by shifting resources from food production into cloth production. Thus, the slope of the production possibility frontier is sometimes called the marginal rate of transformation – in this case, of food into cloth. The marginal rate of transformation is a concept we use later in the book, particularly when we deal with welfare economics in Ch. 8. Notice that in Fig. 1.1, where the production possibility frontier is drawn as a straight line, the opportunity cost and the marginal rate of transformation remain unchanged no matter how much cloth is produced. This is said to be the case of *constant* opportunity costs.

Marginal rate of transformation *The marginal rate of transformation (MRT) is the rate at which one product can be transformed or converted into another product by reallocating resources*

The assumption of constant opportunity costs is very unrealistic. It implies that all factors of production can be used equally efficiently in either the production of food or the production of cloth. It is much more likely that some factors are more efficient in the production of cloth. To illustrate the effects of this on the production possibility frontier, suppose that the country is once again using all of its resources in the production of food; that is, production is taking place at point A′ in Fig. 1.2. If the country now decides to produce some cloth, we might expect the opportunity cost of the first few metres of cloth to be relatively small as those resources which are more efficient in the production of cloth move from food production into cloth production. As more and more metres of cloth are produced, however, it becomes necessary to move into cloth production those factors which are more efficient in the production of food. As this happens, the opportunity cost of the extra metres of cloth produced will get larger and larger. This is the case of *increasing* opportunity costs.

Fig. 1.2. A country's production possibility frontier with increasing opportunity cost. As additional units of cloth are produced, the opportunity cost of cloth in terms of food increases.

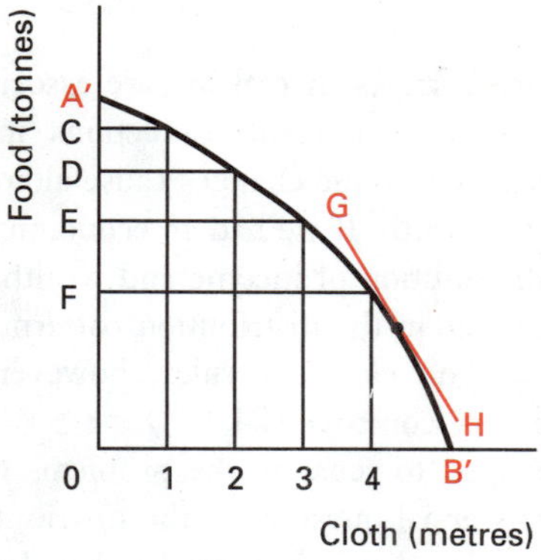

In Fig. 1.2, the production possibility frontier A′B′ is concave to the origin. Starting from point A′, the production of 1 metres of cloth requires that A′C tonnes of food be given up. The production of a second metre of cloth requires that an additional CD tonnes of food be given up. A third requires that DE be given up, and so on. From the concavity of the production possibility frontier, it must be true that EF > DE > CD > A′C. In other words, the opportunity cost of cloth in terms of food increases as more and more cloth is produced. It is also true, of course, that the opportunity cost of food in terms of cloth increases as more and more food is produced. Just as with the straight line production possibility frontier, the opportunity cost of cloth in terms of food and the marginal rate of transformation of food into cloth are measured by the absolute value of the slope of the production possibility frontier. This time, however, the slope is not constant, but increases as more and more cloth is produced. The actual slope of the production possibility frontier can be measured at any point by drawing a tangent to the curve at that point (like GH in Fig. 1.2) and measuring the slope of the tangent.

The production possibility frontier thus provides us with an illustration of the problem of scarcity and choice facing a country when deciding what goods and services to provide. The analysis of production is dealt with in greater detail in Ch. 2.

To ensure that resources are devoted to those uses which result in maximum welfare for a society, we need to be able to judge the production and consumption of wealth by some rules of efficiency and equity. So we turn now to a preliminary consideration of these two important concepts.

Efficiency and equity

Welfare economics
The study of the impact of the pattern of resource allocation on society's well-being (or welfare)

One of the major aims of this textbook is to introduce the reader, at an early stage, to the study of welfare economics at the heart of which are the concepts of efficiency and equity. It is with the aid of these concepts that economists are able to judge whether the existing arrangements about: (a) the methods of production; (b) the types and quantities of goods and services produced and consumed; and (c) the relative share of goods and services going to each household, are satisfactory. A 'satisfactory' situation may be said to exist when no rearrangement of the systems of production, consumption and distribution can increase the welfare of one person or group of persons without hurting someone else. Envy apart, many people would agree that a change which increases the welfare of one individual without harming others is desirable.

However, most welfare changes in real life are associated with gains and losses accruing to different people as a result of actions initiated by producers and consumers. In other words, economic changes cause alterations in the pattern of the distribution of income and wealth. If we had an economic theory which told us what the 'optimal' or 'ideal' distribution of income and wealth was, we should be able to judge whether a given change in the distribution pattern would be socially desirable or undesirable. There are no clear-cut rules, however, and so the problem of distribution has become very controversial.

Economists have managed to separate the problems of an efficient allocation of resources from the controversial question of the distribution of income and wealth. The latter is concerned with value judgements and is dealt with under the heading 'equity'. In order to facilitate understanding, in what follows the efficiency and equity aspects of welfare are treated separately. It should be emphasised, however, that questions of economic policy can scarcely be settled satisfactorily by relying on efficiency or equity considerations alone.

Efficiency

The famous Italian economist Vilfredo Pareto (1848–1923) concentrated on the efficiency aspects of welfare because he believed that welfare was a highly subjective concept. He argued that it was impossible to measure and compare welfare gains and losses between individuals or groups – that is to say, he excluded all 'interpersonal comparisons of welfare' from his analysis. To illustrate this point, suppose that two workers in a company both receive a pay increase of £5,000 a year. The resultant increase in welfare (or satisfaction) that each individual experiences from spending this money on goods and services is extremely unlikely to be the same. But it is not possible to measure objectively the respective welfare gains of the two individuals. Therefore, from Pareto's viewpoint, one cannot make comparisons of welfare gains (or losses) between individuals.

Pareto efficiency *A situation in which it is not possible to make someone better off without making someone else worse off*

For a situation to be described as Pareto efficient it must be impossible to increase the production of one good without reducing the production of another, or to increase the consumption of one household without reducing the consumption of another. In Ch. 8, we show that such a situation results when the following three conditions are satisfied.

(a) *The given stock of resources must be allocated in the production of goods and services in such a way that no re-allocation can increase the output of one good without decreasing the output of any other.*

(b) *The combination of goods and the proportions in which they are produced must be in response to the tastes and preferences of the community – i.e. the goods produced must be the ones that the community wants.*

(c) *The distribution of goods and services must be in conformity with consumers' preferences, given their tastes and incomes.*

As we have already mentioned, however, a Pareto better situation (that is, one which is reached by moving from a Pareto inefficient point to a Pareto efficient one) necessarily involves both gains and losses in real life. This has led to the development of compensation tests in welfare economics. Consider a situation where a gain to group A is worth, say, £100 million while the loss to group B is valued at £80 million. If A compensates B, the latter is restored to the original position whereas A is left with a gain of £20 million. Some economists say that for a Pareto better situation to exist the compensation should actually be paid to the losers, while others contend that it is sufficient to show that compensation could be paid.

Equity

Equity *Is concerned with the fairness of the treatment of different individuals or groups in society*

The word equity means fairness or justice. Questions about what is equitable are moral and ethical ones which have their basis in the norms of society. Individual members of society are bound to have differing and often conflicting views about what is equitable. For instance, what is a fair distribution of wealth and income? How do we judge whether a monopolist is or is not acting in the public interest? Economists have shown increased interest in such questions of equity over the last fifty years. According to one argument, economists are able to give expert advice on issues related to economic efficiency, but equity considerations are outside the purview of economics and should be left to philosophers, politicians and social reformers.

A counter-argument is that the economist is as good a judge as anyone else in society and by the very nature of his or her role cannot neglect equity considerations. Balanced, expert advice involves appraising the system of production and consumption on the grounds of both efficiency and equity. According to this argument, equity considerations are important because every policy action, like building a road or raising a tariff, makes some people better off and others worse off.

Unfortunately, efficiency and equity criteria often conflict. The protection of employment in loss-making industries by government assistance, for example, may be equitable, but at the same time it may be inefficient to prevent the movement of labour and capital out of the loss-making industries. Nevertheless, governments often do use subsidies (or other protectionist measures) to assist unprofitable producers on social grounds. In 1992, for example, the EC imposed restrictions on imports of steel from Eastern Europe, alleging that it was being sold at artificially low prices. The intention was to protect the EC steel industry which was suffering at the time from a depressed market and experiencing job losses from the introduction of new technology.

As a further example, consider the removal of regulatory and administrative barriers to trade which has been undertaken in many industries in the attempt to achieve a single market in the EC. This can be defended on efficiency grounds as it should have the effect of shifting production to lower-cost sources. However, some firms may be harmed by the exposure to foreign competition and some workers may be laid off as a result.

Equilibrium and disequilibrium

Market equilibrium
Exists when the price and quantity of a commodity match both consumers' and producers' expectations. In this case, the quantity demanded and supplied are equal, and the market clears

Market disequilibrium
Exists when the price and quantity of a commodity fail to match consumers' and producers' expectations

Most economics textbooks stress the idea of an equilibrium. Unfortunately, in the real world, equilibria are hardly ever achieved and even when they are, they are not easy to identify.

An equilibrium is a state of rest. In economics, it comes to be established when there is a single price for identical products in a market and when no economic forces are being set up to change that price. In other words, in equilibrium, the price and quantity of a commodity match both consumers' and producers' *expectations* and thus there is no discrepancy between the *actual* and *desired* prices and quantities. Consequently, the market is cleared and there are no involuntary holdings of unsold stocks. The equilibrium behaviour of consumers and producers, whether in a single market or in the economy as a whole, is characterised by the fact that there exists no feeling of urgency on the part of buyers and sellers to change their behaviour.

In contrast, a disequilibrium position is one in which some buyers and sellers feel impelled to change their behaviour because forces are at work that change their circumstances. By changing their behaviour, however, they unwittingly change the circumstances of other producers and consumers who may initially have been in equilibrium. A disequilibrium, then, sets in motion a chain of *adjustment* and *readjustment* processes: for example, on the London commodity markets and on stock exchanges, buyers and sellers change their behaviour daily in response to changing circumstances.

An important point is that the adjustment of output and employment takes time and there are wide variations in time-lags in different lines of production and consumption activities. Disequilibrium economics is concerned with the investigation of the time-lags involved in the path to equilibrium as well as the *speed* and *direction* of the adjustment to equilibrium. Unfortunately, it is very difficult to identify time-lags in every conceivable circumstance: producers and consumers react differently to changed situations and the rate of response tends to vary between different classes of consumers and different groups of producers. One possible reaction to a changed situation may be to 'wait and see'. For instance, an unemployed worker may wait and *search* for work over a period of time before deciding to accept an offer of a job at a reduced money wage. Similarly, producers may, despite a slump in their sales, continue to maintain existing levels of output and employment before eventually deciding to cut back on their production plans.

Apart from the time-lag in diagnosing a disequilibrium, there is a time-lag in deciding to implement a particular policy action. It then takes time for the effects of the action to work through the system. By the time all these things have happened, the original situation may have changed in such a way that the selected policy action is no longer appropriate. It follows that, to formulate an effective policy measure, it is essential to have *sufficient information* about time-lags and the speed and direction of the adjustment process. In practice, buyers and sellers generally trade goods and services with insufficient information: that is to say, they transact business in disequilibrium. This point is well illustrated by the market for housing in the United Kingdom where actual house prices frequently diverge from desired (or expected) prices and consequently supply and demand conditions overshoot or undershoot the equilibrium position. The unsold 'mountains' of butter, meat and cereals in the EC further illustrate disequilibrium conditions in the real world.

The distinction between microeconomics and macroeconomics

Over the past twenty-five years or so, economists have divided their subject matter into two main branches, microeconomics and macroeconomics. This book maintains that tradition by dealing with microeconomics in Chs 2–17 and macroeconomics in Chs 18–32. It must be pointed out, however, that these two branches of economics can never be completely separated from each other – there are many linkages between them.

Microeconomics, broadly speaking, is concerned with the behaviour of individual firms, industries and consumers (or households) and deals with the effects of individual taxes and specific public spending programmes. A study of the determination of the level of output and employment in the British textile industry, for example, would belong to microeconomics. Also, an examination of the activities of a firm by the Monopolies and Mergers Commission or the Office of Fair Trading would also come within the purview of microeconomics. Similarly, an investigation into the working of the Common Agricultural Policy in the EC would be a microeconomic study. Microeconomics deals with the problems of resource allocation, considers problems of income distribution, and is chiefly interested in the determination of the *relative* prices of goods and services.

Macroeconomics, on the other hand, concerns itself with large aggregates, particularly for the economy as a whole. It deals with the factors which determine national output and employment, the general price level, total spending and saving in the economy, total imports and exports, and the demand for and supply of money and other financial assets. For example, an international comparison of the causes of inflation and unemployment is a macroeconomic study. Similarly, the problem of stabilising exchange rates within the European Monetary System is a macroeconomic policy issue.

Economic methodology

The term 'methodology' refers to the way in which economists go about the study of their subject matter. Broadly, they have followed two main lines of approach: *positive* economics and *normative* economics.

Positive economics
This is concerned with propositions that can be tested by reference to empirical evidence. It relates to statements of **what is, was or will be**

Positive economics is concerned with the investigation of the ways in which the different economic agents in society seek to achieve their goals. For example, positive economists may analyse how a firm behaves in trying to make as much profit as it can or how a household behaves in trying to reach the highest attainable level of satisfaction from consumption. Positive statements, therefore, are concerned with *what is, was or will be* and are statements whose validity can be tested against the available evidence. The statement 'an increased budget deficit *will* bring down the present high level of unemployment but *will* increase the rate of inflation' belongs to positive economics.

Normative economics
This is concerned with propositions that are based on value judgments, that is statements which are expressions of opinions. Normative economics, therefore, relates to statements of what **should** *or* **ought to be** *the case*

Normative economics is concerned with making suggestions about the ways in which society's goals might be more efficiently realised. From the standpoint of policy recommendations, this approach involves economists in ethical questions of what *should or ought to be*, so much so that they may take up strong moral positions on the propriety of goals themselves. For example, the statements 'the present high level of unemployment and inflation in Britain *ought to be* reduced' and 'the distribution of income in Britain *should* be made more equal' are normative statements.

The basic economic theories, problems and policies set out in this book include both the positive and normative approaches, though it must be pointed out that it is not always easy to draw a clear line of demarcation between the two. For instance, if the goal is to eliminate poverty, then the question of whether to give cash or help in kind (like free medical care or free school meals) to low-income families is an issue of both positive and normative economics.

Deduction and empirical testing

The process of deduction and empirical testing is the most important method of approach followed by modern economists. It is illustrated in Fig. 1.3. The starting point is an *a priori* proposition or theory. (Note that an *a priori* proposition is one which seems reasonable to the investigator and is based on innate ideas and not derived directly from statistical evidence.) This proposition or theory is then demonstrated logically in the context of a simple model which is set up by specifying a number of assumptions concerning the behaviour of the economic variables under investigation. This logical reasoning (called deduction) may yield in turn a number of predictions or testable hypotheses and it is these which can be subjected to empirical (or statistical) testing. If the evidence supports the theory, we cannot simply accept it: instead, we say that the theory is not rejected but that continued testing is required. This is essential because economic events are rarely sufficiently stable for us to be certain that a theory that is thought to be satisfactory in one period of history will

Fig. 1.3. *Deduction and empirical testing.*

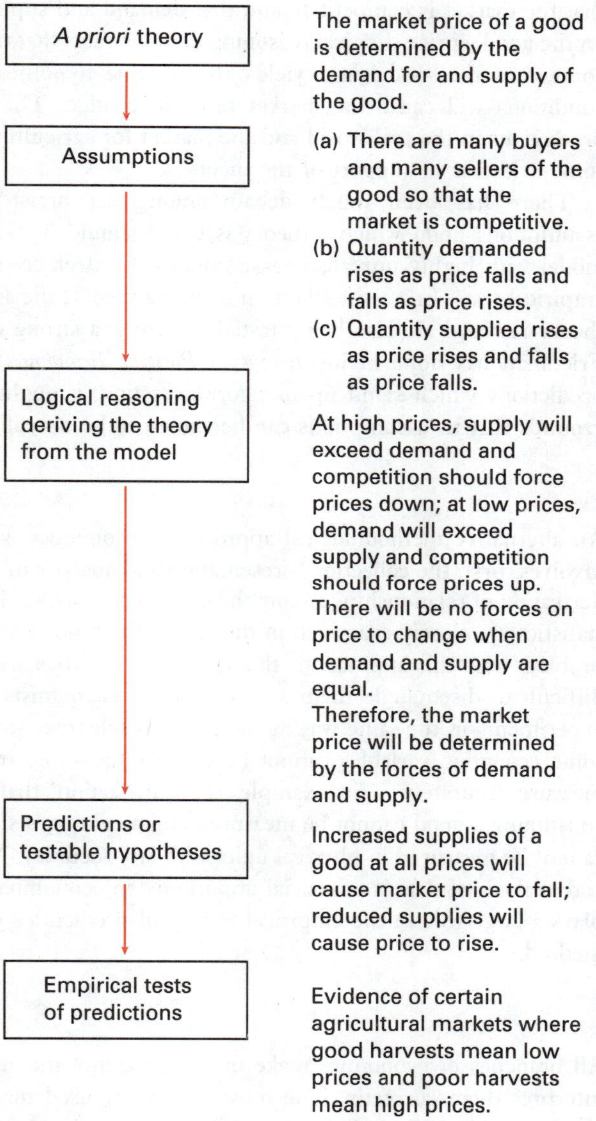

continue to be satisfactory in later periods. If, on the other hand, the evidence fails to support the theory, it must be rejected and either replaced by a new theory or modified in some way which improves its predictive power.

It is through this process, carried out rigorously by economists and statisticians, that economics progresses – unsatisfactory theories are rejected, whilst more satisfactory ones are continually subjected to empirical testing.

Figure 1.3 also provides a specific example of the way in which the deductive method works. The reader should find the example more illuminating after reading Ch. 6, but for now it provides a good illustration of modern economic methodology. First, the reasonable proposition is stated that a good's market price is determined by the demand for and supply of it. A simple model is then set up in which it is assumed that the market is competitive and that demand and supply themselves both depend on the good's price. Logical reasoning demonstrates that the proposition is true in the context of the model and yields the testable hypothesis that changes in supply conditions will cause the market price to change. The final step is to test these predictions in the real world and the market for agricultural goods is seen to provide some evidence in support of the theory.

There has been much debate among economists about how realistic the assumptions upon which a theory is based should be. Let us just state here that a model with highly unrealistic assumptions is extremely unlikely to perform well in empirical tests. In a sense, then, in testing a theory, the assumptions upon which the theory is based are also being tested. There is a strong case for arguing (as Milton Friedman has done in his *Essays in Positive Economics*) that if a model is giving predictions which stand up to rigorous testing, it ought not to be rejected on the grounds that its assumptions can be shown to be unrealistic.

Induction

An alternative methodological approach in economics is known as induction. This involves, first, the collection, presentation and analysis of economic data and then the derivation of relationships among the observed variables. In other words, the available statistics are closely examined in the search for general economic principles. A major problem with this approach is that economic statistics are so complex that it is often difficult to disentangle them and, of course, economists cannot perform laboratory experiments in the same way as the physical scientists can. Another difficulty is that some economic variables cannot be directly measured or are extremely difficult to measure accurately – for example, the 'satisfaction' that a household derives from consuming a good cannot be measured and a country's stock of plant and machinery cannot be measured in physical units with any accuracy. None the less, the collection and analysis of data is of crucial importance in economics, and, as mentioned above, plays a large role in the empirical testing of predictions derived from the deductive method.

The use of diagrams in economics

All branches of economics make use of diagrams and it is important to be able to interpret them correctly. The most frequently used diagrams in this book are: (a) graphs which depict relationships between two variables, usually on the assumption that some other variables remain unchanged; (b) graphs which show the combinations of two variables at which some condition is achieved; and (c) time-series graphs. Consider these three types of diagram in greater detail.

(a) Graphs illustrating relationships between two variables Suppose that economic theory suggests that a rise in after-tax personal income (Y_d) will cause a rise in household saving (S) assuming that all other factors which might influence the household saving decision remain unchanged. This assumption that other influencing factors should remain unchanged is the important *ceteris paribus* assumption which is used so widely in all branches of economics. (*Ceteris paribus* is a Latin phrase meaning 'other things being equal'.) A very convenient way of illustrating the relationship between Y_d and S is by means of the graph shown in Fig. 1.4. Household saving (in millions of pounds per year) is measured on the vertical

Fig. 1.4. ***The relationship between saving and after-tax personal income.*** In this linear relationship, a £100 million increase in after-tax income will always lead to a £20 million increase in saving.

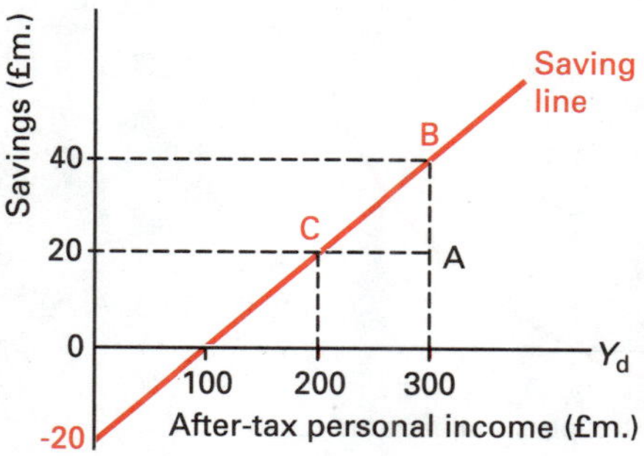

axis and after-tax personal income (also in millions of pounds per year) is measured on the horizontal axis. Note that in this illustration, household saving is termed the *dependent* variable and after-tax personal income the *independent* (or *explanatory*) variable.

It can be seen from the graph that when Y_d is £100 million per year, S is zero (in other words, at this low income level, households spend all of their after-tax income and save nothing). As Y_d rises to £200 million per year, S rises from zero to £20 million per year; and as Y_d rises to £300 million per year, S rises to £40 million per year. In fact, since we have represented the relationship between S and Y_d as a straight line (that is, we have assumed that the relationship is *linear*), it must be true that whenever Y_d rises by £100 million, S will rise by exactly £20 million.

The *slope* (or gradient) of a straight line measures the line's steepness and so tells us the increase in saving (the variable on the vertical axis in our example) which will be associated with a one-unit increase in after-tax personal income (the variable on the horizontal axis in our example). The slope of the saving line in Fig. 1.4 is 0.2. This can be calculated by taking any two points on the line (say, C and B) and then dividing the vertical distance (AB) by the associated horizontal distance (CA). Note that the equation of the saving line is

$$S = -20 + 0.2Y_d$$

where −20 represents the intercept on the vertical axis and, as stated above, 0.2 represents the slope of the line. It should be evident that all straight lines have constant slopes.

The assumption that the relationship between two variables is linear is often very convenient, but it is sometimes highly unrealistic. For example, we may have good reasons for believing that at high income levels, the increase in S associated with a given increase in Y_d will be larger than at low income levels. In this case, the saving line will be non-linear and will become steeper and steeper as Y_d rises. This is illustrated in Fig. 1.5. Non-linear relationships have slopes which change from one point to another along the line. In this book, examples of both linear and non-linear relationships can be found in most of the following chapters.

(b) Graphs which show combinations of two variables at which some condition is achieved The production possibility frontiers shown in Figs 1.1 and

Fig. 1.5. A non-linear saving line. In this non-linear relationship, the increase in saving associated with a given increase in income is larger at high income levels than at low income levels.

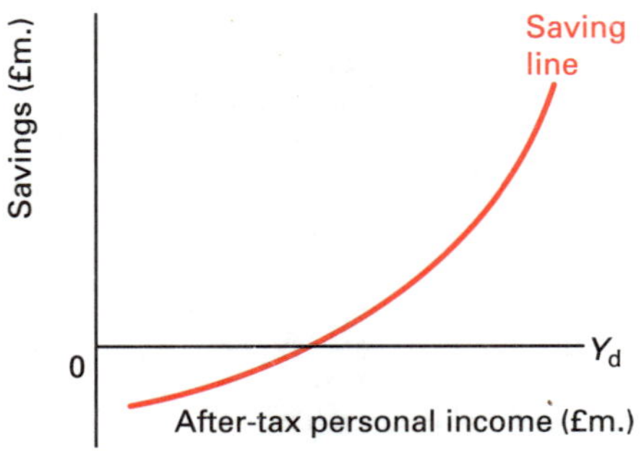

1.2 are examples of graphs of this kind. There is no causal relationship between the two variables measured on the two axes. Instead, the lines on the graph are simply loci of points which join together combinations of the two goods (food and cloth) which can be produced when a certain condition is satisfied: the condition is that all the country's resources should be used efficiently in the production of the two goods.

Two more examples of this kind of diagram are to be found in Ch. 2: the *isoquant* and the *isocost line*. An isoquant is a locus of points which joins together combinations of two factors of production which, when used efficiently, can just produce a certain quantity of a particular good. An isocost line joins together combinations of two factors of production which can be bought for the same monetary outlay (or which have the same cost). Other examples of this kind of diagram are budget lines and indifference curves (see Ch. 4) and IS and LM curves (see Ch. 23).

(c) Time-series graphs Time-series graphs are convenient ways of illustrating how an economic variable has changed over time. Time is usually plotted (in weeks, months or years) along the horizontal axis and the variable in question is plotted along the vertical axis. Figure 24.1 in Ch. 24 is a good example of a time-series graph: it shows how the unemployment percentage in the UK has varied during the period 1878–1992.

Introducing econometrics

The use of statistical methods to test or derive economic theories has developed into a growing branch of economics, known as econometrics. The main concern of econometrics is the investigation of the direction and strength of relationships among economic variables. A serious problem, though, is that economic relationships can never be precisely quantified. One important macroeconomic variable (which we consider in detail in Ch. 22) is households' consumption spending: according to one theory, this depends on current after-tax income. If we plot combinations of total consumption and after-tax income for a period of years on a graph, we find that they do not lie on a straight line or along any well-defined curve: instead, the points are scattered as shown in the *scatter* diagram in Fig. 1.6.

Econometrics makes particular use of the statistical methods of *regression* and *correlation* analysis to estimate the equation of the line or curve of 'best fit' through the points and to measure the closeness of the points to the line. A common measure

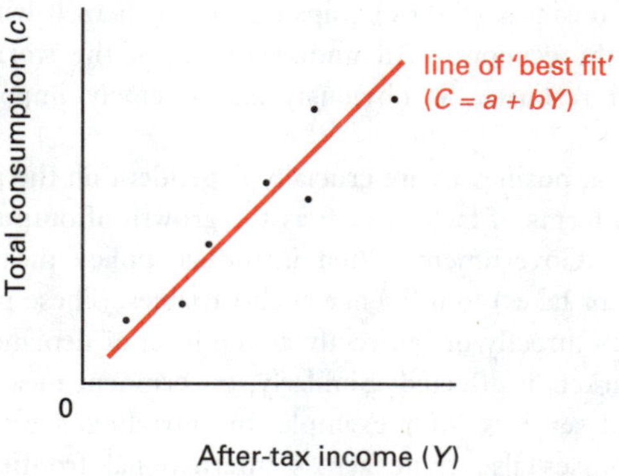

Fig. 1.6. *A scatter diagram.* The least-squares regression line (or line of 'best fit') is the one which minimises the sum of the squared deviations of the actual observations from the line.

of the strength of the relationship between variables is the *correlation coefficient* (r): this is expressed as a figure between -1 and $+1$. A result close to $r = -1$ would indicate strong *inverse* correlation; a result close to $r = +1$ would indicate strong *direct* correlation; a result close to $r = 0$ would indicate that there was no correlation at all. More commonly used is the square of the correlation coefficient, known as the *coefficient of determination* (r^2) which measures the fraction of the variation in one variable which is explained by the variation in another. It has to be emphasised here that a high degree of correlation does not necessarily imply causation: in other words, just because two variables tend to move in the same direction does not necessarily mean that changes in one are causing changes in the other.

Furthermore, it is possible that an observed relationship between two variables may only have occurred by chance and so may not be generally applicable. Statistical techniques are available, making use of probability theory, to enable us to test the *significance* of any relationship. For example, our confidence in a relationship is increased if we can show that the chances of observing such a relationship would be extremely small (say, one in a thousand) if there were in reality no relationship between the variables in question.

Finally, in our examples, we have restricted ourselves to relationships between two variables only. It is possible, though, for a relationship to exist among more than two variables. The analysis of such relationships is called *multiple regression* analysis.

Although not essential for the study of this introductory textbook, serious students of economics are recommended to follow a course of statistics or introductory econometrics at an early stage.

Economics in the context of business studies

Businesses operate with scarce resources and have to make good use of these resources in order to make profits. Firms have to pay for the resources they use and will make profits only if they can sell their products for more than they cost to produce.

Analysis of business problems shows that they often have a number of dimensions, such as marketing, financial, legal and human resource aspects. Business studies is, therefore, an eclectic subject which makes a call on several disciplines, including economics, accounting, sociology and law. Economics, then, contributes one important dimension to the analysis of business problems. By studying economics, a student of business studies equips himself or herself with a deeper insight into the working of the economy. An understanding of the working of markets for goods, services and resources is obviously an extremely important area for students of business.

In addition, businesses are crucially dependent on the performance of the national economy, in terms of factors such as the growth of output, inflation and the level of employment. Governments often introduce policy measures (such as changes in expenditure or taxes) to influence such variables. These policy measures may impact on businesses directly or indirectly as the level of demand for goods and services in different markets is affected. Similarly, government measures may affect the supply of goods and services – for example, by introducing incentives to save and invest. Many businesses also trade across international frontiers and so are exposed to exchange rate fluctuations and economic developments in other countries. Economics analyses the determination of exchange rates and the impact of international commercial policy on businesses.

For these reasons, we feel that students of business studies, as well as those studying economics as a specialist discipline, will find much of value in the following pages.

Summary

1. This chapter has explained the nature of economics. It highlighted the basic economic problem of scarcity of resources. All societies must have a system for deciding *what* goods and services to produce, *how* to produce and *for whom* to produce.

2. The important concept of *opportunity cost* was introduced. This concept stresses that a decision to produce more of one good necessarily means sacrificing the production of something else. The production possibility frontier can be used to depict graphically such a choice between alternatives.

3. A reallocation of resources normally imposes gains and losses on different groups in the economy. Such gains and losses can be judged using the criteria of *efficiency* and *equity*. Efficiency criteria are concerned with the efficient allocation of resources. Equity is concerned with the distribution of income and wealth that results from economic activity.

4. The distinction between microeconomics and macroeconomics was introduced. Microeconomics is concerned with the activities of individual firms, industries and consumers. Macroeconomics, on the other hand, is concerned with broad economic aggregates such as national income, the general price level and unemployment.

5. The section on economic methodology introduced the way in which economists approach their subject matter. *Positive* economics is concerned with testable propositions. In this approach, predictions can be tested against empirical data. *Normative* economics, on the other hand, is concerned with propositions based on value judgements. The process of deduction and empirical testing was introduced. This approach is the most popular method used by modern economists, and results in predictions that can be tested against empirical evidence.
6. The different types of graphs used in economic analysis were outlined. Econometrics is concerned with the use of statistical methods to test economic theories.

Exercises

1. Review your understanding of the following terms:

the basic economic problem	equilibrium
wealth	disequilibrium
welfare	microeconomics
opportunity cost	macroeconomics
production possibility frontier	positive economics
efficiency	normative economics
equity	deductive method
marginal rate of transformation	inductive method

2. Consider a country which, using all its resources efficiently in food production, can just produce 1,000 tonnes and, using all its resources efficiently in cloth production, can just produce 600 metres. Assuming constant opportunity costs:
   (a) draw the production possibility frontier; and
   (b) find the marginal rate of transformation.
   Explain why the production possibility frontier is unlikely in reality to exhibit constant opportunity costs.

3. Discuss the opportunity cost of: (a) your attendance at college for the duration of the course; (b) the construction of an extra mile of motorway; (c) the construction of the Channel Tunnel; (d) the development of nuclear energy in the United Kingdom.

4. Make *positive* and *normative* statements concerning: (a) the level of unemployment; (b) the rate of inflation; (c) the balance of payments; and (d) the distribution of income and wealth in your country.

5. Discuss which of the following can be classified under the heading *microeconomics* and which can be classified under the heading *macroeconomics*:
   (a) the determination of the price of wheat in the European Community;
   (b) the influence of changes in the stock of money on the economy;
   (c) the contribution of oil to the United Kingdom balance of payments;
   (d) the effects on the distribution of income of a reduction in the basic rate of income tax.

6. Discuss the implications for the demand and supply analysis outlined in Fig. 1.3 of an observation that a bumper crop of apples did not lead to a fall in the price of apples. What evidence would be needed for the theory to be rejected in favour of an alternative theory?

7.** Discuss the meaning of the concept of opportunity cost. Illustrate the concept with practical examples.

** Suggested answers to questions marked with a double asterisk are presented at the end of the book.

2 PRODUCTION

Learning objectives

After reading this chapter, you should be able to:

- identify the types of business units that operate in a market economy
- describe firms' motives for growth and the ways in which they might grow
- explain the changing sectoral pattern of production in the United Kingdom
- identify and categorise the factors of production
- analyse the relationship between the input of factors and the output of goods and services in the short- and in the long-run

Introduction

Production can be defined as the creation of wealth which, in turn, adds to society's welfare. It is a vital link in the process of satisfying wants for, as we saw in Ch. 1, wants are almost unlimited relative to the resources available. It is important in production, then, that the limited resources be used efficiently in order to create the maximum possible welfare.

At a general level, all economies, irrespective of their organisation, face the same basic decisions of *what, how* and *for whom* to produce, subject to their production possibilities. In a mixed economy, such as the United Kingdom, some production decisions are left to private enterprise and the market mechanism whilst others are taken by the government: the production of shoes, for example, is the result of the decisions of private firms, whereas the quantity of police services or military tanks produced is the result of political decisions. In a command economy, such as China, most production decisions are taken by a state planning agency. The allocation of resources by the price mechanism and by a central planning agency, and their respective merits and demerits, is taken up in detail in Ch. 7.

In this chapter, we concentrate on firms operating in a market economy or in the market sector of a mixed economy. We discuss the objectives of such firms and describe the types of business units that exist. We then turn to the growth of firms and consider the motives for growth and the ways in which firms grow. Next, we examine the changing pattern of production in the United Kingdom. Finally, we discuss the characteristics of the factors of production and consider the relationship between the input of factors and the output of goods and services both in the short- and long-run.

The firm and its objectives

A firm *A decision-making production unit which transforms resources into goods and services which are ultimately bought by consumers, the government and other firms*

The total level of output in an economy is, of course, the sum of the outputs of all the individual firms. It is important at the outset, therefore, to explain what is meant by a firm, and to consider some of the main factors which motivate firms to produce goods and services.

Traditional economic theory has assumed that the typical firm has a single objective – to maximise its profits. No distinction is drawn between the objective of a corner-store proprietor and that of the largest firm. The modern theories of the firm, however, do acknowledge that firms may have other objectives, such as sales-revenue maximisation or the maximisation of managerial utility.

The significance of the divorce between the ownership and the control of the modern firm has occupied many economists since it was observed by Berle and Means in their book *The Modern Corporation and Private Property* (1932). They pointed out that, typically, the owners of a large public company, the shareholders, delegate their authority to a board of directors who, in turn, place the effective control of the company in the hands of professional managers. The interests of the shareholders and the managers may diverge. The shareholders are presumably interested in obtaining the maximum dividends possible over a reasonable time period, which implies that the firm should aim to maximise its long-run profits. The managers, though, who do not necessarily share in the profits, may not have profit maximisation as their primary objective: instead, they may aim for an increased market share or greater sales revenue which they feel will bring them more prestige, greater security or a higher salary. The managers cannot forget about profits entirely, however, because they need to earn a satisfactory level of profits in order to declare reasonable dividends to keep the shareholders satisfied.

We consider managerial and other models of the firm in more detail in Ch. 10. In this chapter, we assume in the main that firms have the single objective of profit maximisation – that is to say, they attempt to make as large as possible the excess of revenue over costs.

A firm has to decide what level of output to produce. This decision will in turn determine the firm's purchases of factor inputs and may also influence the price at which its output can be sold. The firm's production decisions will be conditioned by the type of market in which it operates. Some firms operate in highly competitive markets, such as catering, foreign exchange dealing and agriculture. As we see in Ch. 9, a firm operating in a *perfectly competitive* market cannot charge a price higher than that of its competitors, or no one will buy its output.

Other markets are less competitive. In the United Kingdom, for example, commercial banking is dominated by a few large firms, namely the 'Big Four' banks, each of which reacts to each other's actions, thereby constituting an *oligopoly*. The motor-car market is similarly dominated by four large domestic car assemblers, although they also face competition from imports. The market for soap powders is dominated by two large firms, Unilever and Procter and Gamble: such a market is a special case of oligopoly called a *duopoly*. A market dominated by a single firm producing a good for which there are no close substitutes is called a *monopoly*. In the United Kingdom, the Post Office had a monopoly in the supply of telecommunication services.

There are a large number of degrees of competition in the thousands of markets of a modern economy; these can be viewed as a continuum stretching from pure monopoly at one extreme to perfect competition at the other. We consider models of market behaviour in Chs 9 and 10.

Types of business units

Consider now the legal status of the different types of firms to be found in a western economy, such as the United Kingdom.

Sole proprietorship

Sole proprietorship *A sole proprietorship (or one-person business) is a business under the ownership and control of a single individual*

In terms of numbers, sole proprietorship (or the one-person business) is the most common type of firm. Typically, it is a small-scale operation employing at most a handful of people. The proprietor is normally in charge of the operation of the business, and is likely to be highly motivated as he or she benefits directly from any increase in profits. As the one-person business is small, it can provide a personal service to its customers and can respond flexibly to the requirements of the market. Decisions can be taken quickly as the owner does not have to consult with any other directors.

Disadvantages associated with a sole proprietorship are that the owner cannot specialise in particular functions but must be a jack-of-all trades, and that the finance available for the expansion of the business is limited to that which the owner can raise. An even bigger disadvantage is perhaps that there is no legal distinction between the owner and the business. The owner has, therefore, unlimited liability for any debts incurred by the business, so that in the eventuality of bankruptcy all the assets (for example, house and car) are liable to seizure.

One-person businesses are common in retailing, farming, building and personal services, such as hairdressing.

Partnership

Partnership *A partnership is a business under the ownership and control of two or more individuals*

The logical progression from a one-person business is to a partnership. An ordinary partnership contains from two to twenty partners. The main advantages over a one-person business are that more finance is likely to be available with the influx of partners, and that each partner may specialise to some extent (for example, in the marketing, production or personnel functions). The major disadvantage, once again, is that of unlimited liability. As each partner is able to commit the other partners to agreements entered into, all of the others may suffer from the errors of one unreliable or foolhardy partner.

Partnerships are often found in the professions – for example, among doctors, dentists, solicitors and architects. Ultimately, the upper limit on the number of partners is likely to restrict the amount of finance available to the partnership and so place a limit on its growth. This, together with the disadvantage of unlimited liability, means that many growing businesses eventually form joint-stock companies.

Joint-stock company

Joint-stock company *A joint-stock company is a legal entity that carries out business in its own name. The company is owned by its shareholders, whose liability is limited*

The joint-stock company with limited liability developed in the second half of the nineteenth century. It helped to promote the development of large companies by providing a relatively safe vehicle for investment in industry and commerce by a wide cross-section of the community. The liability of the shareholders is limited to the amount they have subscribed to the firm's capital and each shareholder knows the extent of his or her potential loss if the company goes bankrupt. To make information available to potential shareholders, all joint-stock companies are required to file annually with the Registrar of Companies details of their profits, turnover, assets and other relevant financial information, such as the remuneration of the directors.

A joint-stock company can be either a *private limited company* or a *public limited company*. The shares of a *private* company cannot be offered for sale to the public and thus are not traded on the Stock Exchange. The shares cannot be transferred without the consent of the other shareholders. Private companies require a minimum of two and a maximum of fifty shareholders (or members), though the upper limit may be exceeded in the case of employees or former employees of the company.

The shares of a *public* company can be offered for sale to the public. A public company requires a minimum of two shareholders, but there is no upper limit. Shares are freely transferable and the company is required to hold an annual general meeting where shareholders are able to question the directors, to change the company's articles of association, to elect or dismiss the board of directors, to sanction the payment of dividends, to approve the choice of auditors and to fix their remuneration. In practice, attendance at annual general meetings is low, and normally the approval of the directors' recommendations is a formality. Although only about 3 per cent of companies are public companies, most large companies are public companies. Indeed, they account for about two-thirds of the capital employed by all companies.

There are equivalent forms of business organisation in other countries. In France, for example, the *Société à Responsabilité Limitée* (SARL) is the French equivalent of a United Kingdom private limited company.

Co-operatives

Co-operative *A co-operative is an entity owned and controlled by its members on the basis of one-member one-vote*

In the United Kingdom, consumer co-operatives have been relatively successful since the first co-operative was formed at Rochdale in 1844. The movement, which comprises a familiar section of the retail trade, is based on consumer ownership and control, although there is a professional management. In 1992 it was reported that there were over 8 million members of retail co-operative societies in the United Kingdom.

Producer co-operatives, on the other hand, have not generally been successful and are not particularly significant in the United Kingdom. The recessions of the early 1980s, however, led to an upsurge in the number of producer co-operatives. In many cases they sprang from an attempt by workers to continue production and to maintain jobs after a parent company had decided to close or sell a plant. This type of co-operative is sometimes referred to as a 'phoenix co-operative'. The Co-operative Development Agency (abolished in 1990), a government-backed body which promoted the development of producer co-operatives, reported the existence of 911 producer co-operatives with around 20,000 members in 1984. In some other countries of the EC, such as France and Spain, producer co-operatives are of more significance than in the United Kingdom.

Public corporation

Public corporation *A public corporation (or public sector firm) is a business enterprise that is owned by the state*

The public corporation is the form of enterprise that has developed in the United Kingdom for those areas where the government has decided to place production in the hands of the state. Whilst there are early examples of the formation of public corporations, such as the Port of London Authority (1909) and the British Broadcasting Corporation (1927), most were formed in the period of the postwar Labour government of 1945–51. The government appoints the chairman and the board of directors which is responsible to a minister of the Crown for fulfilling the statutory requirements for the public corporation laid down by Parliament. The minister is supposed not to concern himself or herself with the day-to-day running of the company.

Recent government policy has been to return state-owned enterprises to the private sector. Privatisation is the word used when the ownership of a state-owned asset is transferred to private individuals or companies. Examples of privatisation include the sale of British Gas in 1986 and of British Steel in 1988. The issue of privatisation is discussed in Ch. 15.

Public utilities, such as railways, gas, electricity and water supply, are state-owned in a number of countries. There are, for example, state-owned railways in France (the *Société Nationale des Chemins de Fer*) and in Germany (*Deutsches Bundesbahn*). At the beginning of 1992, there were nine airlines with majority government shareholdings in Europe, including Alitalia, Air France and Iberia.

The growth of firms

Motives for growth

A firm may have one or more motives for growth. Some firms may see expansion as a way of ensuring their survival in the long-run: they may fear that if they should stagnate at their present size they may become the target of a take-over bid. Diversification may similarly be seen as a key to survival and the best prospect for growth. It can be argued that a diversified firm will be better able to withstand depressed trading conditions because whilst the markets for some of its products may be stagnating or falling in size, other markets may be growing. In recent years, for example, cigarette and tobacco firms have been faced with relatively stagnant traditional markets, largely because of the publicity given to the health risks of smoking. As a result, they have diversified into new areas: the diversification of the Imperial Group (formally the Imperial Tobacco Group) into areas such as food production, packaging, educational supplies, woollen textiles and distribution was a case in point. In turn, Hanson Industries, the huge conglomerate, made a successful take-over bid for the Imperial Group in 1986. Hanson's subsidiaries include such familiar names as Ever-Ready and the London Brick Company.

Another possible motive for growth is to achieve higher profits. These may result, first, from the likely fall in unit production costs as the firm expands and, secondly, through the firm increasing its market share and, therefore, its ability to control the price of its product. A firm with a dominant position in a market may be acknowledged by other firms as a price leader. Alternatively, if the expansion of firms leads to the market being dominated by a few firms, they may engage in some form of collusion whereby they all charge similar prices – it should be pointed out, though, that this practice of oligopolistic collusion is prohibited in most EC countries.

The ways in which firms grow

A firm can grow as a result of internal or external growth. *Internal growth* occurs when a single firm expands its scale of operation within its original management structure. This process is easier if the markets for the firm's product are expanding rapidly and if the firm is efficient relative to its competitors. The raising of finance may be a constraint on the speed at which a firm can grow. It may be able to plough back some retained profits into the business or it may be able to borrow funds from one or more of the financial institutions. The large public company is able to raise finance by floating a new share issue, but this option is normally too expensive for the smaller firm.

External growth occurs when two or more firms join together to form a larger firm. This may be the result of a take-over where a dominant firm acquires a controlling interest in a smaller firm which then loses its separate identity. Alternatively, two or more firms may agree to a merger to form a new company. We can classify the integration of firms into three categories: vertical, horizontal and conglomerate. Consider these in turn.

Vertical integration *A merger between two firms in the same industry that are involved in different stages of the production process*

Vertical integration This occurs when two or more firms in the same industry, but at different stages in the production process, join together. Most of the major oil companies, for example, do not confine their interest to oil refining: they are also involved in the exploration for the extraction of oil (vertical integration backward) and they own chains of filling stations (vertical integration forward).

Vertical integration backward occurs when a firm acquires another firm which produces at an earlier stage of the production process. Other examples include the acquisition of tea plantations by tea companies and the acquisition of a body-building firm by a motor-car assembler. The motives for this kind of integration might be the desire for greater security of vital supplies or better control over the quality of raw materials. In addition, the company might see the prospect of increased profits by capturing the previous supplier's profit margin. Finally, control over an important supplier might give the company a competitive advantage over other companies who may now be denied access to a source of supplies.

Vertical integration forward occurs when a firm acquires another firm which produces at a stage of the production process nearer the consumer. Examples include the purchase of a rolling mill by a steel producer, and the acquisition of public houses by a brewery. As before, the firm may see the prospect of extra profits which formerly accrued to the acquired firm. Also, it may wish to improve upon the marketing of the final product with a view to increasing its sales.

Vertical integration may lead to a reduction in production costs as, for example, in the iron and steel industry where the location of iron and steel production on a single site enables the molten pig-iron to be transferred directly into the converter with a saving in energy costs. There may also be a saving in transport costs, as when a rolling mill is located adjacent to a steelworks.

Horizontal integration *A merger between two firms in the same industry that are involved in the same stage of the production process*

Horizontal integration This refers to the combining of firms that produce at a similar stage of an industry's production. Examples include Ford's take-over of Jaguar in the motor industry in 1989 and the merger between the Alliance and Leicester Building Societies in 1985. Horizontal integration may be undertaken to achieve economies of scale – that is, a reduction in the average production costs (see Ch. 9). Alternatively, it may be undertaken to carry out the rationalisation of capacity, as in the Tate and Lyle–Manbre and Garton case. If two companies have excess capacity, they may be able to close one or more plants and still be able to meet the market demand.

In practice, horizontal integration does not always result in economies of scale being achieved. The integration of different units may prove difficult, especially in cases where the plants are physically separate, and the increased size of the business may give rise to managerial diseconomies of scale. Rationalisation, too, may prove difficult to achieve as it is painful to close plants and to declare redundancies, especially in the face of concerted trade union opposition.

Conglomerate *A business entity with a number of subsidiaries engaged in a range of different production activities*

Formation of conglomerates Conglomerates result from mergers or take-overs involving firms whose activities are not directly related. Recent years have seen the widespread growth of the *holding company*, which may control a wide range of subsidiary companies. Grand Metropolitan, for example, has interests in hotels, public houses, wine and spirits and betting shops.

It is argued that the possibility of achieving economies of scale is not so great with a conglomerate merger as in the case of horizontal integration. However, even if two companies' operations are not directly related, they may depend *indirectly* on similar marketing or financial expertise. Thus, one justification for a conglomerate merger might be that it has the effect of replacing an inefficient management by a more efficient one. This might in turn lead to a more efficient use of the company's assets.

Because of the difficulty of achieving economies of scale, however, and because conglomerate mergers lead to increased concentration in the ownership of resources, the case for conglomerate mergers has been questioned by some observers. In some cases, the skills required for efficient management have been specific to the industry and the mergers have not been successful as, for example, in the case of the B.A.T. Industries (formerly British-American Tobacco) take-over of International Stores, a supermarket chain, in 1972. The supermarket chain, facing severe competition, was less profitable than hoped for and was sold to the Dee Corporation in 1984. B.A.T. Industries did, on the other hand, see prospects of profitable growth in the field of financial services, as evidenced by the purchase of the insurance company Eagle Star for £968 million in 1984 and Hambro Life Assurance (now renamed Allied Dunbar Assurance) for £664 million in 1985.

Another type of conglomerate merger has occasionally occurred when an ailing company with a depressed stock market valuation has been taken over with a view to 'asset stripping'. This involves the running down of the company and the sale of the company's assets, such as factories, land and machinery, so that the work-force loses its livelihood.

Recent years have seen an upsurge in cross-border mergers as in many sectors competition between producers is increasingly on a European or global scale. Many overseas financial institutions, for example, acquired stakes in London-based stockbroking firms in the build-up to the 'Big Bang' in the securities industry in October 1986. The London Stock Exchange abolished minimum commissions and allowed both British and overseas financial institutions to act as stockbrokers and market-makers.

Similarly, many mergers were stimulated by the Single European Act (1986) as the EC developed the single market strategy prior to 1992. Nestlé, the Swiss multinational, for example, outbid its fellow Swiss competitor, Suchard, to acquire Rowntree Mackintosh, the British confectionery manufacturer, in 1988. This take-over is an example of a non-EC conglomerate seeking to maintain or increase its market share after the development of the single European market.

Quasi-integration It is not always the case that a dominant firm need acquire a controlling interest in a supplier in order to earn higher profits by eroding the supplier's profit margin. It is possible for a firm which purchases a high proportion of a supplier's total output to negotiate extremely keen delivery prices, since the large volume specified in the contracts guarantees the supplier a high degree of capacity utilisation. Marks and Spencer may be said to practise such *backward quasi-integration* when purchasing a large proportion of the output of its major suppliers of textiles.

In order to secure markets for its products without owning retail outlets, a firm may consider *forward quasi-integration*. This may take the form of selling franchises, perhaps requiring the franchisee to purchase supplies or ingredients from the franchisor. It may take the form of financial support to the retail outlets, as with brewers granting low interest loans to public houses or clubs that agree to sell particular brands of beer or spirits. Another example is the granting of a loan by a petroleum company to an independent petrol station to develop new forecourt facilities on condition that the petroleum company's brand of petrol is sold.

The changing pattern of production in the United Kingdom

Primary sector *That part of an economy whose activities are directly related to natural resources, such as agriculture and fishing*

Secondary sector *That part of an economy whose activities are concerned with construction, energy and manufacturing, including the processing of the output of the primary sector*

Tertiary sector *That part of an economy whose activities are concerned with the provision of services, such as banking, insurance and tourism*

In world terms, the United Kingdom ranks as a relatively rich economy. In the early 1990s, the United Kingdom's gross national product per capita was around 46 times that of India, 3 times that of Portugal and similar to that of Italy. Germany's gross national product per capita, on the other hand, was about 40 per cent higher than the United Kingdom's.

Production activities can be categorised into the primary, secondary and tertiary sectors. Consider these in turn.

(a) The primary sector includes those activities directly related to natural resources, such as agriculture, forestry, fishing and mining. The extraction of iron ore is an example.

(b) The secondary sector encompasses all other production of goods, including the processing of the output of the primary sector. Thus, manufacturing, construction and the energy-producing public utilities are part of the secondary sector. The refining of iron ore obtained from the primary sector and the subsequent production of iron and steel which are then used in the manufacture of cars and other consumer products are examples of secondary sector activity.

(c) The tertiary sector includes all activity that results in the provision of services, such as banking, insurance, distribution, education, health and defence. The sale of a motor car by a retail outlet is an illustration of the activity of the tertiary sector.

In the late 1980s, the provision of services employed more than three out of five workers in the United Kingdom. The secondary sector, in contrast, has declined in importance in terms of employment and output since the mid-1960s. The term 'de-industrialisation' has been frequently used to describe the relative decline in manufacturing industry. Other major industrial countries have also experienced a decline in the share of manufacturing in gross domestic product in recent years.

Reasons put forward to explain de-industrialisation in the United Kingdom include the following:

(a) *Poor competitiveness.* Over the long-term, the United Kingdom suffered from a high rate of inflation compared with its major trading partners. This, coupled with low labour productivity and, it is argued, insufficient attention to quality, design and adherence to delivery dates, contributed to weak overseas demand and high levels of import penetration.

(b) *Capital-intensive production techniques.* The decline in manufacturing employment is partially explained by the increasing capital intensity of manufacturing processes. In textiles, for example, a worker may watch over several modern weaving machines, rather than one as in earlier times.

Table 2.1 Industrial branches as a proportion of gross value-added: EC countries 1989.

Country	Agriculture forestry and fishing (%)	Industry (incl. construction) (%)	Services and general government (%)
Belgium	2.1	30.3	65.5
Denmark	4.6	27.1	68.3
W. Germany	1.6	39.4	59.1
Greece	17.0	27.2	55.9
Spain	4.9	35.3	59.7
France	3.6	30.3	66.2
Ireland	10.0	36.7	53.3
Italy	3.6	34.2	62.2
Luxembourg	2.1	35.9	62.1
Netherlands	4.7	32.4	62.8
Portugal	6.3	37.7	56.0
United Kingdom	1.1	34.2	64.8
EC average	3.0	34.4	62.5

Source: European Communities' Commission, Basic Statistics of the Community, 1992.

(c) *Increased competition from newly industrialising countries.* Countries like Brazil, Singapore, Taiwan and South Korea have developed their manufacturing capacities in many industries, thereby introducing keen competition for the older producers. These newly industrialising countries tend to benefit from low wage and non-wage labour costs (such as pension contributions, sickness benefits and holiday pay).

(d) *Changing pattern of demand.* Economists have observed that as an economy becomes richer, people tend to spend a larger proportion of their incomes on services, such as recreation, eating outside the home, education and health care.

Value-added *The difference between the value of output and the cost of inputs that are bought to produce that output. Gross value-added is value-added with no allowance made for depreciation*

Table 2.1 shows that there are significant differences in the structures of the economies of the EC member states. The United Kingdom has the smallest share of gross value-added contributed by 'agriculture, forestry and fishing' (the primary sector) at just 1.1 per cent in 1989. At the other extreme, Greece derived 17.0 per cent of gross value-added from its primary sector in that year. The share of gross value-added contributed by 'industry including construction' (the secondary sector) ranged from 27.1 per cent in Denmark to 39.4 per cent in the former West Germany. Denmark derived the greatest share of gross value-added from 'services and general government' (the tertiary sector) with a figure of 68.3 per cent. It is interesting to note that all member states of the EC derived the major part of their final outputs from the tertiary sector.

The factors of production

There are many different inputs into most production processes. The production of pig-iron, for example, requires a blast furnace, iron ore, coking coal and limestone, in addition to the human effort necessary to control the production process. For the purposes of analysis, economists typically place each of the many different factor inputs into one of three categories – land, labour and capital.

Sometimes a fourth factor of product, *enterprise*, is added to the list. Consider these four factors in turn.

Land

Land *All the natural resources which are used in production*

It is important to note that land as a factor of production includes minerals, forests, water and all other natural resources as well as the land itself used in agriculture and as a site upon which economic activities take place. Unfortunately, the classification of factor inputs is not always clear-cut. Take, for example, the 'land' on which the Southampton container port is built: this land has been reclaimed from the sea and so in fact represents both land and capital. (Perhaps a better known example is that of the Netherlands where large areas have been reclaimed from the sea.) Similar remarks apply to agricultural land which has been cleared of bushes and weeds and fertilised. Indeed, a few economists argue that land should be regarded as a form of capital, and they prefer to distinguish only between labour and capital as separate factors of production.

Labour

Labour *All human attributes, physical and mental, that are used in production*

In many ways, labour is a special factor of production as it refers to human effort and as ultimately all production is carried out to satisfy *human* wants. Clearly, labour is not a homogeneous factor of production as some jobs require little, if any, training (for example, petrol pump attendants and ice-cream salesmen) whilst others require several years of training (for example, surgeons and civil engineers). The education that is invested, or embodied, in trained labour is sometimes referred to as 'human capital', yet another reminder that the distinction between factors of production is not water-tight. The compelling argument for retaining a distinction between labour and capital, however, is that whereas capital yields future services that can be bought and sold, trained labour cannot be bought and sold in a society without slavery.

The labour force in the United Kingdom consists mainly of males aged from sixteen to sixty-five and females aged from sixteen to sixty. Not everybody, of course, in these age groups is either working or actively looking for work. Many women (and a few men) are unable to work because of family commitments; many young people are still in full-time education; some people retire early; and there are many other reasons why some members of the potential work-force are not in a position to work. The characteristics of the labour market and the determination of wages are considered in detail in Chs 16 and 17.

Capital

Capital *Goods which are not for current consumption, but which will assist consumer goods to be produced in the future*

Capital goods (sometimes called investment or producer goods) are not wanted for their own sake, but because of the contribution they make to production. They are goods which produce a flow of services over a time period – it is estimated, for example, that each of the Concorde supersonic airliners will have a working life of at least twenty-five years. Capital, then, includes all plant, machines and industrial buildings that contribute to production. Most definitions of capital also include all intermediate goods (or semi-finished goods) and all unsold stocks of finished and intermediate goods. What all these have in common is that they are not to be consumed in the current period, but they enable a greater flow of consumer goods to be made available in the future.

Capital is a *stock* – that is to say, it exists at a point in time. In principle, the capital stock could be measured at a particular moment. With an army of investigators, a list could be made of all the lathes, cranes, lorries, power-tools – in fact, of every piece of plant and machinery in the economy – together with the stocks of finished and intermediate goods. This list would be extremely long and would make very little sense since all the items contained in it would be measured in different units. A more practical approach is to add up the monetary value of each piece of capital. Unfortunately, estimates of the current value of the different components of the capital stock are notoriously inaccurate. The value of a machine, for example, depends on the expected future demand for the final product. An additional problem in an inflationary world is that the price actually paid for a machine may bear little relationship to its current replacement cost.

The heterogeneity of capital and the problems of valuation have led some economists to argue that the capital stock cannot be measured in any meaningful way. In practice, estimates of the value of the capital stock are made in the United Kingdom using arbitrary rules for tax purposes in order to estimate the extent of *depreciation*. Depreciation (or capital consumption) is a measure of the extent to which the capital stock falls in value as a result of use (or 'wear and tear') during the relevant time period, normally a year.

Note that the purchase of new plant and machinery by firms is called *investment*. Investment is a *flow* – that is to say, it can only be measured as 'so much' per time period. Since part of total (or 'gross') investment is needed to make good the depreciation of the capital stock, it is only *net* investment (that is, gross investment minus depreciation) which represents an addition to the capital stock. Investment is considered in greater detail in Ch. 20.

Enterprise

The entrepreneur *A person who organises the production of goods and services. He or she is a risk-bearer as there is no guarantee of the venture being a success and, therefore, making a profit*

To land, labour and capital, we could add a fourth factor of production – enterprise or entrepreneurship. It is the entrepreneur who organises the other factors of production, and who decides what goods to produce and what quantities of the factors of production to use. The entrepreneur bears the risks of production because he or she incurs the costs of production before receiving any revenue from the sale of the finished product. The risk is whether or not there will be sufficient demand for the product. If the entrepreneur has chosen to produce a successful product, a profit will be made; if not, he or she is likely to make a loss.

It has been argued that this formulation of the role of the entrepreneur was perhaps more appropriate in the nineteenth century when one-person businesses were the typical production units. Since production is dominated now to a large extent by large firms, owned by perhaps thousands of shareholders, the concept of the entrepreneur is often not appropriate as the risks of failure fall mostly on the shareholders. The professional management which makes the day-to-day decisions does not bear all the risks, though it is of course possible that the managers and the other employees will lose their jobs if the firm is unsuccessful. In this book we consider management as a specialized type of labour, thereby allowing the list of factors of production to be reduced to three – land, labour and capital.

The production function

As we saw earlier, production involves the transformation of resources into final goods and services. The relationship between inputs and output is a technological relationship which economists summarise in a production function. Suppose that the production of good X requires inputs of capital, labour and land. Using *functional notation*, we can write:

$$Q_X = f(K, L, L_D)$$

where Q_X is the output of X per time period; f is the functional relationship; and K, L and L_D represent the inputs of the services of capital, labour and land respectively into the production process. This production function states that the output of good X is a function of (or depends on) the inputs of the service of capital, labour and land – that is to say, Q_X depends on all the variables included in the brackets. Note that the precise form of the relationship between Q_X and the variables upon which it depends has not been specified.

Technological efficiency *A production method is technologically efficient if, for a given level of factor inputs, it is impossible to obtain a higher level of output, given existing technology*

In this book, we confine our analysis to the consideration of technologically efficient methods of production. A method of production is said to be technologically efficient if, for a given level of factor inputs, it is impossible to obtain a higher level of output, given the existing state of technology. As we saw in Ch. 1, the existing state of technology acts as a constraint on production possibilities. An improvement in technology, of course, would enable more output to be produced from a given level of inputs and this is a possible source of economic growth. For the purposes of analysis, however, we assume that the state of technology only improves in the *very* long-run.

The short- and long-run

The short-run *That period of time over which the input of at least one factor of production cannot be varied*

The long-run *That period of time over which the input of all factors of production can be varied*

Given the state of technology and assuming technological efficiency, a firm can only increase its level of production by employing more inputs. Very often, though, a firm that wishes to increase production quickly is unable to increase the input of all the factors of production that it employs. For example, a manufacturing firm wishing to increase its output is unable to have a bigger factory built overnight and so in the short-run can only produce more by employing more of its variable factors, such as labour, raw materials and fuel. Those factors which can be varied in the short-run are called variable factors; those which cannot be varied (typically capital and land) are called fixed factors. Only in the long-run can factors such as capital and land be increased.

Note that the actual length of the short-run does not correspond precisely to any particular time period. It varies from industry to industry and from firm to firm. In the North Sea oil industry, for example, it may take several years to install a new platform and to make it operational; meanwhile, output can only be increased by more intensive use of existing capital stock. In the case of a shirt factory, on the other hand, the company can probably acquire extra equipment and have it installed within a few weeks.

Short-run changes in production

The 'law of diminishing returns'

As a firm increases its level of production in the short-run, it eventually comes up against the 'law of diminishing returns'. This 'law' can best be illustrated by means of a simple arithmetic example. Consider a wheat farmer with a given area of land (say, 1 hectare) and a given quantity of capital equipment, and assume that neither the land nor capital can be varied in the short-run – in other words, they are both fixed factors. Assume further that the state of technology is constant and that labour (the variable factor) is homogeneous – that is to say, each worker is exactly like any other worker.

Table 2.2 Wheat production illustrating the law of diminishing returns.

(1) Number of workers (L)	(2) Total product (TP)	(3) Average product (AP)	(4) Marginal product (MP)
1	4	4	4
2	14	7	10
3	25.5	8.5	11.5
4	40	10	14.5
5	60	12	20
6	72	12	12
7	77	11	5
8	80	10	3
9	81	9	1
10	75	7.5	−6

Under these circumstances, the firm's production function for wheat can be written as:

$$Q_W = f(L, \bar{K}, \bar{L}_D)$$

where Q_W is the output of wheat in tonnes per time period. The bars on the last two variables indicate that the inputs of the services of both capital and land are held constant.

Table 2.2 shows how wheat output varies as additional workers are employed on the fixed area of land. Column (2), labelled *total product* (TP), shows what happens to total wheat output as the number of workers is varied. Notice that maximum wheat output is achieved when nine workers are employed. When a tenth worker is added, output falls because there are then too many workers employed on the fixed area of land and they begin to get in each other's way.

Average product *The average product of a factor of production is the total output per unit of the factor input*

Column (3), headed average product (AP), tells us the output per worker. It is found by dividing total product by the number of workers employed, or in symbols,

$$AP = TP/L$$

where L is the number of workers employed by the farmer. Notice that average product is at its highest when six workers are employed. The addition of any more workers causes average product to decline.

Marginal product *The marginal product of a factor of production is the change in total output as a result of a unit change in the factor input*

Column (4) shows the marginal product of labour (MP). This can be defined as the change in total product resulting from the employment of an additional worker. When three workers are employed, for example, the total product is 25.5 tonnes and when four workers are employed, this increases to 40 tonnes; the marginal product of the fourth worker, then, is 14.5 tonnes. The marginal product of labour can be defined more generally (to take account of the fact that the labour input might be altered in terms of man-days or man-hours) as the change in total product divided by the change in the labour input. In symbols, we can write:

$$MP = \Delta TP/\Delta L$$

where ΔTP is the change in total product and ΔL is the change in the labour input. Strictly speaking, this formula is only valid for very small changes in the variables.

From Table 2.2 it is apparent that the marginal product of labour is at a maximum when five workers are employed; the fifth worker adds 20 tonnes to total wheat output. After this point, the marginal product of labour declines.

The result (derived arithmetically from our example) that both the average and marginal products of labour eventually decline as more and more units of labour are added to a fixed amount of other factors is an illustration of the law of diminishing returns.

The 'law of diminishing returns' *As additional units of a variable factor are added to a given quantity of fixed factors, with a given state of technology, the average and marginal products of the variable factor will eventually decline*

Plotting the average and marginal products from our example on a graph, we can see how the 'law' comes into operation. This is shown in Fig. 2.1. Notice that the data for the marginal product are plotted at the mid-points of the class intervals.

The AP and MP 'curves' in Fig. 2.1 are not smooth because of the discrete nature of the data used in our example where the labour input increases by 'whole workers'. If we had used continuous data, so that the labour input could be increased in very small quantities, we would have obtained smooth curves for AP and MP, as shown in Fig. 2.2.

In both Fig. 2.1 and Fig. 2.2, the point at which MP reaches its maximum is point A. This is known as the point of *diminishing marginal returns.* Similarly, the point at which AP reaches its maximum (point B in both diagrams) is known as the point of *diminishing average returns.*

Notice from the graphs that MP begins to fall before AP does. In fact, MP cuts AP at the maximum point on the AP curve. This is an arithmetic relationship: when AP is increasing (up to point B), MP is above AP, pulling it up; when AP is at its maximum and constant (at point B), AP is equal to MP; when AP is falling (after point B), MP is below AP, pulling it down. To clarify this, the analogy with a cricketer's batting average may be helpful: if a batsman's average score is to increase from its present level, his next (or marginal) score must be greater than his present average; if his next score is exactly equal to his present average, the average remains

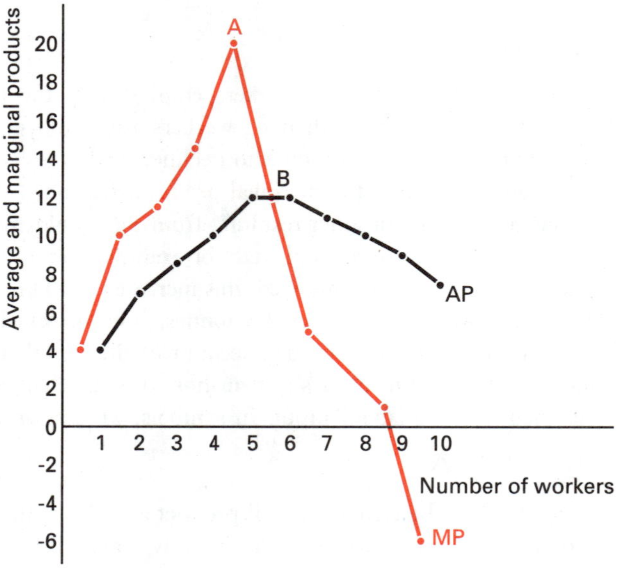

Fig. 2.1. Average and marginal products of labour illustrating the law of diminishing returns. The AP and MP lines drawn on this graph are plotted using the data shown in Table 2.2.

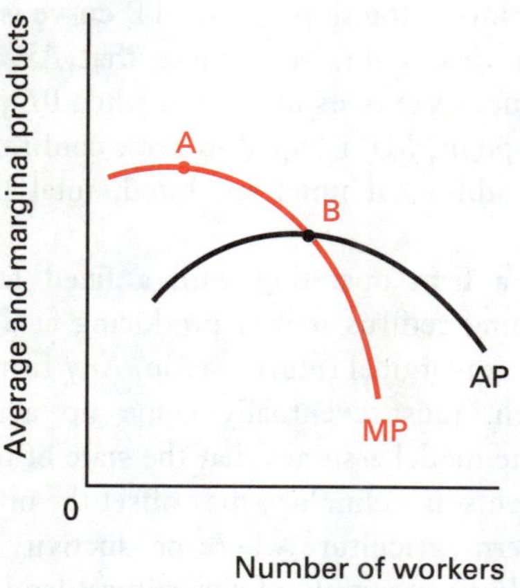

Fig. 2.2. Average and marginal products of labour for continuous data. The AP and MP curves both eventually decline as diminishing returns set in. Notice that MP cuts AP at the maximum point on the AP curve.

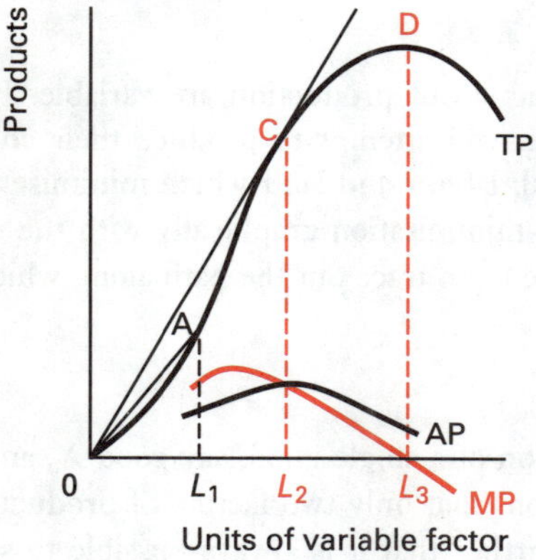

Fig. 2.3. The relationship between total, average and marginal products. The AP and MP curves, and the relationship between them, can be derived from the TP curve.

unchanged; finally, for the average to fall, the batsman's next score must be below his present average.

Total, average and marginal products

The relationship between total, average and marginal products can be illustrated diagrammatically. Consider Fig. 2.3 which presents the TP, AP and MP curves for continuous data.

Since AP is equal to TP divided by the number of units of the variable factor employed, it follows that AP is given by the slope of the ray from the origin to the relevant point on the TP curve. Thus, for example, when $0L_1$ units of the variable factor are used, the AP is equal to the slope of the ray 0A – that is, $AL_1/0L_1$. It is clear from the graph that AP reaches its maximum where the ray from the origin is tangent to the TP curve. In Fig. 2.3, this tangency occurs at point C, indicating that AP is at a maximum when $0L_2$ units of the variable factor are employed. Until $0L_2$ units are employed, we say that there are *increasing average returns to the variable factor*.

We have defined MP as $\Delta TP/\Delta L$, where the changes in the variables are very small. This also measures the slope of the TP curve. Thus, when $0L_2$ units of the variable factor are employed, the slope of the TP curve is given by $CL_2/0L_2$ which also represents AP at that point, confirming that AP = MP when AP is at its maximum. Total product reaches its maximum when $0L_3$ units of the variable factor are employed. At this point, MP is equal to zero, confirmed by the slope of the TP curve at point D. If additional units are hired, total product falls and marginal product is negative.

Finally, note that a firm operating with a fixed factor may not actually be encountering diminishing returns if it is producing at a level of output below the point where diminishing marginal returns set in. Any firm increasing its output with a fixed factor, though, must eventually come up against diminishing returns. Remember also that the model assumes that the state of technology is held constant. In practice, improvements in technology may offset the operation of the law. This has been the case in western agriculture where productivity has greatly increased over time despite a relatively fixed supply of agricultural land.

Long-run changes in production

In the long-run, all factors of production are variable. Firms wishing to maximise their profits, therefore, will attempt to produce their chosen output by employing combinations of capital, labour and land which minimise their production costs. We can illustrate this cost-minimisation graphically with the use of *iosoquants* and *isocost lines*. These also enable us to trace out the path along which a firm can expand in the long-run.

Isoquants

Consider the production of a single good, say good X, and suppose (for purposes of graphical representation) that only two factors of production, labour and capital, are employed. Suppose further that it is always possible to substitute capital for labour and labour for capital continuously in the production process.

Given these assumptions, it follows that a given quantity of good X can be produced using many different combinations of capital and labour. This is shown in Fig. 2.4, where the vertical axis measures units of capital per time period (K) and the horizontal axis measures units of labour per time period (L). Point A, on the isoquant

Fig. 2.4. Isoquant map for good X. Each isoquant shows different combinations of labour and capital which, when used efficiently, can produce a given level of output.

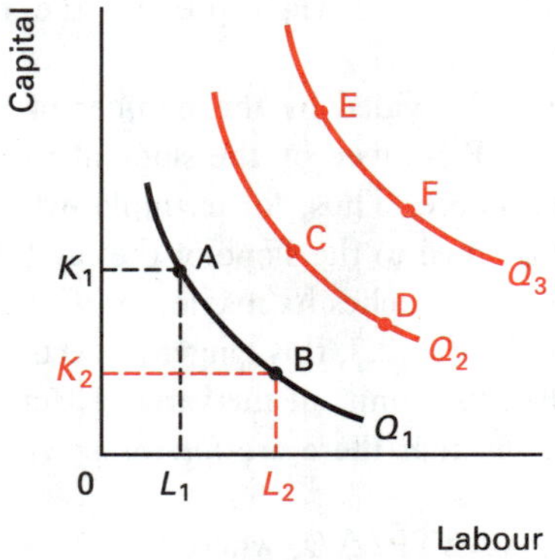

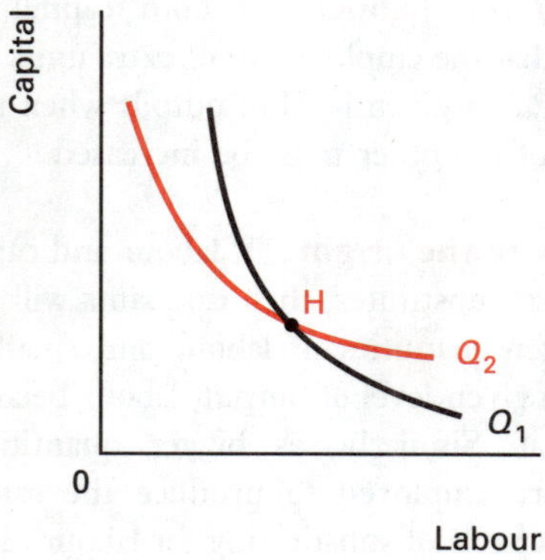

Fig. 2.5. *Two intersecting isoquants for good X.* As drawn, point H is a combination of capital and labour which, when used efficiently, can produce two different quantities Q_1 and Q_2, which is absurd.

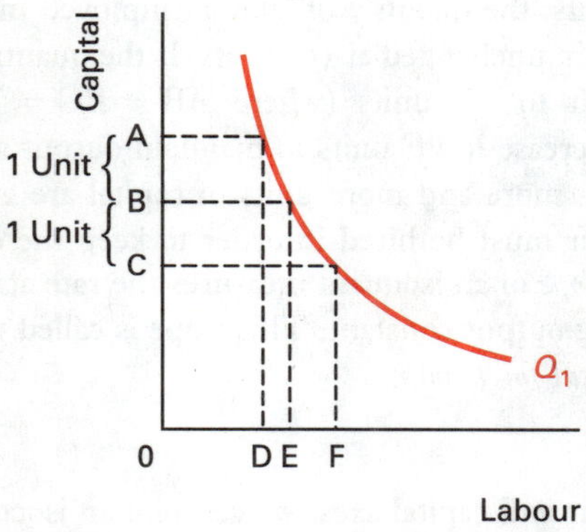

Fig. 2.6. *An isoquant convex to the origin.* As units of capital are given up, successively bigger quantities of labour must be employed to keep the output level unchanged. This makes the isoquant convex to the origin, as shown.

labelled Q_1, represents just one possible combination of capital and labour ($0K_1$ units of capital and $0L_1$ units of labour) which can be used to produce Q_1 units of output. There are in fact an infinite number of other points on the isoquant Q_1 all of which represent different combinations of capital and labour which can be used to produce Q_1 units.

Isoquant *Sometimes called an isoproduct curve, it is a contour line which joins together the different combinations of two factors of production that are just physically able to produce a given quantity of a particular good*

An output of Q_2 units (bigger than Q_1) can be produced using any of the combinations of capital and labour represented by points along the isoquant labelled Q_2, such as points C and D. Similarly, an output of Q_3 (bigger than Q_2) can be produced using any of the combinations of capital and labour represented by points along the isoquant labelled Q_3, such as E and F.

An *isoquant map* is a family of isoquants which illustrates graphically the production function for a good. The isoquants themselves have three important properties: first, no two isoquants can intersect; secondly, isoquants normally slope downwards from left to right (that is to say, they have a negative slope); thirdly, they are convex to the origin. Consider these properties in turn.

Isoquants cannot intersect Fig. 2.5 shows two intersecting isoquants, Q_1 and Q_2. As drawn, point H represents a combination of capital and labour which, when used efficiently, can apparently produce two different quantities of good *X*, Q_1 units and Q_2 units. This absurd result confirms the statement that isoquants cannot intersect.

Isoquants are negatively sloped If both capital and labour have positive marginal products (so that the employment of extra units increases total output), then it follows that to maintain a given level of output when the quantity of one factor is reduced, the quantity of the other must be increased.

Isoquants are convex to the origin If labour and capital are substitutes for each other, though not *perfect* substitutes, then isoquants will be curves which are convex to the origin. As bigger quantities of labour and smaller quantities of capital are employed to produce a given level of output, labour becomes less and less capable of substituting for capital. Similarly, as bigger quantities of capital and smaller quantities of labour are employed to produce the same level of output, capital becomes less and less capable of substituting for labour. This is illustrated in Fig. 2.6. Notice from the graph that as the quantity of capital employed is reduced by one unit from 0A to 0B units, the quantity of labour employed must increase from 0D to 0E for output to remain unchanged at Q_1 units. If the quantity of capital is now reduced again by one unit to 0C units (where AB = BC = 1), the quantity of labour employed must increase to 0F units to maintain output at Q_1. Clearly, EF is bigger than DE. Thus, as more and more units of capital are given up, successively larger quantities of labour must be hired in order to keep the output level unchanged.

Note that the *slope* of an isoquant measures the rate at which capital can substitute for labour, keeping output constant. This slope is called the *marginal rate of technical substitution of capital for labour.*

Isocost lines

Isocost line *Illustrates all the combinations of capital and labour that can be bought for a given monetary outlay*

On the same labour and capital axes, we can plot an isocost line which joins together all those factor combinations which have the *same cost*. This, together with the isoquant map, enables us to identify the cost-minimising combination of factors that a profit-maximising firm will employ to produce its chosen output level.

As an example, suppose that the price of capital is £1 per unit and the price of labour £2 per unit. Table 2.3 shows the combinations of the two factors that can be bought for an outlay (or cost) of £20. These combinations are plotted as the isocost line AB in Fig. 2.7: notice that the slope of the line (0A/0B = 2) represents the relative factor price ratio – in fact, it is the price of labour in terms of capital. The isocost line for an outlay of £40 is plotted as A′B′ on the graph: as might be expected, it is parallel to AB and lies to its right. Similarly, the isocost line for a £10 outlay, A″B″, is also parallel to AB but lies to its left. Isocost lines further to the left represent lower cost factor combinations; those further to the right represent higher cost factor combinations.

Table 2.3 The combinations of labour and capital for a £20 outlay.

Labour (price=£2)	Capital (price=£1)
10	0
8	4
6	8
4	12
2	16
0	20

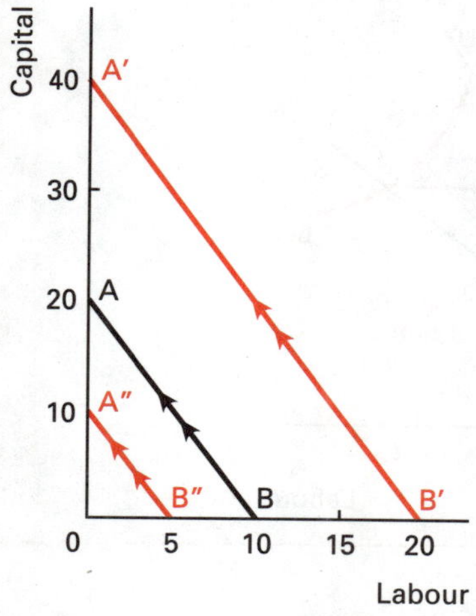

Fig. 2.7. *Isocost lines.* Each isocost line shows combinations of capital and labour that can be bought for a given outlay. The isocost line AB is drawn from the data shown in Table 2.3.

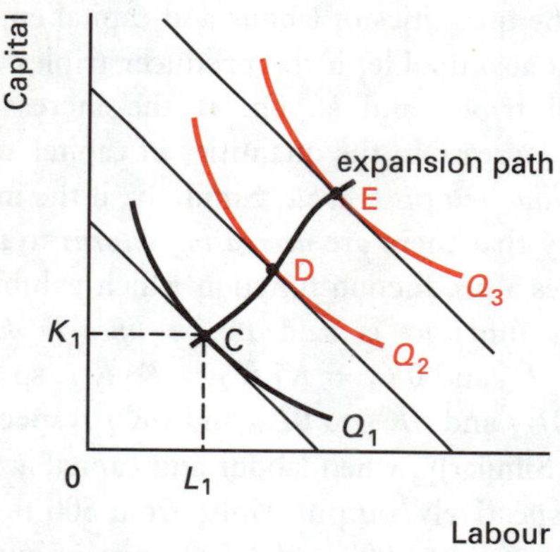

Fig. 2.8. *Cost-minimisation and the firm's expansion path.* Points C, D and E represent the firm's cost-minimising combinations of capital and labour as the firm expands its output from Q_1 to Q_2 to Q_3.

A change in the relative factor price ratio will change the slope of the isocost lines. If the price of capital should rise in terms of labour, the isocost lines in Fig. 2.7 would become less steep; if the price of labour should rise in terms of capital, the lines would become steeper.

Cost-minimisation

To produce a given output of good *X*, say Q_1, at minimum cost, a firm will produce at the point where isoquant Q_1 is just touching, or is tangent to, an isocost line. This is the isocost line nearest to the origin that can be achieved. Point C in Fig. 2.8 represents this point of cost-minimisation: all other combinations of capital and labour along the isoquant Q_1 would involve the firm in a larger monetary outlay. As the firm expands in the long-run, it will continue to attempt to minimise its costs. Thus, production of output Q_2 would be at point D and production of output Q_3 would be at point E. The locus of points CDE is referred to as the firm's long-run *expansion path*.

Returns to scale

In economic theory, it is often found convenient to assume that there are *constant returns to scale* in production. What this means is that when a producer employs more

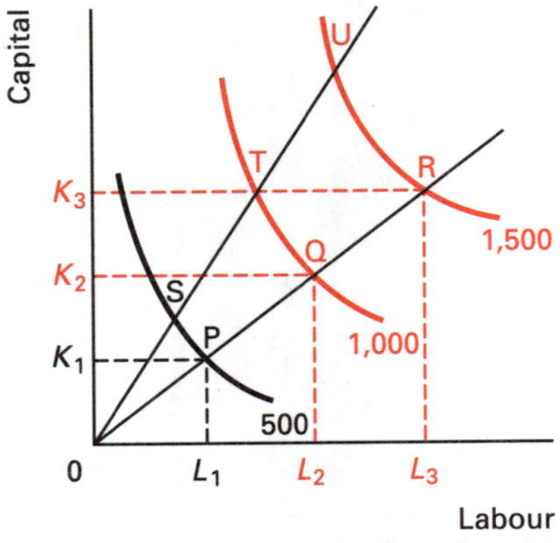

Fig. 2.9. A production function with constant returns to scale. With constant returns to scale, increasing the quantities of capital and labour by a certain proportion will increase output by the same proportion.

labour and more capital, his output increases proportionally. For example, if a producer doubles the quantities of labour and capital employed in the production of good *X*, output will also double; if the producer triples the quantities of capital and labour, output will triple; and so on. If the increase in output is more than proportional to the increase in the quantities of capital and labour employed, we say that there are *increasing returns to scale*. Similarly, if the increase in output is less than proportional, we say that there are *decreasing returns* to scale.

Fig. 2.9 illustrates a production function which exhibits constant returns to scale; such a production function is said to be *linearly homogeneous*. In the graph, $0L_1 = L_1L_2 = L_2L_3$ and $0K_1 = K_1K_2 = K_2K_3$, so that when labour and capital are doubled from $0L_1$ and $0K_1$ to $0L_2$ and $0K_2$ respectively, output doubles from 500 to 1,000 units. Similarly, when labour and capital are tripled from $0L_1$ and $0K_1$ to $0L_3$ and $0K_3$ respectively, output triples from 500 to 1,500 units. Notice that the isoquants representing 500, 1,000 and 1,500 units of output must be equally spaced when there are constant returns, so that 0P = PQ = QR along the ray 0R. The same is true for any other ray from the origin, so that, for example, 0S = ST = TU along the ray 0U.

Although we sometimes find it convenient to assume that there are constant returns to scale, we shall see in Ch. 9 that this is not realistic for most producers. It is more likely that in expanding the scale of operations, a producer will first experience increasing returns to scale, as he or she is able to take advantage of increased specialisation and division of labour. However, when all the inefficiencies of small scale have disappeared, the firm may experience a period of constant returns to scale. Finally, decreasing returns may set in as the scale of production becomes very large.

Summary

1. Production is an activity carried out by the many different types of firms in an economy. Firms may have different objectives, and there are a number of different types of business units found in a market economy: these include sole proprietorships, partnerships, joint-stock companies, co-operatives and public corporations.

2. A firm can grow through internal or external growth. The latter may take the form of vertical or horizontal integration, or the formation of a conglomerate.
3. The relative decline of manufacturing and growth of the tertiary sector has been a common experience of many industrial countries, including the United Kingdom, over the last 20 years or so.
4. The factors of production may be classified into land, labour, capital and enterprise.
5. The short-run is a period of time over which the input of at least one factor of production cannot be changed. In this situation, the law of diminishing returns eventually operates, whereby the marginal and average products of the variable factor begin to decline.
6. The long-run is a period of time over which the input of all factors of production can be varied. In the long-run, therefore, the firm can change the whole scale of production. It may experience constant, increasing or decreasing returns to scale. The firm's production function is illustrated by its isoquant map. The firm's expansion path is given by the points of tangency between isoquants and isocost lines as the firm expands.

Exercises

1. Review your understanding of the following terms:

production	primary sector
firm	secondary sector
one-person business	tertiary sector
partnership	stock variable
joint-stock company	flow variable
co-operative	production function
public corporation	short-run
horizontal integration	long-run
vertical integration	law of diminishing returns
diversification	average product
land	marginal product
labour	returns to scale
capital	isoquants
human capital	isocost line
enterprise	expansion path

2. Using the data in the following table, which shows the variations in the output of good *X* as the labour force is increased, calculate the average and marginal products of labour. Plot these on a graph and indicate the points of diminishing average returns and diminishing marginal returns.

Labour	1	2	3	4	5	6
Total product	100	300	480	560	600	600

3. Suggest reasons why there are many more sole traders in retailing, farming and personal services than in manufacturing industries.
4. Discuss the reasons for the growth in the size of firms and outline the ways in which firms can grow.
5. Indicate the factors which influence the production functions of the textile industries in: (a) rural India; and (b) Japan.
6. Sketch the isoquant maps for a good: (a) where labour and capital are perfect substitutes for each other; (b) where labour and capital have to be used in fixed proportions; (c) where the average and marginal products of one of the factors of production is zero.
7. For a product of your choice, outline the main factors that an entrepreneur would have to take into account in setting up a small business.

DEMAND AND SUPPLY

DEMAND

UTILITY AND DEMAND

SUPPLY

EQUILIBRIUM AND DISEQUILIBRIUM

3 DEMAND

Learning objectives

After reading this chapter, you should be able to:

- define the meaning of the term *demand* and interpret a demand curve
- describe the difference between normal, Giffen and Veblen goods
- identify the factors which bring about *movements along* and *shifts in* a demand curve
- define and understand the concepts of price, income and cross elasticity of demand
- illustrate the practical uses of price, income and cross elasticity of demand

Introduction

We have seen in Chs 1 and 2 that the basic economic problem faced by all societies is that of allocating the scarce resources of land, labour and capital among competing uses in an attempt to satisfy the limitless wants of consumers. Later in this book, in Ch. 7, we examine in some detail the different methods of resource allocation: from the free market economy, where government intervention is kept to a minimum and the forces of demand and supply are left to determine relative prices, to the command economy, where all economic decisions are planned by the central administration. In doing this, we highlight the role played by the *price mechanism* in allocating resources in a market economy.

Before looking in detail at the working of the price mechanism, however, we must examine how the economic forces of demand and supply can interact with each other to determine the market prices of goods and services: this is the objective of the present and the next three chapters. In this chapter, we concentrate on the determinants and measurement of demand, one of the most important concepts in economics. First, we consider an individual's demand and the market demand for a commodity; secondly, we explain the concept of the 'elasticity of demand'; finally, we consider some of the problems which arise in attempting to identify a demand curve statistically and in attempting to measure elasticities.

An individual's demand for a commodity

Individual demand
The quantity of a commodity that an individual is willing and able to buy during a given time period

As a first step, consider the main factors which influence an individual consumer's demand for a particular commodity, say good X. An individual's demand for a good is the quantity of the good that the individual is *willing and able to buy* during some time period.

Suppose we list some of the factors which may be expected to influence this consumer's demand for good X over a given time period (d_X):

- the price of good X (P_X)
- the prices of other goods which are related to good X (P_R)
- the consumer's income (y)
- the consumer's taste for good X (T)
- the consumer's expectations about future prices (E)
- advertising (A)
- other relevant factors (Z)

Using functional notation, we can write the following *demand function*:

$$d_X = f(P_X, P_R, y, T, E, A, Z)$$

This states simply that the individual's demand for X is a function of all the factors listed in the brackets.

Although all the factors are undoubtedly important, the price of a commodity is in many cases the most important factor influencing an individual's demand for it. Economists analyse the relationship between a consumer's demand for X and the price of X by assuming that all the other influencing factors remain unchanged: this is the important *ceteris paribus* assumption which is used so widely in all branches of economics. We can now write:

$$d_X = f(P_X), \textit{ ceteris paribus}$$

This states simply that the individual's demand for X is determined by the price of X, assuming that all the other influencing factors are held constant.

Now look at Table 3.1 where different prices of X are listed together with our consumer's weekly demand for X, *ceteris paribus*. As price rises from 10p per unit to 20p per unit, weekly demand falls from 3 units to 2 units. As price rises from 20p to 30p, demand falls to 1 unit. If the price should rise to 40p, our consumer would choose to buy no units at all.

An individual's demand curve for a good
Shows the relationship between the quantity demanded by the individual and the price of the good, **ceteris paribus**

Demand schedules can be represented most conveniently by using graphs. It has become convenient to represent the price of a commodity on the vertical axis and the quantity demanded per time period on the horizontal axis. Thus, in Fig. 3.1, the vertical axis measures the price of X in pence per unit and the horizontal axis measures the quantity demanded per week. The line DD reproduces the information contained in Table 3.1 and is called the individual's *demand curve* for X.

Table 3.1 Individual consumer's demand schedule for good X.

Price of X (pence per unit)	Consumer's demand (units per week)
10	3
20	2
30	1
40	0

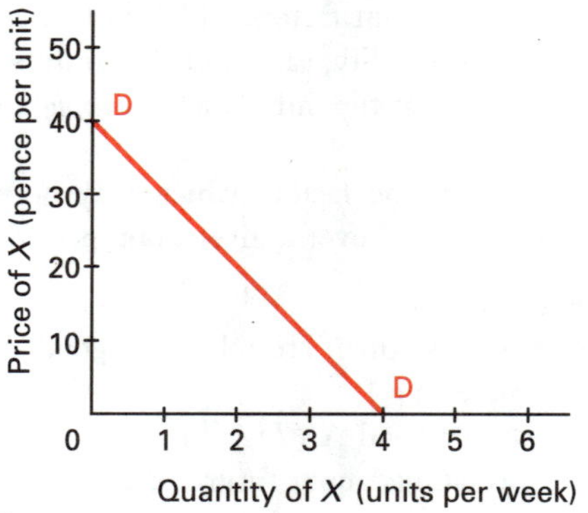

Fig. 3.1. An individual's demand curve for good X. The information contained in Table 3.1 is plotted on a graph to produce a demand curve with a negative slope (equal to −10).

Notice in Fig. 3.1 that the quantity axis is labelled the 'quantity of X *per week*'. Demand is a *flow* concept, so in measuring the quantity of a good demanded, it is imperative to refer to some time period. A demand for 3 units has no meaning whatever unless it is expressed over some specified period of time.

The demand curve for X represented in Fig. 3.1 is a straight line and slopes downwards from left to right (that is to say, it is negatively sloped). It certainly need not be a straight line – it is only a straight line in Fig. 3.1 because of the simple numbers used in our example. The negative slope of the demand curve reflects the reasonable expectation that as the price of X falls, *ceteris paribus*, our consumer's demand for it will rise. This proposition is examined in greater detail in the following chapter where we deal with the theory of consumer behaviour and where we bring the important concept of utility into the analysis.

Market demand

Market *The market for a product is the area in which buyers and sellers come into contact with each other in order to exchange the product*

The market for a good can be thought of as the area in which buyers and sellers of the good come into contact with each other to transact their business. It is important to remember that the limits of a market are not necessarily defined by national or geographical boundaries – the markets for certain goods, like black puddings, are very localised, but the advanced nature of communications these days has enabled the markets for many other commodities, like wheat and gold, to become world-wide. The geographical size of a market depends on such factors as how widely dispersed the demand for the product is, and how easily and cheaply it can be transported. The removal of regulatory and administrative barriers to trade within the EC after 1992 should have the effect of extending the markets for many goods and services which have previously been restricted to the national boundaries of the member states.

Market demand *The market demand for a product is the sum of the demands of the individual consumers in the relevant market*

In this chapter, we assume for simplicity that the market for good X is restricted to the home economy. We can say, therefore, that the market demand for good X is the sum of all the individuals' demands in the economy. As with our individual's demand, we may expect this market demand (D_X) also to be influenced by the price of X (P_X) and the prices of other related goods (P_R). It obviously will not, however, be much influenced by a single consumer's income; this time, instead of the income of an individual, we use the income of the economy as a whole – that is to say, national income (Y). If T represents society's taste for X, A represents advertising

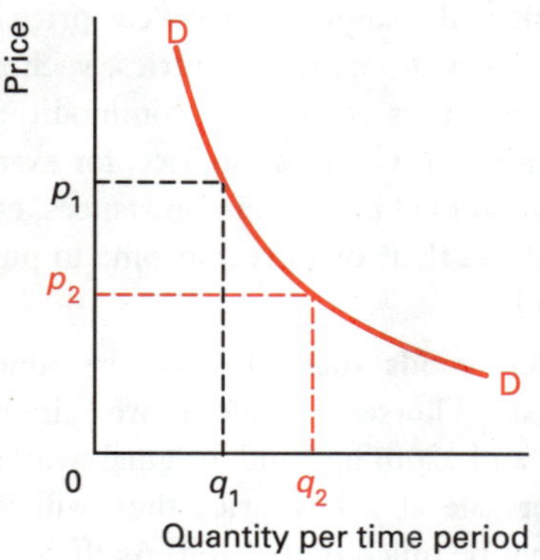

Fig. 3.2. ***Market demand for good X.*** The market demand curve for good X is shown here with a negative slope. This means that as price falls, quantity demanded increases, *ceteris paribus,* and *vice versa.*

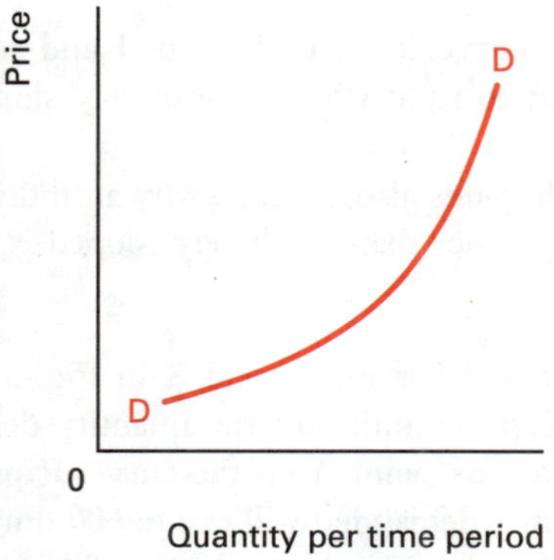

Fig. 3.3. ***The demand curve for a Giffen or Veblen good.*** This demand curve has a positive slope. This means that as price falls, quantity demanded decreases, *ceteris paribus,* and *vice versa.*

and Z represents other relevant factors (including expectations about future price changes), we can write the following *market demand function* for X:

$$D_X = f(P_X, P_R, Y, T, A, Z)$$

Making the *ceteris paribus* assumption and holding all the influencing factors constant except the price of X, we can write:

$$D_X = f(P_X), \textit{ ceteris paribus}$$

Representing this on a graph, and assuming that a fall in the price of X will cause an increase in the total quantity demanded, we have the downward-sloping market demand curve, DD, shown in Fig. 3.2. As price falls from $0p_1$ to $0p_2$, the total quantity demanded in the market rises from $0q_1$ to $0q_2$; if price should rise back to $0p_1$, quantity demanded would fall back to $0q_1$. This inverse relationship between the price of a commodity and the quantity demanded in the market is summed up in the so-called law of demand.

Law of Demand *A rise in the price of a good leads to a fall in the total quantity demanded. A fall in the price of a good leads to a rise in the total quantity demanded*

It must be emphasised, however, that this 'law' is not an unassailable truth. There are two major exceptions to it.

(a) *Giffen goods.* A Giffen good (named after the nineteenth-century economist Sir Robert Giffen) is a very inferior good for which quantity demanded increases as price rises, and quantity demanded decreases as price falls. This is possible when consumers in certain less developed countries, such as Bangladesh, are so poor that most of their income is spent on a commodity necessary for subsistence. Suppose that the commodity in question, rice, for example, is traded in a market. If the price of rice should fall in such circumstances, consumers may reduce their demand for rice and use their extra real income to purchase meat or some other more nutritious food.

(b) *Veblen goods.* Veblen goods (named after the nineteenth-century American economist-sociologist, Thorsein Veblen) are 'luxury' goods like jewellery, designer perfumes and clothing, and original works of art. If goods of this type are put up for sale at a low price they will lack snob-appeal and, as a consequence, may not be much in demand. As their price rises then snob-appeal rises too and a marked strengthening of demand may well follow – again in contradiction to the law of demand.

The market demand curve for a Giffen good and for a Veblen good will be upward-sloping from left to right (that is, positively sloped). This is illustrated in Fig. 3.3

The existence of such goods also explains why an individual consumer's demand curve may be positively, rather than negatively, sloped.

Movements along and shifts of the demand curve

Consider the market demand curve for good X in Fig. 3.4. To start with, suppose that the price of X is 20p per unit and the quantity demanded is 500 units: this combination is represented by point A on the curve. If price should fall to 10p per unit, *ceteris paribus*, quantity demanded will rise to 600 units. This fall in price means that we have simply *moved along* the demand curve from point A to point B. If price should rise to 30p per unit, quantity demanded will fall to 400 units. Again, we have simply moved along the demand curve – this time from point B to point C. Such movements along a demand curve are sometimes called *extensions* of demand (for an increase in quantity demanded following a price change) or *contractions* of demand (for a decrease in quantity demanded following a price change).

Result: *The effect of a change in the price of good X,* ceteris paribus, *can be traced by moving along the market demand curve for good X.*

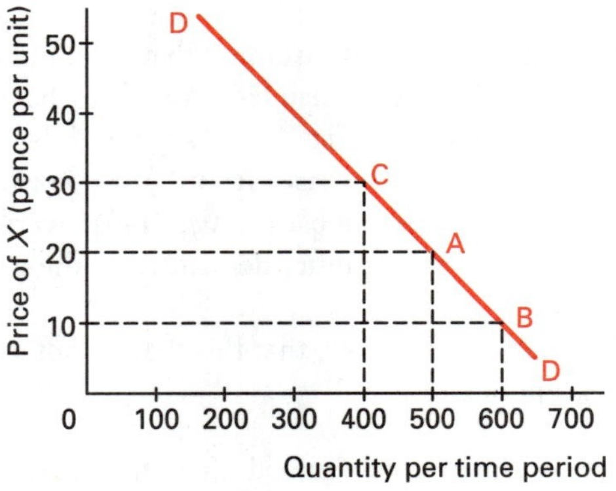

Fig. 3.4. *Movements along a demand curve.* Other things being equal, the effect of a change in the price of good X can be seen by moving along the demand curve.

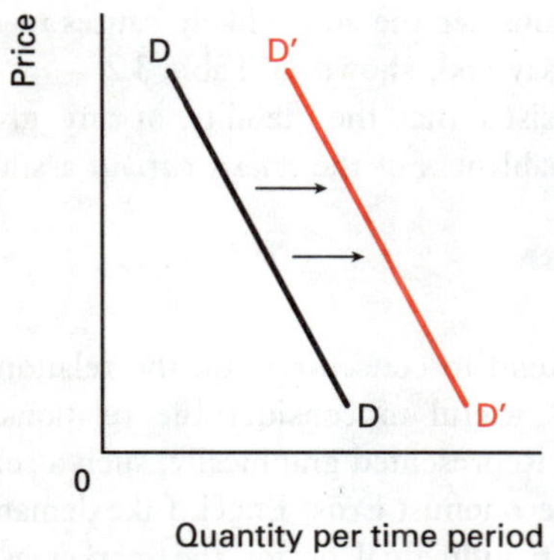

Fig. 3.5. **A shift in the** ***demand curve.*** **For a normal good, a rise in income causes the demand curve to shift to the right.**

Starting once again at point A on the demand curve, suppose now that one of the other influencing factors changes. Suppose in fact that real national income increases so that every one has more to spend on all goods. The market demand for good *X* will now increase *at all prices*. In other words, we must draw a new demand curve to represent the new relationship between quantity demanded and price. Figure 3.5 shows the original demand curve, DD, together with the new one, D′D′, which lies above and to the right of the original one.

Result: *A change in any of the influencing factors except the price of X causes a shift in the demand curve for X.*

Table 3.2 **Likely causes of shifts in the demand curve for cod.**

	Cause	Effect
1.	Increase in national income.	Increase in demand for cod at all prices. Demand curve shifts *right*.
2.	Decrease in national income.	Decrease in demand for cod at all prices. Demand curve shifts *left*.
3.	Rise in the price of substitute goods (such as haddock or plaice).	Demand curve for cod shifts *right*.
4.	Fall in the price of substitute goods.	Demand curve for cod shifts *left*.
5.	Rise in the price of complementary goods (such as chips).	Demand curve for cod shifts *left*.
6.	Fall in the price of complementary goods.	Demand curve for cod shifts *right*.
7.	Change in tastes in favour of cod.	Demand curve shifts *right*.
8.	Change in tastes against cod.	Demand curve shifts *left*.
9.	Increase in cod advertising.	Demand curve shifts *right*.
10.	Decrease in cod advertising.	Demand curve shifts *left*.
11.	Expectation of a rise in the future price of cod.	Demand curve shifts *right*.
12.	Expectation of a fall in the future price of cod.	Demand curve shifts left.

To illustrate this, consider the above likely causes of shifts in the demand curve for a particular good, say cod, shown in Table 3.2.

It must be emphasised that the stability of any given market demand curve depends on the reasonableness of the *ceteris paribus* assumption.

Engel curves

Although economists tend to concentrate on the relationship between demand and price, it is sometimes useful to consider the relationship between demand and income, *ceteris paribus*. Represented graphically, such a relationship is called an *Engel curve*, named after the economist Ernst Engel. Like demand curves, Engel curves can be drawn either for an individual or for the market as a whole. As an example, consider an individual consumer's Engel curve for good *X*. Table 3.3 shows different levels of income for the consumer together with his demands for good *X* on the assumption that the price of *X* and all other influencing factors (except, of course, the consumer's income) remain constant. Plotting this information on a graph with income on the vertical axis and quantity demanded on the horizontal axis, we obtain the consumer's Engel curve for good *X*. This is shown in Fig. 3.6.

Note that Engel curves can also be drawn for the economy as a whole – in that case, though, the vertical axis must be labelled 'national income' and the horizontal axis the 'total quantity demanded in the market'.

Engel curves are useful for distinguishing between *normal* and *inferior* goods. When income rises, the quantity demanded of a normal good increases (as in our simple example) and this is indeed the result one would normally expect. But the quantity demanded of an inferior good falls. To explain this, consider the market

Table 3.3 Consumer's income and demand for good *X*.

Consumer's income (£ per week)	Quantity demanded (units per week)
50	1
60	2
70	4
80	7

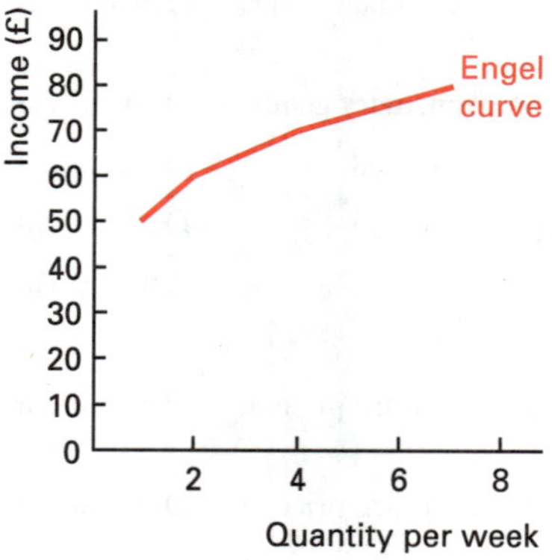

Fig. 3.6. Engel curve for good X. The information contained in Table 3.3 is plotted on a graph to produce an Engel curve with a positive slope.

demand for black and white television sets. As real national income rises, more and more people may find that they can afford to buy colour sets so that the demand for black and white sets falls. If this is the case, black and white television sets are said to be inferior goods and will have an Engel curve which slopes downwards from left to right.

Finally, it is important to note that inferior goods and Giffen goods are not exactly the same. The difference between them is explained in the next chapter.

The role of advertising and publicity

As indicated in Table 3.2, the effect of an increase in advertising expenditure on a particular good is to shift the good's demand curve to the right. This is illustrated in Fig. 3.7 where D_1D_1 represents the demand curve for good X for a given level of weekly advertising expenditure and D_2D_2 represents the demand curve after a rise in the level of weekly advertising expenditure. If the price of the good remained constant at $0p_1$, the quantity demanded would increase from $0q_1$ to $0q_2$. Advertising may also have the effect of reducing the elasticity of demand for the product by creating brand loyalty.

Why is advertising usually effective in increasing the demand for a product? There are two possible reasons:

(a) *Advertising is informative.* The lack of information concerning the price and the availability and performance of a good is one of the factors which may prevent the good from reaching those consumers who would benefit from it. Although consumers can search for this information themselves, it can be made more accessible to them by means of advertising paid for by the sellers and, in part, by buyers via a higher price. In this way both sellers and buyers share the cost of information and both groups benefit.

(b) *Advertising is persuasive.* As well as providing information, most advertising is intended to *persuade* consumers to buy a particular brand name rather than rival brands. This is done by attempting to convince consumers that the good in question is of a higher quality than its rivals, even though in many instances they are of very similar or equal quality. It can be argued that this form of advertising in many cases does little more than raise the firms' costs. If all sellers

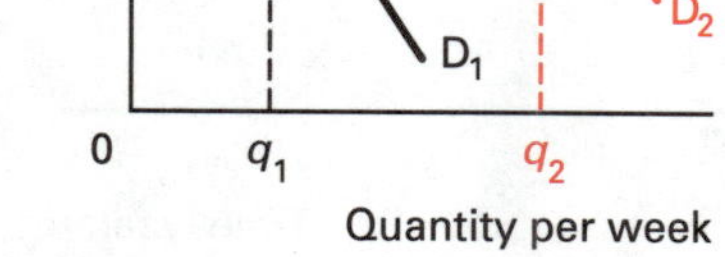

Fig. 3.7. The effect of an increase in advertising expenditure. Successful advertising of good X should shift its demand curve to the right. This means that more units can be sold at the same price $0p_1$.

in a market have similar advertising campaigns, they may each succeed only in holding their respective market shares. No firm dare reduce its advertising expenditure for fear of losing its market share, but the total market for the product may not be expanded at all by the 'persuasive' advertising. This form of advertising becomes part of each firm's costs of production and causes product prices to be higher than they otherwise would be.

Some advertisers have concentrated on pointing out the weaknesses of competitors' products. For example, some advertisements for cars compare the attributes of the cars in question with those of near competitors, emphasising the faults that have been found in the competitors' products. This form of 'knocking' advertising appears to be becoming increasingly popular.

As well as planned advertising, publicity in general can have a considerable effect on the market for a good. A product which gains a reputation for unreliability or lack of safety will soon lose sales – for example, bad publicity concerning new timber-framed houses in the United Kingdom undoubtedly caused a fall in demand for such houses. Similarly, a producer who gains a good reputation through publicity (whether organised or spontaneous) will experience rising sales.

Product life-cycles

Product life-cycle *The product life-cycle model illustrates the time-pattern of demand for a product during its life*

According to the product life-cycle model, certain products pass through a number of stages with changing patterns of demand throughout their lifetimes. The life-cycle pattern illustrated in Fig. 3.8 is fairly typical of products such as black and white television sets, home computers and models of cars. Thus, another possible determinant of the market demand for a product is the stage reached in the product's life-cycle.

When a new product is first introduced, it may experience a gradually increasing level of demand. As it becomes more widely known and accepted by consumers and before new rival brands are fully developed, it will pass through a 'growth' stage during which demand will rise rapidly. Eventually, the product will reach its 'maturity' stage and then, as innovations and new products are developed by competitors, demand will begin to decline.

Fig. 3.8. A typical product life-cycle. This diagram shows how a product may pass through a number of stages over time – from its introduction and acceptance to its eventual decline as new competing products are developed.

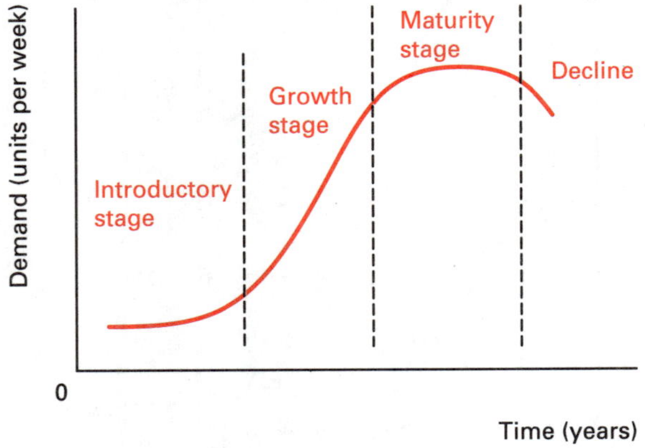

Elasticity of demand

Price elasticity of demand *A measure of responsiveness of quantity demanded to a change in the price of a good,* **ceteris paribus**

The 'elasticity of demand' is a measure of the extent to which the quantity demanded of a good responds to changes in one of the influencing factors. The main measures are the price elasticity of demand (which is a measure of the responsiveness of quantity demanded to a change in price); *income* elasticity of demand (which measures the responsiveness of quantity demanded to a change in income); and *cross* elasticity of demand (which measures the responsiveness of quantity demanded to a change in the price of some related good). Of these, the price elasticity is the most commonly used. It is calculated by using the following general formula:

$$\text{Price elasticity of demand, } E_D = -\frac{\text{Proportionate change in quantity demanded}}{\text{Proportionate change in price}}$$

Inelastic demand *The quantity demanded changes less than proportionately in response to a given change in price*

Elastic demand *The quantity demanded changes more than proportionately in response to a given change in price*

This means that if the price of good X should rise by 10 per cent (or 0.1) and the quantity demanded should fall in consequence by less than 10 per cent, say 5 per cent (or 0.05), then the price elasticity of demand would be $0.05/0.1 = 0.5$. In this case, since the elasticity is less than 1, we say that the demand for X is inelastic: *a given percentage change in price gives rise to a smaller percentage change in quantity demanded.* Now suppose that when the price of X increases by 10 per cent, the quantity demanded falls by more than 10 per cent, say 20 per cent (or 0.2). The price elasticity of demand will now be $0.2/0.1 = 2$. This time, since the elasticity is greater than 1, we say that the demand for X is elastic: *a given percentage change in price gives rise to a bigger percentage change in quantity demanded.* If, when the price of X increases by 10 per cent, the quantity demanded should fall by exactly 10 per cent, the price elasticity of demand would be exactly equal to 1 – this is called *unitary elasticity*.

Now consider what happens to the total sales of good X when its price falls by 10 per cent. If the demand is elastic, total sales value (which is the price of X multiplied by the total quantity sold) will rise – this must be so because, although price has gone down, quantity has risen by a bigger proportion. If the demand for X has unitary elasticity, then total sales value will be unchanged – this is because, although price has fallen, quantity sold has risen by exactly the same proportion. Finally, if the demand for X is inelastic, then total sales value will fall when the price of X falls.

To illustrate these points, consider the example shown in Table 3.4. As the price of X falls from 8p to 0p, quantity demanded increases steadily from 0 to 40. The third column of the table shows the total sales value of X at each price. All this information is reproduced in graphical form in Fig. 3.9. The market demand curve, which reproduces the information contained in the first two columns of Table 3.4,

Table 3.4 The quantity demanded and total sales value of good X at different prices.

Price of X	Quantity demanded	Total sales value
8	0	0
7	5	35
6	10	60
5	15	75
4	20	80
3	25	75
2	30	60
1	35	35
0	40	0

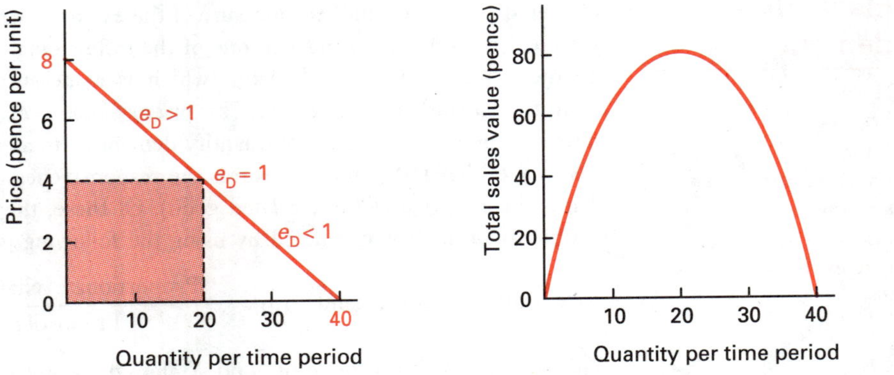

Fig. 3.9. Demand curve and total sales revenue curve. These graphs reproduce the information shown in Table 3.4. Good *X* has a straight-line demand curve with a negative slope. As the price of *X* falls and quantity demanded increases, the total sales revenue curve rises at first, reaches a maximum, and then declines. Demand is price elastic at prices above 4 pence per unit, inelastic at prices below 4 pence, and has unitary elasticity at 4 pence exactly.

turns out to be a straight line. The total sales value curve starts at the origin, rises to a maximum of 80p when price is 4p and quantity sold is 20, then falls off to zero again when price is zero and quantity sold is 40. It should be clear that demand is elastic in the price range greater than 4p, inelastic for all prices less than 4p, and of unitary elasticity when price is exactly 4p.

Point price elasticity of demand *A measurement of price elasticity at a particular point on the demand curve*

Arc price elasticity of demand *A measurement of price elasticity between two points on a demand curve*

It is only possible to calculate price elasticity with complete accuracy *at a point* on a demand curve. Such a calculation yields what is called the point elasticity of demand. An estimate of the elasticity along a range of a demand curve is called the arc elasticity of demand. Consider these in turn.

For a straight-line demand curve, *point elasticity* can be found using the following formula:

$$\text{Point } e_D = -\frac{\Delta q/q}{\Delta p/p} = -\frac{\Delta q}{\Delta p}\frac{p}{q}$$

In this formula, p/q is the price divided by the quantity at the point and $\Delta q/\Delta p$ is the reciprocal of the slope of the line. The minus sign is conventional: it ensures that the elasticity of demand for a normal good is positive.

Examples:
From Table 3.4 find the price elasticity of demand when price = 6p.
The slope of the line, $\Delta p/\Delta q = -8/40 = -1/5$

Reciprocal of the slope, $\Delta q/\Delta p = -5$
Point elasticity, $e_D = -(-5) \times 6/10 = 3$.

From Table 3.4, find the elasticity when price = 4p.
Point elasticity, $e_D = -(-5) \times 4/20 = 1$.

The same formula can be used to find the elasticity of demand at a point on a non-linear demand curve, but this time $\Delta q/\Delta p$ refers to the reciprocal of the slope of the tangent to the curve at the point. This is illustrated in Fig. 3.10, where the elasticity at point A is:

$$e_D = -\frac{\Delta q}{\Delta p}\frac{p_1}{q_1}$$

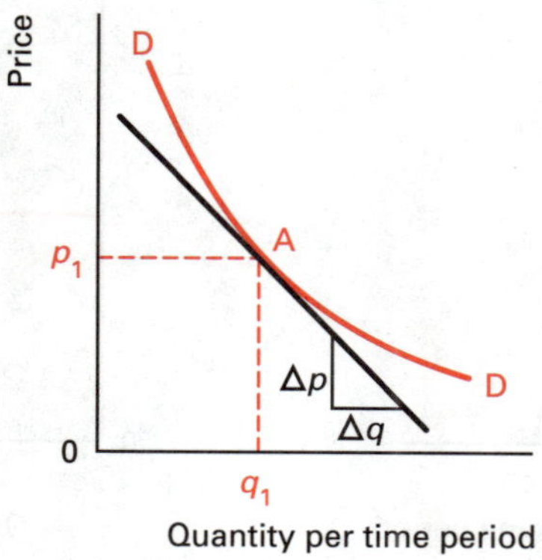

Fig. 3.10. Point elasticity on a non-linear demand curve. The point elasticity at A is measured as the negative of the reciprocal of the slope of the tangent at point A, multiplied by the ratio of price to quantity demanded at that point.

Note that the slope of the tangent is the same as the slope of the curve at point A. This slope (written as dp/dq) can only be determined exactly using differential calculus and is not pursued in this book.

Arc elasticity is an estimate of the elasticity along a range of a demand curve. It can be calculated for both linear and non-linear demand curves using the following formula:

$$\text{Arc } e_D = -\frac{\Delta q}{\Delta p}\,\frac{(p_1 + p_2)/2}{(q_1 + q_2)/2}$$

In this formula, p_1 and q_1 represent the initial price and quantity, and p_2 and q_2 represent the new price and quantity. This means that $(p_1 + p_2)/2$ is a measure of the average price in the range along the demand curve and $(q_1 + q_2)/2$ is the average quantity in that range.

Examples:
From Table 3.4, estimate the elasticity of the demand curve in the price range from 5p to 6p.

$$\text{Arc } e_D = -[(-5)/1] \times \frac{11/2}{25/2} = 11/5$$

From Table 3.4, estimate the elasticity in the price range from 1p to 2p.

$$\text{Arc } e_D = -(-5) \times \frac{3/2}{65/2} = 3/13.$$

Determinants of price elasticity Since the price elasticity of demand changes as we move along a demand curve, it follows that the initial price of a good is one of the determinants of its price elasticity. Other factors which influence the price elasticity of demand are: (a) *The availability of substitutes*: the more substitutes a good has, the more elastic the demand for it is likely to be. (b) *The proportion of consumers' incomes spent on the good*: goods, like cars, which take up a large proportion of consumers' incomes tend to have a more elastic demand than goods, like salt, which take up only a very small proportion of consumers' incomes. (c) *Time*: since it may take time for buyers to react to changes in price, the demand for many goods may be inelastic in the short-run but more elastic in the longer-run.

Fig. 3.11. Perfect elasticity and perfect inelasticity. Graph (a) shows a demand curve which is perfectly price inelastic over its entire length. Graph (b) shows a demand curve which is perfectly price elastic over its entire length.

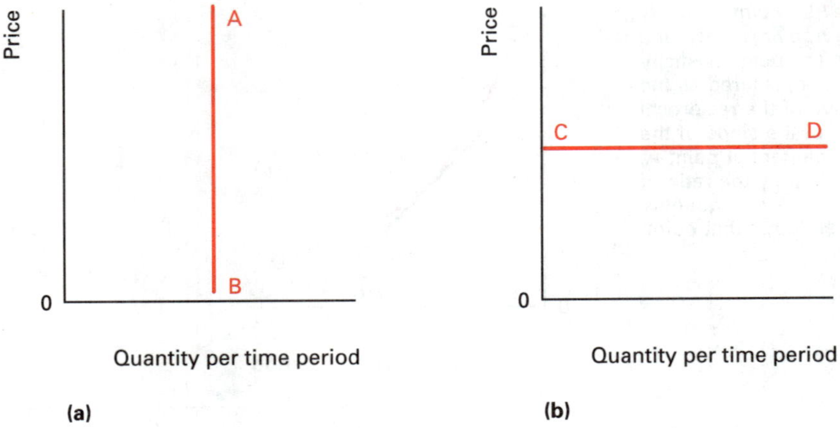

Fig. 3.12. Unitary elasticity. A demand curve which is a rectangular hyperbola has price elasticity equal to one over its entire length. This means that the areas of the rectangles $0p_1Aq_1$ and $0p_2Bq_2$ must be equal.

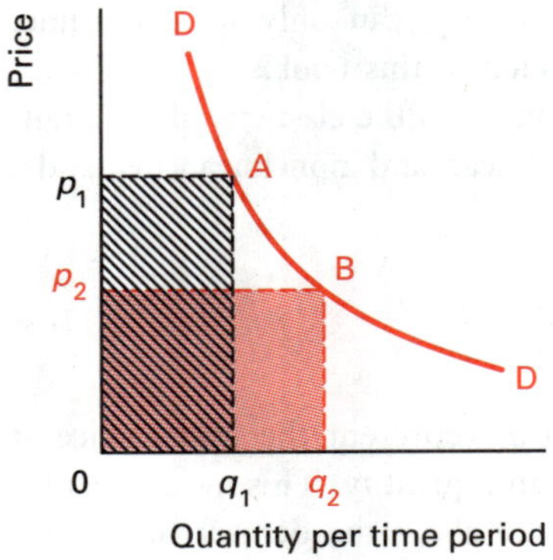

A demand curve is said to be *perfectly inelastic* ($e_D = 0$) when changes in price cause no change in quantity demanded; the vertical straight line AB in Fig. 3.11(a) depicts such a perfectly inelastic demand curve. A demand curve is said to be *perfectly elastic* ($e_D = \infty$) when any quantity will be bought at the prevailing price, but any rise in price will cause quantity demanded to fall to zero; the horizontal straight line CD in Fig. 3.11(b) depicts a perfectly elastic demand curve.

A demand curve is said to exhibit *unitary elasticity* ($e_D = 1$) when changes in price cause equi-proportionate changes in quantity in the opposite direction, so that total sales revenue remains unchanged. Fig. 3.12 depicts a demand curve which exhibits unitary elasticity along its entire length. This curve is a rectangular hyperbola so that price × quantity is the same at every point along the curve: for example, at points A and B on the demand curve DD, it must be true $p_1 q_1 = p_2 q_2$.

Other elasticity formulae

To calculate the *income* elasticity of demand, the following general formula can be used:

$$\text{Income } e_D = \frac{\text{Proportionate change in quantity demanded}}{\text{Proportionate change in income}}$$

An income elasticity of demand greater than 1 means that a given proportionate increase in national income will cause a bigger proportionate increase in quantity demanded. It follows that producers of such goods may need to plan extra capacity in times of rising incomes.

To calculate the *cross* elasticity of demand, the following general formula can be used:

$$\text{Cross } e_D = \frac{\text{Proportionate change in quantity demanded}}{\text{Proportionate change in the price of a related good}}$$

This will be positive if the related good is a substitute good and negative if the related good is a complement.

Problems of measurements

Suppose that we were to collect some actual sales figures for a particular good, say potatoes, and plot the quantities sold at different prices on a graph. Table 3.5 shows some hypothetical statistics of the quantity of potatoes sold at different prices and these are plotted as a scatter of points on the graph in Fig. 3.13. Can the best-fitting line through the scatter diagram be properly called the demand curve for potatoes and can we use it to calculate the price elasticity of demand for potatoes? The answer to both questions is likely to be no for three main reasons:

(a) The figures can only have been collected over time and we cannot be certain that the other influencing factors all remained unchanged during that time

Table 3.5 Hypothetical figures of the quantity of potatoes demanded at different prices.

Price of potatoes (pence per kg)	Quantity demanded (tonnes per week)
5	10
10	6
15	7
20	4
25	3

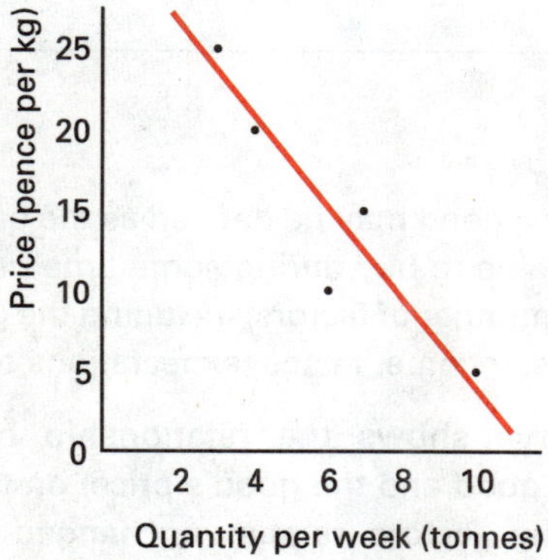

*Fig. 3.13. **Best-fitting line through a scatter diagram**.* The information contained in Table 3.5 is plotted as a scatter diagram. Does the best-fitting (regression) line represent a reasonable estimate of the demand curve for potatoes?

period. If any single one of them did change, then the best-fitting line will not trace out a demand curve and any calculations we make of the price elasticity of demand will be unreliable. Since controlled experiments are usually impossible to perform in economics, we have to rely instead on the statistical techniques of multiple regression analysis to estimate the influences of individual variables on the quantity demanded of a good. As we pointed out in Ch. 1, such techniques are the subject matter of a branch of economics called econometrics and are beyond the scope of this book.

(b) As we shall see in Ch. 5, the supply of a good also depends on the price of the good. Thus, when we plot our observed combinations of prices and quantities sold of potatoes on a graph (even assuming *ceteris paribus*), we cannot be certain whether we are plotting the demand curve or the supply curve, or even some combination of the two. This problem of identifying the demand curve separately from the supply curve is called the *identification problem*. It is a problem which can also be overcome to some extent by using econometric techniques, but it does illustrate the danger of drawing inferences about demand curves from observed price–quantity changes.

(c) Supposing that all the other influencing factors remain constant and that the identification problem is satisfactorily solved, can we now describe our best-fitting line as the demand curve for potatoes? Assuming that a sufficiently large sample has been taken, then it certainly does provide an estimate of the demand curve *at the time the study was made*. But is it a good estimate of that relationship today, and will it still be a good estimate next year, and in ten years' time? This depends on how long the *ceteris paribus* assumption holds over time. The stability of the relationship can only be determined by continuous empirical testing.

Practical uses of demand measurement

In the remainder of the book, we shall see that demand is a very important variable in economic analysis. It plays a crucial role in allocating resources via the price mechanism (see Ch. 7). Knowledge of demand and the elasticity of demand is of great importance to firms in planning how much to produce and in setting their prices (see Chs 9 and 10). It is also of importance to governments in many areas: for example, in formulating their taxation policies (see Ch. 14) and in estimating the effectiveness of exchange rate changes in correcting a balance of trade deficit (see Ch. 29).

Summary

1. The demand for a good may be defined as the quantity that consumers are willing and able to buy during some time period. Demand is likely to depend on a number of factors, including the good's price, the prices of related goods, income, tastes, expectations and advertising.
2. A demand curve shows the relationship between the quantity demanded of a good and the good's price, on the assumption that all other influencing factors remain unchanged (i.e. *ceteris paribus*).

According to the 'law of demand', demand curves have negative slopes, meaning that a rise in price, *ceteris paribus*, leads to a fall in demand and *vice versa*. Giffen goods and Veblen goods represent exceptions to this 'law'.

3. The effect on quantity demanded of a change in a good's price can be traced out by moving along the good's demand curve. The demand curve will shift if any of the other influencing factors should change.
4. An Engel curve shows the relationship between quantity demanded and income, *ceteris paribus*. A normal good has an Engel curve with a positive slope. An inferior good has an Engel curve with a negative slope.
5. Advertising may be informative and/or persuasive. Successful advertising will shift the demand curve to the right.
6. The price elasticity of demand measures the responsiveness of quantity demanded to a change in price. Income elasticity measures the responsiveness to a change in income, and cross elasticity measures the responsiveness to a change in the price of a related good.
7. The problem of identifying a demand curve separately from a supply curve represents one of the main difficulties of estimating the demand for a good statistically.

Exercises

1. Review your understanding of the following terms:

demand function	Engel curve
demand curve	price elasticity of demand
ceteris paribus	point elasticity
market	arc elasticity
normal good	income elasticity
inferior good	cross elasticity
Giffen good	substitutes
Veblen good	complements

2. Consider the following price and quantity demanded data for good X:

Price (£)	2	4	6	8	10	12
Quantity demanded	100	80	60	40	20	0

(a) Plot the demand curve and sales revenue curve on separate graphs.
(b) Calculate the point elasticity of demand at price = £4 and at price = £10.
(c) Estimate the elasticity between the prices of £6 and £8.
(d) Suppose now that a rise in real income causes quantity demanded to increase by 50 units at every price. Repeat exercises (a), (b) and (c).

(e) Given that the new demand curve is parallel to the original one, explain why the elasticities have changed.

3. Discuss the main determinants of the market demand for: (a) ice creams; (b) holidays in the United Kingdom; and (c) fashionable clothes.

4. Explain what is depicted by a demand curve and sketch demand curves which exhibit: (a) negative price elasticity; (b) perfect price elasticity; and (c) perfect price inelasticity.

5. What are the main determinants of the price elasticity of demand? How elastic would you expect the demand to be for: (a) salt; (b) petrol; (c) cigarettes; (d) sausages; and (e) black and white television sets?

6. In drawing the market demand curve for butter, what other things do we assume to remain unchanged?

7.** Explain the various measures of elasticity of demand and consider their practical uses.

Appendix

Demand functions and point elasticity

The demand function, $q = f(p)$, *ceteris paribus*, states that the quantity demanded of a good depends on the price of the good, other things being equal. If the demand 'curve' is a straight line with a negative slope, we can express the demand function by the linear equation:

$$q = a - bp$$

where a and b are constants. As an example, consider the following linear demand equation:

$$q = 100 - 2p \tag{1}$$

From this demand function, we can determine the quantity demanded at any price by substituting an appropriate value for p in the equation. For example, if $p = 0$, then $q = 100$; if $p = 10$, then $q = 80$; if $p = 20$, then $q = 60$; and so on. Alternatively, the function may be re-written as:

$$p = 50 - 0.5q$$

From this, we can determine the price at which a given quantity will be demanded. For example, if a quantity demanded of 50 was desired, a price of 25 would have to be charged.

The *elasticity of demand* at a point on a linear demand function can easily be found using simple differentiation and the general formula:

$$\text{Point } e_D = -\frac{dq}{dp}\frac{p}{q}$$

The expression dq/dp is the derivative of the quantity demanded with respect to price. Applying the rules of differentiation to the demand equation (1), we find that $dq/dp = -2$. We can now calculate elasticity at any point on the demand curve. For example, at $p = 10$ and $q = 80$,

$$e_D = -(-2) \times 10/80 = 0.25$$

Similarly, at $p = 40$ and $q = 20$,

$$e_D = -(-2) \times 40/20 = 4$$

For a non-linear demand curve, the same formula for point elasticity may be used. For example, consider the demand function:

$$q = 100 - 2p + 100/p$$

Using the rules of differentiation,

$$\frac{dq}{dp} = -2 - 100/p^2$$

At $p = 10$ and $q = 90$,

$$e_D = -\left(-2 - \frac{100}{100}\right)\frac{10}{90} = 0.33$$

Now confirm that for a demand curve which is a rectangular hyperbola with an equation

$$q = 1/p$$

the first derivative equals $-(1/p^2)$, and point elasticity of demand equals one. This is the case illustrated in Fig. 3.12. Note that it can similarly be shown that for a demand curve with an equation

$$q = 1/p^{\beta}$$

the point elasticity of demand equals β.

4 UTILITY AND DEMAND

Learning objectives

After reading this chapter you should be able to:

- define the term utility, and explain the difference between cardinal and ordinal utility
- define marginal utility and outline the cardinalists' explanation of why an individual's demand curve normally slopes downwards from left to right
- define an indifference curve and set out the three main properties of indifference curves consistent with the assumption of consumer rationality
- derive a budget line from knowledge of the prices of two goods and the consumer's income
- show how a consumer will maximise utility in choosing between two goods by equating the marginal rate of substitution (the slope of the individual's indifference curve) to the ratio of the prices of the two goods (the slope of the budget line)
- trace out the income-consumption line by analysing the effects of changes in the consumer's income, and the price-consumption line by analysing the effects of changes in the good's price
- use indifference curve analysis to distinguish between normal, inferior and Giffen goods, and to explain the meaning of consumer surplus
- outline the basics of the revealed preference theory and the 'characteristics of goods' approach to demand theory

Introduction

In the last chapter, we considered a consumer's demand and the market demand for a single good only. In reality, of course, consumers have to choose from the many thousands of different goods available on the market. In other words, consumers are faced with the problem of choice. In examining the shape of a demand curve for a single good, therefore, we must look closely at the behaviour of consumers when faced with this problem of choice. The 'theory of consumer behaviour' or 'theory of consumer choice' has developed into one of the major branches of microeconomics.

In this chapter, we first explain the important concept of *utility* and discuss whether or not it can be measured. Secondly, we set out, rather briefly, the 'cardinalist' or 'marginal utility' approach to the theory of demand. Thirdly, and in much greater detail, we set out the 'ordinalist' or 'indifference curve' approach – this is a very important section since it introduces concepts and techniques which are now widely used in all branches of modern economics. Finally, we consider two of the more recent developments in the theory of consumer behaviour: Samuelson's 'revealed preference' approach and Lancaster's 'characteristics of goods' approach.

Cardinal and ordinal utility

Utility *The satisfaction derived from the consumption of a good*

When a good is consumed, the consumer presumably derives some benefit or satisfaction from the activity. Economists have called this benefit or satisfaction utility, and have assumed that, in choosing among goods, a consumer will attempt to gain the greatest possible utility, subject to the size of his or her income.

Some nineteenth-century economists thought that utility might be measurable as if it were a physical commodity. In other words, just as coal can be measured in tonnes, they believed that utility could similarly be measured in its own units (like utils). These economists (among whom Alfred Marshall figured prominently) have become known as *cardinalists* because they believed that cardinal numbers could be used to express utility measurements. For example, a consumer may obtain 20 utils of utility from a helping of carrots, but only 10 utils from a helping of beans. The cardinalists would conclude from this that the consumer obtains twice as much utility from the carrots as from the beans and that the absolute difference between the utility derived from the carrots and that derived from the beans is 10 utils.

Utility, however, is an abstract, subjective concept and there are two major problems involved in trying to measure it for an individual:

(a) It is difficult to find an appropriate unit of measurement. If we call the unit a util, what is a util? How do we calculate the number of utils enjoyed by an individual at a moment in time? Are 10 utils enjoyed by one individual equivalent to 10 utils enjoyed by another – in other words, can we make *interpersonal comparisons of utility*?

(b) To measure the utility derived by an individual in consuming a good requires that all the other factors which affect his or her level of satisfaction be held constant and it is clearly impossible to carry out such a controlled experiment. There are too many other factors (economic, social and psychological) which influence an individual's level of utility.

By the 1930s, many economists were coming to the view that utility could not be measured cardinally and that cardinal measurement was not essential for a theory of consumer behaviour. These economists (who included Hicks and Allen, who in turn were influenced by the earlier work of Pareto and Slutsky) have become known as *ordinalists*. This is because they claimed that an individual can rank bundles of goods in order of preference and say that he or she derives more utility from one bundle than from another, or that the consumer derives equal utility from two or more bundles. It is impossible, though, to measure by how much one bundle is preferred to another. For example, a consumer may prefer carrots to beans but, according to the ordinalists, will be completely unable to attach a numerical measure to the degree of preference. In this case, only ordinal numbers (first, second, third and so on) can be used to 'measure' utility and these say nothing about the absolute difference or any other relationship between utilities. Indifference curves and budget lines are the means of illustrating this ordinalist approach to demand theory and these are now widely used in all branches of modern economics.

The cardinalist approach

Marginal utility *The extra utility derived from the consumption of one more unit of a good, the consumption of all other goods remaining unchanged*

Marginal utility per penny *The extra utility derived from consuming one extra penny's worth of a good*

The hypothesis of diminishing marginal utility *States that as the quantity of a good consumed by an individual increases, the marginal utility of the good will eventually decrease*

The objective of this section is to outline the cardinalists' explanation of why an individual's demand curve normally slopes downwards from left to right. Central to this approach are the concept of marginal utility and the *hypothesis of diminishing marginal utility*.

Consider an individual's consumption of good X over a particular time period, say a week. Table 4.1 shows what happens to the consumer's total utility and marginal utility (both measured in utils) as he or she consumes more and more units of the good in the week. When the individual consumes no units of X at all, no utility is derived from the activity. Consuming one unit, though, yields 20 utils. Apparently, this whets the consumer's appetite for the good because when two units are consumed in the week, the total utility rises to 50 utils so that the second unit adds more to the consumer's total utility than the first. Adding further units up to the fourth continues to increase total utility, but at a decreasing rate so that marginal utility is falling. Finally, consuming a fifth unit actually causes total utility to fall so that marginal utility is negative.

This example illustrates the reasonable proposition that as more and more units of a good are consumed in a given time period, the extra utility derived from the consumption of additional units *eventually* falls. This is called the hypothesis of diminishing marginal utility.

To illustrate this hypothesis further, consider the utility derived by a thirsty consumer from successive cups of tea. The first cup will yield a great deal of utility: in other words, the marginal utility of the first cup is very high. A second cup may also be very welcome, but is unlikely to yield as much utility as the first, and a third cup is likely to yield even less utility. Once the consumer's thirst has been quenched, he or she may have no further desire for liquid refreshment: we say that any more tea would yield *disutility*. It seems reasonable to regard this hypothesis as a valid generalisation about consumer behaviour: the more a consumer has of a commodity, the less utility he or she is likely to derive from the consumption of an additional unit.

Now consider a consumer who has to choose between two goods, X and Y, which have prices P_X and P_Y respectively. Assume that the individual is rational and so

Table 4.1 An example illustrating diminishing marginal utility.

Quantity of X consumed per week	Total utility (units per week)	Marginal utility (units)
0	0	
1	20	20
2	50	30
3	60	10
4	62	2
5	60	−2

wishes to maximise total utility subject to the size of his or her income. The consumer will be maximising total utility when his or her income has been allocated in such a way that the utility to be derived from the consumption of one extra penny's worth of X is equal to the utility to be derived from the consumption of one extra penny's worth of Y. In other words, when the marginal utility per penny of X is equal to the marginal utility per penny of Y. Only when this is true will it not be possible to increase total utility by switching expenditure from one good to the other. The condition for *consumer equilibrium* can be written as follows:

$$\frac{\text{MU}_X}{P_X} = \frac{\text{MU}_Y}{P_Y}$$

where MU_X and MU_Y are the marginal utilities of X and Y respectively and P_X and P_Y are the prices (in pence) of X and Y respectively. In order to derive the individual's demand curve for good X, consider what happens to this condition when the price of X falls. It must be true (assuming that the price of Y remains unchanged) that:

$$\frac{\text{MU}_X}{P_X} > \frac{\text{MU}_Y}{P_Y}$$

The consumer can now increase his or her total utility by consuming more units of good X. This will have the effect of decreasing the marginal utility of X (because of the hypothesis of diminishing marginal utility) and the consumer will continue increasing his or her expenditure on X until the equality is restored. We now have the result we have been seeking: that a fall in the price of a good will, *ceteris paribus*, give rise to an increase in a consumer's demand for it – that is to say, the demand curve slopes downwards from left to right.

As an illustration of this suppose initially that $\text{MU}_X = 20$ utils, $\text{MU}_Y = 25$ utils, $P_X = 4\text{p}$ and $P_Y = 5\text{p}$, so that the condition is satisfied:

$$\frac{\text{MU}_X}{P_X} = \frac{\text{MU}_Y}{P_Y} = 5 \text{ utils per penny.}$$

Now let the price of X fall to 2p. With consumption unchanged, the MU per penny of X rises to 10 utils and exceeds the MU per penny of Y. How will the consumer respond to this? By spending an extra penny on good X, 10 utils of utility are derived; by spending an extra penny on good Y, only 5 utils are derived. Clearly, the consumer will buy more units of good X, thus reducing their MU until the MUs per penny for X and Y are once again equal.

The ordinalist approach

To simplify the analysis of the ordinal utility approach so that it can be represented graphically in two dimensions, consider again a consumer's choice between two commodities only, say X and Y. The consumer's preferences for X and Y are represented by the indifference map in Fig. 4.1 where I_1, I_2 and I_3 are three of the indifference curves.

Indifference curves

In Fig. 4.1, the vertical axis measures the quantity of good Y and the horizontal axis measures the quantity of good X. Thus, every point on the graph represents some combination of X and Y. Points very close to the origin, like point A, represent

Fig. 4.1. ***An indifference map.*** This graph shows three of the infinite number of indifference curves which make up an individual's indifference map.

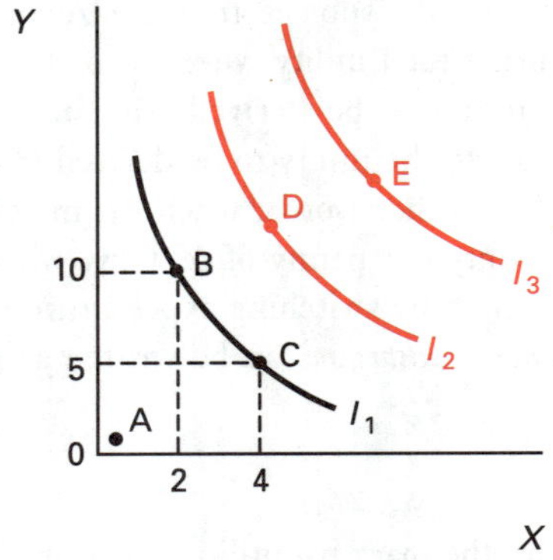

very small quantities of X and Y; points further away from the origin represent bigger quantities. Since combinations B (10 units of Y and 2 units of X) and C (5 units of Y and 4 units of X) are on the same indifference curve, the consumer is said to be indifferent between them – that is to say, both combinations yield the same utility to the consumer. Combination D, however, is on a higher indifference curve than B or C. We say that he or she prefers D to either B or C. Similarly, the consumer prefers combination E to A, B, C, or D.

Indifference curve *A curve which joins together all the different combinations of two goods which yield the same utility to the consumer*

We assume that the consumer is able to rank his or her preferences over the entire field of choice. This means that the consumer must be able to consider any two possible combinations of X and Y and say either that he or she prefers one to the other, or that he or she is indifferent between them. It should be clear from this that there must exist an indifference curve passing through every possible combination of X and Y – that is, through every point on the graph. This means that, although we have only drawn three of them in Fig. 4.1, there are an infinite number of indifference curves making up the indifference map.

Note at this stage the similarity between indifference curves and isoquants (see Ch. 2). There is, though, an important difference between them: this is that whereas an isoquant represents a given level of output which is *cardinally* measurable, an indifference curve represents a given level of utility which is only *ordinally* measurable.

Before taking the analysis further, we need to make the assumption that our consumer is rational. To be rational, he or she must satisfy the following conditions:

(a) To be able to rank his or her preferences over the entire field of choice.
(b) Behaviour must be *transitive*: this means that if the consumer prefers combination A to combination B, and combination B to combination C, then he or she must also prefer A to C.
(c) Never to have all he or she wants of all goods – the consumer must always want some more of at least one good.

For a rational consumer, indifference curves have three important properties:

Indifference curves can never intersect To show this, consider Fig. 4.2 which shows two intersecting indifference curves. Since both combinations A and C are on

Fig. 4.2. ***Intersecting indifference curves.*** The individual is indifferent between A and C, and between B and C and should, therefore, also be indifferent between A and B. But this would be irrational as A contains more *Y* than B and the same amount of *X*. We conclude that to be consistent with rationality, indifference curves cannot intersect.

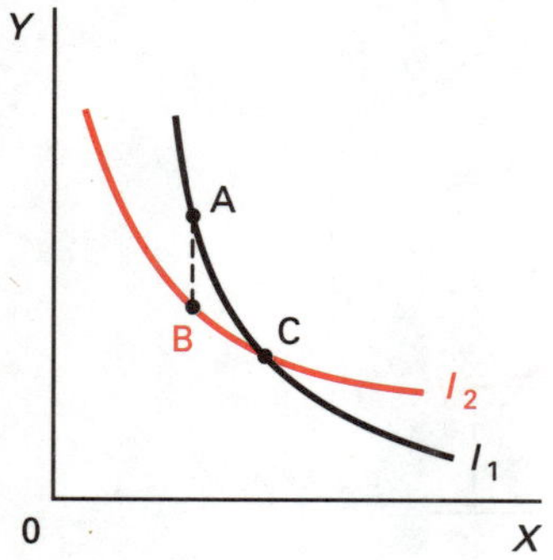

Fig. 4.3. ***The negative slope of an indifference curve.*** For utility to remain unchanged as units of *Y* are given up, additional units of *X* must be obtained. It is for this reason that indifference curves slope downwards from left to right.

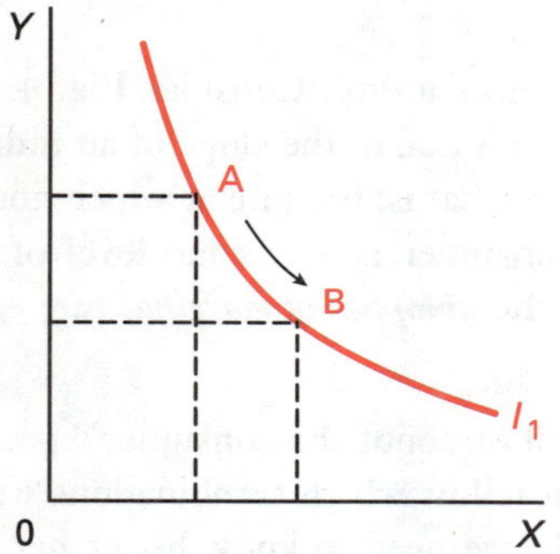

the same indifference curve, the consumer must be indifferent between them. Combinations B and C, however, are also on the same indifference curve, so the consumer must be indifferent between them as well. If the consumer is indifferent between A and C, and between B and C, he or she must (by the rule of transitivity) be indifferent between A and B. This, however, is absurd because A contains more *Y* and the same amount of *X* as B and so must be preferred to it. This kind of absurd result occurs whenever indifference curves cross. We conclude, therefore, that indifference curves can never intersect each other.

Indifference curves slope downwards from left to right If both *X* and *Y* are goods (so that the consumer derives utility rather than disutility from them) and if the consumer is not satiated with either *X* or *Y*, then as some of the good is given up, more units of the other good must be obtained if the consumer is to remain at the same level of utility. Consider Fig. 4.3. In moving from point A to B, as units of *Y* are given up, more units of *X* are obtained and the utility derived is unchanged. For this to be true, the indifference curve must slope downwards from left to right.

Indifference curves are convex to the origin As more and more units of one good, say *Y*, are given up, it is reasonable to suppose that successively bigger quantities of *X* must be obtained to compensate the consumer for the loss and leave

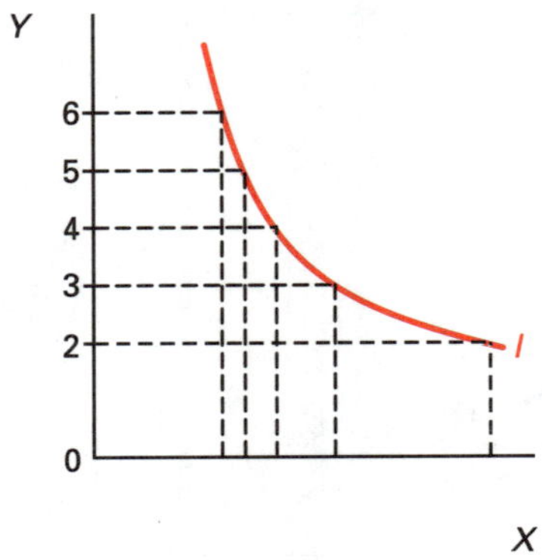

Fig. 4.4. The convexity of an indifference curve. As more and more units of *Y* are given up, successively bigger quantitites of *X* must be obtained to compensate the consumer for this loss.

him or her at the same level of utility. Consider Fig. 4.4 where this proposition is illustrated. Since the absolute value of the slope of an indifference curve is called the marginal rate of substitution (that is, the rate at which good *Y* can be substituted for by good *X*, leaving the consumer at the same level of utility), the proposition is sometimes summed up as the *diminishing marginal rate of substitution.*

Budget lines and 'consumer equilibrium'

Indifference curves only tell us about the consumer's preferences for the two goods. By themselves, they cannot tell us which combinations will be chosen. In addition to the consumer's preferences, we need to know his or her *income* and the *prices of the two goods.* Given this information, and assuming that the consumer will choose the combination of the two goods which will yield the greatest utility (that is, put the consumer on the highest attainable indifference curve), we can determine the combination of *X* and *Y* that the consumer will choose.

Budget line *Shows the different combinations of two goods that can be bought with a given money income*

As an example, suppose the price of *X* is £20, the price of *Y* is £10, and suppose the consumer's income is £100. Table 4.2 shows the combinations of *X* and *Y* that he or she can just afford to buy. Plotting these points on the same graph as the indifference map, we obtain what is called the budget line. This is illustrated in Fig. 4.5; it shows the combinations of the two goods that can just be afforded with an income of £100. The (absolute) slope of the budget line (10/5 = 2) measures the relative price of *X* in terms of *Y* – that is, two units of *Y* must be given up in order to buy one unit of *X*. If we let P_X denote the price of *X* and P_Y the price of *Y*, then we can write the slope of the budget line as equal to P_X/P_Y.

Consumer equilibrium point *Refers to the combination of goods that yield the maximum utility or satisfaction to the consumer, given the consumer's budget constraint*

Fig. 4.6 shows the indifference map and budget line on the same graph. Assuming that all the consumer's income is spent on *X* and *Y*, he or she will choose the combination represented by point A. This is the point where the budget line is just tangent to an indifference curve – the indifference curve I_2 is the highest one that can be reached. Point A is called the consumer equilibrium point. The consumer is said to be *maximising utility subject to budget constraint.*

Since the budget line is tangent to the indifference curve at point A, it must be true that the slope of the indifference curve (the marginal rate of substitution) is equal to the slope of the budget line at that point. Thus, we can write that, at the 'consumer equilibrium' point,

$$\text{Absolute slope of budget line} = \frac{P_X}{P_Y} = \text{Marginal rate of substitution.}$$

Table 4.2 The combinations of *X* and *Y* that the consumer can just afford to buy with an income of £100.

Quantity of *X* (price=£20)	Quantity of *Y* (price=£10)
0	10
1	8
2	6
3	4
4	2
5	0

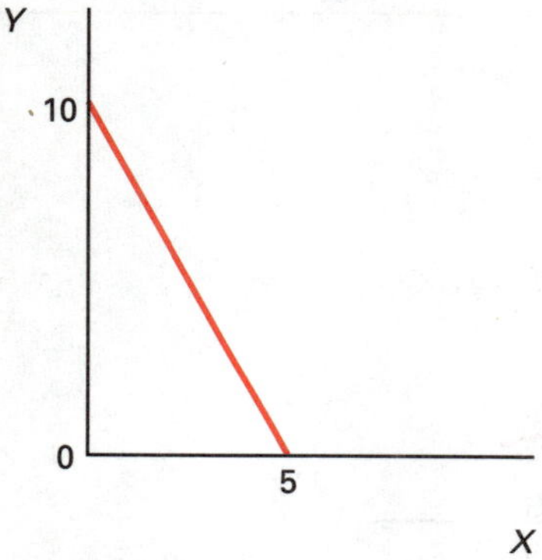

Fig. 4.5. ***A budget line.*** Assuming that the consumer's income is £100 and that the prices of *X* and *Y* are £20 and £10 per unit respectively, this budget line shows the combinations of the two goods that the consumer can just afford to buy.

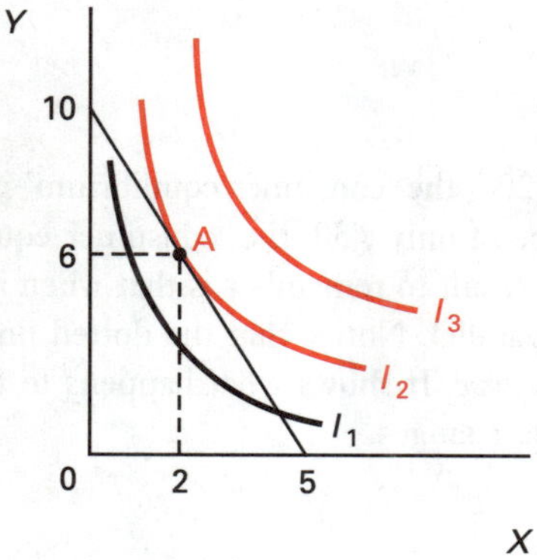

Fig. 4.6. ***Consumer equilibrium.*** The consumer maximises utility subject to the budget constraint at point A where the budget line is tangent to the indifference curve I_2.

Effect of an income change

If the consumer's income increases, his or her budget line will shift upwards remaining parallel to the original one. Similarly, if the consumer's income falls, the budget line will shift downwards remaining parallel. To show this, suppose that the consumer's income rises from £100 to £200. Table 4.3 (a) shows the combinations of *X* and *Y* that can be afforded after the income rise; the new budget line FG, together with the original one DE, is shown in Fig. 4.7. Now suppose that the consumer's income falls to £50: the combinations that can just be afforded are shown in Table 4.3(b) and the new budget line HJ is shown with the others in Fig. 4.7.

Table 4.3 The combinations of *X* and *Y* that the consumer can afford to buy with different incomes.

(a) Income=£200		(b) Income=£50	
Quantity of *X* (price=£20)	Quantity of *Y* (price=£10)	Quantity of *X* (price=£20)	Quantity of *Y* (price=£10)
0	20	0	5
2	16	$\frac{1}{2}$	4
4	12	1	3
6	8	$1\frac{1}{2}$	2
8	4	2	1
10	0	$2\frac{1}{2}$	0

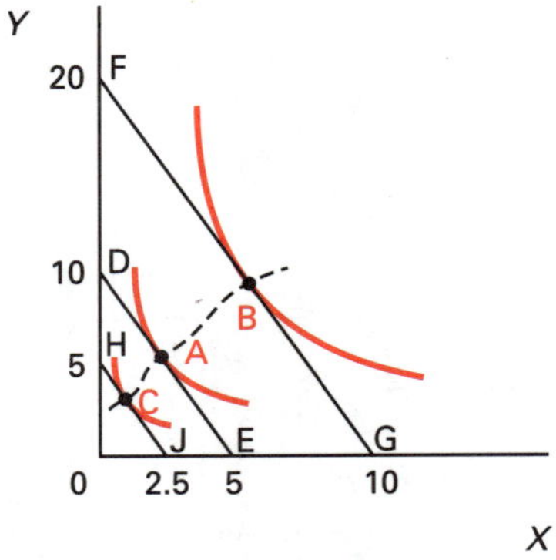

Fig. 4.7. Effects of an income change. As income increases, the consumer moves from point C to A to B, tracing out the income-consumption curve.

With an income of £200, the 'consumer equilibrium' point is shown as point B in Fig. 4.7. With an income of only £50, the 'consumer equilibrium' point is shown as point C. The important result to remember is that when income changes, the budget line shifts but remains parallel. Notice that the dotted line CAB in Fig. 4.7 is called the *income–consumption curve*. It shows what happens to the consumer's demand for the two goods as income changes.

Effects of a price change

To examine the effect of a price change, suppose that the price of *X* falls, *ceteris paribus*. Table 4.4 shows the combinations that the consumer can just afford to buy when his or her income is £100, the price of *Y* is £10 and the price of *X* has fallen to £10. The new budget line DE′ is graphed, together with the original one DE, in Fig. 4.8. Notice that when the price of one of the goods falls, the budget line shifts, but this time it *pivots* and so does not remain parallel to the original one. It becomes less steep, reflecting the fall in the relative price of *X*.

The effect of the price fall on the 'consumer equilibrium' point is shown in Fig. 4.9: it moves from point A to point B. The dotted line AB is called the *price–consumption curve*. In Fig. 4.9, the fall in the price of *X* causes the consumer's demand for it to expand from two to six units. There are two possible reasons for

Table 4.4 The combinations of X and Y that the consumer can afford to buy after a price change.

Quantity of X (price=£10)	Quantity of Y (price=£10)
0	10
2	8
4	6
6	4
8	2
10	0

Fig. 4.8. *Effect of a price change.* As the price of X falls, the budget line pivots around point D from DE to DE′.

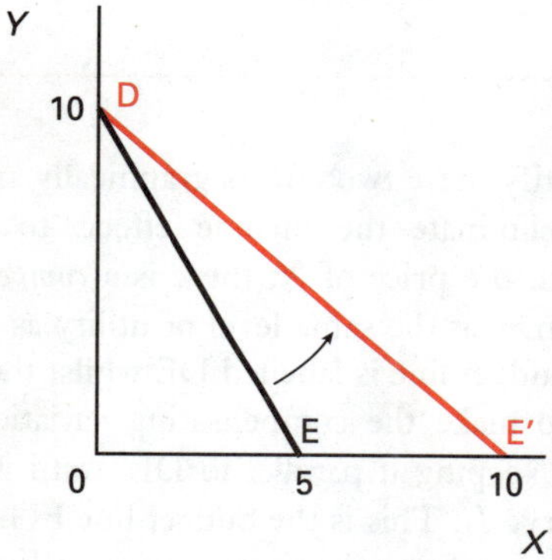

Fig. 4.9. *The price-consumption curve.* As the price of X falls, the consumer moves from point A to point B, tracing out the price-consumption curve.

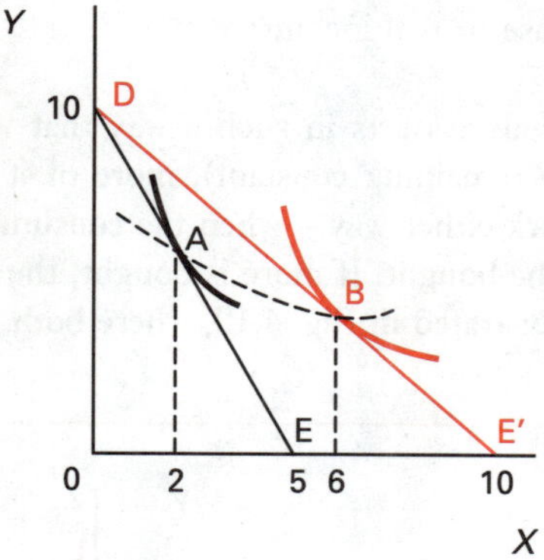

this:

(a) As the price of X falls, it becomes relatively cheaper and Y becomes relatively more expensive. The consumer is therefore induced to substitute X for Y. This is called the *substitution effect* of the price change.

(b) As the price of X falls, the consumer is made better off – i.e. experiences an increase in real income. This may induce the consumer to buy more X, although he or she may use the extra income to buy more Y. This is called the *income* effect of the price change.

Fig. 4.10. *Income and substitution effects.* The movement from A_1 to A_3 represents the substitution effect of the fall in the price of *X*. The movement from A_3 to A_2 is the income effect.

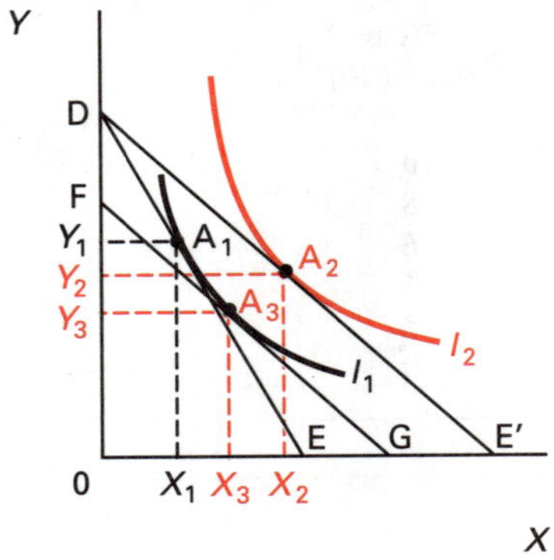

It is possible to identify these two effects graphically and this is done in Fig. 4.10. The first step is to eliminate the income effect: to do this, we assume that, accompanying the fall in the price of *X*, there is a *compensating variation* in income which leaves the consumer at the same level of utility as before the price change. In Fig. 4.10, the original budget line is labelled DE whilst the budget line after the price fall is labelled DE′. To make the compensating variation in income, we shift the budget line to the left, keeping it parallel to DE′ until it becomes tangential to the original indifference curve I_1. This is the budget line FG. The movement from point A_1 to A_3 is the *substitution effect* – the consumer is no better off, but has substituted X_1X_3 of *X* for Y_1Y_3 of *Y* because of the change in relative prices. The movement from point A_3 to A_2 is the *income effect* – the consumer buys X_3X_2 of *X* and Y_3Y_2 of *Y* because of the increase in real income.

Normal, inferior and Giffen goods

Normal good *One for which an increase in consumers' real income leads to an increase in demand*

The substitution effect always acts in such a way that when the relative price of a good falls (real income remaining constant), more of it is purchased. The income effect, however, can work either way – when the consumer's real income rises, more or less of good *X* may be bought. If more is bought, the good is said to be a normal good; this is the case illustrated in Fig. 4.10, where both *X* and *Y* are normal goods.

Fig. 4.11. *The case of an inferior good and a Giffen good. (a) Inferior good.* The negative income effect is smaller than the substitution effect. *(b) Giffen good.* The negative income effect is bigger than the substitution effect so that the net effect of a fall in the price of *X* is a fall in quantity demanded.

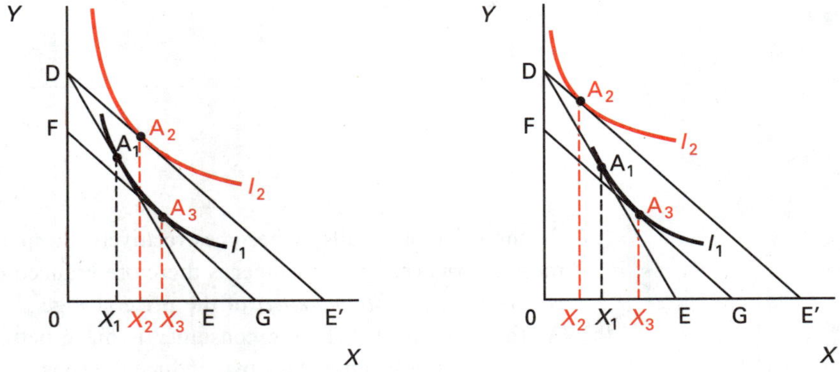

(a) Inferior good **(b)** Giffen good

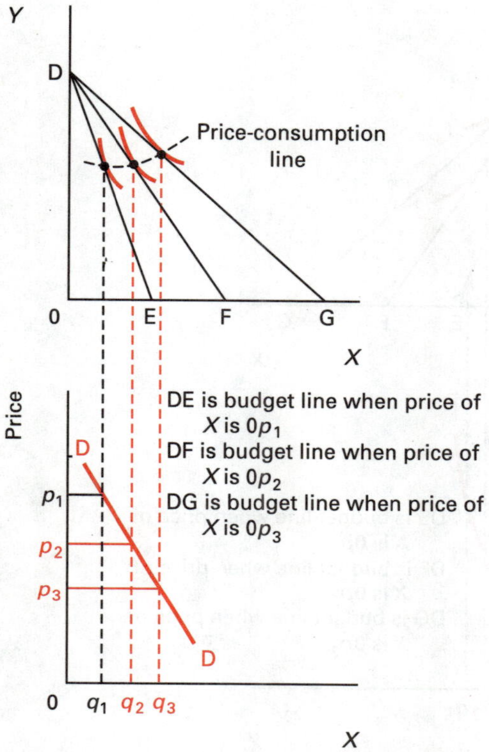

Fig. 4.12. Derivation of the demand curve for a normal good. As the price of *X* falls, the budget line pivots outwards and the quantity demanded increases. Transferring this result to a price-quantity graph yields the negatively sloped demand curve, DD.

Inferior good *One for which an increase in consumers' real income leads to a fall in demand*

Giffen good *A strongly inferior good with an upward sloping demand curve*

If less is bought, the good is said to be an inferior good; this is illustrated in Fig. 4.11(a) where the movement from A_3 to A_2 is the negative income effect. If the consumer buys less, and the income effect is actually bigger than the substitution effect so that the overall effect of the price fall is a decrease in consumption, then the good is said to be a Giffen good; this is illustrated in Fig. 4.11(b) where the negative income effect (A_3 to A_2) is bigger than the substitution effect (A_1 to A_3).

The demand curve again

The preceding analysis can be used to derive a consumer's demand curve. The price-consumption curve in Fig. 4.9 shows the different points of 'consumer equilibrium' as the price of *X* is varied, *ceteris paribus*. It gives us enough information, therefore, to draw the consumer's demand curve. This is done in Fig. 4.12 where *X* is a normal good: as the price of *X* is reduced from $0p_1$ to $0p_2$ to $0p_3$, the quantity of *X* demanded expands from $0q_1$ to $0q_2$ to $0q_3$. The resulting demand curve is downward-sloping from left to right. The same analysis is carried out in Fig. 4.13 where *X* is a Giffen good and the resulting demand curve is upward-sloping from left to right.

We have now completed a full circle. Having started by considering an individual consumer's demand curve in isolation in Ch. 3, we have now looked at the concept of utility and the theory of consumer behaviour which underlies demand. Furthermore, we have seen that by making certain assumptions about the consumer's preferences

Fig. 4.13. ***Derivation of the demand curve for a Giffen good.*** As the price of *X* falls, the budget line pivots outwards and the quantity demanded falls. Transferring this result to a price-quantity graph yields the positively sloped demand curve, DD.

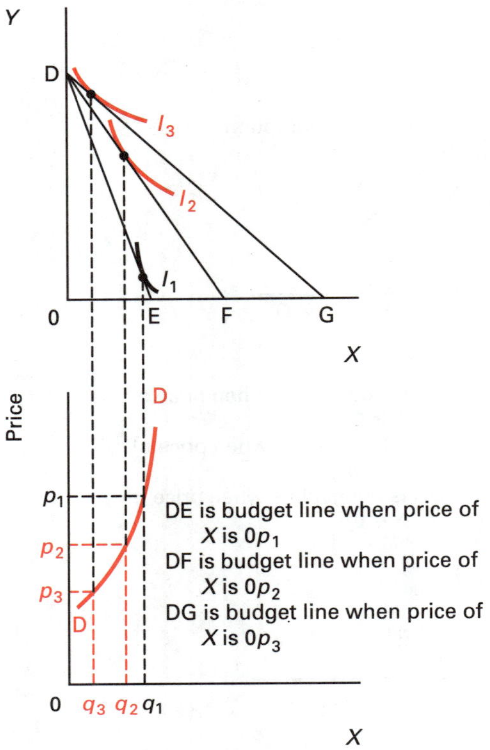

and assuming *ceteris paribus*, we can derive a demand curve which slopes downwards from left to right. We have also seen that under certain exceptional circumstances, a demand curve which slopes upwards from left to right can be derived.

Consumer surplus

Consider now an individual's demand curve for good *X* as shown in Fig. 4.14 and suppose that the prevailing market price is £4. The graph indicates that the individual will buy 6 units of the good per week, paying out a total of £24. We have

Fig. 4.14. ***Consumer's surplus.*** The consumer is willing to pay £9 for the first unit of the good, £8 for the second unit, £7 for the third and so on. If the actual price is £4 per unit, the consumer earns a surplus on the first five units consumed. For continuous demand curves, consumer's surplus can be measured by the area under the demand curve and above the price (ECD in the graph).

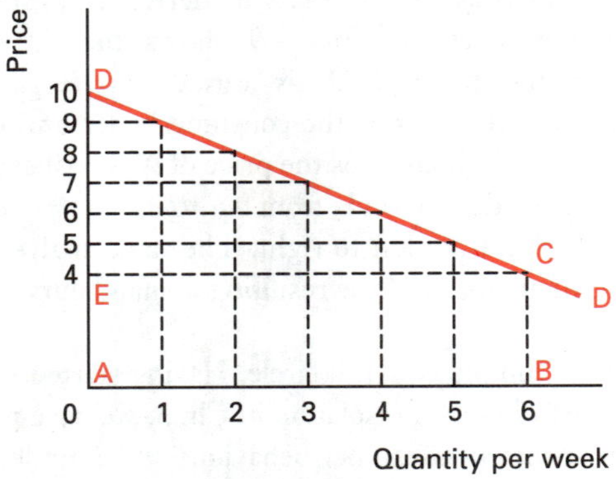

seen in the foregoing analysis that the individual's utility will be maximised by these purchases. Consider, though, the first unit of good X that the individual buys – it yields so much utility that he or she would have been prepared to pay as much as £9 for it. Similarly, he or she would have been prepared to pay as much as £8 for the second unit, £7 for the third unit, and so on. Since a single price of £4 prevails in the market, the individual has only had to pay £24 for the six units (area ABCE), instead of $£(9+8+7+6+5+4) = £39$ which he or she would have been prepared to pay – for continuous data, this is equal to the area under the demand curve, ABCD. The £15 difference can be thought of as the consumer's surplus and is represented by the area under the demand curve and above the price line (ECD in Fig. 4.14).

Consumer surplus *A measure of the difference between the actual price paid and the price that a consumer is willing to pay for a given good*

For a market demand curve, *consumer surplus* is a monetary indicator of the gap between the total utility that society derives from a good and the good's actual market value. We see in later chapters that it is a useful concept in illustrating the welfare effects on an economy of taxes, quotas and certain elements of imperfect competition.

Other developments in demand theory

The 'theory of revealed preference' is based on the reasonable proposition that a consumer will actually choose to consume that collection of goods that he or she prefers. Paul Samuelson used this proposition to derive a consumer's downward-sloping demand curve in such a way that required neither the subjectivity of the utility concept used in both the ordinal and cardinal utility approaches, nor the assumption of diminishing marginal utility of the cardinal utility approach. All that was required was that the consumer behaved consistently.

The 'revealed preference' theory can demonstrate that the consumer's demand curve for a good will be downward-sloping from left to right so long as the consumer is observed to increase purchases of the good when his or her income increases. Consider Fig. 4.15. Suppose that the line AB is a consumer's budget line and that point C is the combination of X and Y that the consumer reveals preferred to all the other attainable combinations in the triangle A0B. If the price of X falls, the budget line will shift to AB′. We can eliminate the income effect of this price change, as before, by shifting the budget line back to A′B″ (parallel to AB′). Having revealed point C preferred to all other points in the triangle A0B, the consumer will clearly not now choose any points along the section A′C. The consumer must, therefore, choose

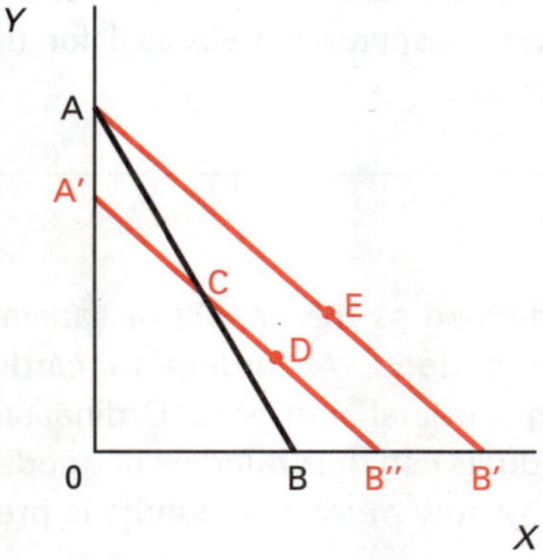

Fig. 4.15. The revealed preference approach. A fall in the price of good X shifts the budget line from AB to AB′. Applying a compensating variation in income shifts the budget line to A′B″. The revealed preference approach enables us to predict (without reference to the concept of utility) that the substitution effect of the price fall will induce the consumer to move from his or her original choice at point C to a point on the line CB″, such as D. With a positive income effect, the consumer's final position will be a point on the budget line AB′ to the right of D, such as E.

a point on the line CB″, say point D. The movement from C to D is the substitution effect of the price fall; according to this effect, the consumer purchases more of X following the price fall. If, as we have assumed, the income effect also causes the consumer to buy more of X, then he or she must end up at a point on the budget line AB′ somewhere to the right of point D, say at E. Since the fall in the price of X has caused the consumer to buy more, *ceteris paribus*, we can conclude that the consumer's demand curve slopes downwards from left to right.

It is important to notice that, in arriving at this conclusion, no mention was made of the abstract concept of utility. The 'revealed preference' approach can be described as a more objective approach to the theory of consumer behaviour. However, it cannot be denied that some subjective evaluation is implicit when consumers reveal their preferences for goods.

The 'characteristics of goods' approach

So far in this chapter, we have been concerned with consumers' choice between different goods on the assumption that a consumer will make a choice which will maximise his or her utility (whether cardinal or ordinal), subject to his or her income constraint. In this traditional approach, however, it is difficult to analyse a consumer's choice between different brands of the same product. One good must be treated either as the same as another or as a different good altogether. How then can we analyse a consumer's choice between two different brands of, say, a car? Is a Mini the same as a Jaguar or are they to be treated as completely different products? Lancaster's approach to demand theory helps us to overcome this problem.

Lancaster argues that it is the *characteristics* or attributes of goods which yield utility to the consumer, rather than the goods themselves. Thus, a car can be viewed as a collection of a number of different attributes – for example, engine size, seating capacity, body style, colour and so on, each of which yields utility to the consumer. Although different cars will clearly have similar characteristics, they will also vary in a number of respects. According to Lancaster's approach, we should analyse a consumer's choice between different brands on the assumption that the consumer (subject as always to income constraint) is attempting to maximise the utility to be derived from the characteristics possessed by the goods, rather than from the goods themselves.

In the United Kingdom, there are a large number of so-called differentiated products – that is, products which are very similar but not identical. In Lancaster's terminology, we say that such goods have similar characteristics. Clearly, traditional economics can be criticised for its inability to analyse a consumer's choice between these goods, and Lancaster's approach welcomed for throwing some light on this previously untrodden ground.

Summary

1. Utility may be defined as the benefit or satisfaction derived from the consumption of a good. According to cardinalists, utility can be measured using cardinal numbers. Ordinalists, on the other hand, claim that individuals can rank bundles of goods in order of preference, but cannot say *by how much* one bundle is preferred to another.

2. To cardinalists, different individuals' utility levels can be measured and compared. But to ordinalists, interpersonal comparisons of utility are impossible because of the subjective nature of utility.
3. The ordinalist approach relies on indifference analysis. An indifference curve links all the combinations of two goods which yield the same utility to the consumer, and an indifference map illustrates the individual's preferences for the two goods. Indifference curves slope downwards from left to right, are convex to the origin and can never intersect.
4. A budget line shows the combinations of two goods that a consumer can just afford to buy.
5. The consumer is assumed to maximise utility subject to a budget constraint. This means that the 'consumer equilibrium' point is found at the point of tangency between the budget line and an indifference curve. Indifference analysis may be used to examine the effects on consumer demand of changes in income and price.
6. Consumer's surplus may be defined as the difference between the price the consumer is willing to pay for a good and the good's actual market price.
7. Other developments in demand theory include the 'revealed preference' approach and the 'characteristics of goods' approach.

Exercises

1. Review your understanding of the following terms:

cardinal utility	income–consumption curve
ordinal utility	price–consumption curve
marginal utility	income effect
indifference map	substitution effect
budget line	compensating variation
marginal rate of substitution	consumer surplus
consumer equilibrium	revealed preference

2. Suppose all of an individual's weekly income is spent on two goods, *X* and *Y*. Draw the individual's budget line if his or her income is £150 per week, the price of *X* is £10 per unit and the price of *Y* is £15 per unit. Draw the new budget lines: (a) if the price of *X* doubles; (b) if the price of *Y* halves; (c) if the individual's income rises to £250 per week.

3. Draw an individual's indifference maps for two goods, *X* and *Y*:
   (a) where the individual regards *X* and *Y* as perfect complements;
   (b) where the individual regards *X* and *Y* as perfect substitutes;
   (c) where the individual derives utility from good *X*, but disutility from good *Y*.

4. Suppose that X is a normal good, but that Y is an inferior good. Illustrate graphically the income and substitution effects following: (a) a fall in the price of X; (b) a fall in the price of Y.

5. Discuss the precise meaning of the term 'utility'. To what extent can it be measured cardinally?

6. 'The revealed preference approach eliminates the abstract concept of utility from the theory of demand.' Discuss.

5 SUPPLY

Learning objectives

After reading this chapter, you should be able to:

- define the meaning of the term *supply* and interpret a supply curve
- describe the main determinants of supply and interpret the meaning of a supply function
- identify the factors which bring about *movements along* and *shifts in* a supply curve
- define and explain the meaning of the term *producer surplus*
- define and describe the determinants of the elasticity of supply

Introduction

As we saw in Ch. 2, it is the primary function of firms to hire and organise factors of production in order to produce goods and services which are then offered for sale. Firms, then, whether sole traders, partnerships, limited companies or public corporations, are the economic agents responsible for the supply of goods and services.

Market supply *The sum of the quantities of a good that individual firms are willing and able to offer for sale over a given time period*

The market supply of a good may be defined as the sum of the quantities of the good that firms are willing and able to offer for sale over some time period. To give a full treatment of supply, it is necessary to analyse in detail how firms under different market structures make their price and quantity decisions. Firms in highly competitive industries, for example, operate differently from those with some monopoly power. This detailed analysis, however, is left for Chs 9 and 10. In this short chapter, a preliminary discussion of supply is presented. This includes an outline of some of the problems facing all suppliers, the main factors likely to influence the market supply of a good *under competitive conditions*, the supply curve and the elasticity of supply.

Problems facing suppliers

Whatever its objectives, every firm needs to earn sufficient revenues to cover its costs if it is to remain in business in the long-run. In Ch. 2, we saw that a profit-maximising firm attempts to produce that quantity which will yield biggest possible profits and, of course, firms with other objectives must aim at least for some satisfactory level of profits (if only to keep their shareholders happy). In striving to achieve their objectives, then, firms would like to be able to estimate their current and future *sales revenues* and their current and future *production costs* with a reasonable degree of accuracy. It is this estimation of revenues and costs which represents a major problem to many firms.

Consider a firm which is thinking of expanding its output. To determine whether or not such a policy will be profitable, the firm has to *search* for a certain amount of information. In particular, the firm must be able to estimate the profitability of employing extra labour and capital, the cost of acquiring additional raw materials and the future demand for its product. In an uncertain world with imperfect knowledge, none of this information is easy to obtain.

The *profitability of employing extra labour*, for example, depends on the productivity of that labour and the new wage rates required to attract it to the firm, bearing in mind that the wage levels paid to newly employed labour will in most cases also have to be paid to the existing work-force. The productivity of extra labour is not known with certainty by the firm. Similarly, the wage rates and any overtime rates which the firm may have to pay to expand its output are also initially unknown – they depend to some extent on the rates prevailing in the market and will in many cases be the result of negotiations with trade unions.

Similarly, the *profitability of employing more capital*, say a new machine, depends on the price of the machine and the rate of interest which has to be paid on money borrowed to finance its purchase. This cost (which presumably can be estimated with a reasonable degree of accuracy) must then be compared with the estimated future yield of the machine, and this is not so easy to determine – it depends on future demand conditions and future prices which are not known with any certainty by the firm.

Even the *cost of acquiring additional raw materials* may not be known with certainty as it depends on future raw material prices. In the 1970s, for example, the unanticipated and very rapid rise in oil prices, together with the difficulty of finding alternative sources of energy, posed many problems for firms throughout the world. If a firm is a very large one, its own increased demand for raw materials as it expands may push prices upwards unexpectedly. On the other hand, of course, a new discovery of raw materials may cause their prices to fall substantially.

Finally, the *future demand for a firm's product* depends (as we saw in Ch. 3) not only on the future price of the product, but also on many factors which are not under the firm's control, like the prices of related goods, family income, tastes and expectations. These can be very volatile and therefore difficult to predict. Firms receive information about the demand for their product through price changes, changes in their stocks and market research. They have to use this information to estimate future trends.

Imperfect knowledge and uncertainty in the modern business world mean that firms have to employ time and resources searching for current information. The more information that is collected, the greater are the potential future profits but, of course, the more time-consuming and costly is the search.

In spite of the fact that firms face some quite severe problems in making their price and quantity decisions, it is still possible to isolate some of the factors which are likely to influence the total market supply of a good. In doing this, however, it is important to bear in mind that firms make their quantity decisions in the light of imperfect knowledge, and having determined their preferred output may even fail to produce it because of factors outside their control. In the following section, we list the likely determinants of the total supply of a *competitive* industry – that is, one in which there are many firms competing with each other and where there is relatively free entry into and exit from the industry.

Determinants of supply

The main determinants of the market supply of a good, say good X, are (a) the objectives of the firms in the industry; (b) the price of good X; (c) the prices of certain other goods; (d) the prices of factors of production; (e) the state of technology; and (f) expectations. Consider these in turn.

Objectives of the firms (O) We saw in Ch. 2 that firms can have different objectives. The nature of a firm's objectives will affect the decisions it takes. A firm which aims to maximise its sales revenue, for example, will generally supply a greater quantity than a firm aiming to maximise profits. This is illustrated in Fig. 5.1 where a single firm's total costs and total revenues are plotted against quantity supplied – the difference between the two curves representing the firm's profits. Sales revenue is maximised at output $0q_1$ where the total revenue curve reaches its maximum. Profits are maximised at output $0q_2$ where the difference between the total revenue and total cost curves is greatest: on the graph, this is also the point where the profits curve reaches its maximum. It follows from this that the total market supply of good X depends on the primary objectives of all the firms in the industry. Changes in these objectives will usually lead to changes in the quantity supplied.

Price of good X (P_X) As the price of good X rises, with all costs and the prices of all other goods unchanged, production of X becomes more profitable. Existing firms are likely, therefore, to expand their outputs and eventually new firms will be attracted into the industry. Hence total market supply will expand when price increases. This is also illustrated in Fig. 5.1 where the price rise causes the total revenue curve to shift upwards and the profit-maximising quantity to increase to $0q_3$. For example, a rise in the price of wheat, *ceteris paribus*, will create an incentive for cereal farmers to shift resources from barley and maize production into wheat production.

Fig. 5.1. ***Different objectives yielding different outputs.*** Profit is maximised at quantity $0q_2$. Total revenue is maximised at quantity $0q_1$. A rise in price causes the total revenue curve to shift upwards and raises the profit-maximising quantity to $0q_3$.

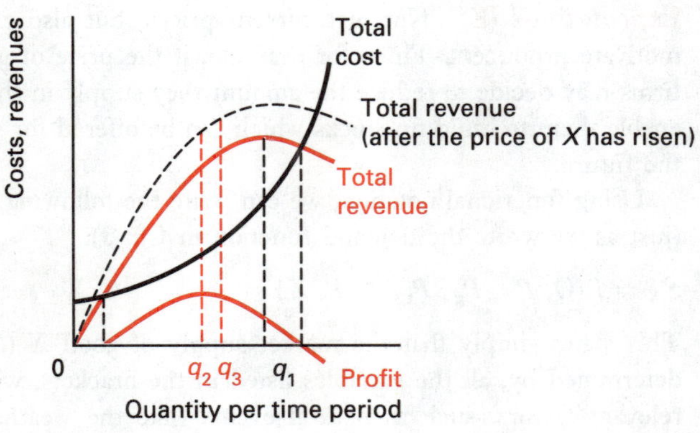

Prices of certain other goods (P_g) If the price of some other good, say Y, should rise, with the price of X unchanged, some of the firms now producing X may be tempted to move into Y production, motivated by their search for profits. A producer of wheat, for example, who sees that the price of barley has risen may decide to use more land for barley production and so reduce wheat output. Wheat and barley are said to be *substitutes in production* and in this case there is an inverse relationship between the supply of one good and the price of the other.

However, this is not the result we should expect for goods which are *complements* (like cars and petrol) or *jointly supplied* (like petrol and paraffin). An increase in the demand for, and therefore the price of, cars will lead to an increased demand for petrol: this should raise the price of petrol and so lead to an expansion rather than a contraction of supply. With petrol and paraffin, increasing the supply of one necessarily increases the supply of the other. Thus, if the demand for and price of petrol should rise, the supply of petrol should expand leading at the same time to an increase in the supply of paraffin.

It is also true, of course, that the extent to which firms can move from one industry to another in search of higher profits depends on the ease with which resources can be shifted from one use to another.

Prices of factors of production (P_f) As the prices of those factors of production used intensively by X producers rise, so do the firms' costs. This will cause supply to fall as some firms reduce output and other, less efficient, firms make losses and eventually leave the industry. Similarly, if the price of one factor of production should rise (say, land), some firms may be tempted to move out of the production of land-intensive products, like wheat, into the production of a good which is intensive in some other factor of production.

The state of technology (T) This is another factor which influences the firms' costs. Technological improvements (such as the invention of a new machine or the development of a more efficient technique of production) will reduce costs and increase the profit margin on each unit sold. Total supply can, therefore, be expected to increase.

Expectations (E) Not just current prices, but also expected future prices, will motivate producers. Thus, for example, if the price of good X is expected to rise, firms may decide to reduce the amount they supply in the current period. This will enable them to build up stocks which can be offered for sale when the price rises in the future.

Using functional notation, we can write the following *supply function* for good X (just as we wrote the demand function in Ch. 3):

$$S_X = f(O, P_X, P_g, P_f, T, E, Z)$$

This states simply that the market supply of good X (S_X) is a function of, or is determined by, all the variables listed in the brackets, where Z represents all other relevant factors, such as natural events (like the weather or an invasion of pests which destroys an agricultural crop) and the levels of taxes and subsidies.

Table 5.1 Quantities supplied of good *X* at different prices.

Price of good X (pence per unit)	Quantity supplied (units)
10	0
20	100
30	200
40	400

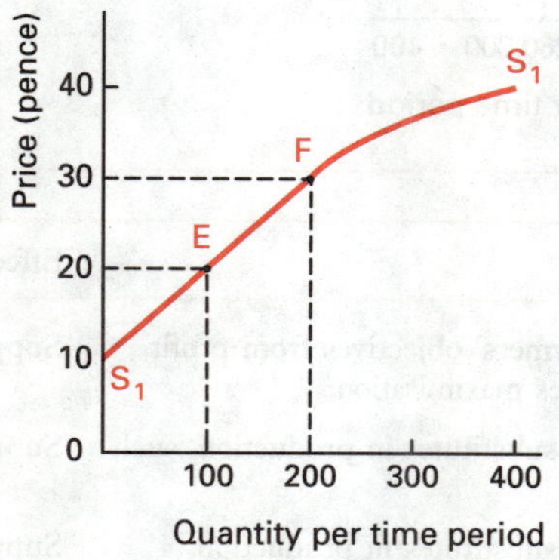

Fig. 5.2. *Supply curve.* This supply curve is constructed using the price and quantity data in Table 5.1.

The supply curve

Supply curve *The supply curve for good X shows the relationship between the prices of X and the quantities that firms are willing and able to sell at those prices,* **ceteris paribus**

In order to isolate the relationship between the supply of good *X* and its price, we need to make the *ceteris paribus* assumption and hold all the other influencing factors unchanged. We can then write:

$S_X = f(P_X)$, *ceteris paribus.*

As stated above, in a competitive market where the profit motive is a major objective of firms, this relationship between supply and price is likely to be a positive one. When plotted on a graph, then the supply curve will slope upwards from left to right so that as the price of the good increases, so does the quantity that firms are willing to supply. Table 5.1 shows some figures for the price and quantity supplied of good *X* which reflect this proposition. The corresponding supply curve is graphed in Fig. 5.2. Note that in plotting a supply curve, it is most important to specify the time period under consideration along the horizontal axis.

Movements along and shifts in the supply curve

Consider the market supply curve S_1S_1 in Fig. 5.2. Suppose that the price of *X* is 20p per unit so that the total quantity that firms are willing to supply is 100 units: that is, the combination represented by point E on the curve. If the price should rise to 30p per unit, *ceteris paribus*, quantity supplied will expand to 200 units. The change in price means that we have simply moved along the supply curve from point E to point F. (Note that this is similar to the movement along the demand curve described in Ch. 3.)

Result: *The effect of a change in the price of good X,* ceteris paribus, *can be traced by moving along good X's market supply curve.*

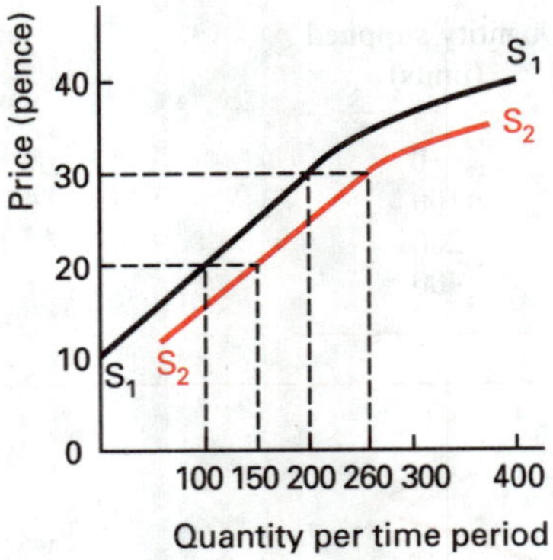

Fig. 5.3. *A shift of a supply curve.* An improvement in technology shifts the supply curve to the right from S_1S_1 to S_2S_2.

Table 5.2 Likely causes of shifts in the supply curve of wheat.

	Cause	Effect
1.	Change in cereal farmers' objectives from profit maximisation to sales maximisation.	Supply curve shifts *right*.
2.	Rise in the price of substitutes in production, such as barley.	Supply curve shifts *left*.
3.	Fall in the price of substitutes in production.	Supply curve shifts *right*.
4.	Expected rise in the price of a substitute in production.	Supply curve shifts *left*.
5.	Expected fall in the price of a substitute in production.	Supply curve shifts *right*.
6.	Rise (or expected rise) in the price of those factors used intensively in wheat production, such as land, fertiliser and seeds.	Supply curve shifts *left*.
7.	Fall (or expected fall) in the price of those factors used intensively in wheat production.	Supply curve shifts *right*.
8.	Improvement in technology which, for example, increases the speed of operation of combine harvesters.	Supply curve shifts *right*.

The whole supply curve will shift if any of the other influencing factors should change. For example, an improvement in technology which reduces the firms' costs of production will cause an increase in supply at every price and the supply curve will shift to the right. This is illustrated in Fig. 5.3 where the original supply curve for *X*, S_1S_1, is reproduced. After the improvement in technology, the curve shifts to S_2S_2, so that now at a price of 20p per unit, quantity supplied has risen to 150 units and at price 30p per unit, quantity supplied has risen to 260 units.

Result: *A change in any of the influencing factors, except the price of X, causes a shift in good X's market supply curve.*

The most likely causes of shifts in the supply curve of wheat are summarised in Table 5.2.

Fig. 5.4. Producer surplus. Producer surplus is measured by the area above the supply curve and below the prevailing market price.

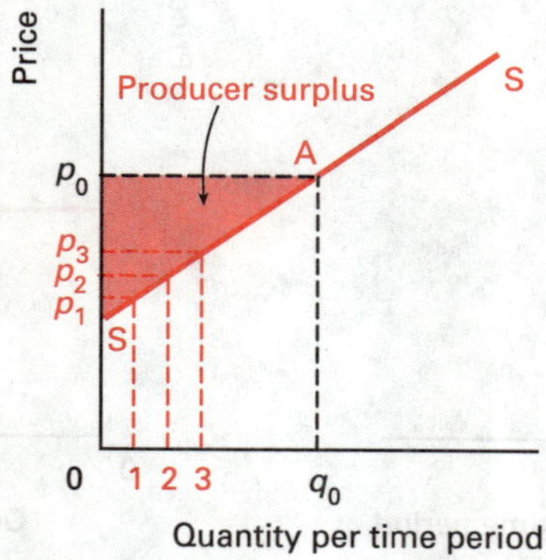

Producer surplus

Producer surplus *A measure of the difference between the actual price received and the price at which producers are willing to supply a given good*

Consider the market supply curve SS in Fig. 5.4. Recall that it shows the quantity of good X that producers are willing and able to supply over a given time period at different prices. Suppose that the prevailing market price is actually $0p_0$, so that quantity $0q_0$ is being supplied. The firms in the industry are receiving a total revenue of $0p_0 \times 0q_0$, represented by the total area $0p_0Aq_0$. It can be seen from the graph that the producers in the industry would have been prepared to supply the first unit at the much lower price of $0p_1$, the second unit at price $0p_2$, the third at $0p_3$ and so on. Since all the firms are receiving the same price ($0p_0$) for each unit sold, the area above the supply curve and below the price line, Sp_0A, can be interpreted as a gain to the producers over and above that required to keep them in business. This area is therefore sometimes called *producer surplus*. Like the related concept of consumer surplus (discussed in Ch. 4), it is useful in examining the effects of taxes and subsidies.

Elasticity of supply

The *elasticity of supply* is a measure of the extent to which the quantity supplied of a good responds to changes in one of the influencing factors. In this chapter, we concentrate on the *price* elasticity of supply (which is a measure of the responsiveness of quantity supplied to a change in the good's own price, *ceteris paribus*). It can be calculated by using the following formula:

Inelastic supply *The quantity supplied changes less than proportionately in response to a given change in price*

$$\text{Price elasticity of supply} = \frac{\text{Proportionate change in quantity supplied}}{\text{Proportionate change in price}}$$

Or in symbols, $$e_s = \frac{\Delta q/q}{\Delta p/p}$$

Elastic supply *The quantity supplied changes more than proportionately in response to a given change in price*

where $\Delta q/q$ represents the proportionate change in quantity supplied and $\Delta p/p$ represents the proportionate change in the good's price.

Supply is said to be inelastic ($e_s < 1$) when a given percentage change in price causes a smaller percentage change in quantity. It is said to be elastic ($e_s > 1$) when a given percentage change in price causes a bigger percentage change in quantity. Figure 5.5(a) illustrates perfect supply inelasticity ($e_s = 0$). This means that the fixed quantity Oq_1 will be supplied at any price; it will be supplied even at a zero

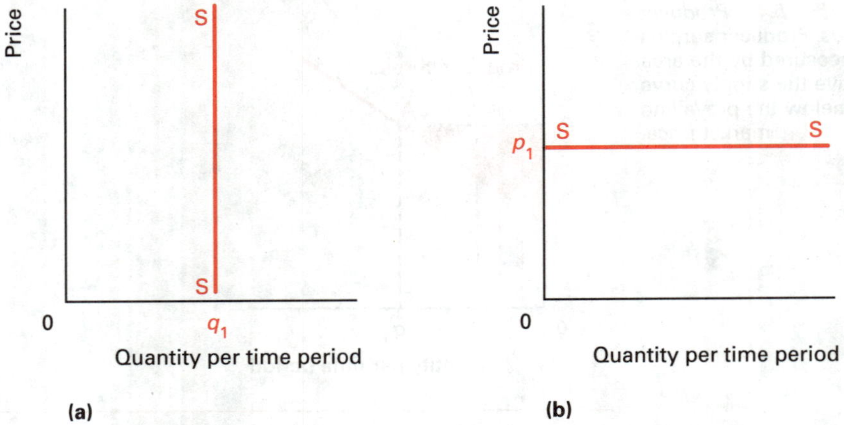

Fig. 5.5. ***Perfectly inelastic and elastic supply curves.*** (a) A vertical supply curve exhibits perfectly inelastic supply. (b) A horizontal supply curve exhibits perfectly elastic supply.

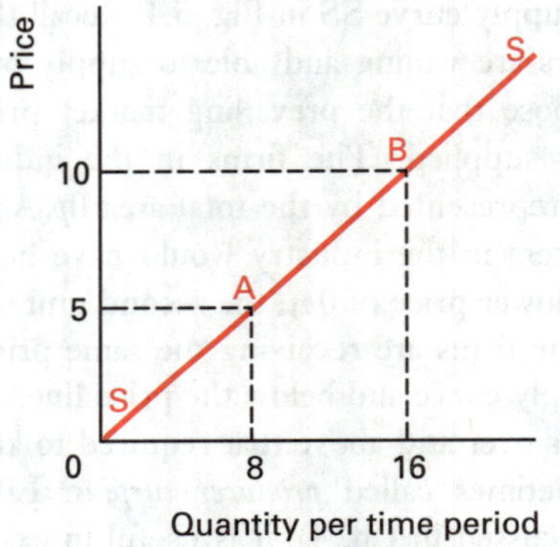

Fig. 5.6. ***Unitary supply elasticity.*** A straight-line supply curve passing through the origin has an elasticity equal to one at every point.

price. The total supply of land in the world may be regarded as being perfectly inelastic (unless, that is, we take into account the possibility of reclamation schemes). Now consider the other extreme illustrated in Fig. 5.5(b): that of perfect supply elasticity ($e_s = \infty$). In this case, nothing at all will be supplied at prices below $0p_1$; any amount will be supplied at $0P_1$; presumably (unless the supply curve eventually turns upwards) an infinite quantity will be supplied at prices above $0p_1$. Although these extremes of elasticity are possible over a certain range of prices or quantities, they are extremely unlikely over the entire range of a supply curve.

Figure 5.6 illustrates unitary elasticity of supply ($e_s = 1$). This is the case where the percentage change in quantity supplied is exactly equal to the percentage change in price. Thus, in moving from point A to point B along the supply curve in Fig. 5.6, a 100 per cent rise in price causes a 100 per cent rise in the quantity supplied. In fact, it can be demonstrated that any straight-line supply curve passing through the origin has an elasticity equal to 1.

Determinants of the elasticity of supply

Consider in turn the following three main factors which are likely to influence the elasticity of supply: (a) time; (b) excess capacity and unsold stocks; (c) the ease with which resources can shift from one industry to another.

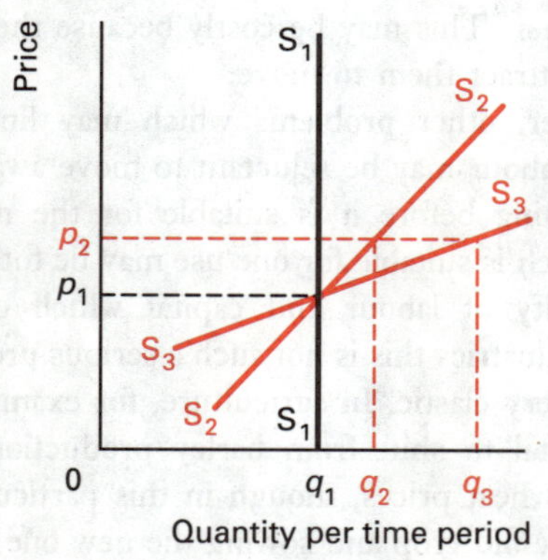

Fig. 5.7. Momentary, short- and long-run supply curves. The long-run supply curve, S_3S_3, is more elastic than the short-run supply curve, S_2S_2, in the price range p_1 to p_2. The momentary period supply curve, S_1S_1, is perfectly inelastic.

Time Since it takes time for firms to adjust the quantities they produce, the supply of a good is likely to be more elastic the longer the period of time under consideration.

In the *momentary period*, supply is limited to the quantities already available in the market and it cannot be increased even if a substantial rise in price occurs. Supply is, therefore, perfectly inelastic and is represented by supply curve S_1S_1 in Fig. 5.7 – a rise in price from $0p_1$ to $0p_2$ leaves the quantity supplied unchanged at $0q_1$. For example, the supply of bread in a single day is limited to the quantities delivered to bread shops.

In the *short-run*, supply can be increased by employing more variable factors of production. For example, more bread can be produced (in response to a rise in price) by encouraging bakers to work overtime or by employing more bakers. In this case, the supply curve will slope upwards from left to right exhibiting some degree of elasticity, but there is a limit to the increase in supply that is possible without an expansion of the scale of operations. The short-run supply curve is illustrated by S_2S_2 in Fig. 5.7 and this time a rise in price from $0p_1$ to $0p_2$ brings forth an increase in supply from $0q_1$ to $0q_2$.

In the *long-run*, the quantities of all factors of production can be increased. Existing firms can be expanded and new firms may enter the industry. In our example of bread production, existing bakeries can be expanded and new ovens and other forms of capital equipment can be installed; new bakeries may also be set up. Supply in the long-run, then, is likely to be much more elastic than in the short-run and the long-run supply curve is illustrated by S_3S_3 in Fig. 5.7. A rise in price from $0p_1$ to $0p_2$ this time brings forth an increase in supply from $0q_1$ to $0q_3$.

Excess capacity and unsold stocks In the short-run, it may be possible to increase supplies considerably if there is a pool of unemployed labour and unused machinery (known as *excess capacity*) in the industry. Similarly, if the industry has accumulated a large stock of unsold goods, supplies can quickly be increased. It follows that supply will be more elastic the greater the excess capacity in the industry and the higher the level of unsold stocks.

The ease with which resources can be shifted from one industry to another In both the short- and long-runs, in the absence of excess capacity and unsold stocks, an increase in supply requires the shifting of factors of production from one use to another. This may be costly because the prices of the factors may have to be raised to attract them to move.

There are, however, other problems which may limit the *mobility* of factors between industries. Labour may be reluctant to move away from family and friends and may need retraining before it is suitable for the new occupation. Similarly, capital equipment which is suitable for one use may be totally unsuitable for another. It is this heterogeneity of labour and capital which can severely restrict their mobility. In certain industries this is not such a serious problem and, given sufficient time, supply can be very elastic. In agriculture, for example, it is quite possible for both labour and capital to shift from barley production to wheat production in response to a rise in wheat prices, though in this particular example time must be allowed for reaping the old crop and sowing the new one. In many other industries, however, labour may have to be completely retrained and new capital equipment may have to be acquired. In such cases, supply will be inelastic, except over a very long time period.

Note that the mobility of labour is discussed in greater detail in Ch. 16.

Summary

1. The market supply of a good may be defined as the sum of the quantities that individual firms are willing and able to offer for sale over a given time period.
2. Supply is likely to depend on a number of factors, including the good's price, the prices of certain related goods, the objectives of the firms in the industry, the prices of factors of production, the state of technology and expectations.
3. A supply curve shows the relationship between the quantity supplied of a good and the good's price, on the assumption that all the other influencing factors remain unchanged (that is *ceteris paribus*). In competitive markets where the profit motive is paramount, the supply curve is likely to have a positive slope.
4. The effect on quantity supplied of a change in a good's price can be traced out by moving along the good's supply curve. The supply curve will shift if any of the other influencing factors should change.
5. Producer surplus may be defined as the difference between the total amount that producers receive for any given quantity of a good and the minimum amount they would have been willing to accept for it.
6. Price elasticity of supply measures the extent to which the quantity supplied of a good responds to changes in the good's price, *ceteris paribus*. The main determinants of the elasticity of supply are time, the existence of excess capacity, and the ease with which resources can be shifted from one use to another.

Exercises

1. Review your understanding of the following terms:

market supply	elasticity of supply
supply function	momentary period
supply curve	short-run
joint supply	long-run
producer surplus	

2. Consider the following price and quantity supplied data for good X:

Price	2	4	6	8	10	12
Quantity supplied	25	35	45	55	65	75

   (a) Plot the supply curve on a graph.
   (b) Calculate the elasticity of supply at price = £4 and at price = £10.
   (c) Suppose that a rise in raw material costs causes the producer to reduce supply by 15 units at every price. Repeat exercises (a) and (b).

3. Discuss the main determinants in the United Kingdom of the market supply of: (a) beef; and (b) guest house accommodation in a holiday resort.

4. Discuss the main determinants of the elasticity of supply of: (a) oil; and (b) shoes.

5. Describe the likely effect on the market supply of wheat of:
   (a) a prolonged drought;
   (b) the introduction of a cost-reducing combine harvester;
   (c) an increase in the demand for barley;
   (d) a reduction in the demand for bread. Be careful to distinguish between *movements along* and *shifts in* the supply curve in your answers.

6 EQUILIBRIUM AND DISEQUILIBRIUM

Learning objectives

After reading this chapter, you should be able to:

- define the meaning of an equilibrium in a market and distinguish between stable and unstable equilibria
- apply simple demand and supply analysis to illustrate the interaction that occurs between the markets for substitutes, complements and jointly-supplied goods
- analyse the effects on a good's equilibrium price and quantity of the imposition of a sales tax
- show the effects of imposing artificial restrictions in a market, such as price ceilings or floors
- describe other situations in which disequilibrium prices and quantities may be expected to persist
- trace out a time-path from a disequilibrium position towards an equilibrium position in the cobweb model
- show that in practice, given imperfect knowledge and uncertainty, equilibrium values may be approached only after an extensive period of search

Introduction

Equilibrium *A state of rest in which no economic forces are being generated to change the situation*

In Chs 3–5, we have analysed separately the important concepts of demand and supply. Our next task is to bring these two concepts together and see how interaction between them can determine the market price of a good. We start by explaining the meaning of an equilibrium in economics and by considering some applications of equilibrium analysis. By examining the effects of shifts in the demand and supply curves, we are able to make predictions about the effects of certain changes in the economy on the equilibrium price and equilibrium quantity of particular goods and services.

In the second half of the chapter, the more modern approach to demand and supply analysis is considered. This takes us into the area of disequilibrium economics and search theory where we study the dynamics of the movement from one equilibrium to another.

Equilibrium

Equilibrium market price *The price at which the quantity demanded is equal to the quantity supplied. It is also known as the market clearing price*

Figure 6.1 shows the demand and supply curves of a 'normal' good *X* on the same graph. Remember that these curves are drawn on the assumption that all influencing factors except price remain unchanged (that is, *ceteris paribus*). When the price of *X* is $0p_e$, the demand for *X* and the supply of *X* are just equal: this is called an equilibrium position and $0p_e$ is called the equilibrium market price. At this price, the amount that producers are willing and able to supply to the market is just equal to the amount that buyers are willing and able to buy: both producers and buyers can be satisfied and there will be no pressure on the price to change.

Now consider Fig. 6.2. When the price of *X* is $0p_1$, quantity demanded is $0q_1$, but producers are willing to supply $0q_2$. There is an *excess supply* of *X* equal to q_1q_2. Note that an excess supply exists whenever quantity demanded is less than quantity supplied at the prevailing market price. Producers may react to this by reducing price in an attempt to sell off their unsold stocks – excess supply, then, represents an economic force which exerts downward pressure on price. When the price of *X* is $0p_2$, however, quantity demanded is $0q_4$ but producers are only willing to supply $0q_3$. Now there is *excess demand* for *X* equal to q_3q_4. Excess demand exists whenever quantity demanded is greater than quantity supplied at the prevailing market price. This time it is not unreasonable to suppose that competition amongst buyers will bid the price upwards. Producers are in a position where they can sell all they are producing and more at higher prices. Excess demand, then, is an economic force which exerts upward pressure on price. Prices $0p_1$ and $0p_2$ and all other prices except $0p_e$ are called *disequilibrium* prices.

Comparative static equilibrium analysis *A method of analysis that compares different equilibrium situations when the initial equilibrium is disturbed by a change in a variable*

Since much work in economics has been concerned with comparing one equilibrium state with another at a moment in time (often called comparative static equilibrium analysis), it is very important to understand what is meant by an equilibrium.

In the market for a good, such a state of rest can be said to exist when there is neither any excess demand for nor any excess supply of the good. In other words, the general rule for an equilibrium to exist in a market is that *demand should be equal to supply*.

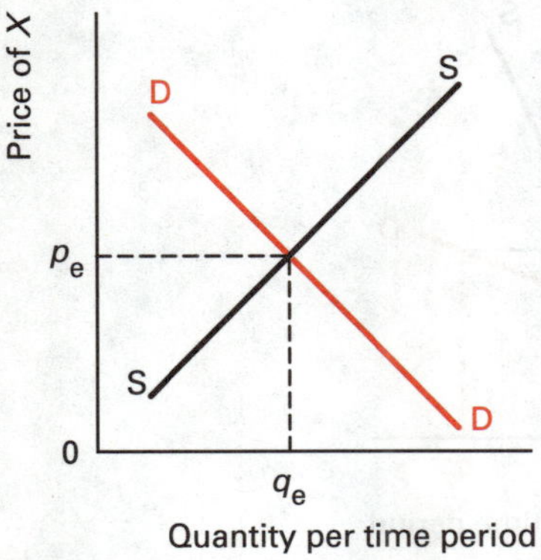

Fig. 6.1. Equilibrium in the market for good *X*. The point at which the demand and supply curves intersect determines the equilibrium price, $0p_e$, and quantity, $0q_e$.

Fig. 6.2. Graph illustrating excess demand and excess supply. At prices above $0p_e$, there is an excess supply which pushes the price down. At prices below $0p_e$, there is an excess demand which pushes the price up.

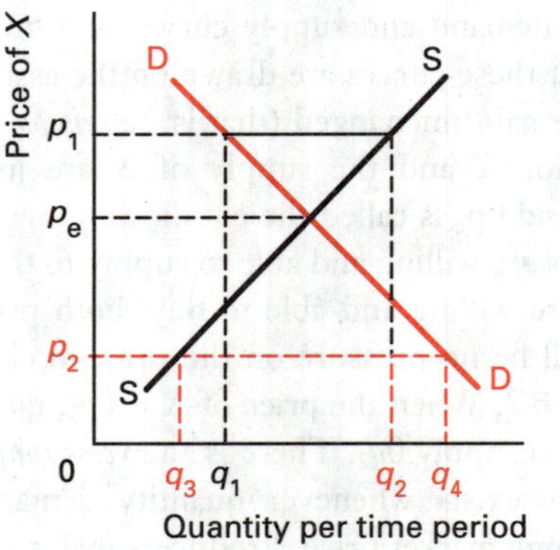

Stable and unstable equilibria

Stable equilibrium *One, such that any divergence from the equilibrium sets up forces which restore the equilibrium*

Unstable equilibrium *One, such that any divergence from the equilibrium sets up forces which push the price further away from the equilibrium price*

An equilibrium is said to be a stable equilibrium when economic forces tend to push the market towards it. In other words, any divergence from the equilibrium position sets up forces which tend to restore the equilibrium. This is the case in the market for good *X* illustrated in Fig. 6.1 and Fig. 6.2. The equilibrium at price $0p_e$ is stable because the establishment of any disequilibrium price, like $0p_1$ or $0p_2$, sets up economic forces (excess supply in the case of $0p_1$ and excess demand in the case of $0p_2$) which, given competition among buyers and sellers, tend to push the price back towards $0p_e$.

Now consider Fig. 6.3 which illustrates the market for good *Y*, which has a demand curve sloping upwards from left to right. Good *Y* might be a Giffen or a Veblen good. Price $0p_e$ is the equilibrium price and quantity $0q_e$ is the equilibrium quantity. This equilibrium, however, is an unstable one. To show this, suppose the disequilibrium price, $0p_1$, is established. This creates excess demand equal to q_1q_2 which pushes the price upwards, even further away from $0p_e$. Similarly, if the price were $0p_2$, the excess supply equal to q_3q_4 would tend to push the price even further downwards.

Fig. 6.3. An unstable equilibrium. The 'abnormal' demand curve means that at prices above $0p_e$, there is excess demand which pushes the price upwards and away from the equilibrium. Similarly, at prices below $0p_e$, there is excess supply which pushes the price even further down.

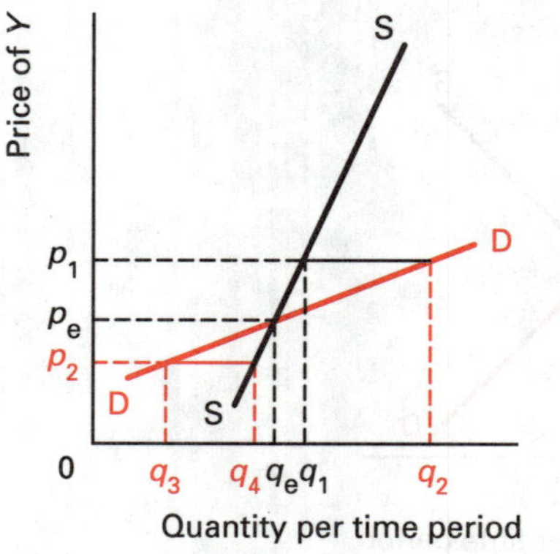

Thus, although equilibria are states of rest at which no economic forces exist to change the situation, it is important to remember that not all equilibria are stable. The equilibrium in Fig. 6.3 is sometimes called a *knife-edge* equilibrium, because a small change in price sends the system well away from equilibrium.

Some applications of equilibrium analysis

In this section, we consider two main applications of equilibrium analysis: the first enables us to analyse the interaction which can occur among the markets for related goods; the second illustrates the effects of a sales tax on a good.

Substitutes, complements and jointly supplied goods

Substitutes *Products, such as butter and margarine, which are similar in that they satisfy the same wants*

Complementary (or jointly demanded) goods *Products which are used together to satisfy a want*

Jointly supplied goods *Products, such as oil and gas, that result from the same production activity*

As a simple illustration of the interaction that can occur between markets, consider the market for *cod* in the United Kingdom. Cod is a fish which can be bought by consumers in a number of different forms: for example, it is available fresh from fishmongers, frozen from supermarkets and cooked in batter and served with chips from the famous English fish and chip shops! It has a number of close substitutes, like haddock, and a number of less close substitutes, like hamburgers. It also has a number of complementary goods like batter, bread-crumbs, chips and cooking-oil, the demands for which tend to increase as the demand for cod increases. These are all demanded jointly with cod. (Other examples of jointly demanded or complementary goods include cars and petrol, and right and left shoes.)

A by-product of cod is cod-liver oil. Since an increase in the supply of cod also increases the supply of cod-liver oil, they are said to be *jointly supplied* goods. (Other examples of jointly supplied goods are petrol and paraffin, and coal gas and coke.)

Now suppose that the supply of cod to the United Kingdom is reduced following a political decision to restrict access to fishing grounds. Consider the likely effects of this on the market for cod, the market for a *substitute good* (say, haddock), the market for a complementary good (say, chips) and the market for a jointly supplied good (cod-liver oil). Figure 6.4 illustrates the likely effect on the market for cod itself. The restriction of access to fishing grounds causes the supply curve to shift from SS to

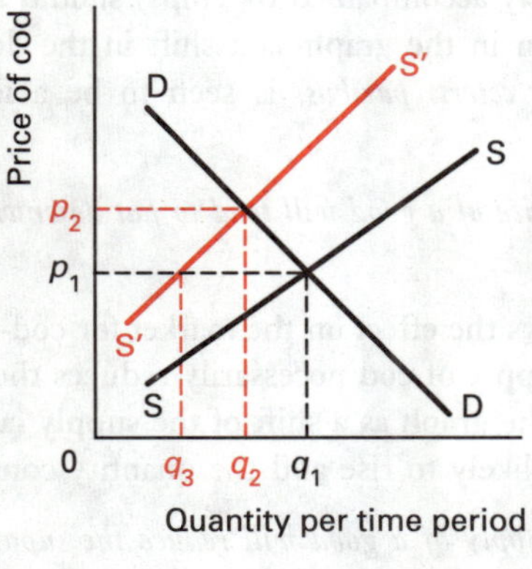

Fig. 6.4. *The market for cod.* A decrease in the supply of cod causes the supply curve to shift from SS to S′S′. Equilibrium price rises from $0p_1$ to $0p_2$ and equilibrium quantity falls from $0p_1$ to $0p_2$.

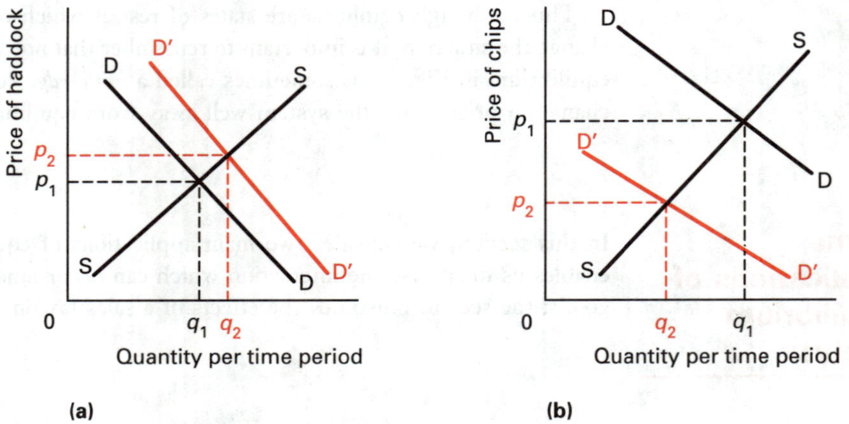

Fig. 6.5. (a) The market for haddock (a substitute for cod). Demand increases causing a rise in price from $0p_1$ to $0p_2$ and a rise in quantity from $0q_1$ to $0q_2$. *(b) The market for chips (a complement to cod).* Demand falls causing a fall in price from $0p_1$ to $0p_2$ and a fall in quantity from $0q_1$ to $0q_2$.

S′S′. Excess demand of q_3q_1 at price $0p_1$ then exerts upward pressure on price until it rises to the new equilibrium level of $0p_2$. Quantity demanded will fall from $0q_1$ to $0q_2$ because of the price rise. So the overall effect on the market for cod, *ceteris paribus*, is a rise in price and a reduction in quantity consumed.

Figure 6.5(a) shows the likely effect on the market for haddock. The rise in the price of cod causes consumers to shift their spending on to a variety of substitute goods, including haddock. Thus there will be an increase in the demand for haddock, shown in the graph as a shift in the demand curve from DD to D′D′. This will push up the price of haddock from $0p_1$ to $0p_2$. The total quantity supplied will also expand (because of the price rise) from $0q_1$ to $0q_2$. So the overall effect on the market for haddock, *ceteris paribus*, is a rise in price and an increase in quantity consumed.

Result: *A rise in a good's price will tend to put upward pressure on the price of substitutes.*

Figure 6.5(b) shows the likely effect on the market for chips. The fall in the consumption of cod and the increase in the consumption of substitute goods (some of which are not normally accompanied by chips) should reduce the overall demand for chips. This is shown in the graph as a shift in the demand curve from DD to D′D′. The final effect, *ceteris paribus*, is seen to be a fall in both the price and quantity consumed.

Result: *A rise in the price of a good will tend to put downward pressure on the prices of complementary goods.*

Finally, Fig. 6.6 shows the effect on the market for cod-liver oil, a jointly supplied good. The fall in the supply of cod necessarily reduces the supply of cod-liver oil as well. This is shown in the graph as a shift of the supply curve from SS to S′S′. The price of cod-liver oil is likely to rise and the quantity consumed fall.

Result: *A fall in the supply of a good will reduce the supply of jointly supplied goods, thereby raising their prices.*

Fig. 6.6. The market for cod-liver oil (a good jointly supplied with cod). The supply of cod-liver oil falls causing a rise in price from $0p_1$ to $0p_2$ and a fall in quantity from $0q_1$ to $0q_2$.

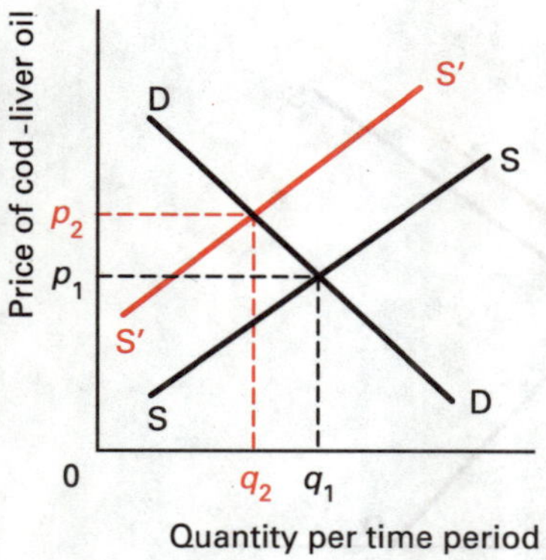

Notice that the above analysis represents a preliminary approach to 'general equilibrium' analysis – that is, instead of merely examining a single market in isolation, we have attempted to show some of the interaction that occurs among markets. Our analysis does not show all the interaction, though. When the price of haddock rises, for example, this will have a secondary repercussion on the market for cod which we have not taken into account.

The effects of a sales tax

Consider Table 6.1 on the next page which shows the quantities demanded and supplied of good *X* at different prices. The demand and supply curves are shown as DD and SS respectively in Fig. 6.7. The initial equilibrium price is £30 per unit and the equilibrium quantity is 60,000 units.

Sales tax *A type of indirect tax imposed on the sale of a product. A specific or per unit sales tax refers to the imposition of a tax equal to a given sum of money on each unit sold*

Now suppose that a sales tax of £5 per unit sold is imposed on good *X* and collected from the suppliers: i.e. for every unit of *X* sold, the suppliers have to pay £5 in tax to the government. The supply curve shows the amounts per unit that suppliers must *receive* to induce them to supply different quantities. Thus, before the tax was imposed, suppliers were willing to supply 30,000 units at a price of £20 per unit and 60,000 units at a price of £30 per unit. After the sales tax is imposed, however, they will only be willing to supply 30,000 units at a price of £25 and 60,000 units at a price of £35. In other words, the supply curve will have shifted vertically upwards *by the full amount of the tax*. The new supply curve is S_TS_T in Fig. 6.7: the new equilibrium price is £33 per unit and the new equilibrium quantity is 54,000 units.

Notice that consumers are paying £3 per unit more than before: this represents their share of the tax. The suppliers are paying the remaining share of the tax (£2 per unit). The distribution of the tax between demanders and suppliers is called the *effective incidence* of the tax. Tax incidence is discussed further in Ch. 14.

The effective incidence depends on the elasticities of demand and supply. To take extreme examples, if the demand curve were perfectly elastic or if the supply curve were perfectly inelastic, the tax incidence would be entirely on the suppliers. These

Fig. 6.7. *The effect of a sales tax.* The demand and supply curves, DD and SS, are constructed from the data in Table 6.1. A sales tax of £5 per unit shifts the supply curve vertically upwards by £5 to S_TS_T.

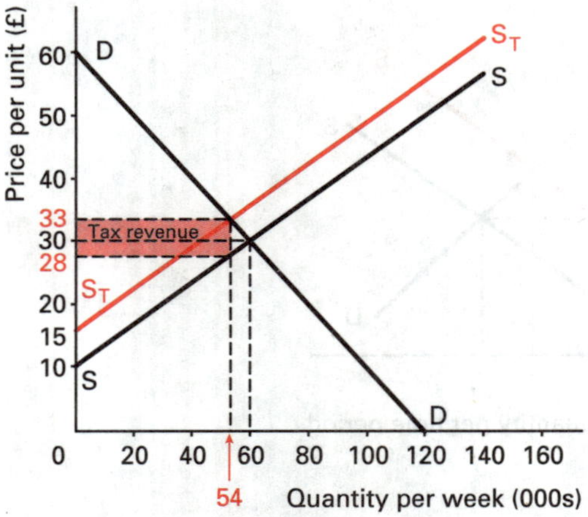

Table 6.1 Quantities demanded and supplied at different prices.

Price per unit (£)	10	20	30	40	50	60
Quantity demanded per week (000s)	100	80	60	40	20	0
Quantity supplied per week (000s)	0	30	60	90	120	150

cases are shown in Fig. 6.8(a) and (b). In both cases, the price paid by the consumer remains unchanged at $0p$ when the tax is imposed. Notice that in Fig. 6.8(b), the vertical supply curve remains unaffected by the tax: suppliers are willing to sell $0q$ units at *any* price.

If the demand curve were perfectly inelastic or the supply curve perfectly elastic, the tax incidence would fall entirely on the buyers of the good. These cases are shown in Fig. 6.9(a) and (b). In both cases, the equilibrium market price paid by consumers rises by the full amount of the tax, from $0p$ to $0p'$.

In general, we can say that the more *inelastic* is the demand curve and the more *elastic* is the supply curve, the greater will be the share of the sales tax falling on *consumers*. Similarly, the more *elastic* is the demand curve and the more *inelastic* is the supply curve, the greater will be the share of the tax falling on *suppliers*.

Subsidy *A cash sum given by a government to producers. A subsidy may take the form of a given cash sum for each unit produced*

A similar analysis may be used to examine the effects of a subsidy. A subsidy of £5 per unit paid to the producers of good *X* would cause the supply curve to shift vertically downwards by the full amount of the subsidy. As in the case of a sales tax, the effect on price and quantity depends on the elasticity of both demand and supply.

Disequilibrium analysis

A disequilibrium is said to exist in a market when the quantity demanded is not equal to the quantity supplied. In other words, it is a state in which either excess demand or excess supply exists.

Fig. 6.8. ***The cases where the incidence of a sales tax falls entirely on suppliers.*** In both cases, the sales tax leaves the market price unchanged, so that suppliers have to bear the entire burden of the tax.

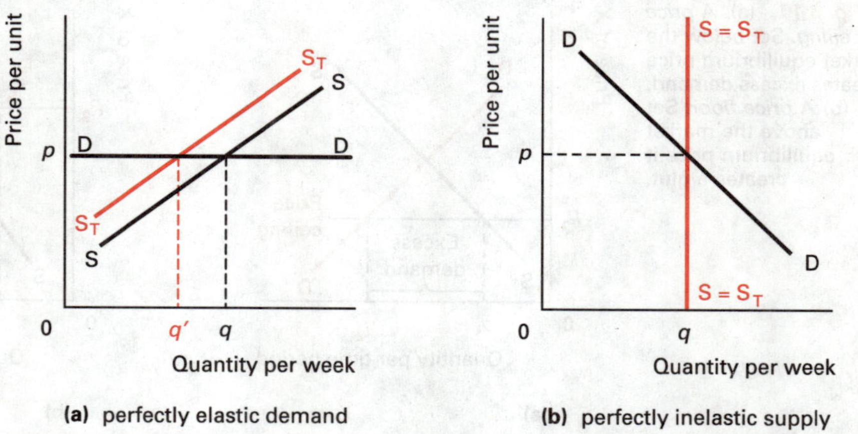

Fig. 6.9. ***The cases where the incidence of a sales tax falls entirely on consumers.*** In these cases, the market price rises by the full amount of the tax, so that consumers have to bear the entire tax burden.

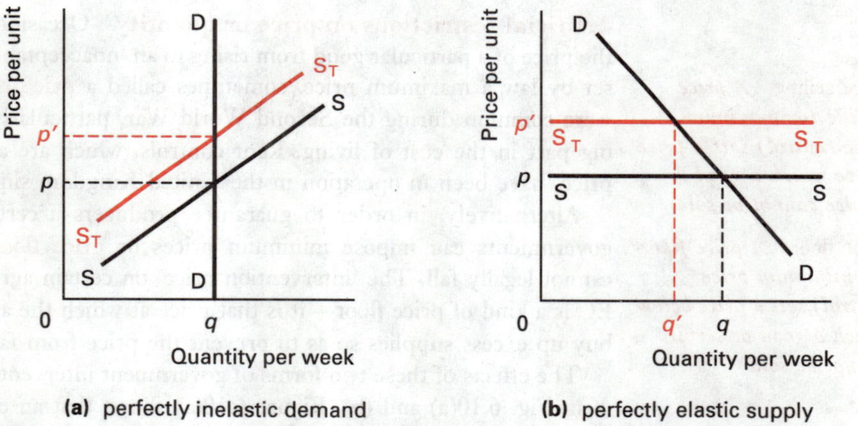

Disequilibrium *A situation in which the expectations of buyers and sellers in a market are not realised. Therefore, the market is in a state of flux, and economic forces are being generated to change the situation*

In our analysis so far, we have assumed that when either of these two economic forces exists, equilibrium will quickly be restored. For example, if we start from an equilibrium position and the supply of good *X* is reduced for any reason, excess demand in the market exerts upward pressure on price until a new equilibrium position is reached. If this return to equilibrium were instantaneous, or at least very speedy, there would be little point in studying disequilibrium economics. If the disequilibrium state should persist for any length of time, however, disequilibrium analysis would perhaps be more important and relevant than equilibrium analysis. Disequilibria can, and do, persist in markets in the following circumstances:

(a) where the government or other bodies impose artificial restrictions on either price or quantity;
(b) where the market equilibrium is an unstable one;
(c) where production plans are not realised;
(d) where there are lagged responses.

Consider these in turn.

Fig. 6.10. (a). *A price ceiling.* Set below the market equilibrium price it creates excess demand. (b) *A price floor.* Set above the market equilibrium price it creates a glut.

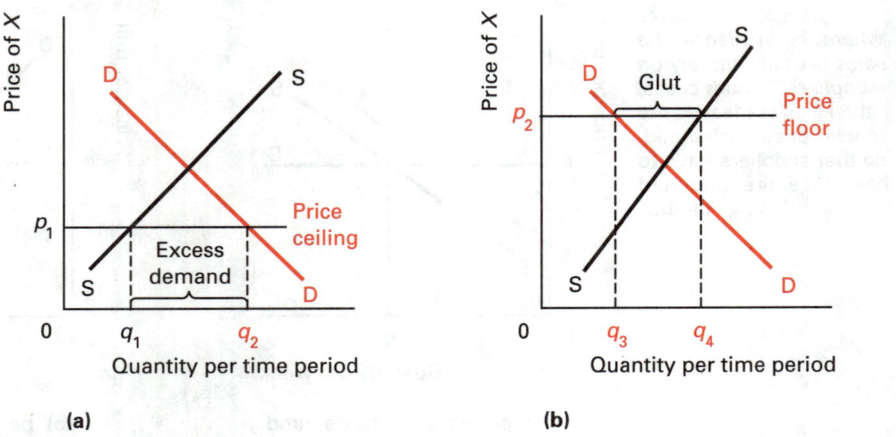

Artificial restrictions on price or quantity Occasionally, in an attempt to stop the price of a particular good from rising to an 'unacceptable' level, governments have set by law a maximum price, sometimes called a price ceiling. Such price ceilings were common during the Second World War, particularly on items which played a big part in the cost of living. Rent controls, which are another form of maximum price, have been in operation in the United Kingdom since 1917.

Price ceiling *A price ceiling (or maximum price control) sets a price above which a good or service cannot be sold*

Alternatively, in order to guarantee producers a certain return on their sales, governments can impose minimum prices or price floors below which the price cannot legally fall. The 'intervention price' on certain agricultural goods sold in the EC is a kind of price floor – it is that price at which the authorities will intervene to buy up excess supplies so as to prevent the price from falling any further.

Price floor *A price floor (or minimum price control) sets a price below which a good or service cannot be sold*

The effects of these two forms of government intervention are illustrated for good *X* in Fig. 6.10(a) and (b). Figure 6.10(a) shows that an excess demand for good *X* occurs when a price ceiling is imposed at $0p_1$ which is below the equilibrium price. Since the price is not allowed to rise back towards the equilibrium, unsatisfied demand exists and this will show itself in queues forming.

At first, *X* may be allocated on a 'first come, first served' basis, but often sellers start to restrict sales to 'so many' per customer, or even to serve only their regular customers. Eventually a 'black market' may develop. In an attempt to allocate the limited supplies fairly, the government may adopt a system of *rationing* – with ration coupons being issued which enable the recipients to buy a limited quantity at the maximum price. Rationing (which involves restricting quantity as well as price) is never entirely satisfactory because many buyers are still unable to obtain the good in the quantities they desire, but it can be argued that it is fairer than simply controlling price.

Figure 6.10(b) shows the effects of a price floor at $0p_2$ which is above the equilibrium price. This time, there is an excess supply of good *X*, sometimes called a *glut*. Where the price floor is established by the authorities intervening to purchase excess supplies, the glut will show itself mainly in an increase in the authorities' stocks of the good. This is the origin of the so-called 'butter mountains' and 'wine lakes' of the EC. In the event of a price ceiling or price floor being set on a good at a price which is not the equilibrium one, the economic forces of excess demand and excess supply will not be able to restore the equilibrium. The disequilibrium will persist, then, for as long as the restrictions are maintained.

Unstable equilibria Where an equilibrium is unstable so that any divergence from it generates an economic force which pushes the market even further away from it, disequilibrium positions may be expected to persist. As an example, consider Fig. 6.11 which shows the market for a Giffen good, like rice in a country where most people spend most of their income on rice. Suppose that at price $0p_e$ (an equilibrium price) people are able to afford a small quantity of more expensive food products, like meat, in addition to rice. If a disturbance occurs so that the price of rice should rise above $0p_e$, consumers will find that they can no longer afford so much meat and have to spend a bigger and bigger proportion of their incomes on rice. The rising price, therefore, creates excess demand and so no pressure is being generated which will restore the original equilibrium. In other words, the equilibrium at point A in Fig. 6.11 is an unstable one.

How long a disequilibrium position of this kind can persist will depend on how abnormal the demand curve for the good is. In the case of a Giffen good, there must be some point beyond which demand will fall if price continues to rise. Eventually, when rice is the only food being eaten, it will no longer be possible to substitute rice for meat and, at that price ($0p_1$ in the graph), total consumption of rice must be cut back. A new equilibrium will then be restored, as at point B in Fig. 6.11. Notice that point B represents a stable equilibrium.

Failure of production plans to be realised In some industries, because of the possibility of unforeseen events happening, the quantities that producers *plan* to supply may fail to be achieved for a variety of reasons. On the one hand, *actual* supply can fall short of *planned* supply if events not under the producers' control (for example, strikes) mean that production targets cannot be met. On the other hand, *actual* supply may exceed *planned* supply if producers underestimate the productive capacity of their resources. Unplanned fluctuations in supply will affect the market price and also, therefore, the producers' incomes.

This problem of fluctuating supply from one period of time to another has been particularly severe in the case of *agriculture*, and this explains why the prices of

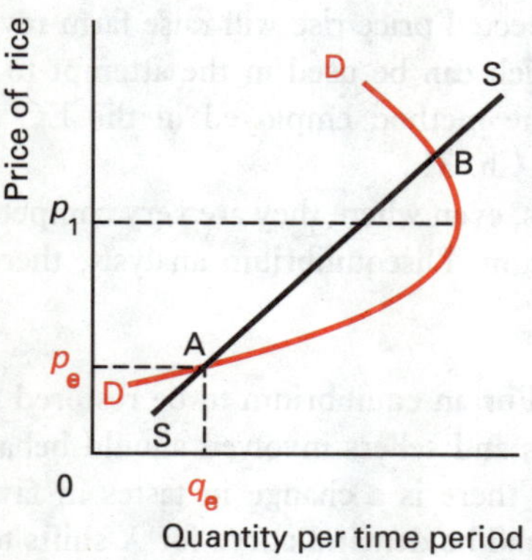

Fig. 6.11. The market for rice, a Giffen good. DD is an 'abnormal' demand curve and point A represents an unstable equilibrium. Point B represents a stable equilibrium.

Fig. 6.12. ***The market for an agricultural product.*** **Unforeseen events can cause the actual quantity produced to fall short of or exceed planned supply, leading to price fluctuations.**

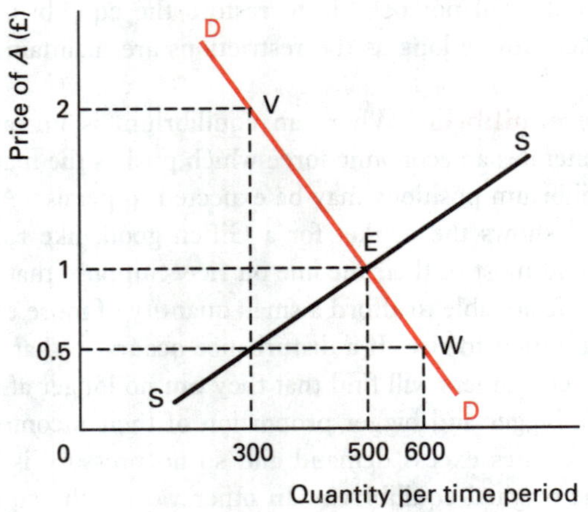

agricultural products tend to fluctuate more than the prices of manufactured goods. To show this, consider the graph in Fig. 6.12 which illustrates the market for the agricultural good *A*. Suppose that at the equilibrium price of £1 per unit, farmers plan to produce 500 units (point E on the supply curve). Assume, however, that because of unexpectedly unfavourable weather conditions or an unexpected attack by destructive insects, actual production is only 300 units. At price £1 per unit, excess demand will exist and this will exert upward pressure on price until it reaches £2 per unit (point V on the demand curve).

Another possibility is that there may be unexpectedly favourable weather conditions or an unusual absence of pests, so that actual production exceeds the planned 500 units – say, 600 units as shown in Fig. 6.12. This time, at a price of £1 per unit, excess supply will put downward pressure on price until it reaches 50p (point W on the demand curve).

In this example, points V and W cannot be regarded as equilibrium points even though quantity demanded is equal to the actual quantity supplied. The reason is that in the next period, producers would plan to increase production if price remained at £2, and reduce production if price remained at 50p. Quantity supplied would then not equal quantity demanded at those prices.

These price fluctuations will, of course, affect farmers' revenues and therefore farmers' incomes. With inelastic demand, an unexpected price fall will lower farm revenues and an unexpected price rise will raise farm revenues. There are a number of policy measures which can be used in the attempt to stabilise agricultural prices and farm incomes. The method employed in the EC (the Common Agricultural Policy) is described in Ch. 31.

Agricultural markets, even where they are very competitive, are extremely unlikely ever to be in equilibrium. Disequilibrium analysis, therefore, is very important in such markets.

Lagged responses For an equilibrium to be restored following a disturbance, we require that the buyers and sellers involved should behave in a particular way. For example, suppose that there is a change in tastes in favour of good *X* so that the demand for it increases. The demand curve for *X* shifts to the right as shown in Fig. 6.13 and the equilibrium point shifts from A to B. For the movement from A to B to

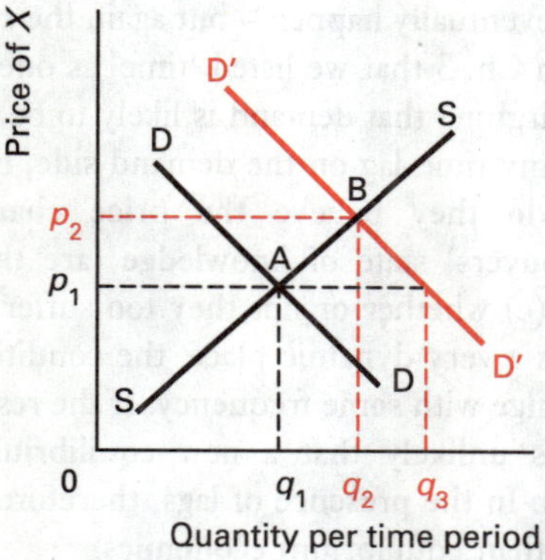

Fig. 6.13. *An increase in demand for good X.* When demand increases from DD to D′D′, the movement from A to the new equilibrium at B may be delayed by lagged responses.

be a swift one, the following behaviour is necessary: (a) the excess demand q_1q_3 must cause sellers to raise their prices from $0p_1$ to $0p_2$; (b) the higher prices must cause sellers to expand quantity supplied from $0q_1$ to $0q_2$; and (c) the higher prices must cause buyers to contract their purchases from $0q_3$ to $0q_2$. These responses are indeed the most likely ones, but they may not occur instantaneously – instead, there may be *lags* which will cause the market to remain in disequilibrium for some period of time. Lags may occur because of *imperfect information, expectations, inertia* or for *technological reasons*.

Lags on the supply side For firms to respond to the increased demand they have to be aware that it has occurred. Since they only have *imperfect information*, it may take some time before increased sales figures or an increased number of enquiries concerning their product convinces them that an actual increase in demand has taken place. Even then, they will not necessarily increase price immediately – it depends upon whether they expect the increased demand to be permanent or temporary. Only if their *expectations* are optimistic will price finally be raised and, as we shall see later, the formation of expectations can be very time-consuming. Apart from the formation of expectations, some firms may respond very slowly because they suffer from *psychological inertia* – that is, they are set in their ways and insensitive to changing conditions. Assuming that firms do eventually recognise the increase in demand, do expect it to be permanent and are not suffering from inertia, the price of the product will be raised. Our model next predicts an expansion of quantity supplied, but in many industries this will only be possible after a time-lag for technological reasons. This kind of lag is sometimes called a *production lag*. It arises because it takes time for firms to organise the additional factors of production necessary to increase output and this will be particularly difficult if the economy as a whole is close to full employment – then additional labour and capital will be scarce and expensive to acquire. Agriculture provides a good example of a production lag – output can only be increased after one whole season because time has to be allowed for the growing of the new crop.

Lags on the demand side For the equilibrium in Fig. 6.13 to be restored quickly, we require that buyers should reduce their demand from $0q_3$ to $0q_2$ as price rises from $0p_1$ to $0p_2$. Assuming that the demand curve D′D′ is an accurate and stable relationship, this must eventually happen – but again the crucial question is: how long will it take? Recall from Ch. 3 that we listed 'time' as one of the determinants of the 'elasticity of demand', arguing that demand is likely to be less elastic in the short-run than in the long-run. Any time-lag on the demand side, then, will depend on (a) the buyers' *expectations* (do they believe the price change to be permanent or temporary?); (b) the buyers' state of knowledge (are they aware of the prices of available substitutes?); (c) whether or not they too suffer from inertia.

Since an economy is a very dynamic place, the conditions of demand and supply may be expected to change with some frequency. If the responses to any given change are lagged, it becomes unlikely that a new equilibrium will be reached before something else changes. In the presence of lags, therefore, disequilibrium economics may be more valuable than equilibrium economics.

An application of disequilibrium analysis

A very simple model which enables us to trace out a time-path from a disequilibrium position towards an equilibrium position, given the presence of a production lag, is the so-called *cobweb model*. This was originally used to analyse the market for hogs in the United States, but it is a rather oversimplified theory and is presented here only as an illustration of dynamic, disequilibrium analysis. More complex versions of the cobweb model are unfortunately outside the scope of this book.

Suppose that the demand for hogs depends on this year's market price, but that this year's supply depends on *last* year's price. This is not unreasonable because if prices were high last year, farmers would have reared many hogs in the expectation of high prices this year; if prices were low last year, farmers would have reared fewer hogs in the expectation of low prices this year. Using functional notation, we can write:

$$D_h = f(p_t)$$
$$S_h = f(p_e), \text{ where } \quad p_e = p_{t-1}$$

D_h and S_h represent the demand for and supply of hogs respectively, p_t is this year's price, p_e is the price which farmers last year expected would prevail this year, and p_{t-1} is last year's price. The important point to remember is that any change in price leads to an immediate change in quantity demanded, but only a lagged change in quantity supplied, the production lag being one year. Consider Fig. 6.14. Suppose we start in year 1 with a disequilibrium price of $0p_1$. The quantity supplied in year 2 (which depends on the price in year 1) will be $0q_2$, but to sell this quantity of hogs the price in year 2 will have to be reduced to $0p_2$. This price will bring forth a supply of $0q_3$ in year 3. This quantity can, however, be sold at the higher price $0p_3$ and this will bring forth a supply of $0q_4$ in year 4. This process will continue year after year, tracing out a cobweb pattern on the graph, with the market slowly approaching the equilibrium position. As drawn in Fig. 6.14 and assuming *ceteris paribus*, the equilibrium will eventually be reached. This is an example of a damped cobweb. The *ceteris paribus* assumption is rather unrealistic in this case since the path to equilibrium takes several years. It is also possible for the cobweb pattern to be explosive so that instead of moving closer and closer to the equilibrium each year, the market moves further and further away from it.

Damped cobweb *This depicts a market that moves over a number of periods towards the equilibrium price and quantity*

Explosive cobweb *This depicts a market that moves over a number of periods away from the equilibrium price and quantity*

It must be emphasised that the above cobweb model represents a very simple approach to disequilibrium analysis. It only introduces a production lag – it does not

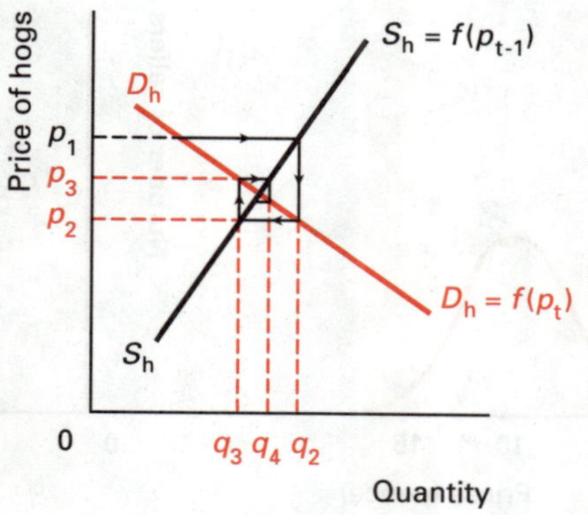

Fig. 6.14. The cobweb model. The graph shows how an agricultuural market may move from a disequilibrium price $0p_1$ towards the equilibrium, tracing out a cobweb pattern.

take any account of inertia, expectations or imperfect knowledge on the demand side. Expectations are introduced on the supply side in a very simple form with no learning. It does, however, enable us to trace out a dynamic time-path and is therefore a useful starting-point for disequilibrium economics.

Introduction to search theory

It can be seen from the foregoing discussion that one of the major reasons for the persistence of disequilibrium states is the existence of *imperfect knowledge*. This term can be used to explain the inability of producers to predict both their own output and the demand for their product, and is one of the main reasons for lagged responses.

Search theory *Search theory is concerned with the analysis of the costs of gathering information about relevant prices and quantities*

Imperfect knowledge of equilibrium values means that the economic agents involved (that is firms and consumers) have to *search* for the relevant prices and quantities. The analysis of this search process has been called search theory. For equilibrium analysis to be perfectly accurate, we require that all transactions should take place in equilibrium and that no transactions should be allowed to take place in disequilibrium. To this end, 'classical' economists (in particular, Leon Walras) constructed a fable, known as the '*tâtonnement*' *process* which is admittedly unrealistic but which at least provides us with an illustration of how an economy would have to work if equilibrium economics were to be completely acceptable. Here is a summary of that fable:

> Consider an economy which consists of firms and households and which is ruled by an all-powerful *auctioneer*. Before any transactions can take place, the auctioneer has to call out a set of prices for all goods and services and command all willing buyers and sellers to indicate their demands and supplies. If the demand for any good is not equal to its supply, *no* transactions are allowed to take place. Instead, the auctioneer calls out a new, revised set of prices and again counts the demands and supplies. This process of 'groping towards' the general equilibrium position continues until the demand for each good and service is just equal to its supply. Then, and only then, are transactions allowed to take place. Should any change in demand or supply occur, all transactions must stop and the whole process of *tâtonnement* be repeated.

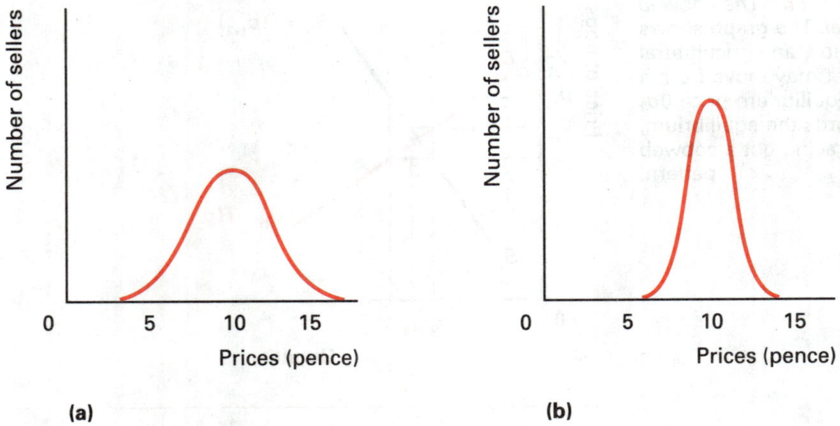

Fig 6.15. **Distribution of prices among different sellers.** (a) A distribution of prices *before* consumers have had time to search for more information. (b) A distribution of prices *after* a period of search.

Clearly, no economies operate in this highly simplified way. Indeed, many transactions take place at disequilibrium values – sometimes called 'false trading' at 'false prices'. Since there is no omnipotent auctioneer controlling economic systems, both firms and households themselves have to search for the equilibrium values in their attempts to clear markets. Buyers have to search for the most favourably priced goods and sellers have to search for that set of prices at which they can just sell their output.

As different sellers of the same good are searching for information to help them in their pricing decisions, buyers often find themselves faced with different prices for the same good. An initial distribution of prices facing consumers of good *X* may look like that represented in Fig. 6.15(a). A few sellers are offering good *X* for sale at only 5p per unit and a few for as much as 15p, but most are offering it for the middle prices, like 9p or 10p. After a while, though, when buyers have had time to search for information concerning prices in the market, those sellers charging 15p will have difficulty in selling the good, and those charging 5p will experience an excess demand for their product. Because of this, the distribution of prices will eventually tend to cluster around the middle prices as shown in Fig. 6.15(b).

Only if perfect information is available will a single equilibrium price be determined and such an equilibrium can only be achieved immediately if perfect information is available costlessly and without the need for searching. Such single equilibrium prices are hardly ever achieved because search processes are costly and time-consuming and even after a long period of searching, only improved (not perfect) information is acquired.

Summary

1. An equilibrium is defined as a state of rest in which no economic forces are generated to change the situation. In the market for a good or service, an equilibrium is said to exist when the market demand for the good or service is equal to its market supply.

2. In a *stable* equilibrium, economic forces tend to push the market towards the equilibrium. In an *unstable*, or knife-edge, equilibrium, any divergence from the equilibrium creates economic forces which tend to push the market further away from the equilibrium.

3. Demand and supply analysis can be used to illustrate the interaction between markets. For example, a fall in supply which raises a good's price will tend to put upward pressure on the price of substitute goods and downward pressure on the price of complementary goods. The fall in supply will also reduce the availability of jointly supplied goods and so raise their prices.

4. The imposition of a sales tax on a good has the effect of shifting the supply curve vertically upwards by the full amount of the tax. The effect on both the equilibrium price and quantity depends on the elasticities of demand and supply. In general, the more inelastic is the demand curve and the more elastic is the supply curve, the greater is the share of the sales tax falling on consumers.

5. A market will tend to remain in disequilibrium in the following circumstances: where artificial restrictions are placed on price or quantity; where the market equilibrium is unstable; where production plans cannot be realised; and where there are lagged responses.

6. Imperfect knowledge means that economic agents have to search for equilibrium values. In general, the longer the search period, the less dispersed will be the distribution of prices for a particular good.

Exercises

1. Review your understanding of the following terms:

equilibrium	free good
disequilibrium	price ceiling
equilibrium market price	price floor
equilibrium market quantity	rationing
excess demand	lagged response
excess supply	cobweb model
stable equilibrium	search theory
jointly supplied goods	*tâtonnement*

2. Consider the following price, quantity demanded and quantity supplied data for good X:

Price (£)	2	4	6	8	10	12
Quantity demanded	100	80	60	40	20	0
Quantity supplied	25	35	45	55	65	75

(a) Plot the demand and supply curves on the same graph and identify the equilibrium price and quantity.

(b) Calculate the elasticities of demand and supply at the equilibrium.
(c) Suppose a sales tax of £2 per unit is imposed on good X. Show the effect of this on the graph and identify the new equilibrium price and quantity.

3. Suppose good X and good Y are substitutes. Show the effects in the market for good X of:
(a) a new discovery which increases the supply of good Y;
(b) an industrial dispute which reduces the supply of good Y.
Repeat (a) and (b) on the assumption that X and Y are complements.

4. Explain why the prices of agricultural goods usually fluctuate more than the prices of manufactured goods. How has the EC attempted to stabilise the prices of agricultural goods?

5. Consider a competitive agricultural market with the following demand and supply curves respectively:

$$q_t^d = 1000 - 2p_t$$
$$q_t^s = 3p_{t-1}$$

where q_t^d and q_t^s represent the quantities demanded and supplied in the current period, p_t represents the current price and p_{t-1} is the price in the previous period.
(a) Draw the demand and supply curves on a graph and find the equilibrium price and quantity.
(b) From the graph, estimate the prices in the first four periods following a disturbance which moves the price 50 units below its equilibrium.
(c) Comment on the stability of the adjustment to a disturbance in the market.

6. Discuss the characteristics that would indicate that the market for a good or service was in disequilibrium.

7.** Discuss the economic effects of: (a) a maximum price; (b) a minimum price in the potato market.

Appendix

Demand and supply functions and the determination of equilibrium price and quantity The appendix to Ch. 3 introduced the concept of a demand function expressed as an equation. Supply functions may also be expressed as equations, and the demand and supply functions together enable us to determine the equilibrium price and quantity in a simple market by solving a pair of simultaneous equations.

As an example, consider a market described by the following equations:

Demand function, $$q^d = 100 - 2p \quad (1)$$

Supply function, $$q^s = 4 + 4p \quad (2)$$

Equilibrium condition, $$q^d = q^s \quad (3)$$

where q^d is the quantity demanded and q^s is the quantity supplied over some time period. Equation (1) is a linear demand function with a negative slope. Equation (2) is a linear supply function with a positive slope. Equation (3) is simply a statement of the equilibrium condition that the quantity demanded should equal quantity supplied. This system of simultaneous equations can easily be solved by setting the right-hand sides of (1) and (2) equal to each other. This gives:

$$100 - 2p = 4 + 4p$$

$$6p = 96$$

$$p = 16$$

So the equilibrium price is 16. At this price, the equilibrium quantity demanded and supplied can be determined by substituting $p = 16$ into either the demand or supply equation. Using the demand equation (1):

$$q^{d} = 100 - (2 \times 16) = 68$$

Using the supply function (2):

$$q^{s} = 4 + (4 \times 16) = 68$$

This confirms that at $p = 16$, quantity demanded and quantity supplied are equal, as required by equation (3).

In general terms, the model may be written as:

$$q^{d} = a + bp \qquad b < 0$$

$$q^{s} = c + dp \qquad d > 0$$

$$q^{d} = q^{s}$$

To find the equilibrium price, we require that:

$$a + bp = c + dp$$

Re-arranging gives:

$$bp - dp = c - a$$

$$p = \frac{c - a}{b - d}$$

Now the equilibrium quantity can be obtained from either the demand or supply equation. Using the demand equation, we have:

$$q^{d} = a + b\left(\frac{c - a}{b - d}\right)$$

$$= \frac{a(b - d) + b(c - a)}{b - d}$$

$$= \frac{ab - ad + bc - ba}{b - d}$$

i.e. $$q^{d} = \frac{bc - ad}{b - d}$$

You should be able to confirm that this equilibrium quantity can also be derived by substituting the equilibrium value of p into the supply function.

GENERAL EQUILIBRIUM AND WELFARE

RESOURCE ALLOCATION

INTRODUCTION TO WELFARE ECONOMICS

7 RESOURCE ALLOCATION

Learning objectives

After reading this chapter, you should be able to:

- illustrate the concept of social welfare maximisation in a simple two-good economy where the given distribution of income is the socially desired one
- identify the nature of allocation decisions in an economy
- distinguish between alternative methods of resource allocation and assess their relative merits and demerits
- describe circumstances that may constitute a case for government intervention in a mixed economy
- identify the key elements of reform in the transition from a command to a market economy

Introduction

The aim of this chapter is to analyse society's decisions about resource allocation and to consider the different methods societies use to allocate resources. Chapter 1 introduced the fundamental economic problem of allocating scarce resources among the competing wants of society. Although resources like labour and capital have increased over time and technology has made steady advances, society's wants have continuously exceeded the means to satisfy them.

Positive economics does not pronounce judgement on the desirability of wants – society's wants and scales of preferences are assumed to be given. This means that efforts have to be directed towards making the most efficient use of scarce resources. With given scales of preferences, the problem of scarcity imposes choices on society. Decisions have to be taken as to which set of wants society must forgo in order to satisfy that set of wants which will maximise the welfare of its members. Such decisions essentially belong to the branch of economics known as general equilibrium analysis which is concerned with the allocation of resources in the production of commodities and with the distribution of those commodities among the members of society.

General equilibrium analysis *The study of the processes by which equilibrium is achieved in the markets for all commodities and resources simultaneously*

We propose in this chapter to focus attention on the following aspects of the allocation problem: (a) the meaning of general equilibrium and its relation to resource allocation; (b) the types of allocation decisions in a general equilibrium system; (c) the methods of resource allocation in a *closed* economy (that is, one with no international trade); (d) the advantages and disadvantages of the different methods of allocation.

General equilibrium and welfare maximisation

The term general equilibrium refers to equilibrium in the markets for all commodities and resources simultaneously throughout the economic system. Such an equilibrium is reached when no forces exist to compel buyers and sellers in these markets to change their behaviour. The equilibrium behaviour of every individual is then compatible with the equilibrium behaviour of all the other members of society. It can be seen that a general equilibrium is in sharp contrast with a partial equilibrium in the analysis of which no attempt is made to relate the market under consideration to the rest of the economic system.

Economists are interested in general equilibrium because all markets are interdependent. Given full employment, a decision to shift resources to one industry to meet an increased demand for one commodity means a reduced quantity of resources in other industries and reduced supplies of other commodities. Consider, for example, the limited stock of energy resources in an economy: if it is decided to use more energy to produce goods for future consumption, there will be less energy available to produce goods for current consumption.

It follows that the level of output of one industry cannot be determined in isolation, but only in relation to the output levels of other industries which compete for society's limited stock of resources and available technology. These interrelationships are illustrated in Fig. 7.1 for a simple closed economy, producing only two goods (food and cloth) with two factors of production (labour and capital). The curve AB is the production possibility frontier with the output of food measured along the vertical axis in tonnes and that of cloth measured along the horizontal axis in metres.

The absolute value of the slope of AB measures the amount by which the production of food must be reduced to increase the production of cloth by 1 metre. As we saw in Ch. 1, this is called the *marginal rate of transformation*. If all resources are transformed into food, the largest possible output is 0A tonnes; if, on the other hannd, all resources are transformed into cloth, the largest possible output is 0B metres. Between these two extremes is a range of possible combinations of food and

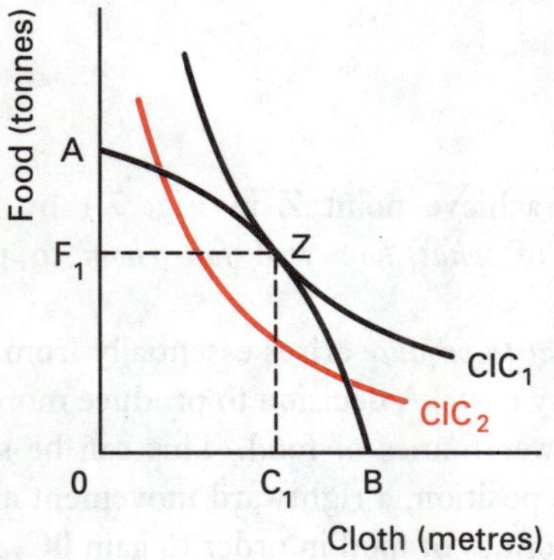

Fig. 7.1. Social welfare maximisation. Social welfare is maximised by producing at the tangency point between a community indifference curve, CIC_1, and the production possibility frontier, AB.

cloth along AB that can just be produced using all resources efficiently. Point Z is one such combination with $0C_1$ metres of cloth and $0F_1$ tonnes of food being produced. At this point and at all other points on the frontier, it is not possible to increase the output of one of the goods without reducing the output of the other. Recall from Ch. 1 that points inside the frontier imply either that there are unused resources or that resources are being used inefficiently – at such points, it is always possible to increase the output of one good without reducing the output of the other.

Assuming that the country can reach its production possibility frontier, the problem then is which combination of food and cloth actually to produce. The 'desired' combination is the one that maximises social welfare. To find this, we have to know something about consumers' preferences for the two goods. Just as we were able to express an individual's preferences for two goods by means of an indifference map in Ch. 4, so we can express a community's preferences for two goods by using a *community* indifference map. In Fig. 7.1, CIC_1 and CIC_2 are two of the community indifference curves which make up such a map for our hypothetical economy.

Community indifference curve *A curve which joins together all the different combinations of two goods which yield the same utility to a community*

Note that a community indifference curve can only be drawn on the important assumption that the distribution of output amongst the members of the community *remains unchanged* so that all individuals remain on their original indifference curves. This heroic assumption is essential because, as we have stressed, community welfare (or utility) depends not only on the quantities of the two goods available for consumption, but also on the distribution of those goods. Thus, as we move from one point to another along an indifference curve, community welfare will only be unchanged if neither individual is made better off at the expense of the other – an unlikely event. As might be expected, this assumption severely restricts the analytical usefulness of the community indifference curves.

The highest attainable community indifference curve in Fig. 7.1 is CIC_1 which is tangential to the production possibility frontier at point Z. If we further assume that the given distribution of output is the socially desired one, then we can say that the combination of food and cloth represented by point Z is the one that will maximise social welfare. However, if that given distribution is not the socially desired one, we can only go so far as to say that point Z satisfies the criteria for economic *efficiency* and not equity. These welfare considerations and the conflict between efficiency and equity are considered more fully in the next chapter. In the remainder of this chapter, we concentrate on the actual *methods* of resource allocation that different societies employ in their attempts to maximise social welfare.

Social welfare maximisation *This is achieved, given the socially desirable distribution of income, when resources are allocated to achieve the highest possible level of utility for the community*

Types of allocation decisions

All societies strive to achieve point Z in Fig. 7.1 by making the three types of interrelated decisions of *what, how* and *for whom* to produce. Consider these in turn.

The question of *what to produce* arises essentially from scarcity and choice and the existence of opportunity costs. A decision to produce more cloth, for instance, has the opportunity cost of fewer tonnes of food. This can be seen from Fig. 7.1: starting at point A, an extreme position, a rightward movement along the frontier to point Z means giving up AF_1 tonnes of food in order to gain $0C_1$ metres of cloth. Similarly, a leftward movement along the frontier means giving up cloth in order to gain more food. Note that the problem of what to produce is a general one – it applies to all human societies.

The second question of *how to produce* arises because every country, apart from the limited technological know-how at its disposal, possesses a mixture of relatively cheap and expensive resources. India, for example, has relatively abundant (and therefore cheap) labour but a shortage of capital. The United States has relatively cheap capital but expensive labour. Such differences in 'factor endowments' between countries influence the factor combinations used to produce the chosen output mix at minimum cost. An efficient combination of factors is one which makes greater use of the relatively cheap resources and more sparing use of the relatively expensive ones.

The third question of *for whom to produce* leads us into normative economics because it involves value judgements concerning the pattern of the distribution of income and wealth. This is undoubtedly the most difficult question of all as it reflects societies' attitudes to fairness and economic equality. Unlike positive economics, normative economics does pronounce judgements on the desirability of different distributional patterns on the basis of interpersonal comparisons of welfare. This means that normative economics is concerned with public sector redistribution policy decisions whose aim it is to maximise social welfare. In terms of Fig. 7.1, we said that point Z was the social welfare maximising point *only so long as the given distribution underlying the community indifference map was the socially desired one*. This implies that all societies have to decide in some way what it is that they regard as an equitable distribution and then what method to use to achieve it. In practice, a decision to have more equity may mean forgoing some efficiency – in this case, societies have to decide how much efficiency they are prepared to give up in order to gain more equity.

It should be clear from the foregoing account that the problem of resource allocation is that of making decisions in a general equilibrium system about efficiency and equity. These decisions (*what, how* and *for whom*) all arise from the universal problem of scarcity and choice. Thus, all societies, irrespective of their political complexions and stages of development, have to tackle the same basic economic problem. It is the *methods* of allocation that differ between countries and, in what follows, we outline and appraise these different methods of allocation.

Methods of resource allocation in a closed economy

In this section, we consider three methods of resource allocation, assuming for now that there is no international trade: (a) the hypothetical case of the price mechanism under *perfect conditions* – an economy characterised by this method is sometimes referred to as a *pure market economy*; (b) the price mechanism under imperfect conditions, as employed by the *mixed economies* of the western industrialised countries; (c) central planning, as used by the *command economies*, such as China.

The price mechanism under perfect conditions

With a freely operating price mechanism, the economy's decisions of what, how and for whom to produce are not taken consciously by individual consumers and firms. There is no central authority for fixing prices or setting output targets, so that both prices and output levels are determined by the interaction of the free forces of demand and supply. Firms supply goods and services motivated by their desire for profits, and consumers demand those goods and services which will maximise their utilities.

By the phrase *perfect conditions*, we mean a situation in which there are so many buyers and sellers competing freely with each other in the markets for *homogeneous* goods and services that no individual buyer or seller is in a position to influence any market price by his or her own actions. Also, there is perfect information, so that a single price can be established for identical goods, and there are no restrictions on the movement of resources between industries or between firms in the same industry. Buyers and sellers are said to be *price takers* in the sense that all prices are market-determined.

Under these (admittedly unrealistic) conditions, *what* to produce is determined by consumers' preferences expressed freely in the market. This power of consumers to determine the allocation of resources in the production of different goods and services has been called consumer sovereignty. Consumers make their preferences known to producers through money 'votes'. In fact, there is a sort of general election every day where consumers cast their money 'votes' for the millions of different commodities on the market. Note that this general election, though, is unlike a political election of 'one man, one vote' because a rich person has more money 'votes' than a poor person and so has a bigger say in what is produced.

Consumer sovereignty
A situation in which the preferences of consumers have a dominant influence in determining what is produced

The decision *how* to produce is determined by competition among firms for the available factors of production whose prices are determined by demand and supply conditions. Profit-maximising firms can only achieve their objective by keeping their costs at a minimum and making use of the most efficient methods of production. This means, for example, that if a change in demand or supply conditions in the labour market should lead to a fall in the price of labour relative to other factors, firms who can do so will adopt more labour-intensive methods of production. It is the demand for and supply of the different factors of production which determine their relative prices and so influence the factor combinations which profit-maximising firms employ.

The decision *for whom* to produce in a market economy is also determined by demand and supply conditions in the factor markets. Households can be thought of as the owners of factors of production, the services of which they sell to firms to earn their incomes. The distribution of these incomes, therefore, depends on the distribution of the ownership of factor services and the prices of the factors. If we take the distribution of the ownership of factors as given, then the distribution of incomes depends on factor prices. The majority of households, of course, own little land and capital, so that the command they have over goods and services depends largely on the wage rate that they can earn by selling labour services. In a market economy under perfect conditions, this wage rate will depend on the demand for and supply of labour. The important topic of the distribution of income is taken up in Chs 16 and 17.

To illustrate the working of the price mechanism under perfect conditions, consider the following simple example. Suppose that goods X and Y are substitutes for each other and are produced using two factors of production, labour and capital. Suppose further that X is a labour-intensive good and that Y is a capital-intensive good. Now let consumers in general suddenly develop an increased preference for good X so that the demand for X increases and the demand for Y correspondingly falls. The effects of these shifts in demand in the markets for the goods are illustrated in Fig. 7.2(a) and (b), where the demand curve for X (DD_X) shifts to the right to

A labour-intensive good
A good in the production of which the ratio of labour to capital is high.

A capital-intensive good
A good in the production of which the ratio of capital to labour is high

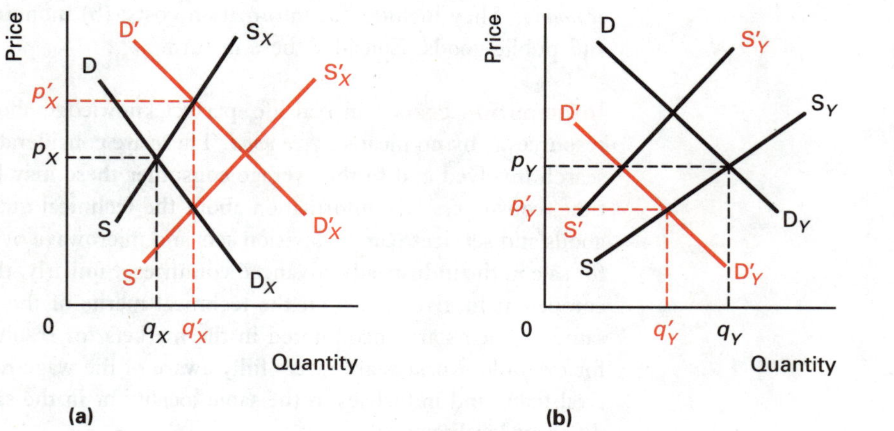

Fig. 7.2. Interaction between the markets for goods X and Y. A change in tastes increases the demand for good *X*, resulting in a rise in its price. Profit-seeking producers of *X* respond to this price signal by increasing the output of *X*. At the same time, the demand for *Y* falls, resulting in a fall in its price. Producers of *Y* respond by reducing the output of *Y*. In the long-run, the supply curve of *X* shifts to the right, whilst the supply curve of *Y* shifts to the left.

$D'D'_X$ and the demand curve for *Y* (DD_Y) shifts to the left to $D'D'_Y$. The supply curves illustrated in Fig. 7.2 are short-run supply curves. The result in the short-run is that the price of *X* rises from $0p_X$ to $0p'_X$ and the price of *Y* falls from $0p_Y$ to $0p'_Y$. These price changes now act as signals to producers. The production of good *X* is seen to be more profitable, so existing producers expand their supplies (from $0q_X$ to $0q'_X$ in Fig. 7.2) and in the long-run new firms are attracted into the industry, causing the supply curve to shift from SS_X to $S'S'_X$. The production of Y, though, is seen to be less profitable, so existing firms contract their supplies (from $0q_Y$ to $0q'_Y$) and some are eventually forced to leave the industry, causing the supply curve to shift from SS_Y to $S'S'_Y$. It is in this way that the price mechanism automatically responds to changes in consumers' demand to ensure that what is demanded is produced.

In the factor markets, similar automatic forces are at work. The expanding labour-intensive *X*-industry is demanding more labour than is being released by the contracting capital-intensive *Y*-industry. This puts upward pressure on the price of labour. At the same time, more capital is being released by the contracting *Y*-industry than is being demanded by the expanding *X*-industry. This puts downward pressure on the price of capital. Thus, the distribution of income is affected as the owners of labour gain at the expense of the owners of capital. This change in the distribution of income in turn affects the pattern of consumer demand for good *X* and good *Y*. Adjustments continue to take place until all markets are back in equilibrium.

The important point to notice is that the price mechanism under perfect conditions operates automatically. Price changes, the profit motive and the self-interest of consumers all interact to channel resources away from unprofitable lines of production and into the more profitable ones.

The price mechanism under imperfect conditions

The term *imperfect conditions* refers to the frictions or impediments which prevent a free market economy from reaching an otherwise attainable point on its production possibility frontier. There are several types of impediments to perfect allocational efficiency and these are all features of the mixed economies of the western industrial countries. *These impediments constitute a case for government intervention in the economy*. They include: (a) information costs; (b) monopoly power; (c) externalities and public goods. Consider these in turn.

Information costs In real life, perfect knowledge about the prices of goods and resources is by no means a *free good*. There are considerable costs of information and search involved and to the average consumer these may be prohibitive. At the same time, consumers lack information about the technical qualities of the many complex goods and services (cars, television sets and microwave ovens, for example) which are for sale in the industrially advanced countries. Similarly, the average seller may not be competent to give advice on the technical merits of the goods he or she sells. The same problems are encountered in the markets for resources. In the labour market, for example, workers are rarely fully aware of the wage rates and career prospects in rival firms and industries in the same locality or in the same firms and industries in different localities.

Monopoly power Monopoly power is the ability of a firm to control its prices. It can be achieved through collusion or mergers which give a firm a substantial market share and can be maintained by making it difficult for new rival firms to enter the industry or by differentiating the product through branding, labelling and advertising. Some firms are *natural* monopolies – these occur where the nature of the industry requires a single supplier in order to avoid overlapping and duplication of activities. The supply of water is an example of a natural monopoly, for it would clearly be wasteful to have more than one company supplying water to the same town. Other examples include the distribution of gas and electricity.

Given the motive to maximise profits, a firm with monopoly power is likely to set price above competitive levels and, as we see in Ch. 10, this will lead to a misallocation of resources. The control of monopoly profit is part of the explanation for government intervention in the price mechanism through legislation and nationalisation, as discussed in Ch. 15.

Externalities and public goods The economic organisation of every human society is characterised by certain social costs (such as pollution and noise) and certain social benefits (such as the panoramic view of a row of beautiful houses) which are not taken into account by firms in determining their price levels. Such social costs and benefits are called *externalities* and their existence means that the price mechanism fails to reflect the true opportunity cost of resources. Externalities are tackled in mixed economies by government measures such as taxes, subsidies and legislation. These are discussed in Ch. 12.

Also, the price mechanism by its very nature is not well equipped to provide certain types of goods whose benefits cannot be attributed to individual users. These goods are called *public goods*: examples include defence, the police service and roads. Such goods are produced and consumed in great 'lumps' and the users cannot easily be charged through the pricing system. This explains why the state intervenes to provide these types of goods in mixed economies.

Resource allocation in a command economy

A command economy is one in which decisions about production and distribution are taken by a central planning authority (CPA). This CPA is generally made up of a large administrative machinery responsible for issuing directives to factory managers about: (a) what to produce; (b) where to get the supply of resources; (c) what techniques of production to use; (d) where to dispose of the finished product. Thus, the CPA is a centralised decision-making body concerned with allocating resources. This method of allocation was common in eastern European countries and persists in socialist countries, such as China and Cuba. Although allocation by a CPA is the most common method in these countries, they cannot be described as *pure* command economies.

In a pure command economy, there would be no place for money and prices. People would most probably be issued with ration cards telling them to which commodities they were entitled and at what distribution centres they could obtain them. Moreover, a pure command economy would be likely to direct labour to occupations and industries decided upon by the CPA. Judging by these criteria, it is clear that the present-day command economies are far from being pure command economies. Like the economies of the western industrialised countries, they depend on the use of money for allocational decisions. China, for instance, has developed markets designed to mirror consumers' choices more accurately.

Advantages and disadvantages of the different methods of resource allocation

The mixed economies of western industrialised countries depend upon the price mechanism as the principal instrument of allocating resources. Several advantages can be claimed for this method of allocation. Consider the following.

Advantages of the price mechanism

Economic efficiency Given that consumers are the best judges of their interests, it can be shown that the price system working under perfect conditions ensures economic efficiency in the sense that no one can be made better off without making someone else worse off. *This important result is demonstrated in Ch. 9.* It is argued that the impersonal and sensitive price mechanism fulfils consumers' choices more accurately than central planning.

Greater freedom of choice The pricing system of completely free and unregulated markets is a vehicle for communicating consumers' decisions to producers about the preferred output combinations of goods and services. Given that firms enjoy freedom of entry into industries, competition amongst firms gives rise to a large number of goods and services being offered for sale. This means that consumers, in seeking to maximise their utilities, have the freedom to choose from a much wider range of goods and services than would be made available in a centrally planned economy.

Greater responsiveness to changes in the world economic environment It is argued that a market economy responds more quickly to changing economic conditions in world markets than does a command economy. Because profit-maximising firms are exposed to much greater competition in international markets, they have an incentive to respond rapidly to changes in the relative prices of goods and raw materials. For instance, the enormous increase in oil prices in the 1970s compelled firms in the chemical and related industries to use fuels more efficiently. Additionally, it encouraged firms to develop alternative sources of energy. Similarly, the rapid advances in high-technology products in the 1980s and 1990s, together with relatively open markets, have led to even more competition in world markets. This in turn has intensified the pressure on firms to innovate in order to maintain their market shares.

Greater incentives to bear risks It is possible that free markets with minimum state intervention will encourage competition and thus stimulate the incentive to take business risks. If this, in turn, leads to a faster rate of technological advance, it may result in a higher rate of economic growth.

Disadvantages of the price mechanism

Critics of the free forces of markets point to the following disadvantages.

Inequalities of income and wealth It is maintained that the price system operates in the face of extreme inequalities of income and wealth. As goods and services are produced in response to money 'votes' cast in their favour, scarce resources are diverted to the production of luxuries for the rich who have more money 'votes' before an adequate output of goods for the poor is produced. The pricing system, therefore, ignores the equity objective of resource allocation.

Unemployment It is claimed that the free market mechanism subjects an economy to cyclical unemployment when production and consumption decisions get out of line. Experience has shown that the total demand for output (in the absence of government intervention) periodically falls short of the total supply of goods. As a result, unsold stocks of goods accumulate, forcing producers to cut back on production plans and to lay off workers. Labour market imperfections, such as the immobility of labour, may also result in a form of unemployment known as structural unemployment. The different types of unemployment are described in Ch. 27.

Inflation Experience of the 1970s and 1980s has led many economists to argue that, in spite of government intervention in market economies, the price system is prone to severe inflation. Most of the industrialised and less developed countries have experienced persistently rapid rises in prices in their economies. This has in turn led to social and political tensions in many of these countries.

Contrived demand Recall that a result of the operation of the price mechanism under perfect conditions is that the consumer is sovereign. It can be argued, though, that the advertising and sales promotion media which have evolved over the years in western capitalist societies have actually created new wants. Thus, consumers' demand is contrived by advertising and this has resulted in a substantial loss of consumer sovereignty.

Market imperfections As mentioned above, market imperfections (such as information costs, monopoly power, externalities and public goods) are inherent in a price mechanism. With such imperfections, price and output levels are unlikely to satisfy the conditions for economic efficiency.

Advantages of a command economy

Some of the disadvantages of allocation by the price mechanism disappear when allocation decisions are made by a CPA. In particular, it has been argued that allocation by a CPA has the following advantages.

Full employment The CPA enables a command economy to achieve full employment of resources by directing labour to production activities even if those activities are not profitable.

Low rate of inflation Given that a command economy is characterised by a whole range of administered prices for goods and services, a much lower rate of inflation can be maintained than in an economy subject to the price mechanism. If the CPA should fail to match its production and consumption decisions, shortages would lead to queues forming, black markets and possibly social unrest, rather than rising prices.

Minimum waste of resources Compared with private monopolies seeking to maximise profits in a market economy, state monopolies operating in the public interest may mean less waste of resources in a command economy. However, a CPA would only achieve economic efficiency if it set prices which reflected the true social marginal costs.

Greater ability to tackle externalities The CPA operating in the public interest is well placed to take negative externalities, such as environmental pollution, into account when deciding upon the pattern of production. This means that a command economy can more easily deal with the harmful effects of production activities, all of which are under the direct control of the CPA. In practice, however, many of the former command economies in Eastern Europe had a poor record in tackling externalities such as pollution.

Minimum inequalities of income and wealth As the CPA determines the prices of all factors of production, it is able to minimise inequalities in the distribution of income and wealth. Unlike a market economy, individuals are not able to accumulate large amounts of capital as all major production enterprises are owned by the state. At the same time, the state can aim to achieve desired standards of housing, health and education for all members of the society.

Disadvantages of a command economy

Several criticisms can be levelled against centralised decision-making as a means of achieving efficiency in resource allocation. Consider the following.

Information costs It is pointed out that the cost of gathering information about *what*, *how* and *for whom* to produce is likely to be very high as it requires an army of experts in several fields, such as statisticians, engineers, planners and administrators. The collection of sufficient information on the three interrelated decisions is, however, unavoidable given that the objective of a CPA is to achieve efficiency in resource allocation. In contrast, the device of casting money 'votes' under the free market mechanism is a costless source of information, provided that society is prepared to tolerate the existing distribution of income and wealth.

Difficulty of estimating demand Without price signals, it is immensely difficult to estimate the existing and future pattern of demand for goods and services.

Consequently, shortages and gluts have been recurring features of command economies.

Lags in the implementation of plans Even if the required information about allocation decisions is collected, the pattern of consumers' preferences and society's composition of resources might well change before production and distribution plans are implemented. There is a time-lag between the collection of information and the formulation of production plans based upon that information. Then, there is a further time-lag between the implementation of production plans and the realisation of production targets.

Possible lack of incentives As we saw above, the price mechanism stimulates incentives to greater effort and to take business risks. In a command economy, with administered prices and wages and the absence of profits, workers and managers may lack such motivation.

Restricted choice and dull conformity Because demand is manipulated to match the limited range of goods available on the market, consumers can be said to have restricted choice. Also, the goods produced tend to be standardised with practically no regard for individual tastes.

The transition from a command economy to a market economy

Following the political changes in the former Soviet Union that led to its break-up, several countries in eastern Europe embarked on major programmes of economic reform. This reform is intended to convert their economies from centrally planned to market economies. The countries undertaking these reforms include Poland, Czechoslovakia, Hungary and Bulgaria. The overall objective is to gain the benefits of the higher living standards which the market economies of the west have already achieved.

Key elements of reform

The reform programmes generally involve the following key elements:

- freeing of prices and withdrawal of subsidies.
- privatisation of industries and other property formerly owned by the state.
- elimination or reduction of government budget deficits.
- development of budgetary and fiscal systems.

Consider these elements in turn.

Freeing of prices and withdrawal of subsidies In a command economy limited use is made of the price system in the process of resource allocation. Typically, prices of some consumer goods would be held constant for long periods of time and would not be closely related to production costs. In some instances, substantial subsidies would be provided in order to keep the prices of these goods artificially low. In the former Soviet Union, for example, bread prices in 1987 were only one-fifth of the price of bread in the United States. As a result, much bread was simply thrown away and wasted.

In a market economy, on the other hand, the prices of goods and services are freely determined by the interaction of supply and demand. In the case of goods and services which attracted subsidies in a command economy, the freeing of prices would mean a rapid increase in prices which now have to reflect the real costs of production. When Russia, for example, introduced price liberalisation at the beginning of 1992, overnight the price of bread rose more than threefold and taxi fares rose tenfold.

Privatisation of state-owned industries In a command economy, most resources (other than labour) and most production units are state-owned. In a market economy, on the other hand, these resources and production units are generally privately-owned. The transfer of ownership necessary to convert a command economy to a market economy is a major task. It involves the development of a legal system to enforce contracts between buyers and sellers of goods and resources. Also, it requires the development of financial institutions and financial markets that facilitate transactions and perform the functions of financial intermediation.

As part of a reform programme, state-owned banks are privatised to become profit-motivated commercial banks. It is necessary for all privately-owned companies in such a reformed economy to focus on the need to make a profit. Hitherto, the concept of profit played an insignificant role in the command economy as the CPA decided on what was produced. In a market economy, on the other hand, profitability plays a vital role in determining the allocation of resources to alternative uses, rewarding risk-taking and as an important source of funds for investment.

Development of budgetary and fiscal systems In a command economy, budgeting and fiscal measures are not used to influence production and consumption decisions. The transition to a market economy requires the development of budgetary and fiscal systems. These systems involve the setting up of a machinery to administer and implement government spending and tax-collection.

A government in a command economy typically runs a budget deficit. This means that its expenditure is greater than its income. Such a deficit is normally financed by printing money. As noted above, the inflationary effects of a budget deficit are suppressed in a command economy through price-fixing and the use of subsidies. In the transition to a market economy the government needs to take into account the potential inflationary effects of a continued budget deficit. As part of the reform programme it becomes necessary to develop the role of the central bank. Such a bank would have the responsibility to regulate the supply of money to control inflation and to stabilise the country's exchange rate.

The role of international institutions The major international institutions, such as the International Monetary Fund and the World Bank, are providing financial and technical assistance to the countries of central and eastern Europe which are making the transition to market economies. There is universal agreement on the objectives of the transition. These include higher living standards, faster economic growth, efficient resource allocation, economic freedom and political stability. Nevertheless, there is a continuing debate about the speed with which the transition can be achieved. Two opposing schools of thought can be identified. The *radical* school believes in a rapid transformation from a command to a market economy. Its supporters would recommend:

(a) the speedy elimination of subsidies on goods and services;
(b) rapid large-scale privatisation of state-owned industries, allowing production decisions to be taken by entrepreneurs;
(c) large scale privatisation of residential property.

The radical school, therefore, supports the widespread use of markets, and minimum state intervention.

The *gradualist* school of thought supports a slower pace of reform. Its followers would recommend:

(a) a gradual reduction of subsidies together with an indefinite retention of subsidies on essential consumer goods for social reasons;
(b) a slower pace of privatisation, together with continued state ownership of key industries. This school fears that rapid privatisation might mean a large-scale transfer of ownership to foreign investors at knock-down prices.

The gradualist school, therefore, is of the view that the unchecked use of the price mechanism may lead to undesirable consequences, such as the development of monopoly power and an inequitable distribution of income and wealth.

Resource allocation in less developed countries

In less developed countries, the method of allocation is normally a blend of the price mechanism and central planning. The governments of these countries are typically active interventionists in the markets for both commodities and resources with a view to promoting the objectives of economic growth and development.

The policy instruments employed by the governments of such countries typically include: (a) subsidies to capital and exports; (b) import controls; (c) taxes on labour and capital in selected industries and occupations; (d) rationing of foreign exchange to capital and food imports; (e) price controls on essential foods; (f) licensing of industrial and residential buildings, plant and equipment; (g) land reforms, redistributing the ownership of land and fixing the optimum size of holdings. These policy instruments are a reflection of these countries' dissatisfaction with the unfettered working of the price system. Indeed, certain features of a CPA can be observed from the fact that almost all the less developed countries have comprehensive economic plans where the public sector is assigned a key role in influencing decisions about production and distribution.

Such economic plans assess the availability of total domestic and overseas resources over the plan period (typically, five years). In the light of this information about resources, the plans then set *production targets* and the *strategy* – that is, the way in which the public and private sectors are expected to contribute to the realisation of the plan. A typical development plan of a less developed country reviews the performance, targets and availability of resources in its third year of implementation and, in the light of experience and new information, identifies bottlenecks and revises its expectations accordingly.

Unfortunately, a number of difficulties arise in implementing development plans. In particular, there are great problems of estimating and then acquiring the foreign exchange component of investment expenditures. In the agricultural sector, natural factors, such as droughts and floods, militate against the implementation of production plans.

Summary

1. All methods of resource allocation have social welfare maximisation as their overriding aim. The criteria necessary for social welfare maximisation can be illustrated with the aid of a community indifference map and a production possibility frontier, on the assumption that the existing distribution of income is the socially desired one.
2. Resource allocation involves deciding *what, how* and *for whom* to produce. A market economy under 'perfect conditions' would rely on prices as signals to consumers and producers. Consumers express their preferences for goods and services to producers through their spending decisions, which may be viewed as money 'votes'. The more money is spent on a particular good, the greater will be the incentive for producers to supply that good. This is the notion of *consumer sovereignty*.
3. The frictions or imperfections which exist in real economies prevent free-market economies from attaining otherwise attainable points on their production possibility frontiers. They include information costs, monopoly power, externalities and public goods, and constitute a case for government intervention in a mixed economy.
4. Resource allocation in a command economy is determined by a centralised decision-making process.
5. There are advantages and disadvantages associated with the two main alternative methods of resource allocation. This explains why all modern economies exhibit characteristics from both.
6. The transition from a command to a market economy is a major economic reform which poses a number of serious problems for the countries involved.

Exercises

1. Review your understanding of the following terms:

general equilibrium	central planning
community indifference map	command economy
allocation decisions	mixed economy
price mechanism	consumer sovereignty
market economy	money 'votes'

2. 'The price mechanism operating under perfectly free conditions allocates resources to the production of those goods and services for which consumers

have expressed their preferences through money votes in the market place.' Explain and criticise this statement.

3. Outline the circumstances under which you think government intervention in the working of the pricing system can be justified in: (a) an industrially advanced country; (b) a less developed country.

4. 'It is the method of allocation rather than the nature of allocation decisions that distinguishes command economies from the mixed economies of western industrialised countries.' Do you agree?

5. Assess the achievements and failures of the allocation methods of the USA and the former USSR during the post-war years until 1990.

6. Do capitalist countries necessarily have market economies? Do socialist countries necessarily have planned economies? Can you think of an example of a socialist market economy and a capitalist planned economy?

7.** 'The price mechanism is an efficient method of allocating resources.' Discuss.

8 INTRODUCTION TO WELFARE ECONOMICS

Learning objectives

After reading this chapter, you should be able to:

- outline the main requirements for Pareto efficiency and illustrate them using Edgeworth-Bowley box diagrams in the context of a simple 2 × 2 × 2 model
- distinguish between efficiency and equity criteria
- give examples of the conflict between efficiency and equity which often faces policy-makers
- show how compensation tests might be used to reconcile the conflict between efficiency and equity
- show how cost-benefit analysis can be used as a practical application of compensation tests

Introduction

Welfare economics has grown in recent years into a complex body of analysis. It is our intention in this chapter to introduce the reader to the subject in as simple a way as possible and, later in the book, to show how welfare economics may be applied in the theory of the firm, in the analysis of the public sector and in the theory of distribution.

We saw in the last chapter and to some extent in Ch. 1 that economic systems, in whatever way they are organised, all face the same problem of resource allocation, and we examined the different ways in which the free market economies and the planned economies tackle this problem. This chapter is concerned not with the actual methods of allocation, but with identifying those allocations which are *efficient* and *equitable*.

First, then, we must decide what is meant by *social welfare*. It can be thought of as being synonymous with the level of satisfaction or utility enjoyed by the members of society. It includes, therefore, a variety of objective and subjective factors. In Ch. 1, we pointed out that it has two main aspects – economic efficiency and equity. A given allocation can be said to be *economically efficient* in the Pareto sense when no reallocation is possible which makes anyone better off without making someone else worse off. In addition, an allocation can be said to be *equitable* when it is associated with a 'fair' distribution of income and wealth. Clearly, there is a good deal more subjectivity in equity than in efficiency considerations.

Social welfare function *A statement of the factors that influence the utility or well-being of the members of a society*

A social welfare function is a statement of the factors which determine social welfare (SW) and might include the total quantity of goods and services produced (Q) and some measure of the way in which these goods and services are distributed (D). Such a function might also include factors such as the health of the community (H), the amount of leisure time (L), the degree of environmental pollution (P), political stability (S) and even the quantity of rainfall (R). Thus, letting Z denote other relevant factors, we could write:

$$\text{SW} = f(Q, D, H, L, P, S, R, Z).$$

Alternatively, we could suppose that the welfare of society as a whole depends on the welfare or utilities of the individuals who make up society – in which case, we could write:

$$\text{SW} = f(U_1, U_2, \ldots, U_N)$$

where $U_1, U_2, \ldots, U_N$ are the utilities of the N individuals who make up a society. This is known as the Bergson-Samuelson social welfare function.

Unfortunately, writing the social welfare function in either of these forms does not enable us to determine whether any specific change in the economy which makes some people better off and others worse off will increase or decrease social welfare. It is the purpose of this chapter to move us a step closer to being able to make such judgements. First, we consider economic efficiency in the Pareto sense and derive the conditions necessary for Pareto optimality in the context of a very simple model. Secondly, we consider some equity criteria for judging welfare. Thirdly, we examine the possible conflict which can arise between efficiency and equity and, finally, consider the use of 'compensation tests' and 'cost-benefit' analysis to reconcile this conflict.

Economic efficiency

It has been stated a number of times in this book that economic efficiency in the Pareto sense can be said to exist when it is not possible to change the allocation of resources in any way which makes someone better off without at the same time making someone else worse off. In Ch. 1, we explained the implications of this in greater detail, pointing out that in *production*, it must be impossible to increase the output of one good without reducing the output of any other and in exchange, it must be impossible to increase the consumption of one household without reducing the consumption of some other.

For this state of Pareto efficiency or *Pareto optimality* to be achieved, there are three main requirements.

(a) *Efficiency in production.* This means that the economy must be employing all of its factors of production in efficient combinations so that it is on and not inside its production possibility frontier.

(b) *Efficiency in exchange.* This means that it must be impossible to redistribute a given stock of goods and services in such a way that benefits someone without at the same time harming someone else.

(c) *Efficient output mix.* This means that it must be impossible to change the actual combination of goods and services produced in such a way that will benefit someone without harming someone else.

In order to derive the main conditions for Pareto optimality, consider these three requirements in the context of a very simple model. To set up the model, the following assumptions are made.

(a) The economy is a barter economy where one good is simply exchanged for another and there is no international trade.
(b) There are only two goods, food and cloth.
(c) There are only two factors of production, capital and labour, which are fixed in supply.
(d) There are only two people, A and B, making up the society.

This model with its two goods, two factors and two individuals is sometimes called a $2 \times 2 \times 2$ model. Obviously, it is highly unrealistic. It does, however, enable us to derive results which can be generalised to more realistic situations and it has the advantage that it can be analysed using graphs. Consider now the above three requirements for Pareto optimality in turn.

Efficiency in production

Recall that our simplified economy has fixed supplies of the two factors of production. Suppose that the total supply of labour is fixed at $0L$ units per time period; this is said to be the country's *total endowment* of labour. Suppose further that the country's total endowment of capital is equal to $0K$ units. These endowments are indicated on the axes of the graphs in Fig. 8.1. Fig. 8.1(a) shows the isoquant map illustrating the production function for food and Fig. 8.1(b) shows the isoquant map illustrating the production function for cloth. Since the production function for food is unlikely to be the same as the production function for cloth, the isoquant map for food (of which F_1, F_2 and F_3 are representative isoquants) is not likely to have the same shape as the isoquant map for cloth (of which C_1, C_2 and C_3 are representative isoquants).

Suppose now that we turn the graph showing the cloth isoquant map (Fig. 8.1(b)) upside down, so that it looks like Fig. 8.2. Notice that Fig. 8.2 shows exactly the same information as Fig. 8.1(b).

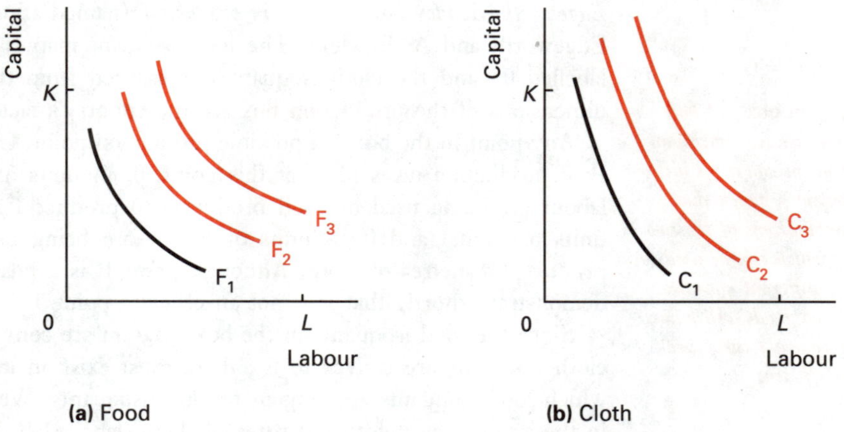

Fig. 8.1. Isoquant maps for food and cloth. The two isoquant maps illustrate the production functions for food and cloth respectively.

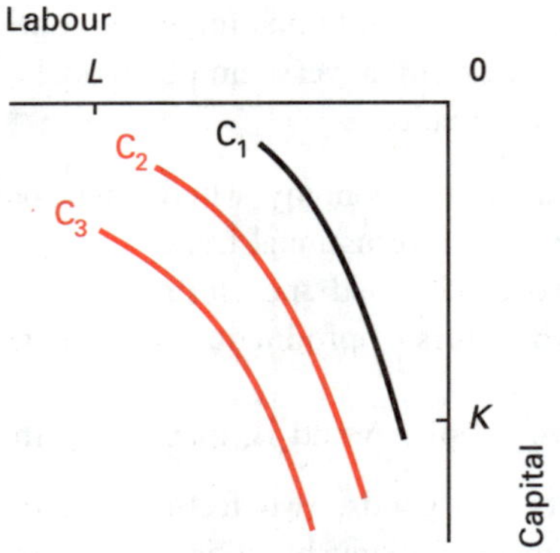

Fig. 8.2. The cloth isoquant map upside down. This graph is identical to Fig. 8.1(b), but is drawn upside down.

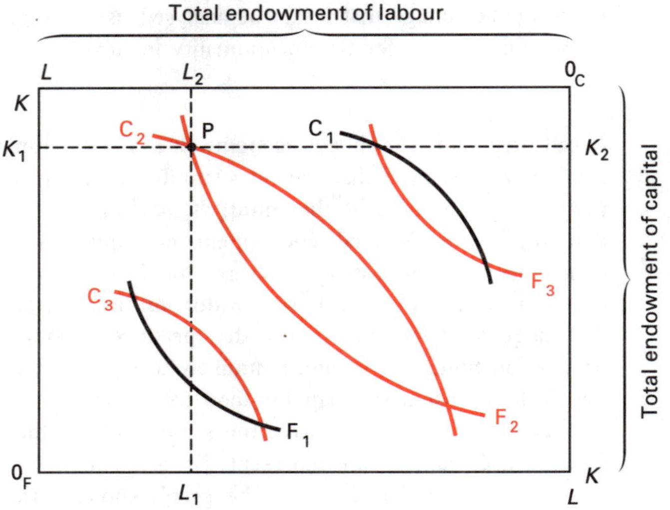

Fig. 8.3. The production box diagram. The food isoquant map is measured from 0_F and the cloth isoquant map is measured from 0_C. The dimension of the box are the country's factor endowments.

Suppose further that we join the axes of the graphs in Fig. 8.2 and Fig. 8.1(a) together so that they form a box, as shown in Fig. 8.3. This is the country's *Edgeworth–Bowley box diagram in production* (named after the British economists F. Edgeworth and A. Bowley). The food isoquant map is measured from the origin labelled 0_F and the cloth isoquant is measured from the origin labelled 0_C. The dimensions of the production box are the country's factor endowments.

Production box *A box diagram (whose dimensions represent the country's factor endowments) which shows the combinations of the two factors which can be used to produce different quantities of the two goods. All points on the contract curve are Pareto efficient*

Any point in the box is a possible production point. Consider, for example, point P: if production takes place at this point, $0_F K_1$ units of capital and $0_F L_1$ units of labour are being used by food producers to produce F_2 tonnes of food and $0_C K_2$ units of capital and $0_C L_2$ units of labour are being used by cloth producers to produce C_2 metres of cloth. Although point P is a possible production point, we demonstrate shortly that it is not an efficient point.

Since the food isoquants in the box diagram are convex to the origin 0_F and the cloth isoquants are convex to 0_C, there must exist an infinite number of points at which food isoquants are tangent to cloth isoquants. We are particularly interested in these tangency points and three of them (labelled S, R and T) are illustrated in

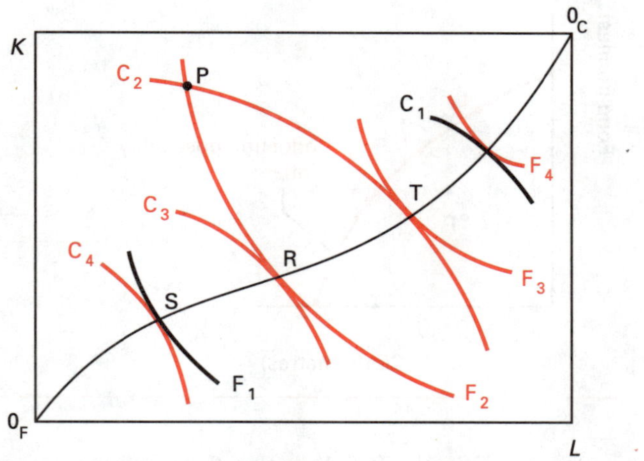

Fig. 8.4. The production box diagram and contract curve. The contract curve, 0_FSRT0_C, joins together all the points of tangency of food isoquants with cloth isoquants. All these tangency points are technically efficient.

Fig. 8.4. The curve, 0_F0_C, which joins together all the tangency points, is called the *contract curve* and we can show that all the production points on the contract curve are *technically efficient*, whereas all points which are not on the contract curve are *technically inefficient*. Consider point P in Fig. 8.4. At this point, C_2 metres of cloth and F_2 tonnes of food are being produced. Notice, however, that by moving from point P to point R (which is on the contract curve) food output remains unchanged (because production is still taking place on isoquant F_2), but cloth output increases to C_3 metres. Point P, then, cannot be an efficient production point because it is possible to reallocate factors of production in such a way that more cloth is produced while food production remains unchanged. This is true of all points which are not on the contract curve.

Once a point on the contract curve is reached, however, it is no longer possible to increase the production of one good without reducing the production of the other. To show this, consider point R which is on the contract curve: any movement which increases food production (say, to point T) has the effect of reducing cloth production, and any movement which increases cloth production (say, to point S) has the effect of reducing food production.

The contract curve joins together all the points of tangency of food isoquants with cloth isoquants and all these points are technically efficient. Recall from Ch. 2 that the absolute value of the slope of an isoquant is equal to the marginal rate of technical substitution of capital for labour ($MRTS_{KL}$). It follows that *for efficiency in production, the $MRTS_{KL}$ in food production must be equal to the $MRTS_{KL}$ in cloth production*. More formally, we can write that, for efficiency in production, we require that:

$$(MRTS_{KL})_{food} = (MRTS_{KL})_{cloth} \qquad [1]$$

When this condition is not satisfied, it is possible to reallocate resources in such a way that more of at least one of the goods can be produced without having to reduce the output of either of the goods.

We should note at this point the relationship between the contract curve and the production possibility frontier (the graphical technique introduced in Ch. 1). Points on the contract curve can only be reached when the country is using all of its

Fig. 8.5. The production possibility frontier. Points s, r and t on the production possibility frontier correspond to points S, R and T on the contract curve shown in Fig. 8.4.

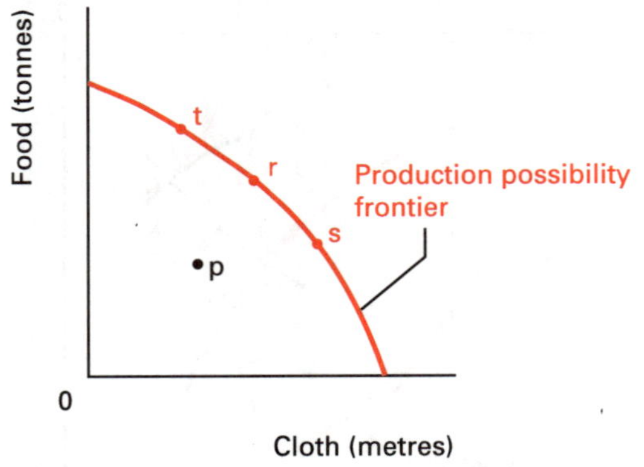

resources efficiently. It follows that these points must correspond to the points on the country's production possibility frontier. This is illustrated in Fig. 8.5, where points s, r and t correspond to the points S, R and T in Fig. 8.4. Point p inside the production possibility frontier corresponds to the inefficient production point P in the box diagram.

Efficiency in exchange

Having used the two factors of production efficiently to produce a given amount of food and cloth, the next problem is how to distribute the two goods to the two individuals in an efficient way. Notice that we are concerned here only with the *efficient* distribution of the goods – as we show later, this will not necessarily be an equitable distribution.

To derive a condition for efficiency in exchange, consider Fig. 8.6(a) and (b) which shows the two individuals' indifference maps for the two goods. Since A and B are likely to have different preferences, the indifference maps have different shapes. As with the isoquant maps in the previous section, we can invert one of the indifference maps (in this case, B's) and join it on to the other one so that they form

Fig. 8.6. The indifference maps for individuals A and B. The two indifference maps illustrate the two individuals' preferences for the two goods.

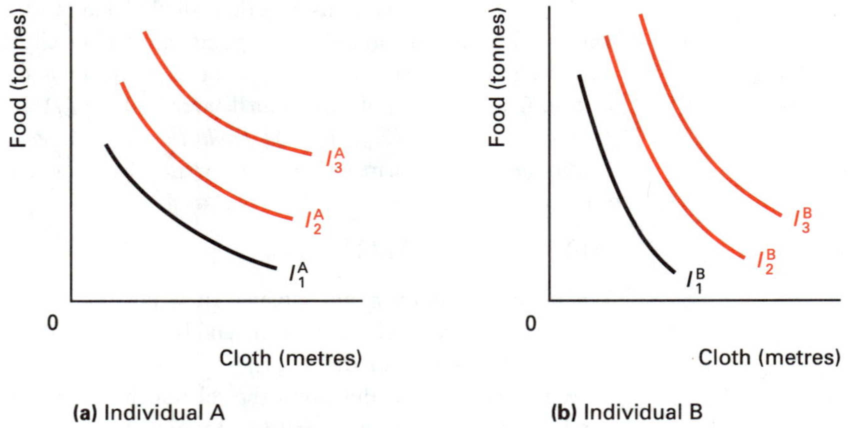

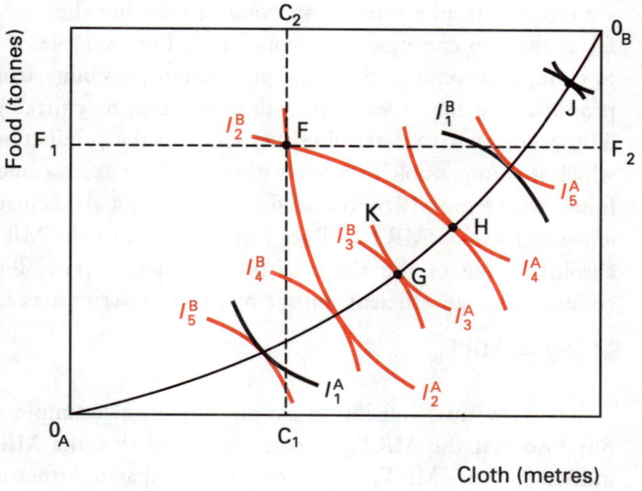

Fig. 8.7. *The exchange box diagram.* The contract curve, $0_A GHJ 0_B$, joins together all the points of tangency between A's and B's indifference curves. All these tangency points are efficient exchange points.

Exchange box *A box diagram which shows combinations of the two goods which the two individuals can consume. Only points along the contract curve are Pareto efficient*

a box, as in Fig. 8.7. This is the exchange box. A's indifference map is measured from the origin labelled 0_A and B's is measured from the origin labelled 0_B. The dimensions of the box are the quantities of food and cloth which the country has produced.

Any point in the box represents a possible allocation of the two goods to the two individuals. Consider, for example, point F. At this point, A consumes 0_AF_1 tonnes of food and 0_AC_1 metres of cloth, and B consumes 0_BF_2 tonnes of food and 0_BC_2 metres of cloth. Point F is inefficient because it is possible to move to another point, like G, in such a way that both individuals are made better off (that is, reach higher indifference curves) or at least to move to a point, like H, where A is better off and B no worse off.

As in the production box diagram, all the efficient points lie along a *contract curve* which this time joins together all the points of tangency between A's indifference curves and B's indifference curves. Once a point on the contract curve is reached, it is no longer possible to move to any other point without making at least one of the individuals worse off. As we showed in Ch. 4, the absolute value of the slope of an indifference curve is the *marginal rate of substitution* of one good for another (in this case, food for cloth). It follows that *for efficiency in exchange, the marginal rate of substitution of food for cloth (MRS_{fc}) for individual A must be equal to the MRS_{fc} for individual B.* More formally, we can write the condition for efficiency in exchange as:

$$(MRS_{fc})_A = (MRS_{fc})_B \quad [2]$$

When this condition is not satisfied, it is possible to reallocate the two goods to the two individuals in such a way that at least one of them is made better off without making the other worse off.

Efficient output mix

When conditions (1) and (2) are satisfied, the economy will be producing at a point on its production possibility frontier and the two goods will be allocated to the two individuals in an efficient way. All the points on the production possibility frontier are efficient from a production point of view but they are not all equally efficient as far as the two consumers are concerned. For example, if both A and B prefer food to cloth, a movement along the production possibility frontier which increases food production at the expense of cloth production may make both consumers better off. The problem is to determine the point on the production possibility frontier from which it is impossible to move without making at least one individual worse off. It is found where the MRS_{fc} (equal for both individuals) is just equal to the *marginal rate of transformation* (MRT_{fc}). Recall from Ch. 1 that the MRT is the name given to the absolute value of the slope of the production possibility frontier. Formally, the condition for an efficient output mix can be written as follows:

$$MRS_{fc} = MRT_{fc} \qquad [3]$$

To show this, consider a simple numerical example where they are not equal. Suppose that the MRT_{fc} is equal to $\frac{1}{4}$ and that the MRS_{fc} is equal to $\frac{1}{8}$ for both individuals. An MRT_{fc} equal to $\frac{1}{4}$ means that if 1 metre of cloth is sacrificed, an additional $\frac{1}{4}$ tonne of food can be produced. An MRS_{fc} equal to $\frac{1}{8}$ means that 1 metre of cloth can be taken from either individual and substituted for by $\frac{1}{8}$ tonne of food, leaving the individual at the same level of utility. Suppose, then, that 1 metre of cloth is sacrificed in production and an additional $\frac{1}{4}$ tonne of food is produced. Both individuals can now be made better off. For example, A will stay at the same level of utility if the metre of cloth is given up in exchange for $\frac{1}{8}$ tonne of food. But an additional $\frac{1}{4}$ tonne of food has been produced, so the extra $\frac{1}{8}$ tonne can be allocated to the two individuals, raising them both on to higher indifference curves. This kind of reallocation is possible whenever $MRT \neq MRS$. Only when $MRT = MRS$ is no such reallocation possible.

Summary

We can say that in our very simple model the three conditions for economic efficiency in the Pareto sense are that:

(a) *the MRTS of one factor of production for the other should be the same for both goods*;
(b) *the MRS of one good for the other should be the same for both individuals*;
(c) *the common MRS should be equal to the MRT*.

The above are the conditions for Pareto optimality in the $2 \times 2 \times 2$ model. The conditions in the completely general situation of *many* factors, individuals and goods can be expressed as follows:

(a) *the MRTS of every factor for every other factor should be the same for all goods*;
(b) *the MRS of every good for every other good should be the same for all individuals*;
(c) *the common MRS should be equal to the MRT for all pairs of goods.*

We show in Ch. 9 that a perfectly competitive economy with no externalities (that is, one operating under the perfect conditions described in Ch. 7) satisfies the above three conditions for Pareto optimality.

Welfare criteria

We are now ready to discuss several criteria which have been proposed for judging whether a particular change in the way in which production and distribution are organised will increase social welfare.

Efficiency criterion

This criterion, which is based on the concept of Pareto efficiency, states that any change in the organisation of production and distribution which benefits someone *without harming anyone else* will increase social welfare. Whether or not a given change possesses this characteristic can be verified by examining it in relation to the three conditions for Pareto efficiency. Suppose that, before the change, some of these conditions are not satisfied and that these violations of the conditions will *all* be removed by the change. Then the change will have the effect of transforming a situation which is inefficient in the Pareto sense into one which is efficient. In other words, it will benefit someone without harming anyone else. Hence it will increase social welfare on the efficiency criterion.

What if the change will remove some, *but not all*, of the existing violations of the conditions for Pareto efficiency? In this case, it will not necessarily increase welfare on the efficiency criterion – indeed, it may reduce it. This is a corollary of the theory of second best. The theory states that if one of the conditions for Pareto efficiency cannot be fulfilled, then the other conditions, although attainable, are no longer in general desirable. An example of the theory of second best is outlined in Ch. 12 where Pigou's tax-subsidy solution to externalities is discussed.

The theory of second best *If one of the conditions necessary for Pareto efficiency cannot be fulfilled, then the other conditions, even if attainable, are no longer in general desirable*

It is important to emphasise that the efficiency criterion relates only to changes *which benefit someone without harming anyone else*. It has nothing to say about the welfare consequences of changes which are not of this type – changes from which someone gains and someone else loses. This is a serious limitation of the efficiency criterion because the changes on which it remains silent are by far the most common. Most reorganisations of production and distribution are such that some people benefit while others are harmed. For this reason, several other criteria have been devised and it is to these that we now turn our attention.

Equity criteria

The concept of equity is concerned with the allocation question of 'for whom to produce' and so belongs to normative rather than positive economics. This is because decisions about how the national income and national wealth *should be* shared out among the different members of society are necessarily based on value judgements. One can only argue subjectively about the existence of a *'socially desirable'* distribution of income and wealth and economists are as good as (though not necessarily better than) anyone else when it comes to making moral judgements concerned with equity. Indeed, it is true to say that there are no real experts on equity in society.

It follows that if the economist ignored equity considerations when giving expert advice on economic policy, the impression might be given that he or she regarded economic efficiency as a more important criterion of social welfare than equity. Besides, there is a real danger that the economist's advice on efficiency would be given greater weight by the policy-maker than society's vague views about the equitable distribution of income and wealth.

It has, therefore, become increasingly acceptable for the economist to judge social welfare in terms of both efficiency and equity. Clearly, most of the economist's recommendations in the fields of international trade, taxation, government spending, industry and so on are bound to affect the distribution of welfare between individuals and different income groups. This means that the economist should have a sense of 'fairness' and 'economic justice'. In order to analyse welfare in terms of equity, it is necessary to develop some criteria for judging an equitable distribution of income and wealth. The following standards have been suggested:

Egalitarian standard This standard stems from a belief in the equal worth of every human being in society. Thus, an egalitarian society is one which cares equally about every member. According to the egalitarian standard, one distribution of income and wealth is to be regarded as more equitable than another if it is closer to the 'ideal' of absolute equality.

Consider once again our simple economy with two individuals, A and B, and suppose that all income (say, £10,000) is earned by A while B is a sick person with no income. To ensure absolute equality, a 50 per cent tax rate would have to be imposed on A's income and the entire tax revenue transferred to B. Unfortunately, such a high tax rate may adversely affect A's willingness to work and so reduce total income (say, to £6,000). A lower rate of tax with less adverse effects on incentives to work would result in a larger total income for society (that is, more for both A and B). It follows that in order to maximise B's income, the egalitarian standard may necessitate taking into account the effects that income transfers have on people's willingness to work, save and take business risks.

The egalitarian standard may be criticised on the grounds that it assumes that all individuuals in a society have an equal capacity to enjoy. Utility, though, is a subjective concept and individuals may well differ in their abilities to experience satisfaction from a given amount of income. Furthermore, there are severe difficulties in measuring individual utilities and in adding up the utilities of individuals so as to be able to say whether society's welfare is greater in one situation than in another.

To overcome these difficulties, some economists have suggested a *social evaluation* approach. According to this, the total cost and benefit to society of a policy decision has to be estimated. As long as the social cost is less than the social benefit, the policy will increase society's welfare. This explains the growing importance of the cost-benefit approach to decisions in the public sector.

'Social conscience' standard This standard is based upon the idea of the interdependence of individuals' utilities. A rich man's welfare may not only be dependent on his own collection of goods and services but also upon the amount of goods and services available to a poor man. In other words the rich man may have a 'social conscience' so that, once he has attained a certain level of welfare, he may enhance his own welfare by giving voluntarily to the less well off.

It follows that not all taxes are necessarily involuntary payments. A rich man might voluntarily contribute towards government programmes intended to reduce poverty levels. This helps to explain the existence of contributions to charities. Thus, according to this standard, one distribution of income and wealth is to be viewed as more equitable than another if it more clearly reflects the 'social conscience'.

'Under-dog' standard In this case, equity is judged by taking into account the relative share of the 'lower' income groups in the national income. Consequently, poverty levels have to be defined and the family incomes of those living below the poverty line have to be raised. This standard involves weights being assigned to the welfare of different income groups – it is by no means obvious how these weights could be devised.

'Inter-generation' standard It is becoming increasingly realised that decisions about what and how to produce by one generation may affect, adversely or favourably, the welfare of future generations. When, for example, the present generation expedites the exploitation of irreplaceable natural resources and causes the destruction of part of the environment, this results in a loss of welfare for future generations. On the other hand, future generations may experience a gain in welfare if they are bequeathed advances in science and technology and an accumulated stock of capital. An application of the inter-generation standard means taking into account temporal changes in the distribution of income and wealth.

Conflict between efficiency and equity

It is clear from the foregoing discussion that applying policies based on equity criteria means making some people better off and others worse off. Earlier in this chapter, however, we observed that judging society's welfare by efficiency criteria alone means dodging all questions of equity – efficiency criteria cannot be applied to a situation where a policy change benefits some people and harms others. It is nearly always the case that policy measures involve value judgements and thus some kind of interpersonal comparisons of welfare. It is impossible, therefore, to judge them on the basis of efficiency criteria alone because these dispense with both value judgements and interpersonal comparisons.

To illustrate the possible conflict between efficiency and equity, reconsider Fig. 8.7 which shows the exchange box diagram. All the points on the contract curve are efficient in the Pareto sense; they cannot all be described as equitable, however. At point J, for example, individual A has a very large quantity of both cloth and food while individual B has hardly any. It is impossible to make B any better off without making A worse off and so J is an efficient point, but it is still highly inequitable. Now consider point K: this is an inefficient point (off the contract curve) but, being in the centre of the box, represents a perfectly equal distribution of the two goods to the two individuals.

Practical examples of the conflict between efficiency and equity Consider the following two examples which illustrate the problems facing policy-makers because of the potential conflict between efficiency and equity.

(a) *The rationalisation of the British coal industry* Over several decades, successive British governments have given substantial subsidies to protect jobs in the coal mining industry. Many of the regions in which the coal mines were located were heavily dependent on employment in the coal industry, and the life of whole communities in these regions revolved around the mines. Closure of mines, therefore, would result not only in a loss of jobs, but also in a break-up of the affected communities.

One view is that subsidies to coal mining are justified on grounds of equity, to protect miners' jobs and the mining communities. The alternative view, however, is that subsidies encourage labour immobility and prop up loss-making activities by keeping in operation mines which are unable to cover their full production costs. According to this latter view, a subsidy is contrary to the attainment of efficiency in coal-mining. The application of efficiency criteria alone would require the closing down of loss-making activities and the re-allocation of resources to activities where the full production costs may be covered.

In this example, there is clearly a trade-off between efficiency and equity, and this gave rise to an intense political debate in 1992–3. The British government proposed the closure of thirty-one out of a total of fifty remaining coal-mines on efficiency grounds. But the proposal resulted in a political controversy which eventually caused the government to review the planned closures. The debate was between the government view which stressed efficiency and the opposing view which stressed equity and emphasised the need to maintain employment and keep community life intact.

Some observers pointed to the contrast between the policy approaches of the British and German governments in relation to subsidising mines. Subsidies to German coal come not only from the local and state governments, but also from power users who pay artificially high prices for German coal. From an EC perspective, a quest for efficiency would require closure of some high-cost German mines rather than lower-cost British mines. The German government appears to have placed greater emphasis on the equity criterion in this context than the British government.

(b) *The GATT Uruguay Round of trade negotiations* Another well-publicised case that illustrates the conflict between efficiency and equity concerns the recent world trade negotiations (known as the Uruguay Round) by the members of the General Agreement on Tariffs and Trade (GATT). The agreement aims to reduce barriers to international trade, thereby allowing *efficient* producers to expand through access to new markets. The lowering of trade barriers will normally result in a fall in prices to consumers and a greater incentive to efficient production. Thus, trade policy designed to lower trade barriers is based on the efficiency criterion.

The EC Common Agricultural Policy (CAP), on the other hand, aims to promote *equity* by subsidising EC farmers and keeping up farmers' incomes. In 1993, the French government was reluctant to accept an agreement reached between the EC and the United States which required a reduction in aid to EC farmers through the CAP as part of world trade liberalisation. The French government, being influenced by considerations of equity, was reluctant to agree to a change which would make French farmers worse off. Of course, it is possible that the French government was also partly influenced by political considerations, namely a desire to win French farmers' votes.

Estimates published by the Organisation for Economic Co-operation and Development (OECD) indicated that in 1990 each agricultural job preserved by farm subsidies in the EC cost about $20,000 in lost household income. In these and many other examples, the problem facing policy-makers is how to reconcile the conflict between efficiency and equity.

Reconciling the conflict One way of reconciling the conflict between efficiency and equity is to choose from all the Pareto efficient points that one which is regarded as the most equitable and then attempt to reach it through redistribution

Fig. 8.8. **The maximisation of social welfare.** UU is the 'grand utility frontier'. Point Z is the 'bliss point' which maximises social welfare.

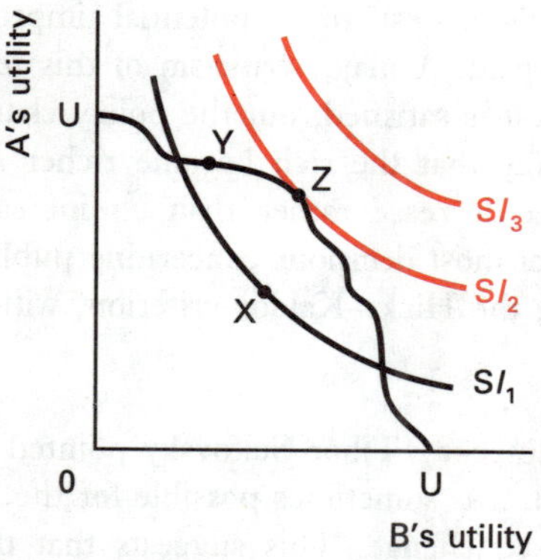

policies. To illustrate this theoretically, consider Fig. 8.8 where the vertical axis measures A's utility and the horizontal axis measures B's utility. The curve UU is called the community's 'grand utility frontier' – every point on it is Pareto efficient (that is, all three marginal conditions are satisfied at every point). The 'grand utility frontier' shows all those combinations of utilities which can be attained when resource allocation is Pareto optimal – notice that since utility is assumed only to be ordinally measurable, the frontier cannot be drawn on a smooth curve. How can we decide which point is the most equitable and so maximise social welfare? One way is to return to the Bergson–Samuelson social welfare function in which the welfare of society depends on the utilities of the individuals, A and B. Such a function can be represented on the graph by a set of *social* indifference curves, three of which (SI_1, SI_2 and SI_3) are shown in Fig. 8.8. The one point on the grand utility frontier which maximises social welfare (that is, puts the community on its highest social indifference curve) is point Z, sometimes called a 'bliss point'.

The difficulty is how to reach point Z. Suppose that initially the community is at point Y. The imposition of taxes to change the distribution of income in an attempt to reach point Z may create an unwillingness to work hard and so reduce efficiency. It may, therefore, only be possible to reach a point like X, inside the grand utility frontier. In other words, there is likely to be a trade-off between efficiency and equity which makes point Z unattainable.

Compensation tests

Compensation test *A method of determining whether a given policy change will increase or decrease net social welfare*

The world is imperfect. The production, consumption and distribution of goods and services are neither efficient nor (most people believe) equitable. How, then, can we determine whether any given policy change will increase or decrease social welfare? Consider the following three compensation tests:

Hicks–Kaldor test According to this test, devised by the British economists Sir John Hicks and Lord Kaldor, there is a net improvement in the welfare of the community if those who gain from a policy measure place higher monetary values on their gains than the losers place on their losses. In these circumstances, the gainers could (hypothetically) compensate the losers and still have some gain left over. Note that this is a test of a potential improvement in welfare since compensation is rarely paid. A major criticism of this test is that it ignores equity considerations. If the test is satisfied, but the policy change affects the distribution of income in such a way that the rich become richer and the poor poorer, then overall there may be a decrease rather than an increase in social welfare. It is probably true to say that most decisions concerning public projects have been taken in practice by applying the Hicks–Kaldor criterion, with little or no compensation being paid.

The Scitovsky double test Tibor Scitovsky pointed out that where compensation is not actually paid, it is sometimes possible for the losers to 'bribe' the gainers to abandon the proposed change. This suggests that the change from the initial situation A to the new situation B and the reverse change from B to A would *both* satisfy the Hicks-Kaldor test. To cover this possibility, Scitovsky suggested a two-part test for a welfare improvement:

(a) confirm that the proposed change satisfies the Hicks–Kaldor test;
(b) confirm that the return to the initial position would *not* satisfy the Hicks–Kaldor test. Notice that both sets of test operate on an implicit value judgement and assume no actual payment of compensation. If compensation were paid, there would be a welfare improvement in the Pareto sense.

Little's test I.M.D. Little, in his book *A Critique of Welfare Economics* in 1957, pointed out several theoretical and practical shortcomings in the above two compensation tests. He thus devised the following stricter tests: first, apply the Hicks–Kaldor and Scitovsky tests; secondly, check that the policy proposal does not adversely affect the distribution of income or wealth. By arguing that explicit value judgements should be attached to what happens to the distribution of income following a change in policy, Little incorporated equity considerations into the social welfare function.

In practice, though, not all policy prescriptions have taken income distribution considerations explicitly into account. Instead, economists have frequently reverted to the Hicks–Kaldor test.

Cost-benefit analysis

Cost-benefit analysis
This seeks to identify the social costs and benefits of a project. It also attempts to quantify these costs and benefits by expressing them in a common monetary unit

This can be regarded as the practical illustration of the uses and limitations of compensation tests. As a technique, cost-benefit analysis is widely applied to public expenditure policies (for example, in transport, education, health and defence).

A public body aiming to maximise social welfare will take account of the *social* costs and benefits of individual projects, as opposed to a private firm which takes account only of its private costs and benefits. The cost-benefit technique attempts to identify the social costs and benefits associated with a scheme over a long period of time and tries to quantify them by expressing them in a common monetary unit. Consider, for example, the building of a motorway. Its social costs include construction and maintenance costs, noise, pollution from dirt and exhaust fumes, loss of landscape and general disfigurement of the environment. Its social benefits include savings in journey time to existing and new road users, possibly fewer accidents and deaths and a smaller fleet of commercial vehicles needed to meet the same demand.

Much the same set of costs and benefits apply to the construction of the Channel Tunnel and the new rail link between London and Paris. A thorough cost-benefit study of this major project would take into account, among other things, the building and maintenance costs of the tunnel and associated rail links; the possible loss of jobs on cross-channel ferries and at ferry ports; the compensation paid to land-owners and householders directly affected by the laying of track for the high-speed trains; and environmental damage caused by the new railway and tunnel terminals. Benefits would include the time saved for travellers; the possible reduction in congestion on roads and at airports; and the additional jobs created to run the system and to build the new trains and infrastructure.

The underlying principle of the technique is to maximise social benefits in relation to social costs, both usually expressed in a common monetary unit. Social benefits include all those effects of a policy change that increase social welfare, and social costs include all those that reduce social welfare. An increase in net social welfare can be written as equal to gross social benefits minus gross social costs.

Viewed in this way, cost-benefit analysis is an alternative technique for resource allocation in the public sector to that of allocation by the market mechanism. It enables the decision maker to choose from the alternative projects that which maximises net social benefit. This narrow objective of the maximisation of net social benefit of a given project should in principle, however, be consistent with the broader objectives of allocation and distribution.

Cost-benefit analysis provides a wide scope for public expenditure decisions which are not made in aggregate but for the provision of a specific good or service. In the United Kingdom, several central government departments have tried to apply cost-benefit techniques – for example, the Home Office, the Departments of the Environment and Transport and the Ministry of Defence. Some local authorities have also made use of it in particular fields of expenditure. However, a far greater use seems to have been made by the Departments of the Environment and Transport in connection with town planning, urban transport, commuter train services and the siting of airports.

Shadow pricing

Shadow price *An artificial or estimated price used by cost-benefit analysts to reflect the 'true' social costs and benefits of a project*

The existence of externalities and monopolistic elements in the market mechanism means that prevailing market prices do not reflect the true social marginal cost of resources in alternative uses. This leads the cost-benefit practitioner to resort to the device of using shadow prices which are imputed prices designed to reflect the 'true' social costs and benefits of a project. For instance, the journey time saved by motorists as the result of the building of a motorway may be valued at an appropriate average hourly wage rate. Similarly, savings from a reduction in the number of accidents can be estimated in terms of the reduced cost of medical treatment. The foreign exchange costs of a project can be imputed if, for example, the prevailing exchange rate in the market overvalues the domestic currency, perhaps because of government reluctance to devalue.

The discounting process

The costs and benefits of a project, once given monetary values through shadow pricing, must be *discounted* before the *present worth* of the project can be determined.

This is necessary because people generally prefer present consumption to future consumption. A sum of £100 received today, for example, is worth more to a person than the same sum received in two years' time: this is because by investing the £100 at, say, a 10 per cent rate of interest compounded annually, both the principal (£100) and the accumulated interest (£21) would be received at the end of the two-year period. Reversing this process, we can say that the present value of £121 to be received in two years' time (given a current rate of interest of 10 per cent) is £100. The same discounting process has to be applied to the costs and benefits of a capital project.

Present value *The present value of a future sum of money is that present sum which when placed with a bank, will grow to that future sum at the given rate of interest*

There are two well-known rules for discounting the costs and benefits associated with a project. These are the net discounted present value (NDPV) rule and the internal rate of return (IRR) rule. Consider these two rules in turn.

The net discounted present value rule This refers to the process of discounting back to the present the streams of costs and benefits associated with a project during its lifetime. According to this rule, *a project is acceptable if the NDPV is greater than zero.* The NDPV can be calculated by applying the following generalised formula:

$$\text{NDPV} = \left[\frac{B_1}{(1+i)} + \frac{B_2}{(1+i)^2} + \ldots + \frac{B_t}{(1+i)^t}\right] - \left[\frac{C_1}{(1+i)} + \frac{C_2}{(1+i)^2} + \ldots + \frac{C_t}{(1+i)^t}\right]$$

where $B_1, B_2, \ldots, B_t$ and $C_1, C_2, \ldots, C_t$ are the gross benefits and costs accruing in years 1 to t, and i is the rate of interest.

As an example, consider a hypothetical project which has a useful life of two years. Suppose for simplicity that it has no maintenance costs and no scrap value at the end of its life, so that all costs are incurred at the initial stage. Suppose in fact that the initial capital outlay is £10 million and that benefits of £6 million and £7.25 million accrue in years 1 and 2 respectively. Applying the above formula with a rate of discount of 10 per cent, we have:

$$\text{NDPV} = \left[\frac{6\text{ m.}}{1+0.1} + \frac{7.25\text{ m.}}{(1+0.1)^2}\right] - 10\text{ m.}$$

$$= £1.4\text{ m.}$$

Since the NDPV > 0, the project is acceptable.

Internal rate of return *The discount rate that equates the present value of a project's benefits with the present value of the project's costs*

The internal rate of return rule The IRR is the estimated rate of return achieved by investing in the project. Since both costs and benefits are involved, it can be calculated as that rate of discount which equates the present value of the project's benefits with the present value of the project's costs. The project can then be regarded as acceptable *if the IRR exceeds the current market rate of interest.* In terms of a generalised formula, the IRR is that rate of discount, r, which solves the following equation:

$$\left[\frac{B_1}{(1+r)}+\frac{B_2}{(1+r)^2}+\ldots+\frac{B_t}{(1+r)^t}\right]-\left[\frac{C_1}{(1+r)}+\frac{C_2}{(1+r)^2}+\ldots+\frac{C_t}{(1+r)^t}\right]=0$$

Applying this to the above example of a project which has a present cost of £10 million and benefits of £6 million after one year and £7.25 million after the second year, we have

$$\left[\frac{6\text{ m.}}{(1+r)}+\frac{7.25\text{ m.}}{(1+r)^2}\right]-10\text{ m.}=0$$

$$r=0.2 \text{ or } 20 \text{ per cent.}$$

Thus, the IRR is 20 per cent which is greater than the rate of interest of 10 per cent. So the project proves to be acceptable by this rule too.

The NDPV rule versus the IRR rule An important question is which of these rules should be applied in determining whether or not a given project is economically viable. As the above examples suggest, a capital project which passes the NDPV test will also pass the IRR test and one which fails the NDPV test will also fail the IRR test; so in that sense, the two rules are consistent.

However, a conflict can arise between the two rules when they are used to compare *alternative* projects both of which may be economically viable. This is illustrated in the example summarised in Table 8.1, where the initial costs of projects A and B are the same (£100m.), but project A is a more capital-intensive project so that only £2 million of benefit accrues in year 1, but £125 million accrues in year 2. Project B is a less capital-intensive project so that bigger benefits accrue in year 1 (£110m.) and smaller benefits accrue in year 2 (£4m.). With an interest rate of 10 per cent, the NDPV rule favours project A, but the IRR rule favours project B.

In cases of conflicting results, the appropriate solution is to apply the NDPV rule. This rule produces the conceptually 'correct' result. The IRR rule is deemed to be less appropriate because it discriminates against capital-intensive projects which yield benefits in the more distant future. Public sector projects, of course, are typically of this type.

Table 8.1 Conflict between IRR and NDPV rules in comparing two projects.

	Present cost	Benefits Yr I	Yr II	IRR	NDPV (i=10%)
Project A	£100m.	£2m.	£125m.	12%	£5m.
Project B	£100m.	£110m.	£4m.	14%	£3m.

Limitations of cost-benefit analysis

The technique attempts to measure the social costs and benefits of a project, but fails to take account satisfactorily of income distribution effects and 'intangibles'. Consider the following limitations:

(a) Some studies ignore the income distribution effects in that they avoid the crucial issue of the actual distribution of the gains and losses of the projects under consideration. This is partly because the technique itself depends upon the Hicks–Kaldor hypothetical compensation tests initially devised to preserve the notion of a Pareto improvement. Pearce and Nash showed, in connection with the Portswood Link Urban Motorway (Southampton), that although total benefits exceeded total costs, the analysis ignored the question of the distribution of gains and losses. One way to overcome this problem might be to give different weights to the gains and losses of different income groups in the population: the main problem with this, though, would be the difficulty of devising appropriate weights. Alternatively, the gains and losses accruing to different groups may be shown separately (as in the Roskill Commission Study on the siting of the third London airport), leaving the final decision to the policy-maker.

(b) The forecasting of the flows of benefits and costs during the lifetime of a project is an extremely hazardous business. It requires predictions of supply and demand patterns over a period of perhaps twenty or thirty years, estimates of future rates of inflation, population growth and spatial movements of population, all of which are extremely difficult to assess accurately.

(c) Intangibles, such as pollution and the general disfigurement of the landscape, are difficult to measure. For example, the environmental damage caused by a motorway in an area of scenic beauty is impossible to evaluate objectively. The extension of the M3 motorway over Twyford Down, near Winchester, for example, will cause environmental damage to an area of great beauty with important archaeological sites. Evaluating the cost of this damage clearly involves making value judgements, and the decision to proceed with the road across the Down (rather than through a tunnel) caused a major controversy.

(d) Cost-benefit analysis aids decision makers to choose between different methods of achieving a *particular* objective, but not to choose between different objectives. For example, if the objective is to reduce traffic congestion in a city, the technique helps the decision makers to choose between, say, an urban motorway system and an underground railway system. The technique does not, however, help the government to choose between, say, education projects and defence projects.

Cost-benefit analysis in less developed countries

The application of cost-benefit analysis to resource allocation is important in less developed countries since public investment plays a key role in the development process – for example, in health, road transport and irrigation schemes. Moreover, the governments of many of these countries provide subsidies directly to private investment. The purpose of public investment and the government support for private investment is to generate widespread external benefits and thus try to overcome the problem of structural imbalances.

However, the scarcity of foreign exchange, domestic savings, technical knowledge and entrepreneurial abilities imposes severe limits on the speed of the development process. By the same token, markets may not reflect the true social cost of resources. For instance, market prices tend to overvalue labour if there is widespread unemployment so that the market wage rate exceeds the social opportunity cost of labour.

It follows that in order to allocate scarce resources amongst the competing claims of different sectors, it is necessary for economic planners to use shadow prices when engaged in estimating the social costs and benefits of development projects. More importantly, it is necessary that in the design of development plans the distribution of gains and losses is given explicit consideration, for the basic philosophy of planned development is to increase the welfare of the individual members of a group by raising their incomes and thus their living standards.

Summary

1. A social welfare function is a statement of the factors which influence social welfare. It includes a measure of the quantity of goods and services available for consumption and a measure of the way in which these goods and services are distributed.
2. Pareto efficiency requires that three main conditions be achieved: efficiency in production; efficiency in exchange; and an efficient output mix.
3. In a simple $2 \times 2 \times 2$ model, efficiency in production requires that the MRTS of one factor of production for the other should be the same for both goods. Efficiency in exchange requires that the MRS of one good for the other should be equal for both individuals. An efficient output mix requires that the common MRS should equal the MRT.
4. Equity criteria can be based on a number of different standards: the egalitarian standard; the 'social conscience' standard; the 'under-dog' standard; and the 'inter-generation' standard.
5. Compensation tests are one way of attempting to reconcile the conflict between efficiency and equity. The tests include the Hicks–Kaldor test, the Scitovsky double test and Little's test.
6. Cost-benefit analysis is concerned with evaluating the social costs and benefits associated with a public project. It may be described as a practical application of compensation tests. It is a method of judging the desirability of a policy where some groups gain and others lose.

Exercises

1. Review your understanding of the following terms:

social welfare function	egalitarian standard
Pareto optimality	social conscience standard
efficiency in production	inter-generation standard

efficiency in exchange
efficient output mix
Edgeworth–Bowley box diagram
contract curve
marginal rate of technical substitution
marginal rate of substitution
marginal rate of transformation
equity
social indifference curve
'bliss point'
theory of second best
Hicks–Kaldor test
Scitovsky double test
Little's test
cost-benefit analysis
shadow pricing

2. Consider a country producing two goods (bread and ale), with two factors of production (labour and capital) and two individuals (Adam and Eve). Draw the box diagrams in production and exchange, showing clearly the contract curves. Explain why points off the contract curves fail to satisfy the marginal conditions (a) and (b) derived in this chapter. Suppose that the MRT of bread into ale is equal to 2 and that the common MRS of ale for bread is equal to 4. Suggest a reallocation which will make both Adam and Eve better off.

3. 'Pareto efficiency and equity are conflicting objectives.' What welfare policy could be used in the attempt to reconcile these conflicting objectives?

4. 'The rapid depletion of the Earth's natural resources by the present generation means that less is available for future generations.' Discuss this statement in terms of equity criteria. Comment on the applicability of compensation tests to this problem.

5. What variables might be included in the social welfare functions of: (a) the government of a developed country; and (b) the government of a less developed country? What problems might be encountered in the measurement of these variables?

6. Consider the proposal to introduce night flights into an airport which will result in noise disturbance to nearby residents. Discuss how the relevant authority might employ cost-benefit analysis and compensation tests to determine the desirability of implementing the proposal.

7. Discuss the problems involved in using cost-benefit analysis to evaluate the construction of the Channel tunnel.

PRIVATE SECTOR FIRMS

9 THEORY OF THE FIRM – I

Learning objectives

After reading this chapter, you should be able to:

- recognise that, in economics, production costs are based on the concept of opportunity cost, and explain the distinction between accounting and opportunity cost
- define fixed and variable cost and show that in the short-run, average and marginal costs will eventually rise as 'diminishing returns' come into operation
- explain the role of economies and diseconomies of scale in determining the shape of a firm's long-run average cost curve
- show that a firm's profit will be maximised at the point where the marginal cost curve cuts the marginal revenue curve from below
- outline the assumptions upon which the model of perfect competition is based
- illustrate and explain the short-run and long-run equilibrium positions of a perfectly competitive firm and industry
- show that, in the absence of externalities, perfect competition will lead to a Pareto optimal allocation of resources

Introduction

The theory of the firm is concerned with the analysis of firms' output and pricing decisions. Such decisions are influenced by the objectives that the firms set themselves and by the structure of the industries to which the firms belong. In this chapter, after examining the behaviour of firms' production costs in the short- and long-run, we consider price and output determination under conditions of *perfect competition*, assuming throughout that firms attempt to maximise their profits. We demonstrate the important result that *an economy characterised by perfect competition in all markets and with no externalities satisfies the marginal conditions for Pareto efficiency*.

The models of imperfect competition and alternatives to the assumption of profit maximisation are considered in Ch. 10.

Costs of production

It is important to note that economists base their estimate of production costs on the concept of *opportunity cost* which, as we saw in Ch. 1, is measured in terms of forgone alternatives. In this context, the opportunity cost to a firm of using resources in the production of a good is the revenue forgone by not using those resources in their next best alternative use.

In estimating opportunity costs, economists take a wider view of costs than accountants. In the economist's view, there is no necessary connection between the price originally paid for a factor of production and the cost of using that factor in production. Consider an extreme case of a firm that owns a specialised piece of machinery which can only be used in one production process, has no alternative use and no scrap value. The opportunity cost of using this machine in production is zero, whatever price was originally paid for the machine. If a firm buys a factor of production and uses it up entirely within the relevant production period, then the price actually paid is normally a good estimate of the opportunity cost. If, for example, a firm buys some fuel-oil for £1,000, the outlay of £1,000 represents the alternative resources that the firm has given up by spending that sum on fuel-oil. Similarly, if a firm hires the services of a factor (for example, labour), then the money cost of hiring that factor is a good estimate of opportunity cost.

In the case of factors owned outright by a firm, it is necessary to *impute* (or estimate) the opportunity cost. In this case, the estimate of opportunity cost is normally based on the amount for which the firm could hire out the services of the factor. If, for example, a firm uses money which it already owns, the cost is the interest given up by not lending that money to someone else at the market rate of interest. Analogously, an entrepreneur has the alternative of hiring out his labour services and working for another employer, who might pay him, say £30,000 per annum. Thus, in estimating production costs when the entrepreneur is in business alone, he or she should include the sum of £30,000 per annum to reflect his or her own efforts.

Distinction between accounting and opportunity costs

To illustrate the distinction between accounting costs and opportunity costs, consider the case of a market trader who sells umbrellas. For simplicity assume that the trader sells all the umbrellas he or she purchases during the relevant period. The trader's accountant might prepare the following simplified accounts for a particular year.

In Table 9.1 the cost of sales of £30,000 worth of umbrellas reflects the purchase price of the umbrellas and the quantity purchased (say 5,000 umbrellas at £4 each). The expenses are the overheads incurred by the trader, say hire of market stall and cost of transport. From the accountant's viewpoint, therefore, the trader has made a net profit of £6,000.

The economist, adopting the opportunity cost principle, would argue that account must also be taken of the opportunity cost to the market trader of using capital and labour in this particular way. Suppose that the trader has funds worth £5,000 tied up in the business. The trades could have lent the £5,000 at the market rate of interest, say 10 per cent per annum. In this case, he or she would have received £500 per annum in interest payments, and this sum represents the opportunity cost of tying up funds in the business of selling umbrellas.

The trader might have taken up employment elsewhere and earned, perhaps, £8,000 per annum. These additional opportunity costs, totalling £8,500 per annum,

Table 9.1 Trading and profit and loss account for the year ended 31 December 199X.

		£
	Sales	30,000
Less	Cost of sales	20,000
	Gross profit	10,000
Less	Expenses	4,000
	Net profit	6,000

which are not included in the accountant's calculations, are added to the cost of sales and expenses in the *economist's* calculation of opportunity costs. Thus, the total *opportunity cost* of being a market trader is £32,500 per annum. With revenue from sales of only £30,000, from the economist's point of view the trader has made a loss of £2,500 over the relevant period. On the basis of the information given, the economist's advice must be to consider seriously whether it is worthwhile to continue as a market trader. At this stage, of course, the trader might claim that the calculations do not take full account of personal preferences. The trader might place a considerable, subjective value on continuing in the way of life of a market trader with the independence it confers.

Short-run costs

When we discussed production in Ch. 2, we distinguished between two production periods: the short- and long-run. Recall that the *short-run* was defined as that period of time over which the input of at least one factor of production cannot be increased. If the quantity of a factor cannot be increased in the short-run, it is called a *fixed factor*. A factor whose quantity can be increased in the short-run is known as a *variable factor*.

Total costs *The sum of total fixed costs and total variable costs*

Fixed costs *Costs which do not vary as the level of output varies*

Variable costs *Costs which vary with the level of output*

Corresponding to this division, total costs can be broken down into fixed costs and variable costs. As the firm has to pay the costs associated with the fixed factors whether or not the firm produces, these costs are called fixed costs. Examples are rents and rates on buildings, interest payments on loans, and licence fees contracted for manufacture under licence from a patent holder. It must be emphasised that fixed costs do not vary as the level of output varies: they are the same whether output is zero or a thousand units per week. Those costs that do change as the level of output varies are known as variable costs. Examples include the cost of raw materials, components, labour and power. Total variable costs increase as the level of output increases.

To summarise we have:

total costs = *total fixed costs* + *total variable costs*, or in symbols:

$$TC = TFC + TVC$$

Now consider the costs of a hypothetical firm producing good X, shown in Table 9.2. Suppose that labour is the only variable factor. Recall that, with a fixed capital stock, this firm will eventually encounter the law of diminishing returns and the average productivity of labour will begin to fall. Assuming that the firm buys its factors of production in perfectly competitive factor markets, factor prices will be constant however much the firm buys. This implies that the eventual decline in the

Table 9.2 The cost of production of a hypothetical firm in the short run.

(1) Output (units)	(2) Total fixed cost (£)	(3) Total variable cost (£)	(4) Total cost (£)	(5) Average fixed cost (£)	(6) Average variable cost (£)	(7) Average total cost (£)	(8) Marginal cost (£)
0	5	0	5	∞	-	∞	-
1	5	4	9	5	4	9	4
2	5	7.5	12.5	2.5	3.75	6.25	3.5
3	5	10.8	15.8	1.67	3.60	5.27	3.3
4	5	13.8	18.8	1.25	3.45	4.70	3.0
5	5	17.0	22.0	1.00	3.40	4.40	3.2
6	5	20.5	25.5	0.83	3.42	4.25	3.5
7	5	24.3	29.3	0.71	3.47	4.18	3.8
8	5	28.6	33.6	0.63	3.57	4.20	4.3
9	5	33.5	38.5	0.56	3.72	4.28	4.9
10	5	39.0	44.0	0.50	3.90	4.40	5.5

average productivity of labour must push up the average variable cost of production, as average variable cost and average labour productivity are opposite sides of the same coin.

Average variable cost (AVC) *The variable cost per unit of output*

In Table 9.2, column (6) is headed average variable cost (AVC). This is obtained by dividing total variable cost by the quantity produced, or in symbols:

$$\text{AVC} = \frac{\text{TVC}}{Q}$$

From Table 9.2 we see that AVC reaches a minimum when output is 5 units per production period. This is the level of output at which average productivity of labour is at a maximum. In other words, at this level of output, the proportions between the fixed factor and the variable factor are at an optimum.

At levels of output above 5 units, the variable factor has progressively less of the fixed factor to work with and its average productivity declines. This results in higher AVC as output increases. Conversely, AVC falls until output reaches 5 units because at low levels of output the variable factor has too much of the fixed factor to work with. Thus, if we plot AVC on a graph against output we obtain a U-shaped curve (see Fig. 9.1). Note that if a firm encountered diminishing returns as soon as it started production, it would have an upward-sloping AVC curve.

Average fixed cost (AFC) *The fixed cost per unit of output*

Column (5) is headed average fixed cost (AFC). This is obtained by dividing total fixed cost by the quantity produced, or in symbols:

$$\text{AFC} = \frac{\text{TFC}}{Q}$$

Clearly, AFC must decline continuously as output increases because the given level of fixed cost will be spread over a bigger level of output. The 'tooling-up' costs of establishing a car assembly line are an example. The tooling-up costs per car decline as the volume of output increases. This is sometimes described as 'spreading the overheads'.

Fig. 9.1. Short-run cost curves plotted from Table 9.2. Both the MC and AVC curves eventually rise as predicted by the law of diminishing returns.

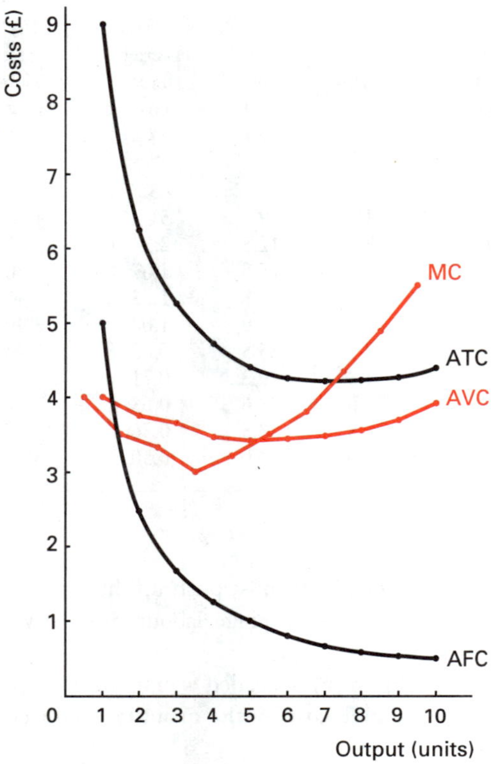

Average total cost (ATC) *The total cost per unit of output*

Column (7) is headed average total cost (ATC). ATC is obtained by adding together average fixed cost and average variable cost, or in symbols:

$$\text{ATC} = \text{AFC} + \text{AVC}$$

Alternatively, ATC can be obtained by dividing total cost by the level of output, or in symbols:

$$\text{ATC} = \frac{\text{TC}}{Q}$$

In Table 9.2, ATC declines until output reaches 7 units as the fixed costs are spread over a larger output and initially the firm benefits from increasing returns to the variable factor. Above the level of output of 7 units, ATC increases as the influence of diminishing returns, which is pushing up AVC, outweighs the decline in AFC. Thus if we plot ATC on a graph against output, we obtain another U-shaped curve (see Fig. 9.1).

Marginal cost (MC) *The change in total cost as a result of changing the level of output by one unit*

Column (8) is headed marginal cost (MC). This is defined as *the change in total cost resulting from changing the level of output by one unit*, or in symbols:

$$\text{MC} = \frac{\Delta\text{TC}}{\Delta Q}$$

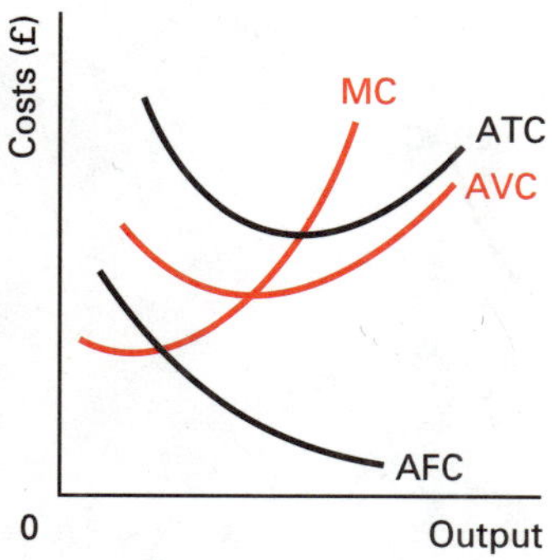

Fig. 9.2. Short-run cost curves for continuous data. The MC curve cuts the AVC and ATC curves at their lowest points.

From Table 9.2, we see that producing 3 units of X costs £15.80, and producing 4 units costs £18.80. To work out the MC of producing the fourth unit, we have

$$MC = \frac{18.80 - 15.80}{1} = £3$$

The shape of the MC curve is related to the behaviour of the marginal product (MP) curve, which we encountered in Ch. 2. If at low levels of output a firm benefits from increasing marginal returns to the variable factor (that is increasing MP), MC will be declining. MC reaches a minimum at the level of output at which MP is at a maximum. When the firm encounters diminishing marginal returns, so that MP is falling, MC begins to rise. Whenever there is a fixed factor, so that the law of diminishing returns comes into operation, the MC curve will eventually start to rise. If we plot the MC curve on a graph against output, we see that it is a U-shaped curve (see Fig. 9.1). Note that in Fig. 9.1, the MC is plotted at the mid-point of the class interval.

The MC curve cuts the AVC and ATC curves at their minimum points for arithmetical reasons similar to those which meant that the MP curve cut the AP curve at its maximum. In Table 9.2, MC does not exactly equal ATC when ATC is at a minimum because of the discrete nature of the data. It is also for this reason that MC does not exactly equal AVC when AVC is at a minimum. If we had continuous data, we would obtain smooth cost curves as drawn in Fig. 9.2.

Long-run costs

Recall from Ch. 2, that we defined the *long-run* as that period of time over which the input of all factors of production can be varied. Thus, all factors are variable factors in the long-run. Recall also that profit-maximising firms will wish to minimise their costs of production.

Traditionally, when deriving the long-run average cost (LRAC) curve, elementary economic theory has assumed that a firm can build an infinite number of plants of different capacities. In some industries, this is clearly an unrealistic assumption; if only a limited number of plants of different capacities can be constructed, the firm's LRAC curve will not be continuously smooth.

The LRAC curve shows the lowest possible cost of producing different levels of output given the production function and factor prices, as reflected in the firm's

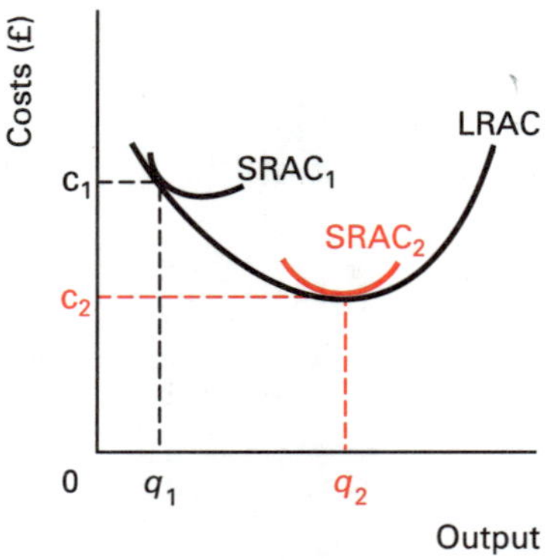

Fig. 9.3. *Long-run average cost curve.* The LRAC curve shows the lowest cost of producing different levels of output, given the firm's production function and factor prices. The LRAC curve is an envelope curve to the firm's SRAC curves.

isocost curves. Note that a cost-minimising firm will only produce at points along its *expansion path* as explained in Ch. 2. An LRAC curve is illustrated in Fig. 9.3. It indicates the minimum possible average cost of producing any level of output on the assumption that all factors are variable. Thus, the LRAC curve in Fig. 9.3 indicates the minimum average cost of production for each level of output, given that the plant of the appropriate capacity has been constructed. The minimum average cost of producing output $0q_1$ is shown to be $0c_1$.

The LRAC curve reaches a minimum when $0q_2$ units of output are produced. Up to this level of output, the LRAC curve is declining; the firm is experiencing economies of scale. Assuming fixed factor prices, this must be because the firm has increasing returns to scale. As output is increased above $0q_2$, the LRAC curve rises, indicating that the firm is facing diseconomies of scale. With fixed factor prices, this is because at these levels of output the firm has decreasing returns of scale. If factor prices are constant and long-run average cost is also constant, the firm is said to have constant returns to scale.

Economies of scale
Falling long-run average cost as the scale of output increases

Diseconomies of scale
Rising long-run average cost as the scale of output increases

Note that if, having built a plant appropriate to minimum long-run average cost at a given level of output, the firm varies its output, it will move along a short-run average cost (SRAC) curve. In Fig. 9.3 as the firm changes its level of output with the plant appropriate for minimum long-run average cost of production at output $0q_1$, it moves along $SRAC_1$. There is an SRAC curve at a tangent at every point along the LRAC curve. Each SRAC curve lies above the LRAC curve except at the point at which it is at a tangent. For this reason, the LRAC curve is sometimes known as an *envelope curve.*

Now consider the factors which influence the shape of a firm's LRAC curve. The factors leading to declining long-run average cost (economies of scale) and to rising long-run average cost (diseconomies of scale) are discussed in turn.

Economies of scale

Economies of scale can be either internal or external.

Internal economies are those factors which bring about a reduction in average cost as the scale of production of the individual firm rises. Many types of production processes benefit from this phenomenon, particularly processing industries and certain manufacturing operations. Economies of scale can help to explain the trend towards larger production units in some industries. Consider the followin economies.

Technical economies (a) *Increased specialisation.* The larger is the scale of production, the greater is the scope for the specialisation of both labour and machinery. Where a production process is broken down into a number of tasks, with each worker performing a single task, this arrangement is referred to as the division of labour. Consider, for instance, the large-scale assembly of washing machines in a factory. One worker might assemble the panels, another the motor, yet another the drum, and so on. By performing the same actions repeatedly, labour can become very skilled and perform with speed and dexterity. If the production process is broken down into many different stages, machines can be designed specifically for each stage. This process is well advanced in a modern car-assembly plant, for example, where many of the different stages in assembly are completed by computer-controlled machines.

Specialisation *A situation where factors of production are employed in the provision of a single good or service on a continuous basis*

Division of labour *A situation where the production process is broken down into a number of tasks, and workers specialise in one of these tasks*

(b) *Economies of increased dimensions.* If the external dimensions of a container are increased, the cubic capacity increases more than proportionately. This means that the unit storage or transport costs of liquids or gases may fall as larger containers are used. This has, for example, led to bigger tanks at oil-refineries and chemical works. C.F. Pratten reported that chemical engineers developed a rule that if the capacity of a chemical plant is doubled, the capital cost is increased by only 52 per cent and the average fixed cost falls by 24 per cent. An additional economy of increased dimensions has become more significant since the increase in energy costs. If the dimensions of a container holding heated material are doubled, the cubic capacity increases eight times, but the surface area only fourfold, resulting in a smaller heat loss per unit.

(c) *Factor indivisibility.* Certain pieces of capital equipment have to be of a certain minimum size or capacity to justify their manufacture. An automated car-assembly line, for example, is not a viable proposition for low-volume manufacture as much of the capital would lie idle for long periods. By using indivisible pieces of capital, larger firms may be able to achieve lower average costs than small firms.

(d) *Principle of multiples.* If a production process involves the use of different types of machinery, a large firm can arrange to have more of the machines with a small output and fewer of the machines with a high output, thus achieving a high utilisation rate. A small firm, on the other hand, with only one of each type of machine would find the high-capacity machines standing idle for much of the time.

(e) *Research and development.* A large firm may be able to support its own research and development programme which can result in cost-reducing innovations.

Financial economies Large firms are normally able to obtain finance at lower rates of interest than small firms. Large firms can often provide more collateral as security for loans and investors may be more likely to place money with a well-known, rather than with a small firm. The administrative costs of arranging a large loan will not be twice those of arranging a loan half as large. In addition, large companies have the option of making a new share issue on the stock exchanges. The expenses of a new share issue are such that it is not a practical proposition for raising small sums.

Marketing economies Marketing economies arise from the large-scale purchase of factors of production and from marketing and distributing the finished product in large quantities. A company selling a large volume may be able to use more expensive, but more cost-effective, advertising. Large companies often receive quantity discounts in the purchase of raw materials. Important users of a component are in a strong bargaining position as they can threaten to start production of the component themselves. The distribution and administrative costs of an order for 1,000 units are unlikely to be ten times the costs of an order for 100 units.

Risk-bearing economies A large company that has diversified into several markets is likely to be better placed to withstand adverse trading conditions in one particular market. At the same time, other markets may have buoyant trading conditions. If a company is better able to withstand risks, this may mean that it becomes more willing to take risks than smaller companies. In recent years, many large companies have attempted to diversify their interests, such as the large tobacco companies.

A company has to hold stocks in order to meet fluctuations in orders. Stocks have to be financed and also incur storage costs. As the volume of orders increases because of an increased number of customers, the company will find that the required volume of stocks will increase less than proportionately, as individual changes in orders will tend to offset one another.

Diseconomies of scale

It has been argued that diseconomies of scale are unlikely to occur for purely technical reasons for if a company wishes to expand it can always duplicate its existing plant. As organisations become larger, however, managerial functions become increasingly difficult to perform effectively. In a large organisation, there are likely to be several departments so that more time and effort have to be devoted to communication and consultation. This may lead to delays in decision-making. In areas where consumers' tastes change rapidly, a small firm which can make decisions quickly may have an advantage over a larger firm.

If production is concentrated into one or more production units, the average transport costs of raw materials, components and the finished articles are likely to increase. Indeed, transport costs may place an effective limit on the concentration of production. There is some evidence that larger production units suffer from more strikes and other labour disputes. This may be because workers in a large plant feel themselves to be a 'cog in a machine' with no individual identity. Workers in a typical large manufacturing plant are likely to be far removed from the centre of decision-making and are unlikely to feel highly committed to the firm. A related problem with large integrated plants, such as a steelworks, is that an industrial dispute involving only a few key workers may lead to a complete halt in production, as all the stages in the production process are interdependent.

For these and other reasons, a feeling that 'small is beautiful' and in favour of small firms developed in some quarters in the 1960s and 1970s. It is, of course, true that in many markets small firms can compete effectively, particularly as they can respond quickly to the requirements of consumers. Competition amongst small firms can result in good service for consumers.

External economies of scale

External economies result from the simultaneous growth or interaction of a number of firms in the same or related industries. External economies are available to *all* firms in the industry no matter what their size. It can be noted that particular geographical areas often specialise in the production of particular products. Examples in the United Kingdom include the production of ceramics around Stoke-on-Trent and motor-vehicle production in the West Midlands. When an industry is concentrated in a particular area, all firms can benefit from the specialist services that develop. These include the specialist companies for supplying and repairing machinery, the provision of relevant training courses by local colleges and the facilities of the financial institutions. The specific labour skills developed in the industry will encourage new firms entering the industry to locate in the same region.

Typically, the expansion of an industry leads to the establishment of many firms specialising in particular stages of the production process. This is termed *disintegration*. The example of the textile industry is well known. By specialising in a particular operation, a firm can benefit from internal economies of scale and other firms in the industry can have this operation performed for them at lower cost. Note that external economies of scale are also referred to as externalities, which are considered in detail in Ch. 12.

Economies of scope

A firm may be able to achieve cost reductions as a result of producing two or more products at the same time rather than producing these products separately. If so, the firm is said to benefit from *economies of scope*.

A bank, for example, when providing banking services to a customer, is also able to offer a range of insurance products. It may, therefore, be less costly for the bank to offer both banking and insurance services together than it would be for a bank and insurance company to offer these services separately. This is because a single bank employee can deal with both transactions. If these services were to be offered by a separate bank and insurance company, two employees would have to transact the business, resulting in higher costs. Consider another example of a petrol station with a grocery shop attached. The cashier handles both petrol and grocery transactions with obvious cost savings.

Profit maximisation

Profit maximisation
A situation in which a producer earns the highest possible level of profit. This is achieved by producing the level of output at which marginal cost and marginal revenue are equal

Profit is defined as the difference between total revenue and total cost, or in symbols:

$$\pi = \text{TR} - \text{TC}$$

where π represents profit, TR total revenue and TC total cost. As total revenue is the income to the firm from the sales of its output, it is calculated by multiplying price (or average revenue) by the number of units sold (or quantity). Thus we have

$$\text{TR} = p \times q$$

where p is price and q quantity.

Recall that we assume that firms attempt to maximise their profits. How does a firm achieve profit maximisation? We can answer this question by utilising the concepts of *marginal cost* and *marginal revenue*.

When we considered a firm's marginal cost (MC) curve earlier, we saw that the short-run MC curve must eventually slope upwards because of the law of diminishing returns.

Marginal revenue
The change in total revenue as a result of changing the level of sales by one unit

Marginal revenue is defined as *the change in total revenue resulting from altering the level of output by one unit*. The marginal revenue (MR) curve facing the firm is derived from the average revenue (or demand) curve. Assume for the moment that the firm faces a downward-sloping demand curve which, as we shall see in the next chapter, means that the firm also faces a downward-sloping MR curve, as in Fig. 9.4.

Consider whether the firm is maximising profit if it produces quantity $0q_1$. It clearly is not, as at this level of output MR equals q_1A and MC is q_1B. As MR is greater than MC, by producing an additional unit of output, the firm will add more to revenue than to costs, and profit will increase. In general, we can state that if, for a profit-maximising firm, MR is greater than MC, the firm should increase output.

Now consider whether the firm is maximising profit if it produces output $0q_3$. At this level of output, MC equals q_3C and MR is q_3D. As MC is greater than MR, by producing the last unit the firm has actually reduced profit. As long as MC is greater than MR, by producing less the firm can reduce cost more than revenue. Thus, in general, we can state that if MC is greater than MR, a profit-maximising firm should reduce output.

Taken together our two general statements imply that *in order to maximise profit, a firm should produce that quantity at which MC and MR are equal*. Referring back to Fig. 9.4, in order to maximise profit the firm should produce quantity $0q_2$, at which point both MC and MR equal q_2E.

If we use the simple MC = MR rule for profit maximisation, what is the profit-maximising level of output in Fig. 9.5 where the MC curve cuts the MR curve twice at points A and B? The simple MC = MR rule does not enable us to determine whether $0q_1$ or $0q_2$ is the profit-maximising level of output.

Consider output $0q_1$: if the firm increased output to $0q_3$, say, profit would increase as the MR of the additional units is greater than MC. Thus, output $0q_1$ is clearly not the profit-maximising level.

Now consider output $0q_2$: if the firm reduced output to $0q_4$, say, profit would fall as MR is greater than MC. Conversely, if the firm increased output above $0q_2$, profit

Fig. 9.4. *Profit maximisation.* A firm maximises profit by producing output $0q_2$ where its MC curve cuts its MR curve from below.

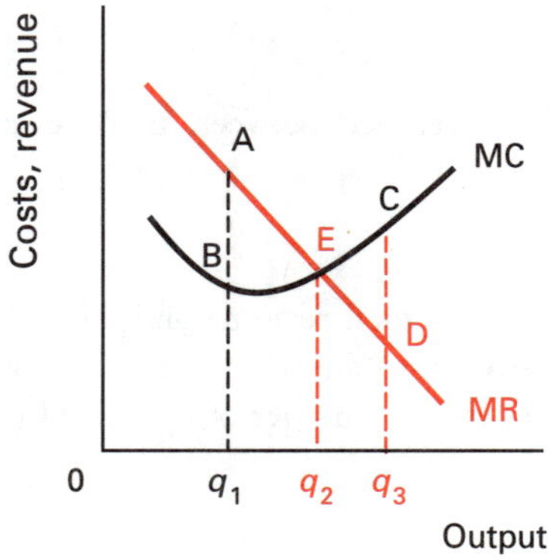

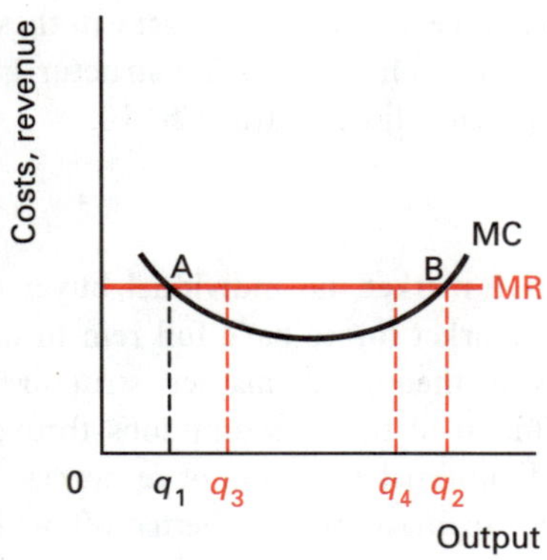

Fig. 9.5. *Profit maximisation where MC cuts MR twice.* Output $0q_2$ is the profit-maximising level of output, determined at the point where the MC curve cuts the MR curve from below.

would also fall as MC is greater than MR. Output $0q_2$, therefore, is the profit-maximising level of output. At this level of output the MC curve is rising and cuts the MR curve from below. At output $0q_1$, on the other hand, the MC curve is falling and cuts the MR curve from above. Thus, the profit maximisation rule requires some refinement. It now states that to *maximise profit a firm should produce that quantity at which MR = MC, provided the MC curve is rising so that it cuts the MR curve from below at this point.*

Any firm which is maximising profit must be producing where MR = MC even if it does not intentionally plan to equate MR and MC. The MR = MC rule applies no matter in what form of market structure the firm operates.

Market structures

Market structure refers to the nature and degree of competition within a particular market. Capitalist economies are characterised by a range of different market structures. These include the following:

Perfect competition This is a theoretical market structure in which there are many buyers and sellers with no individual power to influence market price.

Monopolistic competition In this market there are many firms producing *differentiated* products, such as clothing and hairdressing services. This market structure is sometimes also called *competition among the many*.

Oligopoly Here, a few interdependent firms dominate the market. Examples include the major oil companies in the petroleum industry and the major clearing banks in the United Kingdom.

Duopoly In this case two firms dominate the market for the product, such as British Telecom and Mercury in the telecommunications industry. Duopoly is a special case of oligopoly.

Monopoly This refers to a single supplier for the whole market. Under current legislation British Gas, for example, is the sole supplier of gas to households in the United Kingdom.

Clearly, the nature and degree of competition vary in these markets. We now turn to an analysis of perfect competition. The market structures of monopoly, monopolistic competition and oligopoly are discussed in Ch. 10.

The model of perfect competition

In a perfectly competitive market, no individual buyer or seller has any influence over the market so that market forces have full rein to determine price and output. Perfect competition is a theoretical market structure based on a number of assumptions. The fulfilment of these assumptions throughout the economy can be shown to lead to a Pareto optimal allocation of resources. As we saw in Ch. 8, in this situation it is impossible to make anyone better off without making someone else worse off.

Assumptions of the model

Perfect competition is used by economists as a yardstick against which other market structures are compared and evaluated. The model, however, cannot be realistically expected to exist in totality in everyday life. Nevertheless, some real world markets do contain a number of features of the perfectly competitive model as, for example, in the case of some agricultural markets.

The assumptions of the model of perfect competition model can be summarised as follows:

(a) many buyers and sellers;
(b) freedom of entry and exit;
(c) perfect mobility of factors of production;
(d) perfect knowledge;
(e) homogeneous product.

It should be pointed out that the fulfilment of these assumptions in the absence of externalities satisfies the operation of the price mechanism under 'perfect conditions' as discussed in Ch. 7. The existence of many sellers means that no individuual firm is able to have a significant effect on the market. Each firm is small in relation to the size of the whole market and can effectively be regarded as facing a *perfectly elastic* demand curve for, at the ruling market price, it can sell whatever it produces. Such a firm is described as a *price taker*. If the firm tried to set a price above the ruling market price, it would sell nothing as, with their perfect knowledge, consumers would buy from the other producers. Similarly, the firm would not set a lower price as this would reduce its total revenue. Note that while the individual firm faces a perfectly elastic demand curve, the *market* demand curve for the product will normally be downward-sloping. The existence of many buyers means that no individual buyer has any influence over the market. Any collusion between buyers and/or sellers is also ruled out.

The assumption of freedom of entry and exit is almost self-explanatory. It means that there are no barriers to new firms entering the industry nor to existing firms leaving the industry. In addition to this mobility of firms, there is the assumption of perfect mobility of factors of production. It is assumed that land, labour and capital can switch immediately from one line of production to another.

We have already referred to the assumption of perfect knowledge on the part of both buyers and sellers. It is assumed that all participants in the market are perfectly well informed about prices, quality, output levels and all other market conditions. As

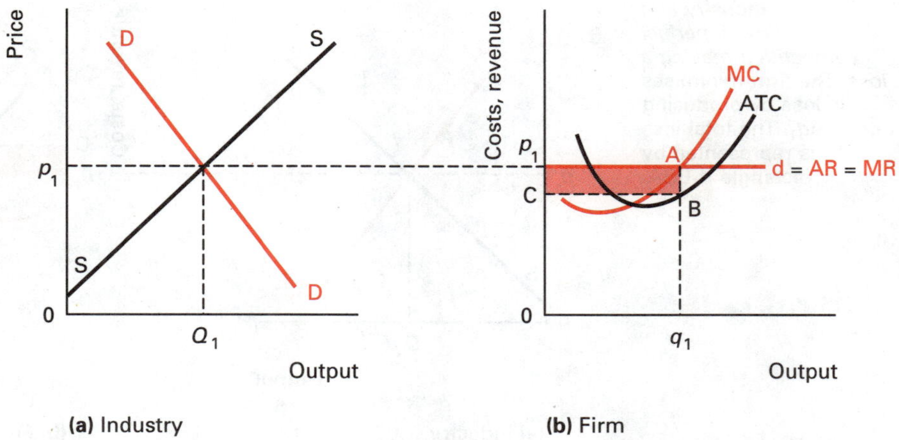

Fig. 9.6. Industry and firm in perfect competition earning above-normal profits. The equilibrium price and output for the industry are determined by the interaction of market demand and supply. The firm is a price taker and has to accept the ruling market price.

a consequence, there are neither advertising costs for sellers nor search costs for buyers. This assumption is a sharp reminder of the theoretical nature of perfect competition, as in reality the collection of information is often a costly and time-consuming chore.

The assumption of a homogeneous product implies that each unit produced is identical, so that buyers can have no preferences between different units. Perfect knowledge and a homogeneous product together imply that there must be a single market price for all units of output.

Prices and output determination in the short-run

Now consider the determination of price and output in the short-run for an individual perfectly competitive firm and for the whole industry, assuming profit maximisation. The equilibrium price is determined in the market for the good (say good X) by the interaction of supply and demand. Figure 9.6(a) shows the market demand curve (DD) and the market supply curve (SS) which intersect to give an equilibrium price $0p_1$ and an equilibrium industry output $0Q_1$.

Figure 9.6(b), drawn on a much bigger scale, illustrates the costs and revenues of a typical firm earning above-normal profit. The firm faces a perfectly elastic demand curve (d), indicating that it can sell all that it produces at the ruling market price $0p_1$. The price the firm receives per unit is given by total revenue divided by the number of units produced, and is, therefore, the same as average revenue (AR). In symbols, we have:

$$p = \frac{\mathrm{TR}}{q} = \mathrm{AR}$$

As the firm receives a constant price $0p_1$, its AR is also constant. In addition, since an *extra* unit of output can always be sold without reducing price, MR must also be equal to price. Thus, in Fig. 9.6(b) the demand curve facing the firm is labelled d = AR = MR.

To find the equilibrium quantity that the firm will produce, we apply the MR = MC rule. The MR and MC curves in the diagram intersect at the point where MC cuts MR from below. The profit-maximising level of output, therefore, is $0q_1$. Note that the equilibrium price $0p_1$ is equal to MC at the equilibrium level of

Fig. 9.7 *Industry and firm in perfect competition making a loss.* The firm minimises its loss by producing output $0q_1$. The total loss is represented by rectangle p_1DBA.

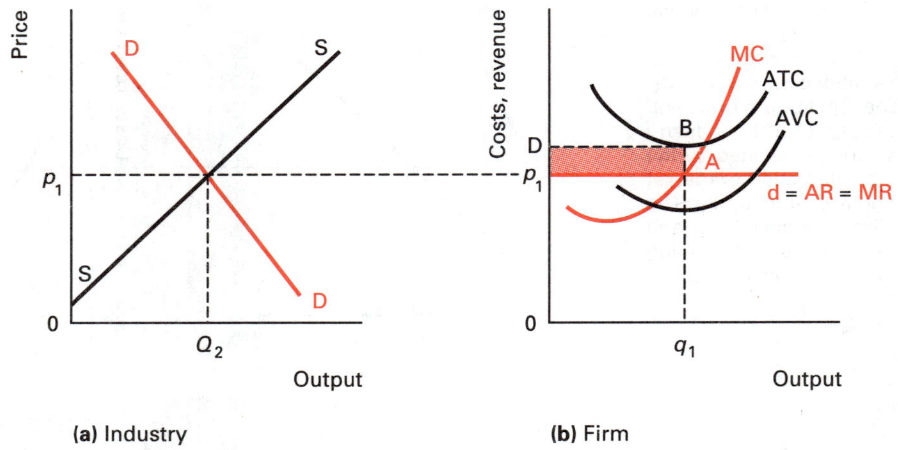

output $0q_1$. Since in perfect competition price and MR are equal, profit-maximising firms which equate MR and MC will also necessarily equate price and MC. The equality of price and MC is the most significant feature of perfect competition and its welfare implications are discussed below.

In Fig. 9.6(b), average total cost at output level $0q_1$ is q_1B. Total cost which is given by average total cost multiplied by quantity is thus represented by the rectangle $0q_1$BC. The cost curves already incorporate an allowance for normal profit, which is the rate of return necessary to keep the factors of production in their present use.

Normal profit *The level of profit necessary to keep factors of production in their present use*

At the equilibrium level of output, total revenue is represented by the area of rectangle $0p_1$Aq_1. Thus, this firm is earning revenue in excess of total cost. It is said to be earning above-normal profit equal to the area of rectangle p_1ABC. In the long-run, the high level of profits in this industry will attract new firms to enter the industry. The increased production will eventually push down the price of the output, thus eliminating the above-normal profits.

Above-normal profit *Also known as super-normal profit, this is the level of profit in excess of normal profit*

Firm making a loss Consider now another perfectly competitive firm whose situation is illustrated in Fig. 9.7.

Figure 9.7(a) again illustrates the determination of the equilibrium price ($0p_1$) in the market. The cost and revenue curves of a typical firm are illustrated in Fig. 9.7(b). Note that the ATC curve lies completely above the AR curve, indicating that this firm cannot cover its full opportunity costs. The intersection of the MR and MC curves at point A now indicates that the *loss-minimising* level of output is $0q_1$. At this output, ATC equals Bq_1, which is greater than AR (= price) or Aq_1. The loss per unit of output is equal to BA so that the total loss is represented by the area of rectangle p_1DBA.

As the price is above average variable cost (AVC) at output $0q_1$, the firm will continue to produce in the short-run, as it thereby minimises its loss. If it shut down production entirely, its loss would be equal to its total fixed cost. By producing and selling output $0q_1$ at price $0p_1$, the firm more than covers its variable cost and can pay for part of its fixed cost.

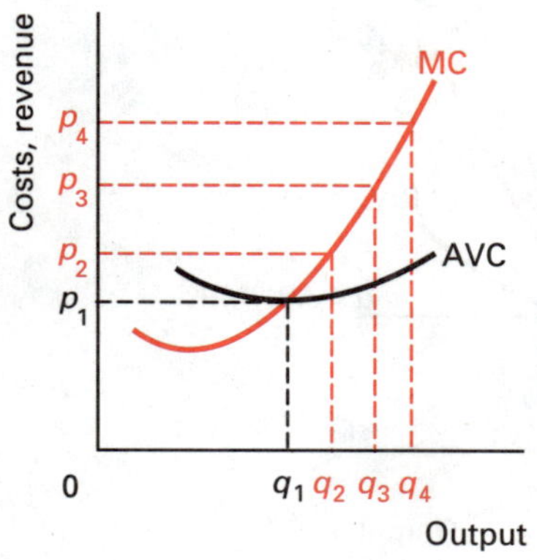

Fig. 9.8. A firm's short-run supply curve. The firm's short-run MC curve indicates how much it is willing to supply at different prices. Below price $0p_1$, the firm cannot cover its variable costs and is forced to shut down.

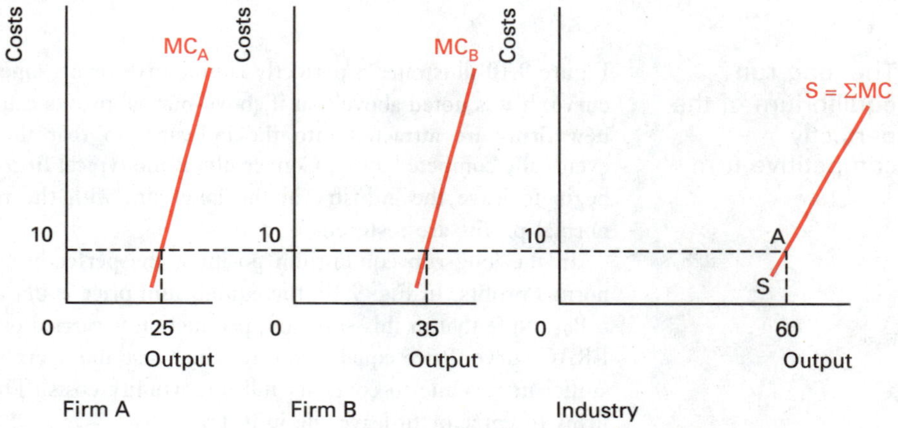

Fig. 9.9. The derivation of the industry supply curve. The industry supply curve is obtained by the horizontal summation of the individual firms' MC curves.

The firm's short-run supply curve

We can note from the foregoing analysis that the perfectly competitive firm which aims to maximise profit produces at the intersection of its horizontal MR curve with the MC curve provided this is above the shut-down point. This is illustrated for different prices in Fig. 9.8. For example, the firm offers for sale quantity $0q_2$ at price $0p_2$. If price rises to $0p_3$, the quantity supplied by the firm increases to $0q_3$. We can see that the short-run supply curve of the perfectly competitive firm is its MC curve above the intersection with the AVC curve.

The short-run *industry* supply curve is obtained by the horizontal summation of the MC curves of the firms comprising the industry. This is illustrated in Fig. 9.9 for an industry containing only two firms.

The two left-hand diagrams illustrate the MC curves of firms A and B respectively. At a price of £10, firm A produces 25 units and firm B 35 units of output per time period. Industry output at this price, therefore, is 60 units and A is one point on the industry supply curve. Summing the firms' outputs at other prices enables the industry short-run supply curve, SS, to be derived. This is the supply curve which (together with the market demand curve for the good) determines the market price which all the individual firms have to take as given.

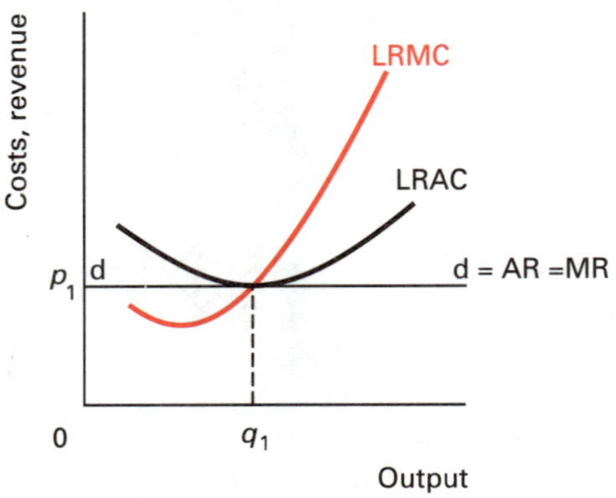

Fig. 9.10. The long-run equilibrium of a perfectly competitive firm. The firm is productively efficient as it produces at the lowest point on the LRAC curve. The firm also exhibits allocative efficiency as $p = \text{MC}$.

The long-run equilibrium of the perfectly competitive firm

Figure 9.10 illustrates a perfectly competitive firm's long-run average cost (LRAC) curve. It was noted above that if above-normal profits can be earned, in the long-run new firms are attracted into the industry, so that the above-normal profits are eventually competed away. Conversely, if the typical firm is making losses, firms will begin to leave the industry in the long-run, with the result that price rises until normal profits are restored.

In the long-run equilibrium position, the perfectly competitive firm earns only normal profits. In Fig. 9.10, the equilibrium price is $0p_1$ and the equilibrium output is $0q_1$. Note that in this situation, production is carried on at the lowest point on the LRAC curve. Price equals both marginal cost and average cost. The firm is earning sufficient revenue to cover its full opportunity costs. There exists no incentive for firms to enter or to leave the industry.

Note that in this long-run equilibrium position, the perfectly competitive firm exhibits both *productive* and *allocative efficiency*. Productive efficiency is achieved when a firm produces at the lowest possible long-run average cost. As seen above, productive efficiency obtains in Fig. 9.10 at the equilibrium output level $0q_1$. Allocative efficiency is achieved when price is equal to the marginal cost of production, given that marginal private cost accurately reflects marginal social cost. This means that allocative efficiency will be achieved by perfectly competitive markets in the absence of externalities, as shown below.

Perfect competition and welfare

One of the arguments in favour of a competitive market structure is that perfect competition leads to an efficient, or Pareto optimal, allocation of resources. Indeed it can be demonstrated that an economy with perfect competition in all markets and with no externalities satisfies all three of the marginal conditions for Pareto optimality that we derived in Ch. 8.

Assume once again that we are dealing with an economy with only two goods (food and cloth), two factors (capital and labour) and two individuals (A and B). Consider the three marginal conditions in turn.

The MRTS of one factor of production for another should be equal for all goods Recall from Ch. 2 that a profit-maximising firm will choose that

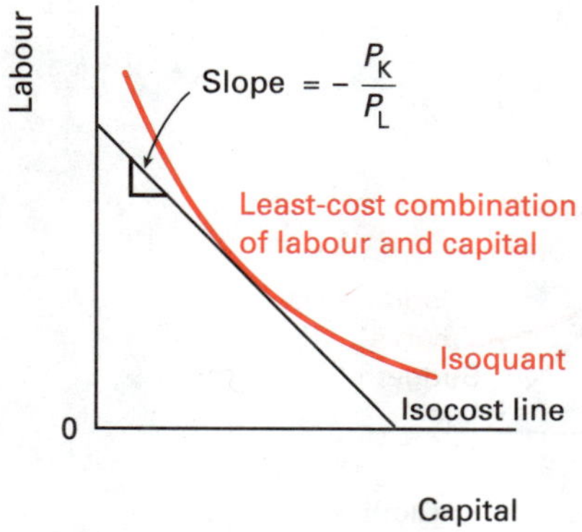

Fig. 9.11. ***A firm's least-cost combination of factors.*** This is given by the point of tangency between an isocost line and an isoquant.

combination of factors at which the firm's isocost line is tangent to an isoquant, as illustrated in Fig. 9.11: this ensures that the chosen output level is produced at minimum cost. Since the absolute value of the slope of the isocost line is equal to the ratio of the prices of the two factors and the absolute value of the slope of the isoquant is the MRTS, we can say that if the food producers are profit-maximisers, they will employ that combination of factors at which

$$MRTS_F = \frac{P_K}{P_L}$$

where $MRTS_F$ is the MRTS in food production, P_K is the price of capital and P_L is the price of labour.

Similarly, if the cloth producers are also profit-maximisers, they will employ that combination of factors at which

$$MRTS_C = \frac{P_K}{P_L}$$

where $MRTS_C$ is the MRTS in cloth production.

In perfect competition, all firms face the same prices for capital and labour, so it must follow that

$$MRTS_F = MRTS_C$$

and the first condition is satisfied.

The MRS for every pair of goods should be equal for all individuals Recall from Ch. 4 that a utility-maximising consumer will choose that combination of goods at which the budget line is tangent to an indifference curve, as illustrated in Fig. 9.12: this ensures that the consumer is on the highest attainable indifference curve. Since the absolute value of the slope of the budget line is equal to the ratio of the prices of the two goods and the absolute value of the slope of the indifference curve is the MRS, we can say that if A is a utility-maximising consumer, he or she will allocate income in such a way that

$$MRS_A = \frac{P_c}{P_f}$$

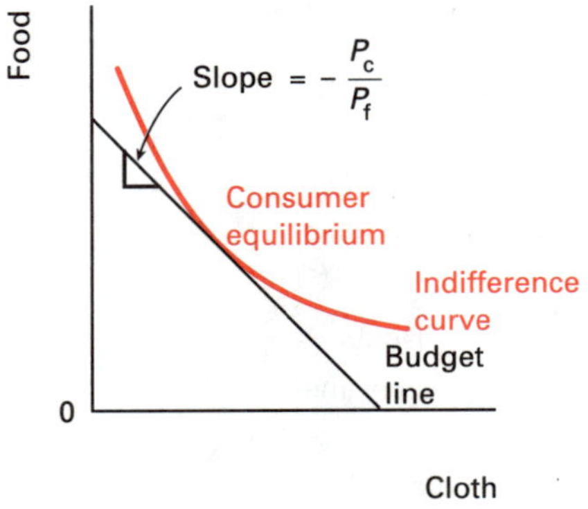

Fig. 9.12. *Consumer equilibrium.* This is given by the point of tangency between a budget line and an indifference curve.

where MRS_A is consumer A's MRS, P_c is the price of cloth and P_f the price of food.

Similarly, if B is also a utility-maximising consumer, he or she will allocate income in such a way that

$$MRS_B = \frac{P_c}{P_f}$$

where MRS_B is consumer B's MRS.

Assuming, as *we must do* in perfect competition, that both A and B face the same prices for food and cloth, it follows that

$$MRS_A = MRS_B$$

so that the second condition is satisfied.

The common MRS should equal the MRT for all pairs of goods We have seen that each consumer's MRS will be equal to the ratio of the goods' prices. That is,

$$MRS_A = MRS_B = \frac{P_c}{P_f} \qquad (1)$$

Recall that the marginal rate of transformation (MRT) is given by the absolute value of the slope of the production possibility frontier. As such, it can also be regarded as the ratio of the marginal costs of producing the two goods. That is,

$$MRT = \frac{MC_c}{MC_f} \qquad (2)$$

This result is illustrated in Fig. 9.13 where, in making a small movement along the frontier from A to B, Δc of cloth is given up in order to produce Δf of extra food. Since moving along the frontier leaves total cost unchanged (because *all* resources are fully employed at every point), it must be true that

$$\Delta c \times MC_c = \Delta f \times MC_f$$

$$\text{The absolute value of the slope of the frontier} = \frac{\Delta f}{\Delta c} = \frac{MC_c}{MC_f} = MRT$$

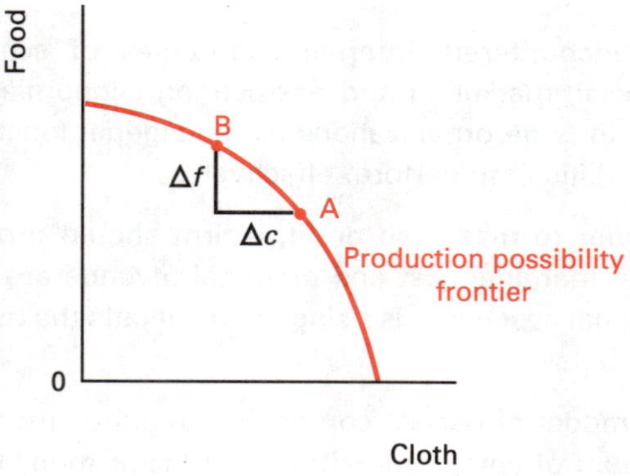

Fig. 9.13. The production possibility frontier and the marginal rate of transformation. The slope of the production possibility frontier is the marginal rate of transformation (MRT). The MRT measures the rate at which cloth can be transformed into food by shifting resources from cloth production into food production.

From (1) and (2) above, we can say that for MRS to be equal to MRT, it is necessary that

$$\frac{P_c}{P_f} = \frac{MC_c}{MC_f}$$

In perfect competition, where the food-producing and cloth-producing firms set their prices equal to their marginal costs of production, this condition must be satisfied.

We can conclude from the above that an economy with perfect competition in all markets and with no externalities will be efficient in the Pareto sense. Of course, this does not necessarily mean that such an economy will have an equitable distribution of income.

Summary

1. Economists base their estimate of production costs on the concept of opportunity cost (that is cost measured in terms of forgone alternatives). This is a wider definition of cost than that employed by accountants.

2. In the short-run, some costs are fixed and others variable. Average cost is total cost divided by the quantity produced. Marginal cost is the change in total cost resulting from changing the level of output by one unit. The U-shapes of the short-run average and marginal cost curves are determined by the operation of 'diminishing returns' in production.

3. In the long-run, all factors are variable. The long-run average cost curve shows the lowest possible cost of producing different levels of output, given the production function and factor prices.

4. As a firm's scale of operations increases, it may at first experience declining long-run average costs because of the existence of economies of scale. Beyond a certain point, however, increasing long-run average costs may be experienced as diseconomies of scale

are encountered. Internal economies of scale include technical, financial, marketing and risk-bearing economies. Diseconomies may arise in large organisations as managerial functions become increasingly difficult to perform effectively.

5. In order to maximise profit, a firm should produce that quantity at which marginal cost and marginal revenue are equal, as long as the marginal cost curve is rising so that it cuts the marginal revenue curve from below.
6. The model of perfect competition requires many buyers and sellers; freedom of entry and exit; perfect factor mobility; perfect knowledge; and a homogeneous product. Under these assumptions, a typical firm may make excess profits (or losses) in the short-run only. In the long-run, only normal profit will be earned.
7. In an economy with perfect competition in all markets and with no externalities, all three marginal conditions for Pareto optimality will be satisfied.

Exercises

1. Review your understanding of the following terms:

opportunity cost
fixed costs
variable costs
average variable cost
average fixed cost
average total cost
marginal cost
long-run average cost
expansion path
normal profit
economies of scale
diseconomies of scale
internal economies
external economies
economies of scope
marginal revenue
profit maximisation
perfect competition
price taker

2. Consider the following data on a firm's total costs of production.

Quantity produced:	1	2	3	4	5	6
Total cost (£):	10	16	18	28	45	66

Given that total fixed cost is £8, calculate average total cost, average variable cost, average fixed cost and marginal cost and plot them all on the same graph. Comment on the relationships between the four cost curves.

3. Explain the circumstances under which a firm's long-run average cost curve may be: (a) U-shaped; (b) L-shaped.
4. Compare the scope for the attainment of economies of scale in the steel industry with that in hairdressing.

5. 'The model of perfect competition is based on such unreal assumptions that it has little relevance to modern market structures.' Discuss.
6. Outline the factors that determine the level of normal profits in a perfectly competitive industry. Under what conditions will a perfectly competitive firm close down: (a) in the short-run; (b) in the long-run?
7. Under what circumstances will the long-run supply curve of an industry in perfect competition be horizontal?

Appendix

Profit maximisation A firm's profit (π) is defined as the firm's total revenue (TR) minus the firm's total cost (TC). Both total revenue and total cost are functions of quantity produced (q). Thus, we can write:

$$\pi = \text{TR}(q) - \text{TC}(q) \tag{1}$$

To find the profit-maximising level of output, we differentiate this function with respect to q and set the first derivative equal to zero. This gives:

$$\frac{d\pi}{dq} = \frac{d\text{TR}}{dq} - \frac{d\text{TC}}{dq} = 0 \tag{2}$$

The terms $d\text{TR}/dq$ and $d\text{TC}/dq$ are, of course, MR and MC respectively. So this confirms the result presented in the chapter that profit maximisation requires that MR should equal MC. If the firm is operating under conditions of perfect competition, MR will be constant and equal to the price of the product (p). Thus, the rule for profit maximisation for a perfectly competitive firm is that p should equal MC.

Condition (2) above is referred to as the *first-order condition* for profit maximisation. To be sure that we have identified a maximum (rather than minimum) value for the profit function, we also require that the value of the second derivative be negative. This is the *second-order condition* for profit maximisation and may be written as:

$$\frac{d^2\pi}{dq^2} = \frac{d^2\text{TR}}{dq^2} - \frac{d^2\text{TC}}{dq^2} < 0 \tag{3}$$

The terms $d^2\text{TR}/dq^2$ and $d^2\text{TC}/dq^2$ are the slopes of the MR and MC curves respectively. Thus, condition (3) states that the slope of the MR curve must be less than the slope of the MC curve at the point where they are equal. In other words, as stated in the chapter, the MC curve must cut the MR curve from below, as shown at point B in Fig. 9.5. The second-order condition ensures that MC is less than MR at points below the profit-maximising quantity.

Example Consider a profit maximising firm operating under conditions of perfect competition. Suppose the market price is £50 and the firm faces a total cost function given by:

$$\text{TC} = 10 + 5q^2$$

The firm's total revenue is simply equal to price times quantity, i.e.

$$\mathrm{TR} = pq = 50q$$

Profit is given by:

$$\pi = \mathrm{TR} - \mathrm{TC}$$
$$= 50q - 10 - 5q^2$$

To maximise this function, we differentiate it with respect to q and set the result equal to zero. *Note that this is equivalent to setting price equal to MC, as shown above.* This gives:

$$\frac{d\pi}{dq} = 50 - 10q = 0$$

$$q = 5$$

Taking the second derivative to check the second-order condition gives:

$$\frac{d^2\pi}{dq^2} = -10$$

As the second derivative is negative, a maximum has been identified.

10 THEORY OF THE FIRM – II

Learning objectives

After reading this chapter, you should be able to:

- define the term monopoly and draw a diagram showing the short-run equilibrium of a profit-maximising monopolist
- contrast the long-run equilibrium positions of monopoly and perfect competition and draw policy conclusions for social welfare
- identify the conditions under which price discrimination can be practised and the reasons for its widespread use
- define the term monopolistic competition and produce diagrams showing the short- and long-run equilibrium positions of firms in this market structure
- state the reasons why oligopolies dominate many markets and illustrate alternative models of oligopolistic behaviour
- appreciate the game theory approach to the analysis of oligopolies

Introduction

In the previous chapter, we considered the model of perfect competition under the traditional assumption of profit maximisation. Perfect competition can be thought of as being at one end of the spectrum of market structures with pure monopoly (in which an industry is dominated by a single firm) at the other end. Between these two extremes, there is an infinite number of market structures with differing degrees of competition. In this chapter, we first consider the price and output determination of a profit-maximising monopolist. Secondly, we consider two of the intermediate forms of market structure – monopolistic competition and oligopoly. Finally, we examine alternatives to the assumption of profit maximisation and briefly outline some of the views of the American economist, J.K. Galbraith.

Monopoly

Problems of defining a monopoly

A pure monopolist is a single supplier of a good or service for which there is no close substitute. In general terms, we can say that the cross-elasticity of demand between the pure monopolist's product and all other products is low – in other words, a rise in the price of the monopolist's product leads to no significant increase in the demand for any other product. The definition of a 'close substitute' is, however, somewhat arbitrary. For example, are gas and oil close substitutes for electricity?

Pure monopolist *A single supplier of a good or service for which there is no close substitute*

The answer is likely to depend on the use to which the fuel is put. Electricity suppliers may have a monopoly in the market for domestic and industrial lighting, but they face stiff competition from gas and oil in the heating market.

Pure monopoly can best be regarded as a theoretical model as it is unusual to find a single firm with a 100 per cent market share. In the United Kingdom, the Monopolies and Mergers Commission can be asked to investigate a monopoly to determine whether or not it is operating in the public interest; for this purpose, a monopoly is defined as a single firm or interrelated group of firms controlling 25 per cent or more of a market. The United Kingdom policy towards monopoly is discussed in Ch. 15.

It is possible for a group of firms or countries to engage in collusion over prices or production levels and hence act as a monopolist. Such a situation is described as a *cartel.* Examples of cartels in the United Kingdom include the Milk Marketing Board and the Potato Marketing Board. Similarly, the Organisation of Petroleum Exporting Countries (OPEC), which attempts to support oil prices, is an example of an international cartel. In what follows, we confine our attention to a single-firm monopoly.

The monopolist's demand curve

As the monopolist is the sole supplier of a good, the firm is, in effect, the industry. The monopolist thus faces the *market* demand curve which is normally downward-sloping from left to right. The demand curve tells us the prices at which the producer can sell different levels of output.

Recall that average revenue (AR) is equal to total revenue (TR) divided by the quantity sold and so is also equal to the price of the good. The demand curve can, therefore, also be called the AR curve. Faced with a downward-sloping AR curve, the monopolist has to reduce the price of *all units sold* in order to sell an extra unit of output. This means that marginal revenue (MR), which is the revenue earned by selling an extra unit, must be less than AR (or price).

Consider the data in Table 10.1. Columns (1) and (2) represent the demand schedule for the product of a monopolist, say good *X*. Column (3) shows total revenue, obtained by multiplying together columns (1) and (2). Column (4) shows marginal revenue and it can be seen that MR falls faster than and is less than AR

Table 10.1 The revenue of a monopolist.

(1) Quantity	(2) Price (=average revenue) (£)	(3) Total revenue (£)	(4) Marginal revenue (£)
1	25	25	–
2	23	46	21
3	21	63	17
4	19	76	13
5	17	85	9
6	15	90	5
7	13	91	1
8	11	88	– 3
9	9	81	– 7
10	7	70	–11

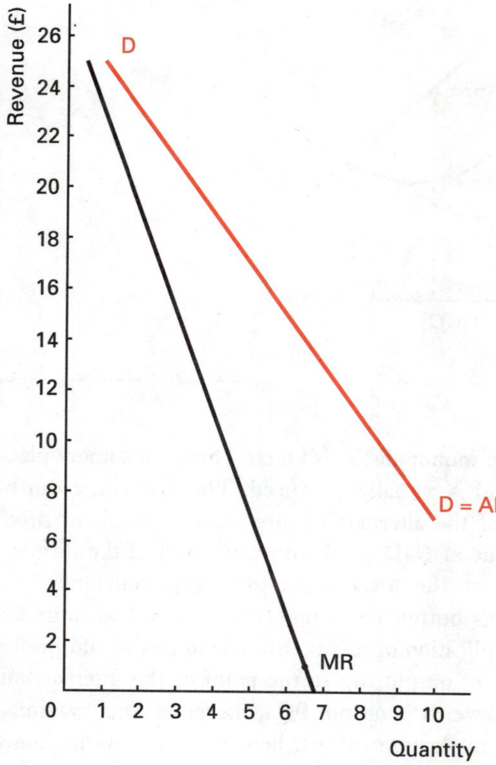

Fig. 10.1. The monopolist's revenue curves. The monopolist faces the market demand curve which is also its AR curve. The MR curve lies below the AR curve because the monopolist has to reduce price to sell extra units.

over its entire length. The monopolist's AR and MR curves are plotted in Fig. 10.1 which illustrates graphically the result that whenever a firm's AR curve is downward sloping, the MR curve lies below the AR curve.

From Table 10.1, we can see that at first as the monopolist sells more, TR increases and reaches a maximum of £91 when seven units are sold. Beyond this level of output, TR begins to fall and MR becomes negative. Clearly, a profit-maximising monopolist would never produce where MR was negative, unless MC were also negative – a highly unlikely event.

Output and price determination of a profit-maximising monopolist

As with any other profit-maximising firm, the monopolist will equate MC with MR. This is illustrated in Fig. 10.2 where the monopolist is producing quantity $0Q_1$ and charging a price of $0P_1$ ($=$ AQ_1). This monopolist is making above-normal profit. Total revenue is given by the area of the rectangle $0P_1$AQ_1. Total cost is given by the area of the rectangle 0CBQ_1. Thus, the smaller rectangle CP_1AB represents the above-normal profit.

Welfare implications and criticisms of monopoly

Note from Fig. 10.2 that the price (AQ_1) is greater than MC which is equal to Q_1D. This underlies the charge that monopoly leads to a *Pareto sub-optimal allocation of resources*. The following rationale can be given for this charge of resource misallocation. The demand curve DD tells us the consumers' valuation of marginal

Fig. 10.2. The equilibrium position of a monopolist. The monopolist maximises profit by equating MR and MC. Thus, the profit-maximising quantity is $0Q_1$ which is sold at price $0P_1$. Total profit is given by the area of the shaded rectangle.

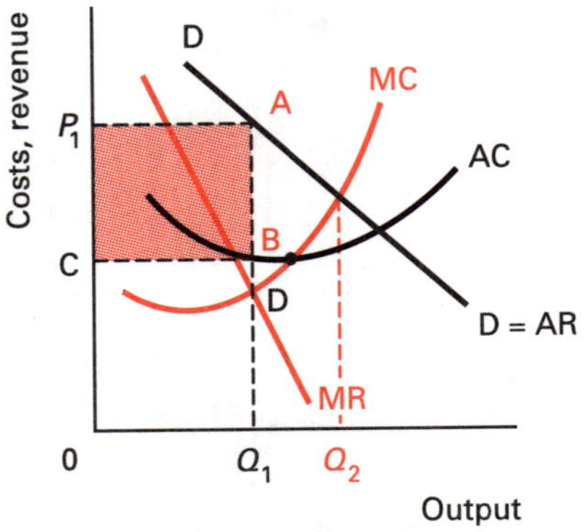

units of the monopolist's product. Thus, consumers place a value of AQ_1 on the last unit of good X actually produced. The MC curve can be viewed as the consumers' valuation of the alternatives forgone as a result of producing good X. Thus, they place a value of Q_1D on the marginal unit of the forgone alternative. It can be seen, then, that at the level of output $0Q_1$, consumers value marginal units of the monopolist's output more highly than marginal units of the forgone alternative.

The implication of this is that consumers would prefer the monopolist to produce extra units of output, up to the point of the intersection of the demand curve with the MC curve. It is output $0Q_2$, therefore, that maximises society's welfare because at this output level, marginal benefit (given by the demand curve) is equal to MC. Here we are judging welfare by efficiency criteria alone and are ignoring equity questions. We are also assuming that the firm's MC curve accurately reflects marginal *social* cost – that is to say, no externalities are present.

We saw in Ch. 9 that, with no externalities, Pareto optimality would result under perfect competition where price is equal to MC. In monopoly, though, output is restricted and price is set above MC. This means that the third marginal condition for Pareto optimality (that MRS should equal MRT) cannot be satisfied, except by an unlikely coincidence. Recall from Chs 8 and 9 that this condition can be written as follows:

$$\text{MRS} = \frac{P_X}{P_Y} = \frac{\text{MC}_X}{\text{MC}_Y} = \text{MRT}$$

where X and Y represent any pair of goods. Clearly, if both the X and Y industries are perfectly competitive, so that $P_X = \text{MC}_X$ and $P_Y = \text{MC}_Y$, the condition must be satisfied. But if the X-industry is a monopoly, so that $P_X > \text{MC}_X$, the condition will not be satisfied and a misallocation of resources will result. Only if both industries are monopolised to exactly the same extent and in such a way that P_X exceeds MC_X by the same proportion as P_Y exceeds MC_Y, will the condition be satisfied in the absence of perfect competition: this is highly unlikely.

Our analysis leads to the prediction that if a perfectly competitive industry is taken over by a profit-maximising monopolist, and production costs do not change, output will fall and price will rise. This result is illustrated in Fig. 10.3. For simplicity, we assume constant average and marginal production costs. Price and output in perfect competition are $0P_c$ and $0Q_c$ respectively, as determined by the

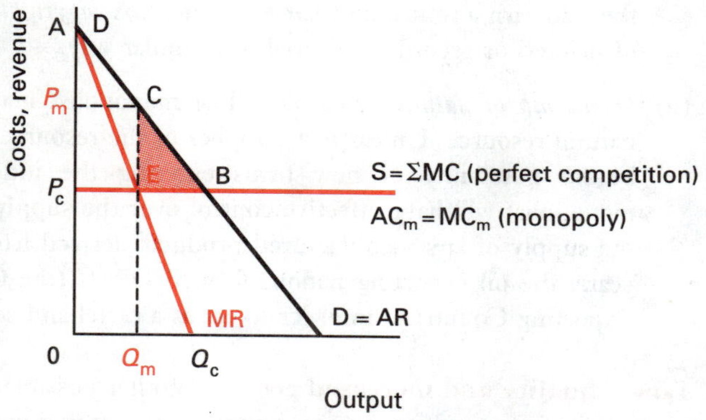

Fig. 10.3. The welfare loss under monopoly. When a perfectly competitive industry is taken over by a monopolist, with unchanged costs, price rises from $0P_c$ to $0P_m$ and quantity falls from $0Q_c$ to $0Q_m$. The deadweight welfare loss is represented by the area CBE.

intersection of the demand curve DD and the industry supply curve which, in this case, is horizontal. Consumer surplus is represented by the triangle ABP_c. Now suppose that the industry is taken over by a monopolist and that costs do not change so that the industry supply curve becomes the monopolist's MC curve. To maximise profits, the monopolist will equate MR and MC and so produce the lower quantity $0Q_m$ at the higher price $0P_m$. Consumer surplus falls to the triangle ACP_m. Part of the original consumer surplus (rectangle P_cP_mCE) is the monopolist's gain, but the triangle CBE represents a net fall in welfare and is sometimes called the deadweight loss of the monopoly. Representing the welfare loss in terms of the triangle CBE is, however, a little misleading as it ignores the equity aspects of the redistribution of income from consumers to the monopolist.

Deadweight loss *Refers to the net fall in welfare as a result of the monopolist's restriction of output*

Long-run profits resulting from barriers to entry A monopolist may be criticised on the grounds that he or she may be able to maintain above-normal profits in the long-run because of barriers to the entry of new firms. As we have seen, this might result in a redistribution of income that is not desirable on equity grounds. There are several entry barriers which may have the effect of preventing the emergence of competitive firms. Consider the following.

(a) *High entry costs.* An existing monopolist, producing a large volume of output, may be benefiting from economies of scale. This may mean that a new competitor, probably producing a low volume of output, would be faced with higher per unit production costs and so would not be able to compete effectively in the market. If the new firm were faced with heavy initial losses, it might never be able to produce at a volume sufficient for it to enjoy comparable economies of scale.

(b) *Legal monopolies.* In some cases, the state has created monopolies by law as, for example, with the Post Office in the United Kingdom. In cases like these, it is illegal for rival firms to enter the industry.

(c) *Patents and copyrights.* A monopoly may result from the holding of a *patent* on an invention or innovation. A patent confers sole production rights for a given time period on those who have invested in research and development to enable them to earn a return on their investment. A *copyright* restricts the reproduction of printed or recorded material in a similar way.

(d) *Ownership of natural resources.* The monopolist may be the sole owner of a natural resource. Unless new supplies of the resource are discovered, there will be no possibility of new firms entering the industry. Consequently, the monopolist will have effective control over the supply of the resource and over the supply of any manufactured products derived from the resource. In recent years, the oil exporting nations formed OPEC (the Organisation of Petroleum Exporting Countries) in order to act as a cartel and so drive up the price of oil.

Lower quality and increased costs Another possible criticism is that because a monopolist is not subject to conventional competitive pressures, the quality of the good or service may decline as the consumer cannot take custom elsewhere. This charge, in fact, was made against motorway service areas in the United Kingdom and a committee was set up by the government to investigate their operation: the committee reported in 1978 and made a number of suggestions about how to improve the operation of these areas. It can further be argued that a monopolist may 'settle for an easy life' and allow costs to rise unnecessarily. The market power of the monopolist enables him or her to pursue objectives other than profit maximisation and still survive in the long-run.

Possible benefits of monopoly

It should be recognised that monopoly can in certain circumstances have some beneficial effects. Indeed, as we see in detail in Ch. 15, the approach to monopoly policy in the United Kingdom is to judge each case on its merits. So consider now the following possible advantages of monopoly.

Economies of single ownership As we have seen, the standard prediction that a monopolist restricts output and raises price rests on the assumption that costs remain unchanged when a perfectly competitive industry is taken over by a monopolist. It is most unlikely, however, that costs would remain unchanged in such a situation. A monopolist may be able to benefit from economies of scale that are not attainable by the individual perfectly competitive firms. It is even possible for costs to fall so much that price will actually fall and output rise in the new monopoly situation.

This is illustrated in Fig. 10.4. The supply curve under conditions of perfect competition (SS) is the sum of the individual firms' marginal cost curves. Competitive price is $0P_c$ and output $0Q_c$. After the industry is taken over by the monopolist, the monopolist's marginal cost curve is MC_m and lies below the competitive supply curve. As a result of equating MR with MC, the monopolist will produce the larger quantity $0Q_m$ and charge the lower price $0P_m$. It can thus be argued that the monopolisation of the industry benefits the consumer in this instance; the misallocation of resources still remains, however, as price is greater than the new MC.

As mentioned in Ch. 7, the economies of scale are so large in the cases of some public utilities that monopoly is the natural production unit. These are described as *natural monopolies*. There would clearly be an unnecessary duplication of resources if two gas companies served the same district with two sets of pipes under each road.

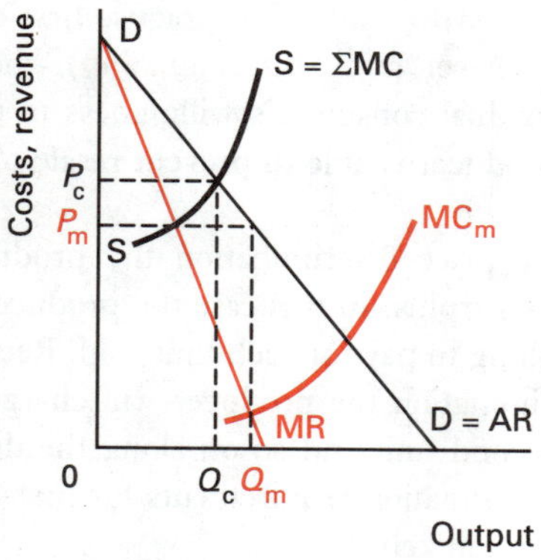

Fig. 10.4. *The case of a monopolist reducing price and increasing output.* When the monopolist takes over the competitive industry, the monopolist benefits from economies of scale. In this case, price falls from $0P_c$ to $0P_m$ and quantity increases from $0Q_c$ to $0Q_m$

In the case of two separate water companies serving the same district, there would be a similar waste of resources. With natural monopolies, the United Kingdom approach used to be to place them in public ownership (see Ch. 15). An alternative approach (common in the United States) is to allow the existence of a private monopoly, but to establish a regulatory agency to monitor and control the monopolist's prices and profits. Following the policy of privatisation in the 1980s, the United Kingdom has also adopted this alternative approach.

Technical progress It has been claimed that the existence of high profits and larger resources allows the monopolist to devote a large amount of expenditure to research and development. This may be beneficial to society as it can lead to an increased rate of technical progress and thus economic growth. The monopolist's position is often more secure than that of a competitive firm and he is thus able to devote more resources to innovative activity over a long period.

Schumpeter was a notable proponent of the view that the *dynamic gains* to society from monopoly through increased technical progress outweighed the costs of resource misallocation. Whether or not monopoly actually does lead to increased technical progress, however, is not clear. Studies for the United Kingdom have found no conclusive evidence of a link between the levels of concentration and the rate of innovative activity.

Discriminating monopoly

Price discrimination
A situation in which a supplier charges different prices to different consumers for the same or similar product, and where the price differences do not reflect differences in the costs of supply

A monopolist may be able to charge different prices to different consumers of similar goods and services *in different markets* and in this way increase total profits. The markets may be separated from each other in a number of different ways. First, they may be separated *geographically*, as when an exporter charges a different price in the overseas market than in the home market. Secondly, the markets may be separated by the *type of demand*, as in the market for milk where the household demand for liquid milk differs from the industrial demand for milk for cheesemaking. Thirdly, they may be separated by *time*, where typically a lower price is charged in off-peak periods – this is the case in the electricity, telephone and travel industries. Finally, they may be separated by the *nature of the product*, as with medical treatment where if one person is treated that person is unable to resell that treatment to another. The important point is that, for successful price discrimination, the monopolist must be able to prevent resale of the product, otherwise the purchasers at the lower price might sell directly to other customers.

Perrfect price discrimination *Perfect price discrimination occurs when a producer charges a consumer the highest price he or she is willing to pay for each unit sold*

First-degree price discrimination To practise first-degree price discrimination (sometimes known as perfect price discrimination), the monopolist has to have knowledge of each individual consumer's willingness to pay or demand curve. It is also essential that the producer is able to prevent resale of the product by individual consumers.

Through first-degree price discrimination the producer is able to extract the whole of the consumer's surplus. In this case the producer charges the highest price that the consumer is willing to pay for each unit sold. Recall Fig. 4.14 in Ch. 4. With first-degree price discrimination the producer will charge the consumer £9 for the first unit, £8 for the second unit and so on along the downward-sloping curve. In practice, however, the information requirements for first-degree price discrimination make its implementation unlikely.

Second-degree price discrimination This involves charging different prices for different blocks of consumption. The aim of the monopolist, say a public utility, is to charge a relatively high price for the first block of consumption, a lower price for the next block and so on. Second-degree price discrimination is illustrated in Fig. 10.5 in which the demand curve for a product, say electricity, is given by D_1D_1. The producer charges price $0P_1$ for units up to quantity $0Q_1$. For units above $0Q_1$ but below $0Q_2$, the producer charges price $0P_2$. For units above $0Q_2$ but below $0Q_3$, the producer charges price $0P_3$. In this way, the monopolist is able to extract more of the consumer surplus compared with the alternative case of charging a single price. In the case above, the discriminating monopolist earns a total revenue given by the areas of $0P_1AQ_1 + Q_1BCQ_2 + Q_2DEQ_3$ for selling output $0Q_3$. Without the use of second-degree price discrimination the revenue earned would be given by the area $0P_3EQ_3$.

Third-degree price discrimination In this case, the monopolist is able to separate two or more markets with differing elasticities of demand and charge different prices in the separate markets. As an example, consider the profit-maximising outputs and prices of a discriminating monopolist who operates in two completely independent markets. In Fig. 10.6(a), AR_A and MR_A are the relevant average and marginal revenue curves in market A. Similarly, Fig. 10.6(b) illustrates the monopolist's average and marginal revenue curves in market B. Notice that, at

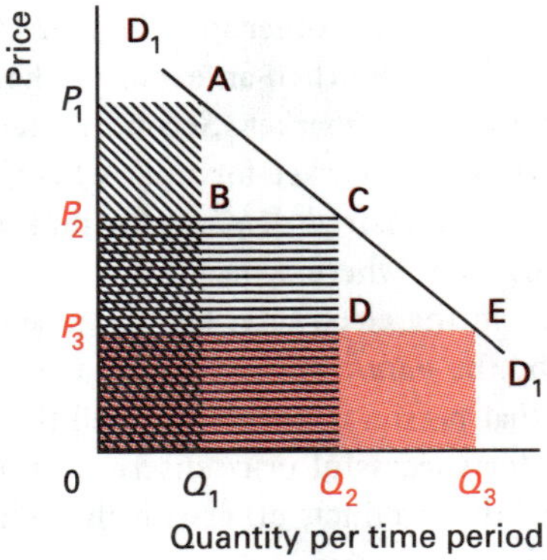

Fig. 10.5. *Second-degree price discrimination.* The monopolist charges different prices for different blocks of consumption.

Fig. 10.6. ***Price discrimination in two separate markets.*** The monopolist equates the combined MR with MC to determine the profit-maximising quantity. This is then allocated to the two markets such that $MR_A = MR_B$.

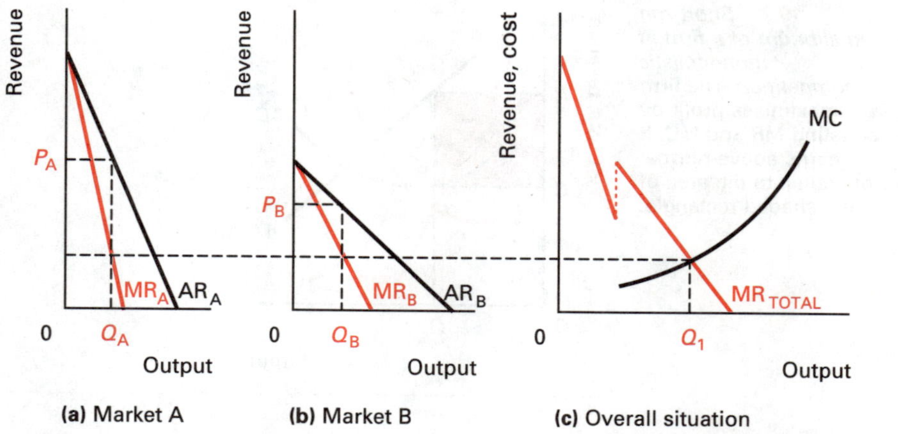

given prices, the elasticity of demand is greater in market B than in market A – this is, therefore, a situation in which price discrimination can be profitable to the monopolist. Figure 10.6(c) shows the combined marginal revenue curve for both markets (MR_{TOTAL}).

For profit maximisation, MR_A and MR_B *must be equal.* If this were not so, then profits could be increased by selling extra units of output in the market with the higher marginal revenue. As is usual, the profit-maximising level of output, $0Q_1$, is found where MR_{TOTAL} is equal to marginal cost. This output is then divided between the two markets with $0Q_A$ being sold in market A at price $0P_A$, and $0Q_B$ being sold in market B at price $0P_B$. Notice that $0Q_A + 0Q_B = 0Q_1$.

Price discrimination is sometimes criticised on the grounds that it confers on the monopolist the power to decide which groups of consumers should pay higher prices. Also, in terms of the welfare criteria outlined in Ch. 8, we can say that, since with price discrimination all consumers do not face the same prices, it must follow that the first marginal condition for Pareto optimality (that the marginal rates of substitution should be equal for all pairs of individuals) will no longer be satisfied.

Monopolistic competition

The model of monopolistic competition was originally developed by E.H. Chamberlin in his book *The Theory of Monopolistic Competition* in 1933. The assumptions of the model are similar to those of perfect competition with one exception. It is assumed that there are a large number of producers of similar, but *differentiated*, products. An example might be food retailing where a large number of competing stores offer a similar range of goods, but differ as regards location and service. Within the model, there is freedom of entry and exit for firms.

Product differentiation
A set of marketing strategies designed to capture and to retain particular market segments by producing a range of related products. These products may be differentiated in terms of packaging, design and advertising

Product differentiation implies that while each firm is likely to face a relatively elastic demand curve, it will not face a *perfectly* elastic demand curve. This is because if a single firm should raise its price, it would not lose all of its sales, as would be the case in perfect competition. Some customers would continue to buy the product because of the qualities that differentiate it from the competing products. In other words, brand loyalties exist.

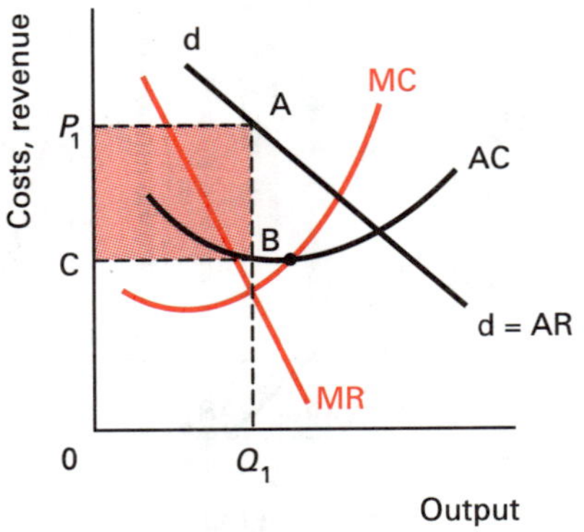

Fig. 10.7. Short-run equilibrium of a firm in monopolistic competition. The firm maximises profit by equating MR and MC. It earns above-normal profit equal to the area of the shaded rectangle.

Short-run equilibrium

Non-price competition *Strategies adopted by producers to give their products a competitive advantage, other than a price cut*

Consider now the short-run equilibrium position of a firm operating in monopolistic competition. This is illustrated in Fig. 10.7. The curve dd = AR is the demand curve facing the firm on the assumption that all other firms hold their prices constant. To achieve maximum profit, the firm will equate MC with MR and so produce quantity $0Q_1$ and charge a price of $0P_1$. The firm is making above-normal profit in the short-run equal to the area of the rectangle P_1ABC. The firm may try to retain or increase its above-normal profit by engaging in some form of non-price competition – this might include advertising or further expenditure on packaging to make the good appear more attractive to consumers.

Long-run equilibrium

As long as the monopolistically competitive firms are earning above-normal profits, there exists an incentive for new firms to enter the industry. If we assume that the total demand for the product does not change, this implies that the demand for any single firm's product will fall. The demand curve will shift to the left until the above-normal profits are eliminated, at which point there will exist no further incentive for new firms to enter the industry. The long-run equilibrium position of a firm in monopolistic competition is illustrated in Fig. 10.8. Notice that the above-normal profit is completely eliminated when the demand curve facing the firm is

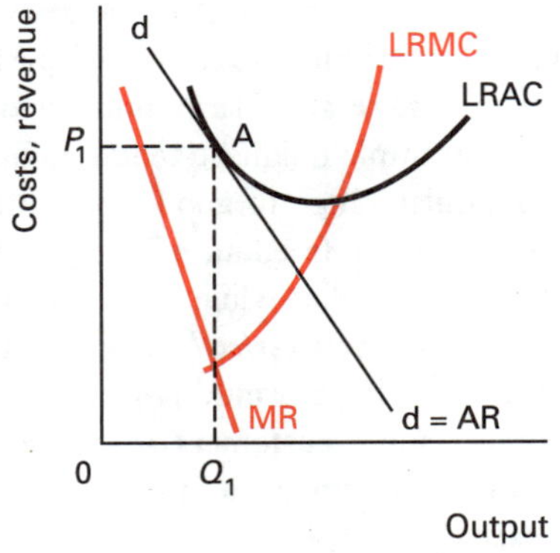

Fig. 10.8. Long-run equilibrium of a firm in monopolistic competition. The firm maximises profit by equating MR and LRMC. It earns normal profit in the long-run as the entry of new firms competes away any short-run above-normal profit.

tangential to the long-run average cost curve. As the demand curve is not perfectly elastic, this point of tangency must be above the lowest point on the LRAC curve (it is at point A in Fig. 10.8). Equating MR with MC, the firm produces quantity $0Q_1$ and sells it at price $0P_1$. Since AR and AC are equal, only normal profit is earned in the long-run.

Welfare implications

The model of monopolistic competition clearly does *not* lead to an optimal allocation of resources. As can be seen from Fig. 10.7 and Fig. 10.8, price exceeds marginal cost in both the short-run and the long-run. We have discussed the ensuing misallocation of resources earlier in this chapter.

As we noted above, production in monopolistic competition is conducted above the minimum point on the LRAC curve. This means that the consumer pays a higher price relative to that paid in the long-run in perfect competition. This prediction is sometimes called the *excess capacity theorem*, indicating that the monopolistically competitive firm could achieve lower-cost production if it increased its output. The consumer has to pay for the wasteful over-provision of capacity through higher prices.

Oligopoly

Oligopolistic interdependence
The recognition by an oligopolist that if it changes its price or non-price stategies, its rivals will react

Many markets that at first sight appear to be monopolistically competitive are in reality dominated by a few major producers who each manufacture a large number of different brands. These markets can best be described as *oligopolies*. In an oligopoly, the number of firms is small enough for each seller to take account of the actions of other sellers in the market. Sellers realise that they are mutually dependent. The model is sometimes called 'competition among the few' and is relatively common in manufacturing industries, such as automobile production and the tobacco industry. The special case of a market dominated by two firms is called a *duopoly*.

The recognition of oligopolistic interdependence means that a comprehensive theory of oligopoly would have to take account of the oligopolist's view of how rivals would react to any price or production change. Because of the uncertainties involved, there is no satisfactory comprehensive theory of oligopoly. Nevertheless, many models of oligopolistic behaviour have been developed, including 'market sharing' and 'dominant firm' models.

Kinked demand curve model

P. Sweezy developed a model in 1939 to explain the relative stability observed in the pricing policies of oligopolists. To illustrate this, consider a single firm operating in a market in which there are also several rival firms producing similar products. Suppose that, as shown in Fig. 10.9(a), the oligopolist is selling quantity $0q_1$ at a price of $0p_1$. Based on past experience, the oligopolist might believe that if it lowered its price, its rivals would also reduce their prices in order to maintain their market shares. Thus, for prices below $0p_1$, the oligopolist believes that it is effectively facing a relatively *inelastic* demand curve, as indicated by the segment AD_1. The line D_1D_1 is the demand curve facing the oligopolist when its rivals match its price changes. (MR_1 is the associated marginal revenue curve.) The line D_2D_2, on the other hand, is the demand curve facing the oligopolist if its rivals do not match its price changes. (MR_2 is the associated marginal revenue curve.) If the oligopolist believes that when

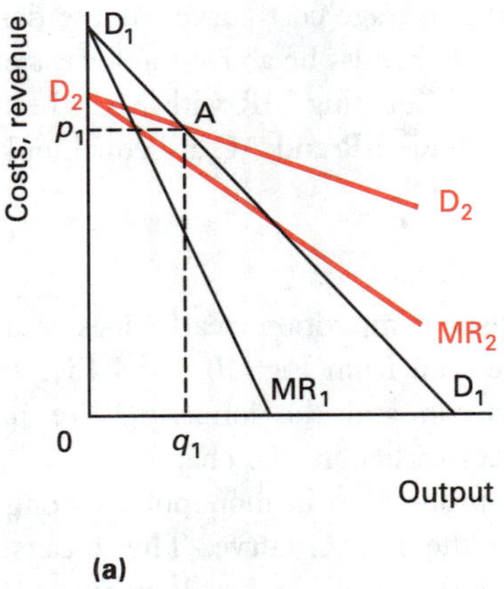

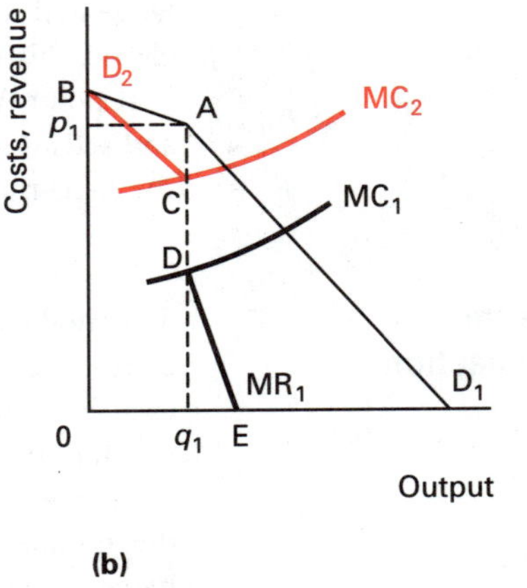

Fig. 10.9. The oligopolist's kinked demand curve. The oligopolist produces quantity $0q_1$, at price $0p_1$. The firm believes that if it increased price, its rivals would not follow suit – therefore, the firm believes it faces a relatively elastic demand curve above $0p_1$. If the firm were to reduce price, however, it believes that its rivals would follow suit. It believes, therefore, that it faces a relatively inelastic demand curve below $0p_1$.

it increases its price, its rivals will keep their prices constant to increase their market shares, then the oligopolist will believe that it is effectively facing the demand curve D_2A at prices above $0p_1$.

For simplicity, the demand curve that the oligopolist thinks it is facing is reproduced in Fig. 10.9(b). It is D_2AD_1 and because it has a kink at point A, it has been called the oligopolist's *kinked demand curve*. Also transferred to Fig. 10.9(b) is the effective marginal revenue curve that the oligopolist faces. It is given by the curve BCDE, with a discontinuity at CD. Since the firm's profit-maximising price and output are Op_1 and Oq_1 respectively, it must be true that the marginal cost curve cuts the marginal revenue curve somewhere in this area of discontinuity. It follows that quite large changes in the firm's marginal costs are possible (from MC_1 to MC_2 in fact) which will *not* induce the firm to change either its price or quantity.

Whilst this theory may help to explain the relative stability of prices in oligopoly, it is of limited value. It does not explain what factors determine the profit-maximising price and output initially. Indeed, we need to know the profit-maximising price and output in order to find the kink in the demand curve.

Oligopolists may engage in *non-price* competition. This behaviour may be particularly attractive in those oligopolistic markets with a high degree of excess capacity where a price war might force price down to such a low level that losses would result.

Non-price competition may, as in the case of monopolistic competition above, include product differentiation by means of brand-image advertising, packaging, styling or after-sales service. By this non-price competition, firms may attempt to capture a particular market segment (based perhaps on age or income characteristics) or to generate consumer brand loyalty through actual or perceived differences in the product offered.

Cartels

It is possible for a group of oligopolists to engage in collusion – that is, to make an agreement relating to the prices to be charged and/or the level of output to be produced. The objective of a collusive oligopoly is to act like a monopolist, by

Fig. 10.10. *A cartel operating as a monopoly.* In the extreme case, a cartel is able to achieve the level of profit that a pure monopolist is able to earn. Monopoly profit is represented by the shaded rectangle.

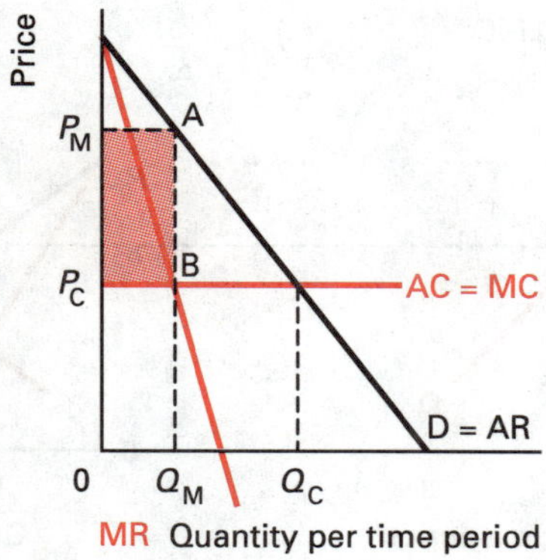

Collusive oligopoly
An oligopoly in which there is an explicit agreement between the oligopolists with respect to the levels of price and output

restricting output and raising price, thereby earning the maximum profits that can be attained in the industry. The cartel agreement may be *overt* so that the terms of the agreement are generally known, as in the case of OPEC. More likely, however, the cartel agreement will be *covert* (that is, known only to the participants) since such agreements are in general prohibited by the legislation relating to competition. In practice, the members of the cartel will have to set up a central authority with power to fix the price and quotas for individual producers.

Cartels, it is argued, are likely to break down in the long run as individual producers have an incentive to cheat by producing in excess of their quota and by undercutting the agreed price. In Fig. 10.10 it is assumed that oligopolists have combined to act as a cartel. The cartel sets total production at $0Q_M$ which is sold at the price $0P_M$. Note that this is also the result that would be obtained in the case of a pure monopoly.

The price $0P_M$ exceeds the marginal cost, and the *individual* oligopolist who believes that other producers will adhere to the cartel agreement has an incentive to increase profit by producing more output at a lower price. But the individual firm can only increase profit at the expense of its competitors, as the original situation represents the maximum profit situation for the *industry*. In the case of a homogeneous product for which the price cuts of the individual firm become known to others, then the market price may be driven down to the competitive price $0P_C$ if rival firms also increase their outputs and reduce their prices.

On the other hand, it can be argued that if a cartel member *expects* other member firms to follow price reductions which are against the rules of the cartel, then there exists little or no incentive for any individual member of the cartel to try to cheat. In the long run the breaking of the cartel agreement will, if practised by all cartel members, result in lower profits for *all* members.

Dominant firm model

Another model that can represent an oligopolistic market is the *dominant firm model.* Assume that an industry consists of a large dominant firm and a number of smaller firms. The dominant firm sets the price which is then accepted by the smaller firms who act as price takers.

In Fig. 10.11, DD represents the market demand curve and SS represents the sum of the MC curves of the smaller firms. The effective demand curve facing the

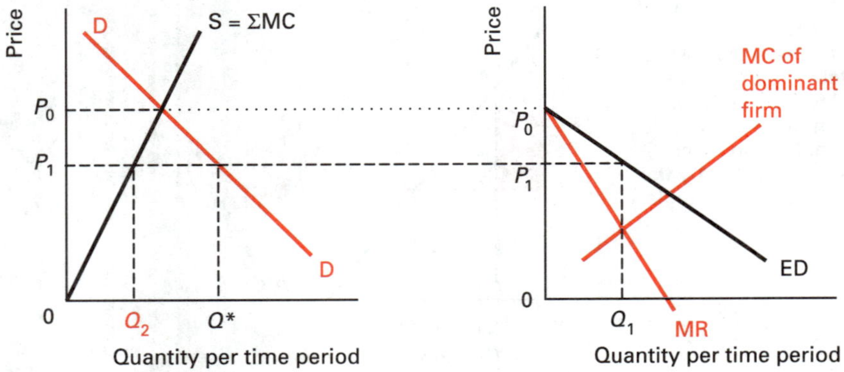

Fig. 10.11. The dominant firm model. The dominant firm maximises profit by producing quantity $0Q_1$ at price $0P_1$. The smaller firms accept the price set by the dominant firm and produce quantity $0Q_2$.

Dominant firm *A firm that acts as a market leader and effectively sets the market price*

dominant firm is obtained by subtracting from DD at each price the quantity that the smaller firms would be willing to supply at that price. The resulting *excess demand curve* is labelled ED in the right-hand diagram. Note that above price $0P_0$, the small firms are willing to supply all that the market demands.

The dominant firm maximises profits by producing where its MC is equal to its MR. Thus, it produces output $0Q_1$ and sets a price of $0P_1$. The smaller producers accept price $0P_1$ and produce up to the point at which this price equals their MC. The smaller firms, therefore, produce in total an output $0Q_2$ as shown in the left-hand diagram. Note that $0Q_1 + 0Q_2 = 0Q^*$, the total market demand at price $0P_1$.

As drawn in Fig. 10.11, the result is *not* efficient because at the margin of production, the MC of the dominant firm is less than the MC of the smaller firms. Total output could, therefore, be produced at a lower total cost by a shift away from the smaller producers to the dominant firm.

Whilst the dominant firm model may be useful in the short run, in which the number of firms is given, in the long run it is likely that the entry of *new* producers would erode the power of the dominant firm.

Oligopoly and game theory

The *interdependence* of firms in oligopolistic (or duopolistic) industries and, in particular, the fact that each firm has to take account of its rivals' likely responses to any of its own actions, has led to the application of *game theory* in the analysis of oligopolistic behaviour. Game theory was developed by the mathematician John von Neumann in 1937 and extended by the economist Oskar Morgenstern in the 1940s. It can be used to analyse conflicts of interest among rival firms. Oligopolists may engage in various *strategic* activities, such as price cutting or advertising, when competing with their rivals in the market place. Game theorists liken their behaviour to that of players in a game, like chess.

In a typical game, we find *strategies, pay-offs, a pay-off matrix* and *a dominant strategy*. Consider these in turn.

(a) *Strategies.* These are the players' plans of moves and counter-moves. A player's strategy has to set out not only the preferred course of action, but also to anticipate the possible reactions of opponents.

(b) *Pay-offs.* These are the possible outcomes of each strategy, or combination of strategies for a player, given the rivals' counter-strategies.

(c) *The pay-off matrix.* This is a table which illustrates the pay-offs for every possible action by each player for every possible reaction by the other players.

(d) *Dominant strategy.* This refers to each player's best strategy, given the rivals' counter-strategies.

Armed with these concepts, it is possible to analyse the behaviour of firms in an oligopolistic (or duopolistic) industry. Consider, for example, the case of a duopolist, firm A, which has a single rival, firm B. Suppose in fact that A is a motor company which wishes to increase the market share of one of its models. It is considering two alternative strategies: a price cut, or an increase in advertising. Firm A anticipates that B will react to either of these strategies in like manner: that is, either with a price cut of its own, or with an increase in its advertising. We can thus construct a pay-off matrix showing two strategies each for A and B with four possible outcomes (in terms of market shares). This is shown in Table 10.2.

Row 1 shows the two possible outcomes when A adopts the price cutting strategy: A will achieve a market share of 60 per cent if B also goes for a price cutting strategy, and a market share of 75 per cent if B responds with extra advertising. Row 2 shows the two possible outcomes when A adopts the extra advertising strategy: in this case, A will achieve a 50 per cent market share if B responds with a price cutting strategy, and a 65 per cent market share if B also goes for extra advertising.

We assume that A will proceed in the belief that B is also aware of the pay-off matrix. This being so, it is clear that in this example, B will respond to either of A's strategies by cutting price as this gives B a higher market share than could be achieved by extra advertising. Knowing this, A will also opt for the price cutting strategy and so achieve a market share of 60 per cent. Price cutting is the *dominant strategy* for both A and B.

Zero-sum game *A game in which the gains of one player are necessarily the losses of another player*

Notice that in this example, the market is shared between A and B only, so one firm's gain is necessarily the other firm's loss. This situation is referred to as zero-sum game by game theorists.

Nash equilibrium

This is named after John Nash, who argued that competitive behaviour might result in a situation in which no firm could improve its pay-off, given the other firms' strategies. If this were achieved in our two-firm example, firm A would not be able to improve its position, given B's strategy, and B would not be able to improve its position, given A's strategy. Such a situation is called a *Nash equilibrium.*

Table 10.2 Pay-off matrix: percentage market shares.

		Firm B: Price cut		Firm B: Extra advertising	
		A	B	A	B
Firm A	Price cut	60	40	75	25
	Extra advertising	50	50	65	30

Table 10.3 **Pay-off matrix: profits (£m).**

		Firm L: Low Price	Firm L: High Price
Firm P	Low Price	P 0, L 0	P 60, L −15
	High Price	P −10, L 55	P 70, L 50

Consider, for example, a duopoly in the soap market (say, firms P and L). Suppose that each firm is seeking to maximise profits with the use of high or low price strategies. Assume that a high price strategy by both firms would yield above-normal profits, while a low price strategy by both firms would yield normal profits. The pay-off matrix in Table 10.3 illustrates the outcomes of each combination of these strategies. Note that 'normal' profits are recorded as zero profits in the table as normal profits are assumed to be included in each firm's costs.

It can be seen that collusion by both firms to charge high prices results in the highest pay-offs: that is, £70 million and £50 million profit for P and L respectively. This outcome is illustrated in the bottom right cell of the matrix. But suppose each firm is not able to trust its rival. Firm L, for example, may be tempted to engage in a low price strategy in order to increase its profit to £55 million, given that P adheres to charging high prices. If this happens, P would sustain a £10 million loss, as shown in the bottom left cell. Note that in a similar manner, firm L would also sustain a loss (of £15 million) if P cut prices whilst L maintained high prices. Because of a constant fear that the rival may adopt such a damaging strategy, it is in the interests of both firms to adopt a low price strategy. Thus, the equilibrium position in this example is the outcome illustrated in the top left cell, where normal profits will prevail. In this case, P and L follow a maximin strategy, according to which (given the rival's low price strategy) neither firm can do any better than earn normal profit. Since neither firm can do any better, given its rival's strategy, a Nash equilibrium has been achieved.

Maximin strategy *A strategy that results in the maximum pay-off to the player adopting the strategy, on the assumption that the other player is seeking to inflict the maximum damage*

The prisoner's dilemma

This is a special type of game which shows that sometimes, under specific circumstances, *co-operation* is beneficial to the participants. In oligopolies or other market structures, when producers behave selfishly, their strategies may lead to a greater loss to themselves and to their rivals than if they had behaved co-operatively.

The essential premise of the *prisoner's dilemma* is the mistrust of other participants which creates an incentive to cheat. In this game, the behaviour of firms is likened to that of prisoners faced with the dilemma of whether or not to confess to a crime of which they are accused.

Prisoner's dilemma *A situation in which the players would be better off through co-operation. But, as a result of mistrust they pursue a non-co-operative stategy and consequently are worse off*

Consider, for example, two individuals A and B whom the police arrest on suspicion of burglary and possession of stolen goods. Each is locked up in a separate room and the police then offer the following deal: 'If you confess while your partner does not confess, you will get a three-month jail sentence while your partner will get three years'. In addition, each knows that if they both co-operate with the police and confess to the burglary, each will get two years. But if neither makes a confession, the evidence is such that each will be convicted of possessing stolen goods and get

Table 10.4 Prisoner's dilemma.

		Individual B: Confess		Individual B: Don't confess	
		A	B	A	B
Individual A	Confess	2 yrs	2 yrs	3 mths	3 yrs
	Don't confess	3 yrs	3 mths	9 mths	9 mths

nine months in prison. The two strategies available to A and B and the four possible outcomes are illustrated in the pay-off matrix in Table 10.4.

Inspection of the matrix shows that if A and B trust each other and co-operate between themselves, they can each get a 9 month sentence by not confessing. But both individuals feel unable to trust the other not to confess. Each fears that the other might confess, in order to get a short 3 month sentence, so resulting in a 3 year sentence for the one who does not confess. Consequently, in this position of mistrust, each prisoner will tend to adopt a strategy of confessing to the crime. Thus, the final outcome is given by the top left cell in which each prisoner confesses and receives a 2 year sentence.

Notice, this is also a Nash equilibrium as both A and B act in their own self-interest. This outcome displays competitive behaviour. The pursuit of self-interest, therefore, does not produce the optimal outcome from the point of view of the prisoners. It will be noted that many of the examples of negative externalities, especially environmental pollution, exhibit the characteristics of the *prisoner's dilemma.* Mistrust and the competitive behaviour of producers tend to exacerbate the harmful effects of externalities, while co-operation might lead to reduced levels of damage.

Contestable markets

Perfectly contestable market *A market where the costs of entry and exit by new competitors are zero*

A new theory, called the theory of contestable markets, which challenges many of the conclusions of the traditional theory of monopoly has been developed. This theory points out that a market with only one or two established producers may, in fact, represent a market in which firms have no effective monopoly power to dictate price or quantity. The key aspect is the *ease of entry into* or *exit from the market.* If such entry is easy, so that there are a number of potential competitors, then the theory predicts that the actual market price will be kept down to near the competitive level, where P = MC. If the costs of entry and exit by new competitors are zero, the market is said to be perfectly contestable.

If above-normal profits emerge (perhaps due to an increase in demand, or improvements in technology) this will attract potential competitors into the market. The ease of entering a contestable market implies that the required technical knowledge and production techniques can be easily acquired by new entrants. Similarly, the ease with which firms can leave a contestable market implies that the sunk or irrecoverable costs of production are low. This means that if a firm decides to leave the market it can recoup most of its outlay by transferring capital equipment to other lines of production or, alternatively, sell the equipment.

Sunk cost *A cost that cannot be recouped in the event of exit from a market*

This theory may be applied, for example, to airline routes with only one or two airlines currently operating. The argument is that if potential competitors are able to commence operations on the route easily, the fares will be kept down to competitive levels even though there are only one or two operators. This is because existing operators will be aware of the *threat of entry* from potential rivals if above-normal profits are being earned. Just as important as the ease of entry is the ease of exit. If new airlines begin to operate on a new route, with the result that they make losses and so decide to withdraw, the sunk costs will be low. This is because the expensive aircraft can be switched quite easily from the loss-making route to a potentially profitable one.

However, the extent to which the theory of contestable markets may be applied is limited. As noted, two key conditions must be satisfied for a contestable market to exist. The first is that the potential entrants must have low sunk costs, should they decide to withdraw from the market. In many cases, the sunk or irrecoverable costs of entering a market tend to be quite high. Consider the case of Nissan, which has invested substantial sums in constructing assembly plants in the United Kingdom. Exit from this market would probably involve very significant sunk costs for Nissan.

The second necessary condition is that the requisite technical knowledge and production techniques must be widely available to new entrants. In reality, many monopolies and oligopolies are firmly based on technical knowledge which is their exclusive preserve. Examples include patented drugs developed by pharmaceutical companies. Nevertheless, this important theory illustrates a principle with far-reaching implications. The mere fact that there are only one or two producers in a market does not necessarily mean the existence of market power in such cases.

Alternatives to profit maximisation

Managerial models

In perfect competition, profit maximisation is a necessary condition for survival in the long-run. However, once we turn to other models in which firms do not face a perfectly elastic demand curve, an area of discretion becomes available to firms in their behaviour. The growing recognition of the possible divergence of interest between the owners of large companies (the shareholders) and the day-to-day controllers (the managers) was remarked upon in Ch. 2. The awareness that managers may be interested in maximising variables other than profits has led to the development of several managerial models of the firm.

These models implicitly or explicitly assume that the managers aim to maximise a managerial utility function containing at least one variable besides profit. Suggestions of variables for inclusion in this function have included the market share of the firm, the complexity of the corporate structure and the growth of the firm. Most of the models specify a constraint, such as a minimum profit constraint or a constraint on the value of the firm's shares. The argument is that some minimum level of profit is necessary to ensure the survival of the firm and its managers because shareholders expect a minimum return on their investment if they are to continue to hold the firm's shares. It is only when the firm has earned this required level of profit that it can turn its attention to other objectives.

The sales-maximisation model In this model, originally developed by Baumol, it is assumed that the firm attempts to maximise the revenue obtained from sales

Fig. 10.12. **Sales maximisation with a profit constraint.** The firm maximises total sales revenue by producing quantity $0Q_3$. If a minimum profit constraint of $0Z$ is introduced, the firm is forced to reduce output to $0Q_2$.

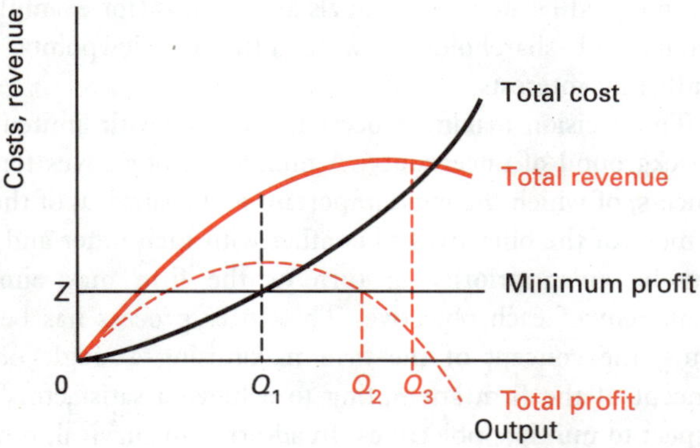

Sales maximisation *An objective of a firm that is achieved by producing the level of output at which sales revenue is maximised*

Profit constraint *The minimum level of profit considered necessary to satisfy the shareholders of the firm*

either subject to or without a profit constraint. A possible motive is the managers' belief that their salaries are related to the size of the firm.

In Fig. 10.12, the total cost and total revenue curves of a firm are shown. From these, the total profit curve is derived and it can be seen that the profit-maximising level of output is $0Q_1$. If the firm should attempt to maximise sales revenue without any profit constraint, it would produce quantity $0Q_3$, which is bigger than $0Q_1$. Now assume that the firm attempts to maximise sales revenue subject to a minimum profit constraint of $0Z$. The sales-maximising quantity $0Q_3$ does not meet the profit constraint and so output has to be reduced to $0Q_2$, the largest volume of output that meets the constraint. Notice that in general the sales-maximising level of output is greater than the profit-maximising level. The two output levels would be identical only in the exceptional case where the maximum attainable level of profits was just equal to the profit constraint.

The sales-maximising model subject to a profit constraint leads to a prediction about a firm's reaction to an increase in fixed costs different from that of the profit-maximising model. In the profit-maximising model, as an increase in fixed costs does not affect marginal cost, the firm's equilibrium output remains unchanged. But now reconsider the firm in Fig. 10.12 which is maximising its sales revenue at output $0Q_2$, subject to the profit constraint $0Z$. If fixed costs increase, profits will fall, so that in the diagram the total profit curve will shift downwards. The firm will now have to reduce output to meet the profit constraint.

An unresolved problem with this model is what determines the minimum acceptable level of profit. Indeed, one might ask why, in the face of the increase in fixed costs in the above example, the minimum acceptable level of profit was not reduced to accommodate the new situation.

Behavioural models

The behavioural school emphasises that the internal organisational structure of firms is likely to influence their behaviour. Behavioural models, such as those of Cyert and March, suggest that the decision-making process within the firm results in the pursuit of a number of objectives. Each objective acts as a constraint on the future activity of the firm.

The behavioural approach points out that decision-making results from a bargaining process among members of the firm (or *coalition*); the bargaining process is conducted between individuals and groups (for example, managers, workers, trade unions and shareholders) with differing viewpoints, bargaining strengths and conflicting interests.

The decision-making process takes place with limited information and subject to a background of uncertainty. A number of objectives for the firm emerge from this process, of which the most important is the survival of the firm. It is possible for two or more of the objectives to conflict with each other and, in this case, the objectives may be given priority in turn or the firm may aim for satisfactory levels of attainment of each objective. This latter process has been described as satisficing. Thus, the concept of the firm maximising a single objective is replaced by the concept of the firm attempting to achieve a satisfactory level of performance with respect to multiple objectives. In addition to survival, other objectives include target levels of profit, sales, rate of return on capital, growth and market share

Satisficing *An attempt by a firm to achieve a satisfactory level of attainment of a number of objectives*

The target level of attainment of these objectives is influenced by both the past level of attainment and by what is thought to be currently attainable. If the target level is achieved too easily, it is subsequently raised; if it proves impossible to reach, it is lowered. If a target level is not achieved, the firm may pursue problem-oriented search procedures. Information is gathered and alternative courses of action are considered sequentially, beginning with alternatives that involve a small change from existing policies. If the target level is still not achieved, strategies that involve greater changes may be introduced.

As an example, consider a firm which has a minimum market share as one of its objectives, but which is no longer achieving its desired target. The firm may conduct market research to find out why consumers are turning away from its products. It may also increase its advertising expenditure and search for information on what new products may help to restore the market share. It may analyse carefully the products of its competitors to see if they include features popular with consumers. In addition, the firm may instigate a long-run research programme to develop possible new products. Search procedures are satisficing rather than maximising, so that the first satisfactory course of action is selected.

Another feature associated with the behaviour models is the concept of *organisational slack*. Members of the coalition receive side-payments in the form of monetary awards or as commitments to specific policies. Typically, the level of side-payments distributed exceeds that necessary to maintain the coalition and this gives rise to the concept of organisational slack.

Whilst behavioural models provide useful insights, they are of limited value at present as detailed knowledge of the internal bargaining process of the firm is required in order to derive precise predictions. This is an area where economics comes into close contact with the disciplines of psychology and sociology. Indeed, progress was recognised by the award of the Nobel Prize for economics to H.A. Simon in 1978 for work in this field.

Cost-plus pricing

Cost-plus pricing *Involves the addition of a mark-up to the unit cost of production*

An attack on the profit-maximisation theory resulted after a number of surveys reported that many business people did not employ, or were not familiar with, the concepts of marginal cost and marginal revenue. How then, it was argued, could these business people achieve profit maximisation? It was claimed that in practice cost-plus (or full cost) pricing was pursued. According to this approach, business people request their accountants to estimate the full cost of production per unit of output (including both fixed and variable costs). The final price is then determined by adding on a mark-up to ensure the achievement of the required profit level.

A possible explanation for this procedure is that the typical firm may be unable to estimate its demand curve (and hence its marginal revenue curve) accurately. Similar problems of estimating marginal cost also arise. Moreover, it has been claimed that cost-plus pricing using a flexible mark-up can result in relatively infrequent price changes which will appeal to customers. If price is held constant and costs vary, this implies a variable profit margin.

Later observers have pointed out that the survey results were not necessarily a challenge to the traditional theory of the firm which does not claim to predict how prices are actually fixed. The MR = MC rule for profit maximisation does not imply that business people must consciously calculate and equate the two variables. Indeed, cost-plus pricing could result in the same price and output decisions as profit maximisation. This possibility is highlighted by some of the business people questioned who stated explicitly that the actual size of the mark-up is determined with reference to the state of competitive pressures. In those cases where the size of the mark-up is rigid and is not varied in response to competition, however, the outcomes are likely to differ from those derived in the traditional theory.

Some critics have questioned whether the cost-plus approach does constitute a theory. A theory is expected to yield testable predictions, but the cost-plus approach does not appear to result in predictions that can be subjected to empirical tests.

The economics of J.K. Galbraith

One of the most controversial figures in modern economics is the American economist, John Kenneth Galbraith. His ideas, particularly those on the role of large companies, have been influential with the general public. His critics, though, argue that he propagates his ideas without sufficient regard as to whether evidence exists to support his theories. Galbraith is certainly one of the most literate economists and he has introduced several striking phrases into the literature, such as countervailing power. This expresses the idea that any power centre is eventually likely to come up against another power centre that may have grown up in response to the initial exercise of power. An example is a large company faced with the countervailing power of the trade unions.

Countervailing power
The notion that a power centre (such as a large company) is likely to be opposed by another power centre (such as a trade union) that attempts to soften the impact of the initial power centre

In his later writings, Galbraith analysed the consequences of the concentration of economic activity in the hands of large companies. He argued that large companies are not subservient to market pressures. By generating internal funds for investment, they are no longer subject to the disciplines imposed by the capital market and to a large extent they can create markets for their products through advertising, so that consumers are no longer 'sovereign'.

The large company is controlled by what Galbraith calls the *technostructure* – that is, the groups of specialists whose skills and information are vital to the continued functioning of the company. The technostructure includes technologists, scientists, computer programmers, accountants and managers. The technostructure aims to ensure the stability of the company and, therefore, of itself. Thus, the resources of the company are not used to maximise profits, but to promote growth and stability. Galbraith argues that the large company is forced to plan and in this way performs society's planning function.

As mentioned earlier, the ideas of Galbraith have been subjected to much criticism. It has often been pointed out that in contrast to the Galbraithian model, large companies are indeed subject to market pressures. Examples of United Kingdom companies that hit major crises in the 1970s and 1980s include Rolls-Royce, Burmah Oil, Chrysler UK, Laker Airways and British Leyland. The 1990s has seen the demise of Coloroll and the International Leisure Group. Similar crises have been experienced by companies in Europe and the United States. The Galbraithian idea that the technostructure controls the large company has also been challenged. It is argued that in many cases large shareholders or those in control of the shareholders' votes are in effective control. In addition, many top executives have large shareholdings in their company which might act as a powerful incentive towards profit maximisation (and consequently large dividends for the executives) rather than towards the stability of the company.

Galbraith has admitted that market pressures do operate effectively in those parts of the economy where small businesses predominate, such as hairdressing, agriculture, household and personal services: this is the *market sector*. The world of the large companies is the *planning sector*. Where the dividing line between the two should be drawn is not made clear. To ensure a compatible level of economic development, not only in the market and planning sectors but also in the public sector, Galbraith is in favour of a high level of public expenditure. Because of the relatively low level of public expenditure in the United States, Galbraith has pointed to the contrast between 'private affluence and public squalor': by this, he is referring to the waste of resources in the affluent private sector and the consequent underprovision of public services required to deal with pressing social needs. It is because Galbraith favours more government intervention that he has been widely criticised by right-wing economists who favour the operation of the market mechanism in as many fields as possible.

Multinational companies

Multinational company
A business organisation whose production activities are located in more than one country

In recent years, increasing attention has been paid to the international nature of production in many industries. A multinational company is usually a large company which is heavily committed to the international ownership and control of production. Well-known examples include British Petroleum, Ford, Unilever, Philips and Mitsubishi.

There are a number of reasons why a company might decide to set up production facilities overseas. With the uneven distribution of natural resources between countries, the motive may be to gain control over the supplies of raw materials found in abundance in particular locations. Oil provides a familiar example. By gaining control over its raw materials, a firm may be able to erect *entry barriers* against other firms.

Cost advantages may be another motive. The company may take the view that it is most cost effective to supply a local market with local production. There are many examples of companies establishing overseas production facilities to take advantage of low labour costs. Some United States electronic companies, for example, have located in Hong Kong and Singapore.

A multinational company may set up a plant in a country as a defensive measure if its market share is threatened by the entry of a local firm. Alternatively, the government of a country may erect trade barriers (such as tariffs and quotas). These may act as an incentive for a foreign producer to set up local production facilities in order to avoid the barriers. The Japanese car manufacturer, Nissan, is an example of a company which has set up plants in several countries (including Italy, the United States and the United Kingdom) in an attempt to jump over trade barriers. The United Kingdom car industry negotiated voluntary restrictions on the Japanese share of the market for many years. France and Italy have also imposed restrictions on imports of Japanese cars. Once the EC content of Nissan cars produced in the United Kingdom reached a specified proportion, they became, under EC regulations, exempt from the trade barriers within the rest of the EC. More recently, Toyota and Honda have built assembly plants in the United Kingdom, partly to gain unrestricted access to the EC market.

Summary

1. Monopoly has both costs and benefits. In terms of costs, it results in resource misallocation and new competition may be stifled through entry barriers. On the other hand, monopoly may confer benefits in terms of economies of single ownership and technical progress.
2. A monopolist may attempt to increase profits through practising price discrimination. This normally involves charging different prices to different consumers.
3. Monopolistic competition, or competition among the many, results in resource misallocation, but may be said to benefit consumers by providing them with a wide variety of goods and services.
4. Oligopoly, or competition among the few, may result in a range of market behaviour by firms. A number of models have been developed to analyse the behaviour of firms in such markets, including the kinked demand curve and dominant firm models. In recent years, increasing use has been made of game theory to analyse the behaviour of oligopolists.
5. Whilst the assumption of profit maximisation is an important feature of the theory of the firm in economics, it is increasingly recognised that firms may pursue a range of objectives. A number of alternative models of the firm have been developed, including the sales-maximisation model and behavioural models.

Exercises

1. Review your understanding of the following terms:

monopoly	zero-sum game
cartel	Nash equilibrium
resource misallocation	maximin strategy
barriers to entry	prisoner's dilemma
natural monopoly	contestable market
price discrimination	sales maximisation
monopolistic competition	satisficing

product differentiation	cost-plus pricing
oligopoly	countervailing power
kinked demand curve	technostructure
pay-off matrix	multinational company
dominant strategy	deadweight loss

2. The following data represent the cost and revenue schedules of a pure monopolist.

Quantity	Total revenue (£)	Total cost (£)
5	500	350
10	900	550
15	1,200	675
20	1,400	800
25	1,500	1,125
30	1,500	1,800
35	1,400	2,800

(a) Calculate AR, MR, ATC and MC.
(b) Plot the AR, MR, ATC and MC schedules on the same graph and estimate the profit-maximising price and quantity.
(c) Estimate the firm's total profit.

3. Explain why a profit-maximising monopolist is unlikely to operate on the inelastic part of the demand curve facing him or her.

4. Consider the scope for price discrimination in the following cases: (a) British Rail; (b) a single wheat farmer; (c) a doctor with private patients.

5. Explain the unusual shape given to the combined MR curve (MR_{TOTAL}) in Fig. 10.6(c).

6. 'Monopolistic competition provides a wide variety of products for consumers at the cost of some resource misallocation.' Discuss.

7. Consider the view that an oligopolistic market structure provides a higher incentive to innovate than other market structures.

8. Given the following pay-off matrix for duopolists A and B with two alternative strategies (low- or high-cost marketing), determine the best strategy for each firm:

		Firm B: Low-cost marketing		Firm B: High-cost marketing	
		A	B	A	B
Firm A	Low-cost marketing	4	6	0	9
	High-cost marketing	8	0	2	4

where the entries in the table represent net profits in £m.

9. What criticisms can be levelled against the assumption of profit maximisation in the traditional theory of the firm? Describe two alternative models that have been developed in response to these criticisms.

Appendix

An example of profit maximisation, sales revenue maximisation and sales revenue maximisation with a profit constraint Consider a monopolist who faces the following demand (or average revenue) function:

$$p = 140 - 2q \qquad (1)$$

In addition, suppose that the monopolist's total cost function is given by:

$$\mathrm{TC} = 10 + 5q^2 \qquad (2)$$

The firm's total revenue equals price times quantity, that is

$$\mathrm{TR} = pq = 140q - 2q^2 \qquad (3)$$

Profit maximisation Suppose first that the firm wishes to maximise profit. Profit is given by:

$$\begin{aligned} \pi &= \mathrm{TR} - \mathrm{TC} \\ &= 140q - 2q^2 - 10 - 5q^2 \\ &= -10 + 140q - 7q^2 \qquad (4) \end{aligned}$$

For profit maximisation, we take the first derivative and set it equal to zero. *This is equivalent to setting marginal cost equal to marginal revenue.*

$$\frac{d\pi}{dq} = 140 - 14q = 0$$

$$14q = 140$$

$$q = 10$$

The second derivative of the profit function is equal to -14. As this is negative, a maximum has been identified.

To find the profit-maximising price, we substitute $q = 10$ into the demand function (1):

$$\begin{aligned} p &= 140 - 2(10) \\ &= 120 \end{aligned}$$

Finally, the maximum level of profit can be determined by substituting $q = 10$ into the profit function (4):

$$\begin{aligned} \pi &= -10 + 140(10) - 7(10)^2 \\ &= -10 + 1400 - 700 \\ &= 690 \end{aligned}$$

Sales revenue maximisation Assume now that the firm wishes to maximise the value of its sales (i.e. maximise TR). The first derivative of TR with respect to q is MR, so the condition for TR maximisation is simply that *MR should equal zero*. In our example, TR is given by (3). Differentiating TR with respect to q and setting the result equal to zero gives:

$$\frac{d\,\mathrm{TR}}{dq} = \mathrm{MR} = 140 - 4q = 0$$

$$q = 35$$

To find the sales revenue maximising price, simply substitute $q = 35$ into the demand function (1). This gives:

$$p = 140 - 2(35)$$
$$= 140 - 70 = 70$$

The maximum level of TR is $70 \times 35 = 2{,}450$. Finally, the level of profit/loss can be found by substituting $q = 35$ into the profit function (4). This gives:

$$\pi = -10 + 140(35) - 7(35)^2$$
$$= -3{,}685$$

So maximising sales revenue would in this case mean that the firm would make a *loss* of 3,685.

Sales revenue maximisation with a profit constraint Suppose now that the firm wishes to maximise its sales revenue, but only so long as a certain level of profit is earned. Let the profit constraint be 20. So the firm's problem is to maximise TR, subject to making a profit of at least 20. We know that as q increases from 0 to 35, TR rises from 0 to its maximum of 2,450: in this range, therefore, we know that higher values of q mean higher values of TR. We can solve the firm's problem by finding the highest value of q at which π equals 20. Setting the profit function (4) equal to 20, we get:

$$-10 + 140q - 7q^2 = 20$$

or

$$-7q^2 + 140q - 30 = 0 \qquad (5)$$

The formula for solving a quadratic equation of the form $ax^2 + bx + c = 0$ is:

$$x = \frac{-b \pm \sqrt{(b^2 - 4ac)}}{2a}$$

Applying this to the π constraint (5) gives:

$$q = \frac{-140 \pm \sqrt{(19{,}600 - 840)}}{-14}$$
$$= 19.78 \text{ or } 0.22$$

An output of 19.78 will sell at a price of 100.44 and yield a TR of 1,986.7. This is the maximum TR that can be achieved given the firm's profit constraint. Note that an output of 0.22 also yields a profit of 20, but with a much lower sales revenue.

THE PUBLIC SECTOR

INTRODUCING THE PUBLIC SECTOR

PUBLIC GOODS AND EXTERNALITIES

ENVIRONMENTAL ECONOMICS

FINANCING THE PUBLIC SECTOR

ISSUES OF PUBLIC POLICY

11 INTRODUCING THE PUBLIC SECTOR

Learning objectives

After reading this chapter, you should be able to:

- outline the main reasons why an economy needs a public sector
- explain the theoretical and practical difficulties of determining the size of the public sector that maximises social welfare
- make international comparisons of the relative sizes of public sectors, using public expenditure and taxation ratios
- understand the main components of public expenditure and government revenues
- discuss the main causes of the long-term growth of public expenditure

Introduction

Public sector *The public sector is made up of the activities of government, its agencies and public corporations*

The aim of the next four chapters is to consider the role of the public sector in an economy. By the term 'public sector', we mean that part of the national economy for which the government has some direct responsibility; it includes both central and local government, public corporations and other public enterprise activities. Economists are interested in the behaviour of the public sector because the government's decisions affect individuals and institutions in many different ways. The most important decisions are concerned with public spending, taxation and various rules and regulations that have an influence on social welfare. It is appropriate, therefore, that we should examine the basis of these decisions and indicate the principles of state policy on welfare.

Our major task in the present chapter is to highlight the objectives of the public sector, to examine the 'optimum' size of the public sector and to indicate the difficulties associated with measuring state activity. In this connection, we consider the structure and growth of public expenditure and taxation in the United Kingdom and other selected countries; we also outline some of the theories of the growth of public expenditure.

A fundamental point that must be made at the outset is that the public and private sectors in an economy constantly interact. This process of interaction tends to increase with imperfections in the market mechanism as public action is frequently called for to compensate for market failure. It is hardly surprising to note that in most of the present-day major western industrial nations, about 30 per cent (and in many cases, including the United Kingdom, more than 30 per cent) of the gross national product is made up of public sector activity. Note that the gross national product (or GNP) can be defined as the total monetary value of a country's annual output of final goods and services. The related measurement of gross domestic product (or GDP) is equal to gross national product minus net property income from abroad.

Why do we need a public sector?

In a national economy, the market mechanism cannot perform all those functions required to attain an efficient and equitable allocation of resources. There are a number of reasons, therefore, why a public sector may be needed. Consider the following:

To promote competition The claim that the price system leads to an efficient use of resources depends on a most important condition: that there should be competition in the markets for both resources and finished goods. This means that there should be no restrictions on the free entry of firms into industries and consumers and producers should have complete information about prices and profit-making opportunities. To promote competitive conditions and to prevent potential abuse of monopoly power, government measures such as taxes, subsidies and rules and regulations may be used.

To ensure the provision of goods not adequately provided by the private sector Even if we had perfect markets, there are certain types of goods which could not be provided adequately by private firms. For example, in Ch. 7 we noted that *public goods* (like defence and lighthouses) and *natural monopolies* (like the distribution of gas) would lead to an inefficient use of resources if production were left to private enterprise.

To tackle externalities Connected with market failure are the problems of *externalities*, such as noise and pollution, which require public action. Generally, private sector decisions take into account only the *private costs* and *benefits* connected with production and consumption and in this way ignore the wider implications of such decisions for others in society or for future generations. A public sector can seek to weigh the benefits and costs of the future, and take a wider view of the effects of producers and consumers on others.

To enforce contracts To make the market mechanism work, government rules and regulations are required to enforce contracts entered into between buyers and sellers of goods and resources.

To redistribute income and wealth Given that the government's goal is to maximise social welfare, public policy may be required in the attempt to achieve a more equitable distribution of income and wealth.

To promote macroeconomic objectives Public policy may be required in market economies where the price system is prone to high unemployment, inflation and balance of payments difficulties. In such economies, governments are concerned to implement policies designed to achieve a high level of employment, a low rate of inflation, a satisfactory balance of payments position, a desired rate of economic growth and balanced regional development. In this part of the book, we are concerned only with the government's microeconomic policy objectives. Macroeconomic theory and policy are dealt with from Ch. 18 onwards.

The microeconomic objectives of government

Governments are primarily concerned with maximising social welfare and in seeking to achieve this, they aim to influence both the allocation and distribution of resources. Microeconomic policies, then, may be said to have an allocation function and a distribution function. Consider these in turn.

The allocation function In its allocation function, the major objective of the public sector is to achieve Pareto efficiency in resource allocation. In order to implement public decisions about allocation, the government's *budget* (that is, its receipts and expenditures) plays an important role in switching resources from private to public consumption and vice versa. Budgetary policy, in fact, is at the heart of the government's allocation function. For example, it is through its budget that a government is able to ensure the provision of public goods, like defence and law and order. However, to make the market mechanism work, we mentioned above that the government also lays down rules and regulations (such as anti-pollution and anti-monopoly legislation); these must be regarded as part of the state's allocation function as well.

It is important to distinguish between the state *production* and the state *provision* of goods. Some goods (for example, gas, electricity, rail, air travel and municipal transport) are actually produced by state agencies and rationed through prices. Such state production occurs, for example, in many western European countries. Public provision refers to those goods and services generally produced by private firms, but financed through the budget and paid for indirectly by the community in the form of taxation. Examples of publicly provided goods in the United Kingdom include pharmaceutical supplies to the National Health Service and defence equipment to the armed forces.

The distribution function In its distribution function, the overriding aim of the state is to promote equity – that is to say, to achieve a 'fair' distribution of income and wealth. For this purpose, budgets are usually designed to impose higher rates of taxation on higher incomes and to try and secure a fair distribution of tax burdens in the community. On the expenditure side of the budget, spending can be channelled into those areas (such as health, education and social security benefits) which directly benefit the lower-income groups.

Difficulties arise, however, in deciding whether income, spending power or wealth is the most equitable base for taxation. Added to this is the problem of defining income, capital and wealth and the difficulty of valuing assets.

Conflict of objectives

It is argued that the public sector's objectives cannot all be attained simultaneously. Conflicts arise partly because, unlike private individuals, governments strive to achieve a multiplicity of objectives. For example, the policy of maintaining low council house rents on equity grounds results in long waiting lists; this may be undesirable on efficiency grounds as it acts as a barrier to labour mobility and this in turn may increase unemployment. Likewise, policies to combat inflation might call for a cut in public expenditure which in the short-run may lead to a higher rate of unemployment and a less equitable distribution of income and wealth.

The size of the public sector in theory

Since the government plays such an important role in a mixed economy, the next question we must ask is what size of public sector will maximise social welfare, a question which concerns both economic efficiency and equity. There are two main ways of illustrating conceptually the most efficient and equitable size of the public sector. These are (a) by identifying the social welfare maximising point on the production possibility frontier; and (b) by determining the *optimum-size fiscal community*. Consider these in turn.

Identifying the social welfare maximising point This approach starts from the division of the given stock of a country's resources between the private and public sectors. The resources allocated to the public sector have to be determined by the political process as there exists no market mechanism by which people can express their preferences for goods for collective consumption. On the other hand, the resources used for private goods are allocated by the price mechanism where consumers bid for those assortments which they want most.

When resources have been divided between the two sectors in such a way that enables the community to reach its highest attainable community indifference curve, then that community can be said to have reached a Pareto optimal intersectoral allocation of resources. This is illustrated in Fig. 11.1, where AB is the production possibility frontier and CIC_1 and CIC_2 are two of the community indifference curves drawn on the assumption of a given socially desired distribution of income. CIC_2 is the highest attainable community indifference curve; point Z is the social welfare maximising point and 0T is the most efficient and equitable size of the public sector.

The optimum-size fiscal community The phrase 'optimum-size fiscal community' refers to that level of government activity at which the social marginal benefit from public spending is equal to the social marginal cost imposed on the community by taxation. The social marginal benefit from public spending can be defined as the extra utility to society resulting from each additional pound spent by

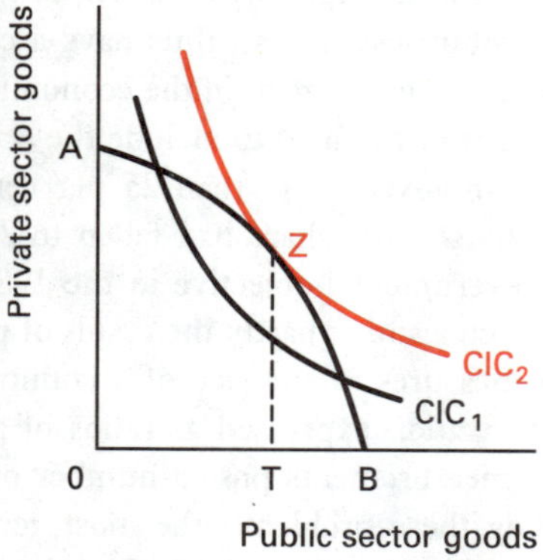

Fig. 11.1. The choice between public and private goods. Point *Z* is the social welfare maximising point, where AB is the production possibility frontier and CIC_2 is the highest attainable indifference curve.

Fig. 11.2. The social marginal benefit and cost of state activity. When the level of government activity equals 0B, the social marginal benefit from public spending (AB) equals the social marginal cost of taxation (BC).

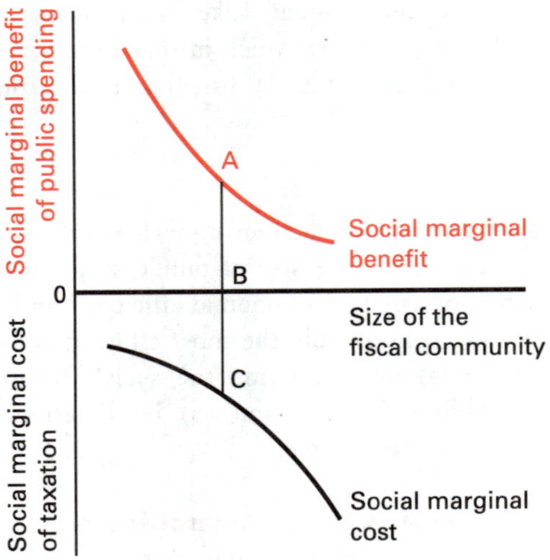

the government; assuming that it obeys the law of diminishing marginal utility, we can expect it to fall as government activity increases. The social marginal cost of taxation, however, which includes both the loss of command over purchasing power and such things as disincentives to work and save, is likely to increase as government activity (and therefore taxation) increases.

These relationships are illustrated in Fig. 11.2 where government expenditure and taxation are measured along the horizontal axis (labelled 'size of the fiscal community'). Notice that the quadrant in which the social marginal cost of taxation is plotted has been inverted for ease of comparison. Assuming that government expenditure and taxation are kept equal, the optimal scale of government activity is shown by 0B, where AB = BC. Points to the left of B would call for an expansion of government activity because such an expansion would increase total benefit to society by more than it would increase total cost. For the opposite reason, points to the right of B would call for a contraction of government activity. 0B, then, is called the optimum-size fiscal community.

The size of the public sector in practice

Measuring the size of the public sector

The public sector, regarded as a single organisation, is the largest employer of the work-force in developed countries and can thus have a considerable impact on the level of wages, productivity and investment in the economic system. For instance, the United Kingdom's public sector (defined to include the central and local government and public corporations) employed more than 25 per cent of the country's labour force in 1975. By 1990, the sector's share had fallen to 22.3 per cent of the labour force. This reflects the government's objective in the 1980s to shift resources from the public to the private sector and is partly the result of privatisation. However, the most frequently applied measures of the size of a country's public sector are total public expendituure and taxation expressed as ratios of gross national product. As will be seen below, these measurements pose a number of conceptual and statistical problems. Notwithstanding these problems, the most general point to make at this stage is that in both the industrially advanced nations and the less developed

Table 11.1 Total outlays of government[a] as a percentage of GDP: selected countries.

Country	1980	1990
United States	33.7	36.1
Japan	32.6	32.3
West Germany	48.3	46.0
France	46.1	49.9
United Kingdom	45.0	42.1
Italy	41.6	53.1
Canada	40.5	46.9
Denmark	56.2	58.4
Netherlands	57.5	55.6
Sweden	61.6	61.4
EC average	45.6	48.7

Source: Economic Outlook, OECD, December 1992.

[a] Government outlays consist of current disbursements plus gross capital formation.

Table 11.2 Current receipts of government[a] as a percentage of GDP: selected countries.

Country	1980	1990
United States	30.8	31.8
Japan	27.6	34.6
West Germany	44.7	43.4
France	44.5	46.5
United Kingdom	40.1	40.0
Italy	32.9	42.1
Canada	36.2	41.6
Denmark	52.2	56.1
Netherlands	52.8	49.5
Sweden	56.6	63.9
EC average	41.4	43.9

Source: Economic Outlook, OECD, December 1992.

[a] Government receipts consist of direct and indirect taxes and social security contributions.

countries, the share of the public sector has increased both relatively as a proportion of GNP and absolutely over time.

In the United Kingdom, as in other countries, attempts are often made at international comparisons of the relative size of the public sector. Tables 11.1 and 11.2 show the relative size of the United Kingdom's public sector compared with other industrialised countries.

One conclusion that can be drawn from Table 11.1 is that the United Kingdom, which was close to the EC average in 1980, was well below the EC average in 1990. Notice that Italy's government spending ratio increased significantly during the 1980s, reaching more than 53 per cent of GDP in 1990. However, Sweden maintained the largest public expenditure ratio of the countries listed during 1980–90. Within the EC, Denmark had the largest ratio in 1990, closely followed by the Netherlands.

According to the taxation ratios, shown in Table 11.2, the United Kingdom government raised 40 per cent of GDP in taxes in 1990, which is lower than the EC average of 43.9 per cent. In contrast, France, the Netherlands and Denmark had taxation ratios higher than the EC average in 1990. Not surprisingly, of the countries listed, Sweden had the largest taxation ratio and the United States and Japan had the lowest.

Tables 11.1 and 11.2 show that the 1980s have witnessed quite marked variations in the public expenditure and taxation ratios. Within the EC, notice the declining expenditure and taxation ratios of the United Kingdom and the former West Germany since 1980. The fall in these ratios reflects the view held by these two countries' governments that public expenditure, particularly if debt-financed, adversely affects private saving and capital formation, and weakens incentives.

Conceptual and statistical problems of measurement

We see in Ch. 18 that a major difficulty arises in estimating the GNP: only goods which are subject to the measuring rod of money are included. So, for example, leisure, pollution, noise and the domestic services of housewives are excluded. As far as international comparisons are concerned, the differing needs and tastes of different income groups within and between nations are not taken into account.

When we turn to public expenditure, the main difficulty is whether or not to include *transfer payments* – that is, payments for which no direct service is rendered (for example, pensions and social security payments). On the one hand, it can be argued that transfers do not result in the direct absorption of resources by the government. On the other hand, they do help to redistribute incomes and so are part of the government's distribution function. A more important difficulty arises from the fact that transfer payments are always excluded from GNP; if they were included in the measurement of public expenditure, the ratio of total public expenditure to GNP (or GDP) would tend to overstate the size of the public sector.

A number of problems also arise in using taxation as a measure of government activity. First, should social security contributions (called national insurance contributions in the United Kingdom) be included as taxes? If a tax is defined as a compulsory payment without direct benefit to the payer, then social security contributions are not taxes because they confer entitlements to direct benefit. Secondly, it can be argued that it is the taxable capacity of a taxpayer (that is, the taxpayer's ability to pay and not the actual tax payment) that most reflects the tax effort of the community. Such a tax effort may be judged by the extent to which a community is capable of earning, accumulating or spending its income and wealth. Finally, using the taxation ratio alone would tend to hide the extent to which a government borrows money to finance a budget deficit or the extent to which privatisation proceeds might be used to cover the shortfall in taxation revenues.

We can conclude from this section that public expenditure and taxation expressed as ratios of GNP or GDP are but crude measures of the impact of public sector decisions on the economy.

The growth of public expenditure in the United Kingdom

In the 1880s, the German economist Adolph Wagner advanced his *law of ever rising public expenditures,* basing his observations on a statistical study of major European countries, including Britain. He maintained that, with industrialisation giving rise to 'social progress', there would be greater public pressure for increased public expenditures over the next fifty to a hundred years. The long-term trend would be

Table 11.3 The growth of public expenditure in the United Kingdom, 1981 and 1991.

		1981	1991
1.	Total government expenditure in current prices (£m).	112,995	236,682
2.	Total government expenditure in constant 1985 prices (£m.)	142,850	167,740
3.	GNP at factor cost in current prices (£m.)	220,006	497,329
4.	Total government expenditure as a percentage of GNP in current prices.	51.4	47.6

Source: UK National Accounts, 1992.

one of an increase in public spending at a faster rate than the increase in GNP. Has this law been borne out by United Kingdom data?

Line 1 of Table 11.3 shows that, between 1981 and 1991, government expenditure in current prices more than doubled. However, this is not a very useful way of looking at the growth of public expenditure because the general level of prices increased during the same period. From line 2, it is clear that the rise in government expenditure in constant (1985) prices was much more moderate. Line 4 shows that, as a percentage of GNP, public expenditure fell between 1981 and 1991 from 51.4 per cent to 47.6 per cent. This downturn is attributable to the government's policy of reducing the share of public spending by means of setting annual cash targets for the spending of central and local government.

It is instructive to note that there has been an *upward long-term trend* in total government expenditure in most industrialised countries and in less developed countries. Peacock and Wiseman undertook a major statistical study of the growth of public expenditure in the United Kingdom for the period 1890–1955. The study showed that total public expenditure in current prices rose from 8.9 per cent of GNP in 1890 to 36.6 per cent of GNP in 1955. This indicates a considerable increase in the relative size of the United Kingdom's public sector since 1890. Additionally, Peacock and Wiseman observed a marked change in the composition of government expenditure. In particular, they pointed to the growing share of expenditure on education, health and transport and the growing importance of transfers, such as social security payments, subsidies and debt interest.

There is a major difficulty in trying to draw worthwhile conclusions from secular increases in total government expenditure. This difficulty stems from the problem of maintaining a consistent definition of public expenditure. Definitions tend to change over time. In the United Kingdom, for instance, the official definition of 'total public expenditure' included the entire capital expenditure of nationalised industries and other public corporations for many years. But part of the capital expenditure of nationalised industries was financed from internal surpluses and from domestic and overseas borrowing. This meant that the definition overstated the extent to which the government had to finance the activities of the public sector by taxation and through its own borrowing requirement. Consequently, a new definition of public expenditure was adopted in 1976 which included only loans and grants by the public sector to the nationalised industries and other public corporations, rather than the total capital expenditure of these bodies.

Whatever definition of public expenditure is adopted, the essential point is that public expenditure represents the cost to society of satisfying collective wants, such as those for defence, education and health. There is a belief in some quarters that public budgets have an inherent bias towards waste through overspending. It is argued that this bias arises because publicly provided goods are not subjected to the rigours of market discipline which force decision-makers to equate the marginal resource cost with the marginal benefit of these goods to members of the community. Public expenditure decisions are concerned with 'non-marketed' goods and services – that is, those paid for indirectly, outside the market place, with taxes. The 1980s witnessed positive government measures, with varying degrees of success in OECD countries including the United Kingdom, to reduce public expenditure both absolutely and as a proportion of GNP. There is now a strong belief among the governments of many industrialised nations that a public expenditure growth rate which exceeds the GNP growth rate poses a potential threat to the success of supply-side economic policies.

The composition of public expenditure

Table 11.4 shows the composition of public expenditure in the United Kingdom in 1981 and 1991. Consider the various categories of expenditure in turn.

Total final expenditure on goods and services (line 1) is by far the biggest item and rose from 47.9 per cent of the total in 1981 to 51.5 per cent in 1991. This category includes spending on the wages and salaries of the armed forces, the police, teachers and civil servants as well as the supply of provisions to the armed forces, schools and hospitals.

Total capital expenditure (line 2) rose from 6.1 per cent of the total in 1981 to 8.1 per cent in 1991. This category is in fact subject to quite large fluctuations over time largely because changes in *capital expenditure* are politically less unpopular. Examples of capital expenditure include spending on roads, bridges, hospitals and school buildings.

Capital expenditure
Spending on the creation of assets that yield a flow of services over a period of time

Note that these first two categories of public expenditure (lines 1 and 2) are the *resource-using expenditures* of the public sector. Resources used to produce goods like roads, education and defence are no longer available for the production of goods and services by the private sector. It might be argued, however, that some of the real resource-using public expenditures provide goods which are complementary to those provided by the private sector. For example, government expenditure on roads, traffic lights and street lighting complement private sector goods, such as cars and bicycles. Similarly, education, defined as investment in 'human capital', can be

Table 11.4 The composition of government expenditure in the United Kingdom, 1981 and 1991.

	1981 £m.	1981 % of total	1991 £m.	1991 % of total
1. Total final expenditure on goods and services	54,100	47.9	121,798	51.5
2. Total capital expenditure	6,948	6.1	19,093	8.1
3. Subsidies	6,369	5.6	5,878	2.5
4. Grants to personal sector	31,242	27.7	71,767	30.3
5. Grants abroad	1,607	1.4	1,049	0.4
6. Debt interest	12,719	11.3	17,097	7.2
Total government expenditure	112,995	100.0	236,682	100.0

Source: UK National Accounts, 1992.

regarded as being complementary to investment in plant and machinery by the private sector.

Subsidies (line 3) represent unrequited payments by both central and local government to the nationalised industries, other public corporations and private firms.

Grants to personal sector (line 4) include pensions, unemployment benefits, student grants and other social security payments. This is a growing category of public expenditure in the United Kingdom and rose from 27.7 per cent of the total in 1981 to 30.3 per cent in 1991. Indeed, this category is one of the most important indicators of the extent to which the government is attempting to carry out its redistribution function.

Grants abroad (line 5) include mainly development aid to the less developed countries.

Debt interest (line 6) represents payment of interest on the national debt, including interest on the amount of money borrowed annually to cover any budget deficit. The increase in debt interest during the period 1981–91 was largely due to budget deficits having to be financed by borrowing.

It should be noted that the public expenditure categories from lines 3 to 6 differ from those in lines 1 and 2. The items in lines 3 to 6 do not involve the absorption of real resources by the public sector itself. Spending on these items fell from 46 per cent of the total in 1981 to 40.4 per cent in 1991.

The composition of the public sector's revenue

It can be seen from Table 11.5 that taxes on incomes make the largest contribution to the government's total revenues in the United Kingdom. Taxes on expenditure and social security contributions are the second and third largest contributors respectively. Notice the rise in social security contributions during the period 1981–91 and the relatively small importance of rates and the community charge as a means of raising revenue. The shortfall in revenues (lines 1–7 in Table 11.5) required to finance total public expenditure (lines 1–6 in Table 11.4) is made up through borrowing and proceeds from other sources, such as privatisation and the sale of council houses. In 1991, government borrowing amounted to £16.3 billion and this is

Table 11.5 The composition of total government revenue in the United Kingdom, 1981 and 1991.

	1981		1991	
	£m.	% of total	£m.	% of total
1. Taxes on income	36,134	32.0	75,105	31.7
2. Taxes on capital	278	0.2	3,687	1.6
3. Taxes on expenditure	32,271	28.6	76,861	32.5
4. Rates/community charge	10,194	9.0	6,162	2.6
5. Social security contributions	15,916	14.1	36,643	15.5
6. Total taxes	94,793	83.9	198,458	83.9
7. Government property income	9,584	8.5	10,766	4.5
8. Financial receipts	8,618	7.6	27,458	11.6
Total government revenue	112,995	100.0	236,682	100.0

Source: UK National Accounts, 1992.

included in the 'financial receipts' shown in line 8 of Table 11.5. The borrowing forecast of £50 billion for the 1993–4 financial year will account for about 8 per cent of GDP, the largest percentage recorded in the postwar years.

Government budget deficit *The difference between government spending and revenue, in a situation where spending exceeds revenue*

Government budget balance The amount of money which the public sector has to borrow during a given financial year is called the government's budget deficit and is known as the *public sector borrowing requirement* (PSBR) in the United Kingdom. The size of the PSBR is determined by the following factors:

(a) the size of the deficit of the central and local governments;
(b) the size of the deficit of the nationalised industries and other public corporations;
(c) the amount of net lending to the private sector and overseas;
(d) the public sector's receipts from the sale of financial assets and other financial transactions.
(e) the public sector's receipts from the sale of real assets (for example, privatisation and council house sales).

In recent years, a distinction has been made between the 'cyclically-adjusted government budget balance' and the 'structural budget balance'. Consider these in turn.

(a) *Cyclically-adjusted budget balance.* Even if public expenditure programmes, tax rates and social security benefits are held constant, the government budget balance will alter as the level of economic activity goes up or down. For example, the *budget deficit* will increase in a recession as tax revenues fall and social security expenditure increases as a result of lower incomes and higher unemployment. The cyclically-adjusted budget balance attempts to remove the effects of the economic cycle from the figures for the budget balance. The resulting figures are then estimates of what the budget balance would be at given tax rates and levels of social security if the economy maintained its trend rate of growth. Movements in the cyclically-adjusted budget balance can be used as an indicator of the government's discretionary changes in fiscal policy.

(b) *Structural budget balance.* This is determined by government policy decisions about planned levels of taxation and expenditure in the medium term of, say, five or six years. Such policy decisions are influenced by economic, political and demographic factors, such as a rising, ageing population leading to rising public expenditure on pensions and health. Some economists have expressed concern that an increasing structural budget deficit, combined with a cyclical budget deficit during a recession, might lead to a large increase in total government indebtedness. In such a case, government borrowing might get out of hand and lead to high interest rates in financial markets and possibly rapid monetary growth and inflation in the country concerned.

Causes of the long-term growth of public expenditure

Studies of public expenditure in both developed and less developed countries suggest that there has been a long-term upward trend in government spending during this century. Several demand and supply factors have been proposed as explanations for this growth.

Demand factors

(a) *Growth in per capita incomes.* As an economy grows, there is normally a rise in income per head of the population. This results in a growth of consumer demand for services provided by the public sector, such as education and health. The argument is that the demands for these services are income elastic so that government spending on them tends to grow faster than the growth of GNP over time.

(b) *Population growth.* A growing population makes an ever-expanding demand on basic government services. So population growth represents a simple explanation for the growth in public expenditure. In particular, the growth of new towns makes demands on the public provision of transport and communications, water and sewerage services, and other civic amenities. Similarly, an increase in the proportion of people in the older age groups generally means increased spending on health and pensions.

(c) *Public expectations of non-marketed goods.* In a representative democracy, politicians who wish to maximise their stay in office may build up voters' expectations about increased spending on a variety of programmes. Whilst voters may be able to make consistent choices on a single issue (such as more or less defence expenditure), they are unable to make consistent choices when faced with a multiplicity of issues (such as the level of spending on defence, health, education and the environment). To fulfil voters' expectations, therefore, political decisions about the size and composition of public budgets have to reconcile competing expenditure and interest groups. This process exerts upward pressure on public spending. Moreover, it is argued that the public tends to pay greater attention to the benefits of increased public expenditure than to the burden of additional taxation.

Supply factors

(a) *Relative price effect.* It is now increasingly recognised that public expenditure rises partly because *input prices* in the public sector tend to rise faster than input prices in the private sector. For example, the above-average rises in the prices of drugs and medical equipment in recent years have contributed to the rapidly rising costs of the National Health Service in the United Kingdom.

(b) *High unit labour costs.* Compared with the private sector, there is only limited scope for the application of new technology in the public sector. This is because most public sector output (with the exception of defence, crime prevention and fire-fighting) is overwhelmingly labour-intensive. Rising labour costs, therefore, mean a rise in the cost of supplying the same level of public service.

The role of the public sector in less developed countries

The market mechanism in less developed countries operates in far less perfect conditions than that in industrially developed countries. In particular, the price incentives which might otherwise be engendered by demand and supply conditions in the markets for goods and services are usually hampered by such factors as the lack of developed means of communications, lack of specialisation and exchange, customs and traditions and general inertia on the part of producers and consumers. This places the public sector in a position to initiate and influence the pattern of economic development through its expenditure and taxation policies. For example, government budgets can help to break the 'vicious circle' of poverty by stimulating investment and developing the infrastructure. Thus, investment in health, education, transport and the development of natural resources very often falls into the 'social overhead' investment category which becomes the spearhead of budgetary policy.

As regards the financing of economic development, the budgets are frequently deficit-financed by borrowing or printing money because the revenue side of the budget has only meagre taxation income. Furthermore, unlike developed countries where progressive income taxes are a principal instrument for redistributing incomes, less developed countries depend mainly on selected indirect taxes, such as import and export duties and sales taxes, with the result that the development objective takes precedence over the distribution and other objectives. Note that a broadly based indirect tax is difficult to apply in less developed countries because of the problem of identifying the origins and destinations of many goods since many firms keep incomplete records of their accounts. In addition, the subsistence level of income and the absence of an efficient administrative machinery to discover incomes above the subsistence level mean that it is extremely difficult to put into practice an equitable system of progressive income taxation.

Summary

1. In mixed economies, a public sector is needed to carry out important allocative and distributive functions, including the promotion of competition; the provision of goods and services not adequately provided by the private sector; dealing with externalities; enforcing contracts; the redistribution of income and wealth; and the promotion of macroeconomic objectives. The attempt to achieve the public sector's objectives may give rise to policy conflicts.

2. Given that the overall aim of government is the maximisation of social welfare, efficiency and equity criteria are needed to judge the success of government policies. As part of its decision-making process, a government must determine the optimum-size fiscal community – that is, the size of the public sector that maximises social welfare.

3. There are practical difficulties in measuring the size of the public sector. International comparisons of the size of a country's public sector can be undertaken using public expenditure and taxation ratios.

4. Over the long-run, the relative share of the public sector has tended to increase in most mixed economies. This may have been caused by such factors as the high income elasticity of demand for services, such as health and education, and by demographic trends, such as the growing proportion of elderly people in the population.

Exercises

1. Review your understanding of the following terms:

public sector	government revenue
allocation function	optimum-size fiscal community
distribution function	Wagner's 'law'
state production	non-marketed goods
state provision	public sector borrowing requirement
government expenditure	cyclically-adjusted budget balance
structural budget balance	

2. Consider the following data on the United Kingdom's public sector borrowing requirement (PSBR):

1988	−£5.8 billion
1989	−£4.7 billion
1990	£2.2 billion
1991	£16.3 billion

Source: Financial Statistics, 1993.

(a) Explain what is meant by the PSBR.
(b) When negative (as in 1988 and 1989), the figure is sometimes called *public sector debt repayment* (PSDR). Make up a definition of the PSDR.
(c) Suggest reasons for the size of the PSBR/PSDR in these years.
(d) In what ways might changes in the PSBR/PSDR affect the level of planned government expenditure?

3. Discuss the meaning of the 'optimum size' of a country's public sector. What conditions should be satisfied before a public sector can be described as being of 'optimum size'?
4. Discuss the main difficulties which arise in attempting to measure the size of a country's public sector and in comparing it with that of other countries.
5. Which, in your view, is the most plausible explanation of the long-run growth of public expenditure in the United Kingdom?
6. What theoretical and practical arguments are there in favour of reducing the size of a country's public sector?

12 PUBLIC GOODS AND EXTERNALITIES

Learning objectives

After reading this chapter, you should be able to:

- define a pure public good, a private good, a merit good and a mixed good and illustrate them with practical examples
- define an externality and distinguish between positive and negative externalities
- identify the characteristics of public and private goods and show, with the aid of examples, the linkages between them
- differentiate, on the basis of their characteristics, between the demand patterns of public and private goods
- identify the causes of externalities and the methods of dealing with externalities

Introduction

The aim of this chapter is to explore the basis of public expenditure policies concerned with public goods and externalities. Economists have striven to explain public expenditure decisions in terms of the concepts of public goods and externalities because these form the basis of many government decisions about the size and composition of public expenditures. We propose in this chapter, after establishing certain definitions, to focus attention on the following areas: (a) the nature of public goods; (b) the links and differences between public goods and private goods; (c) the nature and causes of externalities and some suggested solutions.

Public goods, private goods, mixed goods and externalities

Public good *A good the consumption of which by one individual does not prevent its consumption by other individuals*

A pure public good is a good or service, such as defence, the consumption of which by one person does not reduce its availability to others in society. If we let Y denote the total quantity supplied of a pure public good, Y_A the quantity consumed by individual A and Y_B the quantity consumed by individual B, then we can write: $Y = Y_A = Y_B$. The equality signs show that there is no extra cost in supplying a given quantity of a public good to additional people – although, of course, the production of additional units of such a good would involve extra cost.

A private good is a good or service whose consumption by one individual results in the reduction of its supply to others. The more bread is consumed by one individual,

Private good *A good whose consumption by one individual reduces the supply available to others*

the less is left for others to consume; the more petrol this generation uses, the less it leaves for future generations. If we let Z denote the total supply of a pure private good, we can write: $Z = Z_A + Z_B$, where Z_A is the amount consumed by individual A and Z_B is the amount consumed by individual B.

Mixed good *A good with both private and public good content*

A mixed good is a good or service which has both private and public good content, such as a television which can be watched at home on one's own (a private good) but which it is also possible to watch with a group of friends (as a quasi-public good). In real life, there are few *pure* public or private goods. A public good may have some private good content: for example, a motorist crossing a bridge in peak-hour traffic affects the supply of bridge-crossings to other motorists by contributing to congestion and delays; in this case, the marginal cost of supply is zero for low levels of use, but exceeds zero for higher levels. Similarly, a private good may have some 'publicness': for example, watching a television at home (basically, a private good) has some public good content as neighbours and friends may also be invited to watch. Such observations of real life situations show that there are a whole range of mixed goods, whereas pure public and pure private goods are but extremes of these situations. Producers depend upon other producers and upon consumers in their attempts to maximise their profits and thus their behaviour can hardly be described as completely private. Consumers depend upon other consumers and producers in the attempt to maximise their utilities and so their behaviour is not completely private either.

It is because of the interdependence of the behaviour of consumers and producers that considerable interest has been stimulated in the analysis of externalities.

Externalities *Those gains and losses which are sustained by others as a result of actions initiated by producers or consumers or both and for which no compensation is paid*

Externalities are those gains and losses sustained by others as a result of actions initiated by producers or consumers or both, and for which no compensation is paid. Externalities are sometimes called 'third party effects', 'neighbourhood effects' or 'spillovers'. Alfred Marshall, the Victorian economist, used the phrases 'external economies' and 'external diseconomies'. As an example of an externality, consider a chemical firm which discharges noxious wastes into a river estuary, killing all the fish and resulting in the loss of livelihood of a fisherman: no compensation is paid for this loss. Similarly, the discharge of unclean water from an industrial city into a river may result in the loss of recreational activities like swimming, boating and angling. Yet no compensation is claimed for the loss of these pleasures, nor are these external costs included in the cost calculations of the polluting firms and other agents.

As we shall see, the most important externalities are those which affect the environment within which human beings seek to satisfy their economic and biological needs. The most important point to emphasise at this stage, though, is that externalities can arise from *both* production and consumption. A *consumption externality* may be explained in the context of a two-person, two-good economy using the following functional notation:

$$U_A = f(a_1, a_2, \ldots, a_n; b)$$

where U_A denotes the total utility of individual A; a_1 to a_n denote the activities from 1 to n which are directly under the control of individual A; and b denotes the activity of individual B. The equation asserts that A's utility is not only dependent on A's own activities, but also on the activity of individual B. For example, an individual's enjoyment of peace and quiet depends not only on what the individual does, but also on the neighbours' activities.

It must be noted that interdependence alone is not sufficient to constitute an externality. It must also be shown that there has been a failure to pay for or to receive payment on account of any gains or losses. Thus, a consumption externality exists where there is interdependence coupled with an absence of any form of compensation or price paid by the gainers.

A *production externality* can similarly be defined using the following functional notation:

$$P_C = f(c_1, c_2, \ldots, c_n; d)$$

This states that firm C's profit (P_C) depends on the n activities of firm C (that is, c_1 to c_n) and on the activity d of a second firm. Thus, a production externality exists where there is some interdependence among the activities of firms coupled with an absence of any form of price or compensation paid on account of the loss or gain.

The nature of public goods

Pure public goods have two main identifiable characteristics:

(a) *Non-rivalness in consumption.* If a public good is supplied to one individual, it is at the same time made available to others at zero cost. This is true of defence, lighthouses and police protection. Such goods are indivisible in the sense that the benefits that each user derives from them cannot be measured, nor can the actual number of users of such goods be identified.

(b) *Non-exclusion.* Once a public good is supplied to individual A, individual B cannot be excluded from consuming it, whether B wants to or not. This implies that public goods are impossible to reject: a pacifist, for example, cannot fail to be affected by defence provided to other members of society. Note that this characteristic of non-exclusion can also be applied to externalities where, as we noted above, other members of a group cannot be excluded from suffering a loss or deriving some benefit as a result of the action of a producer or consumer.

Only *pure* public goods will exhibit both of the above characteristics. The degree of 'publicness' of other public goods can be restricted by either spatial or capacity limitations. Consider these in turn.

(a) *Spatial limitations.* The degree of 'publicness' may depend on the geographical area which a given public good is able to benefit. For example, fire protection is likely to be non-rival in a compact geographical area, but once the area is enlarged the 'publicness' element disappears. Similarly, the Blackpool illuminations are non-rival only when one is on or near the promenade and certainly not when one is in London.

(b) *Capacity limitations.* The number of people able to enjoy a public good is dictated by the limits of its capacity. For example, a road bridge has a given traffic-carrying capacity beyond which it would become congested and lose its non-rival characteristic.

Table 12.1 Linkages between private and public goods.

	Excludable	Non-excludable
Rival	Case 1	Case 2
Non-rival	Case 3	Case 4

Links between public and private goods

Mixed goods exhibit some of the characteristics of both private and public goods. The possible linkages between private and public goods are summarised in Table 12.1, where the following four cases are identified.

Case 1 (rival and excludable) is a clear-cut example of a pure private good, such as a loaf of bread whose consumption by individual A necessarily reduces its supply to individual B. When A pays the price for the loaf, this entitles A to exclude B from consuming it.

Case 2 (rival and non-excludable) illustrates the case of a private good with some public good content. As an example, consider a bee-keeper and a flower grower: the bee-keeper is unable to select which flowers the bees will pollinate and the flower grower is unable to choose which bees should get the nectar for honey (non-exclusion in both cases). Once a given swarm of bees is engaged in pollinating the nursery of one flower grower, however, they cannot at the same time be expected to benefit another nursery (rival consumption).

Case 3 (non-rival and excludable) illustrates a situation of the private provision of goods which have a public good content and the public provision of goods with a private good content. As an example, consider a football stadium with a capacity crowd of 60,000 spectators. Up to this capacity, watching a match is non-rival. It is made excludable by fencing the ground so that entry can only be gained by payment or by ticket. The same argument applies to theatres and cinemas. As an example of a good provided by the government but which has a private good content, consider the National Health Service: this is non-rival up to its capacity, but excludable in the sense that the beneficiaries of medical care can be identified – this means that the government is able to choose to some extent who shall benefit from the service.

Case 4 (non-rival and non-excludable) typifies a pure public good, like defence and lighthouses, as discussed above.

Merit goods

Merit good *A good which, it is generally believed, should be made widely available because of the social benefits that result from its provision*

A merit good is a good or service which, it is generally believed, should be made widely available because of the social benefits that it provides. One example of a merit good is fire protection. Virtually all communities would consider the provision of a fire brigade as desirable because of the large contribution it makes to social welfare. Thus, in most countries, fire protection is provided by the state as a merit good. Also, a government may take the view that a minimum level of consumption of a particular good or service is desirable regardless of consumers' incomes. The sight of people sleeping on the streets, for example, offends the social conscience of individuals in most countries. Thus, housing may be provided by a government at a low subsidised price as a merit good.

By the same token, some goods and services may be viewed as being socially harmful: these are known as *demerit goods*. Examples include tobacco and other addictive drugs. A government may take measures to discourage consumption of demerit goods by levying taxes or introducing legislation banning their consumption.

Mixed goods and the economic theory of clubs

As mentioned above, not many goods are *pure* private goods or *pure* public goods. It is possible to consider the characteristics of 'mixed' goods as resembling those of clubs, such as sports clubs. Like road-bridges and hospitals, clubs have limitations in terms of both capacity and geographical setting. People voluntarily join clubs which provide indivisible facilities and agree to share the costs. Sharing costs illustrates both a willingness to pay and the principle of the exclusion of non-members from the enjoyment of the facilities. Thus, a club is seen as a mechanism for revealing preferences as regards indivisible mixed goods. In the absence of a club, an entrepreneur or local authority considering the provision of such a facility might encounter problems in discovering the potential demand.

A club is a voluntary group of people with similar tastes. Its purpose is to exploit the economies of scale associated with a particular facility. The cost of provision is therefore similar to the cost of providing a bridge or hospital in that none of these items can usually be afforded by a single person or small group in the area. To achieve efficiency, the management of a club, like the management of a hospital, has to determine *either* the optimum size of the facility *or* the optimum size of the club's membership. In either case, the total cost and the share of the cost to each member will be determined simultaneously.

Differences in the demand for private and public goods

Demand for a private good Since consumers of private goods buy different quantities but normally pay the same price, the market demand curve for such a good is obtained by summing the individual demand curves *horizontally*.

Figure 12.1 shows the derivation of a market demand curve for good X in a simple two-person economy, with the two individuals A and B. The curve D_AD_A represents A's demand curve for X and the curve D_BD_B represents B's demand for the same good. At price $0P$, A's demand for X is equal to $0q_A$ and B's demand is equal to $0q_B$: the total market demand at price $0P$ must be $0q_A + 0q_B = 0q_M$. The market demand curve, D_MD_M, is found by adding A's and B's demands together at every price – in other words, by horizontal summation.

Notice also that the marginal benefits derived by the two people are the same, indicated on the graph by α and β, and that these in turn are equal to the market marginal valuation δ. These marginal benefits are all equal to the prevailing price $0P$.

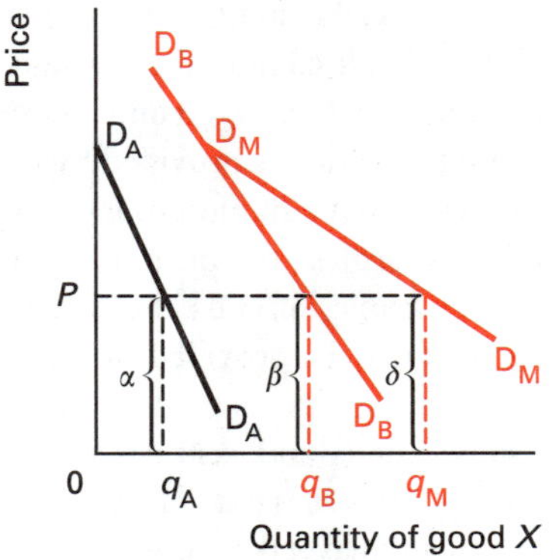

Fig. 12.1. *Horizontal summation of individual demand curves.* The market demand curve, D_MD_M is obtained by the horizontal summation of the individual demand curves D_AD_A and D_BD_B.

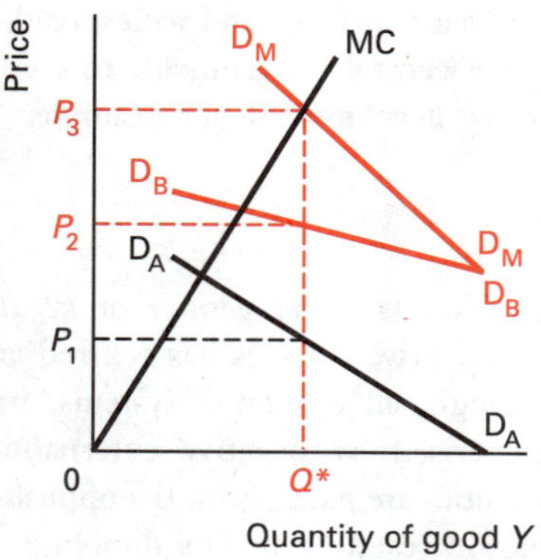

Fig. 12.2. Vertical summation of individual demand curves. The market demand D_MD_M, for a public good is obtained by the vertical summation of the individual demand curves, D_AD_A and D_BD_B. Individuals may place different valuations on the same quantity of a public good. In this case, A and B are willing to pay the prices $0P_1$ and $0P_2$ respectively for the quantity $0Q^*$.

Demand for a public good Since each additional unit of a public good benefits everyone, we must add all the individuals' valuations placed on extra units of such a good in order to obtain its market demand curve. To find society's *willingness to pay*, the prices individuals would be willing to pay if they revealed their true preferences must be added. Graphically, this means that individual demand curves must be summed *vertically*, as shown in Fig. 12.2. The graph again portrays an economy with two persons, A and B. The curves D_AD_A and D_BD_B represent the two individuals' demand curves for the public good Y. The market demand curve is represented by D_MD_M. Consider the quantity $0Q^*$: Individual A is willing to pay the price $0P_1$ for this quantity and B is willing to pay the price $0P_2$. The marginal benefits derived from the good by the two individuals differ. Thus, the price which society as a whole is prepared to pay for the quantity $0Q^*$ is $0P_3 = 0P_1 + 0P_2$. If MC represents the social and private marginal cost of producing the public good, then the interaction of MC and D_MD_M determines the *socially optimal output* of the public good ($0Q^*$ in the diagram).

The number of people participating in the enjoyment of non-excludable and non-rival consumption goods is generally very large. As a result, each individual has little incentive to reveal his or her true preference for public goods. Members of large groups are aware that it is impossible to exclude them from enjoying the benefits of public goods and so they may try to be *free riders* and avoid payment. The potential existence of free riders makes the estimation of the market demand for public goods exceedingly difficult. Furthermore, unlike most private goods whose quantities demanded are measurable, there exists no identifiable unit of measurement for many public goods. For example, defence is not a single concept, but is made up of disparate elements of personnel, equipment and strategy. The same is true of the police, education and health.

One important policy conclusion emerging from our discussion of the demand patterns of the two types of goods is worth noting. Given the goal of social welfare maximisation, it must be determined whether the most efficient unit of supply of public goods is the central government, a local authority, a public corporation or even a private sector firm. For example, street lighting and public parks are probably most efficiently supplied by local authorities: they are in a better position to estimate the demand for these amenities and can more easily compare the relevant costs and benefits. Where the benefits are diffused and widespread, however, the most efficient unit of supply may be the central government: this is so in the cases of external security and nuclear energy development, for example.

Externalities – public goods and public bads

The nature of externalities

Externalities can be classified as either *positive* or *negative*. Most of the foregoing discussion about public and private goods has centred around positive externalities. In addition to these, though, all economic systems, irrespective of their state of development, are characterised by negative externalities of differing degrees of severity. Negative externalities are *public bads*, the opposite of public goods. Examples include international tension resulting from a doubling of defence spending by one country; smoke and noise from vehicles, aeroplanes and factories creating air pollution and discomfort; nuclear tests polluting the environment and exposing human life to radioactive fallout.

A close examination of any economic activity is likely to reveal both positive and negative externalities and a web of initiating agents and affected parties, as illustrated in Fig. 12.3. The arrows in the diagram indicate the direction of the effects the initiating agents produce on firms or consumers. As an example, consider an asbestos factory. It may provide jobs to local residents, thereby raising their living standards (a positive production externality benefiting consumers). At the same time, the emission of asbestos dust may endanger the health of the employees and local residents (a negative production externality harming consumers). Yet again, the factory may provide work to local building and catering firms (a positive production externality benefiting other producers). By the same token, the factory may discharge its wastes into a river, thereby affecting the profit levels of firms downstream dependent on the supply of clean water from the river (a negative production externality harming producers).

We note from this that externalities, positive or negative, can run from production to production and from production to consumption. In addition, they can run from consumption to production and from consumption to consumption.

An important problem is how to determine whether a given externality-generating activity is one of net external costs (that is, a negative externality) or net external benefits (that is, a positive externality). Broadly speaking, if the externality leads to a net increase in the total of consumer and producer surplus, it can be said to be a

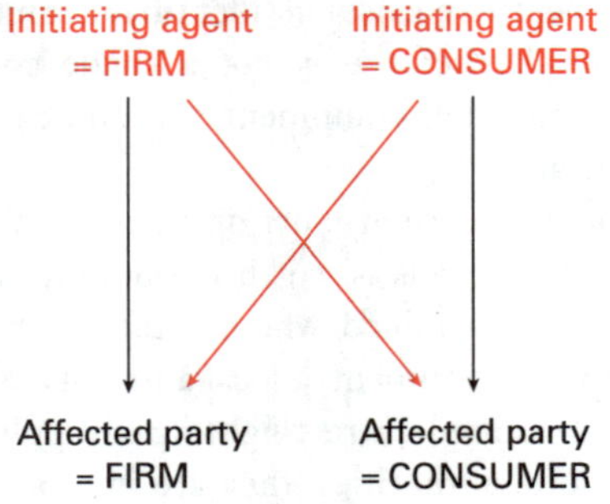

Fig. 12.3. *Externalities.* Firms and consumers may generate and be affected by externalities.

positive externality and, in that case, state action might be called for to encourage it. Conversely, if the externality leads to a net reduction in the total of consumer and producer surplus, government action may be called for to curtail it or even to ban it completely.

The divergence between private and social costs

Private cost Costs incurred by the producer of a commodity

Social cost Costs incurred by the whole society as a result of the production of a commodity. Social costs are equal to the sum of private costs and external costs

Where there is a negative externality, we can say that there exists a divergence between private and social costs. To illustrate this graphically, consider a firm which is polluting a river with noxious chemical wastes. This pollution creates an *external* marginal cost which is imposed on society, but which is not included in the firm's own *private* marginal cost. This is shown in Fig. 12.4. The *social* marginal cost curve (SMC) represents the extra cost to society of producing an additional unit of the good; it lies above the private marginal cost curve (PMC) because private producers fail to take account of the external marginal cost (EMC). Notice that the infinitely elastic demand curve facing the firm, DD, implies that the market is assumed for convenience to be perfectly competitive. It can be seen that Oq_1 is the Pareto optimal level of output where SMC intersects DD at point h. A profit-maximising firm, however, will produce the larger quantity Oq_2 at which point social marginal cost (equal to q_2j) exceeds private marginal cost (equal to q_2g). Thus, the good in question may be said to be *oversupplied*.

Causes of externalities

Consider the following four possible reasons for the existence of externalities.

Interaction between the economic system and the environment A most important reason for the existence of externalities is that every economic activity begins and ends with the environment. All initiating agents draw resources, such as air, water and raw materials, from the environment. They then transform these resources partly directly into consumption, and partly into the production of intermediate and finished goods. The resources are then returned to the environment as wastes – for example, in the form of polluted air, unclean water, empty tins and bottles. This constant interaction between the economic system and the environment is illustrated in Fig. 12.5. The direction of the arrows indicates flows to initiating agents in the top half of the diagram. The bottom half of the diagram shows the waste disposal flows from initiating agents into the environment which then recycles these

Fig 12.4. The divergence between private and social costs. External marginal cost (EMC) represents the difference between social marginal cost (SMC) and private marginal cost (PMC).

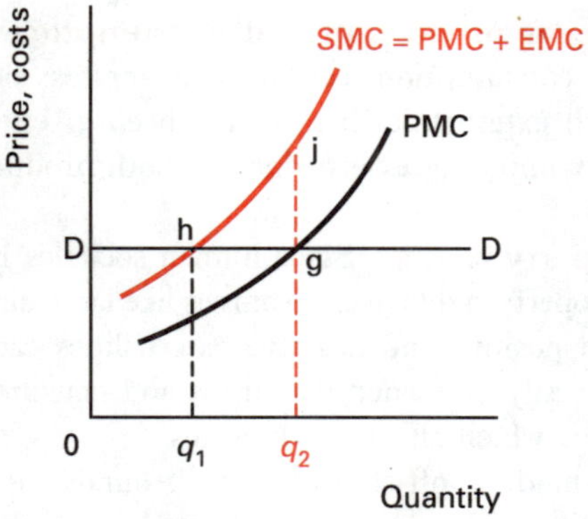

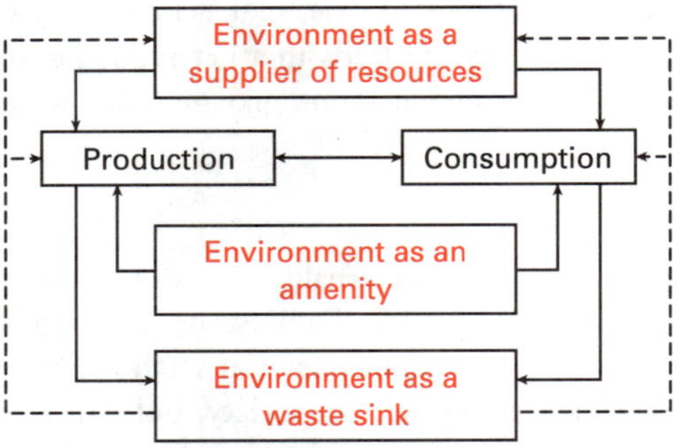

Fig. 12.5. The economic system and the environment.

flows back to producers and consumers. The recycling process is shown by the dotted arrows from the environment as a waste sink.

The left-hand arrow running from the box entitled 'environment as an amenity' to the production box represents the use of environmental amenities, like scenic beauty, in the course of production activities, like tourism. The arrow running from this box to the consumption box represents the use of environmental amenities, such as beaches and the countryside, which yield satisfaction to consumers.

Externalities arise because the environment has only a limited *assimilative capacity* as a waste disposal sink. Given the existing state of technological knowledge, the environment has a zero assimilative capacity for certain types of wastes – for example, cumulative pollutants such as cadmium and mercury. For wastes like polluted water, the assimilation process takes time, the length of time depending on the biochemical and organic composition of the waste substances.

Lack of developed markets Most societies have developed markets for intermediate and finished goods and services. They also have labour markets for human resources. Markets for some environmental resources, however, are non-existent – for example, there can be no market for fresh air. In other instances, markets do not take account of the full social cost to future generations: this may be the case in markets for *non-renewable resources* like oil, coal and copper. Glaring deficiencies exist in the markets for waste disposal; indeed, producers and consumers often regard the environment as a free good for waste disposal.

Interdependence of production and consumption The interdependence of production and consumption activities generates potential externalities. An illustration of such externalities has already been given above in the discussion of an asbestos factory imposing externalities on both producers and consumers.

Property rights *The legal title that confers ownership of an asset. Such property rights enable the owner to practise exclusion over the asset*

Incomplete property rights Since human societies have less developed private and communal property rights over resources like land, air, space and water than over other goods, both positive and negative externalities can arise. It is because these resources cannot easily be owned that firms and consumers are not excluded from using them in ways which affect third parties.

An example would be off-shore fishing grounds in the oceans over which no country has jurisdiction. No property rights exist over these waters, so fishing fleets from different countries cannot be excluded. In this situation, the fishing fleets may display insufficient regard for the long-term consequences of their actions. Overfishing may occur with the result that fish stocks are seriously depleted. This may, in turn, threaten the livelihood of all those who depend on these fishing grounds for their livelihood.

Methods of dealing with externalities

A number of methods have been suggested for dealing with externalities. Consider the following.

Pigou's tax – subsidy solution Pigou suggested that a *tax* be imposed on generators of negative externalities and a *subsidy* be given to generators of positive externalities.

First, consider the tax solution to a negative externality such as river pollution caused by a perfectly competitive chemical industry, as shown in Fig. 12.6. DD is the market demand curve and SS is the supply curve for the industry's product, reflecting only the industry's private marginal costs (ΣPMC). The price 0*P* and quantity 0*Q* are determined by market forces. Suppose, however, that the industry's production imposes an external marginal cost on society in the form of river pollution, shown by the EMC curve in the graph. Thus, at output 0*Q*, the external marginal cost is equal to *Q*A. The level of output 0*Q* is not socially optimal, however. The market demand curve, DD, represents the social marginal benefit derived from consuming the chemicals. The social marginal cost of chemical production (SMC) is given by the sum of EMC and the supply curve, SS. The supply curve in turn is given by the sum of the producers' private marginal costs (ΣPMC). The social marginal benefit of the output of chemicals in the range $0Q_1$ to 0*Q* units is less than the social marginal cost. Thus, the free market level of output results in a deadweight welfare loss, represented by the area of triangle FGH. To allow for this, the government can impose an excise tax equal to EMC at each level of output, which shifts the supply curve upwards from SS to S+T. This induces the industry to reduce its level of activity to the optimal level $0Q_1$, where price equals social marginal cost (SMC). Notice that this method of pollution control is generally one of reducing the level of pollution rather than eliminating it completely. This is shown in Fig. 12.6 where the post-tax EMC, equal to Q_1B, is less than the pre-tax EMC, *Q*A.

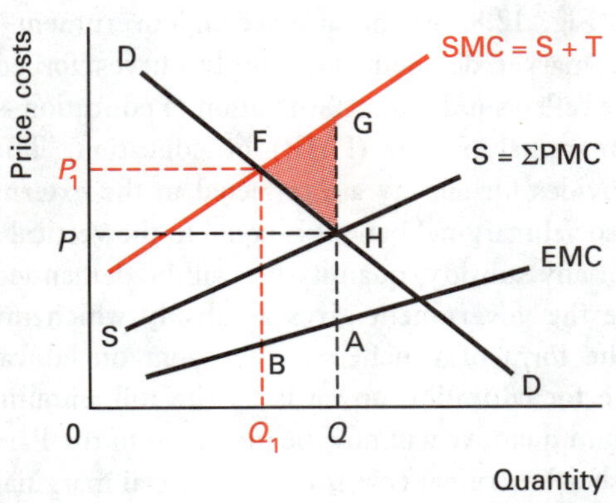

Fig. 12.6. *Tax solution to a negative externality.* In a perfectly competitive industry, the imposition of a tax equal to EMC shifts the supply curve, SS, upwards to coincide with SMC. This results in the Pareto optimal levels of output.

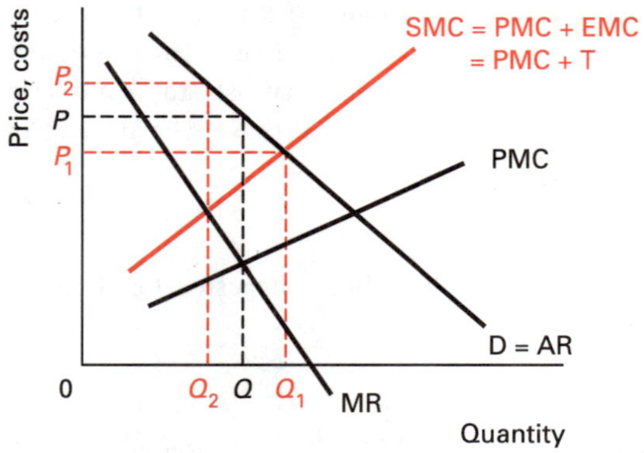

Fig. 12.7. ***Limitations of the tax solution in an imperfect market.*** In an imperfect market, the imposition of a tax equal to EMC results in a move away from the Pareto optimal level of output, $0Q_1$.

The tax remedy, however, is not entirely satisfactory when we come to consider the scale of activity of a firm under conditions of *imperfect competition*. To show this, consider Fig. 12.7 which illustrates a monopolistic firm maximising profit (where MR equals PMC) by producing output $0Q$ at price $0P$ before any tax is imposed. The Pareto optimal price and output, though, are found where price equals social marginal cost – that is, price $0P_1$ (lower than $0P$) and output $0Q_1$ (greater than $0Q$). The imposition of an excise tax which shifts the firm's PMC curve upwards to PMC + T, causes the firm to produce a reduced quantity $0Q_2$ and charge a higher price $0P_2$. In this case, therefore, the tax causes the firm to move in the opposite direction to that required to achieve a Pareto optimum. The reason for this is that the negative externality causes overproduction which tends to offset the profit-maximising monopolist's restriction of output. Notice that this is a clear example of the *theory of second best* because there are two imperfections and even after tackling the externality, the market imperfection persists.

Now consider the subsidy solution to a positive externality and take the external benefits of *education* as an example. Education directly increases the earning power of those individuals who receive it and they in turn benefit those who come into contact with them socially and at work. For example, their increased knowledge and skill may increase the productivity of the economy and so raise other people's incomes. From the standpoint of society as a whole, the number of people likely to benefit is large and this means that, for social welfare maximisation, education cannot be left to the ordinary bargaining process of the market. The case for subsidising education is illustrated in Fig. 12.8. In the absence of government intervention, DD and SS represent the market demand and supply curves for education respectively. The demand curve reflects individuals' valuation of education – that is to say, it represents the private marginal benefit (PMB) of education. The external benefits which education provides for society are reflected in the external marginal benefit (EMB) curve. Total social marginal benefit is equal to the vertical sum of PMB and EMB. In the absence of any subsidy, quantity $0Q$ will be demanded and supplied at price $0P$. Now suppose the government gives a subsidy which mirrors EMB. This subsidy might take the form of vouchers to be spent on education and so will shift the demand curve for education upwards by the full amount of the subsidy (to D′D′). The equilibrium quantity will now be increased to the Pareto optimal level of $0Q_1$, at which point social marginal cost is equal to social marginal benefit. At this point, the subsidy paid is equal to AB. The net increase in social welfare brought about by

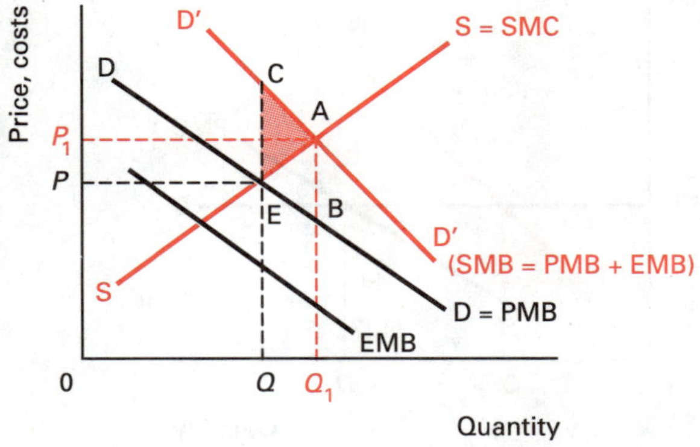

Fig. 12.8. ***A subsidy on education.*** The social marginal benefit (SMB) of education is the sum of the private marginal benefit (PMB) and the external marginal benefit (EMB). A subsidy equal to EMB enables the Pareto optimal output to be achieved.

raising the level of output of education from $0Q$ to $0Q_1$ is represented by the area of the triangle ACE.

If society considered that the external benefits of education outweighed the private benefits, then the government might decide to subsidise the entire quantity, making it available free of charge to all, as with compulsory education in the United Kingdom. In that case, it would become analogous to a pure public good benefiting large groups of people.

Bargaining solution According to the *Coase theorem*, if property rights are well defined, then government intervention to tackle problems caused by externalities may not be required. Instead, *voluntary bargaining* between the affected parties may lead to the Pareto efficient outcome.

Consider the case of a factory that emits air pollution which adversely affects the environment of the surrounding residents. Suppose that the residents form an association to negotiate with the factory owner. The Coase theorem suggests that the outcome of the agreement negotiated between the factory owner and the residents will not depend on the initial allocation of property rights. If the factory has the prior right to pollute the environment, the residents' association can negotiate and offer financial inducements to the polluter to reduce the level of pollution. If, on the other hand, the residents have the prior right to enjoy an uncontaminated environment the polluter can offer the residents compensation. The actual outcome of the negotiations will depend on the relative values of the right to pollute to the factory owners and of the right of a pollution-free environment to the residents. Suppose the residents have the prior right to a pollution-free environment. If the right to pollute is worth more to the factory owner than stopping the pollution is to the residents, then the factory owner will buy the right to pollute from the residents. In this case the pollution will continue.

Now consider the alternative situation where the factory owner has the prior right to pollute. But, as before, this right to pollute is still worth more to the factory owner than a pollution-free environment is worth to the residents. In this situation the right to pollute will not be sold, and the pollution will continue. The Coase theorem, therefore, states that the initial allocation of property rights does not influence the amount of resources devoted to reducing pollution.

The bargaining solution is generally only appropriate where small numbers of people are involved, otherwise the transaction and administration costs may be so high that they outweigh the benefits of bargaining.

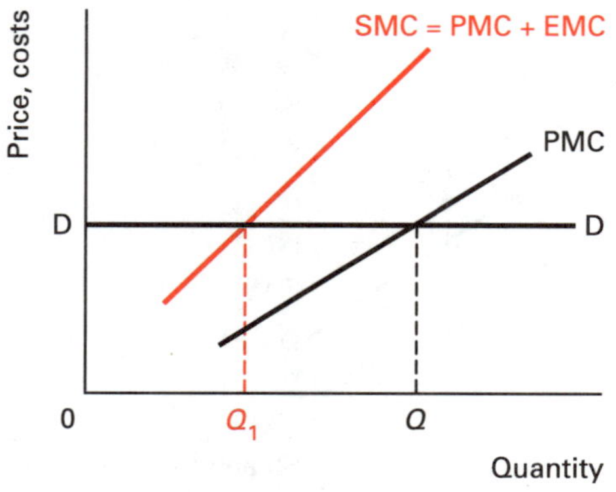

Fig. 12.9. The merger solution. When firms A and B are independent entities, A imposes external costs on B. After a merger, the external cost is internalised.

Merger solution Where one firm imposes an external cost on another, it may be possible to *internalise* the externality by merging the two firms into one. Consider two competitive firms, A and B, where A imposes a negative externality on B. This effectively means that A's social marginal cost of production exceeds its private marginal cost, as shown in Fig. 12.9. DD is the demand curve for firm A's product. Before the merger, A will be producing output OQ, ignoring the external cost which it is imposing on B. After the merger, though, the combined management of A and B will reduce the level of output of firm A to OQ_1, the Pareto optimal quantity. This is so because what was previously an external cost to firm A has become a *private* cost to the larger, merged firm and must, therefore, be taken into account in determining the profit-maximising output level.

Legislation to impose minimum standards This method of dealing with externalities belongs to the wider field of legal rules and regulations. For instance, factory owners could be legally obliged to raise the height of their chimneys or to install noise abatement equipment. Motor-car manufacturers may be compelled to fit exhaust systems that reduce emissions from vehicles and to develop fuel-efficient engines. Aeroplanes might be required to fly at certain minimum heights over residential areas.

It can be seen that these methods stipulate environmental standards of minimum desirable quality. There are, however, major difficulties associated with ascertaining the costs of pollution control and measuring the benefits from pollution control. There are as yet no precise measurements of the extent of damage caused by environmental pollution.

The interaction between economic activities and the environment is of such significance in both the national and international contexts that we devote the next chapter to an analysis of some important aspects of environmental economics.

Summary

1. A community consumes pure public goods, private goods, merit goods and mixed goods.

2. A pure public good is one, the consumption of which by one person does not reduce its supply to others in the community. This contrasts with a private good, the consumption of which by one person does reduce supply to others. Many goods and services have both public and private good content: these are known as mixed goods.
3. Merit goods are goods which the government believes people should be encouraged to consume because of the social benefits that result from their consumption.
4. Pure public goods possess two identifiable characteristics: non-rivalness in consumption and non-exclusion. The degree of 'public-ness' of other public goods can be restricted by either spatial or capacity limitations.
5. Externalities are all-pervasive because the production and consumption of many goods and services result in spillover effects. Policy actions may be called for to identify and deal with positive and negative externalities.

Exercises

1. Review your understanding of the following terms:

public good	non-exclusion
private good	initiating agents
mixed good	affected parties
positive externality	social cost
negative externality	private cost
consumption externality	external cost
production externality	Coase theorem
non-rivalness	

2. Consider the two individuals, A and B, who have truly revealed their preferences for a particular *public* good. The following data represent the two demand schedules:

Price (£):	10	20	30	40	50	60
A's demand:	50	45	40	35	30	25
B's demand:	20	18	16	14	12	10

   (a) Draw the two demand curves on a graph.
   (b) Aggregate them and draw the total demand curve for the public good on the same graph.
   (c) Now draw the total demand curve on the assumption that the good is a pure private good.

3. 'Education cuts can be criticised because education is a public good.' 'Increases in tuition fees can be justified because education is a private good.' Discuss these two statements.

4. To what extent is an open-air pop concert a public good in the same sense as defence and police protection?

5. How do externalities arise? Suggest methods for dealing with: (a) environmental pollution; and (b) the benefits of a national health service.

6. Consider two neighbours, one of whom has a garden which is unattended and unsightly, thereby imposing a negative externality on the other, whose garden is well stocked with flowers. In what ways might the two neighbours bargain with each other to overcome the externality? What other solutions are possible?

Appendix

Private and public goods

In this appendix, we consider in more detail the welfare implications resulting from the existence of public goods. Consider first, however, the case where all commodities are private goods. As we saw in Ch. 8, a condition for optimality is that consumers demanding the same commodities give these commodities the same relative valuations. For example, suppose that in order to be persuaded to give up a hamburger, I need five pieces of chocolate. The five pieces of chocolate will keep me just as happy as I was before. Optimality requires this trade-off to be the same for every consumer of these two goods. In this example, the hamburger and the chocolate are both private goods: in both cases, consumption is *rival* and *excludable*.

In the welfare theory outlined in Ch. 8, we assume that all commodities are private goods. This means that consumer A's total utility is derived from the commodities which that individual consumes. The consumer does not and, in fact, cannot share these commodities with any other person. Similarly, the consumer derives no utility whatever from private goods consumed by other individuals.

To be a little more technical, optimality requires the same marginal rate of substitution (MRS) for any pair of goods consumed by A, B and others. Individuals consume the commodities in different proportions, but all end up with bundles implying the same slope of their indifference curves.

The case of a public good

For a large range of goods and services, however, the assumptions behind the condition of equality between the MRS's of consumers are not satisfied. Consider a street sign, for example. All persons passing by are offered the information on the sign, and the information in no way deteriorates because of such usage. Naturally, in this case, it follows that the demands of many persons for the same commodity must be added to find the total demand.

Let us approach this problem using indifference curve analysis. Fig. 12.10 shows an indifference curve for each of two consumers, A and B. The horizontal axis measures the consumption of a good of the street sign type. It is a *pure public good* and it is designated by S. The vertical axis measures the consumption of good X, an ordinary private good (or some bundle of such goods). The interesting point is that, if the quantity S' is supplied, then this quantity of the public good is necessarily consumed by both A and B. The two individuals consume the same quantity of the public good and (apart from coincidence) different quantities of the private good.

Figure 12.10 shows how much of X, A is willing to give up in exchange for the last unit of S to remain on the specific utility level of I_A. This is MRS'_A. Similarly, the same principle applies for consumer B, who is willing to give up MRS'_B for the last

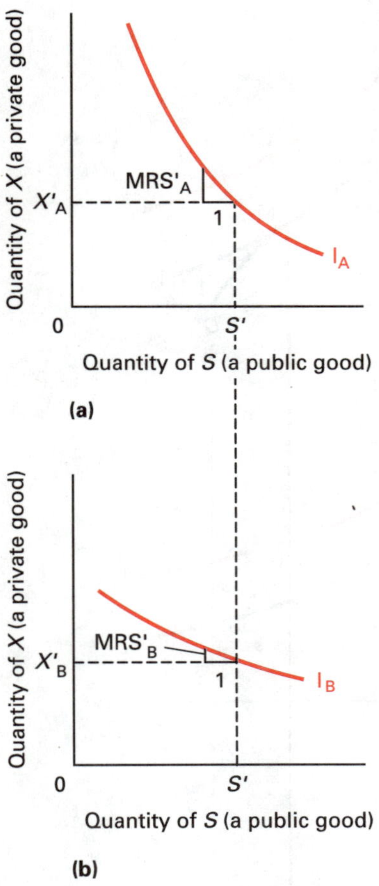

Fig. 12.10. Indifference curves of individuals A and B for a private good (X), and a public good (S). In the case of a pure public good, the two individuals A and B have to consume the same quantity, say, S′. In general, the valuation placed by A and B on the marginal unit of S will differ.

unit of *S*. If, for convenience, we let the price of *X* equal 1, then these two quantities of *X* are the prices that the consumers would be willing to pay for the last unit of *S*. These are their valuations of *S* when supplied together with the specific quantitites of *X* shown in the figure. MRS'_A and MRS'_B will, in general, differ because A and B place different valuations on consumption of the public good. If they are forced to consume the same amount of the public good, the willingness of A and B to pay for it is not necessarily the same. As for the private good, a similar logic applies the other way round. Every consumer is forced to pay the same price and reacts, quite understandably, by consuming, in general, different amounts.

Let us push the analysis a little further by asking under what conditions Pareto optimality would be achieved in a model with two consumers, A and B, and two goods, *X* (a private good) and *S* (a public good). To do this, consider the three graphs shown in Fig. 12.11. In Fig. 12.11(c), FF is the economy's production possibility frontier. Recall that the slope of this frontier is the negative of the marginal rate of transformation (MRT). This can be interpreted as the number of units of *X* that must be given up in order to produce an extra unit of *S*. The consumers' tastes are given by the indifference curves, I_{A_1}, I_{A_2} and so on for consumer A, shown in Fig. 12.11(a), and I_{B_1}, I_{B_2} and so on for consumer B, shown in Fig. 12.11(b).

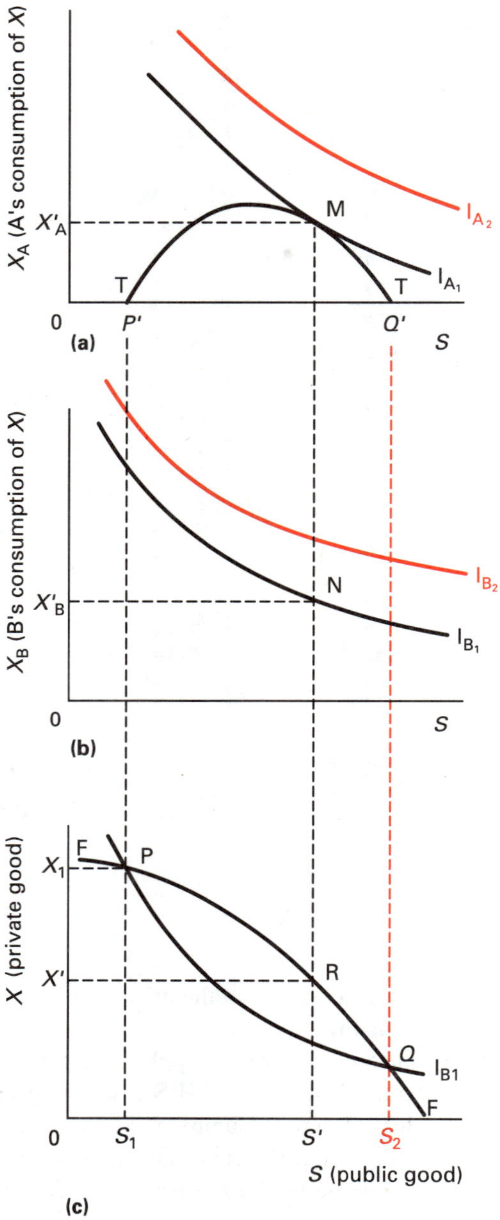

Fig. 12.11. A Pareto optimal allocation of resources in a model with one private and one public good. The distribution of the available quantities of the private good (X) and the public good (S) between consumers A and B, as indicated by points N and M, represents a Pareto optimal allocation of resources.

Assume that B's utility is to be maintained at the level represented by the indifference curve I_{B_1}. Given this assumption, we need to find the highest indifference curve that can be achieved by A, subject to the combinations of the two goods depicted by the production possibility frontier. To do this, the indifference curve I_{B_1} is superimposed on FF in Fig. 12.11(c). TT in Fig. 12.11(a) represents A's consumption possibility frontier, given that B remains on indifference curve I_{B_1}: that is, TT represents the different combinations of the private and public goods that are available for A's consumption, given that B remains on indifference curve I_{B_1}. Note that TT is obtained by subtracting I_{B_1} vertically from FF. Suppose, for example, that individual B is at point P in Fig. 12.11(c), consuming S_1 units of the public goods and X_1 units of the private good. Since X_1 represents the total output of X at point P, this means that no units of X are available for consumption by A. As the public good is available in the same amount to both consumers, A consumes S_1 units of S and no units of X, as depicted by point P' in Fig. 12.11(a). This then is one point on TT. Other points on TT, such as point Q', are derived in a similar way.

Given TT, consumer A maximises utility by consuming at point M on the indifference curve I_{A_1} . At this point, A consumes X'_A of the private good and S' of the public good. With A consuming the quantities represented by point M, consumer B will necessarily consume the quantities represented by point N in Fig. 12.11(b). At point M, A is unable to increase his or her utility without reducing B's utility. Thus, consumption points M and N represent a Pareto efficient allocation of resources.

Note that at point M, the slope of I_{A_1} (that is, MRS'_A) equals the slope of TT. For the level of output of the public good, S', the slope of TT is equal to the slope of the production possibility frontier at point R (that is, MRT′) minus the slope of the indifference curve I_{B_1} (that is, MRS'_B). Formally, it follows that at the Pareto efficient point:

$$MRS'_A + MRS'_B = MRT'.$$

Using absolute values, the sum of the slopes of the indifference curves must equal the slope of the production possibility frontier. As stated earlier, different consumers who have to consume the same amount of S, in our example S', will want to pay different 'prices', and these are MRS'_A and MRS'_B .

It is important to point out that the optimal situation depicted in Fig. 12.11 presupposes the given income distribution that underlies the utility level depicted by I_A and I_B in Fig. 12.10. This should come as no surprise. Any optimum on the contract curve in an Edgeworth-Bowley box, taking the simple example of distributing given quantities of two commodities among two consumers, implies a specific combination of utilities for the consumers.

Having examined the demand for a pure public good in a general equilibrium context, let us look at the ordinary demand functions. Suppose that both consumers voluntarily reveal their true preferences. Demand curves for the public good can be derived for A and B (using the method developed in Ch. 4) on the assumption that A and B are given an initial income measured in terms of X, and budget constraints corresponding to different prices of S can be drawn. Having found the demand curves of the two consumers, the market demand for the public good is obtained by adding the individual curves. However, this time the summation must be vertical, as illustrated above in Fig. 12.2.

In this analysis, the assumption of only two consumers is merely for expository simplification. The principles are general and can be used for any number of consumers.

The demand for and supply of public goods in practice

It is quite easy to list examples of public goods. For a country as a whole, defence is the public good par excellence. The willingness to pay certainly varies a lot across individuals. Nevertheless, the same protection is offered to everybody. Uncongested roads and bridges are other examples of important public goods. In addition, radio and television reception can be used by one more person without interfering with its

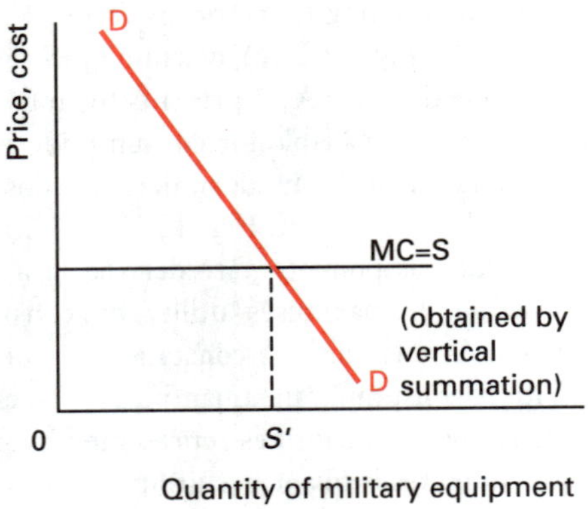

Fig. 12.12. The market for military equipment (a public good). If consumers voluntarily reveal their true preferences, the market demand for a public good (such as military equipment) is given by the vertical summation of individual demand curves. The optimal level of output is determined by the intersection of the market demand and marginal cost curves.

use by others. The list could be extended almost indefinitely, but if you try to find yet more examples, you will almost certainly think of commodities that have characteristics of private, as well as public goods. We will return to this shortly, but first we concentrate on the supply mechanism for a *pure public good.*

Figure 12.12 shows demand and supply curves for military equipment. The market demand curve is the result of a vertical summation, as seen above. The supply curve shows the marginal cost of producing the equipment and putting it into service. It is drawn as a horizontal line, but the analysis in no way depends on the precise shape of the MC curve. Optimality requires quantity S' to be supplied. MC is the society's valuation placed on the amount of other commodities given up to supply the last unit of the public good. It corresponds to the MRT in the exposition above. In fact, under perfect competition, we know that MC represents other commodities, which could alternatively have been produced and sold for just that amount of money (P = MC). The demand price is the sum of the willingness to pay by all consumers for the marginal unit of S. Together they have given up commodities for that amount, which equals the sum of all consumers' MRS's. As a result, the intersection of demand and supply in Fig. 12.12 replicates the optimality condition given above:

$$\text{MRT} = \Sigma\text{MRS}.$$

Sticking to the market for military equipment, in practice, this commodity is not and cannot be bought in small amounts by individual consumers and then be put together for national defence. Furthermore, if there are n consumers and the equipment corresponding to the willingness to pay of the first n-1 consumers is already in service, we could, with almost certainty, expect the nth consumer to be quite happy with this outcome. The nth consumer derives the same utility from the public good whether it is supplied as a result of his or her money or as a result of the money of fellow citizens. But the theoretical idea of asking everybody to reveal their true preferences does not work in practice. Each consumer will be tempted to reveal a very low preference, or none at all, for the public good, if the consequence of such an environment were an obligation to pay a given amount of money. This phenomenon is called the *free rider problem.*

Theorists are working on mechanisms that would make it advantageous for the consumer to reveal true preferences, but generally applicable and reasonably simple methods have not yet been found. We probably have to accept now, and for the forseeable future, that the supply of public goods is decided upon through the political process. Finance is secured by general taxation and, in most countries, taxes are not earmarked for specific public goods.

Typically, there is no market for a pure public good. This is not meant to rule out innovations in the gathering of information on the wants of consumers for public goods and in the use of such information in the provision of public goods. There is, however, a big gulf between the analysis of determining the optimal level of public goods and their provision through a market-type system.

Inter-relationships between the markets for private and public goods

The use of many public goods requires a decision also to use a private good. For example, to make use of television reception through the airwaves, a television is required. Consider an uncongested road as another example. To use the road, a bicycle or car is needed. Let us continue with the example of the road and let the final commodity consumed be trips in a car.

In this example, two markets are involved. One is the size, quality and coverage of the road system which in fact is the market for S, the pure public good analysed above. The other is the market for trips, an ordinary market for a private good. The consumer incurs marginal costs in undertaking trips, consisting of the use of time, petrol, depreciation of the car and so on.

The market for trips is shown in Fig. 12.13(a). DD and ΣMC represent ordinary horizontal summations over the demand and marginal cost curves respectively. Trips are, of course, only possible if there are roads, so the demand for trips must in some way imply a demand for roads, obtained by vertical summation of the individual's demand curves. This *derived* demand for the road system is illustrated in Fig. 12.13(b). (These two markets are interdependent, a matter not elaborated on here, but note that this interdependence becomes even more significant when the imposition of a road toll is discussed below.) Equilibrium and optimality in both markets are obtained at the intersections of the two pairs of demand and marginal cost curves.

Welfare implications of a road toll This analysis enables us to examine the effects of pricing a public good, in this case, imposing a road toll, as shown in Fig. 12.14(a). Assume that trips cause no damage through wear and tear to roads and that

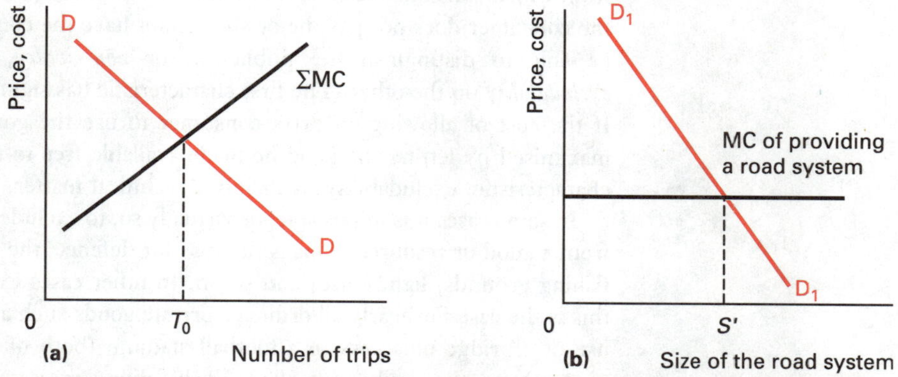

Fig. 12.13. *The interrelated markets for trips and a road system.* Graph (a) illustrates the market for trips. Graph (b) represents the market for a road system, where the demand curve (D_1D_1) is derived from the demand for trips.

Fig. 12.14. The welfare effect of imposing a road toll. In Fig. 12.14(a) the imposition of a toll reduces the number of trips undertaken, and so reduces consumer surplus, as shown in Fig. 12.14(b).

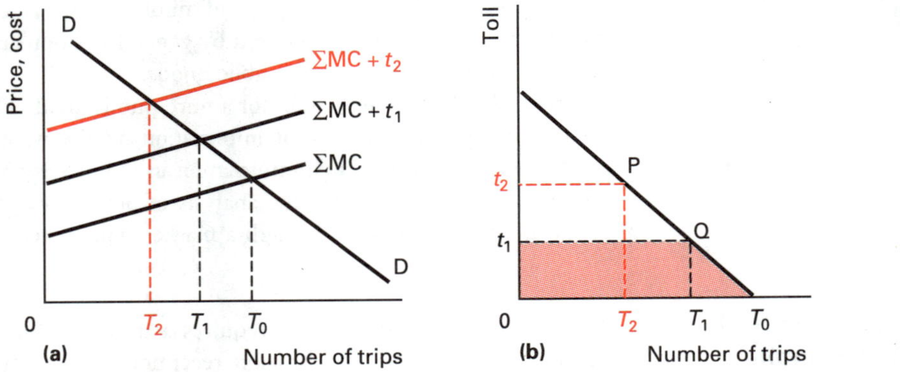

no negative externalities result from the trips. The marginal cost to the road owner (that is, the public) of allowing extra trips is then zero. Now let the authorities impose a toll for the use of the road system. The collection could be difficult or even impossible, but leave this aside. A zero toll leads to the previous situation, and the quantity of trips demanded is T_0. Tolls equal to t_1 and t_2 increase the marginal cost of trips and result in quantities demanded T_1 and T_2 respectively.

In Fig. 12.14(b), the demand for trips is drawn as a function of the toll. By the assumption of zero maintenance costs being incurred by the use of the road, the optimal situation is a zero toll. Levying a toll of t_1 reduces the number of trips to T_1 and so cuts consumer surplus by the lowest shaded trapezium, that is area $0t_1QT_0$. If the toll is increased further to t_2, the surplus is reduced again. Now the welfare loss to society depends only on the number of trips lost. The amount collected in tolls, $T_1 \times t_1$ in the first case, is a transfer of income from consumers to the public agency. Consequently, the net or deadweight losses in the two situations are T_0T_1Q and T_0T_2P respectively. This analysis suggests that *a Pareto optimal situation is achieved when the public good is supplied at a zero price, given that there is no capacity constraint.*

Excludability and goods with a public good content

The analysis of the road system and the possible introduction of a toll leads to a consideration of another dimension in the classification of goods, namely excludability. If the imposition of a toll is feasible, then 'trips' is a commodity from which consumers can be excluded. The mechanism is simply that of a market. If the consumer does not pay, he or she cannot have the commodity. It is important to be able to distinguish the publicness or *non-rivalry*, on the one hand, from *excludability* on the other. The first characteristic has significant welfare implications. If the cost of allowing an extra consumer to use the good is zero, then welfare is maximised by letting the good be made available free to the consumer. The second characteristic, excludability, is mainly a technical matter.

In some cases it is impossible, or virtually so, to exclude consumers or other agents from a good or resource. This is the case for defence, the road system of a large city, fishing grounds, lighthouses and so on. In other cases exclusion is easy to practise: this is the case for nearly all ordinary private goods such as food and clothes. But the use of a bridge or access to a football stadium (both of which have a public good content) are also easily controlled. Excludability in cases such as these is largely a technical matter. Whether it is wise to exclude, in the welfare sense, depends on the first characteristic, the degree of non-rivalry.

From the welfare point of view, the degree of non-rivalry has priority. It is about what ought to be done, whereas excludability is about what can be done. If the good is a pure public one, such as an uncongested bridge, a toll ought not to be levied.

Cumbersome, as it might be, this is not the whole story. Go back to Fig. 12.12 which addresses the question of the optimal supply of a public good. In a long run sense, there is excludability in relation to public goods as well. Through the political process it can be decided to cut, for example, military expenditures by half, so the public excludes itself from that half at the same time as it continues to provide itself with the other half.

Acknowledgement

We are grateful to Lars Lund of the Copenhagen Business School for this appendix.

13 ENVIRONMENTAL ECONOMICS

Learning objectives

After reading this chapter, you should be able to:

- describe alternative approaches to the control of pollution
- assess the strengths and weaknesses of alternative approaches to pollution control in national economies
- analyse the costs and benefits of using pollution taxes
- evaluate the use of direct controls and legislation in combating pollution
- consider the case for and against the use of tradeable allowances
- articulate the global nature of externalities, such as global warming and acid rain
- describe and explain alternative approaches to environmental issues and pollution control in an international context

Introduction

This chapter considers the environmental effects of production and consumption activities, the benefits and costs of which are not fully reflected in the market prices of goods and resources. Effectively, this chapter is an application of the main ideas of Ch. 12 to environmental issues at the micro- and macroeconomic levels.

A recurring theme throughout this book is that markets can be a relatively efficient way of allocating scarce resources to alternative uses. The market mechanism sends signals to both consumers and producers. Through prices, it signals to consumers the costs of producing a given good or service. The market also signals to producers the consumers' valuation of the output of goods and services.

In Ch. 12, it was noted that the constant interaction between economic systems and the environment gives rise to *externalities*. But the existence of externalities means that economic activity in a market economy can have undesirable effects on the environment and on human welfare. This is because some inputs into a production process may not be priced correctly. Some inputs are not priced at all. Consequently, these inputs are treated as 'free goods', even if they are limited in supply. Examples might include clean water and clean air.

Other inputs are priced at levels that do not fully reflect the costs that their use imposes on society. A well-known example is the use of blue asbestos as a lagging material in the construction industry that produced adverse long-term effects on the respiratory system of affected workers.

Environmental pollution

Unfortunately, examples of environmental pollution abound in many parts of the world and it will be a fortunate reader who does not have first-hand knowledge of pollution in his or her own region. In the United Kingdom, as with other developed countries, concern about environmental pollution has grown considerably in recent decades. Membership of environmental pressure groups, such as Greenpeace and Friends of the Earth, has increased in recent years.

Examples of large-scale pollution in the United Kingdom include the discharge of sewage into the surrounding seas; discharges of effluents from factories into rivers; air pollution from motor vehicles and factories; and noise pollution from motor vehicles and aircraft. There have been successes and failures in tackling pollution. The Clean Air Acts, for example, together with changing technology and the disappearance of much heavy industry, have contributed to a massive reduction in the occurrence of smog in major cities, such as London. This has resulted in a significant increase in the hours of winter sunshine recorded in London. On the other hand, in 1992, the Royal Commission on Environmental Pollution reported that the quality of British rivers had deteriorated over the past decade, and warned of extensive pollution to sources of underground water.

In the first part of this chapter, the analysis of the underlying factors and the search for appropriate solutions are conducted in the context of national economies. In the second part of the chapter, attention is focused on the global dimension of externalities. Therefore, the environmental effects of externalities we have in mind in this second section are those that transcend national boundaries. Examples of such externalities with international dimensions include the problems of global warming (often referred to as the *greenhouse effect*), acid rain and the depletion of the ozone layer.

Dealing with pollution at the national level

There are a number of approaches that local or national governments can use in an attempt to control pollution and its effects. These include: pollution taxes; direct controls or legislation; emission allowances (or tradeable permits). Consider these in turn.

Pollution taxes

In the case of a production activity that results in pollution, the price system does not give the producer an incentive to take into account the *external costs* borne by third parties. The rationale of a pollution tax is, therefore, to compel polluting producers to include in the prices of their goods the full *social costs* of production. It can be noted that the use of pollution taxes is an affirmation of the 'polluter pays principle' adopted by the Organisation for Economic Co-operation and Development (OECD) in 1974 and by the EC in 1975.

As demonstrated above in Fig. 12.6, the objective of a pollution tax is not normally to eliminate completely a pollution externality. Pollution of some degree is a virtually inevitable by-product of economic activity. The objective is to compel polluters to reduce the level of emissions to the optimal level.

The 'polluter pays' approach gives the polluter the following choices:

(a) paying a tax that is based on the level of pollution caused by the level of output; or

(b) installing pollution abatement equipment.

Assuming that the polluter seeks to maximise profit, the costs and benefits of the two choices must be weighed before selecting the minimum cost alternative. Ideally, the actual tax rate levied under the polluter pays principle should depend upon the external marginal costs imposed by the pollution.

Achieving the optimal level of pollution through a pollution tax One method of achieving the Pareto optimal level of output in the presence of an externality, such as pollution, was illustrated in Ch. 12. We saw that in the case of a perfectly competitive industry which imposed negative externalities, a solution was to levy a tax equal to the external marginal cost (EMC). As a result, the producers' private marginal cost was brought into line with the social marginal cost of production. The industry then produced the Pareto optimal level of output where price was equal to social marginal cost. The top half of Fig. 13.1 reproduces Fig. 12.6 from Ch. 12 and illustrates the tax solution to a negative externality. Before the imposition of the tax, price is $0P$ and the level of output is $0Q$, determined by the intersection of the demand curve (DD) with the supply curve (SS = ΣPMC). The supply curve reflects the producers' private marginal cost.

By levying the tax, equal to the EMC, the government effectively induces the producers to take account of the external costs that production imposes on society. As a result, price rises to $0P_1$ and the level of output falls to $0Q_1$ which is the Pareto optimal level. This is determined by the intersection of the demand curve and the

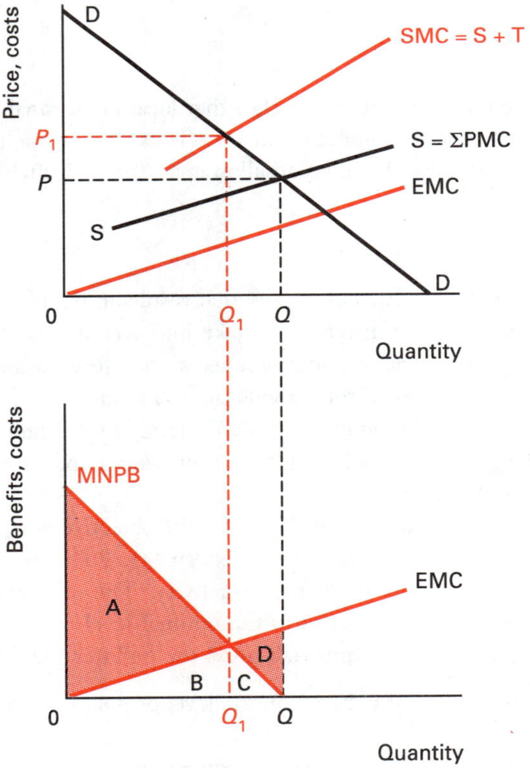

Fig. 13.1. Tax solution to a negative externality. The imposition of a tax (equal to EMC) results in the attainment of the Pareto optimal level of output $0Q_1$.

social marginal cost curve (SMC = S + T). By implication, the level of pollution associated with output $0Q_1$ can be regarded as the optimal level of pollution.

The lower part of Fig. 13.1 illustrates an alternative method of determining the Pareto optimal level of output and pollution. The diagram shows the marginal net private benefit (MNPB) resulting from production. The MNPB curve is derived by subtracting private marginal cost from average revenue or price. Thus, in the perfectly competitive case, the MNPB curve represents the vertical difference between the demand curve and supply curve. As above, EMC represents external marginal cost.

This analysis yields the same result as the previous discussion. The optimal level of output is $0Q_1$ where MNPB intersects EMC. Given that the two curves are marginal curves, the areas beneath them represent total magnitudes. The area under MNPB represents the sum of the producers' net private benefit. The area under EMC represents total external cost. Society's aim can be stated as maximising the difference between total benefits and total costs. The area represented by triangle A is the largest net benefit obtainable.

Note that below output $0Q_1$ the marginal net private benefit from an additional unit of output exceeds the external marginal cost. Increasing output will, therefore, increase total benefit. At output levels above $0Q_1$, on the other hand, the extra net benefit from an additional unit of output is valued less than the extra damage caused by the resultant pollution. Total benefit will be increased in this case by reducing output to $0Q_1$. Thus, reducing output from $0Q$ to $0Q_1$ reduces external cost by the areas of triangles C and D. The corresponding fall in producers' net private benefit is, however, represented by the area of triangle C. Thus, reducing output from $0Q$ to $0Q_1$ by means of the tax results in a net benefit to society equal to the area of triangle D.

For social welfare maximisation, we require that *marginal net private benefit is equal to the external marginal cost of production.* As shown in Fig. 13.1, this is achieved at output level $0Q_1$. Recall that in the absence of a pollution tax, the profit-maximising level of output in Fig. 13.1 is $0Q$. Note that increasing the level of output from $0Q_1$ to $0Q$ increases external costs by more than it increases net private benefit. This increase in output increases external costs by the areas of triangles C and D in the lower part of Fig. 13.1. The corresponding increase in producers' net private benefit is represented by the area of triangle C. Thus, increasing output from $0Q_1$ to $0Q$ imposes a net cost on society, equal to the area of triangle D.

Advantages of pollution taxes It can be argued that using pollution taxes to alter the behaviour of economic agents in the economy is preferable in some respects to the use of environmental standards imposed through legislation. Consider the following claimed advantages of pollution taxes.

(a) *Incentive to reduce pollution.* If a producer has to pay a tax based on the quantity of pollution created, then the producer can pay less tax as a result of emitting less pollution. It is argued, therefore, that a pollution tax can give a producer a *continuing incentive* to reduce pollution. Whether or not the producer chooses to pay the tax or to incur expenditure on installing pollution abatement equipment depends on which option is cheaper. Producers for whom the cost of reducing pollution is high are more likely to choose to pay the pollution tax.

(b) *Demonstration effect.* If the pollution taxes are well publicised to consumers then there may be a *demonstration effect* whereby consumers' attention is drawn to the pollution effects of the relevant products. It is possible that some environmentally conscious consumers may cut back on their usage of these products to a greater extent than suggested by estimates of short-run elasticities of demand.

Cost of pollution taxes It can also be argued that pollution taxes impose some costs. Consider the following.

(a) *Inflation impact.* By pushing up prices, it is said that pollution taxes are inflationary. Clearly, there is some truth in this view as far as the short-run impact on the price level is concerned. But pollution taxes should not be a source of continuing inflation. Indeed, over time the total amount paid in pollution taxes should fall as the level of pollution diminishes.

(b) *Monitoring costs.* It is the case that the effective implementation of pollution taxes will require continuous monitoring of pollution emissions. Such monitoring may prove costly. But it should be noted that such monitoring is also required for effective implementation of physical limits on pollution levels.

Direct controls or legislation

As noted in Ch. 12, another approach to dealing with negative environmental externalities is to introduce direct controls or legislation (often referred to as a *command and control* approach). This approach may specify minimum environmental standards, concerning air or water quality, for example. Alternatively, direct controls may be imposed stipulating a complete ban on the use of particular inputs. For instance, the use of lindane as a wood preservative has been outlawed in several countries.

In some cases, governments require the installation of specific types of anti-pollution equipment, such as flue-gas desulphurisation plants at coal-burning power stations. At the consumer level, new cars sold in the EC from 1993 onwards had to incorporate catalytic converters.

Limitations of anti-pollution legislation In order to enforce specified minimum environmental standards, it is necessary to set up an inspectorate to monitor polluters' activities and to impose penalties on those exceeding permitted levels of pollution. The effluent from a chemical factory, for example, may be permitted to contain up to a specified level of a particular pollutant.

Unfortunately, such standard setting is unlikely to be optimal. This is because standard setting is most unlikely to result in the Pareto optimal level of economic activity. This point is illustrated by Fig. 13.2 where $0Q_1$, the Pareto optimal level, is determined by the intersection of the MNPB and EMC curves.

In the diagram, the horizontal axis represents the level of output for a product whose output generates pollution. The vertical axis measures the costs and benefits resulting from the output. MNPB represents the producers' marginal net private benefit and EMC is the external marginal cost of production. (The Q_2S line represents the maximum level of output compatible with the specified minimum environmental standard.) In the absence of any penalty, the producers would wish to

Fig. 13.2. ***The use of pollution standards.*** The imposition of a pollution standard is unlikely to result in the attainment of the Pareto optimal level of output, $0Q_1$.

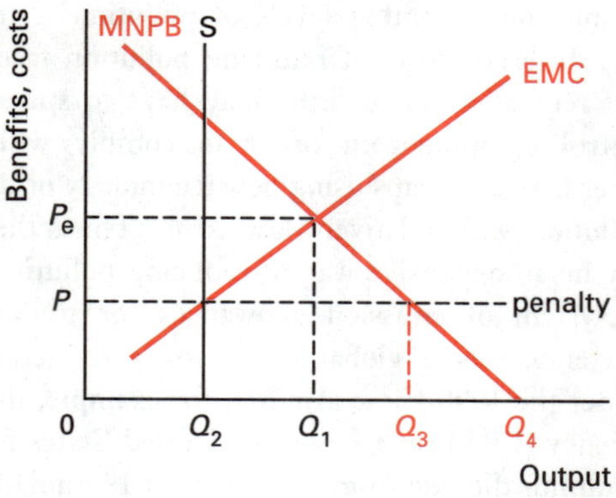

increase output as long as the MNPB is positive. Thus, in the absence of intervention, firms would produce output $0Q_4$.

Suppose now that the inspectorate specifies a maximum permitted level of pollution which, given the existing technology, implies a maximum output of $0Q_2$ which is less than the Pareto optimal level of output $0Q_1$. In general, it is unlikely that specifying a maximum permitted level of pollution will result in the Pareto optimal output and associated level of pollution. Even if the legislation imposes a financial penalty on firms for exceeding the permitted level of output, they may still produce an amount different from the Pareto optimal level. Suppose a penalty of $0P$ per unit is imposed for producing in excess of $0Q_2$ units. In this case, the polluters have an incentive to produce $0Q_3$ units of output, as determined by the intersection between the MNPB curve and the penalty line. Below output $0Q_3$ the MNPB is greater than the penalty of $0P$, thus giving producers the incentive to increase output.

This analysis suggests that for the standard setting approach to be completely effective, the inspectorate must have knowledge of the MNPB curve and the EMC curve in order to determine the Pareto optimal level of output and associated level of pollution. In reality, an inspectorate is most unlikely to have the requisite knowledge. When standards are applied across the board to all firms, the process does not take account of the marginal cost of reducing pollution for individual firms. Some firms may find it costly to reduce pollution, whilst other firms may be able to reduce pollution more cheaply. As a result, standard setting applied to all firms may be an inefficient, expensive way of reducing pollution.

Why then are standards so widespread? It is the case that anti-pollution policy has been (and still is) dominated by standard setting and other direct controls. Politicians may prefer to impose legislation, rather than use market-based incentives, because they wish to be certain of achieving specified objectives. Market-based incentives, such as pollution taxes and tradeable emission allowances, may not work with such speed and certainty as direct controls. Legislation may, therefore, be appropriate when a government wishes to ban completely the use of a dangerous substance on health and safety grounds.

Tradeable emission allowances

In recent years increasing attention has been paid to the use of emission allowances (or tradeable permits) that can be traded between producers whose economic activity results in pollution. As noted above, a major disadvantage of legislation that sets quantitative limits on permitted levels of pollution is that this approach takes no account of the different costs of reducing pollution faced by firms. Under such a crude form of regulation some firms may have to spend large sums of money on pollution control equipment in order to comply with the permitted levels of pollution. Other firms, perhaps using new technology or different inputs, may be able to reduce pollution with relatively low costs. Thus, the introduction of pollution standards may be an expensive way of reducing pollution in terms of resources.

With the system of emission allowances (or tradeable permits) the relevant government agency sets a global target for a reduction in a particular type of pollution. Under the 1990 Clean Air Act, for example, the American Environmental Protection Agency (EPA) set a target for United States power stations to cut annual emissions of sulphur dioxide from an average of 19 million tons in 1980–85 down to 9 million tons by the year 2000. The EPA issued emission allowances for sulphur dioxide in proportion to power plants' existing emissions of the pollutant.

With effect from March 1993, power generators for whom the cost of pollution abatement is high can buy additional allowances in an auction rather than installing flue-gas desulphurisation equipment. Conversely, generating companies for whom the cost of pollution abatement is low can sell some of their allowances to other producers. It is estimated that this market in emission allowances may save up to one-third of the costs of a comparable reduction in sulphur dioxide emissions through a command and control approach.

A graphical analysis The demand for tradeable emission allowances or permits is determined by the marginal cost of pollution abatement. The use of tradeable permits is illustrated in Fig. 13.3 in which for ease of analysis the horizontal axis shows both the amount of pollution associated with units of output and also the number of permits issued. For simplicity, assume that one permit is required to emit one unit of pollution. Thus, an individual firm's demand for permits depends on the number of units of pollution that the firm wishes to emit.

Marginal abatement cost (MAC) ***The additional cost of reducing pollution by one unit by incurring expenditure on pollution abatement equipment***

In the diagram the curve labelled MAC = D is the marginal abatement cost. It shows the extra cost of reducing pollution by one unit by spending on pollution abatement equipment. Thus, the cost of reducing pollution below, say $0Q_1$ units is relatively low and is given by $0C_1$. The marginal cost of reducing pollution is low when there is heavy pollution, as at the level of output associated with $0Q_1$ units of

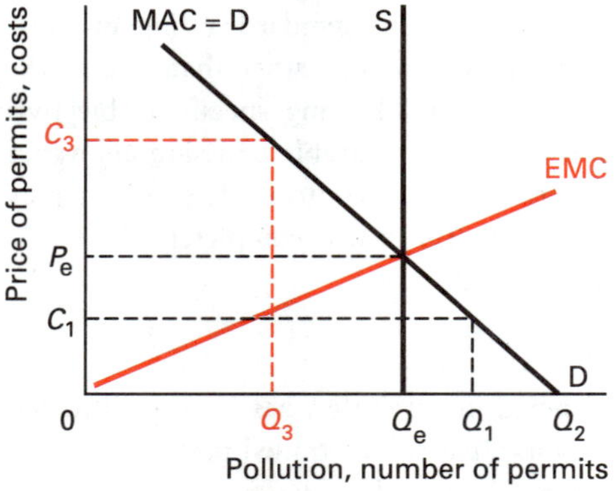

Fig. 13.3. The use of tradeable emission permits. The regulatory agency issues $0Q_e$ number of permits at a price of $0P_e$ per permit in order to attain the Pareto optimal level of pollution.

pollution. But at a lower level of pollution, say $0Q_3$ units, the marginal cost of reducing pollution still further is higher and is given by $0C_3$. In this situation, the reduction of pollution is likely to require the application of expensive, specialist equipment.

The firms' marginal abatement cost curve (MAC) is also the demand curve for permits. This is because a cost-minimising firm will compare the relative price of buying a pollution permit with the cost of reducing pollution through the purchase of pollution abatement equipment.

In Fig. 13.3, the optimal level of pollution is $0Q_e$, given by the intersection of the MAC curve with the EMC curve. The regulatory agency needs to issue $0Q_e$ number of permits in order to achieve the optimal level of pollution. Thus, the optimal price of permits is OP_e.

In the absence of measures to reduce pollution, profit-maximising firms would wish to produce output $0Q_2$. This is the level of output where for a firm marginal revenue is exactly equal to private marginal cost. In other words, it is the level of output where MNPB is equal to zero.

If pollution permits are now introduced, firms will need to purchase a permit for each level of pollution emitted. If permits are priced at $0P_e$, it will pay firms to reduce pollution to the optimal level $0Q_e$ by installing abatement equipment. Once pollution is reduced to $0Q_e$ units, however, it then becomes cheaper to purchase pollution permits (at price $0P_e$) rather than installing more abatement equipment. This is reflected in the MAC curve exceeding the price of permits $0P_e$ for pollution levels below $0Q_e$.

As outlined above, a major advantage of issuing tradeable permits is that firms faced with high costs of reducing pollution can buy permits from other firms which face lower costs of reducing pollution. Fig. 13.4 is similar to Fig. 13.3, but now MAC_A and MAC_B represent the marginal abatement cost curves of two firms, A and B respectively. MAC is the overall marginal abatement cost curve and is the horizontal summation of MAC_A and MAC_B. As before, the regulatory agency issues $0Q_e$ permits which trade at price $0P_e$. To maximise profits in the absence of regulation, firms A and B would wish to produce levels of output associated with $0Q_3$ and in the absence of regulation $0Q_4$ units of pollution respectively.

As can be seen from the diagram, firm A is faced with lower marginal abatement costs than firm B. Therefore, it pays firm A to install abatement equipment to reduce pollution to level $0Q_1$. Consequently, firm A only needs to purchase $0Q_1$ number of

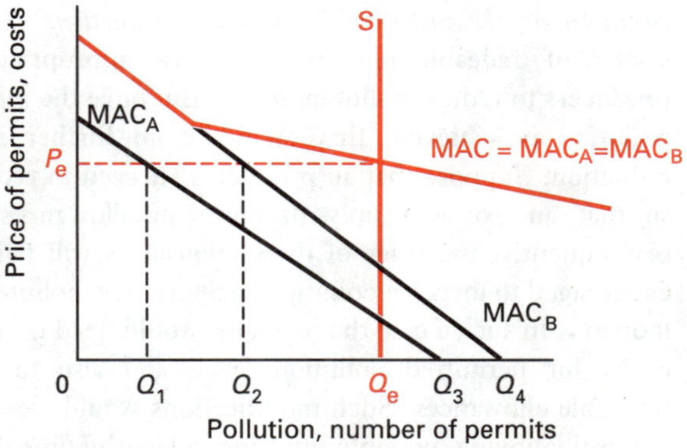

Fig. 13.4. **Minimum cost method of reducing pollution with tradeable permits.** The use of tradeable permits means that pollution abatement is achieved at the lowest possible total cost.

permits. On the other hand, it pays firm B to install abatement equipment to reduce pollution to level $0Q_2$ and to buy the associated larger number of permits.

Both firms install abatement equipment up to the point where the marginal abatement cost is just equal to the price of a permit. As a result, pollution abatement is achieved at the lowest possible total cost. The same result would also be obtained if the regulatory agency sold in an auction the initial allocation of permits to the firms involved.

Advantages of tradeable emission allowances Tradeable allowances can be seen as offering potential advantages for policy purposes. Consider the following:

(a) *Cost effectiveness.* Achieving pollution control in a less costly way is the major potential advantage of tradeable allowances. By issuing emission allowances the regulatory agency emphasises that the right to pollute the environment is a scarce resource and, therefore, should be priced. Tradeable allowances make use of the price system by effectively compelling producers to include the previously unpriced resource of the unpolluted environment in their cost estimations.

(b) *Incentive for pollution reduction.* As with pollution taxes, the introduction of tradeable allowances can give firms an incentive to reduce actual levels of pollution. If a firm can find a way of reducing its emissions cheaply, it may find itself able to increase profits by selling some of its allowances to other firms.

(c) *Flexibility.* This method has the added advantage that if the government alters its policy on the desirable level of pollution, the regulatory agency can buy back permits or alternatively, issue additional permits.

Disadvantages of tradeable emission allowances It can also be noted that there are certain potential disadvantages associated with a system of tradeable allowances:

(a) *Implementation problems.* Criteria for the initial allocation of permits may have to be established if they are not priced at time of issue. It seems likely that such criteria are bound to be somewhat arbitrary. The EPA's system of allocating allowances in proportion to existing emissions of sulphur dioxide, for example, may be seen as rewarding generators which currently are heavy polluters. A mechanism may also have to be established for issuing allowances to new entrants to an industry.

(b) *Maintaining the incentive for pollution reduction.* It was argued above that a system of tradeable allowances can give appropriate incentives for individual producers to reduce pollution levels. But once the initial *total* target reduction in pollution is achieved, there may be no further incentive for a continuing reduction. Suppose that all producers succeed in reducing their pollution levels so that an excess supply of emission allowances develops in the market. Consequently, the price of these allowances will fall so that producers may be encouraged to increase pollution again, or new polluters may be attracted into the industry. In such a case the regulator would need to introduce a new lower global target for permitted pollution levels and also to issue a lower quantity of tradeable allowances. Such modifications would clearly be subject to protracted political lobbying, possibly resulting in lengthy time delays before action is taken.

Externalities and the global environment

We now turn our attention to environmental problems that transcend national boundaries. Acid rain, the threat to the ozone layer from CFCs and global warming are important examples of such problems. These are issues which illustrate the importance of externalities with *global* dimensions.

The fundamental question we wish to consider is: what effects might one economy have on the welfare of other nations when it is using up renewable and non-renewable resources? It is immediately apparent that this question brings into sharp focus the fact that in the global environment, the welfare of one country is inextricably bound up with the welfare of other countries.

In order to deal with this question and to highlight the associated policy issues, we discuss the following areas:

(a) the nature and importance of externalities in the global environment;
(b) the environment as a public good;
(c) methods of dealing with externalities which have both national and international dimensions;
(d) the implications of environmental externalities for the economic growth and development of the world economy.

The nature and importance of externalities in the global environment

The acts of production and consumption undertaken in every country make calls upon:

(a) man-made resources, such as machines, tools, roads and bridges;
(b) natural, renewable resources, such as ocean habitats, wetlands, forests, fishing grounds and the atmosphere;
(c) natural non-renewable resources, such as oil and coal.

Negative externality in the global environment *The loss of welfare sustained by one country without actual or promised compensation as a result of the actions of individuals, firms and national governments in other countries*

Economic activities are undertaken to satisfy individuals' wants for goods like food, shelter, warmth and clothing. Society also has group wants for goods like defence, clean air and rivers. Environmental pollution, such as unclean air and water that transcend national boundaries, is a by-product of economic activities. So environmental pollution on such a large scale is synonymous with negative externalities in the global environment.

Recall from Ch. 8 that environmental pollution is an important factor that affects welfare. Notice the interdependence of the welfare of countries as a result of the impact of global externalities. In the global context, in addition to consumers and producers as generators of externalities, national governments also may be important in the extent to which they contribute to environmental pollution. This might be, for example, either through failure to enforce rules and regulations of minimum environmental standards, or connivance at the discharge of effluents into rivers or seas.

Transboundary externality *An externality that imposes gains or losses across national boundaries*

Transboundary externality Consider, for example, acid rain which is often attributed to the emission of sulphur oxides into the atmosphere in Europe. A *transboundary externality* occurs because sulphur oxides emitted from the burning of fossil fuels in one country may contribute to acid rain in other countries. This externality shows up in detrimental effects on ground and surface water, on fresh-water fish in rivers and lakes, and on forests. Yet, as is explained below, no means exist to ascertain the precise level of damage in the victim country, nor is there a mechanism to enable compensation to be claimed. Nevertheless, acid rain as an environmental externality is an example of *mutual damage*. The emitters of pollutants inflict damage not only on themselves and on other countries, but are themselves damaged by emissions from other countries. The Scandinavian countries, for example, are alleged to be the main sufferers of acid rain discharges from power stations in other West European countries. Emitters themselves (the United Kingdom, for example) sustain damage because not all air-borne pollutants associated with acid rain cross national boundaries. In addition, other countries' power stations may emit gases with sulphur-oxides that also inflict damage on the first set of emitters. As a result, it is impossible to determine the precise sources of the pollution and damage sustained.

So we see that there are *mutual externalities* in the world economy. However, some environmental externalities are *unidirectional*. Consider, for example, the River Rhine in Europe. As it flows through several countries, it receives industrial and toxic wastes, supplies part of their water needs and also acts as a recreational amenity. With the application of sufficient resources, the polluters, the sufferers and the level of damage sustained could all be ascertained due to the unidirectional nature of the pollution. As the OECD reported in 1991, the contributions from each country of 27 out of 42 toxic substances into the Rhine have been identified. Under the Rhine Action Plan, the riparian countries (Switzerland, Germany, France, Luxembourg and the Netherlands) have committed themselves to improving the environmental quality of the River Rhine. Specifically, these countries aim to achieve four objectives by the year 2000: (a) to reduce the level of toxic wastes in the Rhine sediments; (b) to maintain the quality of Rhine water so that it is suitable for the supply of drinking water; (c) to enable important species of fish, such as salmon, to return to the river; and (d) to improve the North Sea eco-system. These improvements are to be achieved by the construction of additional waste treatment plants in the riparian countries.

Global warming *The increase in the earth's average temperature believed by some scientists to be caused by emissions of gases, such as carbon dioxide*

The phenomenon of global warming The phenomenon is so called because of the gradual warming up of the earth's atmosphere and the possibility of associated changes in the global weather pattern as a result of emissions into the atmosphere of such gases as carbon dioxide, carbon monoxide, nitrous oxide and methane. These gases are generally referred to as *greenhouse gases* (GHGs). The emissions of GHGs and their consequent concentration in the atmosphere are the result of production and consumption activities not of a single nation, but of all those nations which burn fossil fuels. The burning of fossil fuels, like coal, oil and gas to generate electricity, is the major contributor to emissions which produce global warming, also referred to as the *greenhouse effect*. The GHGs let in solar heat but, rather like the panes of a greenhouse, trap it when it is reflected back from the earth's surface.

There is, thus, a growing fear that the rise in average temperature of the atmosphere and the possible melting of the polar ice-caps could cause widespread flooding. In addition, the consumption of chlorofluorocarbons (CFCs) is said to be causing a gradual depletion of the ozone layer, thereby posing a threat to life on earth. As is well known, the ozone layer protects people from the harmful rays of the sun. The depletion of the ozone layer may result in an increased incidence of skin cancer.

It is, however, important to point out that in the present state of technological and scientific knowledge, it is by no means easy to ascertain and quantify the long term damage being caused by the emissions of GHGs and CFCs to human and non-

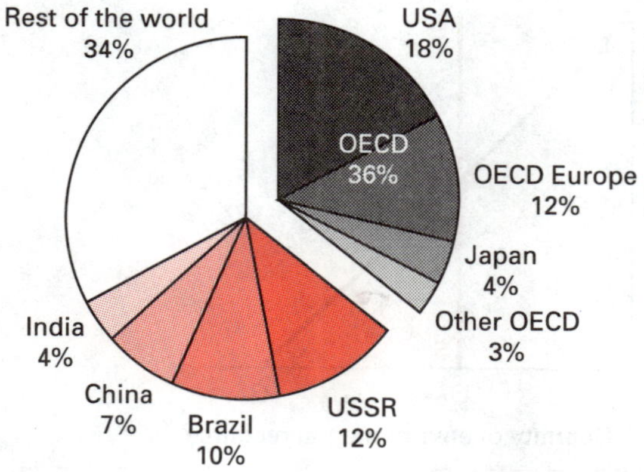

Fig. 13.5. Greenhouse effect. Contribution to annual net emissions of greenhouse gases by different regions of the world.

Source: OECD, *The State of the Environment*, 1992.

human life. Nor can anything definite be said about the magnitude of the effects of GHGs on the amplitude of changes in the global weather patterns in the future. But the fact that there has been a rapid build-up of GHGs in the atmosphere in the past few decades calls for international measures to reduce these emissions and to stabilise their atmospheric concentration. Note that the *greenhouse effect* as an externality crosses national boundaries and that the full costs of GHGs and CFCs are not borne by producers and consumers burning fossil fuels and using CFCs. Fig. 13.5 shows the contributions to net emissions of greenhouses gases by different regions of the world. It can be noted that developed countries are the major contributors of greenhouse gases.

The environment as a global public good Many environmental resources provide a flow of services to producers and consumers over time. The earth's atmosphere, for example, may be viewed as an important public good providing a vital life-support system. More specifically, clean air and the ozone layer are major contributors to the sustenance of life. Many of the resources found in the natural environment are renewable and also have the characteristics of public goods.

Fishing and whaling on the high seas, for example, yield direct benefits to nations which have access to these natural resources. Fish and whales, at the same time, are able to reproduce and multiply themselves. The same is true of animal, bird and plant populations, which are able to reproduce and multiply themselves in their habitats. Amongst the plant populations, the tropical rain forests do not merely yield direct benefits, like timber products and protection against soil erosion, but also provide vital ecosystem services of the biosphere to human populations. These forests are, thus, not merely repositories of biological diversity, such as animal and insect life and plant species, but they also play a significant part in the recycling of carbon dioxide and other gases.

Some environmental resources confer indirect benefits because of their 'existence value'. Nowadays, many people tend to associate their well-being with the preservation of species, which face threats of extinction, on the grounds that every species has a right to exist. On these grounds, people derive welfare when an endangered species is preserved and thus is available for the enjoyment of present

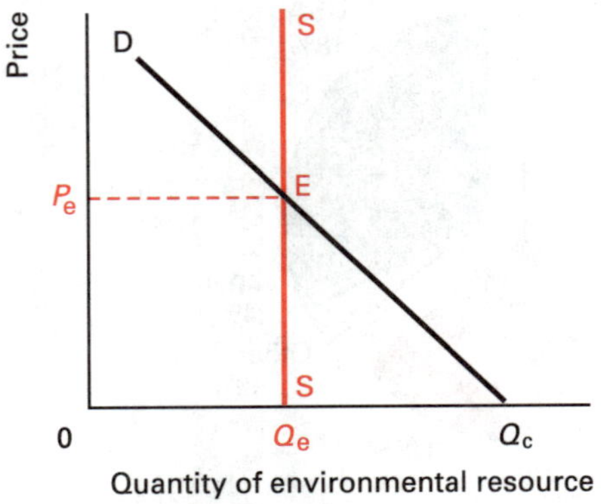

Fig. 13.6. *Consumption of an environmental resource.* At a zero price, the desired level of consumption exceeds the available supply.

and future generations. Note that some of the indirect benefits of this environmental preservation are brought to people's attention through wildlife magazines, videos and television programmes.

The environment as a 'global waste sink' is another important public good shared by all nations. Because of the absence of property rights over the environment as the supplier of renewable resources and as a global waste sink, the environment is sometimes known as global commons. This is because there is no *exclusion principle* in operation, in the sense that, for example, fishing grounds on the high seas (as global commons) are shared freely (without any price for access) by all nations. However, many environmental resources do not belong to the category of 'pure' public goods. In fact, there are *capacity limitations* on the provision of their benefits (that is, positive externalities) to producers and consumers. In spite of their capacity limitations, however, these resources are vulnerable to excessive use. Producers, consumers and national governments tend to regard them as 'free goods'. This is because of the absence of markets for most of these goods. The existence of zero user prices encourages their excessive consumption. This is illustrated in Fig. 13.6 where the quantity $0Q_c$ of the environmental resource is consumed at zero price. If it were possible to create a market, with equilibrium price, $0P_e$ consumption would fall to the equilibrium quantity $0Q_e$, which is less than $0Q_c$. In some cases, then, the absence of markets for environmental resources leads to excessive consumption with the result that the assimilative capacity of the environment as a waste sink is exceeded, thereby giving rise to global negative externalities. In other cases, over-exploitation of renewable resources has led to serious depletion. An example has been provided by the excessive hunting of some types of whales resulting in a threat of extinction.

Global commons *Those environmental resources over which no individual, firm or government has property rights and so cannot exercise exclusion*

Methods of dealing with transfrontier externalities

We now turn to examine alternative methods of dealing with externalities which have both national and international dimensions. Most attention has been directed to the signing of bilateral and multilateral treaties designed to limit the damage from negative environmental externalities. Below, we consider agreements relating to global warming and the use of CFCs.

Agreement on global warming The world's recognition of the importance of global warming is reflected in the signing of the Framework Convention on Climate

Change at the 1992 Earth Summit in Rio. This convention sets a target for all developed countries to stabilise carbon dioxide emissions at 1990 levels by the year 2000. The target is a guide-line to be aimed at rather than a legally binding constraint. Compliance with the convention is, therefore, dependent on the goodwill of the signatories. In reality, there may at times be conflict between national interest and the overall interest of the world community. The attainment of a target on carbon dioxide emissions might in some circumstances, for example, place a constraint on the permitted level of economic activity, in a particular country, with a possible threat to jobs.

Phasing out CFCs As noted above, the use of CFCs depletes the ozone layer and also contributes to global warming. At present, most CFCs are used in developed countries but without government intervention the use of CFCs by developing countries is likely to increase rapidly. Forecasts suggest, for example, an increase in the proportion of Chinese homes with refrigerators (which contain CFCs) from about two per cent in 1985 to around fifty per cent in the year 2000.

The Montreal Protocol relating to the use of CFCs was strengthened in 1990 at a UN conference held in London. The conference agreed to the phasing out of the use of CFCs in developed countries by the year 2000. It also set up a fund, known as the Interim Multilateral Fund, to help developing countries phase out CFCs by the year 2010 and to encourage the transfer of technology from developed to developing countries. The fund was established on a three-year pilot basis to provide up to $200 million in concessional finance to cover the incremental costs of phasing out CFCs in developing countries, such as converting factories to produce CFC substitutes and retooling refrigerator factories. This agreement can be seen as a landmark in international co-operation between developed and developing countries, particularly in respect of the concessional finance made available by developed countries to tackle a global environmental problem. The long-term success of the Protocol will again depend on the co-operative behaviour of the participating countries.

Sustainable development

Conventional national income accounting fails to take into account any decline in a country's stock of natural resources, such as fossil fuels. National income estimates do try to take account of the wear and tear of man-made assets, such as machinery, buildings and roads, through the concept of depreciation. But no equivalent adjustment is made for the loss of environmental resources, such as clean air and beautiful countryside. If adjustments were made for environmental damage, some economists have suggested that the national income figures would be significantly lower – for example, by up to 40 per cent lower in the case of Japan.

Sustainable development
A method of economic growth and development that does not adversely affect future growth potential

The concept of *sustainable development* has grown out of the recognition that current economic activity may have important effects on future generations. The concept stresses the need to maintain the long-term productive capacity of the biosphere.

The concept of sustainable development was made popular by the World Commission on the Environment and Development which defined the concept as 'development that meets the needs of the present without compromising the ability of future generations to meet their own needs'.

Different approaches have been utilised in an attempt to operationalise the concept. One approach is to argue that sustainable development means the preservation of the existing stock of resources, such as clean air, trees, water and so on. An alternative, more realistic, approach stresses the need to maintain the *productive capacity* of the world's resources. Where non-renewable resources (such as oil, for example) are exhausted, this second approach would hold that there would need to be a compensatory increase in the capital stock or an improvement in technology sufficient to maintain productive capacity. The concept of sustainable development, therefore, seeks to take into account the welfare of both present and future generations.

Summary

1. In most economies, the market mechanism is the most important method of allocation. But some inputs with external effects are incorrectly priced. Others, such as clean water and clean air, are not priced at all. Environmental pollution, with national and international dimensions, is an illustration of imperfections in the market mechanism.
2. Measures designed to deal with pollution at the national level include direct controls, pollution taxes and emission allowances (or tradeable permits). Clearly, each one of these measures has its own merits and demerits.
3. Externalities in the global environment have become increasingly important in recent years, calling for national and international measures. Acid rain, the threat to the ozone layer from CFCs and global warming are some of the examples of negative externalities with global dimensions.
4. The environment may be regarded as a 'global public good' providing a flow of services to producers and consumers over time. Examples of resources which provide such services include the atmosphere, the seas, the animal and plant populations and the tropical rain forests. Unfortunately, the existence of zero user prices for most of these resources encourages excessive consumption, possibly resulting in transfrontier negative externalities.
5. International action designed to deal with global externalities must be consistent with the aims and philosophy of sustainable development.

Exercises

1. Review your understanding of the following terms:

command and control approach	greenhouse effect
polluter-pays principle	marginal net private benefit
tradeable permits	pollution tax

marginal abatement cost	CFCs
transboundary externality	mutual externalities
sustainable development	global commons

2. Suppose a wood pulp plant located on a river bank also generates water pollution that imposes costs on a fish farm located downstream. The producer is a price taker and receives £100 per tonne for pulp. Column (3) gives the producer's private marginal cost of production. The external marginal cost in column (4) is the pollution cost resulting from an extra tonne of pulp produced.

(1) Tonnes of pulp produced per hour	(2) Price per tonne (£)	(3) Private marginal cost (£)	(4) External marginal cost (£)
1	100	70	20
2	100	80	20
3	100	100	20
4	100	120	20
5	100	140	20

(a) On the assumption the producer takes account only of private revenue and cost, what is the profit-maximising level of output? Illustrate your answer graphically.
(b) What is the socially optimal level of output?
(c) Suggest how government action might result in the socially optimal level of output.
(d) Discuss how the fish farm might persuade the wood pulp plant to reduce its pollution.

3. Outline the practical difficulties of creating a market in tradeable permits for sulphur dioxide emissions by electricity generators in a country.

4. Suggest alternative methods that a government might use to bring about a reduction in air pollution from the use of motor vehicles in both the short- and the long-run.

5. Consider the obstacles that might be encountered in seeking international co-operation between governments in the attempt to conserve tropical rain forests.

14 FINANCING THE PUBLIC SECTOR

Learning objectives

After reading this chapter, you should be able to:

- distinguish between direct and indirect taxes
- differentiate between proportional, progressive and regressive taxes
- explain the principles according to which taxes may be levied
- identify the advantages and disadvantages of direct and indirect taxes
- analyse the formal and effective incidence of a tax, including the effect on incentives
- describe the structure of taxation in the United Kingdom
- identify other sources of public sector revenues

Introduction

This chapter is concerned with investigating the major sources of the public sector's revenues. Like private individuals, governments need money to finance their spending. But unlike private individuals who, given their incomes and tastes, try to maximise their own utility, the public sector raises revenues to spend in a way that benefits society as a whole. Revenues are collected not merely to meet the public expenditure requirements, but also to serve many other objectives. For example, as pointed out in Ch. 11, taxes are levied on the community by the state to perform its allocation function, to assist its redistribution function, and to implement macroeconomic objectives.

After establishing a definition of taxation, the focus of attention in this chapter is on the following areas: (a) the principles of taxation; (b) the concepts of tax incidence and excess burden; (c) the allocational efficiency and equity of direct and indirect taxes; (d) the structure of taxation in the United Kingdom, together with international comparisons; (e) the financing of government spending by user charges; (f) the financing of government spending by borrowing and the printing of money.

A major emphasis is placed on taxation because most governments in western industrialised countries obtain a substantial proportion of their income from *taxes* (T). The remaining sources from which governments derive revenue are *borrowing* (B), *printing money* (ΔM) and *state trading activities*. Strictly, the profits earned from state trading activities are in the nature of a tax on the community and for the purposes of this chapter are included in taxation. It follows that the methods of financing the public sector can be expressed conveniently by the following identity:

$$G - T \equiv B + \Delta M$$

This tells us that the difference between the level of government expenditure (G) and taxation is met from borrowing and printing money.

Definition of taxation

Taxes *Compulsory transfers of money from private individuals, groups or institutions to the government*

Direct tax *A tax that is imposed on income, wealth or spending power*

Indirect tax *A tax that is imposed on goods and services, and is often included in the price of the product*

Average rate of tax *The percentage of tax paid on each pound of an individual's total income*

Marginal rate of tax *The additional tax paid on an additional pound of income*

Taxes are compulsory transfers of money from individuals, groups or institutions to the government. They may be 'direct' or 'indirect'. Broadly, direct taxes are levied on income, wealth or spending power, or any combination of these three tax *bases*: most tax systems in practice combine the three bases to differing degrees. Indirect taxes are levied on goods and services; in this case, the tax base is the good or service itself and the taxes may be applied *ad valorem* (that is, as a percentage of value), at a *specific rate* (that is, so much per unit sold), or at a *flat rate* (that is, a *lump sum* which does not vary with the quantity or value of the good or service).

Taxes can be *proportional, progressive* or *regressive*. Consider these in turn.

Proportional tax With a proportional tax, the *percentage of income paid in tax remains constant as income rises.* As illustrated in Fig. 14.1, for a proportional tax the average rate of tax (that is, total tax paid divided by income, T/Y) and the marginal rate of tax (that is, the increase in tax brought about by a one pound increase in income, $\Delta T/\Delta Y$) are both constant.

Consider, for example, a proportional tax at a rate of 25 per cent levied on all income. With a monthly income of, say, £1,000 a taxpayer is called upon to pay $0.25 \times 1000 = £250$ in tax. If the taxpayer's income rises by £10, he or she would be liable to pay an extra £2.50 in tax (0.25×10). Thus, it can be seen that both the average and marginal tax rates are constant in this case.

Progressive tax With a progressive tax, the *percentage of income paid in tax increases as income rises.* In other words, the average rate of tax increases with an increase in income. As illustrated in Fig. 14.1, the progressive tax schedule drawn exhibits both a rising average rate and a rising marginal rate of tax.

Note, however, that there is not complete unanimity about the definition of a progressive tax. Many experts argue that a rising marginal tax rate on additional

Fig. 14.1. *Proportional, progressive and regressive taxes.* For a progressive tax, the average rate of tax increases as income rises. For a regressive tax, the average rate of tax falls as income rises.

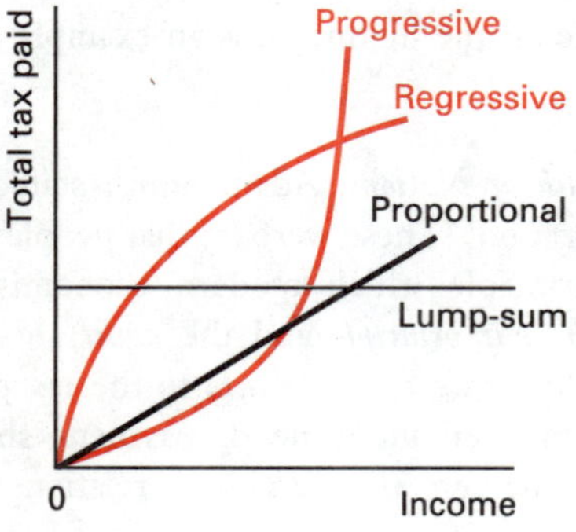

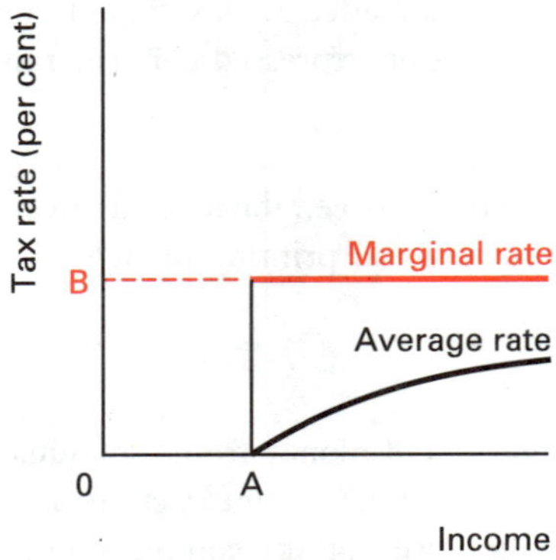

Fig. 14.2. *A progressive tax system.* The average tax rate increases as income rises.

income is not a necessary requirement for a progressive tax. The key requirement is that the marginal rate is above the average rate. Consider, for example, the tax schedule illustrated in Fig. 14.2, which reflects the type of income tax system operated in the United Kingdom.

In Fig. 14.2, note that the vertical axis measures the tax rate in percentage terms. Incomes up to £0A attract no tax because of reliefs and allowances. At incomes above £0A, taxpayers begin to pay tax at a constant marginal rate of 0B per cent. Note that the average rate of tax increases even though the marginal rate is constant above income level £0A.

Consider an example. Suppose that a taxpayer is allowed to earn £500 a month before paying any tax, and that at income levels above £500 a month, tax is levied at a rate of 25 per cent. With a monthly income of £1,000, a taxpayer will be charged tax at 25/100 on £500 taxable income. Thus, the total tax payable will be £125, giving an average tax rate of 125/1000 or 12.5 per cent for this individual.

Now consider the tax position of another individual with a monthly income of £2000. With a tax allowance of £500, taxable income is £1,500 a month. The total tax payable will be 25/100 × 1500, equal to £375. The average tax rate is given by 375/2000, or 18.75 per cent. This example, then, illustrates a progressive tax whereby the average rate of tax increases as income rises.

Regressive tax With a regressive tax, the *percentage of income paid in tax decreases as income rises*. If a poll tax of £100 a month were introduced, this would represent 10 per cent of the income of our individual on an income of £1,000 a month. This poll tax of £100 would, however, represent only 5 per cent of the income of the individual on £2,000 a month. In the United Kingdom, the vehicle excise duty, a fixed sum payable to use a vehicle on the highways, is an example of a regressive tax.

Principles of taxation

In his book, *The Wealth of Nations*, Adam Smith stated four principles which he called the 'canons of taxation'. These were (a) that people should pay taxes according to their abilities (a principle which modern economists have subjected to two interpretations – the *benefit principle* and the *ability-to-pay principle*); (b) that the payment of taxes should be *clear* and *certain* to the tax payer and the tax collector; (c) that the method, manner and time of payment should be *convenient* to the taxpayer; and (d) that the *cost of collection* in relation to the tax-yield should be minimal.

Initially, Smith's canons were propounded to enable governments to raise money to meet their expenditures. In view of the more diverse aims of taxation of modern governments, there are additional criteria by which a tax system should be judged. Consider the following desirable characteristics of a modern tax system.

(a) The finance minister (or Chancellor of the Exchequer) should be able to estimate the *yield* of individual taxes accurately. This will assist the government to control the economy and to plan its future expenditures.

(b) The finance minister should be able to estimate the distribution of the tax burden. That is, the minister should know with some accuracy the different income groups that will bear the burden of the tax. This will assist the government to achieve its equity objective.

(c) Except for equity reasons, taxes should not discriminate between different income groups. Similarly, in the absence of market imperfections, taxes should not distort people's choices between goods or occupations, or reduce the willingness to work and take business risks. Thus, to achieve the efficiency objective, taxes should be *neutral*.

(d) Taxes should have *built-in flexibility* or automatic adjustment. This is the case with a progressive income tax system where, as incomes rise, taxes increase more than proportionately, thereby having a dampening effect on total demand in the economy. This means that less frequent changes in the budget are required to achieve the macroeconomic objectives.

In practice, tax systems try to reconcile the conflicting aims of these different principles of taxation. A tax system can be judged by the extent to which it conforms to the principles. An underlying objective of most tax systems, however, is equity, and this may be achieved by applying either the benefit principle or the ability-to-pay principle.

The benefit principle

The benefit principle *This states that the amount of tax paid by an individual should be directly related to the benefits which that individual derives from government expenditure*

According to the benefit principle, the taxation which people pay should be related to the benefits they derive from public spending. The application of *benefit taxation* requires that both the expenditure and taxation sides of the government's budget be determined at the same time. Whilst it may be feasible to apply this principle to the public provision of certain *excludable private goods*, severe problems arise in trying to apply it to the provision of public goods. To illustrate these problems, consider an economy of two individuals, A and B, who are willing to pay taxes for the supply of a public good, such as defence. The two individuals' demand curves for the public good, D_AD_A and D_BD_B, are shown in Fig. 14.3 together with the cost line CC which shows the cost of producing each unit of the good. To simplify matters, the average and marginal costs are assumed to be constant.

The demand curves, D_AD_A and D_BD_B, measure the different values which A and B put on different levels of output. The market demand curve (the vertical summation of the two individual demand curves) is shown as D_MD_M. In the graph, there is only one output level ($0Q$) at which the sum of the amounts the two individuals are willing to pay is just equal to the average and marginal cost of providing the public good. At any other output level, the total amount that they are willing to pay either exceeds or falls short of this cost. Applying the benefit principle, when $0Q$ units are supplied, A should pay $0S$ per unit in taxes and B should pay $0T$

Fig. 14.3. The determination of tax shares by the benefit principle. The tax on each individual is levied in proportion to the marginal benefit that each individual derives from consumption of the public good.

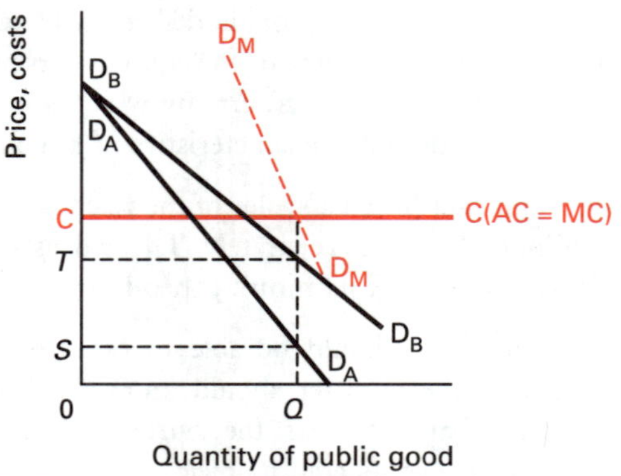

per unit. In spite of the fact that the public good is equally available for both to enjoy, B pays more than A because, given the individual's tastes and income, B derives more benefit from it. The two individuals would only pay equal tax shares if they had identical demand curves for the good – a highly unlikely event.

For such a system to be put into practice, it is necessary that taxpayers should in some way reveal their preferences fully and truthfully for public goods and that they should have equal bargaining skills. Where only a small number of people are involved, this may be possible. In an economy consisting of millions of taxpayers, however, such honest preference revelations are highly unlikely. Indeed, as we saw in Ch. 12, it would pay people to understate their preferences. Furthermore, any changes in individuals' tastes, incomes or the prices of other goods will shift the demand curves and so alter the tax shares. It would be impossible to take account of these changes in practice.

The same difficulties apply, though to a lesser extent, to government expenditure on education, health and other social services. The people who receive these services directly are not the only ones to benefit from them. Such services give rise to *external* benefits which cannot easily be evaluated in money terms. More important, in performing its redistribution function, a government may decide to levy taxes on the rich regardless of direct benefits to them. Only in specific instances where the government supplies *excludable private goods* (with few externalities) is the benefit principle applicable. Social security contributions reflect the application of benefit taxation.

The ability-to-pay principle

Ability-to-pay principle *This states that taxes should be imposed on people according to what they can afford to pay*

Taxes are generally viewed as burdens on taxpayers. The ability-to-pay principle postulates that tax revenues should be raised in such a way that the tax burden is distributed among individuals according to their *taxable capacities* or *abilities to pay*. So the principle shifts the emphasis from levying taxes on the basis of benefits which taxpayers receive from public spending to the basis of how much each individual can afford to pay. Thus, by making the *tax burden* independent of the benefits which individual taxpayers receive directly from public spending, the ability-to-pay principle enables a government to carry out its redistribution function. Recall from Ch. 11 that redistribution of income and wealth is generally one of the important micro-economic objectives of modern governments. But, as we noted in that chapter, there exists at any given time, a multiplicity of micro- and macro-economic objectives. In order to achieve these objectives, modern governments need to raise revenues. Under the ability-to-pay principle each taxpayer is called upon to contribute to the required total revenue on the basis of his or her ability to pay. In this way, the principle seeks to reflect the equity objective, that is, fairness in the distribution of the tax burden.

Equity in the distribution of the tax burden according to the ability-to-pay principle has two identifiable meanings – horizontal equity and vertical equity. Consider these two meanings in turn.

Horizontal equity *Horizontal equity is achieved when taxpayers with similar circumstances and incomes pay the same taxes*

Horizontal equity This implies equal treatment for tax purposes of equivalent or similar circumstances. Most people would agree that two taxpayers of similar circumstances with the same income, wealth or spending power should pay the same amount of tax as they have the same ability to pay. This would be considered to reflect horizontal equity between taxpayers. In this sense, the concept of equity is based upon the equivalent needs and circumstances of taxpayers. For example, the system of reliefs and allowances, under the United Kingdom tax system, is claimed to reflect individual taxpayers' circumstances and, hence, illustrates the concept of horizontal equity. Close inspection shows that it is by no means easy to achieve a socially acceptable definition of similar circumstances. For instance, circumstances are affected by the household composition of taxpayers. Thus, it might be argued in some quarters that the set of reliefs and allowances given to a married couple with children should be more generous than that given to a childless married couple on grounds of horizontal equity. But others, with an opposing viewpoint on the desirability of income redistribution, may come to a different value judgement. Thus, for purposes of horizontal equity, defining 'similar circumstances' in the final analysis is a question of value judgement.

Vertical equity *Vertical equity is achieved when taxpayers with dissimilar circumstances and incomes pay taxes according to their different abilities to pay*

Vertical equity This implies unequal treatment of unequal circumstances. In essence, this is equivalent to saying that people with unequal taxable capacity should be treated fairly. It proceeds from the premise that fairness between two taxpayers faced with different circumstances requires that each should pay different amounts of tax, as they have different abilities to pay. If income or wealth or both are taken as measures of ability to pay, then vertical equity requires that the taxpayer with the higher income and/or wealth should pay more tax. This suggests that vertical equity views progressive taxation as an important instrument of redistribution. The theoretical justification for the redistribution of income and wealth is based on the assumption that the marginal utility of income tends to decline as an individual's income and wealth increase. Thus, an extra pound yields less utility to a rich person than to a poor person. This implies that the rich person should be called upon to pay more tax than a poor person. As we see below, in this sense vertical equity becomes synonymous with the principle of *equality of sacrifice*. Notice the yardstick of justice between taxpayers is the utility loss, that is the welfare loss represented by the amount of tax paid. This assumes that one can measure and compare utility levels enjoyed by different taxpayers.

However, there is a difficulty in the application of the principle of vertical equity to a particular tax system. The principle is by no means clear about which particular graduated pattern of tax rates for different levels of income and wealth might be judged socially desirable. It can be argued that a choice of high marginal rates of tax in order to promote redistribution may cause disincentives. In that event, lowering the marginal tax rates on the rich may lead to an increase in work causing an increase in earnings and, thus, an increase in tax revenues. This is because tax revenues depend on average rates of tax whereas disincentives depend on marginal rates of tax. The practical result of this distinction between average and marginal tax rates is that progressivity in taxation does not necessarily mean that marginal rates should rise with rises in income and wealth. It will be noted that two taxpayers may be subject to the same basic rate of tax, but because of reliefs and allowances the rich taxpayer may pay a bigger proportion of income and wealth in tax. This suggests that there can be an element of progressivity in a regime of a single tax rate accompanied by reliefs and allowances. However, with inconclusive empirical evidence, there is a counter argument that the disincentive effects of high marginal tax rates are exaggerated (and at best are psychological). Besides, society may wish to attach a much greater weight to redistribution than to disincentive effects. The design of a graduated pattern of tax rates that combines redistribution and incentives is a complex question of vertical equity and value judgement.

The ability-to-pay principle and equality of sacrifice

Amongst nineteenth century economists the widely held view was that taxes based on ability-to-pay were to be preferred to those levied on the benefit principle. This was because of their concern for minimising the tax burden to individual taxpayers. In order to achieve this, they sought to popularise the notion of the 'just' distribution of the tax burden among the taxpayers. To these economists, a pattern of distribution of income and wealth in society represented a pattern of utilities enjoyed by owners of income and wealth. Given a particular distribution pattern, individual taxpayers have clearly different abilities to pay taxes, in the sense that tax payments mean loss (or sacrifice) of utilities by taxpayers. In this way, the notion of justice in the distribution of the tax burden based on the ability-to-pay principle has become synonymous with the concept of equality of sacrifice.

The equality of sacrifice is by no means an unambiguous concept and has been subjected to three interpretations: (a) *taxes of equal absolute sacrifice* which impose the same loss of total utility on all taxpayers; (b) *taxes of equal proportional sacrifice* which impose a loss of the same fraction of utility to total utility; (c) *taxes of equal marginal sacrifice* which minimise the loss of total utility to the community by reducing every taxpayer's income to the point where the marginal utility of income of every taxpayer is the same. Consider these in turn.

Equal absolute sacrifice To illustrate this, consider an economy of two individuals, A and B, who both have equal preferences so that they have the same total utility function, represented by 0R in Fig. 14.4. Notice that as income rises, total

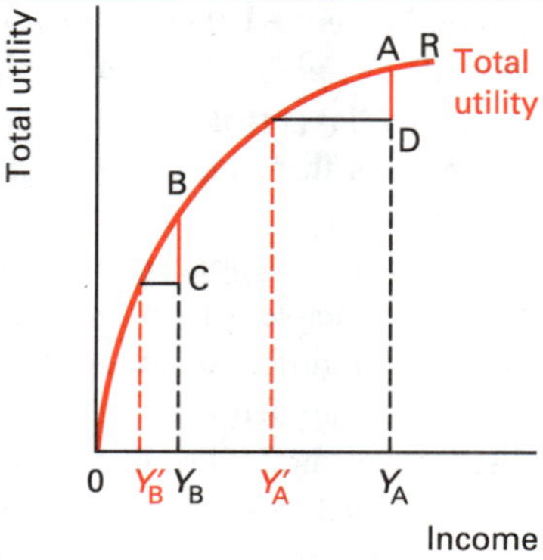

Fig. 14.4. Taxes of equal absolute sacrifice. The tax on each individual is levied in such a way that each individual suffers the same loss of total utility (BC = AD).

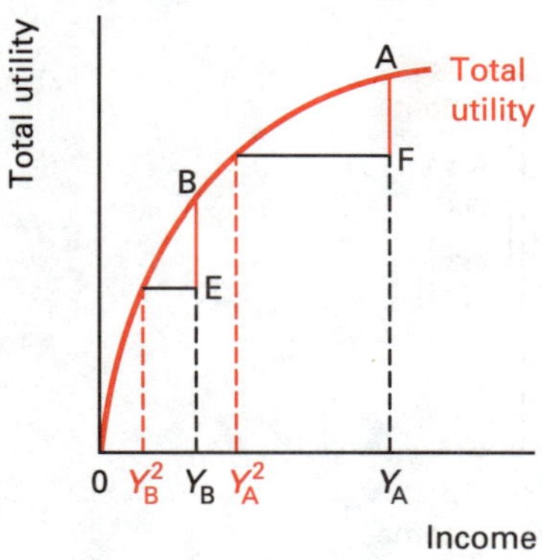

Fig. 14.5. ***Taxes of equal proportional sacrifice.*** The tax on each individual is levied in such a way that each individual suffers an equal proportionate reduction in total utility ($AF/AY_A = BE/BY_B$).

utility rises but at a decreasing rate. This means that the marginal utility of income (given by the slope of the total utility curve) falls as income rises. Now suppose that individual A is a rich man with a pre-tax income of $0Y_A$ and that individual B is a poor man with a pre-tax income of $0Y_B$. A tax which imposes an equal absolute sacrifice is one which reduces both individuals' total utilities by the same amount. An example of such a tax is one which reduces A's income to $0Y'_A$ and B's income to $0Y'_B$. Although A pays more tax than B, they both suffer the same loss of utility (BC = AD). Nothing conclusive, however, can be said about whether this requires a progressive, proportional or regressive tax. The choice of the rate structure depends on the rate of decline of the marginal utility of income.

Equal proportional sacrifice The idea behind this rule is that the tax should have an equal impact on the total utilities of all taxpayers. In terms of the two individuals, A and B, the fraction of total utility lost because of the tax should be the same. This is shown in Fig. 14.5 where the tax reduces A's income to $0Y^2_A$ and B's income to $0Y^2_B$ in such a way that $AF/AY_A = BE/BY_B$. Once again, the choice of rate structure depends on the marginal utility of income schedule.

Equal marginal sacrifice Since the slope of the total utility schedule represents the marginal utility of income, it follows that, in our example, to tax individuals A and B in such a way that equalises their marginal utilities of income, a *progressive* tax has to be imposed which equalises the post-tax incomes. This is shown in Fig. 14.6, where both individuals' post-tax incomes are equal to $0Y_1$.

Apart from the problem of deciding which of the three possible interpretations of equality of sacrifice to adopt, there are a number of practical and conceptual difficulties associated with the ability-to-pay principle: (a) there are severe problems in trying to measure utility; (b) it is by no means certain that the marginal utility of income declines as income rises, nor is it at all clear why income should be the main determinant of utility; and (c) the principle calls for inter-personal comparisons of utility which depend upon cardinal utility measurement.

In seeking to achieve the objective of equality of sacrifice, governments have to decide whether income, wealth or spending power is the appropriate index of ability to pay. Consider these in turn.

Income-based taxes best serve the objective of equality of sacrifice when income is defined broadly in the 'total accretion' sense. This means taking into account income

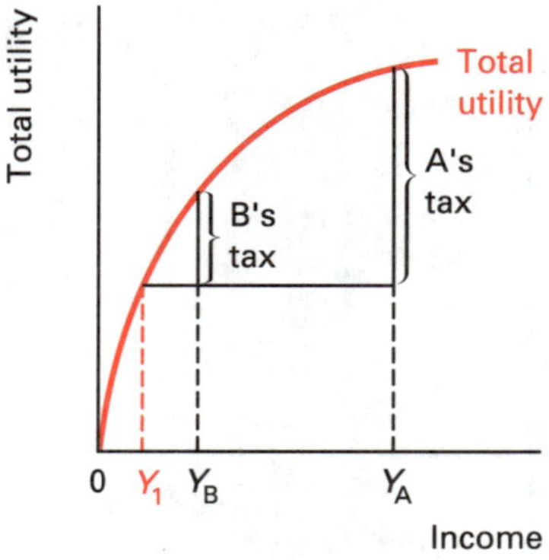

Fig. 14.6. ***Taxes of equal marginal sacrifice.*** The tax on each individual is levied in such a way that the post-tax marginal utility of income is equalised for both individuals.

(monetary and non-monetary) from all sources – for example, income from work, gifts, inheritance and life-time savings; in other words, the increase in net worth valued at market prices during a given tax period. Such a broad definition of income poses many practical difficulties of measurement. Equality of sacrifice also requires the choice of an appropriate *tax period*; for example, should tax liabilities be calculated on a one-year, five-year or life-time basis? The timing of the assessment will affect different taxpayers in different ways. For instance, an individual earning £15,000, £15,000, £10,000 and nothing in four successive years will pay more tax than another individual who earns a steady £10,000 per year if the tax period and tax allowances are annually based.

Wealth-based taxes are sometimes advocated as a way of achieving a more equitable distribution pattern because statistical studies of western industrial societies show that wealth (that is, accumulated assets) tends to be more unevenly distributed than income. It may be objected, however, that wealth-based taxes are unlikely to provide adequate revenues. Furthermore, difficulties arise: (a) in valuing assets to assess tax liability; (b) in adjusting asset values for inflation; and (c) in defining the tax-paying units as wealth may be held in joint names.

Expenditure-based taxes define ability to pay in terms of what a person spends rather than in terms of what a person owns or earns. The use of such taxes dispenses with the need to distinguish between income and wealth since both will be taxed when spent. One way of imposing an expenditure-based tax is to levy taxes on goods and services (that is, indirect taxes). Another (as yet, untried) method would be to estimate an individual's expenditures during a given period and impose a tax on those. The main idea of expenditure-based taxes is to exempt savings which some economists argue are penalised by income- and wealth-based taxes. Indeed, the Meade Report in 1978 favoured the introduction of an expenditure-based tax system in the United Kingdom.

Tax incidence

The concept of incidence is concerned with the question of who bears the tax burden. It can be divided into (a) formal incidence and (b) effective incidence.

(a) *Formal incidence.* Formal incidence refers to the money burden of a tax. For example, a person paying £50 income tax at the basic rate of 25 per cent on a

Formal incidence *This refers to the individual or firm on whom the initial impact of the tax falls*

weekly income of £200 is the one who bears the formal incidence of the tax. Similarly, the formal incidence of excise taxes on tobacco is on the suppliers who have to pay the tax in the first instance. It is possible to calculate the distribution of revenues from all taxes and so arrive at the formal incidence of the tax system on the community. However, from an economic point of view, it is the effective incidence which is important when it comes to the ultimate effect on the distribution of income.

Effective incidence *This refers to the final resting place of the tax after all individuals and firms have adjusted their behaviour*

(b) *Effective incidence.* Effective incidence refers to the final resting place of a tax after all economic agents have adjusted their behaviour in respect of hours of work, spending, saving and investment. For example, the effective incidence of a tax on income is influenced by the extent to which it encourages workers to substitute leisure for work. Similarly, the effective incidence of VAT is influenced by the extent to which it encourages the consumption of exempt and zero-rated goods. It follows that the statistical calculation of effective incidence should provide policy-makers with valuable information about the distributional effects of the tax system. Unfortunately, the complex social and psychological factors which induce taxpayers to alter their behaviour in response to tax changes make it extremely difficult to obtain such a statistical measure in practice.

Effective incidence is closely connected with the attempt by the individual or firm taxed to shift the tax *backward to suppliers* or *forward to consumers*. The extent to which such a shift is possible depends on the following factors:

(a) the relative elasticities of demand and supply in the market for the taxed commodity;
(b) the degree of market power of buyers and sellers;
(c) the coverage of the tax base.

Elasticities of demand and supply As we saw in Ch. 6, the *higher* the supply elasticity, the more an indirect tax is shifted forward to the purchaser of the taxed commodity. In contrast the *lower* the demand elasticity, the more an indirect tax is shifted forward to the purchaser.

In the general case where the demand and supply curves have their usual slopes, we saw that the burden of the tax is shared between the purchaser and the supplier. It can be shown that the relative share of the tax burden depends on the relative elasticities of demand and supply, as indicated by the following formula:

$$\frac{\text{consumers' share of tax}}{\text{producers' share of tax}} = \frac{\text{elasticity of supply}}{\text{elasticity of demand}}$$

Suppose, for example, that the elasticity of demand for wine is 2 and that the elasticity of supply is 1. In this case, the consumers' share of an indirect tax would be half that of the wine producer.

Market power The extent to which a producer can pass on an indirect tax may be related to the producer's market power. A discriminating monopolist, for example, can seek to identify those groups of customers with relatively inelastic demands and, thus, pass most of the tax burden onto them. On the other hand, an individual firm in perfect competition will only be able to pass on a tax to the extent that the market price rises.

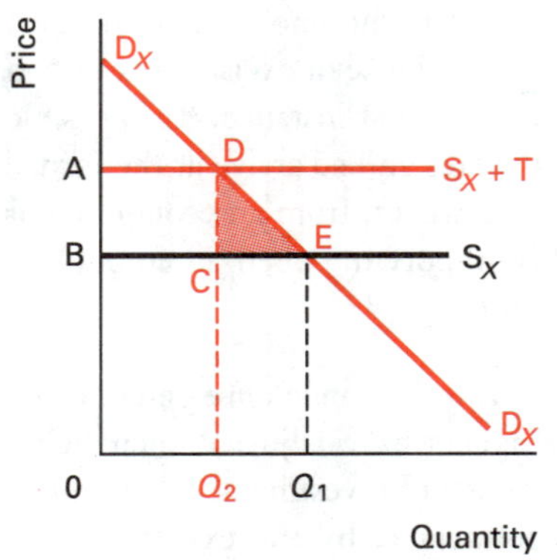

Fig. 14.7. Excess burden of an indirect tax. The area DCE represents the excess burden or deadweight loss of the tax.

The tax base If indirect taxes are applied selectively to a narrow range of goods and services, consumers will tend to substitute untaxed goods and services for those taxed. In contrast, value added tax with its extensive coverage limits the scope for substitution by consumers of untaxed goods and services. It can be argued, therefore, that the effective incidence of value added tax is mainly on consumers. This reflects the wide tax base of value added tax.

Excess burden

Excess burden *The net fall in welfare (or deadweight loss) as a result of the imposition of a tax*

Where a taxpayer incurs costs of adjusting to a change in tax, he or she is said to bear an excess burden. This can be defined as the loss of consumer surplus arising from the imposition of the tax over and above the amount of tax paid. This is illustrated in Fig. 14.7 where D_XD_X is the demand curve for good X and S_X is its supply curve (assumed perfectly elastic for simplicity) before any tax is imposed. Suppose now that a tax is imposed on the supply of X, shifting the supply curve to S_X+T with the result that the quantity consumed falls from $0Q_1$ to $0Q_2$. The tax revenue is ABCD. The loss of consumer surplus over and above that, DCE, is the excess burden or 'deadweight loss' of the tax. This arises because the value that society places on Q_2Q_1 units (given by the area DEQ_1Q_2) is greater than the resource cost of producing these units (given by the area CEQ_1Q_2). Notice that the excess burden will be greater, the more elastic is the demand for the good.

Excess burden is an expression of the idea that taxes on income, capital and commodities distort choices in such a way that the total loss sustained by taxpayers is greater than the money burden of the taxes. Personal income tax, for example, will have an excess burden if it represents a disincentive to work. There will then be a loss of output to society and income to individuals over and above the amount of tax actually paid.

In practice, there are few taxes without an excess burden. Only a head tax, such as the former community charge in Great Britain, is devoid of an excess burden. But this tax may be criticised on equity grounds. A good tax regime may be said to be one that minimises excess burden and improves the allocation of resources.

Taxation and the allocation of resources

The excess burden of an indirect tax, illustrated in Fig. 14.7, results from the distortion of relative prices following the imposition of the tax and it highlights the inefficiency (or misallocation of resources) which results from imposing such a tax. This inefficiency is further illustrated in general equilibrium in Fig. 14.8. The pre-tax

Fig. 14.8. The welfare loss from an indirect tax. The imposition of an indirect tax on good *X* distorts relative prices, raising the relative price of *X* to the consumer. But from the producers' standpoint, the tax-exclusive price falls. As a result, the output of *X* falls.

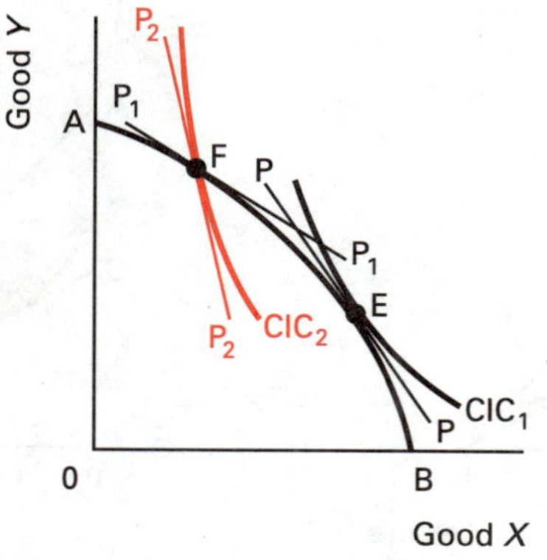

Pareto optimal equilibrium position is at point E where the community indifference curve CIC_1 is tangential to the production possibility frontier, AB. This position will be achieved, with the pre-tax price ratio given by the slope of PP, under conditions of perfect competition with no externalities. If an indirect tax is imposed on good *X*, its price to *consumers* will rise relative to *Y*, shifting the price line to consumers to P_2P_2, say. However, producers' revenues are *exclusive of tax* so that they face the less steep price line P_1P_1. Production will shift to point F and the community will move on to the community indifference curve CIC_2, lower than CIC_1.

We can conclude from the above analysis that an indirect tax, starting from a position of perfect competition with no externalities, spoils the conditions for a Pareto optimum. A *direct tax*, on the other hand, would not distort relative prices and so would not result in such a misallocation of resources. In this way, it is sometimes argued that direct taxes are superior to indirect taxes so far as allocative efficiency is concerned. However, where there are externalities so that social marginal costs exceed private marginal costs, or where there is imperfect competition, it is possible for the imposition of indirect taxes to improve the allocation of resources (as was demonstrated in the case of Pigou's tax solution to externalities in Ch. 12). In a second-best situation such as this, indirect taxes may be superior to direct taxes so far as the allocation of resources is concerned.

Taxation and incentives

A further disadvantage of a direct tax is that it may represent a *disincentive to work*. This is illustrated in Fig. 14.9(a) which shows an individual's choice between income (measured along the vertical axis) and leisure per day (measured along the horizontal axis). The distance 0B represents the maximum amount of leisure possible – that is, twenty-four hours. Before any tax is imposed, the individual's budget line is AB and he or she maximises utility by choosing point E_1 which puts the individual on the highest attainable indifference curve I_1. At this point, the individual is offering HB hours of work per day and taking 0H hours of leisure per day. Now suppose that a 50 per cent income tax is imposed shifting the budget line to CB, so that 0C = CA. The individual will now choose point E_2, offering only H_1B hours of work and taking $0H_1$ hours of leisure. The tax in this case is a disincentive to work and so cannot necessarily be regarded as superior to an indirect tax so far as allocative efficiency is

Fig. 14.9. The effect of a direct tax on the incentive to work. In (a) the imposition of a direct tax acts as a disincentive to work. In (b) the direct tax acts as an incentive to work.

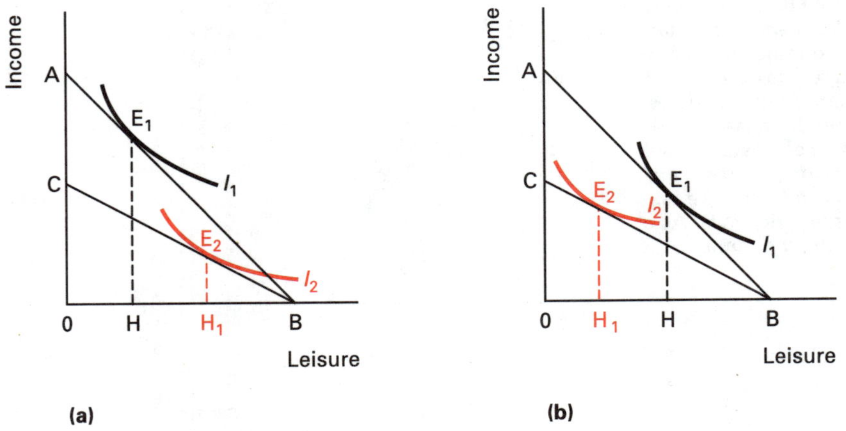

Fig. 14.10. The Laffer curve. The Laffer curve shows how total tax revenue varies as the tax rate changes.

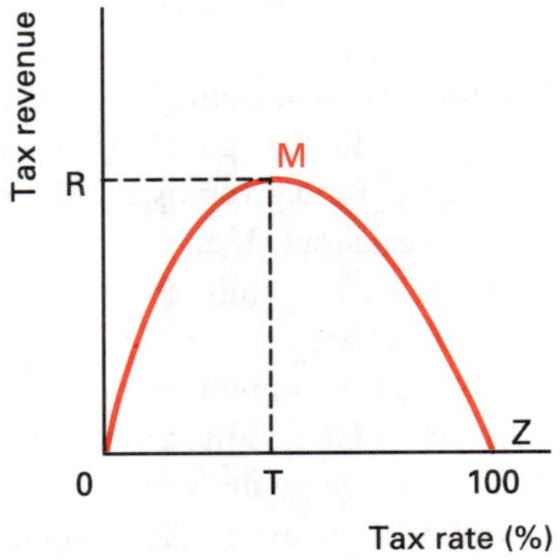

concerned. But now consider Fig. 14.9(b) where the individual has a different preference pattern between income and leisure. In this case, the direct tax induces the individual to offer *more* hours work (H_1B hours as opposed to HB).

Either outcome is possible. Of course, not all workers have much choice about the number of hours of work they can offer. Where there are 'rigidities' in the labour market so that the number of hours worked is institutionally determined and therefore fixed for an individual, an increase in direct taxes, which has a disincentive effect, may cause the individual to work less hard for the same number of hours.

Laffer curve *A curve which depicts the relationship between different income tax rates and the resultant amount of total tax revenue*

Laffer curve If direct taxation does have a disincentive effect which actually reduces the number of hours worked, this will clearly have implications for the value of national output. Higher rates of direct taxation in this case will result in a lower national income. There will also be implications for the amount of tax revenue raised by different tax rates. Suppose, for example, that a government wishes to raise all its revenues from a tax on personal incomes. Such a situation is illustrated in Fig. 14.10 which demonstrates one possible relationship between tax rates and total tax revenue.

As shown in the diagram, a zero tax rate yields zero tax revenue. In the opposite case, a 100 per cent tax rate also yields zero revenue because no one would work if all their earnings were taken away in tax. Between these two extremes, there exists a tax rate (equal to 0T in the diagram) which maximises tax revenues. The maximum revenue is 0R and the curve 0MZ is called the *Laffer curve*, named after the American economist, Professor A. Laffer.

Professor Laffer suggested that a *reduction* in United States direct tax rates would lead to an *increase* in tax revenue. This idea quickly caught on with proponents of supply-side economics. Critics, however, dispute the notion that real economies have tax rates above 0T. These critics contend that a cut in tax rates would in all probability lead to a fall in tax revenue. The backward-bending supply curve of labour implied by the inverted U-shaped Laffer curve is discussed more fully in Ch. 16.

Direct and indirect taxes

The first point to note is that the classification of taxes as *direct* or *indirect* is unsatisfactory. In the context of the British tax system, this classification is based on administrative procedures. When the payment of a tax brings the taxpayer directly into contact with the tax collector, the tax is said to be *direct*. An *indirect* tax is one whose payment does not involve the taxpayer coming directly into contact with the tax collector. Instead, the tax is paid indirectly through an intermediary who acts as a tax gatherer for the authorities.

In the United Kingdom context, income tax, corporation tax, capital gains tax and inheritance tax are the major direct taxes. But examination of the methods of tax collection shows that not all of these taxes fall neatly into the classification outlined above. For example, under the pay-as-you-earn scheme, personal income tax and national insurance contributions are deducted by employers and paid by them to the Inland Revenue. In general, direct taxes are collected by the Board of Inland Revenue.

In the United Kingdom, value-added tax and customs and excise duties are the major indirect taxes. Indirect taxes are generally collected by the Customs and Excise Department. Again, not all indirect taxes fit into the classification outlined above. The vehicle excise duty is generally paid directly to the tax authorities by the owner of the vehicle.

For the purpose of economic analysis, it may be more helpful to think of direct taxes as those which are normally paid on income earned by individuals and businesses. As the concept of direct taxes is also extended to include those on wealth and inherited assets, in this context wealth may be regarded as accumulated income.

Indirect taxes can be defined as those taxes which are paid when money is spent on goods and services. They are sometimes called *outlay* taxes. On this basis, it becomes possible to examine the relative merits and demerits of direct and indirect taxes.

Merits of direct taxes

Attaining horizontal and vertical equity It is often argued that direct taxes reflect the concept of *horizontal equity* better than indirect taxes. Since horizontal equity requires equal treatment of equivalent circumstances, taxes can be levied on individual taxpayers taking into account their personal circumstances. Thus, personal income taxation in the United Kingdom, for example, is applied to an individual's *taxable income*; this is income after deduction of reliefs and allowances. It is also claimed that direct taxes can meet the criteria of *vertical equity*. To redistribute income and wealth, successively higher tax rates can be applied to higher income groups to achieve a degree of progressivity in the tax system.

Low tax avoidance Furthermore, since people generally have to earn a living, they normally incur an unavoidable tax liability when income is earned. Thus, tax avoidance is low in a regime of direct taxes. The formal and effective incidence of a tax is on the same person as the burden of a direct tax cannot be easily shifted forward or backward. A typical worker, for example, cannot shift the tax burden resulting from an income tax on his or her earnings. Note that tax avoidance is the term used to describe legal methods of trying to reduce one's tax bill.

Demerits of direct taxes

Disincentive effects Personal income tax may act as a disincentive to extra hours of work, as shown in Fig. 14.9(a) above. A steeply progressive tax structure may cause a strong disincentive to work. The Laffer curve, illustrated in Fig. 14.10 above, may act as a warning to the tax authorities as to the extent to which they can introduce progressivity in personal taxation.

It is often claimed that high marginal rates of personal income tax may discourage labour mobility and enterprise. Steeply progressive rates of inheritance tax may have similar adverse effects on enterprise and capital accumulation.

Encourage tax evasion It is also claimed that high direct taxes tend to encourage the development of the 'black economy'. The higher the tax rate, the greater is the incentive for tax evasion, and hence, the larger the black economy. Tax evasion is the term used to describe illegal methods of trying to reduce one's tax bill.

Merits of indirect taxes

Less painful for taxpayers Because the effective incidence of most indirect taxes is shifted forward to consumers, these taxes are less transparent as they are included in prices. It is sometimes claimed that hidden taxes inflict less pain on taxpayers. Some taxpayers may suffer from a kind of 'tax illusion' in that they resent handing over part of their income directly to the tax collector. But they may experience a smaller loss of utility in paying the same amount of money in indirect tax to a trader. Such a belief would display a degree of illogicality on the part of the taxpayer.

Increased choice It can be argued that an indirect tax allows an individual the choice of whether or not to pay the tax by choosing whether or not to consume the taxed commodity. There may be a degree of choice for an individual confronted with a particular purchasing decision. But for the community as a whole, if a specific sum of taxation has to be raised, there can be no real choice as to whether to pay the tax or not. Indeed, one of the features of modern indirect taxes, such as value added tax, is that they are levied on a comprehensive range of commodities.

Take account of externalities A government can apply indirect taxes selectively both to commodities and factor services to take account of externalities. Examples include the British government's heavy tax on leaded petrol as an anti-pollution measure. Cigarettes are also taxed heavily in many countries on health grounds. By such means, governments are able to influence the allocation of resources.

Demerits of indirect taxes

Equity considerations Indirect taxes may violate the concept of vertical equity in taxation. This is because both rich and poor taxpayers pay the same rates of tax regardless of differences in their respective 'abilities to pay'.

Table 14.1 Indirect taxes as percentage of disposable income per household, 1989.

Quintile group of households ranked by disposable income	Total Indirect Taxes (Percentage of disposable income)
Bottom fifth	29.9
Next fifth	24.4
Middle fifth	21.8
Next fifth	20.3
Top fifth	15.5

Source: CSO, *Economic Trends*, Jan. 1992.

Table 14.2 Taxes[1] and social security contributions as a percent of GDP in the United Kingdom.

Per cent of total GDP	1987-88	1990-91	1991-92	1992-93 (estimate)
Total taxes[1] and social security contributions	$38\frac{1}{4}$	$36\frac{3}{4}$	36	$34\frac{1}{2}$
of which:				
Income tax	$9\frac{3}{4}$	10	10	$9\frac{1}{4}$
Corporation tax	$3\frac{3}{4}$	$3\frac{3}{4}$	$3\frac{1}{4}$	$2\frac{1}{2}$
VAT	$5\frac{3}{4}$	$5\frac{1}{2}$	$6\frac{1}{4}$	$6\frac{1}{4}$
Excise duties[2]	$4\frac{1}{2}$	4	$4\frac{1}{4}$	$4\frac{1}{4}$
Social security contributions	7	$6\frac{1}{2}$	$6\frac{1}{4}$	$6\frac{1}{4}$
Community charge/council tax and rates	4	$4\frac{1}{4}$	$3\frac{1}{2}$	$3\frac{1}{2}$

Source: Financial statement and budget report, March 1993.
[1] *National accounts definitions, including community charge/council tax.*
[2] *Including vehicle excise duty.*

Low-income groups in society have a higher propensity to consume than high-income groups. Thus, low-income groups bear proportionately a greater burden of indirect taxes in the sense that indirect tax payments comprise a larger percentage of a low-income household's disposable income than that of a high-income household. In other words, indirect taxes tend to be regressive. This is confirmed by the Central Statistical Office figures derived from the 1989 Family Expenditure Survey, shown in Table 14.1.

Notwithstanding the foregoing discussion, in the long run it is doubtful whether there exists a genuine, sustainable distinction between the impact of direct and indirect taxes. In the final analysis, taxes (whether levied on income, wealth or expenditure) are paid by people. Because the effective incidence of taxes may be partially or entirely shifted forward or backward, the determination of the final tax burden borne by a particular group of people is an exceedingly complex matter.

The structure of taxation in the United Kingdom

In the United Kingdom, as in other countries, the tax system is a mixture of direct and indirect taxes. As mentioned above, the main direct taxes are personal income tax, corporation tax, capital gains tax and inheritance tax. The indirect (or outlay) taxes are imposed on goods and services and take the form of value-added tax, customs and excise duties, petrol and oil taxes, betting tax and local taxes.

If we look at the relative contributions of direct and indirect taxes to total tax receipts, we see that direct taxation has always been the major contributor in the United Kingdom. For instance, as shown in Table 14.2, in the financial year 1992–3, direct taxes accounted for 18 per cent of GDP and indirect taxes accounted for 14 per cent of GDP.

In general, the smaller share of indirect taxes may be justified on equity grounds since some of these taxes are levied at flat rates and so are normally regressive. They fail to take into account the personal circumstances or taxable capacities of taxpayers. The larger share of direct taxes, on the other hand, may be justified on the grounds that these taxes reflect the ability-to-pay principle and have enabled the authorities to introduce a certain degree of progression into the tax system.

We turn now to a brief description of the major direct and indirect taxes in the United Kingdom.

Direct taxes

Personal income tax In the United Kingdom, personal income tax applies to taxable income bands. Taxable incomes are calculated net of reliefs and allowances under Schedule E if tax is payable under the pay-as-you-earn scheme, and under Schedule D for self-employed workers. Schedule D is more generous in terms of reliefs and allowances than Schedule E.

Corporation tax This was introduced in 1966 and is levied on the whole of a company's profits net of interest payments and depreciation allowances. Since 1973, the imputation form of corporation tax has been introduced. In this, tax is payable in two parts: (a) advance corporation tax; and (b) mainstream corporation tax. The combined payments add up to the standard rate of taxable profits, but partial relief is given to shareholders against their personal income tax liability.

Capital gains tax The Finance Act of 1965 introduced a comprehensive capital gains tax which applies to gains accruing from the sale of assets, including gifts and trusts. The tax is payable when assets are disposed of and not when gains actually accrue. Since the coming into force of independent taxation in 1990, husband and wife are able to claim a separate capital gains tax allowance. Important exemptions from capital gains tax include owner-occupied houses, national savings certificates, life assurance policies, betting winnings, gifts to charities and government securities.

Inheritance tax The Finance Act of 1975 introduced capital transfer tax to replace estate duty which, under certain circumstances, could be avoided by gifts and bequests. The tax applied at a progressive rate to the capital values of property. The tax rates on death were steeper than those on life-time transfers. A most important exemption was transfer of property between husband and wife during their life-time or at death.

In the 1986 budget, capital transfer tax was replaced by an inheritance tax. This tax is applied to bequests and life-time gifts into discretionary trusts. The exemption limit is set at £150,000 at the time of writing and is normally increased annually in line with inflation.

Indirect taxes

Value-added tax Value-added tax was introduced in 1973 to replace purchase tax and selective employment tax. It can be described as a tax levied on businesses at every stage of production and distribution on the value they add to their purchases of raw materials, fuels and capital goods. It can, therefore, be regarded as a general *turnover* tax on consumption.

To show how it can be calculated, let VA denote value-added, Q the value of output and I the value of inputs (that is, intermediate goods and capital goods). We can write:

$$VA = Q - I$$

Each firm has to calculate its gross tax by applying the appropriate tax rate to its total sales and against this set the tax already paid by supplying firms. This is facilitated by the 'invoice method' which compels each buying firm to insist on the presentation of tax receipts made out to the previous suppliers. The tax applies to a wide range of goods and services, including imported goods but not imported services. Its comprehensive coverage minimises the distortion of choices – that is, it has substantially neutral effects on relative prices. Its wide coverage also means that there is only limited scope for substitution of non-taxed goods and this makes it possible for businesses to shift the tax forward to final consumers.

At the time of writing, the rate of value-added tax is 17.5 per cent. In addition, some goods are zero-rated and others are exempt. The former are those goods which are basic essentials (such as bread, milk, fresh food, new houses, books and children's clothes) and all exports: on these goods, complete tax relief is given and any tax paid on supplies is refunded. The exempt category includes traders with an annual turnover of £37,600 or less at the time of writing and all banking, insurance and stock-broking firms: businesses in this category do not have to charge value-added tax, but they are not entitled to a refund of tax paid on supplies obtained from other firms.

Customs and excise duties Customs duties (or tariffs) are imposed on certain imported goods from all countries. Note, however, that all trade with EC countries is tariff-free and certain preferential rates apply to some products imported from Commonwealth and certain less developed countries. Excise duties are generally imposed on goods which are not subject to value-added tax: in particular, goods such as tobacco, beers, wines and spirits are affected.

International comparisons of taxation

International comparisons of the form of taxation and the composition of tax revenues reflect differences between countries as to the extent to which the governments of these countries carry out:

(a) the allocation and distribution functions; and

(b) the macroeconomic objectives considered in Ch. 11. Hence such comparisons are an indication of the degree of government involvement in the level of provision of 'pure' public goods and 'mixed' goods.

Inspection of the data in Table 14.3 suggests that there is no uniform pattern in the sources of tax revenues between countries. The marked differences in the percentage of tax-take from alternative sources reflect different interpretations of the ability-to-pay principle of taxation in these countries. Considering taxes on household income (excluding social security contributions), of all EC countries, France raised the lowest share of total tax revenues from this source (around 14 per cent in 1991).

Table 14.3 Sources of tax revenue as a percentage of total tax revenue: selected OECD countries 1991.

	Taxes on household income	Taxes on corporate income	Property taxes	Social security contributions	Goods and services
United States	36	7	11	29	16
Japan	27	21	9	29	13
Netherlands	26	7	4	37	25
Germany	29	5	3	34	29
Belgium	32	6	0	34	27
France	14	4	6	44	27
Italy	22	4	4	32	27
United Kingdom	29	10	8	18	32
Denmark	53	4	4	3	33
Sweden	33	2	3	29	28

Percentages for a given country may not sum to 100 because of incomplete coverage.
Source: Lloyds Bank Economic Bulletin, March 1993.

Notice also that within the EC countries reported in Table 14.3, the United Kingdom claimed the lowest share of the total tax-take from the combined sources of taxes on income and social security contributions. It can also be seen that compared with other member countries, the United Kingdom and Denmark have the heaviest reliance on taxes on goods and services. Taxing spending relatively more than taxing incomes may be criticised on the grounds that the United Kingdom government is relatively less concerned with its distribution function. In recent years, increased attention has been paid by the United Kingdom government to the disincentive effects of direct taxes. Consequently, in the 1980s, the United Kingdom experienced a marked shift in the distribution of the tax burden from direct to indirect taxation.

User charges

User charge *The sum which an individual pays for goods and services provided by the public sector according to usage*

Broadly, the term user charge refers to the price charged to an individual user of a facility provided by the public sector and has its origin in the benefit principle of taxation. User charges, then, are an alternative to taxation as a means of financing public spending.

Supporters of user charges maintain that, according to the benefit principle, it is inequitable to raise taxes to finance those public services which benefit identifiable groups. Such services may include education, health services, water supply, civic amenities, sewage disposal, social work and council housing. The supporters go on to allege that governments, local authorities and other public bodies are encouraged to oversupply 'high cost' social services at almost zero prices. In the absence of a price, there is no effective constraint on demand so that queueing, delays, staff shortages and a general deterioration in the standards of these facilities may result. As an example, consider the National Health Service in the United Kingdom: it is argued by some that tax-financed medicine is less efficient than market-financed medicine since only market-financed medicine reflects the true choices of consumers – tax-financed medicine may result in the overconsumption of particular medical services because the consumer-patient does not take into account the full costs of supply.

The main arguments against applying user charges in the fields of education and health are as follows:

(a) The demand for these services may become elastic if high charges are imposed; individuals may find themselves in the onerous position of having to choose between their own health and their children's education.

(b) As far as the National Health Service is concerned, the costs of administering charges may exceed the revenues.

(c) Some medical and educational expenditures are wealth-producing for the economy as a whole; for example, they help to create a healthy and educated labour force. Also, medical expendituure on infectious diseases must be tax-financed because of externalities.

(d) Free education and medical care may be justified on equity grounds as a means of redistributing income and wealth.

Other sources of public sector finance

It is possible for a government to spend more than its tax receipts, covering the resulting *deficit* by borrowing. In the postwar years, loan finance has become one of the major instruments which governments use in connection with their micro- and macroeconomic objectives. This is a marked departure from the classical view that the government's budget should be balanced.

Borrowing

National debt *The total sum of government indebtedness accumulated over a period of time*

Public sector borrowing involves an issue by the government of some sort of security (for example, a treasury bill, a gilt-edged security or a consol). The total amount of securities issued is called the national debt. In the United Kingdom, the national debt dates back to 1694 when the Bank of England was established to lend money to the government to wage war against France. In fact, government borrowing over the centuries has been mainly associated with war finance. Borrowing to finance government expenditure for other purposes has been largely a postwar phenomenon.

There is a popular misconception that government borrowing increases the national debt and therefore 'impoverishes' the nation. But if the debt is *internal*, so that the holders of the government securities are the country's own citizens, then increasing the debt is unlikely to have a significant effect on economic welfare. One effect will be to change the distribution of income as interest payments on the debt are financed from taxation. Another effect may be to reduce the availability of funds for the private sector, but this will only result in a welfare loss if the return on the funds used in the private sector is greater than in the public sector. If the loan is *external*, there is a potential loss of social welfare because then its repayment and interest charges mean that society has to consume less than it has produced. Even so, if external borrowing is used to create assets which expand the economy's productive capacity, then in the long-run, there may be a gain rather than a loss of social welfare.

From the standpoint of equity, if larger government borrowing means less taxation, then it depends upon whether it is direct or indirect taxes which are reduced. Assuming that indirect taxes are regressive and direct taxes progressive, a reduction in indirect taxes will benefit the poor while a reduction in direct taxes will benefit the rich. The financing of interest payments from taxation, however, will represent a transfer of purchasing power from all taxpayers to the richer members of society who own the securities. This effect will be reduced if some part of the interest payments are themselves financed from borrowing.

Finally, government borrowing may be more inflationary than tax finance. This is because, as we see in Ch. 19, raising taxes has the effect of reducing disposable incomes and so curbs consumption spending which offsets to some extent the rise in government spending. Financing government spending by borrowing does not have this offsetting effect.

Printing money

This method of financing public expenditure is as old as a country's central bank – in the case of the United Kingdom, the Bank of England. It has all the characteristics of loan finance discussed above. The issue department of the central bank is in charge of note issue in exchange for government securities which earn interest. Thus, any increase in note issue means an equal increase in the stock of government securities at the issue department. This apparently painless method of finance has ruined many governments in the past through over-issue of notes resulting in a loss of public confidence in the currency in question and serious inflationary consequences. A judicious use of the government's power to print money is necessary for the nation's financial stability.

Summary

1. Governments raise revenue from several sources, such as taxes, borrowing, printing money and user charges. Taxes usually constitute by far the largest source of government finance.
2. Taxes are compulsory contributions to government finances for which taxpayers are unable to claim direct benefits.
3. An underlying principle of most tax systems is equity. This may be achieved by applying either the benefit principle or the ability-to-pay principle.
4. The effective incidence of a tax refers to the final resting place of the tax after all agents have adjusted their economic behaviour in respect of hours of work, spending, saving and investment.
5. The imposition of a tax may result in a misallocation of resources. The resource misallocation cost is referred to as the *excess burden* or *deadweight loss*. A tax may also cause disincentives to effort.
6. Of the other sources of finance, government borrowing has become an important source of revenue for many developed and developing countries. Government borrowing adds to the national debt which has to be serviced through interest payments.

Exercises

1. Review your understanding of the following terms:

taxation	equality of sacrifice
ad valorem tax	'neutral' taxes
specific tax	income-based tax
proportional tax	wealth-based tax
progressive tax	expenditure-based tax
regressive tax	formal incidence
average tax rate	effective incidence
marginal tax rate	excess burden
benefit principle	Laffer curve
ability-to-pay principle	user charges
horizontal equity	direct tax
vertical equity	indirect tax

2. An individual's income rises from £5,000 to £5,200. Calculate the individual's marginal tax rate and original and final average tax rate if the amount of tax the individual pays changes: (a) from £1,000 to £1,050; (b) from £500 to £510; (c) from £1,000 to £1,250; (d) from £2,500 to £2,600. Comment on the relationship between the marginal and average rates of tax in these examples.

3. What principles should govern the design of an efficient and equitable tax system in a country?

4. Consider the view that the most efficient way to increase government revenue is to increase the rate of income tax rather than to increase the rate of tax on spending.

5. In what ways might wealth be regarded as superior to income as a measure of ability to pay?

6. Discuss the advantages and disadvantages of financing government expenditure by: (a) taxation; (b) borrowing; (c) printing money; and (d) user charges.

7.** Distinguish between the various kinds of taxes imposed by governments and explain why governments impose taxes.

15 ISSUES OF PUBLIC POLICY

Learning objectives

After reading this chapter, you should be able to:

- define the meaning of the term 'negative public policy' and trace the evolution of competition policy in the United Kingdom and the EC
- define the meaning of the term 'positive public policy' and consider whether public money should be given to private firms
- explain why some firms are taken into public ownership
- analyse the pricing and investment policies of nationalised industries
- evaluate the case for and against the policy of privatisation

Introduction

The purpose of this final chapter on the public sector is to consider some selected elements of government policy towards: (a) firms and industry in the private sector and (b) the nationalised industries.

One of the aims of the public sector's policies towards the private sector is to improve allocative efficiency. In Ch. 9, we showed that perfect competition with no externalities ensures economic efficiency because firms equate their prices with marginal costs. In contrast, we saw in Ch. 10 that monopolies and firms in other imperfect market structures, such as oligopoly, normally fail to equate prices with marginal costs and so create a misallocation of resources. Such imperfect market structures may therefore adversely affect society's welfare.

In addition to imperfect markets for goods, there are imperfect markets for the nation's resources of labour, capital and land. Also, the rules governing the tendering for government contracts (such as defence contracts and contracts from medical supplies) are not always competitive in practice. We propose in the first part of this chapter to focus attention on the legal regulation of markets for goods and services (called *negative public policy*). Secondly, we consider those measures designed to encourage firms, through financial assistance, voluntarily to change their present and future investment and output decisions (called *positive public policy*). Thirdly, we examine the pricing and investment policies of nationalised industries. Finally, we assess the industrial policy of 'privatisation'.

Negative public policy

By the phrase negative public policy, we mean that set of government measures which is intended: (a) to promote competition and (b) to control monopolies, mergers and restrictive practices. Such measures have developed at a time when concern has

Negative public policy
Those measures introduced by a government designed to prevent the abuse of market power

been expressed about the level of aggregate concentration in British manufacturing. The share of the 100 largest manufacturing firms in Britain, measured in terms of net output, rose from around 25 per cent in 1939 to around 40 per cent by the late 1960s. But from 1978 to 1984, there was a slight decline in the level of aggregate concentration.

It is noteworthy that postwar competition policy in Britain has been built step by step through a series of Acts of Parliament. There has thus been no consistent general policy to promote competition. There has, though, been a presumption that competition is 'good' and monopoly is 'bad'. Assuming that the utility-maximising consumer is the best judge of his or her own interests, competition policy can broadly claim the following benefits to the community:

(a) greater economic efficiency;
(b) wider consumers' choices;
(c) an improved system of information about prices in the markets for goods;
(d) greater incentives to innovate and to develop new products and processes.

However, if we accept that the individual is not always the best judge of his or her own interests, then it is possible to argue that monopolies are not 'bad' *per se*. Indeed, some private sector monopolies and conglomerates may be allowed to operate because they confer special benefits which competition is unable to provide. In the same way, some public sector monopolies, such as the gas, electricity, health and education sectors in some countries, may be justified on the grounds that the private individual's interests do not always coincide with the interests of society. As a result, state monopolies may increase society's welfare whilst competition, if permitted in these spheres, may reduce social welfare.

We discussed the main possible advantages and disadvantages of monopolies in Ch. 10. Recall that advantages might accrue from the monopolist's ability *to reduce costs by benefiting from economies of single ownership* and *to undertake extensive research and development*. The main disadvantages are that the monopolist is likely to set a *higher price* and produce a *lower output* than would be the case under competition and may be able to maintain *above-normal profits in the long-run* because of barriers to the entry of new firms.

Evolution of the control of monopolies, mergers and restrictive practices

In its negative aspect, British government policy is characterised by a series of anti-monopoly legislation designed to curb the disadvantages of monopolies and mergers. The major provisions of some of the more notable Acts of Parliament are outlined below.

The Monopolies and Restrictive Practices (Inquiry and Control) Act 1948 This was the first piece of legislation to encourage competition and curb monopoly in the United Kingdom. The Act established a Monopolies Commission charged with the responsibility for *investigating* and *reporting* on monopoly situations. The Commission was required to determine whether or not a particular monopoly was in the 'public interest'. The Act defined a monopoly as a single firm or group of linked firms controlling one third or more of the market. In course of time, the Commission focused attention on the *market behaviour* of firms more than the *structure*. It found evidence to show that collective restrictive practices were widespread in British industry and this led to the enactment of legislation intended to curb such agreements in 1956.

Restrictive trade practice *An agreement between two or more firms relating to such matters as prices, market sharing and types of goods produced*

The Restrictive Trade Practices Act 1956 This established the Restrictive Practices Court charged with the responsibility for supervising agreements between firms and determining whether or not such agreements were contrary to the public interest. The Act required firms to register restrictive agreements between two or more firms carrying on business in the production or supply of goods. In particular, the agreements required to be registered included the following: (a) those in which the parties accepted restrictions in respect of the prices to be charged or the terms and conditions of sale; (b) those in which the parties accepted restrictions in respect of the quantities or types of goods to be produced or the persons or areas to be supplied.

It can be noted that the major emphasis of the Act is on the behaviour of firms. However, the Act did specify some 'gateways' on the basis of which the parties could justify to the Court the continuation of an agreement. According to these gateways, an agreement may be upheld if it can be shown that:

1. The agreement is necessary to protect the public against injury;
2. Removal of the restriction would result in the loss of specific and substantial benefits to the public;
3. The restriction is necessary against a person or firm not party to the agreement trying to restrict competition;
4. The restriction is necessary to negotiate reasonable and fair terms with another supplier or buyer;
5. Removal of the restriction would result in higher unemployment in areas where the industry in question is heavily concentrated;
6. Removal of the restriction would cause a substantial loss of exports;
7. The restriction is necessary to support some other agreement which the Court finds acceptable.

The Restrictive Trade Practices Act 1968 added an eighth gateway: that an agreement may be acceptable if it does not restrict competition. It should be emphasised that even if an agreement can be shown to satisfy one of the gateway conditions, the Court still has to be convinced that the benefits of the agreement outweigh its disadvantages. The most important cases heard by the Court have been allowed under gateways (2) and (5). For instance, in 1961, the Court accepted the argument of the Cement Makers Federation under gateway (2) that an agreement which restricted competition reduced the risks facing its members and so enabled them to charge lower prices: in making this decision, the Court took into account the efficient performance of the industry prior to the investigation. In 1959, the Court also accepted the arguments of the Yarn Spinners Association under gateway (5), but refused to uphold the agreement after taking into consideration the industry's inefficient performance.

It is interesting that many of the agreements that were registered were in fact voluntarily abandoned or modified. Few agreements actually came before the Court and of these less than a third were upheld.

The Resale Prices Act 1964 The 1956 Act banned collective resale price maintenance (RPM), but made individual RPM legally enforceable. This in turn had

Resale price maintenance
The attempt by producers to lay down prices charged by retailers

adverse effects on the growth of multiple retailers, who were keen to reduce prices in order to achieve a higher volume of turnover. The Resale Prices Act 1964 was, therefore, passed to ban individual RPM in all forms unless the firm could justify it to the Restrictive Practices Court. RPM could be maintained where its abandonment would result in: (a) loss of quality; (b) a substantial reduction in the number of shops; (c) price increases in the long-run; (d) loss of necessary service; (e) danger to health. Even if allowed on any of these grounds, the firm had to show further that the advantages of RPM were in excess of its disadvantages. In course of time, only publishers of books and maps and some manufacturers of drugs and medicines were able to satisfy the Court in this respect.

The Monopolies and Mergers Act 1965 This was passed to deal with the rising industrial concentration caused by mergers and take-overs. The Act gave power to the then Board of Trade to scrutinise and, if thought fit, refer to the Monopolies Commission two categories of mergers: those in which the assets to be acquired exceeded £5 million (£30 million from 1984) and those which created or strengthened a monopoly. The Act also empowered the Monopolies Commission to investigate monopolies in *service* industries.

The Fair Trading Act 1973 This Act created the Office of the Director-General of Fair Trading (DG) with wide powers to protect consumers' interests and to maintain supervision over and to collect information on all types of trading practices in relation to the supply of goods and services.

The Act had the following main provisions:

1. It changed the definition of a monopoly from a firm or group of linked firms controlling one-third of the home market to a firm or group of linked firms controlling *one-quarter* of the home market.

2. The DG was given wide powers to refer monopolies to the renamed Monopolies and Mergers Commission (MMC). However, the minister responsible for prices and consumer protection may also initiate a reference to the Commission. Merger references, though, could only be made by the minister.

3. The provisions of the 1956 Act were extended to cover firms supplying services, such as hairdressers, estate agents and travel agents, requiring them to register their agreements relating to prices, persons and areas with the Office of Fair Trading (OFT).

4. The DG may refer a registered agreement, if considered to be in restraint of competition, to the Restrictive Practices Court for adjudication.

5. The DG can receive complaints from the public and investigates any alleged business malpractices.

The Competition Act 1980 This Act abolished the Price Commission set up by the Labour government. It gave power to the Secretary of State to refer any price or pricing policy causing public concern to the DG for investigation. Also, the Act enabled the DG to investigate the *anti-competitive practices* of single firms, such as a refusal to supply, tie-in sales, full-line forcing and rental-only contracts. An important aim of the Act was to extend the investigation of monopoly situations to certain public sector firms. It enabled the Monopolies and Mergers Commission to enquire into the efficiency of nationalised industries.

EC competition policy

Articles 85 and 86 of the Treaty of Rome set out the regulations for tackling monopolies and restrictive practices within the EC context. The European Commission is responsible for ensuring adherence to the regulations and for investigating alleged transgressions.

The regulations relating to restrictive practices prohibit, under Article 85, all agreements that prevent, restrict or distort competition in the EC and extend over more than one country. Examples include agreements to fix prices, share out markets or to limit production. There are, however, provisions for exemption if it can be shown that such a restrictive agreement improves production or distribution, or promotes progress.

Article 86 bans 'abuses of dominant position' by firms or groups of firms if such abuses affect trade between member states. Such abuses of monopoly power might include the imposition of excessive prices on consumers, price discrimination or attaching extra obligations to contracts.

Government subsidies that distort or threaten to distort competition are outlawed by Articles 92–94 of the Treaty of Rome. Again, certain exemptions are applied, such as aid to depressed regions. Member states are required to notify the European Commission of any planned subsidies. The Commission then decides if the planned aid can be exempted from the Treaty rules.

Regulation of mergers In 1990 a system of regulating merger activity in the EC was introduced. The European Commission has to be notified of any proposed merger involving companies with a combined annual turnover of more than 5 billion Ecu and where each company has annual sales in the EC of more than 250 million Ecu. Such mergers will be disallowed if they create or strengthen a dominant market position.

The Commission made a final decision on sixty cases of notified mergers in 1991, for example. Of these, only one was disallowed, namely the proposed acquisition of DeHavilland by ATR, a manufacturer of turbo-prop aircraft jointly owned by Aerospatiale of France and Alenia of Italy. The proposed acquisition would have given the enlarged company sixty-seven per cent of the EC market for 40–70 seat commuter aircraft.

An example of action taken by the European Commission under Article 86 relates to the supply of right-hand-drive cars on the Continent. In general, new car prices in the United Kingdom in the early 1980s were significantly higher than in West Germany or Belgium. Consequently, a growing number of British purchasers ordered right-hand-drive cars in West Germany and Belgium with the intention of importing them into the United Kingdom. There was evidence that manufacturers, including Ford AG of West Germany, were refusing to supply right-hand-drive cars on the Continent. The European Commission and, after an appeal, the European Court of Justice, instructed Ford AG to supply right-hand-drive cars when ordered in West Germany.

Another example of Commission activity is the imposition in 1980 of fines against Pioneer, a Japanese producer of hi-fi equipment, and three of its distributors. These companies sought to maintain the relatively high prices charged in France by preventing Pioneer products from being imported from other EC countries where prices were lower. Despite an appeal, these fines were upheld by the European Court of Justice in 1983.

Assessment of negative public policy in the United Kingdom

Monopoly If the DG receives a complaint or suspects that a monopolist, with a market share of 25 per cent or more, is abusing its market power, the DG may make a reference to the MMC. In judging whether or not the monopolist is abusing its position, the MMC applies the criterion of the *public interest*. Under the Fair Trading Act (1973), the MMC is required to have regard to, among other things: the desirability of maintaining and promoting competition; the prices, quality and variety of goods and services; the desirability of promoting the use of new techniques, new products and the entry of new competitors into existing markets.

The MMC makes a judgement on a case-by-case basis. In some cases, it concludes *in favour* of a monopolist. In 1991, the MMC decided that Nestlé's technical monopoly in the instant coffee market was not expected to operate against the public interest because there was plenty of competition in the market. Nestlé was found to have a 50 per cent share of the United Kingdom market for instant coffee, a result of its development of successful products and brands that consumers regarded as good value for money. But the MMC found that own-brands from supermarkets provided effective competition, in addition to the branded products of Kraft General Foods and Brooke Bond.

Complex monopoly *A situation in which a group of producers act in concert with the result that they hold monopoly power*

In other cases, the MMC concludes that the monopoly situation is operating *against* the public interest. This was the case in the MMC's report on the supply of beer, published in 1989. This was a complex monopoly where a group of brewers dominated the market for beer in the United Kingdom, controlling around 75 per cent of production. The six major brewers also controlled most retail outlets through their ownership of public houses. The MMC recommended that each brewer should have to sell off their public houses in excess of 2,000. The government eventually decided that a brewer should either have to sell off or lease out half of the public houses in excess of 2,000. The resulting shake-up of the beer market precipitated a degree of turmoil as the big brewers tried to protect their positions. Overall, critics argued, the changes did not benefit customers in terms of increased choice or lower prices.

Mergers Governments are concerned with mergers as they may create firms with excessive market power which may give firms the ability to raise prices or to exploit consumers in other ways. Vertical mergers between firms at different stages of the production process may make it difficult for other suppliers to find outlets. If a brewery takes over a chain of public houses or bars, for example, other brewers may be excluded from selling their products in those outlets.

On the other hand, mergers may result in *benefits*, such as the attainment of economies of scale and scope, or the replacement of an inefficient management. Thus, in order to make a judgement about whether a proposed merger is against the public interest, the prospective benefits and costs must be evaluated carefully.

In the United Kingdom, the Office of Fair Trading (OFT) examines mergers and decides whether or not they qualify for investigation on grounds of size or market share. If a proposed merger does qualify, the OFT identifies the main issues in each case which affect competition, and to a lesser extent, other relevant public interest issues. The OFT also allows requests for confidential guidance on a proposed merger, as a result of which the companies concerned can agree undertakings with the OFT to remove the anti-competitive effects of the merger. A company seeking to take over a rival, for example, may agree to sell some of the rival's brands to other firms to maintain competition.

The Secretary of State has the power to refer proposed mergers to the MMC for investigation. The minister normally follows the advice of the DG in such cases. On occasion, however, the minister may decline to follow the DG's advice that a merger reference is desirable.

The MMC investigates a proposed merger in order to determine whether or not the merger is likely to be against the public interest. After the initial screening of mergers by the DG, in fact, only a small proportion of the qualifying mergers are investigated by the MMC. The MMC publishes its recommendations in a report which it presents to the Secretary of State who then has to decide whether or not to accept them.

There are three main possible outcomes to a merger investigation.

(a) *A merger may be allowed to proceed unconditionally.* This might be the case where a merger would result in only an insignificant reduction in competition, or where a merger would create a more powerful unit that could compete more effectively with other, well-established firms.

(b) *A merger may be allowed to proceed subject to certain conditions.* This applied, for example, when British Airways took over British Caledonian in 1987. The takeover was allowed to proceed subject to British Airways giving up several routes to smaller rivals.

(c) *A merger may be judged to be against the public interest.* This was the MMC's recommendation in 1991 on the proposed merger between Tate and Lyle and British Sugar. The minister accepted the MMC's recommendation. Between them, the two companies accounted for more than 90 per cent of the market for sugar in the United Kingdom.

Restrictive trade practices The OFT is responsible for considering commercial agreements, the details of which have been supplied for registration. If considered necessary, the OFT refers the agreements to the Restrictive Practices Court. Such agreements are lawful and may be adhered to unless and until the court strikes them down. The OFT also attempts to uncover agreements that have been made in secret and whose operation is unlawful. When such secret agreements are uncovered, they are also referred to the Restrictive Practices Court.

Between 1956 and 1991 almost 10,000 agreements were added to the register. Most agreements on the register do not, in the view of the OFT, contain restrictions of such significance for competition that they need to be considered by the court. The court can make orders requiring the parties not to enforce restrictions in the agreement, and not to make any new agreements without registering them with the

OFT. Breaches of orders are contempt of court and may lead to fines, or even to imprisonment for the individuals concerned.

While these procedures may appear sound at first glance, in practice the legislation has been regarded as unsatisfactory by the DG. This is because there is effectively no penalty for a first offence of participating in a secret agreement. Even in cases where court orders are breached, the fines are low. It is widely acknowledged that the existing legislation relating to restrictive practices is weak. A number of proposals designed to strengthen the legislation have been put forward by government for public debate.

Anti-competitive practice *A measure introduced by a single firm that places rival firms at an unfair disadvantage. Examples include refusal to supply, tie-in sales and discriminatory pricing*

Anti-competitive practices The 1980 Act was largely concerned with 'anti-competitive' practices. One example of the government's emphasis on new ways of promoting competition was the decision to allow opticians to advertise and to remove their monopoly in the supply of spectacles. In the financial sector, the DG placed the Stock Exchange's rule book before the Restrictive Practices Court, but an agreement was reached between the government and the Stock Exchange to the effect that the latter would voluntarily amend its rules, for example, to end minimum commissions and to admit new firms to the Stock Exchange.

When the Commission investigated the distribution policy of TI Raleigh in 1981 on grounds of 'anti-competitive' practices under the 1980 Act, it found that the company's practice of refusing to supply bicycles to discount stores was contrary to the Act. The Commission felt that the company's policy of only supplying bicycles to shops which offered after-sales service resulted in restricted consumer choice and kept the bicycles' prices artificially high.

In the case of the Ford Motor Company's refusal to grant licences to manufacturers of replacement car body panels in 1985, the Commission found that, although the practice was against the public interest and constituted an 'anti-competitive' practice, the company's position was protected by the copyright and design laws. Consequently, it merely recommended a change in the law to shorten the period of copyright and design protection.

Consumer protection The DG's record on consumer protection since 1973 has been impressive where the main emphasis has been on the principle of *voluntary agreements*. The DG has wide powers to collect information on trading practices thought to be detrimental to the consumer.

The DG has encouraged the setting up of *codes of practice* by trade associations. These codes cover such wide-ranging areas as package holidays, funeral services, advertising, mail-order trading and new and used car sales.

The principle of voluntary agreements has the obvious advantages of being flexible (as opposed to the rigidity of legal rules) and of being a relatively low cost way of protecting consumers' interests. Whether a code of practice will deal with the case of a 'rogue' trader who does not belong to a trade association is quite another matter.

The DG targets 'rogue' traders with warning letters. In the case of persistent bad business practices that are harmful to consumers, the DG can seek assurances from traders that they will abandon these practices. Failure to give such assurances, or a breach of such an assurance, may result in the DG obtaining a court order. The DG's work in this field has been dominated by traders in the areas of motor cars, home improvements and furnishing, and mail order. The DG has also made increasing use of publicity as a weapon against undesirable business practices. For example, in 1991, the DG obtained widespread publicity about the illusory benefits claimed in advertisements for many home-working schemes.

Positive public policy

Positive public policy
Those measures introduced by a government that seek to induce firms to change voluntarily their investment and output decisions

By the phrase positive public policy, we mean those sets of government measures which are designed to promote faster economic growth through: (a) greater economic efficiency; and (b) the restructuring of industry. In the 1970s, the term 'industrial strategy' was used in relation to the planning of key sectors of the British economy. This strategy referred, first, to those government measures concerned with providing financial assistance to private firms and secondly, to consultations between the government, the Confederation of British Industry and the trade unions as regards the key sectors of the economy.

The Industry Act of 1972 outlined the pattern for regional assistance, with a view to increasing industrial efficiency and protecting jobs. The Act also strengthened the financial help being given already to private firms under previous legislation.

The Industry Act of 1975 established the National Enterprise Board (NEB) with access to funds to enable it to acquire holdings in private firms. It took over existing government holdings in, for example, British Leyland, Rolls-Royce and Ferranti and it acquired stakes in a number of small companies. The NEB's major role was to promote investment in the key economic sectors and to encourage rationalisation into fewer but more efficient units.

A government may hold the view that desirable economic activities will normally result from the working of the market mechanism. Thus, any government assistance to alter the pattern of output will require a strong rationale. This view underlies the basic approach of the British government to industrial policy since 1979. Government financial assistance is concentrated on the following main areas: (a) research and development; (b) information technology; (c) small businesses; and (d) employment and training. Table 15.1 shows the share of funds allocated to different programmes

Table 15.1 General government expenditure on trade, industry, energy and employment, 1987-8 to 1992-3 (selected years).

	1987-88 outturn	1989-90 outturn	1991-92 outturn	£ million 1992-93 estimated outturn
Trade, industry, energy and employment				
Regional and general industrial support	684	719	582	582
Scientific and technological assistance	470	474	525	541
Support for aerospace, shipbuilding, coal, steel and vehicle manufacture	456	708	224	198
Trade and technological support	361	627	567	512
Employment	2,046	861	1,148	1,393
Training	1,390	2,296	2,099	1,996
Departmental administration and other services	695	867	1,103	1,119
Finance for public corporations	132	191	146	171
Nationalised industries' external finance	563	969	736	785
Total trade, industry, energy and employment	6,797	7,712	7,128	7,296

Source: Public Expenditure Analyses to 1995-6, HM Treasury 1993.

in recent years. In real terms, British government spending on industrial policy has declined, reflecting the stance of minimum intervention.

The return of the Conservative government in 1979 led to a considerable curtailment in the activities of the NEB under the Industry Act of 1980, the new government being committed to reducing direct government participation in industry. In 1982, the National Research and Development Corporation (set up in 1948) was merged with the NEB to form the British Technology Group and this became an instrument of the government in providing a system of financial assistance and investment incentives to firms and industries.

Recent British government policy to help small businesses is essentially part of the implementation of the recommendations of the Bolton Committee Report of 1971. The government introduced over a hundred different measures affecting small companies between 1979 and 1984 in pursuit of the government's stated aim 'to establish the conditions for a sustainable growth in output and employment'. The measures include the Business Expansion Scheme which operated from 1983 to 1993. This scheme sought to encourage investors to take up shares in both existing and new unquoted companies and offered a range of tax-relief benefits to investors. The setting up of an Unlisted Securities Market in 1980 made it much easier for potential investors to buy and sell shares in small companies.

The Loan Guarantee Scheme, introduced in 1981, represents further assistance to small firms. Under this scheme, the government encourages 'approved' banks and other financial institutions to lend to small businesses by guaranteeing a proportion of each loan.

The Business Start-up Scheme, formerly the Enterprise Allowance Scheme, is designed to encourage unemployed people to become self-employed by paying a sum in place of unemployment benefit for one year. It has, however, been suggested that up to 50 per cent of those who have benefited from the scheme intended to set up a business in any case, and for this group the subsidy may have been an incidental benefit. Estimates indicate that over 40 per cent of firms set up under the Enterprise Allowance Scheme disappear within three years of commencing trading.

EC industrial policy

A major objective of the EC is to establish a single market across all EC countries. In practice, this means harmonisation of standards and the removal of all artificial barriers to trade between countries. The Single European Act of 1986 set the target date of 1992 for the creation of an area in which there would be freedom of movement for goods, people, services and capital. The elimination of the physical, technical and fiscal barriers to trade in the EC are discussed more fully in Ch. 31.

As pointed out above, subsidies to firms by individual governments are vetted by the Commission to ensure that they do not distort competition between member states. Certain aids are permitted for specific purposes, such as assistance to depressed regions. In 1988, the Commission published a survey which showed that in 1986 about £70 billion had been handed out in government subsidies in EC countries as a whole. The Commission's view was that if these subsidies were allowed to continue, they would negate the economic benefits that could be gained from the completion of the internal market.

In a number of cases, the Commission has required the government of a member country to reduce the amount of state aid. The United Kingdom government, for example, was forced to cut by £250 million the amount of money injected into the state-owned Rover Group prior to its take-over by British Aerospace in 1988.

Why should public money be given to the private sector?

Clearly, government 'cash handouts' to private firms contradict the philosophy of competition that businesses should stand on their own feet and that 'lame ducks' should be left to market forces so that the incentive to be efficient is strengthened.

However there are several arguments in favour of state support to private firms. Consider the following:

(a) Efficiency in resource allocation requires that firms set price equal to marginal cost. However, in a *decreasing cost* industry, this will result in a loss. Efficiency may require a government subsidy to enable the industry to set price equal to marginal cost. This point is illustrated in Fig. 15.3 in the context of a decreasing cost state-owned industry.

(b) Temporary financial assistance may be justified to protect employment in an industry that would otherwise contract or close down, creating serious structural unemployment. In this way, the government will gain time to institute retraining schemes and attract new industries into the affected area. An example of government assistance was provided by the governments of the Netherlands and Belgium which gave financial aid to the Daf company (a lorry producer) in 1993 when its continued existence was threatened.

(c) If there are *externalities* present in the price system, a state subsidy may improve the market performance of firms. For instance, financial help to the British aircraft industry to develop new technology benefits other sectors of private industry, such as electronics, radar, radio and digital computing.

(d) Government financial assistance may be justified to promote exports and save imports, and to strengthen defence. All of these also confer external benefits on other firms.

(e) In less developed countries, financial support from the state may be given to help the growth and development of the private sector. Assistance may be given to *infant industries* which need some temporary aid but which, it is believed, can ultimately become self-supporting. The infant industry argument is further considered in Ch. 30 in the context of international trade policy.

There are, however, counter-arguments about the flow of public money to the private sector. Consider the following:

(a) State support to private firms has an opportunity cost in terms of the forgone benefits in alternative sectors of the economy.

(b) Financial help may encourage the growth of inefficient industries, resulting in a waste of the nation's scarce resources. Such help hinders the outflow of resources from inefficient industries into more productive ones.

(c) On the assumption that the government assistance is financed through taxation, the taxes imposed may have adverse effects on incentives.

(d) Linked with (c) is the effect of the extra taxation on the distribution of income. A redistribution from taxpayers to the owners of the subsidised firms may be judged to be socially undesirable on equity grounds.

Some critics of financial assistance to private firms believe that the market mechanism leads to an efficient allocation of resources and that, therefore, government intervention should be minimised.

Public sector firms

Public sector firm (or public corporation) *A firm that is owned and controlled by the state*

Nationalisation *The transfer of privately-owned assets into the ownership of the state*

A public sector firm may be defined as a nationalised industry. Such an industry is owned by the state and has its own board of directors which is appointed by the minister concerned. In turn, the minister is responsible to Parliament for the efficient operation of the industry.

Historically, in the United Kingdom the nationalised industries have been brought under public ownership and control during the twentieth century. For instance, the Port of London Authority was formed in 1908 and the Central Electricity Board was set up in 1926, whilst the London Passenger Transport Board was established in 1933. During the period 1945–51, a policy of nationalisation by the Labour government brought the railways, the Bank of England and the coal and gas industries into public ownership. The iron and steel industry was nationalised in 1951, denationalised by the Conservative government in 1953 and renationalised by the Labour government in 1967. As we shall see later in this chapter, a further programme of denationalisation (as part of a wider programme of 'privatisation') was commenced after 1979 by the Conservative government.

Reasons for nationalisation

Consider the following reasons for nationalisation.

Economic planning Some economists believe that planning and control of the economy is best achieved through public ownership. In some European countries and many developing countries, this has been an important factor. In the United Kingdom, though, the process of nationalisation cannot be explained solely in terms of economic planning.

Ideology In many western European countries, including the United Kingdom, the nationalisation movement gathered momentum after the Second World War. By and large, the movement seems to have been sparked off by a desire to achieve certain social and political objectives. It was increasingly believed by democratic socialists that nationalisation was an effective method of achieving the transition from capitalism to socialism.

Natural monopolies Economies of scale may result in an industry becoming a natural monopoly in which case the public interest may be best served by putting such a monopoly into public ownership rather than leaving it to private enterprise. Some state monopolies control natural resources, such as water and energy; others are sole producers of goods or services, such as postal services. If these industries were left to private enterprise, this might result in the abuse of monopoly power.

'Lame ducks' Most economists would agree that free market forces do not enable some industries to adjust themselves quickly to changes in tastes, incomes and technology. Given the public sector's macroeconomic objective of full employment, the government may decide that it is socially desirable to nationalise wholly or partly some such industries in order to protect jobs.

Investment and pricing policies of nationalised industries

A pricing policy entails setting price at a level that makes full use of the industry's productive capacity. We saw in Chs 9 and 10 that setting *price equal to marginal cost* would result in an efficient level of output, provided perfect competition prevails in the rest of the economic system with no externalities. Under these conditions, the price consumers have to pay is equal to the cost of resources employed in the production of one additional unit of output.

A 1967 White Paper in the United Kingdom introduced the principle of marginal cost pricing for nationalised industries. We may, however, distinguish between *short-run* and *long-run* marginal cost pricing. In the case of short-run marginal cost pricing, the relevant costs are the *variable* costs of labour, fuel and raw materials, and *not* the costs of capital assets which are fixed in the short-run. As an example, consider the electricity industry. Its capital assets, such as the electric power generating stations, electric cables and so on, are fixed in meeting a given demand for electricity consumption. The only costs it can vary in the short-run are the manning levels of the power stations, supplies of oil, coal, gas and water.

The rule of equating price with short-run marginal cost is illustrated in Fig. 15.1, where SMC is the industry's short-run marginal cost curve and DD is the market demand for electricity consumption. The short-run marginal cost price per unit is 0*P* and 0*Q* is the efficient output level.

It can be seen that at price 0*P*, the industry is producing that level of output at which total benefit (measured by the area under the demand curve, DD) minus total costs (measured by the area under the supply curve, SMC) is maximised. This maximum net benefit is equal to the sum of consumer surplus, *P*DE and producer surplus, H*P*E. Output 0*Q*, then, is the efficient level of output which maximises net social benefit.

However, where the price is unrelated to the costs of capital assets, as in the above analysis of short-run marginal cost pricing, the managers of a nationalised industry are left with an unresolved problem. That is, when should the industry invest in additional productive capacity? The resolution of this problem depends upon whether the existing capacity is larger or smaller than that required to meet future demand at minimum cost. The industry cannot change its capacity in the short-run,

Fig. 15.1. Short-run marginal cost pricing. The firm produces where P = SMC.

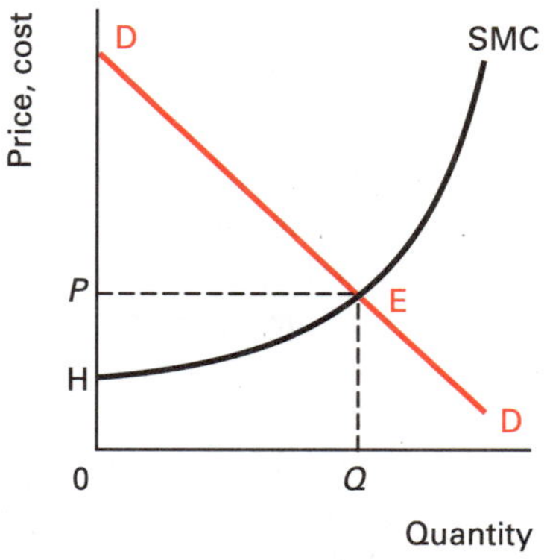

Fig. 15.2. Investment and pricing policy in a decreasing cost industry. In the long-run the firm produces output $0Q_1$ where the price $0P_1$ = SMC = LMC.

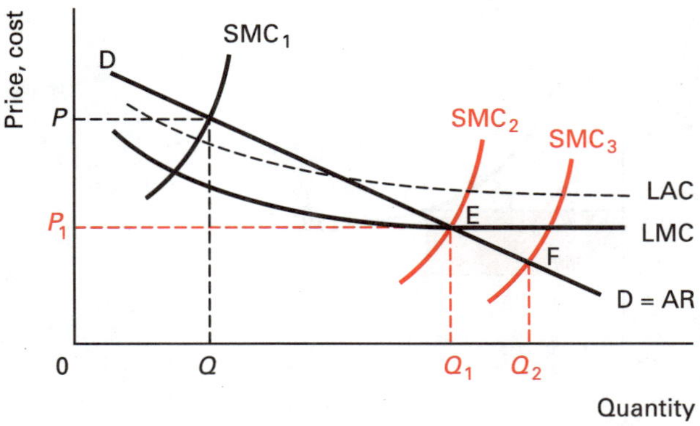

but can undoubtedly increase or decrease capacity in the long-run by changing the volume of investment.

Thus, in the long-run, marginal cost is the *cost of adding to capacity* and, from the point of view of efficiency, prices should be set equal to long-run marginal cost, rather than short-run marginal cost. This gives rise to the basic question: do the two rules (P = SMC and P = LMC) contradict each other? The answer is that they will be consistent so long as the industry is operating at its 'optimum' productive capacity – that is, that capacity at which the given demand can be satisfied at least cost. This is because *when optimum capacity is reached, then prices equal to SMC will also equal LMC*. In that case, the managers of a nationalised concern would find that the cost of increasing output by using existing capacity marginally more intensively equals the cost of expanding output by additions to capacity.

When the industry is not operating at its optimum productive capacity, the two rules will not be consistent. They can, however, be reconciled once again if a particular nationalised industry complies with the following requirement: *where SMC exceeds LMC, construct new productive capacity; where LMC exceeds SMC, cut back on investment and reduce capacity*. In both cases, the investment or disinvestment should be continued until SMC and LMC are equal.

The policy of investment and disinvestment is illustrated in Fig. 15.2 for an industry whose long-run marginal cost (LMC) and long-run average cost (LAC) are falling. DD is the market demand curve for the industry's product. Suppose that the initial position, according to the P = SMC rule, is at price $0P$ and output $0Q$. But at this price, SMC exceeds LMC. The rule outlined above requires the construction of additional capacity until SMC = LMC: that is, up to point E where price will be $0P_1$ and output $0Q_1$. Notice that now $0P_1$ = SMC = LMC, reconciling the short-run and long-run marginal cost pricing rules.

Notice that if a bigger capacity were constructed, LMC would exceed SMC and the two rules would again be inconsistent. This is the case at point F where output $0Q_2$ would be produced. This time, disinvestment and contraction of capacity would be called for.

Practical difficulties of marginal cost pricing There are several difficulties in implementing marginal cost pricing. First, the rule fails to take into account changes in demand: in particular, the demand patterns for gas, electricity, telecommunications and transport vary daily, weekly and from season to season. For example, commuter

Fig. 15.3. ***Marginal cost pricing and decreasing costs.*** By following the long-run marginal cost pricing rule, the firm makes a loss equal to the area of rectangle *P*TJE.

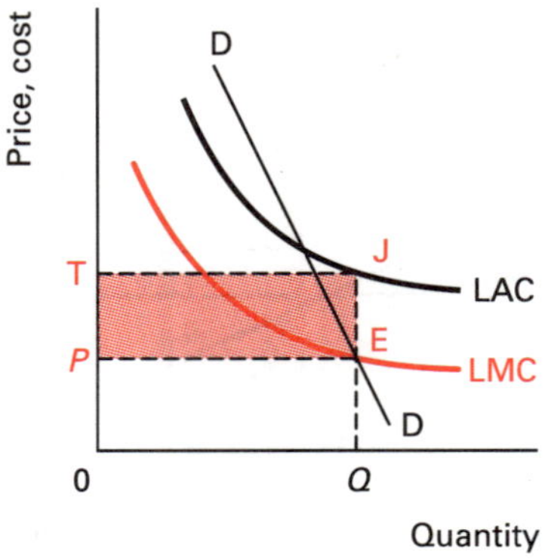

trains are crowded during rush-hours, but have few passengers during the rest of the day: at peak periods, to carry an extra passenger might require an extra train service, whilst at off-peak periods, the marginal cost of carrying an extra passenger is virtually zero. Such variations in demand make it difficult to estimate marginal cost realistically.

Secondly, in integrated systems of production, such as the electricity industry, marginal cost is exceedingly difficult to identify. For example, an increase in the price of oil which raises the marginal cost of generating electricity in oil-fired power stations by, say, 10 per cent does not enable the industry to increase price by exactly 10 per cent. This is because a single consumer, through the grid system, might be consuming electricity generated in nuclear or coal-fired power stations where marginal costs are unchanged. The problem facing the industry is to estimate the overall increase in the marginal cost of the system.

Thirdly, as shown in Fig. 15.3, marginal cost pricing may cause an industry with decreasing long-run costs to encounter financial deficits. Inspection of Fig. 15.3 shows that at price 0*P*, the enterprise sustains a total loss equal to the area *P*TJE.

The loss arises because the enterprise charges a price below long-run average cost and so is unable to generate sufficient revenues to replace worn out plant and equipment. If the deficit were financed by taxes (other than lump-sum taxes), this would distort allocative efficiency in other sectors of the economy and result in a redistribution of income from taxpayers to the consumers of the product of the nationalised industry.

Fourthly, the marginal cost pricing rule is designed to achieve Pareto efficiency in the allocation of resources in the private and public sectors of the economy. But when there are externalities or monopoly elements in the private sector, these will spoil the Pareto 'first best' conditions. Consequently, from the theory of second best, it cannot be concluded whether marginal cost pricing in the public sector will improve or worsen the allocation of resources.

In the light of the difficulties associated with calculating marginal cost, the 1978 White Paper suggested that nationalised industries should set their prices equal to *average incremental cost* (AIC). This can be regarded as an approximation of marginal cost and yet is much easier to calculate. As an example, suppose that the coal industry decides to produce 1,000,000 extra tonnes of coal per week and that this costs an additional £50 million (including the extra labour costs, interest costs and depreciation). We can write

$$AIC = \frac{\Delta TC}{\Delta Q} = \frac{50 \text{ m.}}{1,000,000} = £50$$

The coal industry should set a price of £50 per tonne. The main advantage of AIC pricing is its ease of computation. It will, of course, be closer to marginal cost pricing, the smaller is the increase in output and the nearer the industry is to constant returns to scale.

Privatisation

Privatisation *The transfer of publically-owned assets into the ownership of the private sector*

An important aspect of public policy in the United Kingdom during the 1980s and 1990s has been the large-scale privatisation of certain nationalised industries and other public sector activities. The privatisation programme was designed to achieve the government's stated objective to reduce the size and importance of the public sector in the United Kingdom economy.

Privatisation can take many forms, which include the following:

(a) Contracting out work (for example, local government services, such as refuse collection and the National Health Service laundry and catering services) to private sector firms and financing it with taxes.

(b) Disposing of public sector shareholdings in companies (for example, in ICL and BP).

(c) Denationalising major public sector concerns (such as British Telecom, Britoil and the British Airports Authority) by transferring the public ownership of assets from the state to the private sector.

The major components of the privatisation programme in the United Kingdom are shown in Table 15.2 for the period 1984–91.

The social benefits and social costs of the decision to privatise a particular nationalised industry or public sector activity vary from case to case. Consider the following general social benefits and costs in turn.

The social benefits of privatisation

Increased efficiency Since a privatised concern becomes accountable to private shareholders, it is claimed that this increases the pressure on the organisation to seek to reduce costs and achieve higher profits. Furthermore, a more efficient utilisation of

Table 15.2 The privatisation programme: major sales, 1984-91.

Year	Sale
1984	British Telecom
1986	British Gas
1987	British Airways
	Rolls-Royce
	British Airports Authority (now BAA)
	British Petroleum
1988	British Steel
1989	Water Industry
1990	Regional electricity companies
1991	National Power and Powergen

resources may come about through increased competition in the capital and product markets. For instance, it is argued that investors in the *capital market* will only buy the shares of those companies which are capable of using the funds thus provided most profitably. It is therefore suggested that the capital market's assessment of a firm's performance is superior to the government's non-market criteria for allocating investment funds to nationalised industries. Similarly, it is argued that competition in the *product market* may make the firm more responsive to the changing pattern of consumer preferences.

A reduction in the public sector budget deficit The sale of public assets raises revenue for the government in the year of the sale and so contributes to a reduction in the public sector budget deficit for that year. In addition, the sale of those nationalised industries which tend to earn insufficient profits to finance their investment programmes will help to reduce the deficit in future years. On the other hand, some nationalised industries normally *do* earn sufficient profits to finance their investment programmes and these industries are, therefore, contributors of revenue to the government: the privatisation of these profitable industries will tend to lead to an *increase* in the budget deficit in future years.

Less bureaucratic interference Nationalised industries are sometimes used by governments to influence the level of demand in the economy by bringing forward or postponing investment programmes, or by interfering with their pricing policies. Such interference may lead to less efficient resource allocation. For example, prior to its privatisation, British Telecom's investment programme was impeded by government spending restrictions. After privatisation, the company could determine the level of its investment spending on commercial criteria without political interference.

The social costs of privatisation

Threat to the 'public interest' Nationalised industries have the dual responsibility (a) to operate in the 'public interest' and (b) to seek to achieve profits as commercial undertakings. Making them directly accountable to private shareholders as privatised concerns may mean less regard to their 'public interest' responsibility. For instance, the privatisation of British Telecom was seen by critics as a threat to the rural telephone network and the call-box system. Similarly, the privatisation of bus services may be seen as posing a threat to rural passengers.

Creation of private monopolies Critics maintain that privatisation means, in many instances, a replacement of public monopolies with *private monopolies*. This is because industries such as gas, electricity and telecommunications are close to being 'natural' monopolies. It can thus be argued that these kinds of industries should remain subject to some government control even when privatised. Indeed, it is for this reason that the prices and business operations of British Telecom, for example, are controlled to some extent by the Office of Telecommunications, whose job it is to limit any potential abuse of market power. Similar regulatory agencies have been set up to monitor the operation of the gas, water and electricity industries.

Regulatory agency *A body set up by the government to monitor and influence the behaviour of a privately-owned natural monopoly*

Valuation problems In the absence of a market for the shares of a nationalised industry, it is difficult to determine an appropriate issue price for the shares. This may lead to an over- or under-subscription. Critics of privatisation point to the massive over-subscription which has occurred in some cases at considerable cost to the taxpayer. For instance, Amersham International in 1982 and British Telecom and Jaguar in 1984 were heavily over-subscribed at 'give-away' prices. On the other hand, in 1983 when shares of Cable and Wireless were offered for sale, around 30 per cent were not subscribed for and were taken up by the underwriters to the offer.

Summary

1. Negative public policy includes measures intended to promote competition and control monopolies, mergers and restrictive practices. Dominant firm monopolies may use their market power to raise prices and exploit consumers. Mergers may result in the creation of monopolies or have other adverse effects. Restrictive practices refer to the activities of firms colluding, for example, to fix prices or to share out contracts. Negative public policy tries to control such activities by firms that are judged to be against the public interest.
2. Positive public policy includes those government measures which are designed to foster greater economic efficiency and the restructuring of industry. Most of these measures include financial assistance to private firms and retraining schemes.
3. The main arguments in favour of state support to private firms include improved resource allocation, employment protection and correcting for the existence of externalities.
4. Private firms may be taken into public ownership (or nationalised) for a number of reasons, including improved economic planning, the existence of natural monopolies and employment protection.
5. Nationalised industries may be instructed to employ marginal cost pricing in order to achieve efficient resource allocation, although there are several practical difficulties associated with this pricing policy.
6. Privatisation includes the transfer of state-owned industries to the private sector. The main arguments claimed for privatisation are increased incentives for efficiency, an improved public sector budget balance and less bureaucratic interference in decision-making.

Exercises

1. Review your understanding of the following terms:

negative public policy	privatisation
positive public policy	nationalised industries
consumer protection	'lame duck'
restrictive practice	short-run MC pricing
the eight 'gateways'	long-run MC pricing

resale price maintenance	average incremental cost
dominant firm monopoly	regulatory agency

2. Suppose that a nationalised industry faces the long-run cost and revenue curves shown in Fig. 15.4. Indicate on the graph the price, output and profit levels consistent with: (a) long-run marginal cost pricing; (b) long-run average cost pricing; and (c) long-run profit maximisation.

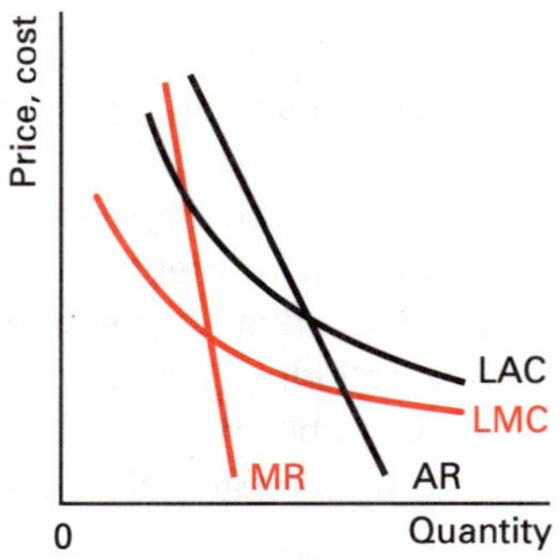

Fig. 15.4. The long-run cost and revenue curves of a nationalised industry.

3. Illustrate the arguments that might lead the Monopolies and Mergers Commission to decide that a particular monopoly is operating in the 'public interest'.
4. What controls would you recommend as necessary to protect the public interest in the case of a privatised 'natural monopoly' such as the telecommunications and gas industries?
5. 'Monopolies are harmful and should be banned!' Discuss.
6. Discuss the case for and against financial help to private industry from the state.
7. Discuss the problems of identifying short- and long-run marginal costs in a nationalised industry which faces demand fluctuations according to the season and the time of day.

THEORY OF DISTRIBUTION

THE DETERMINATION OF WAGES

REWARDS TO FACTORS OF PRODUCTION

16 THE DETERMINATION OF WAGES

Learning objectives

After reading this chapter, you should be able to:

- outline the theory of marginal productivity and assess its usefulness in explaining a firm's and industry's demand for labour
- explain the determinants of the elasticity of the supply of labour and show why an individual's supply curve of labour may bend backwards
- discuss why wage differentials persist in a market economy
- show how wages are determined through the process of collective bargaining in labour markets characterised by imperfect competition
- explain why a disequilibrium may persist in a labour market

Introduction

In Chs 16 and 17, we are concerned with a vitally important topic – the distribution of income among the members of a society. We analyse the factors determining how the output of an economy is divided up, and shared out among the groups and individuals that comprise that society.

We have seen already in Ch. 7 that one method of determining the relative incomes of the factors of production is through a central planning agency. This system operates in a planned or command economy. In a market economy, there are two basic factors influencing the distribution of income to the owners of the factors of production. One is clearly the pattern of ownership of the factors of production; the second is the prices at which the services of the factors of production sell in the factor markets.

The ownership of factors of production can be regarded as given, so that we concentrate on the determination of factor prices. Strictly, it is the determination of the prices of the *services* of the factors that is important as some factors, such as labour, are not used up during the production period. But conventionally, reference is made to the determination of factor prices and we follow that convention.

In a market economy, the major influences on the determination of factor prices are the demand and supply conditions of the factors. In this chapter, we concentrate on labour and examine the variables which influence the determination of wages. But much of what we say can be adapted to the determination of other factor prices. The marginal productivity theory of the demand for a factor of production is, for example, a general theory of the demand for any variable factor. In Ch. 17 we turn specifically to the returns to capital and land.

The demand for a factor

Derived demand *'Derived' demand for a factor of production stems from the consumers' demand for the products which the factor helps to make*

It is important to bear in mind that the demand for a factor of production is a derived demand: it is necessarily derived from the consumers' demand for the products which the factor helps to make. For example, the demand for the services of ice-cream salesmen is derived from the consumers' demand for ice-cream. We start this section by considering a single firm's demand for labour, assuming that labour is a variable factor of production and that all other factors are fixed. This analysis then enables us to determine the total demand for labour of an entire industry.

The demand for labour of a single firm

In Ch. 9, we saw that a firm maximises profit by producing up to the point at which the last unit produced adds just as much to revenue as to cost – that is, at which marginal revenue equals marginal cost. An implication of this is that a firm will hire units of its variable factors of production until the last unit hired adds just as much to revenue as to cost. This result brings us to the important concepts of *marginal revenue product, the value of the marginal product* and *marginal factor cost.*

Marginal revenue product *The change in total revenue caused by employing one more or one less unit of a variable factor*

Marginal revenue product (MRP) of a variable factor is the change in total revenue resulting from the employment of one more or one less unit of the variable factor. It is equal to the marginal physical product (MPP) of the variable factor multiplied by marginal revenue (MR):

$$\mathbf{MRP = MPP \times MR}$$

Note that the term 'marginal physical product' is used in place of marginal product. This is to emphasise that it is measured in *physical* units and to distinguish it from the *value* of the marginal product.

Value of the marginal product *The market value of a factor's marginal physical product*

The value of the marginal product (VMP) of a variable factor is the market value of the marginal physical product of the variable factor. It is equal to the marginal physical product multiplied by the price of the final product (P):

$$\mathbf{VMP = MPP \times P}$$

Marginal factor cost *The change in total cost caused by employing one more or one less unit of a variable factor*

Marginal factor cost (MFC) is the change in total cost resulting from the employment of one more or one less unit of the variable factor.

Notice that if the firm is selling its product in a perfectly competitive market, so that $P =$ MR, then it must also be true that MRP = VMP.

It should be clear from the above definitions that *a profit-maximising firm selling its product in a perfectly competitive market will hire additional units of its variable factor of production up to the point at which MRP (VMP) is equal to MFC.* This is the theory of marginal productivity. If, in addition, we assume that *labour* is the variable factor and that the firm purchases it in a perfectly competitive labour market, then MFC will be the (given) wage rate. The theory of marginal productivity then states that the firm will hire additional units of labour up to the point at which *the wage is just equal to the value of the marginal product of labour.*

Theory of marginal productivity *This states that profit-maximising firms will hire additional units of a variable factor up to the point at which MRP = MFC. This means that under conditions of perfect competition, each factor will receive a payment equal to the value of its marginal product*

To illustrate this, consider the numerical example set out in Table 16.1. The example is that of a wheat farmer who is operating in perfectly competitive factor and product markets and whose only variable factor of production is labour.

Notice that columns (1) and (2) are reproduced from Table 2.3 of Ch. 2. They illustrate the 'law of diminishing returns' because as more and more workers are employed, the marginal physical product of labour eventually declines. Suppose now that the price of wheat is given as £2 per tonne: this enables us to calculate the MRP

Table 16.1 Derivation of marginal revenue product.

(1) No of workers	(2) MPP (tonnes of wheat per week)	(3) MRP = VMP (of labour) (£)
1	4	8
2	10	20
3	11.5	23
4	14.5	29
5	20	40
6	12	24
7	5	10
8	3	6
9	1	2
10	−6	−12

(= VMP). This is shown in column (3) and, since the wage is constant, it follows that this must also eventually decline as more and more workers are hired.

We can state the following general rule for profit-maximisation: *Profit-maximising firms will hire additional units of the variable factors up to the point at which the last unit hired adds just as much to revenue as to cost; that is until the factor's marginal revenue product is equal to its marginal factor cost.* The equilibrium *condition* for a profit-maximising firm is

Marginal revenue product = *Marginal factor cost*

This condition must be fulfilled for *all* variable factors employed if the firm is to maximise its profits.

If a firm purchases its variable factor in a *perfect factor market*, so that it can purchase any quantity without influencing price, the marginal factor cost will be equal to the price of the factor. In this case the equilibrium *condition* becomes

Marginal revenue product = *Price of factor*

The analysis implies that a firm's MRP curve is its demand curve for a variable factor on the assumption that all other factors of production are held constant.

Suppose now that labour is the only variable factor and is sold in a perfect market. A profit-maximising firm will employ additional workers up to the point at which the wage rate equals the marginal revenue product of labour. Consider Table 16.1 again. If the weekly wage is £24, the farmer will maximise profit by employing six workers, as the MRP of the sixth worker is just equal to £24. The farmer would not hire a seventh worker, as this would add only £10 to revenue, but £24 to cost, thus reducing profit by £14.

Now assume that the weekly wage falls to £6. In this situation, the farmer would employ eight workers, once again equating MRP with the wage rate. Consider a diagrammatic representation of the above argument.

Figure 16.1 illustrates the MRP (= VMP) curve of a profit-maximising firm that sells its product in a perfect market. Assume that labour is the only variable factor and that the firm is able to hire any number of workers at the market wage, so that it faces a perfectly elastic supply curve of labour (S_1S_1) at the market wage ($0W_1$).

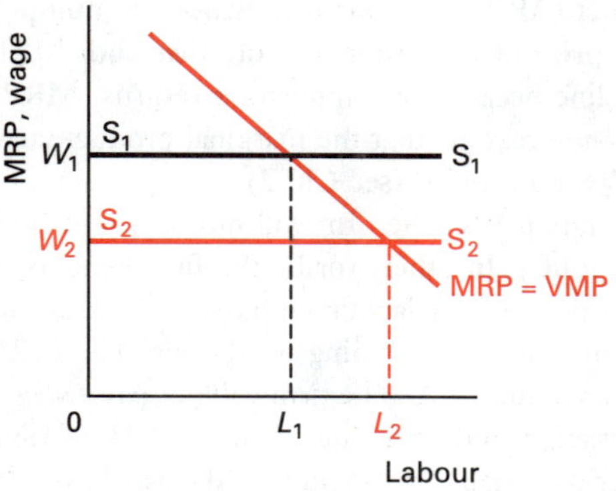

Fig. 16.1. The MRP equals VMP curve of a firm that sells its product in a perfectly competitive market. Initially, the firm maximises profit by hiring $0L_1$ units of labour.

To maximise profit the firm will hire $0L_1$ units of labour, as that equates MRP and the wage. If the firm hired fewer than $0L_1$ units of labour, it could increase profit by hiring additional workers, for MRP would be greater than the wage. Conversely, if the firm hired more units of labour than $0L_1$, it could increase its profit by hiring less labour, for MRP would be less than the wage. Profit is only maximised if the MRP of labour equals the wage rate.

Now consider the quantity of labour the firm will hire if the wage falls to $0W_2$ so that the perfectly elastic supply curve shifts down to S_2S_2. With $0L_1$ workers employed, MRP is now greater than the wage rate, so that the firm will hire additional workers. The MRP and the wage rate are equated if the firm now employs $0L_2$ units of labour. For this firm we have seen that its MRP (= VMP) curve represents its demand for labour curve.

If the producer is selling the product in an imperfect market, he or she will face a downward-sloping demand curve; in order to sell extra units the producer has to accept a lower price. Thus, in this case the increase in revenue from selling an additional unit of output (MR) is less than its price (= AR), as the producer has to reduce the price on all other units sold. In the case of an imperfect competitor MRP must be less than VMP.

It is in fact only the downward-sloping section of the MRP curve that represents the demand for labour. Consider Fig. 16.2 which shows a perfectly competitive firm's MRP curve together with the associated average revenue product curve. The average

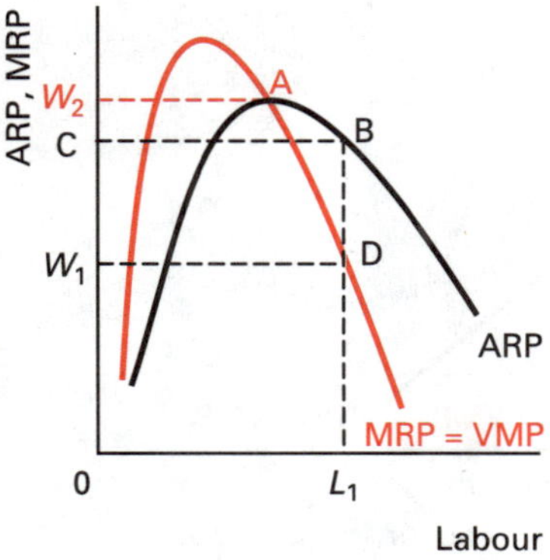

Fig. 16.2. The firm's demand curve for labour. This is given by the section of MRP below the intersection with ARP at point A.

revenue product (ARP) of labour is obtained by multiplying the average product of labour by the price of the product. Note that both MRP and ARP rise at first but eventually decline because of diminishing returns. MRP cuts ARP at its maximum point for the same reasons that the marginal product curve cuts the average product curve at *its* maximum point (see Ch. 2).

If the wage rate is $0W_1$ the firm will hire $0L_1$ units of labour. The ARP of labour will be L_1B (= 0C). In other words, the firm benefits from a monetary surplus of BD (= CW_1) per unit of labour employed. This surplus is available to meet the other costs of production, including fixed costs. The MRP curve cuts the ARP curve at the latter's maximum at A. The firm will not pay a wage rate in excess of $0W_2$, for if it did so, the wage would be greater than the ARP of labour; the firm would then be unable to cover its variable costs and would close down. Thus, it is only the section of the MRP curve below its intersection with the ARP curve that represents the firm's demand for labour.

The industry's demand for labour

We have established that a firm's MRP curve represents its demand for labour when only one factor is variable. In establishing this proposition, we adopted a partial approach assuming *ceteris paribus*, so that when the individual firm increased its output, all other firms held their outputs constant.

However, when considering the demand for labour by the industry as a whole, it has to be recognised that a change in the wage rate will affect each firm's hiring of labour and, therefore, total production. A fall in the wage rate, for example, will induce all firms in the industry to hire more labour, so that total production will increase and the supply curve of the good will shift to the right. With a downward-sloping demand curve, the price of the product will decline. This means that the typical firm's MRP curve will shift towards the origin.

Consider Fig. 16.3 where initially the wage rate is $0W_1$ and the firm operates at point A, hiring $0L_1$ units of labour. MRP_1 is the firm's demand curve for labour on the assumption that the price of the product is fixed.

If there is an exogenous fall in the wage rate to $0W_2$, the firm hires additional units of labour (L_1L_2) until the wage rate and MRP are again equal. However, as all firms hire more labour, total production increases and the price of the product falls. This causes the firm's MRP curve to shift down to MRP_2. From the new MRP curve it can be seen that with a wage rate of $0W_2$ the firm operates at point B and will hire $0L_3$

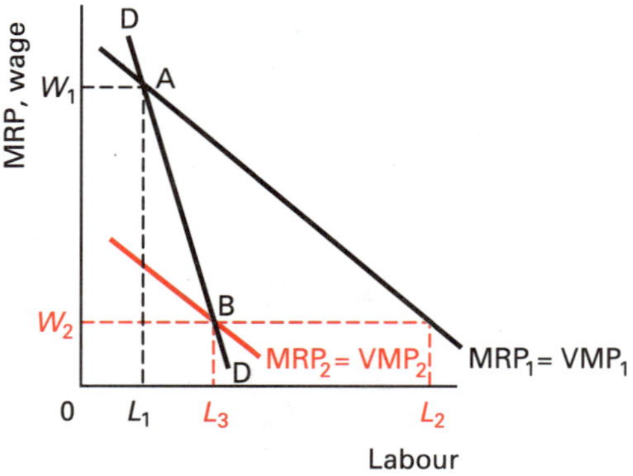

Fig. 16.3. A firm's demand for labour allowing for changes in the price of the product. To obtain the industry's demand curve for labour, the DD curves of all firms in the industry must be horizontally summed.

units of labour. By joining points such as A and B we derive the demand curve DD which is steeper than the firm's MRP curve. To obtain the industry's demand curve for labour, allowing for industry-wide changes in wage rates, we must add together horizontally the DD curves of all the firms in the industry. This industry demand curve will normally, therefore, be downward-sloping.

The elasticity of the demand for labour

Consider now the major influences on the quantity of labour demanded in a particular labour market as a result of a change in wage rates.

(a) The greater the price elasticity of demand for the *product*, the greater will be the elasticity of demand for the labour used to produce that product. To illustrate this, consider a good, such as coal, for which demand is price elastic. A rise in the wage rate for miners will lead to an increase in the price of coal. This rise in price will cause a more than proportionate fall in the quantity of coal demanded, and, therefore, a relatively large fall in the quantity of labour demanded.

(b) The larger the proportion of total cost accounted for by labour cost, the larger will be the elasticity of demand for labour. If the wage bill accounts for a high proportion of total cost, an increase in the wage rate will lead to a substantial rise in total cost. As a result, firms will reduce production substantially and hire fewer workers.

(c) In the *short-run*, the elasticity of demand for labour will be low if it is difficult to substitute other factors for labour. In this case, even if the wage rate rises substantially, the quantity of labour demanded will not be very responsive. In the *long-run*, however, it typically becomes easier to replace labour with capital (in other words, to introduce labour-saving technology) so that the demand for labour is likely to be more elastic.

The limitations of the marginal productivity theory

The analysis outlined above is sometimes referred to as the *marginal productivity theory* of the demand for a variable factor. Since this theory ignores the supply side, it cannot be regarded as a complete theory of factor pricing. Furthermore, to obtain a determinate equilibrium position we assumed that labour is a homogeneous factor, which sells for a single price in a perfectly competitive labour market. In reality, of course, labour is not a homogeneous factor because of differing innate characteristics and skills and labour markets are by no means perfectly competitive.

It was also pointed out earlier that the theory is based on the assumption that firms attempt to maximise profits. We saw in Ch. 10, however, that private firms may have other objectives; for example, public corporations do not normally attempt to maximise profits. In such cases the theory is unlikely to be an adequate explanation of the demand for labour.

The theory also assumes that wage levels and labour productivity are independent. This is not necessarily valid. Increased wages may call forth extra effort from the labour force, so that productivity increases. It is also possible that higher wage costs induce managers to exercise their supervisory function more effectively, which could also result in extra output. Finally, in some countries it is possible that higher wages, which lead to improved nutritional standards, may result in more productive workers in the long-run. Such changes in productivity increase the MPP of labour, and thus shift a firm's MRP curve to the right.

The marginal productivity theory is sometimes criticised on the grounds that firms do not actually sit down to calculate a factor's MRP, perhaps because of insufficient information about the productivity of marginal workers. This criticism, however, is missing the point to some extent; it comes back to the question: is the firm maximising profits? If the answer is in the affirmative, then the firm must be paying factors their marginal revenue products, regardless of whether the firm has specifically set out to calculate the marginal revenue product.

The supply of labour

The total supply of labour in an economy depends on such factors as the size of the population, the age composition of the population and many institutional and social factors. The school-leaving age is one such institutional factor. In the early 1970s in the United Kingdom, for example, the minimum school-leaving age was raised from fifteen to sixteen years. This change clearly reduced the potential labour supply. Currently in the United Kingdom, there is some pressure to increase the normal retirement age for women from sixty to sixty-five. If the retirement age is increased, this will also increase the supply of labour.

Participation rate *The proportion of the potential workforce that is working or actively looking for work*

Other institutional factors, such as the length of the average working week and of holidays, are also of significance. The participation rate (the percentage of the potential work-force working or actively seeking work) is influenced by many factors, such as the level of unemployment benefits relative to wage levels and social attitudes towards the participation of women in the work-force.

The elasticity of the supply of labour

Clearly, the *total* supply of labour is not perfectly inelastic as higher wage rates are likely to draw extra workers into the labour force (for example, students and married women) and will induce some workers to work longer hours.

If we ask what induces the owners of factors of production to allocate them to *particular* uses, the hypothesis of equal net advantage is relevant. This states that the owners of factors of production will move them between different uses until there is no further advantage, monetary or otherwise, in another move. For the owners of *non-human* factors of production, monetary advantage will be of overwhelming importance.

This is not, however, the case with labour, where non-monetary advantages will also be very important. Consider two jobs requiring a similar skill, but where the working conditions for job A are clean and pleasant whilst job B means working in hot and dirty conditions. Most individuals will require higher monetary rewards to accept job B in order to compensate them for the non-monetary disadvantages of the unpleasant working conditions.

The supply of labour to a single industry, then, is likely to be elastic as an increase in the industry's wage rate will induce some workers to transfer from other industries. This elasticity, though, will vary with the length of the time period considered. The longer the time period, the greater will be the elasticity of supply. This is largely because there are barriers to the mobility of labour. These barriers, which may be quite strong in the short-run, can be discussed in terms of occupational and geographical immobility.

Occupational immobility *The difficulties faced by workers wishing to move from one occupation to another*

Occupational immobility Workers are clearly not homogeneous so that natural ability may be a barrier to movement between jobs. Some jobs require an innate ability, such as nimble fingers or an analytical mind, which some workers just do not possess. Many jobs require a period of training, so that a redundant steel-worker, for example, cannot become a television repairman overnight. Workers may be reluctant to undertake retraining as it normally involves a period of low income and starting again at the bottom of the job ladder.

In some cases, artificial barriers to the mobility of labour are erected which have the effect of benefiting special interest groups. For example, there may be '*closed shop*' agreements which require all workers to be members of a trade union. Similarly, membership of some professional bodies, such as the British Medical Association and Law Society, is restricted by high entry requirements.

In the long-run, these barriers to occupational mobility are not likely to be as significant, as new workers enter the labour force and existing workers can be retrained.

Geographical immobility *The difficulties faced by workers wishing to move from one area to another*

Geographical immobility There are several factors which can deter a worker from moving to a job in another part of the country, even if the worker is unemployed. Social ties to family and friends may be strong. There may be problems in obtaining suitable housing in the new location and the monetary costs of transferring a home are significant. A move is also likely to be disruptive to children's education.

Despite the efforts of the employment service in the United Kingdom, it is often difficult to obtain information about vacancies, job conditions and wages in other parts of the country. A further problem is that many workers prefer to remain in their own region even when unemployed and when jobs are available in other regions.

The individual's supply of labour

When we consider an individual's supply of labour, we have to take into account the possibility of a backward-bending supply curve. Consider Fig. 16.4 which shows an individual's indifference map between work and pay. The horizontal axis measures hours of work per day and the vertical axis measures the daily wage. The maximum number of hours the individual is prepared to work is given by $0H_m$ hours. The individual regards the wage as a 'good' and so derives utility from it. However, the individual regards work as a 'bad' and so derives disutility from it.

Each indifference curve joins together those combinations of the daily wage and hours worked per day which yield the same amount of utility to the individual. Clearly, for the individual to stay at the same level of utility, he or she must receive a

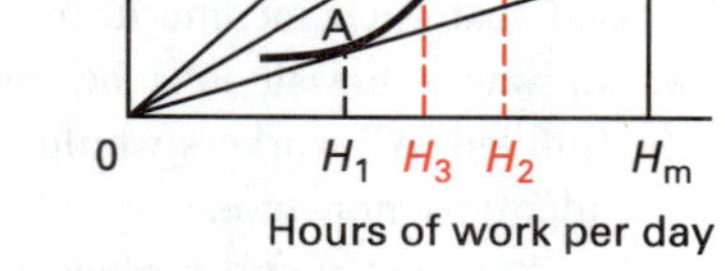

Fig. 16.4. Individual's choice between work and leisure. As the wage rate increases, at first the individual increases hours of work. But further increases in the wage rate result in a fall in the number of hours worked.

Fig. 16.5. Individual's backward-bending supply curve of labour. As the wage rate increases up to $0R_2$, the number of hours the individual works also increases. Above $0R_2$, further increases in the wage rate cause a decrease in the number of hours worked.

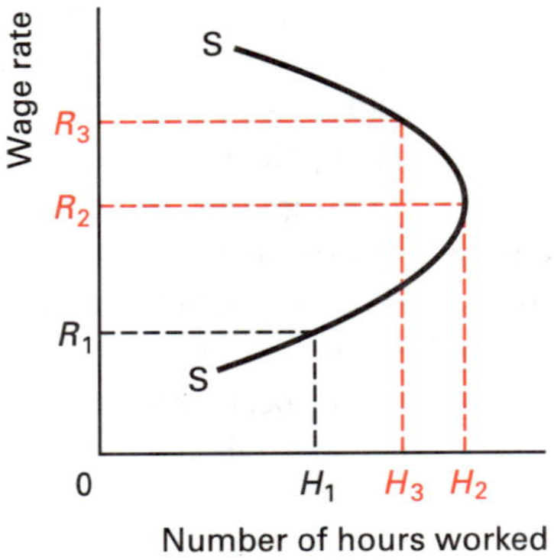

higher daily wage as more hours are worked. This means that the indifference curves must slope upwards from left to right. It also follows that the higher the indifference curve, the greater the level of utility.

Consider the rays $0R_1$, $0R_2$, and $0R_3$, whose slopes represent different wage rates. The slope of $0R_1$ represents a wage rate equal to £$AH_1/0H_1$ per hour. At this wage rate, the individual maximises utility by supplying $0H_1$ hours of work. This puts the individual at point A on the highest attainable indifference curve, I_1. The slope of $0R_2$ (equal to £$BH_2/0H_2$ per hour) represents a higher wage rate than $0R_1$ and the individual will maximise utility by supplying $0H_2$ hours of work. This puts the individual on the indifference curve I_2 at point B. Finally, consider the wage rate $0R_3$ (equal to £$CH_3/0H_3$ per hour) which is higher than $0R_2$. At this wage rate, the individual maximises utility at point C and offers $0H_3$ hours.

If we now plot the individual's supply of labour against the different wage rates, we obtain the backward-bending supply curve, SS, illustrated in Fig. 16.5. As the wage rate increases from $0R_1$ to $0R_2$, the individual offers to work more hours. As the price of labour rises, leisure is becoming more expensive relative to working. The worker substitutes extra hours of work for leisure; this is called the substitution effect.

But as the wage rate rises, the individual's real income also increases. The increase in real income increases the individual's demand for normal goods, including leisure; this is called the income effect. When the wage rate rises above $0R_2$ the income effect predominates over the substitution effect, so that increases in the wage rate reduce the number of hours the individual offers to work. The supply curve becomes backward-bending.

Wage differentials

In a mixed economy, such as the United Kingdom, it is well known that some groups (for example directors of large companies, judges and hospital consultants) earn several times the average wage. In the United Kingdom in 1991, the top fifth of households received 45.5 per cent of pre-tax income. After the deduction of income tax, this share was 43.1 per cent.

We should not be surprised that such income differentials exist. One might ask under what conditions would wages for all jobs be equal? An impressive list of conditions would have to be fulfilled. All workers would have to be homogeneous; all jobs would have to display identical non-monetary advantages and disadvantages; there would have to be perfect knowledge and perfect mobility of labour.

If this demanding list of conditions were fulfilled, wages in all occupations would be equalised. If the wage rate in one industry rose temporarily above the common wage rate, there would be a massive switch by workers who would want to transfer to that industry. The excess supply of labour in the industry would drive down the industry wage rate to that in the other industries. Conversely, if the wage rate in a single industry fell below the general level, there would be a transfer of workers into other industries, resulting in an excess demand for labour in this industry. This would force the industry wage rate up to the level prevalent in the economy as a whole.

It should be recognised that the conditions necessary for the equalisation of wage rates are not fulfilled in practice. In reality, workers are not homogeneous because of differences in natural ability, skills and training. As mentioned above, a steel-worker cannot switch to being a television repairman overnight. Some people do not have the physical requirements or the natural ability required for particular jobs. A policeman, for example, may have to be of a specified minimum height; a lifeguard requires a good swimming ability. Consequently, it can be argued that the labour market is separated into many distinct markets, so that workers can be viewed as comprising non-competing groups.

Non-competing groups
Distinct categories of workers which effectively do not compete with each other for jobs that require specific skills and abilities

Additionally, jobs do not offer identical non-monetary advantages and disadvantages. Some jobs mean working in pleasant conditions with convenient hours of work, as for example, a university professor. Other jobs require working in dirty and unpleasant conditions, perhaps at unsocial hours, as for example, a coal miner.

We know that in practice neither employers nor employees are perfectly well-informed about conditions of service and pay in all occupations. Workers often do not know of all job opportunities that are available, particularly in other areas. This point is further developed below in the section on the 'theory of search'.

Finally, we saw earlier that there are several barriers to the mobility of labour, both geographical and occupational. These may take the form of workers not being willing to move to another part of the country; or barriers may exist because of the differing skill requirements of different jobs. We also saw that trade unions and professional associations sometimes erect entry barriers, perhaps through the requirement of a long apprenticeship or period of training.

Factors such as those outlined above help to explain the differentials that exist between the wages earned in different occupations. But why do certain talented people such as pop-stars and other entertainers earn very high incomes? It all comes back to supply and demand. There is a large demand for the services of 'star' entertainers like Elton John. On the supply side, of course, there is only one Elton John with his particular talents.

As pointed out above, certain jobs and professions require several years' training. Examples include the jobs of doctors, scientists and computer programmers. The above-average earnings of these groups can partly be explained by a scarcity of supply.

Imperfections in labour markets

Labour markets are remarkably imperfect. On the demand side, there are product monopolies, monopsonies (that is, monopoly buyers of labour) and 'collusive oligopsonies' (that is, employers' organisations collectively negotiating wages and

Monopsony *A single buyer of labour services in a particular labour market*

conditions of employment on behalf of member firms). Some large firms may even form labour markets in their own right. On the supply side, there are trade union monopolies which have developed the institution of collective bargaining.

In considering such imperfect markets, the essential point to note is that traditional analysis is merely an extension of the principles of the marginal productivity theory. By comparing the wage rates and levels of employment that would prevail in perfect and imperfect labour markets, we can draw conclusions about the welfare implications of different market structures.

In the following sections, we examine the case of a product monopolist and that of a monopsonist buyer of labour. On the supply side, we consider the influence of trade unions and collective bargaining.

The hiring policy of a profit-maximising product monopolist

A product monopolist faces a downward-sloping demand curve for the good he or she is producing. This means that if the monopolist employs additional workers, he or she must lower the product price to sell the additional output. As shown in Fig. 16.6, the MRP curve lies below the VMP curve for the same reasons as the monopolist's marginal revenue (MR) curve lies below the average revenue (AR) curve (see Ch. 9).

Assume that the monopolist is operating in a perfectly competitive labour market and so faces an infinitely elastic supply curve of labour *WW* paying a fixed wage rate $0W$ per hour as in Fig. 16.6. Then, such a monopolist will employ $0L$ units of labour as indicated by the intersection of MRP with *WW* at point E. Employment of extra units of labour beyond $0L$ would mean that the wage bill would increase by more than the increase in total revenue so reducing profits.

Implications for social welfare The Pareto efficient level of output requires that the level of employment should be pushed up to $0L_1$ where VMP intersects *WW* at point E_1: this is the level of employment which would be achieved under conditions of perfect competition in all markets. It can be seen that a monopolist employs less labour than a perfect competitor. This arises from the monopolist's restriction of output to a level below that required for Pareto efficiency.

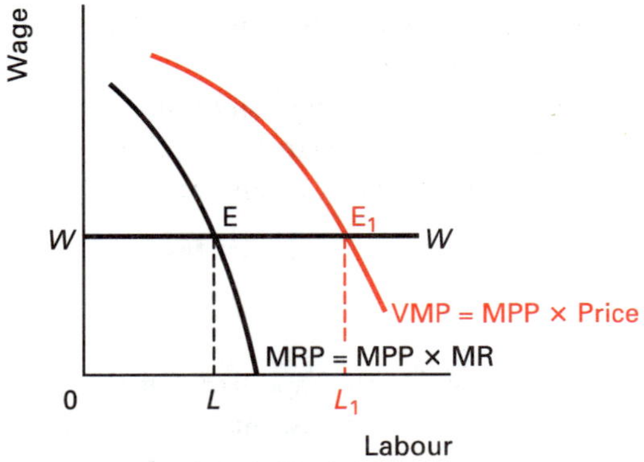

Fig. 16.6. A product monopolist's demand for labour. The monopolist's MRP curve lies below the VMP curve. With wage rate $0W$, the monopolist hires $0L$ units of labour.

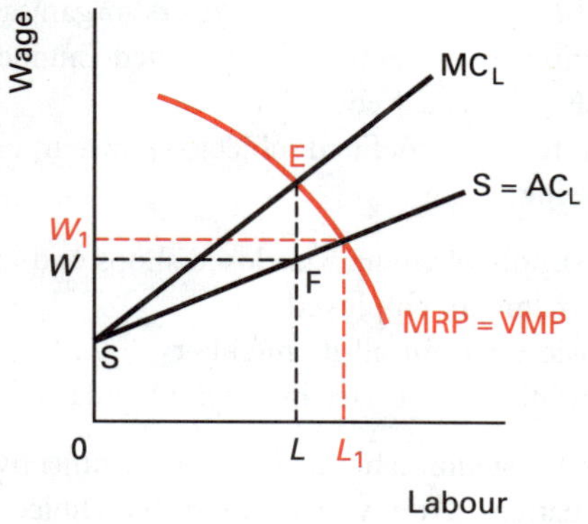

Fig. 16.7. Monopsonist's demand for labour. The marginal cost of labour facing the monopsonist, MC_L, is greater than the average cost of labour, given by the supply curve $SS = AC_L$. The monopsonist maximises profit by equating MRP with MC_L, hiring $0L$ units of labour.

The hiring policy of a monopsonistic buyer of labour

Now consider the case of a monopsonist who sells the finished product in perfect competition. By definition, a monopsonist is the only buyer of labour in a particular market and (unlike the product monopolist or perfect competitor) is in a position to influence the prevailing wage rate and level of employment. The monopsonist's equilibrium level of employment will be influenced by the marginal cost of labour (MC_L) and the marginal revenue product of labour (MRP = VMP). The marginal cost of labour has two components. First, being a monopsonist, the firm can hire additional workers only by offering a higher wage rate. Second, assuming that all workers are paid the same wage, any higher wage offered to attract additional workers will have to be paid to the existing work-force. Thus, the marginal cost of labour exceeds its average cost.

In Fig. 16.7 the upward-sloping supply curve $SS = AC_L$ is in fact the average cost of labour curve: it shows the wage rate that has to be offered to attract a given supply of labour. Given that the monopsonist is a profit-maximiser, then the number of workers the monopsonist is able and willing to employ will be determined by the intersection of the MC_L curve with the MRP = VMP curve. Inspection of Fig. 16.7 shows that the monopsonist employs $0L$ units of labour (as indicated by the intersection of MC_L with MRP at point E). The wage rate $0W$, however, is given by the intersection of the line EL with SS at point F. Contrast this outcome with the perfectly competitive case where a higher wage rate $0W_1$ and level of employment $0L_1$ would prevail.

Implications for social welfare It can be concluded that the monopsonistic buyer of labour pays a wage less than the value of the marginal product of labour. The buyer thus employs a smaller work-force than that required for Pareto efficiency.

The influence of trade unions and collective bargaining on wages and jobs

The institutions of trade unions and collective bargaining play a central role in setting wage levels and determining conditions of service in industrialised countries. In the United Kingdom, for instance, 287 unions with about 10 million members influence the wages and conditions of service for their members, and indirectly for other groups of workers in the economy.

Typically, wage bargaining processes are characterised by *bilateral monopolies* in many trades, occupations and industries. Negotiations are conducted between union

Collective bargaining
The process by which wages and conditions of services are determined by bargaining between the representatives of the workers and employers

representatives and representatives of employers' organisations, as for example in the case of pay negotiations between the Amalgamated Engineering and Electrical Union and the Shipping Employers' Federation.

A union has a few well-defined objectives when bargaining with employers. Consider the following:

(a) to restrict the supply of labour via closed shops and long apprenticeship periods;
(b) to keep all its members employed;
(c) to raise the basic wage for all its members;
(d) to improve conditions of service including holidays, pensions and hours of work.

In practice, unions are seldom able to attain these objectives simultaneously in every round of pay negotiations. At any given time, the choice of objectives is likely to be influenced by such factors as the government's counter-inflation policy, the level of economic activity and the relative bargaining power of the union in question. However, these objectives have different implications for wages and jobs.

Suppose, for example, a union pursues objective (a) and as a result, succeeds in the restriction of the labour supply to a particular occupation or industry. In Fig. 16.8, DD represents the market demand for labour. The restriction of the labour supply leads to the inward shift of the supply curve SS to S_1S_1. This results in a rise in the wage rate from $0W$ to $0W_1$ with a fall in the number of workers employed from $0L$ to $0L_1$.

If, however, the objective is to maintain employment of all its members and total membership is equal to $0L$ as in Fig. 16.8, then the union will have to settle for a lower hourly wage rate than $0W_1$. Any wage rate higher than $0W$ would lead to a cut in the quantity of labour demanded.

The union might consider ways of reducing this trade-off between a higher wage rate and lower employment. This might be achieved by making the demand for labour less elastic through reducing the supply of substitute factors or substitute products. For example, a union may attempt to reduce the supply of non-union labour by enforcing a closed shop. Alternatively, a union may try to restrict the availability of substitute products by campaigning for import controls. A union of textile workers, for example, may call for restrictions on imports of cloth and garments from low-cost countries.

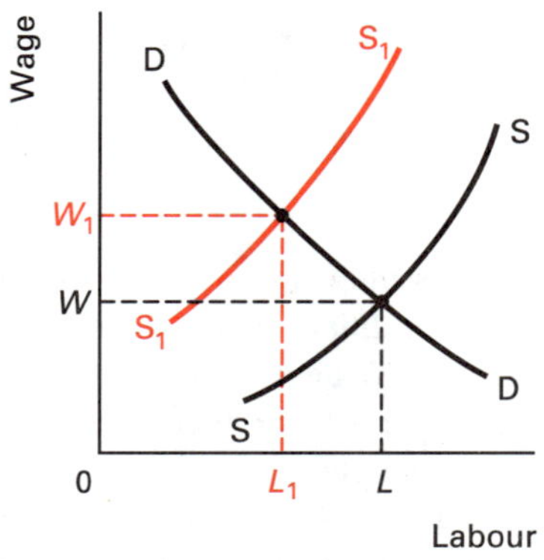

Fig. 16.8. Effects of restriction of labour supply on wages and employment. A trade union forces up the wage rate from $0W$ to $0W_1$ by reducing supply from SS to S_1S_1. The increase in the wage rate is achieved at the expense of a fall in employment from $0L$ to $0L_1$ units of labour.

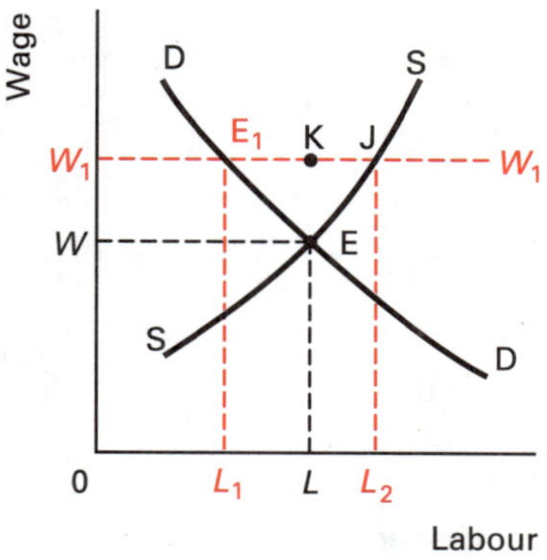

Fig. 16.9. ***Effects of basic minimum wage.*** A minimum wage of $0W_1$ leads to a fall in employment from $0L$ to $0L_1$ units of labour.

Minimum wage Unions may succeed in getting all employers to agree to pay not lower than the basic minimum wage $0W_1$ as in Fig. 16.9, in which case the minimum wage line (W_1W_1) becomes parallel to the horizontal axis. If, as is likely, such a wage rate is set above the equilibrium wage level $0W$, as shown in the diagram, the part of the SS curve below J becomes irrelevant. Instead, the supply curve becomes W_1JS intersecting the DD curve at E_1 with $0L_1$ units of labour employed. At the minimum wage, $0W_1$, there is an excess supply of labour (or unemployment) equal to L_1L_2.

This also explains the view of the opponents of minimum wage legislation that it tends to cause inflation and unemployment. On the other hand, the supporters of the argument for minimum wage legislation (which include some unions) maintain that raising wage rates above the competitive equilibrium level will ultimately lead to an increase in the productivity of labour. If this happens the demand for labour will increase resulting in a higher level of employment and a higher wage rate.

Finally, a union may attempt to force an employer 'off' the demand curve in order to achieve a wage increase without any reduction in employment. In this case the union would be aiming for point K in Fig. 16.9. This strategy is more likely to be successful if the firm is highly profitable.

Disequilibrium in the labour market

The marginal productivity theory of wages is clearly an oversimplification of reality. It asserts that an equilibrium wage rate will be established in the markets for particular grades of labour, skills and occupations. However, labour markets in practice are unlikely to be in equilibrium. The average worker has a narrow view of the market and is not an alert participant in the market able to take advantage of any variations in wage rates.

Consider Fig. 16.10 which shows the demand and supply curves for a particular type of labour. Equilibrium in this market requires that the wage rate be established at $0W_1$ and actual employment be $0L_1$ units of labour.

The market will be in disequilibrium: (a) at any wage rate other than $0W_1$, and (b) where frictions in the labour market prevent the matching up of supply and demand so that, even when the wage rate is $0W_1$, actual employment is less than $0L_1$ (at $0L_2$, say, in Fig. 16.10). Such disequilibria may result for the following reasons:

(a) *Rigidity of wages.* In many trades, occupations and industries, wages are typically rigid, especially in the downward direction. Wage rigidities may arise

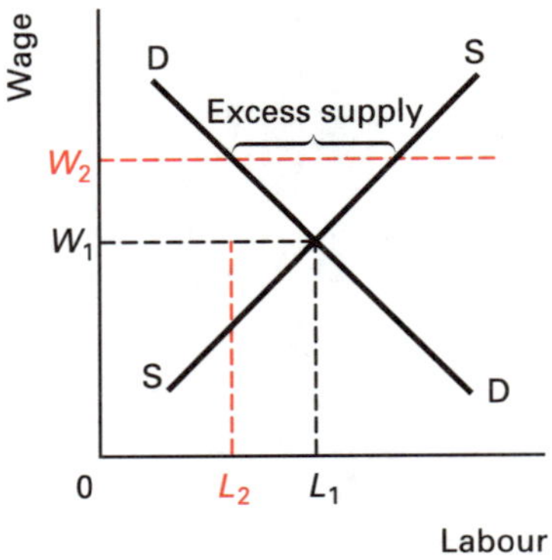

Fig. 16.10. Disequilibrium in a labour market. The market will be in disequilibrium at any wage rate other than $0W_1$. The existence of frictions in the labour market may also prevent the attainment of equilibrium, even though the wage rate is $0W_1$.

from trade union pressures which prevent workers from bargaining individually with their employers. Suppose, for example, a wage rate of $0W_2$ is established in Fig. 16.10 which creates an excess supply of labour. Trade unions may use their monopoly power to resist any cut in wages, so that the disequilibrium persists. Other reasons for wage rigidity, such as implicit contracts and the existence of 'insiders' and 'outsiders' are discussed in Ch. 27.

(b) *Labour as a heterogeneous factor.* Labour is a collection of differing skills, education, training and experience, and so consists of 'non-competing groups'. For instance, mathematics teachers and English teachers are dissimilar in the sense that they do not compete for the same jobs. Even two doctors may differ in their abilities and specialisms, so creating non-competing groups within the medical profession. Consequently, even if the total demand for and supply of doctors are equal, there may be an excess supply of obstetricians at the same time as a shortage of anaesthetists.

(c) *Internal labour markets.* Examination of modern methods of hiring shows that some firms have their own internal labour markets, more or less insulated from outside influences. They generally recruit non-craft and semi-skilled workers at the bottom of the job ladder and employees progress to higher-grade jobs by a system of internal training and promotion based on seniority and ability. Clearly, such a recruitment policy hinders labour mobility since workers can only enter this firm in the lower grades. In addition, these firms develop their own complex methods of job evaluation for the structure of wage differentials. Thus, there are different rates of pay for the range of jobs to be performed within the firm and this makes it difficult for workers to draw comparisons with those of other firms and industries.

(d) *Information costs.* Seeking information about wages and jobs imposes monetary and non-monetary costs on both firms and workers. To obtain a job, an unemployed worker might have to spend a considerable amount of money and time collecting information about job vacancies from newspapers, official employment exchanges, private employment agencies and even by word of mouth. This important point is further developed in the section below on the theory of search.

The theory of search

This theory maintains that given disequilibrium in the labour market, workers and employers engage in a process of search to strike the best possible bargains about wages, terms and conditions of employment including 'fringe benefits'. The longer the process of search for information about wages and job prospects in various firms and industries, the greater are the costs to buyers and sellers of labour. Such costs of search and information gathering have been ignored by the marginal productivity theory of wages which assumed that such activities as bargaining, information collection and labour mobility were costless.

Consider, for example, an employer of labour. On top of the usual wages paid to workers, the hiring transaction includes several costs. The employer has to incur the costs of recruitment which include advertisement costs, employment agency costs, the cost of screening applications and the costs of training workers. In some cases, employers may have to offer inducements to obtain suitably qualified workers. The costs of hiring skilled workers (such as executives and senior managers) will be proportionately higher than the costs of recruiting unskilled and semi-skilled workers. This is because a much more intensive search is called for in order to attract suitable applicants for specialised jobs. In addition, the costs of search are likely to be higher if there are competing firms which are offering terms with considerable variations for more or less similar jobs. The unsuccessful firms may have to readvertise, reassess their relative bargaining positions, improve upon the initial wage offers and lower recruitment standards.

On the other hand, to the seller of labour, the most important cost is the *opportunity cost* of the search. Consider, for example, an unemployed worker with several job offers in hand. Clearly, this person is not likely to strike the best possible bargain, if he or she accepts the first offer. It may be that the unemployed worker can obtain much better terms by intensifying the search for better pay and conditions of work, or it may be that he or she has some ideas beforehand about the minimum acceptable pay. The further the search is intensified, however, the higher is the opportunity cost in terms of the forgone income the unemployed worker could have otherwise earned. Note that the forgone income is measured net of unemployment benefits.

To a dissatisfied worker, who, though already employed, is looking for a job elsewhere, the *loss of leisure time* is the most important cost. Like an unemployed worker, this person may also have preconceived ideas about the lowest acceptable wage, which may be revised upwards or downwards in the light of experience and information gained from continued search. The higher the level of unemployment, the higher is the cost of search because the worker may have to search for much longer before receiving an offer. At the same time there are greater risks involved in search because if the worker does not accept the first offer promptly, he or she may find that it has been taken by someone else. The rising cost of search tends to support the 'discouraged worker hypothesis', according to which searching for work and pay during a period of unemployment could be so disheartening that some of the unemployed may give up looking for work and withdraw from the labour market. A decision to give up the search for a job is obviously influenced by the level of unemployment benefits and the availabilities of such non-market activities as part-time education, sports and recreation facilities, and other social and cultural pursuits.

Equal pay for women

In the United Kingdom, the Equal Pay Act 1970, amended in 1984, and the Sex Discrimination Act 1975 are the major legislative measures designed to achieve equal pay for work of equal value and to provide equal opportunities to males and females in the areas of recruitment, training, promotion, overtime and shift work. Similar legislation has been enacted in other industrialised countries, such as the United States, Australia, New Zealand and Japan.

Since the Second World War, there has been a considerable increase in the overall activity rate of women in the labour force in all the major industrial countries. In the United Kingdom, as in other countries, a large proportion of this increase is in the activity of married women in the age group forty years and over. In 1990, 10.8 million women were employed (that is, 47 per cent of all employees). Of these, about 4.8 million (21 per cent of all employees) were in part-time employment. In fact, about 86 per cent of all part-time employees in the United Kingdom are women and although many are undoubtedly voluntary part-time workers, some (about 5 per cent, according to the Labour Force Survey conducted by the Department of Employment) only accept part-time work because full-time work is not available. It would seem that to achieve sex equality more full-time job opportunities for women are required.

In spite of the increase in the relative size of the female labour force, differences in rates of pay and conditions of service between men and women have persisted. In 1992, the average gross hourly earnings of full-time female workers in Great Britain were 79.3 per cent of the average gross hourly earnings of full-time male workers (up from 63.1 per cent in 1970). Consider the following reasons for this difference:

(a) Women have become concentrated in certain industries and occupations, many of which are not covered by collective agreements and where trade union organisation is weak (for example, clothing, footwear and the service industries).

(b) Traditional attitudes of 'women's work' and 'men's work' have been slow to change and have to some extent created non-competing groups within the labour market. These traditional attitudes have still not been completely eliminated from the education and guidance given in schools and colleges.

(c) Profit-seeking firms look upon training as an investment in 'human capital' and so prefer to invest in workers who are most likely to remain with the firm after the completion of training. If firms believe (rightly or wrongly) that women are more likely to interrupt their careers at an early stage to have children, they will also believe that it is more profitable to train and promote men, rather than women. Of course, this argument does not impress those women who have no intention of interrupting their careers.

It would seem that to achieve the main objectives of the Acts, improved crèche and nursery school facilities and more flexible working hours are required to enable women with small children to continue working. A greater willingness on the part of men to share the day-to-day tasks of bringing up children would also help.

Summary

1. The theory of marginal productivity states that a profit maximising firm selling its product in a perfectly competitive market will hire additional units of its variable factor of production up to the point at which the marginal revenue product of the variable factor is equal to the firm's marginal factor cost. If the variable factor is labour, purchased in a perfectly competitive labour market, the theory states that the firm will hire additional units of labour until the wage is equal to the value of the marginal product of labour.
2. The marginal productivity theory has a number of limitations: it ignores the supply side; it assumes that firms attempt to maximise profit and that labour is a homogeneous factor of production; and it assumes that wage rates and labour productivity are independent.
3. The elasticity of the supply of labour to an industry depends largely on the factors which influence the occupational and geographical mobility of labour. As wage rates rise, an individual's supply curve of labour may bend backwards as the rise in real income increases the individual's demand for leisure.
4. The complete elimination of wage differentials would require all workers to be homogeneous, all jobs to display identical non-monetary advantages and disadvantages, perfect knowledge and perfect labour mobility.
5. In practice, where there are imperfections in labour markets on both the demand and supply sides, wage rates and working conditions are often determined by the process of collective bargaining, in which negotiations take place between employers' and employees' representatives.
6. Disequilibria may persist in labour markets for a number of reasons: wage rigidity; the fact that labour is a heterogeneous factor of production; the existence of internal labour markets; and information costs.
7. In the United Kingdom, the Equal Pay Act and the Sex Discrimination Act have attempted (with only limited success) to achieve equal pay for work of equal value and equal opportunities for men and women, particularly in the areas of recruitment, training and promotion.

Exercises

1. Review your understanding of the following terms:

derived demand	monopsony
marginal revenue product	geographical immobility
marginal physical product	occupational immobility
value of the marginal product	internal labour market
marginal factor cost	search period

2. Given that the price of wheat is £15 per tonne and given the information below about a profit-maximising farmer's output of wheat, calculate the marginal physical product of labour and the marginal revenue product of labour. How many workers will be employed if the wage rate is £150 per week? How many workers will be employed if the wage rate falls to £120?

No. of workers	1	2	3	4	5	6	7
Total product (tonnes of wheat per week)	10	24	34	42	45	46	46

3. Explain in terms of the income and substitution effects the circumstances under which the individual's supply curve of labour will be 'backward-bending'.

4. Discuss the view that a trade union pushing for higher wage rates will inevitably increase the level of unemployment.

5. Discuss the factors influencing the length of the 'search' period during which an unemployed worker is engaged in seeking employment.

6. 'Imperfect competition in labour markets spoils the marginal conditions for Pareto efficiency.' Discuss with reference to: (a) a monopsonistic buyer of labour; (b) a product monopolist; and (c) a trade union.

7. In 1992, the average hourly earnings of women in full-time employment in Great Britain were only 79 per cent of men's average hourly earnings. Explain why, despite the existence of equal pay legislation, women are still paid less than men.

8.** Why are some groups of workers paid more than others?

17 REWARDS TO FACTORS OF PRODUCTION

Learning objectives

After reading this chapter, you should be able to:

- distinguish between the *functional* and *personal* distributions of income
- describe the Ricardian and marginal productivity theories of distribution and discuss the effect of technological progress on the distribution of income
- define *rent* as the price paid for the use of the services of land, and outline and assess the Ricardian theory of rent
- distinguish between the terms *economic rent* and *transfer earnings*
- outline and assess the neo-classical theory of interest and profit

Introduction

In the last chapter, we looked at the labour market and considered how wages are determined in a modern market economy. Our intention in this chapter is to investigate in greater detail the determination of the *relative* shares of the total national income going to the respective owners of the factors of production. Economists are interested in these distributive shares because they represent the most important measures of the welfare of the owners of factors. For instance, a 10 per cent increase in profit income and a corresponding 10 per cent decrease in wage income may mean a redistribution of the total national income from the lower to higher income groups which in turn may represent a deterioration in society's welfare.

First, we develop a general theoretical approach to distribution which focuses attention on: (a) Ricardo's theory of distribution; (b) the marginal productivity theory of distribution; (c) the relation between distributive shares and technical progress. In the second part of the chapter, we investigate theories of rent, profit and interest.

Note, however, a most important point. There is no universally accepted view of why different factors of production get what they receive in payment. This is so because the total value of goods and services produced is a result of the collaboration and co-operative effort of all productive resources. The rewards to factors, therefore, are explicitly or implicitly mingled with property rights which, in turn, are institutionally determined. As a result, a Pareto efficient distribution of income based on *given* property rights may not be the income distribution pattern which maximises society's welfare. As noted earlier, a Pareto efficient allocation of resources can coexist with large-scale poverty which, from the standpoint of social welfare maximisation, may be judged to be undesirable.

Economists have developed two main approaches to distribution: a *functional* distribution approach and a *personal* distribution approach. The former approach is concerned with the *sources* of income (that is, wages, rent, profit, etc.) and seeks to analyse the determination of factor prices; the marginal productivity theory has sprung from this approach. In the second approach, emphasis is placed on the actual size of the income accruing to individuals and families and so is concerned with measuring the inequalities of income and wealth. This aspect of the problem of distribution is dealt with in Ch. 32.

Theories of distribution

Ricardo's theory of distribution

David Ricardo (1772–1823) identified three classes in society – landlords, labourers and capitalists who receive rents, wages and profits respectively. Rents and wages, according to Ricardo, are part of the costs which capitalists must meet so as to be able to carry on production; whatever is left over is the capitalists' profits. In other words, profits are a *residual*.

The central idea of Ricardo's theory is that the demand for investment in the production of commodities comes from the capitalist and is stimulated by the desire to earn profits. Any increase in investment, though, increases the demand for labour and, through competition, pushes the wage rate above what Ricardo called its 'subsistance level'. This subsistence wage level was defined by Ricardo as that which provided the labourers with their customary standard of living. An increase in wages above the subsistence level encourages the population to grow faster through earlier marriages and the resulting increase in the labour supply depresses wages back to the subsistence level. So, in Ricardo's model, the share of wages in the total national income can in the long-run be no higher than that required for mere subsistence.

It also follows that with a rising population (which keeps wage rates down) the demand for land will increase and so tend to raise landlords' rents. Payment of these rising rents by capitalists will squeeze their profits. Since, in the long-run, wages are kept equal to the subsistence level, it follows in Ricardo's model that capitalists will experience *a falling rate of profit* because of ever-rising rents.

The marginal productivity theory again

We saw in the previous chapter that in perfectly competitive markets, factors of production would be paid the value of their marginal products as a reward for their services by profit-maximising firms. The neo-classical or so-called 'marginalist' school of economics argued that all factors made some contribution to production and that it was 'just' that they should receive payments equal to their marginal contributions. This, of course, was quite different from the views of Karl Marx who believed that labour was the source of all production and so should receive the total value of output as payment: anything less he regarded as capitalist 'exploitation' of labour.

The 'marginalist' school owes much to the work of the American economist, John Bates Clark. To outline his views, consider an aggregate production function with only two factors of production, labour (L) and capital (K), which we can write in the following general form:

$Q = f(L, K)$

Clark's views can be summarised in terms of the following propositions:

(a) With perfect competition and no externalities, both labour and capital will be paid the values of their marginal products. For example, as we showed in Ch. 16, profit-maximising firms will go on employing labour up to the point where the marginal product of labour is equal to the real wage (that is, $\Delta Q/\Delta L = W/P$). If the marginal product of labour exceeded the real wage, it would pay the firm to hire more workers; if the marginal product was less than the real wage, it would pay the firm to lay off some workers.

(b) Payments equal to the value of marginal products represent 'fair' and 'just' rewards to factor owners. This is clearly a value judgement based on the belief that *all* factor units should be paid the value of the contribution made by the last unit employed (which is likely to be the least productive unit).

(c) Paying all factors the value of their respective marginal products will just exhaust the value of total output and there will be no residual left over to be seized by the capitalists or by anyone else. This proposition was eventually proved by Leonhard Euler who showed that for a production function ($Q = f(L, K)$) which exhibits *constant returns to scale*,

$$Q = \mathrm{MP_L} . L + \mathrm{MP_K} . K$$

In other words, the total product is exactly used up in making payments to factor owners on the basis of their marginal products. This has become known as Euler's theorem.

Euler's theorem *This states that, given a production function with constant returns to scale, payments to factor owners on the basis of their marginal products will just exhaust the total product*

Critics of the marginal productivity theory have emphasised that the neo-classical views about the rewards to factors hold true only under the restrictive assumptions of constant returns to scale and perfect competition with no externalities.

Testing the marginal productivity theory empirically In the inter-war years, the economists R.W. Cobb and P.H. Douglas attempted to measure the shares of wages and profits in the total national income of the United States using a production function of the form $Q = AL^{\alpha}K^{1-\alpha}$, where A is a constant and α represents the share of labour and $1 - \alpha$ the share of capital in the total product. This has become known as a Cobb-Douglas production function. They found a remarkable constancy in the share of labour and capital for many years. Their empirical results gave a value for α of about 0.75 and hence a value for $1 - \alpha$ of about 0.25. Subsequently, empirical studies for other western industrial countries gave similar results.

A major implication of this is that workers as a whole are powerless to raise their share in the total national income. Any attempt by workers to increase wages will lead capitalists to cut back on their labour force so as to maintain their share of profits.

In the postwar years, however, there has been a tendency for the share of wages to rise. Robert Solow, a supporter of the neo-classical theory, has maintained that the explanation for this is capital accumulation which has increased the amount of capital per head of the labour force and so increased labour productivity. Other possible explanations of the rising share of wages are as follows:

(a) There has been an increase in the size of countries' public sectors in the postwar years. Public sector capital investments (for example, on roads, schools and hospitals) are estimated at cost – that is, they do not include a profit component in the calculation of national income.

(b) There has been a secular decline in the number of self-employed workers. Ceasing to be self-employed and working instead for an employer increases the share of wages.

(c) Technical progress has tended to make the price of capital lower relative to the price of labour. Most technical progress is labour-saving and so increases the productivity of labour.

An assessment of the marginal productivity theory The theory as a whole is an oversimplification of the determination of distributive shares. For one thing, the total income of a factor depends on both its quantity and its marginal productivity; it is by no means easy to identify those changes in income which result from changes in its quantity and those which result from changes in marginal productivity.

Secondly, the theory assumes that all units of factors are homogeneous and are, therefore, capable of being measured; labour, for instance, could be measured in man-hours provided differences in grades and quality were ignored. As we saw in Ch. 16, however, ignoring differences between grades of labour is a serious oversight. The same goes for capital – the quantity of capital can be measured on the basis of what it costs at the time of purchase (that is, its historic cost), but such costs have little bearing on the current value of the capital. Besides, it can be argued that although machines and equipment are productive, it does not follow that the owners of the capital are equally productive.

Technical progress and income distribution

Economists have argued that when technological changes occur in society, these changes can bring about alterations in the relative shares of land, labour and capital. For instance, Marx was one of the first economists to argue that labour-saving technology (for example, automation) would lead to rising unemployment, a decline in the share of wages and conflict between labour and capital.

Broadly speaking, technical progress can be either *neutral* or *non-neutral*. Ignoring land to simplify the argument, neutral technical progress is that which leaves the ratio in which labour and capital are employed unchanged and so does not alter the wage–profit ratio. Non-neutral technical progress, on the other hand, takes the form of a new invention or the development of a new technique of production which is either *labour-saving* or *capital-saving*. It is often argued that labour-saving technical progress tends to lower the share of labour in the national income, whilst capital-saving technical progress tends to lower the share of capital.

An important point must be made here. It is that a labour-saving innovation, instead of raising the share of profits, may actually depress the share of profits and raise the share of wages via the law of diminishing returns. This is possible because, as industries become more capital-intensive, larger units of capital per head of the labour force are employed. This implies greater labour productivity and a decline in the marginal productivity of capital. As a result, we should expect a rise in wages and a fall in profits.

Unfortunately, it is difficult in reality to distinguish changes in output which are due to changes in the capital–labour ratio brought about by technical progress from those which are due to increases in capital and labour (keeping the capital–labour ratio constant). This is because in practice technical progress is inevitably associated with increases in capital. For example, the introduction of jet-engined technology required investment in new aircraft. Consequently, the empirical evidence on the effects of technical progress on the shares of wages and profits is inconclusive.

We turn now to an examination of the rewards to specific factors. Ch. 16 has already dealt with the special problems connected with the reward to labour. In the remainder of this chapter, we focus attention on the issues associated with the rewards to land and capital.

Rent – the reward to land

Rent *The reward for the use of the services of land*

A most important point to note in understanding the economist's conception of rent is that its meaning differs substantially from that in ordinary usage. To the economist, rent is the reward for the use of the services of land; in addition, as we see below, it is a term used for any payment in excess of that needed to keep a particular factor in its current use, whether that factor be land, labour or capital. Whenever rent is used in this second sense, we shall refer to it as *economic rent*. This should be distinguished from the common usage of the term 'rent' which is a payment for the use of property (that is, houses, factories, offices and shops) and which includes a payment for the use of the land, capital and certain labour (for example, for repair and maintenance work). Clearly, this usage of the term 'rent' is much broader than the economist's conception of rent.

Ricardo's theory of rent

Ricardo saw rent as a payment for the 'original and indestructible qualities of the soil' on the assumption that land had only one use: that of growing foodstuffs. He pointed out that, from the standpoint of society, the supply of land is fixed – its supply price is zero in the sense that it is there whether or not it receives any payment. By the same token, it is the community's demand for foodstuffs that determines the demand for land. In other words, the demand for land is a derived demand.

Figure 17.1 illustrates the perfectly inelastic supply of land, SS, intersecting the community's demand for land, DD. The equilibrium rent is 0*R*. Now suppose that a

Fig. 17.1. The determination of rent. Given the inelastic supply of land, the equilibrium level of rent is demand-determined.

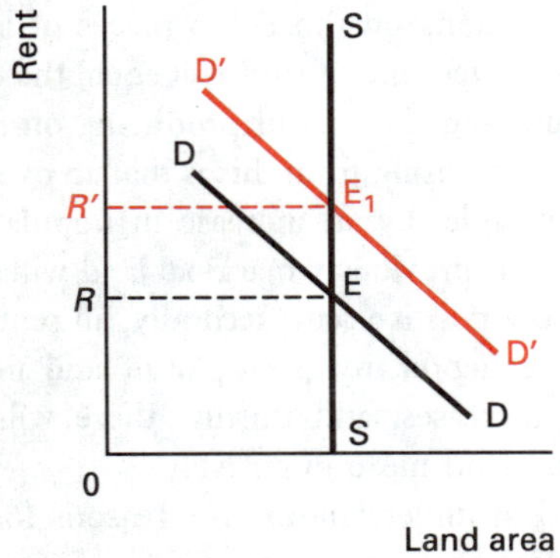

growing population leads to an increase in the demand for land use in general to D′D′. This raises the equilibrium rent from $0R$ to $0R'$. We can say that, given the fixed supply of land, rent is demand-determined.

Henry George, in his most celebrated book *Progress and Poverty* (1880), popularised the notion that rising rents represent 'unearned increments'. From the standpoint of equity, he argued, there is no justification for a few landlords being permitted to receive such 'unearned increments' which arise from the general progress of society and without any effort on the part of the landowners. He therefore campaigned for a 'single tax' system in which land rent regarded as a surplus could be taxed without any adverse effects on incentives. For example, in Fig. 17.1, starting at the equilibrium point E_1, a tax could be imposed which took away from the owners of land the rent equivalent to RR'. Landowners would obviously be made worse off but the demand curve, the supply curve and the equilibrium position would all be left unchanged.

Extending the theory of rent It may be objected that land in fact does not have original and indestructible powers so that rent cannot be regarded as purely demand-determined. Good quality land, after constant cultivation, can lose its fertility considerably. Likewise, natural resources like oil, gas and coal can become permanently exhausted. Furthermore, it is unrealistic to assume that land has only one use. Instead, it has many alternative uses so that the supply of land to a particular use cannot be regarded as perfectly inelastic.

Different tracts of land can *differ* in a number of respects: for example, the fertility of the soil may differ, and some areas of land are closer to markets than others. Some land (such as a desert) may be of such low quality that it is not used at all and so commands no rent. Land which is at the margin of being used in production is called *marginal land* and this too earns no rent. What then determines the different levels of rent on different tracts of land?

Competition should ensure that the same *rate of return* is earned on every piece of land used for productive purposes. To show this, consider two separate plots of land, A and B. Suppose that the cost (excluding rent) of producing a certain quantity of wheat on plot A is £100,000 per year, while the same quantity of wheat can be produced on plot B for only £80,000 per year. It should be true that the rent payable on plot B will be £20,000 per year higher than that on plot A. If the rent on B were not this much higher than the rent on A, farmers would increase their demand for the land on plot B and so drive up its rent. Thus, we can say that the difference between the rents commanded by two separate plots of land should be equal to the difference between the costs of producing on those two pieces of land. This further suggests that the rent payable on a given plot of land will equal the difference between the cost of producing on that land and the cost of producing on marginal land.

An important conclusion arising from this is that an overall increase in the demand for land (caused, for example, by an increase in population) will have three main effects: first, land which was previously marginal land will be brought into productive use and so will command a positive rent; secondly, all rents will rise as the difference between the cost of producing on any given plot of land and the cost of producing on the *new* marginal land increases; and thirdly, there will now be an incentive for producers to use existing land more intensively.

The theory is helpful in understanding the reasons for the rapid rise in rents in developing countries. Most of these countries suffer from over-population which has led to rising food prices and rising rents. Also, because of lack of alternative investment and employment opportunities in the industrial and commercial sectors, land has become a major source of investment as well as employment with a resultant steep rise in land prices and land rents. Many irrigation projects and housing development schemes have provided a great stimulus to large-scale speculative activity in land transactions, pushing up rents even further.

Site rents The above argument applies equally well to different amounts of rent paid for urban sites. Two urban sites may be equally good in all respects other than location and yet command different rents on account of these differences in location. For example, sites in the centre of a city command higher rents than sites on the outskirts of a city. Shops and offices in Oxford Street in London have higher rents than those on the outskirts of London because sites in the centre of London have inelastic supplies in relation to the demand for them.

Economic rent and transfer earnings

The foregoing discussion has shown that Ricardo's theory of rent assumes a fixed supply of land so that all rent is a surplus over and above the cost of keeping land in its present use. Such a surplus has become known as 'economic rent' and it has been pointed out that this concept can be applied not only to land, but also to labour and capital.

Transfer earnings *The payment required to keep a factor in its present use*

Economic rent *Any payment in excess of transfer earnings*

Transfer earnings is the payment required to keep a factor in its present use, while economic rent is any payment in excess of transfer earnings. Consider a doctor employed in private sector medicine and who earns £40,000 per annum. If the same doctor would be paid £30,000 per annum in the National Health Service and assuming that all other conditions of service were identical to those in the present post, transfer earnings would be £30,000 per annum, because this is the payment necessary to keep the doctor in the private sector. The doctor can be regarded as earning an economic rent of £10,000 per annum.

As pointed out above, in the case of perfectly inelastic supply of a factor, all of its earnings are economic rent. This situation was illustrated in Fig. 17.1 in which SS represented the inelastic supply of land. Given the demand curve DD, the factor's earnings (given by $0RES$) are all economic rent.

In the case of an upward-sloping supply curve of a factor, part of its earnings are transfer earnings and part economic rent. Given the demand curve DD and the supply curve SS in Fig. 17.2, the equilibrium price and quantity are $0P_1$ and $0Q_1$ respectively. Total earnings of the factor are thus given by the area of $0P_1EQ_1$. The price paid for the marginal unit of the factor supplied ($0P_1 = Q_1E$) is just equal to the transfer earnings of this unit. All previous units supplied are therefore receiving an economic rent. The area $0SEQ_1$ represents the total transfer earnings of the factor. The remainder of the factor's earnings, that is the area between the supply curve and the line P_1E (triangle SP_1E), represents economic rent.

In some cases, all of the earnings of a factor can represent transfer earnings. Consider the case of a firm that buys a factor in a perfectly competitive market so that it faces a perfectly elastic supply curve. This is represented by the line SS in Fig. 17.3. The factor's total earnings (represented by the area $0P_1EQ_1$) are purely transfer earnings because if the firm offered any price below $0P_1$ it would be unable to purchase any of the factor.

Fig. 17.2. The distinction between transfer earnings and economic rent. The factor's transfer earnings are given by the area $0SEQ_1$. This is the sum of money that needs to be paid to keep the factor in its present use. The remainder of the factor's earnings (area SP_1E) are economic rent.

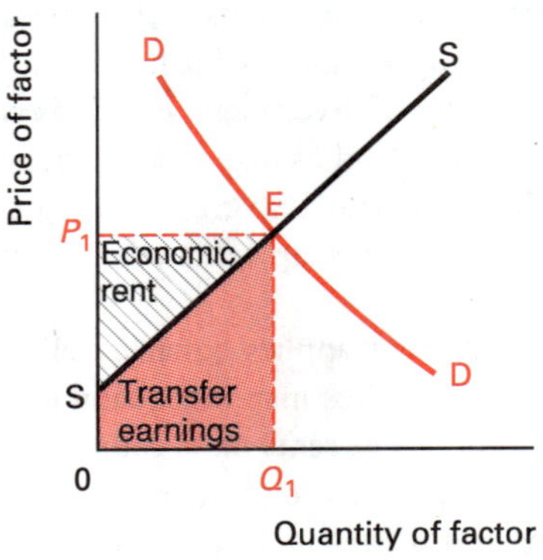

Fig. 17.3. Case in which all of factor's earnings represent transfer earnings. Given the perfectly elastic supply of the factor, all of the payment to the factor is necessary to keep it in its present use.

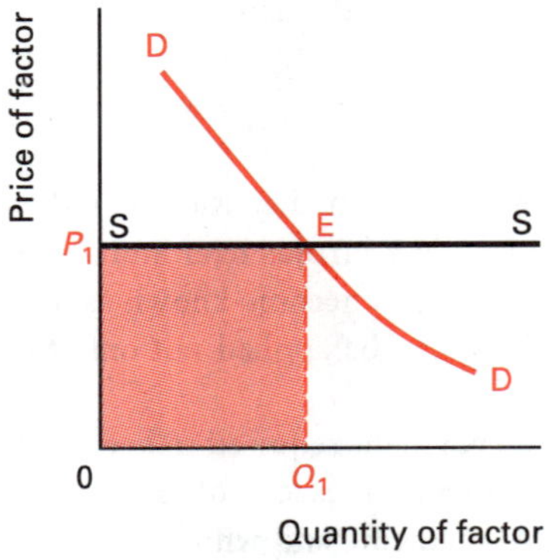

Like land, labour and capital are heterogeneous factors of production – for instance, different grades of workers (teachers, doctors and nurses) have different training and skills. Such grades have an inelastic supply, at least in the short-run. A sudden increase in the demand for doctors cannot be met overnight so existing doctors will earn an economic rent.

Marshall called rent which disappears in the long-run 'quasi-rent'. As an example, consider a machine with only one use, so that in the short-run its transfer earnings are zero and all of its earnings represent economic rent. In the long-run, the machine will depreciate and will only be replaced if it earns a sufficient return to make it worthwhile to the owner. Thus, part of its earnings (regarded as economic rent in the short-run) becomes transfer earnings in the long-run.

In general, because factors of production are heterogeneous, any grade of factor which becomes scarce in relation to the demand for it will earn a surplus in the form of economic rent. Different machines, for example, are designed to do specific jobs and thus have an inelastic supply in the short-run. To take an extreme example, a dust-cart and a computer cannot be expected to perform each other's functions. Changes in the demand for heterogeneous capital inputs, then, will yield differing amounts of economic rent.

To sum up, we can say that economic rent accrues to factors because of factor immobility which results in inelastic supply.

Interest or profit – the reward to capital

Just as wages represent the price of labour and rent is the price of land, so interest (or profit) is the price of capital. Profit can be regarded as the difference between the expected future costs and the expected future returns on investment. Profit is, therefore, the usual term for the reward to capitalists. Interest, on the other hand, represents the cost of capital – if money has to be borrowed to finance an investment, interest has to be paid on it; if a firm uses its own money to finance investment, the interest that could have been earned by lending the money is an *opportunity* cost. In the neo-classical model with perfect competition and perfect foresight, both the cost of capital and the reward to capitalists are equal to the value of the marginal product of capital and there is no surplus. This is equivalent to saying that perfectly competitive firms in long-run equilibrium earn just *normal profit* (or a normal rate of return on investment), where normal profit is defined as the level of profit which provides no incentive for firms to enter or leave the industry. This result was demonstrated in Ch. 9.

Above-normal profit If a firm is a monopolist or oligopolist and so has some degree of market power, it may be able to earn above-normal profit in the long-run by using entry barriers which restrict the entry of new firms (as we showed in Ch. 10).

Also, if a project is *risky*, a prospect of a high profit may be required to attract firms to undertake the project, rather than invest in, for example, risk-free government securities. Projects are risky if they have an uncertain rate of return. For instance, prospecting for oil may or may not result in the discovery of a new oil-field; similarly, developing and launching a new product on to the market may or may not prove popular with consumers. Thus, risk may be associated with the uncertain outcome of both *existing* and *innovative* activities.

One view of profit, then, is as the reward for risk-bearing and innovation. For example, in the pharmaceutical industry, the development of new drugs is highly risky: many research projects do not result in commercially viable drugs, but the prospect of a highly profitable drug provides an incentive for firms to undertake widespread research and development programmes. A successful programme will yield above-normal profit for the innovating firm, at least in the short-run. Of course, if there are no entry barriers, such 'innovation' profit will be competed away in the long-run by imitators.

The neo-classical theory of interest

The central proposition of this theory is that interest is the reward for waiting. Such waiting involves the postponement of current consumption to some future date. The longer the period of waiting, the higher the rate of return on capital because it enables investors to adopt capital-using techniques of production.

According to the neo-classical theory of interest, the price of capital (that is, the interest rate) is determined by the total demand for and the total supply of funds for spending on capital goods. As illustrated in Fig. 17.4, using more resources to produce capital goods means giving up some quantity of consumer goods in the present period. In other words, capital accumulation (or investment) necessitates *refraining from some current consumption* (or saving). In the neo-classical model, savings are seen as providing the supply of loanable funds and releasing resources from the production of current consumer goods into the production of capital goods. Investment, on the other hand, is seen as providing the demand for loanable funds.

Fig. 17.4. ***The choice between capital goods and consumer goods.*** An increase in the output of capital goods from $0K_1$ to $0K_2$ results in the output of consumer goods falling from $0C_1$ to $0C_2$.

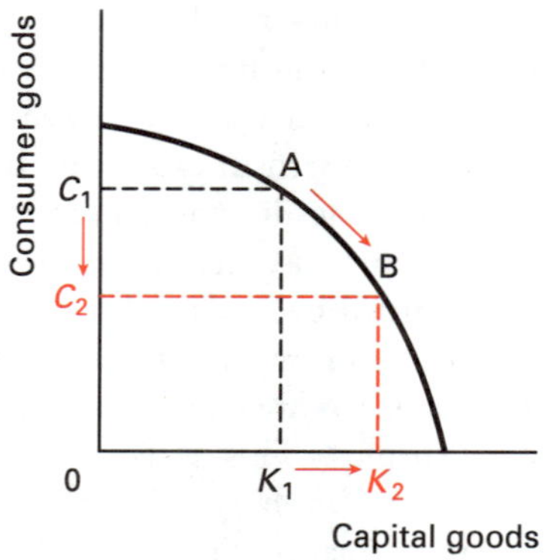

Fig. 17.5. ***The supply of loanable funds.*** An increase in the rate of interest from $0i_1$ to $0i_2$ leads to an increase in the amount of loanable funds supplied from $0L_1$ to $0L_2$.

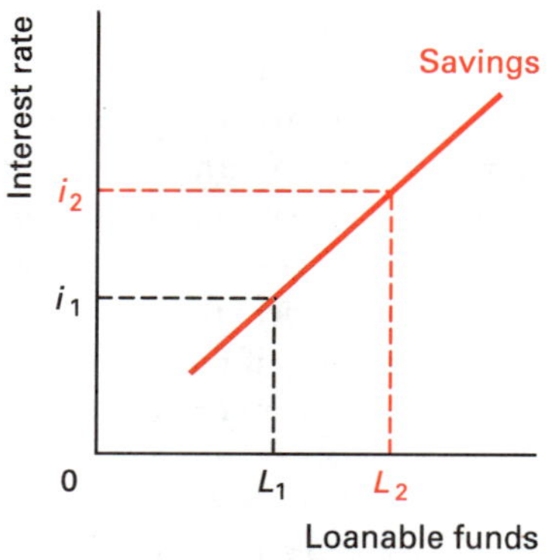

The higher the rate of interest, the more willing households and individuals will be to save and so sacrifice some present consumption for (uncertain) future consumption. This implies that the supply of loanable funds plotted against the rate of interest will yield a curve which slopes upwards from left to right as shown in Fig. 17.5.

The total demand for loanable funds is the sum of all individual firms' demands for capital at different interest rates. It is here that the marginal productivity of capital comes into the analysis. Given perfect competition, the interest rate facing a single firm can be taken as given. To determine how much investment to undertake, therefore, a firm must estimate the marginal productivity of a capital project and compare it with the project's real cost. One way is to estimate the project's *expected internal rate of return* and then compare this with the prevailing market rate of interest, as was shown in Ch. 8. Since a firm will undertake the most profitable capital projects first, the expected rate of return will decline as more and more units of capital are employed (because of diminishing returns). This is illustrated in Fig. 17.6 where the firm in question will invest in capital projects up to $0L_1$ where the expected rate of return is just equal to the market rate of interest $0i_1$. The curve in Fig. 17.6 is sometimes called the *marginal efficiency of capital* curve and can be interpreted as the firm's demand for capital.

Aggregating all firms' demands for capital and drawing the total demand curve against the rate of interest on the same graph as the total supply of loanable funds, we obtain the graph shown in Fig. 17.7. The equilibrium rate of interest (or equilibrium

Fig. 17.6. ***A single firm's demand for capital.*** The marginal efficiency of capital curve shows the expected rate of return on investment.

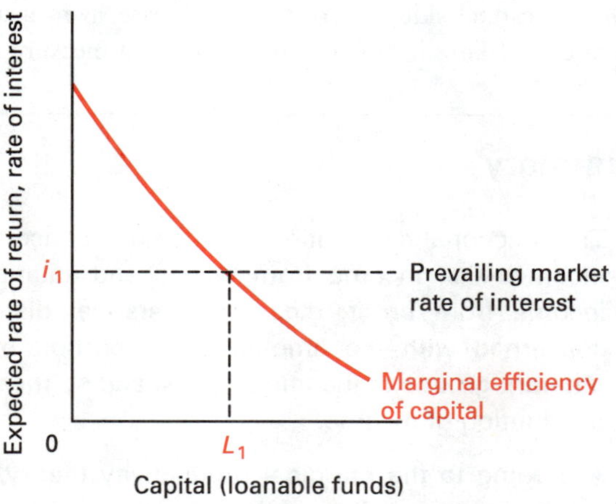

Fig. 17.7. ***The market for loanable funds.*** The equilibrium rate of interest is determined by the interaction of the demand and supply of loanable funds. In this market the equilibrium rate of interest is $0i_1$ and the equilibrium amount of loanable funds is $0L$.

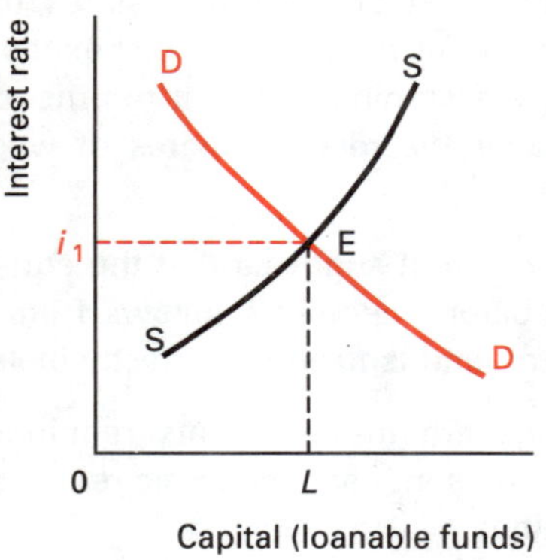

price of capital) is determined at the point where the two curves intersect and is denoted by $0i_1$ in the graph.

Figure 17.7 suggests that if, for some reason, there were an autonomous increase in savings, shifting the supply curve to the right, this would depress interest rates and so reduce the cost of additional investment. Since additional investment yields diminishing returns, a conclusion of the neo-classical theory of interest is that such investment will only be undertaken under conditions of falling interest rates.

Assessing the neo-classical theory of interest Several criticisms can be levelled against the theory. Consider the following:

(a) It ignores the possibility that savers may have a given purpose for which they are saving – to buy a new car or pay for a holiday, for example. In such a case, a higher interest rate may actually reduce savers' willingness to save because rising interest rates raise interest incomes and so reduce the amount of new saving necessary for the given purpose.

(b) A substantial amount of saving in modern industrial societies is done as a matter of habit and custom, independently of interest rate levels.

(c) On the capital side, severe problems arise in measuring the capital stock in a country, making it difficult to identify and measure the reward to capital.

Summary

1. The functional distribution of income is concerned with the *source* of incomes (i.e. income from wages and salaries, income from rent, income from profit, etc.). The personal distribution of income is concerned with the amount or proportion of income accruing to different groups of income earners, and so measures inequality in the distribution of income.
2. According to the marginal productivity theory, factors of production will be paid the values of their marginal products under conditions of perfect competition. Euler's theorem states that paying factors the values of their marginal products will just exhaust national income and leave no surplus (assuming constant returns to scale). Technological progress may alter the relative shares of wages and profits in the national income.
3. Ricardo's theory of rent suggests that the equilibrium level of rent is purely demand-determined. This follows from Ricardo's assumption that the supply of land is fixed or perfectly inelastic.
4. Transfer earnings are the payments required to keep a factor of production in its present use. Economic rent is any payment in excess of transfer earnings.
5. Normal profit in an industry is the level of profit which provides no incentive for firms to enter or leave the industry. Above-normal profits may be earned by firms which have monopoly power and are able to establish barriers to entry. High profits are found in some industries as a reward for risk-taking and innovation.
6. In neo-classical theory, the equilibrium rate of interest is determined by the interaction of the demand for and supply of loanable funds. In this theory, interest is viewed as the reward for saving – that is, for postponing consumption until some future date.

Exercises

1. Review your understanding of the following terms:

functional distribution	rent
personal distribution	economic rent
marginal productivity	transfer earnings
aggregate production function	marginal land
Euler's theorem	normal profit
Cobb–Douglas production function	quasi-rent
neutral technical progress	innovation profit
non-neutral technical progress	subsistence wage

2. Consider the following demand and supply schedules per time period for a homogeneous type of labour:

Wage rate (£)	100	110	120	130	140	150
Quantity demanded	1,000	800	600	400	200	0
Quantity supplied	0	300	600	100	1,200	1,500

   (a) Plot the demand and supply curves on the same graph and identify the equilibrium wage rate.
   (b) Calculate the total wage income at the equilibrium and find the total amount of economic rent and transfer earnings.

3. Discuss the view that since capital is not itself productive and labour is the sole producer of value, the total value of output should be received by labour.

4. Consider the problems involved in measuring a country's capital stock. How do these problems affect the conclusions of the marginal productivity theory of distribution?

5. Explain why office rents are lower in the provinces than in the centre of London.

6. Discuss the effect on the distribution of income of a 20 per cent tax on all land in the UK. What would the effect be if the tax were only imposed on land in the City of London?

7. Consider the factors that will influence the sources of profit in:
   (a) a firm producing pet food in a highly competitive market;
   (b) a computer software company;
   (c) a sugar refining company.

INTRODUCTION TO THE ECONOMY AS A WHOLE

INTRODUCING MACROECONOMICS

18 INTRODUCING MACROECONOMICS

Learning objectives

After reading this chapter, you should be able to:

- explain the meaning of an economic aggregate, particularly the total value of a country's output
- assess the problems involved in aggregation
- define the terms national product, national expenditure, national income, consumption, saving and investment and show how they are linked in the circular flow of income
- explain how the national product, national expenditure and national income are measured in the United Kingdom, and the extent to which national income figures can be used to construct an indicator of economic welfare
- define the terms aggregate demand and aggregate supply, and explain the meaning of macroeconomic equilibrium

Introduction

We now start our study of the economy as a whole and in the remainder of the book we consider many of the world's most pressing macroeconomic problems – problems like persistent unemployment, rapid inflation, balance of payments difficulties, economic stagnation and unequal distributions of income and wealth. In order to analyse these problems, we must first identify, measure and consider the determinants of the main *aggregates* in the economy. The most important aggregates are: (a) the economy's total output of goods and services; (b) the total demand for this output; (c) total employment and unemployment; (d) the general price level; (e) the balance of payments; (f) the rate of economic growth. In this chapter, we concentrate on the meaning and measurement of an economy's total output and the total demand for that output.

All aggregates are made up of their constituent parts – for example, we see later that the total demand for a country's output consists of the sum of individual demands and can be written as follows:

$$AD = C + I + G + X - M$$

Aggregate demand
The sum of the demands for goods and services by consumers, businesses, the government and foreign residents

where AD is aggregate demand, C is the sum of all individual consumers' demands for goods and services, I is the sum of all individual firms' demands for investment goods, G is the government's demand for goods and services, X is the total foreign demand for the country's exports and M is the demand for imports. To analyse the main determinants of aggregates like these, it is necessary first to have an understanding of the behaviour of the individual economic agents. This means that we must be aware of the microeconomic theories of consumer behaviour, of the firm, of public sector activity and of distribution. For this reason, we started the book with microeconomics and only now turn to the study of macroeconomics. Micro- and macroeconomics are intimately linked and, where appropriate, we shall point out the microeconomic foundations of the macroeconomic analyses that we develop and apply.

The problems of aggregation

Problems arise in aggregation largely because of the difficulty of finding an appropriate unit of measurement. In adding up the total output of the United Kingdom, for instance, there is no single physical unit of measurement that can be used: the millions of different types of goods and services are all measured in different units – for example, steel is measured in tonnes and cloth is measured in metres and it is, of course, impossible to add tonnes to metres. The problem is overcome, at least partially, by using money as the unit of measurement – this greatly simplifies the adding up, but it gives rise to the problem of distinguishing between real and nominal values.

If the *value* of total output should double from, say, £10 billion to £20 billion, this does not necessarily mean that total output itself has doubled: part of the increase may indeed be due to an increase in physical output, but part may be due to an increase in *prices*. The problem with value measurements is that they necessarily have a price and quantity component and it is not always easy to separate the two. To estimate real output, it is necessary to deflate the value of total output by an appropriate price index. This converts total output measured in *current* prices to total output measured in *constant* prices. (The actual way in which this calculation is done is illustrated later in this chapter.) There is, however, the problem of deciding which price index to use. In the United Kingdom, two main price indices are calculated: the General Index of Retail Prices and the Producer Price Index. Each one is a weighted average of the prices of a number of selected goods – neither provides a completely true average price of all the goods and services included in the country's total output. Changes in the deflated total output figures, therefore, can really only give us an estimate of the true changes in the nation's physical output.

Real output *The quantity of goods and services produced in an economy. An estimate of the monetary value of real output can be obtained by adjusting the value of output measured in current prices by an appropriate price index*

Price index *This is used to measure changes in the price level by comparing the price of a basket of goods and services in the current year to the price of this basket in a selected base year*

Another problem with aggregates is that they hide their constituent elements. For example, an increase in the economy's total output tells us nothing about who receives that output. Indeed, as we shall see later, a rise in total output accompanied by a change in the distribution of income which makes some people better off and others worse off cannot necessarily be interpreted as an improvement in the country's living standards. Distributional factors should always be borne in mind when considering the effects of changes in aggregate variables.

Total output: national product, national expenditure, national income

In principle, the value of an economy's total output can be measured in three ways. These can be seen by examining Fig. 18.1 which shows the *flow* of income and spending in a simple model of an economy. The two main economic agents in the flow diagram are households and firms. The households can be thought of as the owners of factors of production, the services of which they sell to firms in exchange for income (in the form of wages, salaries, interest, rent and profit). Note that, in the model, all profits are assumed to be distributed to households and not retained by the firms. The firms use the factors of production to produce the many different types of

Fig. 18.1. The circular flow of income and spending. This flow diagram shows the main flows of money around the economy.

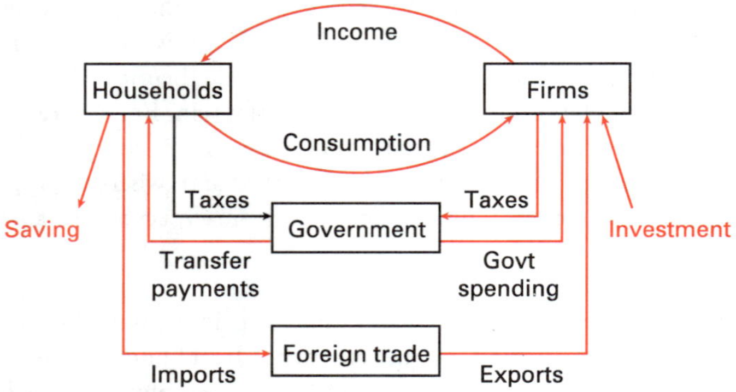

goods and services which they then sell to households (whose spending is called consumption), the government, foreigners (who buy exports) and other firms (whose spending on capital goods is called investment). The diagram also shows that the part of household income which is not spent on consumption is either saved, spent on imports or is taken in taxes by the government. The government itself uses its tax revenue (as well as money from other sources – see Ch. 14) to finance government spending, including transfer payments (such as pensions, unemployment benefits and student grants). Before proceeding we must explain the terms consumption, saving, and investment more fully. Consumption is the total expenditure by households on goods and services which yield utility in the current period. Investment is the production of, or expenditure by firms on goods and services which are not for current consumption; that is, real capital goods like factories, machines, bridges and motorways, all goods which yield a flow of consumer goods and services in future periods. Saving is that part of disposable income (that is, income less taxes) which is not spent in the current period. It follows that disposable income minus saving equals consumption.

Consumption *Total expenditure by households on goods and services which yield utility in the current period*

Investment *The production of goods and services which are not for current consumption*

Saving *That part of disposable income which is not spent in the current period*

The three ways of measuring the annual value of total output in an economy are by calculating its *national product, national expendituure* and *national income*. Consider these in turn.

National product *The total value of all final goods and services produced by firms during a year*

National product This is found by adding up the value of all final goods and services produced by firms during the year. Note that *all* final goods and services produced must be included, whether they are to be sold to consumers or to the government, whether they are to be sold abroad as exports, or whether they are capital goods to be sold to other firms. It is, however, important to include only *final* goods and services: all intermediate goods must be excluded so that double-counting is avoided. For example, in the production of a woollen coat, only the value of the final coat should be counted. The values of the raw wool and the woollen cloth are included in the value of the coat. If we were to count them as well, we should be guilty of double- or even triple-counting. If all intermediate goods were included in the calculation of the national product, therefore, we would seriously overestimate the value of the country's total output.

One way of avoiding double-counting is to sum the *values-added* by all firms at the different stages of production. To illustrate this, consider a simple example in which producing a woollen coat involves the following three stages of production:

1. A sheep farmer produces raw wool and sells it to a mill for £10. This represents an income of £10 for the farmer. *Value-added* = £10.
2. The mill uses the raw wool to produce cloth which it sells to a coat factory for £21. This represents income (including profit) of £11 for the mill – remember that £10 has had to be paid for the raw wool. *Value-added* = £11.
3. The coat factory produces the coat and sells it for £40. This includes £21 to cover the cost of the cloth and £19 to pay incomes, including profits. *Value-added* = £19.

The total value-added in this example (£40) is just equal to the value of the final coat.

National expenditure
The total value of spending on all final goods and services during a year

National expenditure This is found by adding up all the spending on the final goods and services produced by firms. Such an aggregate will only equal the value of total output if those goods which are produced but not sold are also included – this item, which is called 'net changes in stocks and work in progress', is normally counted as part of firms' investment spending (which is logical since such goods are for future rather than current consumption). National expenditure, then, is the sum of consumption of domestically produced goods, investment (including changes in stocks and work in progress), government expenditure and exports. Notice that, as before, in order to avoid double-counting, only spending on *final* goods and services is included.

National income
The total value of all incomes earned by factors of production during a year

National income It is because goods and services are produced by factors of production that income is created in an economy. So another way of calculating the value of total output is to add up all the incomes (that is, wages, salaries, interest, rent and profits) of all factors of production, those producing intermediate goods as well as those producing final goods. It is important in using this method to exclude all transfer payments as these represent nothing more than a redistribution of income from taxpayers to the transfer recipients; including them, therefore, would involve double-counting.

Assuming: (a) that all three measures are calculated accurately; (b) that only *final* goods and services are counted in the national product and national expenditure figures; (c) that any changes in unsold stocks are included in the national expenditure figures; and (d) that *all* incomes, including profits but excluding transfer payments, are counted in the national income figures, then it must follow that all three measures will provide an identical figure for the value of the country's total output. That is,

National product ≡ National expenditure ≡ National income

In principle, then, these three aggregates simply represent different ways of measuring the flow of output or income being created in an economy over a period of time.

Complications

In the attempt to calculate the value of a country's total output using the above methods, a number of complications arise. For example, how to deal with capital depreciation and stock appreciation; whether to value output at market prices or at factor cost; whether to include net property income from abroad. Consider these problems in turn.

Depreciation *An allowance made to take account of the 'wear and tear' of capital*

Depreciation When investment takes place during a year, new capital is created and it is correct that this should be included in our calculation of the value of total output for that year. Some investment occurs, however, simply to replace capital which has worn out during the year – such 'wearing out' of capital is called 'depreciation' or 'capital consumption'. Where no allowance is made for this depreciation in the calculation of investment, the resulting figure is called *gross* investment. When depreciation is deducted from gross investment, we have *net* investment and it is this which measures the true addition to the country's capital stock during the year. Where no allowance is made for depreciation in calculating the value of total output, the resulting figures are also referred to as gross. Thus, we have:

$$\left.\begin{array}{l}\text{Gross national product}\\\text{Gross national expenditure}\\\text{Gross national income}\end{array}\right\} - \text{depreciation} = \left\{\begin{array}{l}\text{Net national product}\\\text{Net national expenditure}\\\text{Net national income}\end{array}\right.$$

For two main reasons, economists are usually quite happy to work with 'gross' rather than 'net' figures: first, depreciation tends to change only slowly over time so that the 'gross' and 'net' figures move closely together over any period of a few years; and secondly, depreciation figures are notoriously difficult to estimate with any accuracy.

Stock appreciation We have noted before that all three measurements of total output include the value of the net change in stocks of unsold goods. If prices are rising, the value of firms' stocks will be rising even if there are no net physical additions to them. To take account of this so-called 'stock appreciation', it is necessary to subtract an appropriate amount in computing the national income.

Market prices and factor cost When national expenditure is computed, it is measured initially in market prices – for example, the total spending on beer is equal to the quantity of beer bought times its average market price. Unfortunately, many market prices are distorted by indirect taxes and subsidies: indirect taxes have the effect of raising the prices of goods above what would otherwise have been set, while subsidies lower such prices. National income and national product, however, are both measured at 'factor cost' – that is, in terms of the sums paid out to the owners of factors of production – and this excludes indirect taxes and subsidies. To ensure that national expenditure is the same as national income and national product, it is necessary to convert market prices to factor cost by *subtracting* indirect taxes and *adding* subsidies. In other words, we can write:

$$\begin{array}{l}\text{National expenditure at}\\\text{market prices}\end{array} - \begin{array}{l}\text{Indirect}\\\text{taxes}\end{array} + \text{Subsidies} = \begin{array}{l}\text{National expenditure}\\\text{at factor cost}\end{array}$$

It is preferable (and usual) to measure the value of total output at factor cost rather than in market prices, otherwise an increase in indirect taxation or a reduction in subsidies would have the effect of raising the estimate of total output even when no greater quantity of goods and services was being produced.

Net property income from abroad Some of the output produced within the United Kingdom is actually produced by firms which are owned by overseas residents. Similarly, some output produced overseas is produced by firms owned by United Kingdom residents or United Kingdom companies. Whether this should be taken into account or not in calculating the value of total output depends on whether we require a measurement of the domestic output of the United Kingdom or a measurement of the output produced by all the factors of production owned by United Kingdom residents. In the former case, we need make no adjustment but the figures are renamed *domestic* product, income and expenditure. In the latter case, 'net property income from abroad' has to be added, where the term 'net property income from abroad' is equal to that income received by United Kingdom residents from the production of output by firms overseas *minus* that income paid to overseas residents from the production of output by domestic firms. We can thus write:

$$\left.\begin{array}{l}\text{Gross domestic product}\\ \text{Gross domestic income}\\ \text{Gross domestic expenditure}\end{array}\right\} + \begin{array}{l}\text{Net property income}\\ \text{from abroad}\end{array}$$

$$= \left\{\begin{array}{l}\text{Gross national product}\\ \text{Gross national income}\\ \text{Gross national expenditure}\end{array}\right.$$

The United Kingdom accounts

A detailed breakdown of the national product, national expenditure and national income figures for the United Kingdom in 1991 is shown in Tables 18.1, 18.2 and 18.3. All the terms used have been explained in the previous section with the exception of the *statistical discrepancy*. This is a figure included to ensure that all three methods yield identical results which, of course, they should do in principle, but which they invariably fail to do in practice because of errors and omissions which arise through imperfect data collection and measurement problems.

Table 18.1 Gross and net national product for the United Kingdom, 1991.

	£ million
Agriculture, forestry, fishing	8,772
Energy and water supply	28,273
Manufacturing	104,283
Construction	33,686
Transport, communications	34,755
Distributive trades	73,024
Insurance, banking, finance and business services	88,179
Ownership of dwellings	34,839
Public administration, defence	34,786
Public health, education	49,643
Other services	33,915
Statistical discrepancy	17
Gross domestic product at factor cost	497,001
Net property income from abroad	328
Gross national product	497,329
Depreciation	−63,968
Net national product	433,361

Source: UK National Accounts, 1992.

Table 18.2 Gross and net national expenditure for the United Kingdom, 1991.

	£ million
Consumers' expenditure	367,853
General government final consumption	121,899
Gross domestic fixed capital formation	95,442
Value of physical increase in stocks and work in progress	–5,303
Total domestic expenditure at market prices	579,891
Exports of goods and services	135,115
Imports of goods and services	–140,415
Taxes on expenditure	–83,023
Subsidies	5,878
Statistical discrepancy	–445
Gross domestic expenditure at factor cost	497,001
Net property income from abroad	328
Gross national expenditure	497,329
Depreciation	–63,968
Net national expenditure	433,361

Source: UK National Accounts, 1992.

Table 18.3 Gross and net national income for the United Kingdom, 1991.

	£ million
Income from employment	329,808
Income from self-employment	57,507
Gross trading profits of companies	60,674
Gross trading surplus of public corporations	3,119
Gross trading surplus of government enterprises	119
Other incomes	48,582
Total domestic income	499,809
Stock appreciation	–2,825
Statistical discrepancy	17
Gross domestic income at factor cost	497,001
Net property income from abroad	328
Gross national income	497,329
Depreciation	–63,968
Net national income	433,361

Source: UK National Accounts, 1992.

The 'black' economy

It should be pointed out that official statistics tend to underestimate the actual volume of economic activity that occurs. This is because of the operation of the so-called 'black' or underground economy. The black economy refers to those unrecorded economic transactions conducted on a cash basis with a view to illegal

Black economy *That part of economic activity that is not recorded in official statistics*

evasion of tax. In 1985, the Liverpool University Research Group estimated that the black economy in the United Kingdom amounted to 14.5 per cent of national income. It appears that in the case of many consumer services (like plumbing, decorating and electrical repairs), it is common for two prices to be quoted. The lower price is quoted on the understanding that payment will be made in cash and that no receipt or other record of the transaction will be issued. The existence of a black economy is, of course, not confined to the United Kingdom. It has been widely reported that in Italy, for example, whole industries operate outside the officially recorded economy. Some estimates suggest that the Italian black economy has an output valued at 30 per cent of national income. In 1987, Italian statisticians added 18 per cent to their estimate of Italy's national income to account for unrecorded economic activity.

The borderline between the officially recorded economy and the black economy is not always clear-cut. If a painter decorates his or her own house, nobody would argue that tax should be paid on the non-existent earnings; but what if a person decorates a friend's house in return for some help with fixing a car? Or what if the painter works for other people at weekends in return for cash? Many would exclude the second example, but would include the third example in a definition of the black economy. By its very nature it is impossible to quantify exactly the extent of the black economy. There is some partial evidence of its existence as the expenditure estimates of gross national product (based on the *Family Expenditure Survey*) regularly exceed the estimates from the income side. Indeed, some estimates have suggested that if the Exchequer received all the tax due to it from the black economy, the basic rate of income tax might be cut by 10 per cent.

National income and economic welfare

Economic welfare *The general level of well-being in a society which depends on such factors as the quantity of goods and services available, the distribution of income, the impact of externalities and the composition of output*

Since the national income of a country is a measurement of the output of the final goods and services produced by that country in a year, can we conclude that if national income rises from one year to the next, economic welfare must also rise? We certainly can make no statements about economic welfare unless we first convert national income into *real* national income *per capita*. In this section, we first show how this is done and secondly, we consider under what circumstances a rise in real output per capita can be interpreted as an *actual*, *potential* or *pseudo*-improvement in economic welfare.

National income and real output per capita To convert national income into real output per capita, it is necessary to make two adjustments: (i) national income must be deflated by an appropriate price index to convert it to real terms; (ii) the figure must then be divided by the population to convert it to per capita terms. To

Table 18.4 Comparing national income figures.

	1988	1992	
National income	£12m.	£24m.	
Price index	100	120	
Real national income (1988 prices)	£12m.	£20m.	(24m. × 100/200)
Population	3,000	4,000	
Real output per capita	£4,000	£5,000	

show how these adjustments are made, consider a simple numerical example. Examine the figures in Table 18.4 where the two years 1988 and 1992 are being compared for a hypothetical economy. Notice that money national income has increased by 100 per cent during the period, but prices have risen by 20 per cent from the base year figure of 100 in 1988 to 120 in 1992, and population has risen by $33\frac{1}{3}$ per cent from 3,000 to 4,000 inhabitants.

The first step is to *deflate* the national income figures to eliminate the effects of the rise in prices. As 1988 is the base year, the money value and the real value of national income are the same in that year. In 1992, though, the price index is 120 and this means that part of the increase in national income is a result of the rise in prices rather than the rise in physical output. This rise in prices is eliminated from the figures by dividing national income by the price index and multiplying by 100. This calculation is called deflating the national income. Comparing the deflated figures, we see that real national income (or national income in constant prices) has increased by $66\frac{2}{3}$ per cent from £12 million to £20 million during the period.

The next step is to take account of the increased size of population because, although real national income has risen, it has to be shared out among more people. Dividing the real national income figures by population for the two years, we obtain a figure for 'real output per capita' of £4,000 in 1988 and £5,000 in 1992, an increase of 25 per cent. So, in this example, although money national income rose by 100 per cent, real output per capita rose by only 25 per cent. We can conclude that an increase in national income will only be equivalent to the same proportionate increase in real output per capita if both prices and the population remain unchanged. Since prices and populations generally change over time, it is crucially important to compare real output per capita figures rather than money national income figures before coming to any conclusions about changes in economic welfare.

Actual, potential and pseudo-improvements in economic welfare Even if real output per capita rises, it is not necessarily true that *actual* economic welfare will have improved. If changes in the distribution of income have also occurred, the improvement may only be a *potential* one. The improvement may only be apparent (or *pseudo*) if, in addition, the increase in real output per capita is accompanied by negative externalities or is caused by increased production of goods and services which are not for current consumption. Consider now these three types of 'improvements' in turn.

An actual improvement. In Ch. 8, where welfare economics was introduced, we stated a very important condition for an increase in economic welfare. This was the Pareto condition that at least one consumer must be made better off without at the same time any others being made worse off. Adopting this condition, we can only interpret an increase in real output per capita as an actual improvement in economic welfare if no distributional changes occur which make any individuals or groups worse off.

A potential improvement. Unfortunately, increases in real output per capita often do leave some individuals or groups in society worse off. For example, suppose that there were a big new discovery of a fuel, like oil, whose production considerably boosted a country's real national income. An unfavourable side-effect of this may be a reduction in demand for some other fuel, like coal. Some coal-workers may then lose their jobs or be put on short-time. These people will have been made worse off by the oil discovery which, on average, increased real output per capita, making many other people better off. By applying the Pareto condition, we cannot say that the oil discovery improves actual economic welfare. What we can do in cases like this is to apply the Hicks–Kaldor condition for a *potential* improvement. Recall from Ch. 8 that, according to the Hicks–Kaldor condition, if any change occurs which redistributes income in such a way that the gainers can potentially compensate the losers and still be better off than they were before, then we can conclude that potential economic welfare has increased. Clearly, when real output per capita rises, it must be theoretically possible for the gainers to compensate any losers, but this could only be interpreted as an actual improvement if full compensation were actually paid. Since workers made unemployed in general find themselves worse off receiving unemployment benefits than they were when working, we can say that only very rarely is full compensation ever paid.

A pseudo-improvement. An increase in real output per capita may not even increase potential economic welfare if it is accompanied by, for example, negative externalities, an increase in the number of hours worked or increased production of investment goods at the expense of consumer goods.

Some *negative externalities*, in the shape of pollution, congestion and less pleasant working conditions, are likely to arise as output expands and these factors will tend to offset the effects of any increase in average income. So although consumers may on average be better off so far as their spending power is concerned, they may be worse off overall when environmental factors are taken into account. As an example, consider the building of a large chemical factory in the heart of the countryside: the extra production may increase real output per capita in the United Kingdom, but the factory may pollute the air and water and cause severe visual pollution in an area of natural beauty. If these external costs offset the increase in real output per capita, then any overall improvement in economic welfare would only be apparent and not real. We call this a *pseudo*-improvement.

The same argument applies if output has been increased only through the workforce taking fewer hours of leisure and putting in *more hours of work*. Again, the improvement in welfare resulting from increased spending power may be offset by a reduction in welfare resulting from loss of leisure. Overall, there may be no real improvement in welfare.

Finally, if the rise in real output per capita is caused by an expansion of investment goods industries and public sector expenditures on the civil service and defence, while at the same time there is a decline in consumer goods industries, then current economic welfare may fall rather than rise. The reason for this is that economic welfare stems from the activity of consumption. The production of investment goods does not in itself add to welfare in the current period, though it should do so in future periods.

Sometimes, a distinction is made between economic welfare and the standard of living. Some economists define an individual's standard of living in terms of the 'basket' of goods and services available for that individual to consume. Clearly, this is narrower than the definition of economic welfare presented above.

Table 18.5
Comparing per capita gross domestic products in the EC in 1990.

Country	Ecu (Purchasing power parities)*
Luxembourg	17,928
Germany	16,954
France	16,157
Denmark	15,539
Belgium	15,207
Italy	14,848
Netherlands	14,614
United Kingdom	14,582
Spain	10,925
Ireland	9,885
Portugal	8,136
Greece	6,823

Source: Eurostat, 1992.
* Adjusted for differences in price levels.

Other uses of the national income statistics

We can conclude from the previous section that a change in national income (even when adjusted for price and population increases) can only be used as an *indicator*, and not an accurate measure, of a change in economic welfare. There are two other possible uses of the national income figures that we should mention.

Making international comparisons Great care should be taken in using real output per capita figures to compare different countries' standards of living. First, a further adjustment is necessary to convert the figures to the same currency using a rate of exchange. This poses problems because the market rate of exchange is not necessarily the ideal measure of the relative values of the goods and services consumed in each country. Secondly, different countries have different needs and tastes which cannot easily be taken into account in making comparisons. Notwithstanding these problems, Table 18.5 compares the per capita gross domestic products at market prices for the twelve EC countries in 1990, measured at current prices and 'purchasing power parities'. For further performance indicators for the EC states, see the comparative unemployment rates in Table 27.2 and the comparative inflation rates in Table 28.3.

Government planning We shall see later that there is a close connection, at least in the short-term, between real national income and the level of employment in an economy. A rising real national income with a fairly constant capital stock will generally be associated with a fall in unemployment. Similarly, there is likely to be a direct relationship between the level of real national income and the rate of inflation – as the *equilibrium* level of national income approaches the 'full employment' level of national income, so inflationary pressure is likely to build up in an economy. To devise appropriate government policies to combat unemployment and inflation and to estimate the effects of such policies, accurate national income statistics are essential.

A rising level of real national income in the long-run is called economic growth and this is yet another policy objective of governments. We can conclude that the national income figures play an important role in the planning of both short- and long-run government policies. Economic growth is dealt with in Ch. 25. Unemployment and inflation are dealt with in Chs 27 and 28 respectively.

Macroeconomic equilibrium

Aggregate demand As we mentioned at the beginning of this chapter, aggregate demand is the total demand for all final goods and services in an economy over a period of time and consists of the sum of the demands of consumers, firms, the government and foreigners. At first sight, it may appear that the value of aggregate demand for a country should be the same as its national expenditure. This, however, is not necessarily so. National expenditure is the *actual* amount of money spent on goods and services over a given period of time, whereas aggregate demand is the total value that households, firms, the government and foreigners *plan* to spend out of their respective incomes over that time period: in other words, it is the total amount they are willing and able to spend. National expenditure, then, can be called *actual* expenditure, while aggregate demand can be called *planned* expenditure. The actual and planned measurements will differ if total output should fall short of or exceed total demand – in the former case, some demand will be unsatisfied because insufficient goods have been produced; in the latter case, some net addition to stocks will occur since too many goods have been produced.

Aggregate supply
The total value of all goods and services that all firms in the economy wish to supply over a given time period

Aggregate supply Aggregate supply may be defined as the total value of all final goods and services that all firms in the economy *wish* to supply over some time period. Clearly this is not necessarily equal to national income. National income is the value of the actual amount produced and so is necessarily equal to the national product and expenditure. Aggregate supply, on the other hand, is the amount that firms want to produce given the general level of wages and prices. The two will only be equal: (a) if wages and price are such that firms plan to produce what is currently being produced; and (b) if firms are able to implement their production plans successfully.

Equilibrium In the microeconomic market for a single good, an equilibrium is said to exist when the demand for the good is equal to the supply of it. Similarly, in macroeconomics, we can say that the equilibrium level of national income has been reached when there are no economic forces operating to change the level of national income. This occurs when the total demand for all goods and services (aggregate demand) is equal to the total supply of these goods and services (aggregate supply). That is, for the equilibrium level of income to be achieved, we require that:

Aggregate demand = Aggregate supply

Only when this condition is satisfied can we say that the total value of goods and services that households and the other economic agents want to buy is equal to the total value that firms want to produce. We shall see in Ch. 23 that one of the main determinants of both aggregate demand and aggregate supply is the *price level.* The relationship between aggregate demand and the price level is likely to be a negative one: in other words, the AD curve will be downward-sloping from left to right, as shown by the curve AD_1 in Fig 18.2. The relationship between aggregate supply and the price level is likely to be a positive one, giving an upward-sloping AS curve, as shown by the curve AS_1 in Fig. 18.2. The point at which the two curves intersect determines the equilibrium level of real national income ($0Y_1$) and the equilibrium price level ($0P_1$). This model, the AD-AS model, is at the heart of modern macroeconomics and it will be fully derived and explained in Ch. 23, and then applied in the chapters which follow Ch. 23.

Fig. 18.2. ***Equilibrium in the macro-economy.*** The intersection of the aggregate demand and aggregate supply curves determines the equilibrium level of real income and the equilibrium price level.

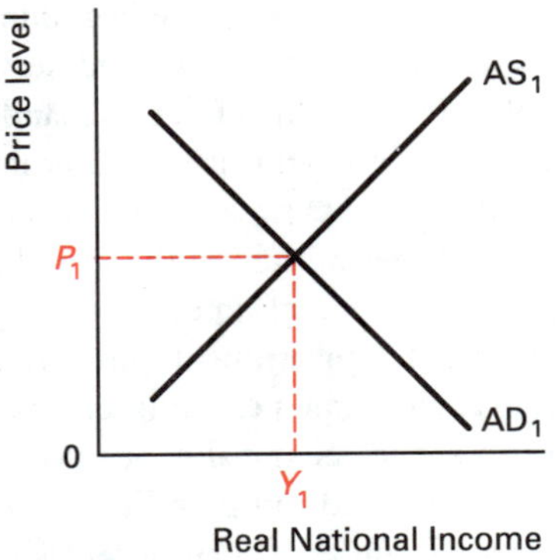

In the Keynesian analysis outlined in the next chapter, however, we shall assume that *the price level remains fixed*. This simplifies the analysis considerably and yet provides us with a useful introduction to macroeconomic theory, at the same time giving some valuable insights into the workings of the macro-economy.

Summary

1. Macroeconomics deals with the economy as a whole and is concerned with the determination of large aggregates, such as national income, consumption and investment.
2. The main problem of aggregation is that of finding an appropriate unit of measurement. Aggregates also hide movements in their constituent parts.
3. National product, national expenditure and national income are different ways of measuring the total value of all final goods and services produced over a period of time. In principle, they should all yield identical results.
4. Official national income statistics tend to underestimate the actual volume of economic activity because of the operation of the 'black' or underground economy.
5. A change in real output per capita may be regarded as an (imperfect) indicator of a change in economic welfare. However, a change in real output per capita does not necessarily represent an actual increase in economic welfare: it does not take into account changes in the distribution of income or the possibility of negative externalities.
6. As we shall see in later chapters, the interaction of aggregate demand and aggregate supply determines the equilibrium level of real national income.

Exercises

1. Review your understanding of the following terms:

economic aggregate	market prices
current prices	factor cost
constant prices	net property income from abroad
national product	gross domestic product
national expenditure	gross national product
national income	residual error
consumption	black economy
savings	actual expenditure
investment	planned expenditure
value-added	aggregate demand
depreciation	aggregate supply
stock appreciation	equilibrium level of income

2. The following data show the national income figures, price indices and population for a hypothetical country in 1991 and 1992:

	1991	1992
National income	£5,000m.	£7,200m.
Price index (1991 = 100)	120	160
Population	10m.	11m.

   (a) Calculate real national income in both years.
   (b) Find real national income per capita in both years.
   (c) Comment on the change in potential economic welfare. What other data would be useful in determining the change in economic welfare?

3. Use the following figures to compute national income (that is, net national product at factor cost):

Value of physical increase in stocks and work in progress	£400m.
Imports of goods and services	£37,000m.
General government final consumption	£27,000m.
Gross domestic fixed capital formation	£23,000m.
Exports of goods and services	£35,000m.
Depreciation	£14,000m.
Taxes on expenditure	£17,000m.
Net property income from abroad	£1,000m.
Consumer expenditure	£74,000m.
Subsidies	£3,000m.

4. Explain the distinction between microeconomics and macroeconomics. Give examples of economic problems that have both microeconomic and macroeconomic dimensions.

5.** Discuss the use of national income statistics as an indicator of living standards and economic well-being within a country and between different countries.

MACROECONOMIC THEORY

19 NATIONAL INCOME AND EMPLOYMENT

Learning objectives

After reading this chapter, you should be able to:

- explain the importance of Say's Law in the classical theory of full employment and outline Keynes' main criticisms of the classical theory
- show how the equilibrium level of national income is determined in the 'simple' Keynesian model, recognising the assumptions upon which the model is based
- illustrate the determination of the equilibrium level of income graphically using either the equality between national income and aggregate demand or between total withdrawals and total injections
- explain and illustrate the multiplier effect and derive simple formulas for calculating the value of the expenditure and taxation multipliers
- appreciate the limitations of the simple Keynesian model

Introduction

In this chapter, we are concerned with the very important question of what determines the level of national income and the level of employment in an economy. We start with a brief summary of the 'classical' economics which J.M. Keynes criticised in his book, *The General Theory of Employment, Interest and Money* in 1936. Secondly, we outline the Keynesian theory of national income determination on the assumption that the price level remains fixed. Thirdly, we develop two extensions of the Keynesian model: the multiplier and gap analysis. Finally, we point out the main limitations of the theory.

The classical theory of full employment

A basic result of classical economics was that, given flexible wages and prices, a competitive market economy would operate at full employment. That is, economic forces would always be generated to ensure that the demand for labour would always equal its supply.

Real wage *The money wage adjusted for changes in the price level*

The equilibrium level of employment is determined in the labour market. The demand curve for labour shows the relationship between the real wage (equal to the value of the marginal product of labour in a competitive economy) and the demand for labour by employers. The relationship is negative: the lower the real wage, the more workers employers will want to employ. The supply curve of labour shows the

Fig. 19.1. ***The labour market and short-run production function.*** The equilibrium level of employment in the labour market, $0L_1$, determines the level of output, $0Q_1$, in the product market.

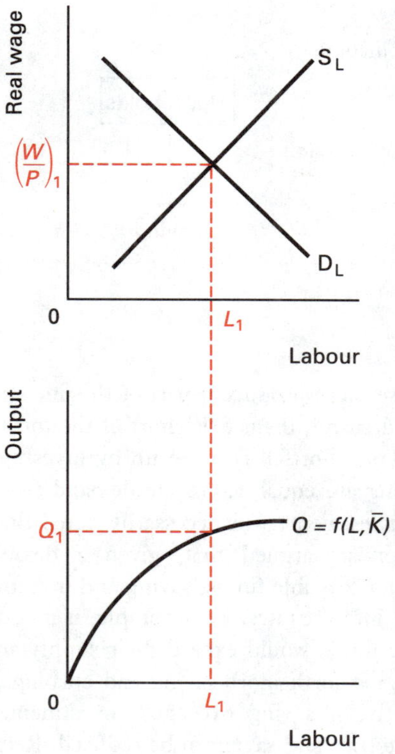

relationship between the real wage and households' supply of labour and this is a positive relationship: the higher the real wage, the greater the quantity of labour supplied.

Now consider Fig. 19.1, where the upper graph shows the aggregate labour market in equilibrium at a real wage of $(W/P)_1$ and a level of employment equal to $0L_1$. The lower graph shows the total output that is produced when different quantities of labour are employed (it illustrates, in fact, the short-run production function). With $0L_1$ units of labour employed, output in the economy will be $0Q_1$. To classical economists, the equilibrium level of employment was the 'full employment' level. So any unemployment which existed at the wage rate $(W/P)_1$ must be due to frictions or restrictive practices in the economy or must be voluntary.

Say's Law *This states that the supply of goods and services in an economy creates its own demand. In other words, the income generated in producing goods and services leads to spending which is just sufficient to purchase the goods produced*

Suppose, then, that the wage rate is flexible and that the economy is sufficiently competitive to ensure that labour market equilibrium is achieved. Can we be certain that aggregate demand will be sufficient to take up the $0Q_1$ units of output produced? The classical economists answered yes – whatever the full employment level of output, the income created in producing it will necessarily lead to spending which will be just sufficient to purchase the goods produced. In other words, *the supply of goods and services creates its own demand* and there can be no overproduction. This became known as Say's Law, named after the French economist Jean Baptiste Say (1767–1832).

To illustrate Say's Law, consider Fig. 19.2 which shows a simplified version of the circular flow of income diagram. It is simplified mainly by the omission of government and foreign trade activities. Households receive income equal to the

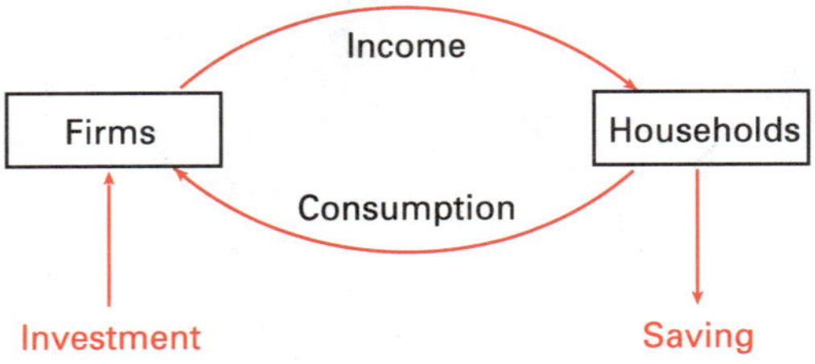

Fig. 19.2. A simplified flow diagram of an economy. Households receive income equal to the value of goods and services produced. Part of this income is saved and part spent. Consumption and investment make up the aggregate demand for the goods and services produced by firms.

value of goods and services produced; part of this income they spend and part they save. Consumption demand, then, falls short of the total value of production by the amount of saving. This shortfall is made up by investment demand and so long as investment and saving are equal, aggregate demand (which in this simple model is consumption plus investment) will necessarily equal the total value of production. The classical economists argued that, given a flexible rate of interest and a competitive market for loanable funds, saving and investment would always be made equal by changes in interest rates. For example, if investment exceeded saving, the demand for loanable funds would exceed their supply and this would push interest rates upwards, bringing forth more saving and curbing investment until they were equal again. Similarly, if saving exceeded investment, interest rates would fall, causing investment to rise and saving to be reduced. Recall that this mechanism was discussed in Ch. 17 and illustrated in Fig. 17.7.

In conclusion, we can say that the classical system depends crucially upon: (a) the dependence of investment and saving on the rate of interest; (b) the upward and downward flexibility of wages, prices and interest rates; (c) the existence of competitive forces in the economy. Given these conditions, there could be no overproduction (or, in other words, no general deficiency of aggregate demand) and full employment would be assured.

Keynes' criticisms of the classical theory

Keynes put forward the following main criticisms of the classical theory:

(a) Saving, he maintained, depends mainly on the level of national income and is not much affected by changes in interest rates. Investment may be influenced by interest rates, but also depends on more volatile factors in the economy like business expectations. Given this, it is no longer possible for the rate of interest to ensure equality between *planned* saving and *planned* investment and so Say's Law will no longer hold.

(b) He argued that, because of monopoly power in both the goods and labour markets, wages and prices will tend to be inflexible, at least in the short-run and particularly in the downward direction. This means that in a situation where saving exceeds investment, so that aggregate demand is less than the total value of production, firms will reduce output and lay off workers. It is in this way that demand-deficient unemployment is created.

The Keynesian theory of employment

The main result of the Keynesian theory is that the level of real national income and therefore employment is determined largely by the level of aggregate demand. This is, of course, very different from the classical model where 'supply created its own demand': in the Keynesian model, it is demand which determines how much is supplied. The argument is that if firms find that they are producing more than is being demanded, they will observe an involuntary increase in their inventories of unsold goods and so will rectify this by cutting back on production and laying off workers. National income will then fall until the value of what is produced is equal to the value of aggregate demand. If firms find that they are not producing enough to satisfy demand, they will experience an unwanted fall in their inventories and so this time will attempt to increase production and hire more workers.

Equilibrium level of income *That level at which aggregate demand is equal to the total value of production*

It follows that there will only be one level of national income at which aggregate demand is equal to the total value of production. This is called the equilibrium level of income. An important point to remember is that in the Keynesian model, the equilibrium level of income is not necessarily the same as the full employment level of income. This is the reason Keynes called his theory a *general* theory – he regarded the classical theory as no more than the 'special case' where the equilibrium and full employment levels of income coincided.

Determination of the equilibrium level of income

In order to set out the Keynesian theory more formally, we must first make a number of assumptions. The following assumptions are intended to conform with the Keynesian view of the economy and to simplify the analysis in such a way that enables us to make useful predictions. Notice in particular that we set out the Keynesian theory more generally than we did the classical theory where we assumed no government and no foreign trade. The reason is that we want to deal with the Keynesian model in greater detail and derive policy implications from it.

Assumption 1: *Wages and prices are fixed.* The model is a short-run model and this assumption means that, in the short-run, producers will respond to changes in demand by changing the quantity they produce rather than price. This implies that the economy is at less than full employment.

Assumption 2: *We ignore the money market.* For now, we concentrate on the real sector of the economy (that is, the markets for goods and services and for labour). We consider the impact of money and the rate of interest in Chs 21–23.

Marginal propensity to consume (mpc) *The change in consumption brought about by a one pound change in income*

Marginal propensity to save (mps) *The change in saving brought about by a one pound change in income*

Assumption 3: *Consumption (C) and saving (S) are both directly related to income (Y).* For simplicity, we assume that both relationships are linear and so can be drawn as straight lines as in Fig. 19.3. The consumption line *C* represents the relationship between *planned* consumption and income. This is the 'absolute income' hypothesis of consumption, outlined in greater detail in Ch. 20.

Notice that the slope of the consumption line measures the increase in consumption brought about by a one pound increase in income – this is called the marginal propensity to consume (mpc). Similarly, the slope of the saving line measures the increase in saving brought about by a one pound increase in income – this is called the marginal propensity to save (mps)

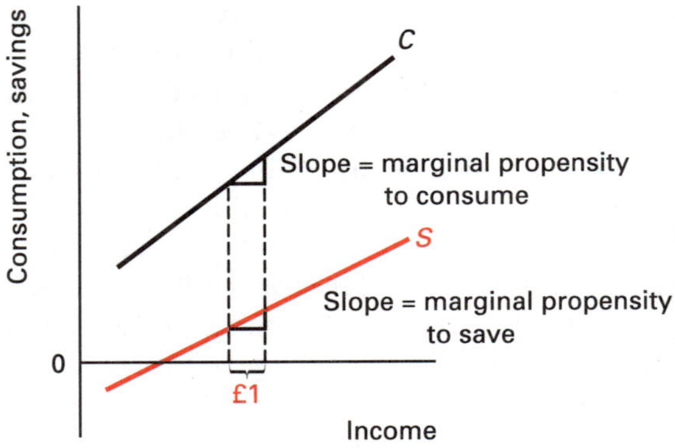

Fig. 19.3. Consumption and saving. As national income rises, both planned consumption and planned saving rise.

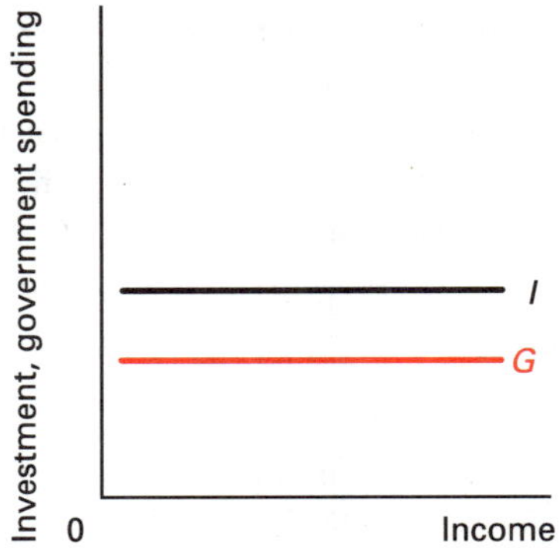

Fig. 19.4. Autonomous government spending and investment. As national income changes, neither planned investment nor planned government spending are affected.

Assumption 4: *Investment (I) and government spending (G) are autonomous.* This means that they are both independent of income changes. Government spending is determined by government policy and investment depends to some extent on the rate of interest (which for now does not appear in the model) and business expectations. Plotted against income on a graph, therefore, they would simply be represented by horizontal straight lines, as shown in Fig. 19.4.

Assumption 5: *Taxation (T) is in the form of lump-sum taxes only.* This is a purely simplifying assumption: it enables us to see the role played by taxes in the model, but at the same time the analysis is kept simple.

Assumption 6: *Exports (X) are autonomous, but imports (M) depend directly on income.* Exports depend on such factors as incomes in other countries and the rate of exchange (which for now we assume fixed). The demand for imports, though, will be directly and, for simplicity, linearly related to income. These relationships are shown in Fig. 19.5. Notice that the slope of the import line is called the marginal propensity to import (mpm), this is the fraction of extra income spent on imports.

Marginal propensity to import (mpm) *The change in imports brought about by a one pound change in income*

Assumption 7: *There is no economic growth.* This assumption is reasonable because the model is concerned with the short-run only. We extend the model into the long-run and take account of economic growth in Ch. 25 where we deal with the Harrod – Domar growth model.

Fig. 19.5. Imports and exports. Imports increase as national income rises, but exports are autonomous.

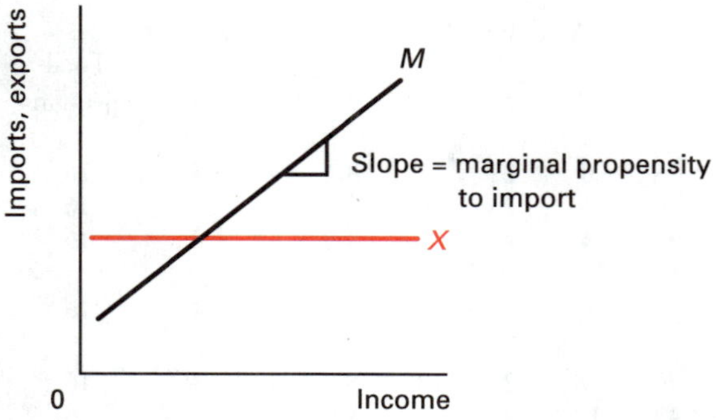

For equilibrium, we require that the aggregate demand for the economy's goods and services should be just equal to the total value of goods and services produced. As we saw in Ch. 18, aggregate demand consists of consumption, investment, government spending, exports minus imports (that is, $AD = C+I+G+X-M$). The total value of goods and services produced is measured by the national income (Y). The income received is either spent on consumer goods, or withdrawn in the form of savings and taxes (that is, $Y = C+S+T$). So, as a condition for equilibrium, we can write:

$$AD = Y$$

$$C+I+G+X-M = C+S+T$$

$$I+G+X = S+T+M$$

Injections *Additional spending items in the circular flow of income that do not begin with household consumption*

Withdrawals *Those parts of national income that are not used to buy domestically-produced consumer goods*

Autonomous variable *An autonomous (or exogenous) variable is one the value of which is determined outside the model under consideration*

Investment, government spending and exports are sometimes called injections (J) into the flow of income, while savings, taxes and imports are sometimes called withdrawals (W) from that flow. Thus, the condition for equilibrium could be written more simply as:

$$J = W$$

We have assumed that all the injections (I, G and X) are autonomous. This means that total injections will also be autonomous so that when plotted against income on a graph, the injections line will be a horizontal straight line. Of the withdrawals, we have assumed that savings and imports are both directly related to income but that taxes are lump-sum taxes. This means that total withdrawals will be directly related to income and when plotted against income on a graph will be an upward-sloping line with a slope equal to the sum of the marginal propensity to save and the marginal propensity to import.

To illustrate these results, consider a simple numerical example. Table 19.1 gives hypothetical figures for consumption, saving, taxes, imports, investment, government spending and exports at different levels of national income for a simple economy. All the relationships conform to the assumptions we have already made. Note that the marginal propensity to consume is 0.8 (because for every £10 million rise in income, consumption rises by £8 million) and the marginal propensity to save is 0.2. The marginal propensity to import is also 0.2, so that for every £10 million rise in income, spending on imports rises by £2 million and the consumption of *home-produced* goods and services rises by £6 million.

Table 19.1 **Hypothetical statistics for a simple economy (£m).**

		Withdrawals			Injections					
Y	*C*	*S*	*T*	*M*	*I*	*G*	*X*	Total injections	Total withdrawals	Aggregate demand
10	8	0	2	2	8	4	4	16	4	22
20	16	2	2	4	8	4	4	16	8	28
30	24	4	2	6	8	4	4	16	12	34
40	32	6	2	8	8	4	4	16	16	40
50	40	8	2	10	8	4	4	16	20	46
60	48	10	2	12	8	4	4	16	24	52

The total injections, total withdrawals and aggregate demand lines for this economy are drawn together with a 45° line in Fig. 19.6. The 45° line joins together all those points which are equidistant from the two axes. The graph shows that there are two ways of identifying the equilibrium level of income: (a) *where aggregate demand is equal to national income* (that is, where the AD line cuts the 45° line); (b) *where total injections equal total withdrawals*. The equilibrium level of income (Y_e) in the example, then, is £40 million. At this level of national income, and only at this level, aggregate demand in the economy is just equal to the total value of goods and services produced. This can also be seen from Table 19.1: when *Y* equals £40 million, *J* and *W* are equal at £16 million, and *AD* equals *Y*.

This equilibrium can also be described as a *stable* one because at any other income level, economic forces will be generated to push the economy back towards the equilibrium position. For example, suppose that the prevailing level of income were £50 million: as can be seen from Table 19.1, this would mean that £50 million worth of goods and services were being produced when aggregate demand was only £46 million. Firms would find their inventories involuntarily building up and so would cut back production thereby reducing national income. Similarly, if income were £30 million, aggregate demand would be £34 million and so would exceed the total value

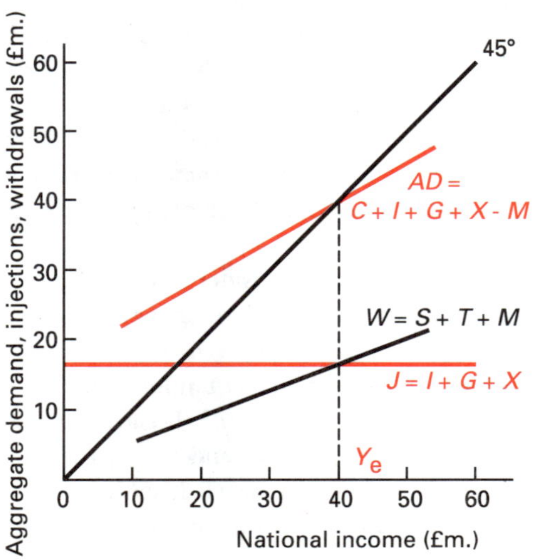

Fig. 19.6. Determination of the equilibrium level of income. The equilibrium level of income is determined at the point where *AD* = *Y* and *W* = *J*.

of production, inventories would be run down causing firms to attempt to step up production and so increase national income. Note that the ability of firms to expand output in this situation depends upon the existence of unemployed resources in the economy.

The multiplier

Multiplier *A measure of the relationship between the change in the equilibrium level of national income and the autonomous change that brings it about*

We have already indicated that investment depends to some extent on the rate of interest and business expectations, government spending depends on government policy and exports depend largely on incomes overseas. If any of these should change, there will be an effect on the equilibrium level of income. Similarly, a change in taxation and autonomous changes in consumption, saving and imports will also affect national income.

Consider first the effects of an increase in one of the injections. Suppose that firms increase their investment spending on new machinery by £2 million (that is, from £8m. to £10m. in our numerical example). The immediate effect of this increased spending will be to raise national income by the full £2 million because the spending of one group in the economy is necessarily the income of some other group. Increased spending on machinery represents higher incomes for those involved in manufacturing the machines. The process does not end here, however, because the increase in income will bring forth additional consumption spending in the next period. In fact, since the mpc is 0.8 and the mpm is 0.2, we know that consumption will rise by £1.6 million of which £0.4 million will be additional expenditure on imports. Thus, consumption of home-produced goods will rise by £1.2 million. This rise in consumption will create a further increase in income in the next period of £1.2 million over and above the initial increase and this in turn will bring forth more consumption spending. This process will continue with both consumption and income rising, but with the actual increases becoming smaller and smaller over time until eventually they become insignificant. The first few stages of this process are summarised in Table 19.2, where C^* represents consumption of home-produced goods and the subscripts refer to time periods.

The total increase in national income ($\Delta Y = \Delta Y_1 + \Delta Y_2 + \Delta Y_3 + \ldots$) will clearly be much bigger than the initial increase in investment spending. To see how much bigger, consider Fig. 19.7 which shows the movement from the original equilibrium position (Y_e = £40 million) to the new one after the entire process has worked itself out. Notice that the increase in investment spending shifts both the injections line and the aggregate demand line vertically upwards by £2 million. We can work out the total increase in income by recalling that the slope of the withdrawals line is equal to the sum of the marginal propensities to save and import (given that, in this model, the marginal propensity to tax is zero). As can be seen

Table 19.2 The first few stages of the multiplier process.

Initial increase in I, ΔI = £2m.	Increase in Y in period, 1, ΔY_1 = £2m.
ΔC_1^* = £1.2m.	ΔY_2 = £1.2m.
ΔC_2^* = £0.72m.	ΔY_3 = £0.72m.
ΔC_3^* = £432,000	ΔY_4 = £432,000
ΔC_4^* = £259,000	ΔY_5 = £259,000
⋮	⋮

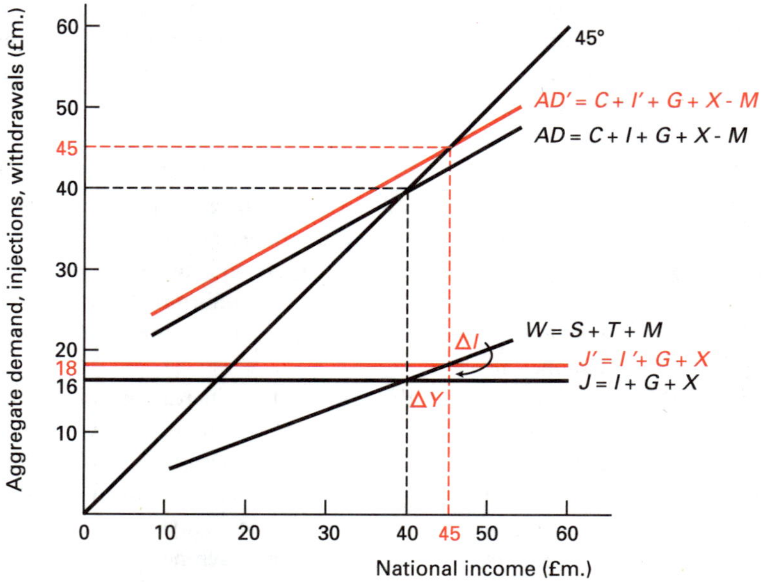

Fig. 19.7. The multiplier effect. An increase in investment of £2m. shifts the injections line and the aggregate demand line upwards by £2m. This gives rise to an increase in national income of £5m.

from Fig. 19.7, this slope can also be written as $\Delta I/\Delta Y$. It follows that if $\Delta I/\Delta Y = \text{mps} + \text{mpm}$, then, by a simple rearrangement, we can write:

$$\Delta Y = \frac{\Delta I}{\text{mps} + \text{mpm}}$$

Substituting the figures from our example, we have:

$$\Delta Y = \frac{\pounds 2 \text{ million}}{0.2 + 0.2} = \pounds 5 \text{ million}$$

In other words, national income rises by £5 million following an increase in investment of only £2 million. This is called the *multiplier effect*, and the multiplier itself is the amount that the change in spending has to be multiplied by to obtain the change in income. That is,

$$\text{Multiplier} = \frac{1}{\text{mps} + \text{mpm}}$$

and this is equal to $2\frac{1}{2}$ in our example. This multiplier is derived algebraically in Appendix I.

An important point to remember is that the size of the multiplier depends on the marginal propensities to save and import. The bigger these withdrawals from increases in income, the smaller will be the multiplier. To take an extreme example, if all the additional income received were withdrawn from the circular flow of income, the multiplier would be equal to 1 and the final rise in income would be just equal to the initial rise in spending and no more.

Now note the following important points about the multiplier:

(a) It comes into operation for any *autonomous* change in spending. So autonomous changes in investment, government spending, exports and consumption will all have the same multiplier effect on an economy's national income.

Fig. 19.8. The multiplier effect of a tax change. An increase in the lump-sum tax of £2m gives rise to a fall in national income of £4m.

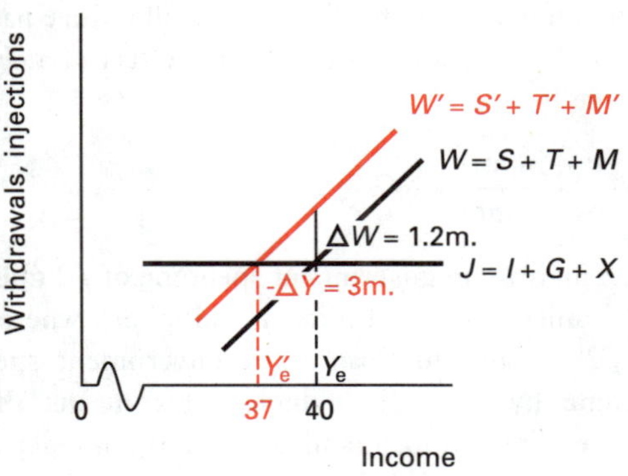

(b) The multiplier, 1/(mps + mpm), is derived on the assumption that taxes are lump-sum only. If we had an income tax in the model so that some part of any extra income received was taken in taxes by the government, total withdrawals would rise and the multiplier would be smaller. This multiplier is derived algebraically in Appendix II.

(c) The multiplier, 1/(mps + mpm), ignores foreign repercussions which could be significant for a country with a large foreign trade sector. Consider the effects of an increase in investment in the United Kingdom. As national income rises, some of it is spent on imports and this is equivalent to a rise in other countries' exports. So incomes in other countries rise (also by a multiplier effect) and some of this rise may in turn be spent on United Kingdom exports. As United Kingdom exports increase, there will be a multiplier effect on national income which we have not so far taken into account.

Disposable income
Income after direct taxes have been deducted

The tax multiplier Finally, we must consider the effect on national income of a change in the lump-sum tax (T) on the assumption that consumption, saving and imports depend on disposable income (Y_d) rather than national income (Y): recall that $Y_d \equiv Y - T$. Suppose that the lump-sum tax is raised by £2 million (from £2m. to £4m.). What will happen to the withdrawals line? The rise in taxes will reduce disposable income by £2 million so that saving will fall at every level of national income by £ (mps × ΔY_d) or 0.2 × £2m. = £0.4 million. Similarly, imports will fall at every level of national income by £ (mpm × ΔY_d) which is also equal to £0.4 million. The withdrawals line, then, which is an aggregation of the saving, taxation and import lines, will be pushed upwards by £2 million because of the tax rise and downwards by £0.8 million because of the fall in saving and imports. Overall, it shifts upwards by only £1.2 million, as shown in Fig. 19.8. Given that $\Delta T = \Delta Y_d$, we can write the change in total withdrawals (ΔW) more generally as

$$\begin{aligned}\Delta W &= \Delta T - (\text{mps} + \text{mpm})\,\Delta T\\ &= [1 - (\text{mps} + \text{mpm})]\,\Delta T\\ &= (\text{mpc} - \text{mpm})\,\Delta T\end{aligned}$$

Notice from the graph that the slope of the withdrawals line is equal to $\Delta W / -\Delta Y = \text{mps} + \text{mpm}$. Rearranging this expression, we have

$$\Delta Y = \frac{-\Delta W}{\text{mps} + \text{mpm}} = \frac{-1.2}{0.2 + 0.2} = -£3 \text{ million}$$

So raising the lump-sum tax by £2 million will reduce national income by £3 million to £37 million. The general formula for the effect of a change in a lump-sum tax on national income is

$$\Delta Y = \frac{-(\text{mpc} - \text{mpm})\Delta T}{\text{mps} + \text{mpm}}$$

Balanced-budget multiplier *This shows the effect on the equilibrium level of national income of an increase in government expenditure that is financed by an equal increase in taxation*

Notice that an increase in government spending of £2 million would increase national income by £5 million (via the ordinary multiplier), whereas an increase in lump-sum taxation of £2 million (to finance the government spending, say) would reduce national income by only £3 million. This means that a policy of increasing government spending but maintaining a balanced budget will have a net expansionary effect on the economy. This is because the government spends all of the tax revenues raised, whereas households would have withdrawn part of this sum in the form of saving and imports. It is no coincidence, either, that increasing both G and T by £2 million raises national income by £2 million also. In other words, in this model, the balanced budget multiplier is equal to 1. This result is derived algebraically in Appendix III.

Gap analysis

Deflationary gap *The amount by which aggregate demand must be increased to raise the equilibrium level of income to the full employment level*

Deflationary gap Gap analysis is a simple way of describing the main policy implications of the Keynesian theory. Consider Fig. 19.9 which illustrates a *deflationary gap*. Since the equilibrium level of income (Y_e) (the one towards which the economy tends) is below the full employment level of income (Y_f), the economy will be suffering from demand-deficient unemployment. The deflationary gap is the amount by which aggregate demand must be increased to push the equilibrium level of income, via the multiplier, to the full employment level. How can this increase in aggregate demand be achieved? The government has a number of possible policy instruments which it can use for this purpose. Consider the following:

(a) *Increase government spending.* This will raise aggregate demand directly and, by increasing total injections, will have a multiplier effect on income. To achieve full employment in Fig. 19.9, it is necessary to shift the AD line upwards by the full amount of the deflationary gap. If taxes are raised to finance the spending, the

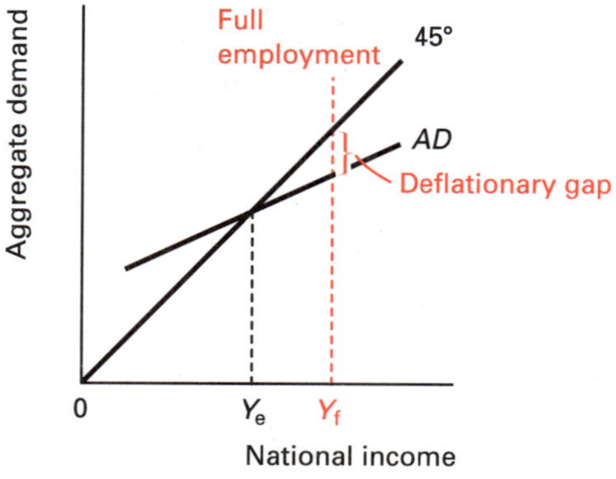

Fig. 19.9. A deflationary gap. The equilibrium level of national income, $0Y_e$, is below the full employment level of income, $0Y_f$.

Fig. 19.10. *An inflationary gap.* The equilibrium level of national income, $0Y_e$, is above the full-employment level, $0Y_f$, causing demand-pull inflation.

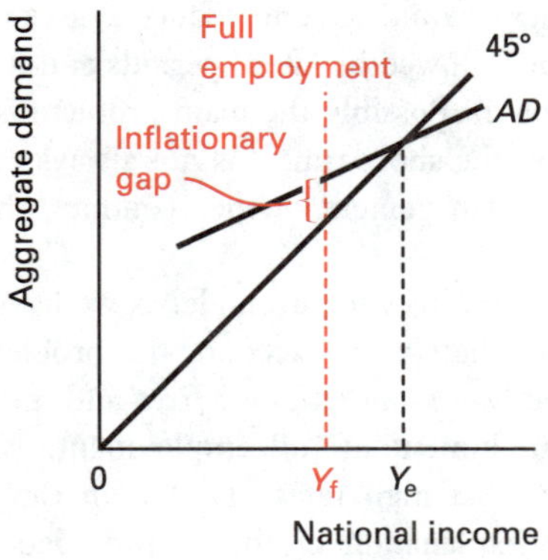

policy will still be expansionary and so reduce unemployment so long as the taxes raised do not exceed the increase in government spending by a certain amount.

(b) *Reduce taxes.* This will increase disposable income so that consumption spending will rise at every level of national income. Once again, the multiplier will come into operation and the equilibrium level of income and employment will rise. To achieve full employment in Fig. 19.9, the *AD* line must be shifted upwards by the full amount of the deflationary gap. Note that, if the government's budget is balanced to start with, cutting taxes while leaving government spending unchanged means running a budget deficit.

Fiscal policy *Changes in the level of government spending or taxation. Such changes may have implications for the government's borrowing needs*

It should be noted that changing the level of government spending and/or taxation is known as fiscal policy. In practice, governments can also use monetary policy and exchange rate policy to influence the level of aggregate demand. Monetary policy is considered in Chs 21–23 and exchange rate policy in Ch. 29.

The major policy implication of the Keynesian theory, then, is that aggregate demand can be increased in order to combat demand-deficient unemployment.

Inflationary gap *The amount by which aggregate demand must be decreased to reduce the equilibrium level of income to the full employment level*

Inflationary gap Now relax the assumption that wages and prices are fixed, and consider Fig. 19.10 which illustrates an *inflationary gap*. This time the equilibrium level of income is above the full employment level and so cannot actually be attained. The economy will be at the full employment level of output, but excess demand (equal to the inflationary gap) will still exist so that the general price level will be forced upwards. Appropriate fiscal policies to combat this *demand-pull* inflation would be a cut in government spending, or an increase in taxation. The objective this time is to shift down the *AD* line by the full amount of the inflationary gap.

Limitations of the Keynesian theory

After the Second World War, Keynesian demand-management policies were used by the governments of most western countries in the attempt to keep unemployment levels down. Generally, these policies were successful in preventing heavy unemployment like that experienced in the 1930s, but unfortunately they tended to give rise to the phenomenon known as 'stop–go'. That is, in periods of high unemployment, the government would expand aggregate demand: this would reduce the unemployment but at the same time tend to create inflationary pressure so that eventually the government would have to reduce aggregate demand again. Thus, all 'go' periods tended to be followed by 'stop' periods and it became difficult to achieve long-term economic growth. Possibly the main problem is that the Keynesian model is only short-term and in the short-run, it is not always easy to predict the effects of policy changes, and the management of the economy, therefore, may become very erratic.

A second limitation of the Keynesian model as we have outlined it in this chapter is that it fails to take adequately into account the problem of inflation. Indeed, the basic model assumes that *wages and prices are fixed* and the only time we allowed them to rise was after the attainment of full employment. Experience in the 1970s in particular has shown us that high rates of inflation can coexist with high rates of unemployment and no explanation of this is provided by the Keynesian theory. Furthermore, the coincidence of inflation and unemployment makes the Keynesian policy recommendations very questionable. For example, if the economy is in the deflationary gap situation illustrated in Fig. 19.9, but is also suffering from a 15 per cent rate of inflation, an increase in government spending or a cut in taxation designed to combat the unemployment is likely to worsen the rate of inflation. We consider the modern theories of unemployment and inflation in Chs 27 and 28 respectively.

A further criticism which has been levelled at the Keynesian model is that it tends to understate the influence of money on the real variables in the economy. Indeed, the model outlined in this chapter has taken no explicit account of the monetary sector and as such is sometimes called the 'simple' Keynesian model. We discuss the role of money in the Keynesian model in Ch. 23 where we see that a change in the money supply, according to this model, only affects national income through its effect on the rate of interest; it is because of this that Keynesians have usually put more faith in fiscal rather than monetary policy.

Monetarists have been particularly concerned to make these three main criticisms of the Keynesian theory. Before we can describe their views in detail, we need to take a closer look at the role of money in the economy. However, we shall see that the upshot of the monetarist position is: (a) that short-term demand management may do more harm than good; (b) that there is a close relationship between changes in the money supply and changes in money national income in the long-run; (c) that without government interference the economy will tend towards its 'natural' rate of unemployment. We are particularly concerned with the views of the monetarists and their policy prescriptions *vis-à-vis* those of the Keynesians in Chs 23, 27 and 28.

Summary

1. According to Say's Law, supply creates its own demand. This is part of the classical theory of full employment, according to which competitive forces and flexible wages and prices ensure that a full employment equilibrium is achieved with no overproduction.
2. In the Keynesian model, aggregate demand determines how much is produced, and the equilibrium level of national income is not necessarily the same as the full employment level.

3. In the 'simple' Keynesian model, the equilibrium level of national income is determined at the point where $AD = Y$ or $J = W$. Any divergence from this equilibrium generates economic forces which push the economy back to the equilibrium.
4. An autonomous increase in spending has a multiplier effect on national income. The size of the multiplier depends on the marginal propensities to save and import. The bigger the 'withdrawals' from increases in income, the smaller the multiplier.
5. The main limitations of the simple Keynesian model are that it fails to pay adequate attention to the effects of changes in wages and prices, and ignores the monetary sector of the economy. These areas will be addressed in Chs 21–23.

Exercises

1. Review your understanding of the following terms:

Say's Law	injections
loanable funds	withdrawals
equilibrium level of income	lump-sum tax
consumption	proportional income tax
savings	multiplier
investment	foreign repercussions
marginal propensity to consume	balanced budget multiplier
marginal propensity to save	inflationary gap
marginal propensity to import	deflationary gap

2. Consider a closed economy in which investment (I) and government spending (G) are assumed to be autonomous and taxes (T) are all lump-sum. Consumption (C) and savings (S) are both directly and linearly related to disposable income (Y_d). You are given the following information:

$C = 22 + 0.6Y_d$
$I = 10$
$G = 20$
$T = 20$

(a) Write down the equations relating consumption and savings to *national* income and plot these relationships on a graph.
(b) On the same graph, plot the $S+T$ and $I+G$ lines and identify the equilibrium level of income.
(c) Calculate the *net* effect on national income of an increase in G of 12 and a simultaneous increase in T of 20. Briefly explain the result.

3. Outline Keynes' criticisms of the classical theory of full employment.
4. Explain why a £10 million increase in government expenditure financed by a £10 million increase in taxation has a net expansionary effect on the economy.
5. Explain why the Keynesian model lost favour with policy-makers in recent years.

6. Discuss the effect on the equilibrium level of income and the level of total savings of an autonomous increase in the community's desire to save.

7.** Discuss the likely economic consequences of a large increase in government expenditure.

Appendix I

Algebraic derivation of the multiplier in a model with a lump-sum tax

The model outlined in this chapter may be expressed in algebraic form using three simple equations:

Equilibrium condition, $Y = C + \bar{I} + \bar{G} + \bar{X} - M$ [1]

Consumption function, $C = a + b(Y - \bar{T})$ [2]

Import function, $M = c + d(Y - \bar{T})$ [3]

where Y represents national income, C is planned consumption expenditure, $\bar{I}$ is planned investment expenditure, $\bar{G}$ is planned government expenditure, $\bar{X}$ is planned exports, M is planned imports and $\bar{T}$ is the lump-sum tax. The constants a, b, c and d specify the positions and shapes of the consumption and import functions: b measures the slope of the consumption line and is the *marginal propensity to consume*; similarly, d measures the slope of the import line and is the *marginal propensity to import*. Of the seven variables, four ($\bar{I}$, $\bar{G}$, $\bar{T}$ and $\bar{X}$) are assumed to be autonomous or *exogenous* (as indicated by the 'bars' over the variables): this means that their values are assumed to be determined by forces *outside* the model. The other three variables (C, M and Y) are said to be *endogenous*: this means that their values are determined by the interaction of the relationships in the model. To be able to solve the system of equations, the number of endogenous variables must be equal to the number of equations. In this case, there are three endogenous variables and three equations.

To find the equilibrium level of national income, we solve the system for Y. This yields an expression called the *reduced-form* of the model. Substituting [2] and [3] into [1], we have

$$Y = a + bY - b\bar{T} + \bar{I} + \bar{G} + \bar{X} - c - dY + d\bar{T}$$

Collecting the Y-terms on the left-hand side, we have

$$Y - bY + dY = a - b\bar{T} + \bar{I} + \bar{G} + \bar{X} - c + d\bar{T}$$

$$Y(1 - b + d) = a - b\bar{T} + \bar{I} + \bar{G} + \bar{X} - c + d\bar{T}$$

Dividing both sides by $(1 - b + d)$ gives the required reduced-form:

$$Y = \frac{a - b\bar{T} + \bar{I} + \bar{G} + \bar{X} - c + d\bar{T}}{1 - b + d}$$

From this expression, we can deduce that the effect on national income of a change in $\bar{I}$, *ceteris paribus*, will be

$$\Delta Y = \frac{\Delta\bar{I}}{1 - b + d}$$

Thus, the injections multiplier in this model is $1/(1-b+d)$, which of course is the same as the expression $1/(\text{mps}+\text{mpm})$, derived graphically in the chapter. Changes in $\bar{G}$ and $\bar{X}$ will have the same multiplier effect on national income as changes in $\bar{I}$. A change in the lump-sum tax will cause the following change in national income:

$$\Delta Y = \frac{-(b-d)\Delta \bar{T}}{1-b-d}$$

This is the same as the formula $-(\text{mpc}-\text{mpm})\Delta \bar{T}/(\text{mps}+\text{mpm})$ derived in the chapter.

Appendix II

Algebraic derivation of the multiplier in a model with an income tax

In equilibrium, $Y = C + \bar{I} + \bar{G} + \bar{X} - M$ [1]

Consumption function, $C = a + b(Y - T)$ [2]

Income tax, $T = tY$ [3]

Import function, $M = c + d(Y - T)$ [4]

where t is a proportional tax rate. Substituting [2]–[4] into [1], we have

$$\begin{aligned} Y &= a + b(Y - tY) + \bar{I} + \bar{G} + \bar{X} - c - d(Y - tY) \\ &= a + bY - btY + \bar{I} + \bar{G} + \bar{X} - c - dY + dtY \end{aligned}$$

$$Y - bY + btY + dY - dtY = a + \bar{I} + \bar{G} + \bar{X} - c$$

$$Y(1 - b + bt + d - dt) = a + \bar{I} + \bar{G} + \bar{X} - c$$

$$Y = \frac{a + \bar{I} + \bar{G} + \bar{X} - c}{1 - b + bt + d - dt}$$

The effect of a change in investment is

$$\Delta Y = \frac{\Delta \bar{I}}{1 - b(1-t) + d(1-t)}$$

Thus, the injections multiplier in this model is $\dfrac{1}{1 - b(1-t) + d(1-t)}$

Appendix III

The 'balanced budget' multiplier

The increase in the equilibrium level of national income following an increase in government spending (in a closed economy with lump-sum taxes only) is

$$\Delta Y_1 = \frac{\Delta \bar{G}}{1-b}$$

where b is the marginal propensity to consume.

The fall in the equilibrium level of income following an increase in lump-sum taxation is

$$\Delta Y_2 = \frac{-b\Delta \bar{T}}{1-b}$$

If the tax and government spending changes occur simultaneously, the combined effect on income is:

$$\Delta Y = \frac{\Delta \bar{G}}{1-b} - \frac{b\Delta \bar{T}}{1-b}$$

But if the budget is kept balanced, so that $\Delta \bar{G} = \Delta \bar{T}$, we can write

$$\Delta Y = \frac{\Delta \bar{G}}{1-b} - \frac{b\Delta \bar{G}}{1-b}$$

$$= \left(\frac{1-b}{1-b}\right)\Delta \bar{G}$$

$$= \Delta \bar{G}$$

The balanced budget multiplier, therefore, is equal to 1.

20 CONSUMPTION AND INVESTMENT

Learning objectives

After reading this chapter, you should be able to:

- define the terms consumption, saving and investment
- explain the 'absolute income' hypothesis, recognising the relationship between consumption and saving
- define the terms marginal propensity to consume (and save) and average propensity to consume (and save)
- outline the results of empirical studies using different types of data and recognise the possible influence of wealth on consumption and saving behaviour
- explain the main features of the 'permanent income' and the 'relative income' hypotheses as alternatives to the 'absolute income' hypothesis
- show how the level of aggregate investment may be inversely related to the rate of interest and discuss the likely strength of this relationship
- explain the 'accelerator' theory of investment and discuss other possible influences on the level of aggregate investment

Introduction

Consumption and investment are two extremely important aggregates in the economy. It should be clear from the last chapter that they both play a role in determining the equilibrium level of income and employment and that a change in either one of them will cause the level of national income to change via the multiplier effect. It follows, therefore, that if we are interested in deriving policies designed to secure full employment, we should first analyse the determinants of these variables. That is the purpose of this chapter.

First, we reconsider the definitions of consumption, saving and investment and discuss the distinction between consumption and investment. Secondly, we examine the Keynesian theory of consumption and saving: that is, the view that consumption and saving are both directly related to current disposable income. Thirdly, we make use of indifference curve analysis to examine the microeconomic foundations of aggregate consumption and we outline the 'permanent income' and 'relative income' hypotheses. Finally, we turn our attention to the determination of investment and outline the views that investment depends on: (a) the rate of interest; (b) changes in national income (that is, the so-called 'accelerator' theory); and (c) profitability.

Definitions

Recall the definitions of consumption, savings and investment given in Ch. 18. Consumption is seen as households' spending on goods and services which yield utility in the current period, while saving is defined as that part of disposable income which is not spent. In a closed economy, it follows that by definition,

$$Y_d \equiv C + S$$

Investment is seen as an activity of firms. It is firms' spending on goods which are not for current consumption but which yield a flow of consumer goods and services in the future.

These definitions enable us to say quite categorically that a household's expenditure on food is consumption – the food will be eaten within a short period of time and that will be an end of the matter. Similarly, we can say that the purchase of a new machine by a firm is investment – the machine itself will not yield utility to anyone in the current period but will produce (or help to produce) consumer goods probably for a long time into the future.

The distinction between consumption and investment is not so clear-cut, however, when we consider household expenditure on consumer durables, like cars and washing machines. These are goods which last for a long time and which yield the household utility-creating services both in the current period and in future periods. In a sense, then, the purchase of consumer durables is both consumption *and* a form of investment. Furthermore, it is sometimes useful to distinguish between consumption spending (meaning the actual amount spent on new consumer goods in the current period) and total consumption (meaning the 'using up' of consumer goods – both those purchased in the current period and those purchased in past periods but which are still providing services to the household).

To keep our analysis fairly simple in this chapter, we adhere to the definitions given above and ignore the complications created by durable consumer goods. For more advanced study, it is important for the reader at least to be aware of these complications.

Consumption and saving

It can be seen from Table 18.2 that consumption spending accounted for over two-thirds of total expenditure in the United Kingdom in 1991 and consequently is a very important component of aggregate demand. Small percentage changes in consumption can have a considerable effect on the equilibrium level of national income and therefore on employment. It is of some importance, therefore, to know what factors determine consumption so that appropriate policies to combat unemployment can be devised.

The 'absolute income' hypothesis

Absolute income hypothesis *The contention that consumption depends on current disposable income*

The Keynesian model we constructed in the last chapter was based on the assumption that both consumption and saving were directly and linearly related to current disposable income. This is sometimes called the absolute income hypothesis to distinguish it from other hypotheses of consumption: in particular, the 'relative' and 'permanent' income hypotheses.

The consumption and saving functions of the 'absolute income' hypothesis can be illustrated either numerically, graphically or algebraically. To show this, consider

Table 20.1 Income, consumption and saving for a hypothetical economy.

Disposable income (£m.)	Consumption (£m.)	Saving (£m.)
250	210	40
200	170	30
150	130	20
100	90	10
50	50	0
0	10	−10

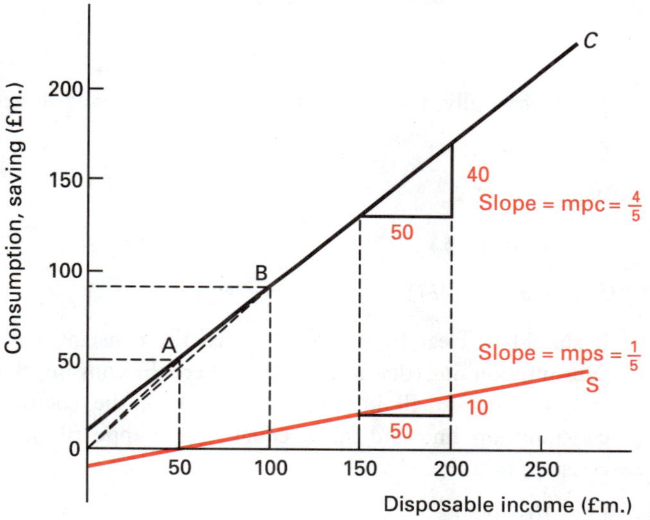

Fig. 20.1. The consumption and saving lines. The consumption line has a positive intercept and a positive slope. The saving line (derived as $Y_d - C$) must have a negative intercept and a positive slope (equal to 1 – mpc).

Table 20.1 which sets out a simple numerical example in which there is a direct linear relationship between disposable income and consumption, and between disposable income and saving. These linear relationships are plotted in Fig. 20.1 where both the consumption and saving relationships are seen to be straight lines. Notice that the slope of the consumption line is 0.8: this represents the fraction of additional disposable income which will be consumed and, as we saw in the last chapter, is called the *marginal propensity to consume* (mpc). Similarly, the slope of the saving line (= 0.2) represents the fraction of additional disposable income that will be saved and is called the *marginal propensity to save* (mps). Since the consumption and saving lines are straight lines and so have constant slopes, the mpc and mps are also constant in this example.

The average propensity to consume (apc) *The proportion of disposable income that is spent on consumption*

The average propensity to save (aps) *The proportion of disposable income that is saved*

The average propensity to consume (apc) is equal to total consumption divided by total disposable income (C/Y_d) and this varies as disposable income varies. At point A on the graph, for example, the apc = 50/50 = 1; but at point B, the apc = 90/100 = 0.9. The apc is in fact equal to the slope of the ray from the origin to the appropriate point on the consumption line, so that at point A, the apc is equal to the slope of OA (= 1) and at point B, the apc is equal to the slope of OB (= 0.9). Exactly the same applies to the average propensity to save (aps) which is equal to total saving divided by total disposal income (S/Y_d).

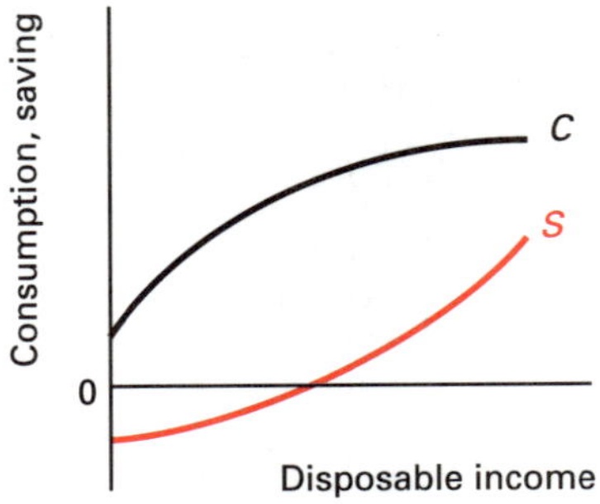

Fig. 20.2. *Non-linear consumption and saving lines.* If the mpc falls as income rises, the mps must rise as income rises.

Algebraically, the relationships can be expressed in general form as follows:

$$C = a + bY_d$$

$$S \equiv Y_d - C$$

$$= Y_d - a - bY_d$$

$$S = -a + (1-b)Y_d$$

It should be clear from Fig. 20.1 that the constant a is the intercept term for the consumption line (that is, the point where the consumption line cuts the vertical axis) and is equal to 10 in the example. Also, the coefficient b is the slope of the consumption line and so is equal to the mpc (0.8). Thus, the equation of the consumption line is

$$C = 10 + 0.8Y_d$$

And the equation of the saving line is

$$S = -10 + 0.2Y_d$$

Notice that it must always be true that mpc + mps = 1.

The following points represent the major characteristics of the 'absolute income' hypothesis:

(a) Consumption and saving are stable functions of current disposable income. The relationships are positive ones.

(b) In our example, the relationships are linear. It is also possible in the 'absolute income' hypothesis for the consumption and saving lines to be curved in such a way that the mpc falls as income rises and the mps rises as income rises. This is illustrated in Fig. 20.2.

(c) The mpc lies between 0 and 1 (0 < mpc < 1). This means that for every additional pound of income received, consumption rises by some fraction of a pound. Of course, it is not impossible for the mps to be greater than 1 or even less than 0, but such values are unlikely.

(d) *The apc falls as income rises and is greater than the mpc.* The hypothesis has this characteristic because the consumption line cuts the vertical axis at some positive point (that is to say, consumption spending actually exceeds income at very low levels of income). This is illustrated in Fig. 20.3 where the slopes of the dashed

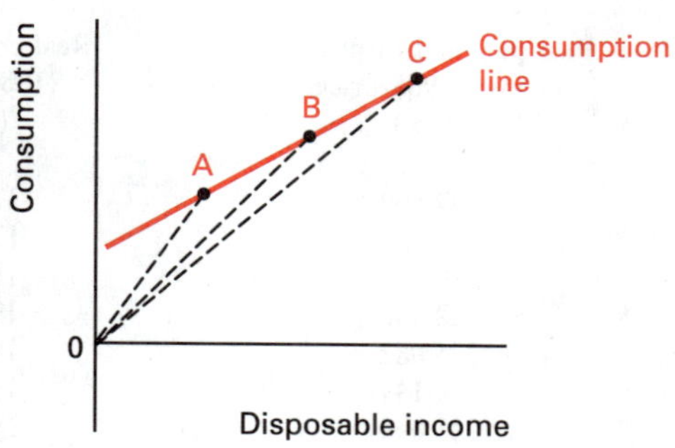

Fig. 20.3. *Comparison of the apc with the mpc.* For a consumption line with a positive slope and positive intercept, apc will fall as income rises and will be greater than the mpc.

Table 20.2 Cross-section budget study for the United Kingdom, 1991.

Weekly income group (£)	Average weekly income (£)	Consumption (£)	apc	mpc
Under 60	49.61	62.97	1.27	
60 and under 100	78.73	92.55	1.18	1.02
100 and under 200	147.39	159.29	1.08	0.97
200 and under 550	308.84	279.70	0.91	0.75
550 or more	651.38	565.43	0.87	0.83

Source: Calculated from CSO *Family Spending*, 1992.

lines 0A, 0B and 0C represent the apc's at points A, B and C respectively and the slope of the consumption line itself represents the mpc. Clearly, the apc's are all greater than the mpc and are diminishing as income rises. This characteristic is an important one because it is empirically testable. We turn now to a consideration of the different types of data that can be collected on the income – consumption relationship.

Different types of data Statistics on the relationship between income and consumption can be collected by means of three main types of empirical study:

(a) *Cross-section budget study.* This involves taking a sample of housholds and classifying them according to their income groups. Dividing the average levels of consumption spending for each income group by the corresponding average level of income gives each group's apc. As can be seen from Table 20.2, which shows figures from the United Kingdom *Family Expenditure Survey* of 1992, the apc has a marked tendency to fall as we move from lower to higher income groups; also, the apc is greater than the mpc in every case. This is a typical result and supports the 'absolute income' hypothesis.

(b) *Short-run time-series study.* This involves collecting annual data of real disposable income and consumption for the economy as a whole. Dividing consumption by disposable income for each year gives the apc and this is done for United Kingdom data (1976–91) in Table 20.3. This time, the results are not quite so clear-cut, particularly in the period 1985–88 when the apc rose steadily in spite of rising incomes. But in the earlier period there is a clear tendency for the apc to fall as income rises and to rise as income falls. These figures, therefore, also tend to support the 'absolute income' hypothesis.

Table 20.3 Short-run time-series study for the United Kingdom, 1976–91.

Year	Real personal disposable income (1985 prices) (£m.)	Real consumption (1985 prices) (£m.)	apc
1976	199,699	178,279	0.89
1977	195,333	177,483	0.91
1978	210,313	187,510	0.89
1979	222,300	195,664	0.88
1980	225,882	195,825	0.87
1981	224,147	196,011	0.87
1982	223,044	197,980	0.89
1983	228,950	206,932	0.90
1984	236,931	210,959	0.89
1985	224,818	218,947	0.89
1986	254,849	232,996	0.91
1987	263,807	245,823	0.93
1988	279,686	264,096	0.94
1989	292,350	272,917	0.93
1990	299,598	274,744	0.92
1991	298,136	269,033	0.90

Source: Economic Trends Annual Supplement, 1992.

Table 20.4 National income and the average propensity to consume in the United States, 1869–1928.

Years	National income ($bn.)	Average propensity to consume
1869–78	9.3	0.86
1874–83	13.6	0.86
1879–88	17.9	0.85
1884–93	21.0	0.84
1889–98	24.2	0.84
1894–1903	29.8	0.85
1899–1908	37.3	0.86
1904–13	45.0	0.87
1909–18	50.6	0.87
1914–23	57.3	0.89
1919–28	69.0	0.89

Source: Simon Kuznets, *National Income: A Summary of Findings*, Princeton University Press, 1946.

(c) *Long-run time-series study*. In this type of study, trend values of consumption and income are collected over a long period of time so that most cyclical fluctuations are smoothed out. The most famous studies of this kind were carried out by Simon Kuznets in the 1940s for the United States (1869–1928). The results of his study tended not to support the 'absolute income' hypothesis as outlined above. Instead, they exhibited an apc which was remarkably constant and had no tendency to fall as income rose or rise as income fell. His results are shown in Table 20.4. According to these results, the long-run consumption function is proportional, as illustrated in Fig. 20.4.

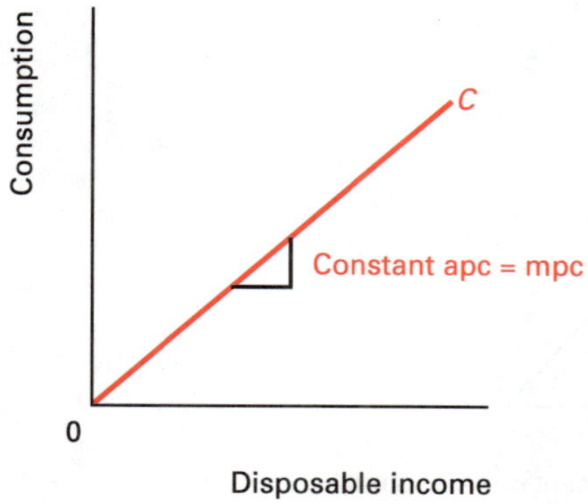

Fig. 20.4. A proportional long-run consumption line. The consumption line 0*C* passes through the origin and has a constant slope.

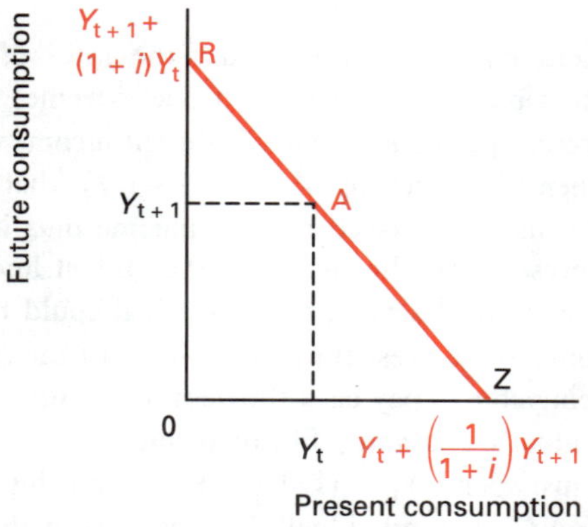

Fig. 20.5. The choice between present and future consumption. The line RAZ represents an individual's budget line for present and future consumption. It shows the individual's consumption possibilities.

The 'absolute income' hypothesis appears to explain the cross-section and short-run time-series data well, but fails to explain the long-run time-series data. One objective of the more recent theories has been to try and reconcile this apparent conflict in the different sets of statistical results.

The influence of wealth on consumption To consider the influence of wealth on aggregate consumption, we should first examine the *microeconomic* analysis of an individual consumer choosing between present and future consumption. (This is, therefore, a good time to review your understanding of budget lines and indifference curves from Ch. 4.)

To simplify, we restrict the analysis to two time periods only: the present period, t, and the future period, $t+1$. Suppose that we denote the individual's present income by Y_t and the expected future income by Y_{t+1}.

Now consider Fig. 20.5 where the individual's present consumption is measured along the horizontal axis and future consumption along the vertical axis. Point A represents the combination of present income (Y_t) and expected future income (Y_{t+1}). This is clearly one consumption possibility for the consumer – i.e. to consume all present income in the present period and all future income in the future period. Point A must, therefore, be on the individual's budget line (or, as it may be called in this case, the individual's consumption possibilities line). Other consumption possibilities exist as well and these are determined by the consumer's

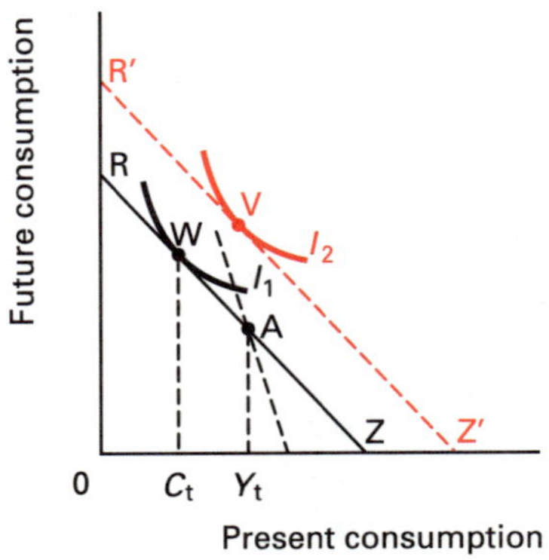

Fig. 20.6. The consumer 'equilibrium' position. Point W is the initial consumer equilibrium. After an increase in the individual's wealth, the new consumer equilibrium is at point V.

ability to lend and borrow. Suppose that the rates of interest for lending and borrowing are the same and equal to i. At one extreme, the consumer could spend nothing in the present period and save all present income so that in the future period he or she can spend as much as $Y_{t+1} + (1+i)Y_t$; that is, the consumer's future income plus the consumer's saved present income plus interest. This is point R in Fig. 20.5 and represents another point on the budget line.

Alternatively, instead of saving, the individual could borrow and so spend more than present income in the present period. The most the consumer could borrow and be sure of just being able to pay back the debt out of future income is $(1/1+i)Y_{t+1}$; this is the individual's *discounted* future income. In the present period then, the individual could just spend $Y_t + (1/1+i)Y_{t+1}$, and this is shown as point Z on the graph. The line RAZ is the individual's budget line – it shows all the combinations of present and future consumption that the individual can just attain, given present and future incomes and the rate of interest. Since *wealth* is the source of the individual's present and future incomes, we can say that the position of the individual's budget line is determined by the individual's wealth and its slope is determined by the rate of interest.

Time preference *The rate at which an individual is willing to forgo current consumption in return for extra consumption in the future*

Which point on the budget line will the consumer choose? This depends on the consumer's time preference for present and future consumption which, to some extent, depends on how patient or impatient he or she is. The consumer's preferences can be illustrated by means of a set of indifference curves which are likely to have the same shape as those depicted in Ch. 4 for the case of an individual choosing between two goods. The rational consumer will choose point W on the budget line which places him or her on the highest attainable indifference curve, I_1, in Fig. 20.6.

At point W, the individual is consuming $0C_t$ and saving C_tY_t in the present period. This consumption and saving will change in the following circumstances:

(a) If there is a change in the individual's wealth which affects present and/or future income. Such a change would cause the budget line to shift but remain parallel to the original one, as shown by line R′Z′ in Fig. 20.6, for an increase in wealth. The new utility-maximising point is V where the increase in wealth has caused present consumption to rise.

(b) If there is a change in the rate of interest which will influence the lending and borrowing possibilities. In this case the budget line would pivot around point A, becoming steeper for an increase in the rate of interest, as shown in Fig. 20.6.

According to this microeconomic analysis of an individual consumer's behaviour, then, present consumption depends on wealth (which is the source of both present and future incomes) and the rate of interest. This result, however, is not reflected in the 'absolute income' hypothesis where consumption depends on present income alone.

To summarise, the 'absolute income' hypothesis may be criticised on two major grounds: (a) for not providing an adequate explanation of the different sets of income–consumption data; (b) for not taking into account the influence of wealth and the rate of interest on consumption, and so for not being consistent with the microeconomic analysis of consumer behaviour. Perhaps the most famous of the theories which attempt to overcome both of these criticisms is Milton Friedman's 'permanent income' hypothesis.

'Permanent income' hypothesis

The basic proposition of Friedman's permanent income hypothesis is that *permanent consumption* (C_p) is proportional to *permanent income* (Y_p): that is, $C_p = kY_p$, where k is constant and equal to the average and marginal propensities to consume. Permanent consumption and permanent income are long-run trend values of consumption and income, so the hypothesis is consistent with long-run time-series data (like that collected by Kuznets) which suggests that the apc is constant.

'Permanent income' hypothesis *The contention that consumption depends on permanent income, which is the present value of the expected flow of long-term income*

Permanent income can be thought of as the present value of the expected flow of income from the existing stock of both 'human' and 'non-human' wealth over a long period of time. Human wealth is the source of income received from the sale of labour services, while non-human wealth is the source of all other incomes (that is, incomes received from the ownership of all kinds of assets, like government bonds, company stocks and shares, and property). Friedman points out that current measured income (Y) for a household or for the economy as a whole could be greater or less than permanent income. The difference between the two he calls transitory income (Y_T), which can be thought of as a temporary, unexpected rise or fall in income (for example, an unexpected increase in income resulting from a win at the races, or a temporary fall in income resulting from a short period of unemployment). Consequently, we can write

Transitory income *A temporary unexpected rise or fall in income*

$$Y = Y_p + Y_T$$

An important assumption of the hypothesis is that Y_T is *not* correlated with Y_p. In other words, a high permanent income is not necessarily associated with a high transitory income and a low permanent income is not necessarily associated with a low transitory income. This means that if we were to take a sufficiently large and completely random sample of households from all income groups, we would expect to find that the negative and positive transitory incomes would just cancel each other out so that the aggregate or *average* transitory income level ($\bar{Y}_T$) would be equal to zero. In this case, of course, the average permanent income would be just equal to the average measured income (that is, $\bar{Y}_p = \bar{Y}$). On the other hand, if we were to take our sample from those families with above-average *measured* incomes, we would expect to find that many of them had only temporarily high incomes so that average transitory income would be positive and $\bar{Y}_p < \bar{Y}$. Similarly, for a sample of families with below-average measured incomes, we should expect to find that $\bar{Y}_T < 0$ and $\bar{Y}_p > \bar{Y}$.

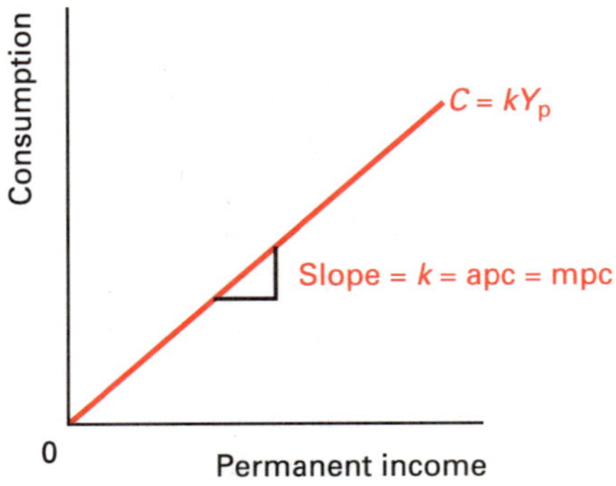

Fig. 20.7. *Friedman's consumption function.* The relationship between consumption and permanent income is represented by a straight line through the origin with a slope equal to the long-run apc and mpc.

Much the same results apply to the economy as a whole. In a normal year (that is, not a boom year or a slump year), we should expect aggregate transitory income to be zero, so that aggregate measured and permanent incomes would be equal. In a boom year, though, when many people would be experiencing unexpectedly high incomes, aggregate measured income should exceed aggregate permanent income. Exactly the opposite would apply in a slump year. All these results are important because, as we see later, they help to explain the cross-section and short-run time-series data.

Permanent consumption can be thought of as the normal or planned level of spending out of permanent income and can differ from measured consumption (C) by any unplanned, temporary increases or decreases in consumer spending, called *transitory consumption* (C_T). We can write

$$C = C_p + C_T$$

Friedman makes two important assumptions about transitory consumption. First, he assumes that it is not correlated with permanent consumption. Secondly, and more questionably, he argues that transitory consumption is not correlated with transitory income – in other words, temporary increases in income do not cause temporary increases in consumption. These assumptions make transitory consumption completely random, so that for any sufficiently large sample from any measured income group or in any year, we can expect the average and aggregate levels of transitory consumption to be zero. This means that average and aggregate levels of measured consumption must equal permanent consumption. Since we are concerned with average or aggregate data in macroeconomics, we need no longer make any distinction between measured consumption and permanent consumption. This means that we can write the basic consumption function in the 'permanent income' hypothesis as

$$C = kY_p$$

This is illustrated in Fig. 20.7.

Friedman, then, has succeeded in introducing wealth into the consumption function, as the source of permanent income upon which consumption depends. The next question to be considered is how he explains the cross-section and short-run time-series data which yield an apc which falls as measured income rises.

Consider first a cross-section budget study in which a sample of families is classified according to their incomes. Recall that in a group of families with above-average measured incomes, $\bar{Y} > \bar{Y}_p$ – this means that the measured apc ($= \bar{C}/\bar{Y}$) will necessarily be less than the long-run apc ($= \bar{C}/\bar{Y}_p$). Now compare this with a sample of families with below-average measured incomes for which $\bar{Y} < \bar{Y}_p$ – in this case, $\bar{C}/\bar{Y}$ will be greater than the long-run $\bar{C}/\bar{Y}_p$. Since the long-run apc is the same for both samples, we would predict that the measured apc of the families with above-average measured incomes would be less than the measured apc of the families with below-average measured incomes. As we have seen, this result is supported by cross-section budget studies.

Next, consider the short-run time-series studies. Recall that in a boom year, aggregate measured income exceeds aggregate permanent income so that the measured apc is less than the long-run apc, while in a slump year (where $Y < Y_p$) the measured apc is greater than the long-run apc. So again we would predict that the measured apc would be higher in a slump year than in a boom year. This is the result supported by short-run time-series data.

In conclusion, we can say that the 'permanent income' hypothesis takes a long-term, wide measure of income as the main determinant of consumption. It proposes that the basic long-run relationship is proportional, yet predicts a non-proportional relationship in the short-run and for cross-section data.

'Relative income' hypothesis

'Relative income' hypothesis *According to the 'relative income' hypothesis, a household's consumption depends not only on its own income, but also on the incomes of other households which it observes*

The relative income hypothesis was proposed by the American economist J.S. Duesenberry in 1949 and this theory can also be used to explain the apparent conflict in income–consumption data. Like Friedman, Duesenberry believed that the basic consumption function was long-run and proportional, as illustrated in Fig. 20.7. How, then, does the theory explain the non-proportionality of cross-section and short-run time-series data? Consider each one in turn.

Cross-section data To explain the observed non-proportionality of cross-section data, such as that in Table 20.2, Duesenberry argues that a household's consumption spending depends not only on its own income, but also on the incomes earned by neighbouring households. In other words, it is the household's *relative* income that determines its consumption spending. It follows that a household will spend more on consumption if it lives in a neighbourhood in which its income is relatively low than if it lives in a neighbourhood in which its income is relatively high. This is because poorer families who see the superior goods being consumed by their richer neighbours will attempt to 'keep up with the Joneses' and so spend a large fraction of their incomes. Duesenberry called this the 'demonstration effect'.

Given the existence of demonstration effects, it is not surprising that households with relatively high incomes have lower apc's and households with relatively low incomes have high apc's. Notice, though, that when all households' incomes rise (keeping each household's *relative* position unchanged) there will be no change in the overall apc. So there is no conflict between the non-proportional cross-section data and the proportional long-run data.

Short-run time-series data To explain the non-proportionality of annual time-series data, such as that in Table 20.3, Duesenberry suggests that aggregate consumption depends not just on current income, but also on the *highest level of*

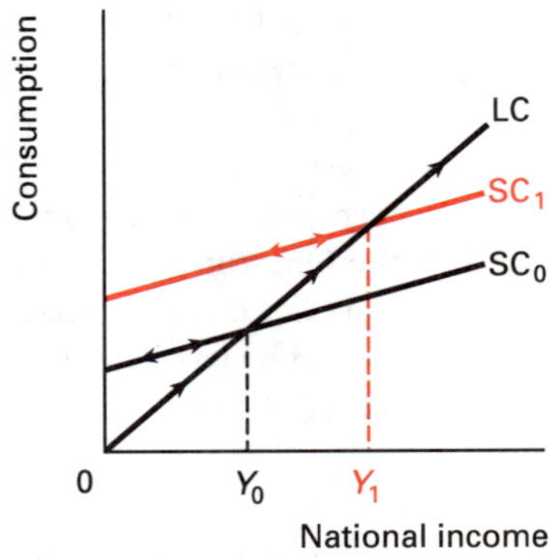

Fig. 20.8. The ratchet effect. If income reaches $0Y_0$ and then falls, consumption will fall along the consumption line SC_0 as consumers try to maintain the standard of living to which they have become accustomed. If income rises above $0Y_0$ consumption will rise along LC.

income previously attained. To illustrate this, consider Fig. 20.8. As national income rises, consumption rises along the long-run consumption line LC. Suppose that national income reaches $0Y_0$ and then begins to fall. Duesenberry argues that consumers (who have become accustomed to the income level of $0Y_0$ and the standard of living that goes with it) will increase their apc in an attempt to maintain their level of consumption and will move down the consumption line SC_0. If national income rises again, consumers will move back along SC_0 until $0Y_0$ is reached.

Now suppose that income reaches $0Y_1$ and then again begins to fall. Consumers again will try to maintain their accustomed standard of living by reducing their spending along the consumption line SC_1. Duesenberry called this the *ratchet effect*. It explains the observed rises in the apc when income falls over the period of a trade cycle.

Investment

Total investment, which includes spending on all types of capital goods by firms, accounts for less than a fifth of total expenditure in the United Kingdom. This is a relatively small proportion, but investment fluctuates more than any other component of national income and these fluctuations generate changes in income through the multiplier. Investment is sometimes thought of as the most dynamic element in the economy – it probably accounts for much of the cyclical instability in the economy and is an important determinant of economic growth (because the creation of new capital increases the economy's potential output level).

All firms have to undertake investment expenditure. New plant, machinery and other equipment must be replaced when they wear out and, at the same time, firms need to acquire additional capital if they are to grow and remain technologically competitive. Purchases of capital goods can be financed from a number of different sources: some firms will earn a sufficient level of profits, a proportion of which can be used for investment purposes; other firms can raise finance by borrowing from the public or from financial institutions, or by taking on new partners or share-holders. Whatever the source of finance, investment always involves an *opportunity cost*. If a firm borrows funds to finance an investment, then the opportunity cost is represented by the interest rate that must be paid on the borrowed funds. If a firm raises finance by bringing in new partners or share-holders, the opportunity cost is the rate of return that must be offered to make it worth their while. Even where a firm uses its own profits to finance new investment spending, there is an opportunity cost in terms of the rate of interest that could have been earned by investing the funds elsewhere.

Investment and the rate of interest

'Classical' economists viewed the rate of interest as the main determinant of investment. To summarise this approach, consider first the microeconomic analysis of a single profit-maximising firm deciding whether or not to undertake an investment (for example, to buy a new machine). When a firm buys a new machine, it expects the *yield* of the investment to exceed its *cost*. Calculating the expected yield from a new machine, however, is not easy because yields are spread over a number of years in the future. Recall from Ch. 8 that an allowance has to be made for the fact that a given sum of money to be received in the future is worth less than the same sum received now.

One way of comparing the expected yield of an investment to its cost is to calculate the *present value* of the investment and to compare that with the *present cost*. If present value > present cost, the investment can be regarded as profitable; otherwise, it is unprofitable.

Example I:
Suppose a machine which has a known life of only two years is expected to yield £242 each year. The machine's present cost is £400 and the rate of interest is 10 per cent. Is the investment profitable?

$$\text{Present value} = \frac{242}{1+0.1} + \frac{242}{(1+0.1)^2}$$

$$= \frac{242}{1.1} + \frac{242}{1.21} = £420$$

Present value > present cost. The investment is profitable.

A second way of comparing the expected yield of an investment to its cost is to calculate the investment's expected *rate of return* and to compare this with the prevailing rate of interest. If the rate of return exceeds the rate of interest, the investment will be profitable.

Example II:
Suppose a machine has a known life of only one year and is expected to yield £450 at the end of that year. The machine's present cost is £400 and the rate of interest is 10 per cent. Is the investment profitable?
We have to find the rate of return, r, which raises £400 to £450 in one year:

$$400(1+r) = 450$$

$$r = \frac{450 - 400}{400}$$

$$r = 0.125 \text{ or } 12\tfrac{1}{2} \text{ per cent}$$

Rate of return > rate of interest. The investment is profitable.

Fig. 20.9. The aggregate investment curve. As the rate of interest falls, more investment projects become potentially profitable and the demand for investment increases.

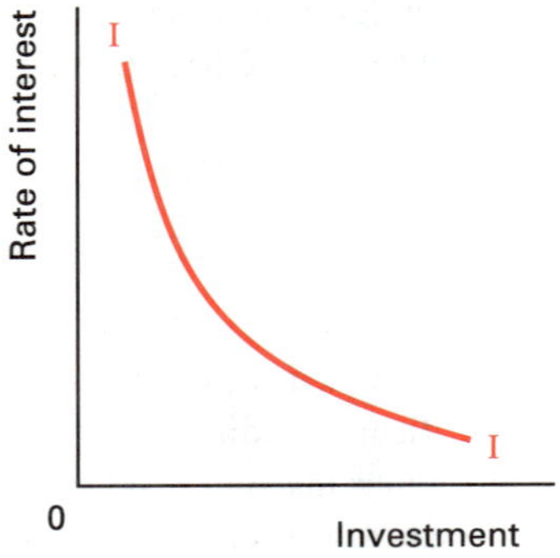

MEI. *The rate of discount which would equate the present value of the expected stream of future income from an investment project to the initial outlay. In other words, it is the expected rate of return from an additional pound of planned investment*

It follows from the above examples that profit-maximising firms, operating under conditions of certainty, will invest in projects where the rate of return on the investment exceeds the market rate of interest. (The rate of return on an additional investment is sometimes called the marginal efficiency of investment or MEI.)

The MEI is likely to decline as more and more investment projects are undertaken for two main reasons: first, because the most profitable projects will normally be undertaken first; and secondly, because as investment increases, the price of investment goods will be bid upwards thereby reducing the expected rate of return.

A fall in the market rate of interest should make profitable some investments in the economy which were previously unprofitable, so that aggregate investment should increase. Similarly, a rise in the market rate of interest should make unprofitable some investments which were previously profitable, so that aggregate investment should fall. In other words, our microeconomic analysis of a single profit-making firm leads us to the conclusion that *aggregate investment is inversely related to the rate of interest.* This is illustrated in Fig. 20.9, where II represents the demand for investment curve for the economy as a whole.

Empirical evidence on aggregate investment tends to confirm that it is indeed *inversely* related to the rate of interest, but most evidence suggests that the relationship is a fairly weak one. For example, in a study in 1989, P. Turner found only a weak negative relationship between the real rate of interest and gross investment in manufacturing in the United Kingdom. Also, the results of many surveys in both the United States and the United Kingdom suggest that only a few firms explicitly take the rate of interest into account in deciding whether or not to carry out an investment project. There are two main reasons why investment tends to be fairly interest-inelastic:

(a) Investment is probably strongly influenced by business *expectations* of future economic activity. If businesses are very pessimistic about the future, it is unlikely that even very low interest rates would induce them to increase their rate of investment. Similarly, if they are generally very optimistic about the future, high interest rates will not discourage them from investing.

(b) Yields on investment projects are notoriously difficult to estimate since they depend on the future demand for the firm's products. It could be that a firm may only be able to say with any certainty that it expects the rate of return on an investment project to be within a particular range, say 10 to 15 per cent. A small

Table 20.5 An example of the accelerator principle.

Year	Demand (D)	Desired capital stock	Net investment (no. of machines)
1	1,000	10	0
2	2,000	20	10
3	3,000	30	10
4	3,500	35	5
5	3,500	35	0

rise in interest rates would be unlikely to dissuade the firm from investing in this case. This would be particularly true if the investment were part of a long-term plan of expansion for the firm.

Now consider a second approach to the theory of investment – the view that it depends on changes in national income.

The accelerator theory

Accelerator theory
The view that the level of current net investment depends on past changes in national income

According to the accelerator theory, the level of current net investment depends on past income changes. In its simplest form, this can be written as follows:

$$I_t = v(Y_t - Y_{t-1})$$

where I_t is net investment in the current period, Y_t is current national income, Y_{t-1} is national income in the previous period and v is a constant known as the 'accelerator coefficient'. Note that v may also be described as the marginal capital-output ratio. Gross investment is equal to net investment plus any replacement investment which takes place because of depreciation. So we can write

$$GI_t = v(Y_t - Y_{t-1}) + R_t$$

Replacement investment
The investment necessary to replace obsolete and worn-out equipment

where GI_t is current gross investment and R_t is current replacement investment.

For the 'accelerator' theory to be valid, it is necessary that firms behave in a particular way. In fact, firms must demand additional capital to meet any increases in demand for their product. Consider the following simplified example.

Consider a single firm which initially has a stock of ten machines each of which is capable of producing 100 units of output per year. To keep the example simple, assume that there is no depreciation so that we do not need to worry about replacement investment. Suppose that to start with the total demand for the firm's product is 1,000 units. This is shown for year 1 in Table 20.5: notice that the *desired* capital stock to meet this demand is ten machines and since the firm already has ten machines, no net investment is necessary. So long as demand stays at 1,000 units, no net investment will take place. But now suppose that in year 2, demand increases to 2,000 units – the desired capital stock will rise to twenty machines and to achieve this, net investment of ten machines is necessary. In year 3, demand has risen to 3,000 units so that the desired capital stock goes up to thirty machines – since the firm already has twenty, another ten must be purchased. Notice here that although demand has risen from year 2 to year 3, net investment has remained the same. In year 4, demand continues to increase, but this time by only 500 units to 3,500 units: the desired capital stock goes up to thirty-five and so net investment of only five machines is necessary. Since demand has risen by a smaller amount than previously, investment has actually fallen. In year 5, demand levels off at 3,500 units – the firm, however, already has the thirty-five machines necessary to meet this demand and so no new investment is necessary.

The example highlights the following important points about the 'accelerator' theory:

(a) To maintain net investment at a constant positive level, demand for the firm's product must be rising at a steady rate.
(b) For net investment to increase, demand must be increasing at an increasing rate.
(c) If demand should level off and remain constant, net investment will fall to zero.

Notice that the relationship expressed in Table 20.5 can be written algebraically as follows:

$$NI = (1/100)(D_t - D_{t-1})$$

where NI is the firm's net investment measured in numbers of machines, D_t is the current demand for the firm's product and D_{t-1} is last year's demand for the firm's product. As each machine is capable of producing 100 units of output, the marginal capital-output ratio (or accelerator coefficient) is equal to 1/100.

If all firms behave in a similar way to this, then we can say that *aggregate* investment in the economy will depend on changes in aggregate demand – both of these have to be measured in value terms and since the value of aggregate demand in equilibrium is the same as national income, we have

$$I_t = v(Y_t - Y_{t-1})$$

which is the expression we started with.

Two main criticisms can be made of the accelerator theory as we have outlined it.

(a) It assumes that firms faced with increased demand for their product will immediately attempt to increase their capital stocks. This implies that there is no excess capacity (that is to say, all existing machines must be fully employed and there must be no possibility of overtime or shift working). This is extremely unrealistic – it is more likely that firms will be able to meet some of the increased demand by working existing machines harder and using whatever excess capacity does exist.

(b) It fails to take into account business expectations. If businesses regard the increase in demand as temporary, they may not respond to it at all: this will be the case if they are generally pessimistic about the future level of economic activity. If, on the other hand, businesses are generally optimistic and see the increase in demand as a signal for further increases, they may actually buy more machines than predicted by the accelerator theory.

Profit as a determinant of investment

Some researchers have argued that higher levels of profit in the economy will lead to higher levels of aggregate investment. The argument is that since profit is one of the cheaper sources of finance, higher profit levels will increase the availability and lower the cost of funds for investment. High profits may also boost business confidence and so raise the expected future income from planned investment projects: this would have the effect of shifting the MEI schedule to the right. Recent empirical evidence published by the European Commission suggests that there has been a statistically significant positive relationship between net investment and the rate of profitability in the EC during the last 30 years. The main problem with such studies, of course, lies in deciding whether the rate of profitability is a true *cause* of the level of investment, or whether both the rate of profitability and the level of investment are affected in the same direction by other factors, such as changes in aggregate demand.

The 'crowding out' effect

Crowding out effect *The displacement of private investment spending by increased public spending*

It is argued by some that the finance required by the government to pay for the growth of public spending has the effect of raising taxes on incomes and profits, and pushing up interest rates. This squeezes the profitability of private firms and raises their investment costs. The argument leads to the conclusion that excessive growth in *public* spending crowds out private investment spending. This view was expressed forcibly by R. Bacon and W. Eltis in their book *Britain's Economic Problem – Too Few Producers* published in 1976. [See Ch. 23 for a further discussion of the 'crowding out' effect.]

Overall view of investment

In conclusion, we can combine the approaches to investment theory and say that the level of net investment in an economy will depend on four major factors: the rate of interest (i), past national income changes, the state of business expectations (B) and the rate of profitability (π). Using functional notation, we can write:

$$I_t = f(t, Y_t - Y_{t-1}, B, \pi)$$

Since it takes time for firms to adjust their capital stocks in response to changes in demand (remember that capital is a variable factor of production only in the long-run), it may be more realistic to introduce a lag into the accelerator part of the function and write:

$$I_t = f(i, Y_{t-1} - Y_{t-2}, B, \pi)$$

Only empirical testing can determine which of the four independent variables is the most important.

Summary

1. Consumption is household expenditure on goods and services which yield utility in the current period. It is the largest of the components of national expenditure, and relatively small changes in consumption spending can have a significant effect on employment.

2. According to the 'absolute income' hypothesis: consumption depends on current disposable income; the mpc lies between 0 and 1; and the apc falls as income rises and is greater than the mpc. The hypothesis appears to explain cross-section and short-run time-series data reasonably well, but fails to explain long-run time-series data.

3. The 'permanent income' hypothesis claims that permanent consumption depends on permanent income, where permanent consumption and income are the long-run trend values.

4. In the 'relative income' hypothesis, a household's consumption spending depends not just on its own income, but also on the incomes earned by neighbouring households. Similarly, aggregate consumption depends not just on current income, but also on the highest level of income previously attained.

5. Investment is spending on capital goods by firms. It is an important component of aggregate demand, as well as being a potentially important source of economic growth. Possible determinants of investment are the rate of interest, *changes* in aggregate demand, profitability and business expectations.

Exercises

1. Review your understanding of the following terms:

absolute income	permanent income
marginal propensity to consume	transitory income
average propensity to consume	permanent consumption
marginal propensity to save	transitory consumption
average propensity to save	relative income
cross-section data	present value
time-series data	marginal efficiency of investment
discounted future income	accelerator
time preference	replacement investment

2. Consider Table 20.6 which shows the results of a cross-section budget study. Calculate the average and marginal propensities to consume for each income group and comment on the significance of your results for the theories of consumption outlined in this chapter.

3. Consider the view that the link between aggregate consumption and current measured income is a tenuous one.

4. In the permanent income hypothesis, Friedman makes a series of assumptions regarding the statistical relationships that exist between permanent and

Table 20.6 Cross-section budget study for the United Kingdom, 1971.

Income group (£ per week)	Average income (£ per week)	Consumption (£ per week)
Under 10	7.89	9.73
10–19.99	14.97	16.46
20–29.99	25.01	23.96
30–39.99	34.97	29.82
40–49.99	44.97	35.90
50–59.99	54.69	42.12
60–79.99	68.14	48.31
80 and over	112.26	70.92

Source: Department of Employment, *Family Expenditure Survey*, 1971.

transitory consumption, permanent and transitory income and transitory income and consumption. Explain these assumptions and discuss their importance to the theory.

5. Consider a firm which initially has a stock of 100 machines, each of which can product 50 units of output per time period. Assume that the 100 machines have been acquired at the rate of ten per time period for the last ten periods, so that from now on depreciation is equal to ten machines per time period. Table 20.7 shows the demand for the firm's product in time periods 0 to 5.

   (a) Calculate the firm's gross investment in time periods 0 to 5.
   (b) Write down the equations of the relationship between gross investment and changes in demand.
   (c) Comment on the applicability of this model to the real world.

6. Discuss the influence of changes in interest rates on aggregate investment in the United Kingdom.

7. Discuss the view that reducing the size of the public sector in the United Kingdom will encourage private investment spending.

Table 20.7 The demand for the firm's product over time.

Time period	Demand
0	5,000
1	6,000
2	10,000
3	12,000
4	12,000
5	10,000

21 MONEY – I

Learning objectives

After reading this chapter, you should be able to:

- explain the concept of money and describe the functions of money
- outline the functions of a central bank
- identify the important role performed by discount houses in the United Kingdom financial system
- understand the way in which a new cash deposit with commercial banks may result in multiple credit creation
- describe the methods which a central bank may use to control the money supply
- explain the meaning of the rate of interest, distinguishing between the nominal and real rate of interest
- identify the factors that lead to the existence of a range of interest rates in financial markets

Introduction

The objectives of this and the following two chapters are, first, to explain the meaning of money in a modern economy; secondly, to show how the supply of money might be influenced by government policy and other factors; and finally, to discuss the role of money in an economy. As we shall see, this is an area which has been central to the most fundamental controversies in macroeconomics. It is in the field of monetary theory and policy that many of the differences between Keynesians and monetarists are debated.

In this chapter, we are concerned primarily with the problems of defining and measuring a country's stock of money and with describing the methods employed in the United Kingdom to influence the money supply. To enable the reader to gain a good understanding of these methods of implementing monetary policy, we also outline the main functions of the more important financial institutions in the United Kingdom.

The nature of money

Money can be defined as any asset that is generally acceptable in transactions and in the settlement of debts. The key word is 'generally' and its interpretation does leave some room for discussion as to exactly which assets should be included as money. In a modern economy, banknotes and coins clearly form part of the money supply as they are generally acceptable in the settlement of all transactions. In addition, many transactions can be settled by the use of cheques drawn on bank deposits. Note that cheques are drawn on bank deposits in *current* accounts (sometimes called sight or demand deposits). Current account deposits, therefore, also form part of the money supply. It must be pointed out, furthermore, that people can readily transfer funds from deposit accounts (sometimes called time deposits) into current accounts or cash. Consequently, it can be argued that deposit accounts with banks and other financial institutions should also be included as part of the stock of money.

Monetary aggregates

For official purposes in the United Kingdom, there are two major alternative definitions of money, namely narrow money and broad money.

Narrow money *Money balances that are held to carry out day-to-day spending*

Narrow money Narrow money refers to money balances which are easily available to finance day-to-day spending, that is, for transactions purposes. It is difficult to give a precise definition of those deposits that are held for transactions purposes. Any definition involves an arbitrary categorisation of deposits at the margin. Note that the narrow definition of money emphasises the medium of exchange function of money.

The main official definitions of narrow money are M0 and M2.

M0 The M0 definition includes notes and coins held by the public *plus* cash in banks' tills *plus* banks' operational balances at the Bank of England. M0 is sometimes called the *wide monetary base* as it includes those assets that are, or could be, used as cash reserves by the banking system. Notes and coins held by the public account for about 90 per cent of M0.

M2 As defined in December 1992, M2 comprises the United Kingdom's non-bank, non-building society (that is, M4) private sector's holding of:

- notes and coins.
- sterling 'retail' deposits with United Kingdom banks and building societies.

Building societies' 'retail' deposits include all shares held by, or sums deposited by, individuals. Also included are shares and deposits with societies of under £50,000 from corporate bodies. Banks' retail deposits are defined as deposits which arise from a customer's acceptance of a particular product. As a general rule, therefore, retail deposits are taken in the banks' branch networks.

Broad money *Money balances that are held as a store of value, in addition to those held for transactions purposes*

Broad money 'Broad' money refers to money held both for transactions purposes and as a form of saving. It includes assets which could be converted with relative ease and without capital loss into spending on goods and services. Thus, the broad definition of money takes into account the store of value function in addition to the medium of exchange function of money.

The main definitions of broad money are:

M4 The M4 aggregate includes:

- the M4 private sector's holdings of notes and coins.
- all sterling deposits (including *certificates of deposit*) at United Kingdom banks and building societies. Note that a certificate of deposit (CD) is documentary evidence that a sum of money has been deposited at a specified interest rate for a given time period. CDs may be sold on the secondary market.

M3H The M3H aggregate contains the same components as M4 with the additions of:

- foreign currency deposits held by the M4 private sector with banks and building societies in the United Kingdom.
- sterling and foreign currency deposits held by United Kingdom public sector corporations with banks and building societies in the United Kingdom.

M3H is the 'harmonised' broad money aggregate, introduced in 1992, designed to facilitate comparisons among member states when analysing monetary developments in EC countries.

In March 1993 M0 totalled £19.3 billion; M2 totalled £379 billion; and M4 was measured at £526 billion. In March 1993, while currency in circulation totalled £19.2 billion, private sector sterling sight deposits totalled £152 billion and private sector sterling time deposits totalled £155 billion. It is obvious from these figures that the financial system operates on the basis of confidence: if all the account holders decided to withdraw their deposits in the form of currency on a particular day (an event with a probability value indistinguishable from zero), there would be a large number of disappointed account holders.

Functions of money

The use of money in a complex economy, such as the United Kingdom, fulfils four main functions.

Medium of exchange Obviously, the use of money greatly eases the carrying out of everyday transactions. Without money, we would have to resort to barter: that is, the exchange of goods for goods. Barter is clearly inefficient and troublesome as it requires a double coincidence of wants. Someone who wishes to obtain some food in return for some clothes, not only has to find someone who has some food, but who is also seeking some clothes. This might involve a prolonged search and thus discourage the specialisation that is so important in increasing output: in a barter economy, an individual would try to be as self-sufficient as possible because of the problems of trading. In a money economy, these problems are considerably reduced: clothes, for example, are exchanged for money which can then be used to purchase food. The food seller is willing to accept money in the knowledge that it in turn can be used in his or her purchases. Thus, with money there is no need for a double coincidence of wants.

Double coincidence of wants *This is the notion that barter necessitates the matching of the wants of both parties to a transaction*

Store of value Money enables individuals to delay a potential purchase to the most convenient time by providing them with a way in which to store their purchasing power. Clearly, if there is inflation, the efficiency of money as a store of value is reduced.

Unit of account The use of money with its units of measurement (pounds and pence in the United Kingdom) enables the prices of all goods to be quoted in these units. This facilitates the quick comparison of the respective values of different goods. In addition, money is the unit used in the financial accounts of all businesses and, for example, in expressing the values of a country's national income and balance of payments.

Standard of deferred payment Many transactions are conducted on the basis of credit. Thus, payment for work carried out now might be made several months later and it is convenient for the debt to be expressed and for the payment to be made in money terms rather than in terms of some commodity. For example, a sub-contractor on a building site may agree to do some work for the developer in return for a certain sum of money to be paid when the work is finished. Both parties to the agreement know how much money will change hands at the agreed date in the future. Once again, if there is inflation, money performs less efficiently as a standard of deferred payment. Some contracts, however, have cost-escalation clauses allowing the passing on of any increased costs.

Inflation and the functions of money

Purchasing power *The basket of goods and services that can be bought with a given sum of money*

The efficiency with which money performs its functions is greatly dependent upon the stability of its purchasing power. Inflation, especially unanticipated inflation, adversely affects the functions of money by undermining wealth-holders' confidence in its ability to be used as a medium of exchange and a store of value. In its medium of exchange role, money provides wealth-holders with a convenience yield in the sense of saving time and effort in undertaking transactions. This yield will fall in a period of inflation because a progressively larger amount of money will be needed to pay for the same quantity of goods and services. Money holders will, therefore, suffer a loss of purchasing power. The store of value function is equally threatened by inflation. As the real value of money falls, wealth-holders are induced to switch to real assets, such as houses, cars and other consumer durables: this will exert upward pressure on the prices of real assets and so make inflationary conditions worse.

The undesirable effects of inflation are considered in greater detail in Ch. 28.

Liquidity

Liquidity *The speed and the possible cost of turning a financial asset into cash*

Liquidity refers to the ease with which a financial asset can be turned into cash. The concept of liquidity has two dimensions. First, there is the speed with which an asset can be converted into spending power. There is no clear-cut dividing line between a liquid and an illiquid asset in this respect: cash, sight deposits and time deposits requiring seven days notice of withdrawal would all generally be regarded as liquid assets. The second dimension of the concept of liquidity is concerned with the *face-value* of the assset. A liquid asset is also one that can be converted into spending power without significant loss of face-value or interest income. As a result, even though it may be possible to sell an asset quickly, that asset will not be regarded as liquid if such a sale involves a risk of a capital loss. Consider, for example, a long-dated government bond that can be sold quickly in the market place. The sale may result in a capital loss for the bond-holder and it should, therefore, be regarded as illiquid.

The development of money

In the course of history, many different commodities have been used as money – for example, shells, animals and metals. Over a period of time, the use of precious metals, such as silver and gold, became increasingly important. In the seventeenth century, goldsmiths acted as depositaries for the gold of the rich. The goldsmiths issued receipts for the gold deposited with them. When individuals wanted to settle debts, they came to realise that rather than withdrawing their gold, they could endorse the receipts instructing the goldsmith to transfer the deposits to the named creditor. In the course of time, the goldsmiths began to issue receipts for gold *payable to the bearer* rather than to any named person. As a consequence, the goldsmiths' receipts began to circulate as generally acceptable means of payment.

The goldsmiths noticed that a large proportion of the gold was not withdrawn from the vaults and as a result they seized the opportunity of making profits by granting loans through the issue of 'receipts' in excess of actual gold deposits. This was the origin of paper currency (or banknotes) as used in modern societies today. Note that by issuing 'receipts' in excess of gold holdings, the goldsmiths were acting as bankers and so laid the foundations of the modern 'fractional reserve' banking system. The goldsmiths learnt from experience what proportion of gold reserves they had to keep in order to meet day-to-day demands for gold withdrawals. Several goldsmiths developed into fully fledged banks and issued banknotes. In the nineteenth century, however, the Bank of England, as the central bank, was granted a monopoly of banknote-issue. In modern times, commercial banks are still able to create money, but only in the form of bank deposits. This process of credit creation by banks is discussed below.

Fractional reserve banking *This describes a bank's practice of maintaining only a small proportion of its deposits as cash reserves*

The central bank

Central bank *A financial institution responsible for ensuring the smooth working of a country's financial system. Its overriding aim is to operate in the public interest*

In most countries, the central bank is at the apex of the financial system. It is responsible for ensuring the smooth working of the banking sector and other financial institutions. The primary aim of the central bank is to work closely with the government and so to operate in the public interest. The Federal Reserve System of the United States, the Bundesbank of Germany and the Reserve Bank of India are all examples of central banks.

The Bank of England is one of the oldest central banks in the world. It was set up in 1694 and nationalised in 1946. Because of its long history and experience, many countries have modelled their central banks on the Bank of England in respect of their duties and responsibilities. Being a nationalised concern, the Bank is subject to the direction of the Treasury. This contrasts with some other central banks which, like the Bundesbank in Germany, are largely independent of political control. However, the primary objective of all central banks, whether nationalised or independent, is the stability of the financial system.

Functions of a central bank

A central bank performs a wide range of functions. In the case of the Bank of England, the most important ones are:

- government's bank
- bankers' bank
- holding the nation's gold and foreign currency reserves
- management of the Exchange Equalisation Account
- management and administration of the national debt
- issuing notes and coins
- implementation of monetary policy
- lender of last resort
- supervision of banks and other financial institutions.

Consider these functions in turn.

Public deposits *The balances of the government held at the central bank*

Government's bank In this role, the Bank of England looks after the finances of the central government. For this purpose, it holds the government's balances which are known as public deposits. Thus, government income from taxes, trading activities and privatisation proceeds is paid into this account. Out of this account, the central government pays for its expenditure on social security, health, education, police and so on.

Bankers' deposits *The balances of the commercial banks held at the central bank for the settlement of claims between themselves*

Bankers' bank The Bank of England holds bankers' deposits which the clearing banks use for the following purposes:

(a) To settle debts with each other. Such debts arise from cheques drawn by customers of one bank in favour of customers of other banks. Thus, bankers' deposits are used to effect inter-bank settlements.

(b) To pay monies to the government. Such debts arise when banks' customers pay taxes or when they buy government securities and so write cheques on their accounts payable to the government.

(c) To receive monies from the government payable to their customers, such as wages and salaries, pensions and interest payments on government securities.

(d) To exchange old and worn out notes and coins for new ones. With bankers' deposits, the clearing banks also buy additional currency to replenish their depleted stocks of till money. During the summer months and at Christmas time, for example, banks experience pressure on their till money because of heavy cash withdrawals by their customers.

The Bank, then, is constantly involved in the daily transfer of funds between the accounts of clearing banks. But much more important is its involvement in the daily transfer of funds between public deposits and bankers' deposits. This enables the Bank to anticipate movements of funds between the government sector and the private sector and to make an accurate forecast of cash shortages or surpluses in the banking system on a daily basis.

Holding the nation's gold and foreign currency reserves and management of the Exchange Equalisation Account These two functions are interlinked. The Exchange Equalisation Account holds the nation's gold and foreign currency reserves. The Bank uses these reserves to intervene in the foreign exchange markets to influence the exchange rate between sterling and other currencies. If sterling's exchange rate is falling faster than the Bank desires, for example, the Bank will use its foreign currency reserves to buy sterling. The ability of the Bank of England to defend a given exchange rate is, however, limited because its reserves are finite. For example, in September 1992, when dealers were selling sterling on the foreign exchange markets, causing its value to fall against other currencies, the Bank of England was ultimately powerless to stabilise sterling's exchange rate in spite of substantial sales of foreign currency reserves to prop up the value of sterling.

Management and administration of the National Debt The Bank is responsible for issuing new government debt and arranging for its redemption. It aims to maintain an orderly market and the public's confidence in government debt. The Bank pays out interest to the holders of the National Debt.

Issuing notes and coins The Bank of England has a monopoly of note-issue in the United Kingdom. Although it is true that some commercial banks in Scotland and Northern Ireland still issue their own notes, these notes have to be backed on a one-to-one basis by Bank of England notes. The Bank is also responsible, on behalf of the government, for the issue of new coins. The public demand for notes and coins is linked with inflation. As the rate of inflation rises, causing the value of currency to fall, the public demand for currency rises to pay for day-to-day needs. Similarly, growth in GDP and a rise in economic activity stimulate individual and business demands for currency. Thus, the Bank has to increase the supply of notes and coins to meet the growing needs of the community.

Monetary policy *A government's decision to control the money supply and/or influence interest rates and the exchange rate*

Implementation of monetary policy This is probably the most important function of any central bank. The level of efficiency and performance of the Bank of England is largely dependent upon the extent to which it successfully executes monetary policy. Being a nationalised concern, the Bank has to carry out the government's monetary policy objectives. However, given its intimate knowledge and experience of the money markets, the foreign exchange markets and the capital markets, at home and abroad, the Bank exercises considerable influence over the formulation of monetary policy objectives and the methods of implementing these objectives.

Monetary policy is essentially concerned with controlling the annual growth of the money supply, and influencing interest rates and the exchange rate. Thus, in this role, the Bank of England is responsible for maintaining both the internal and external value of the currency. Controlling the growth of the money supply may be based on the belief that there is a positive relationship between the growth of the money supply and inflation. It is the responsibility of the Bank of England to ensure that the annual growth rate of the money supply is not so excessive that it causes inflation and erodes the internal and external value of money.

Bills and eligible bills *A bill is a short-term financial instrument issued by a borrower who undertakes to repay the loan after the specified period. An eligible bill is a first-class bill issued or guaranteed by a reputable bank and which the Bank of England is willing to trade in the discount market.*

Open market operation *The process of buying and selling eligible bills by the central bank as part of its monetary policy*

Lender of last resort This function is a recognition of the fact that the central bank is the ultimate source of cash. In other words, an overall cash shortage in the United Kingdom economy can only be relieved by the Bank of England. Cash shortages are initially felt by commercial banks whose liquidity comes under pressure when the movement of funds to public deposits is not compensated by an equivalent reverse movement of funds to bankers' deposits. Unless the Bank wishes to see a rise in short-term interest rates as part of its monetary policy, it relieves cash shortages by buying eligible bills in the money market from discount houses and other authorised dealers at a price that leaves the existing short-term interest rates unaffected. This process of buying bills by the Bank is known as open market operations. The cash paid by the Bank for these bills is credited to bankers' deposits and debited to public deposits, thereby providing the commercial banks with enough cash for their daily business needs.

Note that an individual commercial bank experiencing cash shortages can replenish the shortage by borrowing in the inter-bank market. This market, as the name indicates, exists for lending and borrowing between banks. Last resort lending by the Bank of England is necessary only when there is an *overall* shortage of cash in the banking system.

Supervision of banks and other financial institutions With the removal of exchange controls and the deregulation of financial services, competition has become fiercer amongst banks, building societies and other financial institutions. This has brought into sharper focus the role of the Bank of England as a supervisor and regulator of the banking system. In this role, the Bank has become an important source of guidance and advice to individual commercial banks. It has developed an elaborate system of rules and regulations under the Banking Act (1987) for the solvency of banks and for the protection of their depositors. If a bank were unable to meet its obligations and so became insolvent, this could have a major effect on public confidence in the entire financial system. In its supervisory role, the Bank seeks to maintain public confidence in the stability of banks and other financial institutions.

Commercial banks make profits from taking risks. The Bank of England lays down the liquidity requirements with which individual banks must comply. A bank needs liquidity to meet its customers' demands for cash withdrawals. The Bank of England ensures that banks: (a) have sufficiently strong capital bases to withstand losses from bad debts and falling asset values; (b) maintain a prudent mixture of liquid assets to meet current and future needs of customers; (c) do not take excessive risks by concentrating their lending on too few customers and on too few sectors.

Under the Banking Act (1987) the Bank of England has a statutory right to information about a bank at any time. The Bank also has the power to carry out regular investigations of a bank's business. It is a criminal offence for the directors of a bank to withhold information to which the Bank is entitled as supervisor. A Board of Banking Supervision operates within the Bank of England and advises the governor of the Bank on banking supervisory matters. The Board has the power to revoke the licence of any bank to take deposits. Lending to individual borrowers in excess of 10 per cent of a bank's capital base has to be notified to the Bank; all exposures in excess of 25 per cent require prior notification.

Banking supervision in an international context

The EC Second Banking Co-ordination Directive places legal responsibility for most aspects of supervision of EC banks with the *home country*, rather than with the countries that are hosts to the bank branches. Under this Directive, banks incorporated in one EC country can now carry on business in other member states without having to obtain authorisation from the supervisory authorities in the host country. Henceforth, the host supervisor's prudential responsibility is mainly confined to overseeing local branches in respect of liquidity in consultation with the home supervisor.

Response to the BCCI affair Following the forced closure in 1991 of the Bank of Credit and Commerce International (BCCI) after the discovery of fraud and false accounting, new measures to strengthen supervision were proposed. These included: (a) the setting up of a special investigations unit at the Bank of England to pursue any indication of fraud; (b) measures to ensure more effective supervision of banks by overseas regulators; (c) proposed changes to the Banking Act (1987) that would give the Bank of England explicit power to refuse or revoke the authorisation of banks with group structures that cannot be properly supervised.

Table 21.1 Bank of England's balance sheet, 31 March 1993.

Liabilities	£ million	Assets	£ million
Issue Department			
Notes in circulation	16,447	Government securities	9,283
Notes in Banking Dep.	3	Other securities	7,167
	16,450		16,450
Banking Department			
Capital	14	Government securities	1,265
Public deposits	110	Advances and other accounts	4,889
Special deposits	–	Premises and other securities	454
Bankers' deposits	1,613	Notes and coins	3
Reserves and other accounts	4,874		
	6,611		6,611

Source: Bank of England Quarterly Bulletin, May 1993.

The Bank of England's balance sheet

The weekly return in Table 21.1 illustrates the Bank's assets and liabilities: the division between the Issue Department and Banking Department is largely for historic reasons and has no real economic significance.

The Issue Department is responsible for the note issue. When notes are issued, the Issue Department receives interest-bearing government securities in return. The Issue Department frequently engages in open-market operations as part of the Bank's debt management. In order to avoid large cash payments to the public on a particular date, the Bank purchases government securities before they mature.

If an issue of a government security is under-subscribed the Issue Department will purchase the remainder, which it will gradually sell to the public.

Turning to the Banking Department, *public deposits* refer to the government's account. The balance is kept to a minimum, and any temporary surplus is used to reduce government borrowing.

Special deposits *These refer to the sums of money that the Bank of England may require banks to lodge with it as part of its monetary policy*

Special deposits are deposits of banks from time to time required by the Bank of England to be lodged in addition to normal reserve requirements. The Bank may use them to help control the level of bank lending.

Bankers' deposits are the deposits of the commercial banks, to which reference has already been made. *Other accounts* include the few private accounts the Bank still maintains for historical reasons, the accounts of overseas central banks and the accounts of its own staff.

The discount houses

Discount houses *Financial institutions that seek to make a profit by dealing in short-term securities*

The discount houses are unique to the British monetary system. In a sense, they are intermediaries between the Bank of England and the commercial banks. The discount houses attempt to make profits by creating a market in short-term financial instruments. They borrow short-term funds and use these funds to purchase higher yielding assets, such as Treasury Bills and commercial bills.

The discount houses borrow funds from commercial banks, accepting houses, overseas and other banks and from industrial and commercial companies. The banks are willing to lend funds to the discount houses at call, overnight, or at short notice

Table 21.2
Distribution of discount houses' assets, February 1993.

	£ million
Cash ratio deposits with Bank of England	7
Treasury Bills	31
Other bills	3,358
Sterling investments	193
Funds lent	6,434
Other currencies	174
Total	10,197

Source: Financial Statistics, April 1993.

Treasury bill *An instrument of short-term borrowing by the government, normally having a life of 91 days*

Discounting *The purchase of a financial instrument for less than its face value. In this way, the purchaser earns an implied interest rate*

because the banks earn some interest on these funds, while at the same time retaining a pool of liquidity. The discount houses have an arrangement with the Bank of England whereby they agree to tender for the whole of the weekly Treasury Bill issue. The price at which they bid for these bills determines the Treasury Bill rate. The higher the bid-price the lower is the rate of interest earned by holding them. For example, if the bid-price were £95 for a Bill with a face value of £100, the government would be paying a 3-monthly interest rate of about 5 per cent; if the bid-price rose to £98, the 3-monthly interest rate would fall to about 2 per cent. Note that purchasing an asset for less than its face value is known as discounting.

In return for guaranteeing the sale of the whole Treasury Bill issue, the discount houses have the privilege of borrowing from the Bank of England as 'lender of last resort'. Treasury bills enable the government to cover the difference between its revenues and expenditures on a week to week basis.

If the commercial banks are short of cash they will recall some of their money at call or short notice from the discount houses. As these funds are tied up in Treasury Bills, commercial bills and other assets, the houses may be forced to turn to the lender of last resort – the Bank of England. The Bank will either rediscount (that is, buy) some of the bills or make loans against the security of such bills. The Bank will only deal in 'first class bills' – either Treasury Bills or commercial bills which bear at least two signatures of persons of an acceptable credit standing.

Since 1981, the Bank no longer continuously 'posts' or announces the terms on which it will deal in bills. The Bank has made it clear that the implied interest rate in such deals will be designed to discourage the use of the lender of last resort facility by the discount houses. Thus, when the discount houses offer to sell bills to the Bank, the latter is in a strong position to influence rates of interest in the bill market by refusing to buy at the rates quoted. The implied interest rate charged by the Bank on loans to the discount houses will usually be higher than the market rate on bills. Thus, the discount houses may be making losses on the loans they are repaying to the commercial banks. The discount houses will want to repay the loans from the Bank quickly, and so will reduce the price at which they bid for the next issue of Treasury Bills, thus increasing the Treasury Bill rate. As funds are attracted into the market for Treasury Bills from other parts of the money market, the reduced supply of loanable funds in these other markets will tend to push up other interest rates. This is one way, then, in which the Bank of England can influence interest rates. The discount houses' main assets are shown for February 1993 in Table 21.2.

Commercial banks

Commercial bank A profit-making financial institution that lends at higher interest rates than it pays on deposits

Commercial banks are deposit-taking institutions. They make profits by lending at a higher rate of interest than the rate they pay on deposits. Indeed, banks usually pay no interest on current account deposits. The banks operate the system of payment by cheques which enables them to provide a money transmission service throughout the country to their customers. They also offer a wide range of other financial services to their customers, such as loans, foreign exchange facilities and, increasingly, pensions and insurance products. The commercial banks' assets are illustrated in Table 21.3.

Monetary control arrangements

A commercial bank operating in the United Kingdom has to decide on its desired cash ratio – that is, the ratio of cash to deposit liabilities at which it wishes to operate. All banks need to maintain a cash ratio large enough to meet the cash requirements of their depositors. On the other hand, cash reserves do not earn any return for the bank. Thus, one of the arts of banking is to balance the potential cash requirements of depositors with the bank's desire to hold a spectrum of profit-earning assets, some of which may be relatively illiquid.

Fractional reserve banking

In managing their portfolios, the commercial banks have two aims that may conflict: first, they wish to maintain an adequate stock of liquid assets in case their cash reserves ratio comes under pressure; secondly, they wish to earn a high rate of return on their assets in order to maximise their profits. Generally, banks earn larger profits from long-term loans than from short-term loans as they are able to charge a higher interest rate on long-term loans. Similarly, banks charge higher interest rates to high-risk borrowers than to low-risk borrowers. In general, then, a bank's highest yielding assets tend to be illiquid – for example, a large proportion of advances to customers, though profitable, are illiquid; similarly, equities are illiquid in that any attempt to sell a large amount of stock would depress stock prices and cause capital losses.

Balance between liquidity and profitability In pursuit of profits, banks wish to hold as small a proportion of their assets as possible in liquid form. At the same time, financial prudence requires that they hold adequate cash and other liquid assets to meet customers' demand for cash withdrawals. This means that banks (in common with all other profit-seeking financial institutions) are faced with a conflict between liquidity and profitability.

Table 21.3 United Kingdom banks' sterling assets, March 1993.

	£ million
Notes and coins	3,016
Balances at Bank of England	1,608
Market loans	151,532
Bills	13,693
Advances	380,734
Bank of England Banking Department's lending to central government	324
Investments	39,677
Miscellaneous assets	30,076
Total sterling assets	620,660

Source: Bank of England Quarterly Bulletin, May 1993.

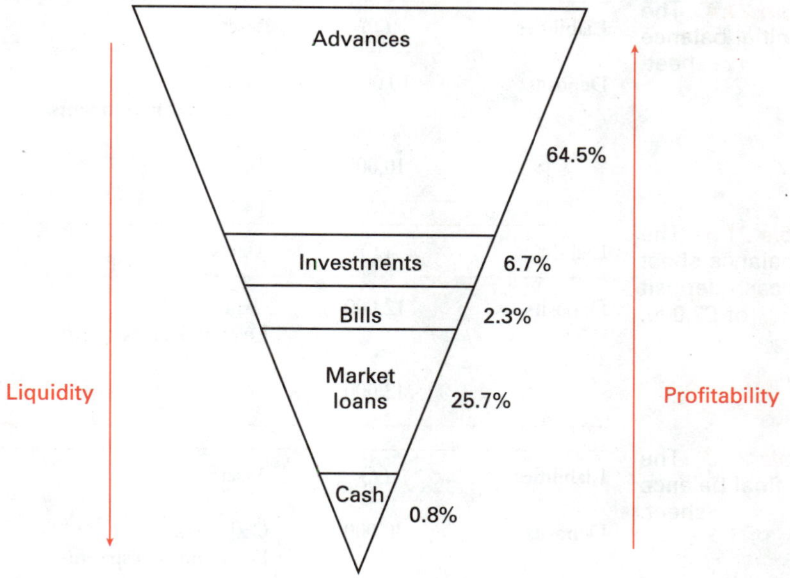

Fig. 21.1. Sterling assets of United Kingdom banks, 1993.

Note: The percentages are merely illustrative and exclude miscellaneous and other currency assets.

Call money *Funds lent by banks to discount houses which are subject to recall at short notice. Call money is included under the heading 'market loans' in Table 21.3*

To reconcile this conflict, commercial prudence dictates that a bank operates an efficient portfolio of assets. As shown in Table 21.3, the most liquid end of the portfolio comprises non-profitable assets, such as till money (notes and coins) and operational balances at the Bank of England. These are followed by other low-profit short-term liquid assets, such as call money, Treasury Bills and trade bills, that ensure a constant stream of cash to meet customers' demands for cash withdrawals. The least liquid end of the portfolio includes high-profit assets, such as loans to individuals and companies. Such a portfolio may be illustrated by an inverted pyramid with the most liquid assets at the base, as shown in Fig. 21.1. The assets are arranged in descending order of liquidity and ascending order of profitability. The figure is illustrated with data for the United Kingdom banks. It might be noted at this point that in recent years there has been a dramatic growth in the volume of business conducted in the inter-bank market and this has become a major source of liquidity for banks.

Credit creation *The process by which banks are able to increase the volume of credit by granting loans. The process results in an increase in the volume of bank deposits and hence in the money supply*

Credit creation The fundamental point about a fractional reserve banking system is that a receipt of *new cash* by the banking system may lead to a multiple expansion of bank lending, and to a multiple increase in the money supply. This is because most of the money lent to one person will, when spent, find its way back to the banking system. The recipients of borrowed money generally deposit it in their own bank accounts. This is the principle of *credit creation.*

To illustrate the *principle* of credit creation, consider a hypothetical example of a closed economy with a *single monopoly bank* which observes a minimum *cash ratio.* Suppose, in fact, that the bank wishes to maintain 10 per cent of its total deposits in cash in order to be able to meet the day-to-day demands of its customers. Table 21.4

Table 21.4 The bank's initial balance sheet.

Liabilities	(£)	Assets	(£)
Deposits	10,000	Cash	1,000
		Loans and investments	9,000
	10,000		10,000

Table 21.5 The bank's balance sheet after new cash deposit of £2,000.

Liabilities	(£)	Assets	(£)
Deposits	12,000	Cash	3,000
		Loan and investments	9,000
	12,000		12,000

Table 21.6 The bank's final balance sheet.

Liabilities	(£)	Assets	(£)
Deposits	30,000	Cash	3,000
		Loan and investments	27,000
	30,000		30,000

shows the bank's initial position; it has total deposits amounting to £10,000 and is just maintaining its 10 per cent cash ratio by holding in its tills £1,000 in cash.

Suppose now that a customer deposits an extra £2,000 in cash. The bank's new balance sheet is shown in Table 21.5. Notice that the ratio of cash to deposits is no longer 10 per cent, but is now as high as 25 per cent. Given that the bank's *desired* cash ratio is 10 per cent and that the bank wishes to maximise its profits, it will increase its total deposits to £30,000 so as to restore the desired ratio. The bank does this by granting new loans amounting to £18,000.

The final position is shown in Table 21.6. The cash deposit of £2,000 has led to an increase in loans and investments of £18,000, so that total deposits have risen by £20,000 – that is, by ten times the amount of the cash deposit. Thus, in this example, the credit multiplier (the figure any increase in cash deposits has to be multiplied by to obtain the increase in total deposits) is ten. This means that every £1 held by the bank in cash is capable of supporting total deposits of £10.

Credit multiplier *The multiple by which total bank deposits increase relative to a new cash deposit*

If, however, the bank's desired cash ratio rose to $12\frac{1}{2}$ per cent, cash holdings of £3,000 would only support total deposits of £24,000 (because £3,000 is $12\frac{1}{2}$ per cent of £24,000). Note that the credit multiplier in this case is only eight. It follows that there is an inverse relationship between the cash ratio and the credit multiplier and, therefore, the volume of bank credit.

Although this important principle of credit creation has been illustrated above for a single bank system, the same principle will operate in an economy with many banks provided that there is an efficient clearing system. When a bank creates a loan in a multi-bank system, the customers may write cheques in favour of customers of other banks and at the end of the day, all the banks have claims against each other. Most of these claims will be offset by counter-claims, so that only the net indebtedness has to be settled by using the banks' balances at the central bank.

Clearing system *The process by which banks settle claims and counter-claims between themselves*

In practice, the credit multiplier in the United Kingdom is not as large as the above example suggests because of *leakages*. As stated above, if an individual bank creates loans, some of the new deposits will end up in different banks. If any individual bank expands lending faster than the other banks in the system, it will experience a drain of its cash reserves. This reduces the bank's capacity to create credit. Other leakages include: (a) the holding of *excess reserves* by banks – that is holding more than the minimum reserve requirement; (b) an increase in the public's desired cash holdings; and (c) a net outflow of currency overseas as a result of a balance of payments deficit.

Control of the money supply

There are several ways in which the Bank of England can seek to control the supply of money and to influence credit conditions.

Open-market operations This refers to sales and purchases of government securities on the open market by the Bank of England. If the Bank wishes to *reduce* the money supply it will sell securities through its broker on the open market. The buyers will pay for these securities with cheques drawn on their accounts with the commercial banks. The Bank of England which now holds these cheques will thus debit the accounts of the commercial banks with itself. This fall in bankers' deposits represents a fall in the commercial banks' cash reserves. If they were previously operating at the desired ratio, the banks will now reduce their deposit liabilities, say, by calling in advances to their customers, by selling assets or by refusing to grant new advances. Such a loss of cash reserves will cause a multiple contraction of bank deposits. Suppose that the banks' desired cash ratio is 10 per cent. Then, if the banks lose £10 million of cash reserves as a result of open-market operations, they will have to reduce their deposits by £100 million.

If the banks were previously operating with a cash reserves ratio above their desired ratio, however, the potential that exists for them to expand their deposits is reduced. Note that in this case if the Bank of England uses open-market operations to reduce the money supply, the official intention may be frustrated as long as the banks' cash reserves ratio remains above the desired level.

Conversely, if the Bank of England wishes to *expand* the money supply, it will instruct its broker to buy securities on the open market and will pay for them with cheques drawn on itself. The sellers of the securities will deposit these cheques with the commercial banks, which will present them for payment to the Bank. The Bank will credit the commercial banks' accounts and this represents an increase in their cash reserves. The commercial banks will now be in a position to undertake a multiple expansion of bank deposits.

Interest rate policy Changes in the rate of interest at which the Bank of England conducts business with the discount houses are often linked with the use of open-market operations. If the Bank wishes to reduce the stock of money, it will sell securities on the open market. The effect of this is to depress securities' prices and force up the yield on securities. Buyers of these securities write cheques on their accounts with commercial banks whose cash reserves with the Bank of England are reduced. This leads commercial banks to recall their loans from the discount houses. The discount houses are now forced to borrow from the Bank of England as lender of last resort. As explained above, in this role, the Bank of England lends to discount houses at a rate of interest of its own choosing. In this way, the Bank may force the desired increase in interest rates in the bill market with repercussions on all other short-term interest rates in the money markets. The effect of this action by the Bank is a rise in the cost of borrowing that may depress the demand for loanable funds, and thus slow down the growth in the money supply.

If the Bank of England wishes to increase the stock of money in the economy, it will *buy* securities on the open market. The chain of events which follows will produce the opposite effects to those described above: that is, a fall in interest rates and a rise in the demand for loanable funds leading to an increase in the money supply.

In the 1980s, the Bank relied mainly on these two techniques of monetary control. There are, however, additional techniques available to central banks which also limit the volume of credit (or the supply of loanable funds). In addition to open-market operations and interest rate policy, the Bank of England has used, from time to time, the following credit control techniques.

Special deposits The Bank of England has the power to require banks to lodge 'special deposits' with it. Calls for special deposits are normally expressed as a uniform percentage of each bank's total eligible liabilities. Special deposits normally earn interest at a rate equivalent to the Treasury Bill rate. As special deposits are compulsory, by using them the Bank can be sure of reducing the bank's liquid assets, and they are equivalent to an open-market sale, in that they reduce the banks' ability to increase credit (and hence the money supply).

Lending ceilings The Bank of England can lay down quantitative limits on the growth of bank assets. While ceilings have been used in the past (for example, in the late 1960s), after the introduction of the Competition and Credit Control System in 1971, their use was discouraged. The banks argued that the overdraft system meant that it was impossible to control bank lending as precisely as quantitative limits would imply. Quantitative limits were also thought to restrict competition as they hampered efficient banks who were in a position to create new deposits.

Funding Funding is the term applied when the Bank of England attempts to lengthen the maturity of outstanding government debt. If the Bank restricts its Treasury Bill issue and sells longer-dated securities, this reduces the commercial banks' cash reserves, and thus restricts their capability of expanding bank deposits.

Requests From time to time, the Bank of England requests banks to channel their lending into or away from certain areas. For example, in April 1978, the Bank of England asked banks to provide finance 'for both working capital and fixed investment by manufacturing industry and for the expansion of exports and the saving of imports'. To achieve these goals, banks were asked to restrain other lending, in particular 'to persons and property companies and for purely financial transactions'.

Changing the cash reserves ratio Of course, it is possible for the Bank of England to control the money supply by changing the minimum cash reserves ratio.

As shown above, an increase in the cash reserves ratio reduces the credit multiplier. In practice, this action is not likely to be taken very often because it may have undesirable disruptive effects on the financial system.

Other sources of changes in the money supply

In addition to the methods of control used by the central bank, there are a number of other sources of changes in the money supply. Consider the following.

Government expenditure financed by borrowing from the central bank When the Bank of England issues new currency it obtains interest-earning government securities in return. The issue of currency may be regarded as helping the government to finance its expenditure. This method of government borrowing is sometimes described as 'turning the printing press'. Customers of commercial banks receiving this new currency as wages, salaries, pensions or unemployment benefits may deposit it in their accounts. As a result, banks' cash reserves will rise, becoming a base for multiple expansion of credit and hence an increase in the money supply.

Government borrowing from the banking system If the public sector is running a deficit, the other sectors of the economy may deposit part of their consequent financial surplus with the banking system. These deposits form part of the money supply. The government might then borrow these funds from the banking system. Suppose, for example, that the government borrows £100 million through government securities to finance its deficit. Cash is initially drained from the banking system to the government sector when banks pay for these securities. But this cash flows back to the banks when the government spends the money on goods and services. Now the banking system will have both the cash and government securities and this may lead to a further expansion of the money supply through increased lending to private sector borrowers. Note that the government securities with banks are a potential source of cash, should banks' liquidity come under pressure in consequence of their increased lending.

It can be noted that government borrowing from the central bank and the banking system could be inflationary. This explains why many central banks try to persuade their governments to search for non-inflationary sources of borrowing. For example, if the government borrows directly from the public, the cash returned to the private sector through government purchases of goods and services is held with the banks. But government securities are held by the private sector and not by banks as a potential source of cash.

A change in the public's desired cash holdings Such a change is dependent, to a large extent, on developments in the financial system. For instance, the introduction of automated teller machines, cheque book facilities by building societies, direct debiting and credit cards all lead to smaller holdings of cash. Likewise, in a less developed country, the growth and development of banks will encourage the use of payments by cheque, thereby resulting in the growth of bank deposits and a reduced demand for cash. If the public decides to hold more cash and smaller bank deposits, the banks will need to replenish the cash in their tills by drawing on their balances at the Bank of England. As cash reserves fall, the banks may be forced to reduce further the level of bank deposits. This mechanism would work in reverse if the public decided to hold less cash and bigger bank deposits.

A change in the banks' demand for excess reserves Most mechanical models of the determination of the money supply assume that the banks will adhere to a constant ratio of cash reserves to deposits. More precisely, it is assumed that the banks will adhere to the minimum legal ratio, on the assumption that the banks will wish to expand bank deposits to the maximum. In practice, however, the banks may decide, or be forced, to hold cash reserves in excess of the legal requirement. This might happen, for example, if there were not enough potential borrowers of a satisfactory credit standing. This means that the Bank of England cannot be sure of success if it uses open-market operations to expand the money supply. The banks may simply allow their cash reserves ratio to rise.

Balance of payments disequilibrium A balance of payments *deficit* involves a net outflow of currency. In effect, the Bank of England has to finance the deficit by providing foreign currencies in exchange for domestic currency. Unless offset by an expansionary open-market operation, this will result in a contraction of the money supply. Conversely, a balance of payments *surplus* involves a net inflow of currency, and unless offset by a contractionary open-market operation, this will result in an expansion of the money supply.

Competition between banks and building societies

Building society *A financial institution that specialises in attracting retail deposits and in lending for home purchase*

In the 1980s and 1990s, competition between banks and building societies has turned out to be a major factor in the development of financial markets in the United Kingdom. The building societies have been very successful in attracting savings from the personal sector. In 1970, building societies accounted for almost 35 per cent of total personal sector liquid assets. They managed to increase this share to almost 53 per cent of the personal sector's liquid assets by the mid-1980s. By 1992, the share of total personal sector liquid assets held by building societies had fallen to around 47 per cent. But this still exceeded the share of banks which was almost 43 per cent. The remainder of personal sector liquid assets took the form of national savings, tax instruments and local authority debt.

There are a number of reasons that help to account for the success of building societies in the retail savings market. First, building societies have developed a friendly image, which they have emphasised in their marketing. Secondly, longer opening hours, including Saturday mornings, gave them a competitive advantage over banks. Thirdly, the composite tax arrangements with the Inland Revenue, whereby a depositor's liability to income tax at the standard rate on interest payments was settled by the society, were attractive to many depositors. This scheme was not applied to tax due on interest earned from bank accounts until 1985. This meant that before 1985 societies were able to offer highly competitive interest rates to the typical saver who was liable to income tax. Another factor that helped societies to offer competitive interest rates was the relative simplicity of their operations, and consequently low administrative costs. An additional attractive feature for savers was the fact that societies did not normally levy transactions charges on accounts.

Faced with this threat from building societies to their share in the savings market, banks have come to attach greater significance to the personal sector and to its importance as a source of profits. As a result, banks have offered a broader range of accounts offering more competitive interest rates. They have also reintroduced selective Saturday opening of branches, together with longer weekday opening. The marketing strategies of banks have been aimed in some cases at attracting young customers, especially the student market.

With the coming into effect in January 1987 of the Building Societies Act (1986), some societies began to offer interest-bearing current accounts. These accounts succeeded in attracting a large number of customers, so that the banks were forced to respond by offering interest-bearing current accounts with effect from 1989.

Apart from intense competition in the retail savings market, banks and building societies also compete strongly in the market for house finance. Banks entered this market in a big way in the early 1980s, after the abolition of the 'corset' scheme, which inhibited the growth of their interest-bearing deposits and made it difficult for them to lend large sums without incurring financial penalties imposed by the Bank of England.

Deregulation of financial institutions and markets

Deregulation *The degregulation of financial services is a process which removes regulations which limit the activities of financial institutions*

During the 1980s, the deregulation of the financial services industry and the *liberalisation* of financial institutions and markets were two major developments that could be observed in the United Kingdom, France, Luxemburg and in other main financial centres in the world. In the United Kingdom, the term *deregulation* can be applied to:

(a) The easing of restrictions which hindered competition between firms dealing in securities on the Stock Exchange. This involved the abolition of the traditional distinction between 'jobbers' and 'brokers' and the ending of the practice of fixed commissions on the sale and purchase of securities. It also included the lowering of barriers to entry into the Stock Exchange by British and overseas banks and other international dealers in securities. These changes, which came into effect on 27 October 1986, were given the name of the *Big Bang*.

(b) The relaxation of restrictions on competition between banks and building societies. The Building Societies Act (1986) conferred a greater degree of freedom on societies to compete with banks for loans and deposits in the personal sector and to offer a wider range of services.

Self-regulation *With self-regulation, a body of practitioners operating in an industry is responsible for ensuring compliance with a code of conduct by its members*

In the field of investment advice, the Financial Services Act (1986) gave legal backing to the principle of self-regulation by industry practitioners. The Act has given rise to the setting up of *self-regulatory organisations* by financial institutions and others concerned with the provision of financial services.

Interest rates

Nominal and real interest rates

Interest rates, defined simply as the cost of borrowing, reflect the market rates prevailing at the time of obtaining a loan. A company seeking to raise funds through a bond issue, for example, will pay a coupon rate (a rate stated on the bond) that corresponds to the current market rate. Similarly, the government, raising money by selling Treasury Bills and gilts, will have to offer interest rates that reflect market rates at the time of borrowing.

Nominal interest rate *The nominal (or money) interest rate is the actual interest rate observed in the market*

The rate of interest on a new loan is referred to as the nominal interest rate. This is the rate of interest expressed in money terms and is also known as the *money* rate of interest. The nominal rate of interest has two components. One is the expected rate of inflation, and the other is the real rate of interest. It is argued that lenders wish to be compensated for future inflation, and that the real rate of interest is a reward for postponing consumption to a future date. So we can write

$$\text{Nominal interest rate} = \text{Real interest rate} + \text{Expected inflation rate}$$

Real interest rate *The nominal interest rate adjusted for changes in the price level*

Index-linked gilt-edged securities *Securities issued by the government which guarantee the holder a given real rate of interest, and maintain the real value of the capital repayment*

In practice, it is not possible to observe the *expected* rate of inflation so, for simplicity, the real interest rate is often defined as the nominal interest rate *minus* the actual inflation rate over a relevant period. As an example, suppose the nominal interest rate is 15 per cent per annum and that the rate of inflation over the past year has been 10 per cent. The real interest rate would be estimated to be 5 per cent per annum. It must be noted that the use of a past inflation rate, rather than the expected future inflation rate, may lead to an incorrect estimate of the real rate of interest to the extent that past inflation rates are not a satisfactory guide to future inflation rates.

In the United Kingdom, one method of estimating the real rate of interest is to note the yield on index-linked gilt-edged securities. Such securities have been issued by the British government since 1981 and enable investors to maintain the value of their investment as well as the real rate of return.

Do interest rates matter?

Amongst the many economic indicators in an economy, interest rates arouse a great deal of public attention. Changes in their general pattern have widespread repercussions on individuals, families, businesses and governments. Interest rate changes affect individuals' decisions to save and spend. Business decisions whether to buy equipment or to build a new factory depend on the relationship between the rate of interest and the expected rate of return on the project. Similarly, a government's decision about the proportion of its budget deficit to be financed by borrowing is affected by interest movements.

In spite of the far-reaching effects of changes in the pattern of interest rates, much of the theory of interest rates starts from the premise that there is *one single* interest rate. This notion is based on the assumption of a perfect financial market, with perfect knowledge and complete certainty about the future. In the imperfect world in which we live, however, there exists a whole range of different interest rates. We have, for instance, mortgage interest rates, banks' and building societies' deposit rates, interest rates on national savings, personal loan rates, Treasury Bill rates, gilt-edged rates and soon. As we see below, one important factor influencing the interest rate charged on a loan is the term or duration of the loan. Although generally short- and long-term interest rates move up and down more or less in unison, this is not always the case.

Observed changes in interest rates are triggered frequently by changes in rates on very short-term (e.g. overnight) loans in the inter-bank market with rippling effects on all other rates. In other cases, the Bank of England may influence very short-term rates through its operations in the discount markets.

Why are there so many different interest rates?

The financial press reports daily a whole range of interest rates. These are the outcome of the flow of funds between and within different sectors of the economy, as well as between the *short-term* and *long-term* financial markets. Different interest rates perform vital economic functions and respond to an array of influencing factors. Consider the following.

Risk This is a most important factor. A lender classifies a borrower on the basis of credit-worthiness which, in turn, depends on the borrower's status, income, current loan commitments, purpose of the loan and so on. These considerations lead lenders to charge different rates for the same amount loaned for a given time period to, say, the government, a commercial company and a private individual. For instance, the default risk on a loan to the United Kingdom government is practically nil. In contrast, lending to a private individual, especially unsecured lending, may be extremely risky and lenders would then wish to be compensated by charging a much higher rate. The risk factor is also significant in relation to the purpose of the loan. Loans for risky projects like North Sea oil exploration, for example, are likely to attract a higher interest rate than the rate on a loan to finance the construction of, say, a foodstore. Likewise, lending abroad may expose the lender to exchange rate risk, so foreign loans, in principle, command a higher interest rate than that on domestic lending.

Duration of loan In general, the longer the term of a loan the higher the interest rate. This means that short-term interest rates on loans due to mature in a year tend to be generally lower than the long-term interest rate on loans of longer maturity. This is because of the greater uncertainty about the future rate of inflation and future interest rate movements.

The implication is that lenders have a myopic outlook with a tendency to discount the future more heavily. A long-term borrower has, therefore, to pay lenders a premium, for loss of liquidity.

If, however, there are strong expectations that the general level of interest rates will fall in the future, it is possible for long-term interest rates to be lower than short-term rates. As a result of these expectations, funds flow from short-term markets to long-term markets, thereby driving down long-term interest rates.

Competition between financial institutions In their intermediation role between savers and borrowers, banks, building societies and other financial institutions earn profits by paying savers a lower rate of interest on deposits and charging a higher rate on loans to customers.

As the competition for deposits between profit-seeking banks and building societies has intensified, these institutions have started to offer a wide range of accounts, with varying terms and conditions, including different interest rates. Similarly, competition in the market for loans results in variations in interest rates on loans.

Range of financial products Closely allied to the above is the availability of different types of financial instruments, such as interest-bearing deposits, bills, bonds, gilts and equities. These instruments meet the differing needs of savers for income, liquidity and tax considerations: for example the National Savings movement pays interest gross to United Kingdom residents. In addition, interest rates on foreign currency deposits might differ from those on sterling deposits, partly because of expectations about future exchange rates.

Size of loans and deposits Wholesale and retail deposits command different interest rates partly because of the relative administrative convenience of handling wholesale funds on a large scale rather than handling large numbers of small deposits. Analogously, large loans attract a lower interest rate than small loans because of the administrative economies of scale.

Money and banking in less developed countries

The role of money

The stock of money has a relatively narrow base in less developed countries (LDCs) as it consists mainly of banknotes and coins in circulation. In these countries, habits of payment by cheque are still in their infancy so that bank deposits constitute a relatively small proportion of the total money supply. As a consequence, the volume of bank deposits has a minor influence on the general price level and total expenditure. The scope of monetary policy measures (such as discount rates, open-market operations and changes in reserve requirements) in regulating total expenditure is therefore limited.

Given the paucity of aggregate savings and the narrow base for taxation, most governments in LDCs resort to budgetary deficits, financed through the printing of money, as a means of speeding up the process of economic development. The resulting increase in the money supply can lead to a faster rate of inflation and a deterioration in the balance of payments. This is because domestic inflationary pressures generally lead to the diversion of foreign currency meant to be spent on imported plant and equipment to the importation of foodstuffs and other consumer goods.

There is, however, a counter-argument that the printing of money within 'safe' limits may not be inflationary. This is because in a growing economy, business units multiply and existing businesses expand, leading to an increased demand for cash holdings for reasons of safety and liquidity. In addition, part of the increased money supply may be hoarded as the non-monetised sector (in some cases as large as 20 to 30 per cent of the economy) is brought within the monetary sector of the LDCs economy. The non-monetised sector is characterised by barter and is known to have high hoarding propensities with respect to both commodities and precious metals.

The role of banking

In several Asian and African countries, central banks have been set up by statute and are based on the model of the Bank of England. Like the Bank of England, these central banks maintain two separate departments for the transaction of business: the banking department concerned purely with banking business; and the issue department concerned with the issue of notes.

In a number of LDCs commercial banks have also followed the British orthodoxy of branch banking. The operations of commercial banks in LDCs, however, are concentrated in major cities and towns. Additionally, loans and advances are concentrated on major industrial borrowers. The banks generally maintain large excess reserves with consequent loss of potential profits. The demand for personal loans and agricultural credit remains largely unsatisfied. Thus, small traders, indigenous producers and small farmers have to depend upon friends, relatives, landlords and money-lenders for loans. It is well known that money-lenders typically charge exorbitant interest rates which are insensitive to interest rates in the organised money markets.

As indicated above, banks and financial institutions in most LDCs have not reached the same stage of development as those in the industrially advanced countries. Therefore, central banks in most LDCs have a statutory responsibility to promote the growth of financial institutions so that the latter can mobilise and channel the community's savings into planned investment. A notable feature of this policy has been the rapid increase in the number of industrial and agricultural banks and finance corporations during the past two decades. Some central banks also give positive encouragement to the growth of co-operative banks and credit societies and thus promote 'thrift' and 'self-help' at local and regional levels in the LDCs.

Summary

1. Money can be defined as any asset that is generally acceptable as a means of payment for goods and services. In a developed financial system, there is a range of financial assets that may be used as a means of payment.
2. A distinction is made between narrow and broad money. Definitions of narrow money stress the medium of exchange function of money, and include those assets which are highly liquid. Definitions of broad money stress the store of value function of money, and also include assets which are less liquid.
3. A central bank performs a number of important functions, including the implementation of monetary policy and the prudential control and supervision of the banking system. In the United Kingdom, the Bank of England influences short-term interest rates through its open-market operations conducted with the discount houses.
4. Commercial banks are profit-making institutions that provide a range of financial services to their customers. By granting loans to customers, banks are able to create new bank deposits that form part of the money supply. At times of inflationary pressure, therefore, the central bank may have to step in to control credit creation. For this purpose, the central bank may use a number of techniques, including open-market operations, interest rate policy and quantitative controls.
5. Since the 1980s, the financial services sector in the United Kingdom and in many other countries has been subject to deregulation. One result has been fierce competition between different types of financial institutions.

6. The interest rate is the cost of borrowing and so it affects the demand for and supply of loanable funds. The real rate of interest is the nominal rate of interest adjusted for inflation. Nominal interest rates are influenced by a wide range of factors, including risk, duration and size of the loan, and competition for funds between financial institutions.

Exercises

1. Review your understanding of the following terms:

'narrow' money	discount houses
'broad' money	Treasury Bills
medium of exchange	open-market operations
store of value	special deposits
unit of account	cash reserves ratio
standard of deferred payment	excess reserves
central bank	real rate of interest

2. A monopoly bank has the following balance sheet. It is required to maintain a ratio of cash to total deposits of 10 per cent.

Liabilities		Assets	
Deposits	2,000	Cash	500
		Bills	500
		Advances	1,000
	2,000		2,000

(a) Illustrate the bank's profit-maximising balance sheet on the assumption that it grants new advances.

(b) Suppose the bank has the original balance sheet and that the minimum cash ratio is increased to $12\frac{1}{2}$ per cent. Illustrate the bank's new profit-maximising balance sheet on the assumption that it wishes to maintain a 50 per cent liquidity ratio – that is, the ratio of cash and bills to total deposits.

3. Discuss the main disadvantages of an economy in which incomes are paid in kind and transactions are carried out by barter.

4. 'Money can only be defined in terms of its functions.' Discuss.

5. Consider the view that no banking and financial system can operate effectively without a central bank.

6.** Describe the methods available to a central bank to control the supply of money in a country. What are the limitations on these methods of controlling the money supply?

22 MONEY – II

Learning objectives

After reading this chapter, you should be able to:

- explain the Fisher and the Cambridge versions of the *quantity theory of money*
- outline the Keynesian theory of money and identify the factors that influence the transactions, precautionary and speculative demands for money
- analyse the effect of a change in the money supply on the equilibrium rate of interest in the Keynesian model
- outline the 'modern quantity theory' of money as the basis of monetarism
- analyse the monetarist view of the effects of a change in the money supply on the rate of interest and level of money national income
- compare the Keynesian and monetarist transmission mechanisms

Introduction

In this chapter, we examine the factors which influence the demand for money and the important question of how the economy reacts to changes in the supply of money. Economists are interested in the economy's reactions to such changes because society's ability to purchase goods and services may be affected. Additionally, changes in the money supply not only affect individual holders of money, but may also lead to inflation and so inject a degree of instability into the economy.

Discussion of the effects of changes in the stock of money goes back hundreds of years. In 1750, David Hume (in his essay, 'Of money') gave an early account of the relationship between a country's stock of money and level of prices. This relationship is generally described as the 'quantity theory of money'. In 1911, an influential exposition of the theory was presented by the American economist, Irving Fisher. In more recent times, there has been a long-running debate between monetarists and Keynesians as to the precise influence of money on individuals, businesses and the economy as a whole.

This chapter starts with a discussion of the quantity theory of money, setting out first the Fisher version and secondly, the Cambridge cash-balance version. The Keynesian theory of money is then considered and the liquidity-preference theory of the determination of the rate of interest is explained. We then consider the 'modern quantity theory' which is the basis of the views put forward by monetarists. Finally, the Keynesian and monetarist transmission mechanisms are discussed.

The quantity theory of money

Fisher's version

Equation of exchange *This denotes the proposition that the value of goods and services sold must equal the amount of money handed over in exchange*

Transactions velocity of circulation *The average number of times the total quantity of money changes hands in transactions.*

Irving Fisher's version of the quantity theory can be explained in terms of the following equation of exchange:

$$MV \equiv PT$$

where M is the nominal stock of money in circulation and V is the transactions velocity of circulation of money (that is, the average number of times the given quantity of money changes hands in transactions); P is the average price of all transactions and T is the number of transactions that take place during the time period. Both MV and PT measure the total value of transactions during the time period and so must be identical. Thus, the 'equation' is really an *identity* which must always be true: it tells us only that the total amount of money handed over in transactions is equal to the value of what is sold. As an example, suppose that during a given time period, the number of transactions (T) is 1,000 and that the average price of these transactions (P) is £5, then it follows that the value of what is sold (PT) is £5,000. If the money stock (M) is only £500, then the average number of times each pound changes hands, the velocity of circulation (V) must be 10. As an identity, the quantity theory is no more than a way of calculating the velocity of circulation.

The identity, however, is converted into a *theory* of the determination of the price level by assuming: (a) that the money supply is determined by the monetary authorities; (b) that the number of transactions is fixed in the short-run because of the classical presumption that the economy operates automatically at full employment; and (c) that the velocity of circulation is also fixed in the short-run because it depends largely on institutional factors (such as whether workers are paid weekly or monthly) which themselves tend to remain constant for long periods of time.

With T and V constant, the identity can be rewritten as follows:

$$M\bar{V} \equiv P\bar{T}$$

It now follows that changes in M, initiated by the monetary authorities, will cause proportionate changes in P. Notice that the direction of causation runs *from* changes in the stock of money *to* changes in the general price level.

Quantity theory of money *This states that the average price of transactions in an economy is proportional to the nominal quantity of money in circulation*

According to the quantity theory, money is held only for the purpose of making payments for current transactions. Thus, the demand for money is called a *transactions demand*. When the money supply is increased, people find themselves holding more than they need for current transactions and so attempt to spend the excess. It is this extra spending which, given full employment and consequent constant *number* of transactions, pushes up the price level. As prices rise, the value of transactions rises and so the demand for money rises. This mechanism ceases when the demand for money and supply of money are equal again.

Cambridge version

A version of the quantity theory which concentrates on the factors that determine the demand for money was developed by economists at the University of

Cambridge. These economists argued that an individual's demand for cash balances (or nominal money) is proportional to the individual's money income. If this were true of all individuals, then the aggregate demand for money (M_D) could be written as proportional to money national income (Y):

$$M_D = kY$$

where k is a constant. Notice that Y in this version represents the money value of spending on all final goods and services produced during the time period. This is much narrower than Fisher's notion of the value of all transactions (PT) which included spending on intermediate goods and financial assets, as well as final goods and services.

Since Y is money national income, it can be divided into its price and quantity components, so that

$$M_D = kPQ$$

Income velocity of circulation *The average number of time each unit of money changes hands in purchasing the commodities that make up national income*

where P is the general price level and Q is real income (or output). Notice that k is the reciprocal of the income velocity of circulation of money (which can be defined as the average number of times the money supply changes hands in financing the national income). This demand for money arises to enable the community to fulfil its planned expenditures during the intervening periods between receipts of wages, salaries or other forms of income.

If we continue to assume that the money supply (M) is under the control of the monetary authorities, we can write that in equilibrium,

$$M = M_D$$

Substituting from above, we have

$$M = kPQ$$

With k constant, and Q fixed because the economy is assumed to remain at full employment, an increase in M will create an excess supply of money. This leads people to increase their spending directly on goods and services so that the general price level is pulled upwards. As this happens, the demand for money increases and eventually becomes equal to the money supply again.

Thus, both the Fisher and Cambridge versions of the quantity theory come to the same important conclusion: *that an increase in the money supply leads directly to an increase in spending and, with full employment, the general price level is proportional to the quantity of money in circulation.*

Keynesian theory of money

Keynes divided the demand for money into three types: (a) the transactions demand, which is the demand by firms and households for holdings of money to finance day-to-day transactions; (b) precautionary demand, which arises out of uncertainty and the desire not to be caught short of ready cash; and (c) the speculative demand, which is the demand for money as a financial asset and therefore part of a wealth portfolio. In (a) and (b), money is clearly held mainly for its role as a medium of exchange. In (c), it is held mainly for its role as a store of wealth.

What factors influence these three demands for money? Consider them in turn.

Fig. 22.1. The transactions demand for money. A household receiving £100 per week has an average money holding of £50. A household receiving £200 per fortnight has an average money holding of £100.

Transactions demand

Transactions demand for money *The amount of money held in order to carry out current transactions*

The transactions demand for money arises because individuals receive their incomes weekly or monthly and yet have to pay for many of the goods and services they buy on a day-to-day basis. The amount of money held by an individual to finance these transactions, therefore, is likely to depend on the size of the individual's money income and on institutional arrangements, such as how often the individual is paid and how often he or she pays bills and engages in monetary transactions. If we assume that these institutional arrangements remain unchanged, then money income is the main determinant. For the economy as a whole, we can expect the total demand for money for transactions purposes to depend directly on *money national income*. Using functional notation, we can write

$$L_t = f(Y)$$

where L_t is the transactions demand for money.

Note that for a given level of income, the transactions demand for money would rise if more households were paid fortnightly or monthly rather than weekly. This is because such households would find themselves holding more money on average to finance the same total value of transactions. This is illustrated in Fig. 22.1 where a household, which at first is paid an income of £100 *per week*, is assumed to spend all of its income in a steady stream until, at the end of each week, it has nothing left until it receives its next £100. The household's average holding of money (that is, its transactions demand for money) is £50. If the household should now be paid £200 fortnightly, it can be seen that its average money holding increases to £100. So the household's demand for money has risen even though its income has remained unchanged.

In what follows, we ignore the possibility of such institutional changes and assume that the transactions demand for money depends only on money national income.

Precautionary demand

The precautionary demand for money arises out of consumers' desires to provide for unexpected, and therefore unplanned, expenditures. For example, a sales representative on a business trip may carry some extra cash, not for expected transactions, but to guard against any unforeseen contingencies, such as a car breakdown, or the possibility of coming across a cash bargain.

Precautionary demand for money *The amount of money held to provide for unplanned expenditures*

This demand for money is also likely to depend on national income: the higher the total value of transactions, the more money will be needed to guard against unexpected transactions. It can be argued that rates of interest may also influence the precautionary demand. The rate of interest is the opportunity cost of holding money: thus, if interest rates rise, consumers and firms may be tempted to reduce their precautionary holdings and hold interest-bearing assets instead.

For simplicity, however, it is convenient to assume that the precautionary demand does not respond to changes in interest rates (that is, it is completely interest-inelastic). This enables us to combine it with the transactions demand and to suppose that the total transactions and precautionary demand for money is a function of money national income. Indeed, in what follows, wherever we refer to the transactions demand, L_t, it should be understood that this includes the precautionary demand.

Speculative demand

Speculative demand for money *The amount of money held to take advantage of profitable opportunities that may arise in financial markets*

It was in his analysis of the speculative demand for money that Keynes differed fundamentally from his predecessors. Before examining the nature of this demand for money, however, we first have to understand the relationship between the price of a bond and the rate of interest. Recall that a bond is an asset that earns a fixed sum of money for its owner each year. In a perfect capital market, the price of a perpetual bond (that is, one which is never redeemed) which earns £5 per annum for its owner will be £100 when the rate of interest is 5 per cent – this is because £100 invested in any other income-earning asset would earn a return of £5. If the market rate of interest now rises to 10 per cent, the price of the bond will fall to £50, because £50 invested in any income-earning asset will now yield £5. Similarly, if the rate of interest should fall to 2 per cent, the price of the bond would rise to £250. There is, then, an *inverse relationship* between the price of a bond and the rate of interest. It follows that an increase in the rate of interest, which reduces the saleable value of a bond, means a potential capital loss for an investor who purchased the bond at a higher price. Similarly, a fall in the rate of interest means a potential capital gain for investors.

Keynes argued that individuals would have some expectation or conception of the 'normal' rate of interest, although each individual's conception of what was normal might differ. If the prevailing rate of interest were greater than an individual's conception of the normal rate, that individual would expect the rate of interest to fall in the near future. It follows that the higher the prevailing rate of interest, the more people will anticipate that the next change will be downwards. Since a fall in the rate of interest implies capital gains for bond-holders, the theory predicts that an abnormally high interest rate will lead to a large demand for bonds and, consequently, a small demand for speculative money balances.

The analysis applies in reverse if the actual rate of interest is thought to be abnormally low. In this case, individuals will expect the rate to rise in the near future and so will expect potential capital losses for bond-holders. In this situation, bonds will appear less attractive and potential buyers will postpone intended purchases and bond-holders themselves will attempt to sell bonds before the fall in bond prices. Thus, if the prevailing interest rate is low, the theory predicts a low demand for bonds and, consequently, a high demand for speculative money balances.

In this way, Keynes derived an *inverse* relationship between the rate of interest and the speculative demand for money, as illustrated in Fig. 22.2. Notice that as the

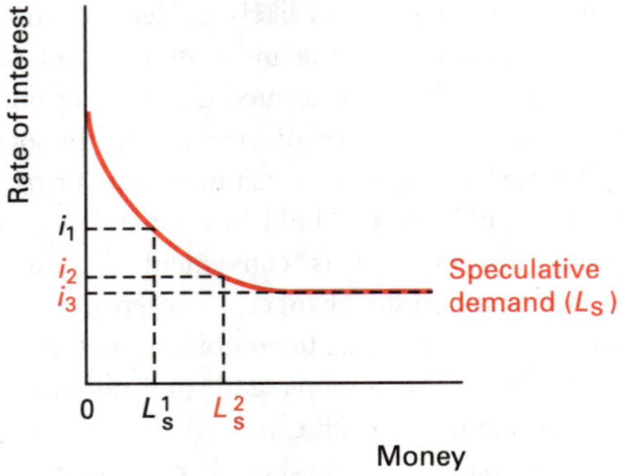

Fig. 22.2. The speculative demand for money. A fall in the rate of interest leads to an increase in the speculative demand for money. At the low interest rate $0i_3$, the speculative demand becomes perfectly elastic.

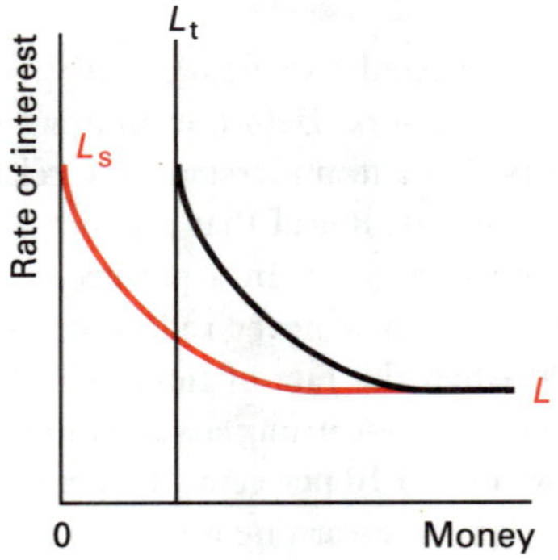

Fig. 22.3. The total demand for money. Adding L_t and L_S at every rate of interest gives the total demand for money curve, L.

rate of interest falls from $0i_1$ to $0i_2$, the speculative demand for money increases from $0L_S^1$ to $0L_S^2$. But at the low interest rate, $0i_3$, bonds become so unattractive (because their prices are high and expected to fall) that the speculative demand for money becomes perfectly elastic.

Total demand for money

The total demand for money (or total liquidity preference) is found by adding together the transactions, precautionary and speculative demands. Figure 22.3 shows the total demand for money plotted against the rate of interest: L_S represents the speculative demand and L_t represents the transactions and precautionary demands for a given level of income. The horizontal summation of L_S and L_t yields the total demand for money curve, L. Note that a rise in income, which would cause L_t to increase, would shift the total demand for money curve to the right. Similarly, a fall income would shift it to the left.

Effects of a change in the money supply

In Fig. 22.4, L represents the total demand for money and M_S^1 the initial supply of money. Given competitive forces in the money market, the interaction of this demand and supply will determine the market rate of interest at its equilibrium level $0i_1$. This is the Keynesian liquidity-preference theory of interest. Should the prevailing interest rate be greater than $0i_1$, there would be an excess supply of

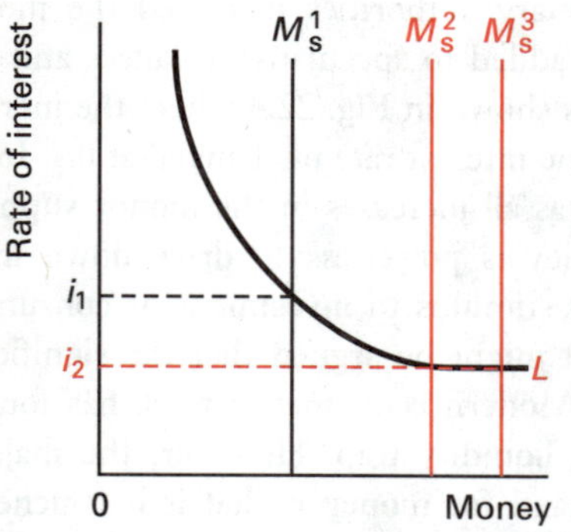

Fig. 22.4. *Effect of a change in the money supply on the rate of interest.* An increase in the money supply from M_S^1 to M_S^2 causes the equilibrium rate of interest to fall from $0i_1$ to $0i_2$. In the liquidity trap, where the demand for money is perfectly elastic, increases in the money supply have no effect on the rate of interest.

Liquidity-preference theory of interest *This states that interaction between the demand for and supply of money determines the equilibrium market rate of interest*

money (or excess demand for bonds) which would push up the price of bonds and push down interest rates, back towards the equilibrium. Similarly, at interest rates below $0i_1$, the excess demand for money exerts upward pressure on interest rates. The equilibrium at $0i_1$ can, therefore, be described as a stable one.

Now suppose that the money supply is increased to M_S^2. This creates an excess supply of money at the interest rate $0i_1$. According to the Keynesian theory, firms and households will attempt to run down the excess money balances they are being forced to hold by buying bonds. But, in the aggregate, they are unable to increase their holdings of bonds and they only succeed in driving up the price of bonds. As we have seen, an increase in the price of bonds implies a fall in the rate of interest. As the rate of interest falls, the speculative demand for money increases. Eventually, the rate of interest will reach $0i_2$ at which point firms and households are induced to hold the increased money supply in speculative balances.

Note that the major effect of the change in the money supply is on the rate of interest. National income and employment will only be affected if the fall in the rate of interest causes a rise in investment and, possibly, consumption. In the Keynesian model, consumption and investment only respond weakly to changes in the rate of interest – that is to say, they are interest-inelastic. This implies that monetary policy is not very powerful as a means of influencing output and employment.

The analysis applies in reverse for a fall in the money supply. This time, firms and households find that their actual money balances are below their desired money balances. They attempt to build them up by selling bonds. In the aggregate, however, the community cannot reduce its bond holdings and the attempt to do so only drives down bond prices and, therefore, leads to an increase in interest rates. As the interest rate rises, the speculative demand for money falls and money market equilibrium is eventually restored.

Liquidity trap *In the liquidity trap, the demand for money is perfectly elastic with respect to the rate of interest. As a result, changes in the money supply have no effect on the rate of interest*

The liquidity trap The horizontal part of the total demand for money curve shown in Fig. 22.4 is sometimes referred to as the liquidity trap, a theoretical possibility pointed out by Keynes in the *General Theory*. The liquidity trap occurs where the demand for money becomes perfectly interest-elastic at some very low interest rate. The argument is that at abnormally low interest rates (at or below Oi_2 in Fig. 22.4) virtually everyone would expect the interest rate to rise towards its normal level in the near future. In this situation, then, virtually everyone would be expecting a fall in the price of bonds and, therefore, capital losses for bond-holders.

Thus, if the monetary authorities increased the money supply, the whole of the increase would be added to speculative balances and the interest rate would remain unchanged. This is shown in Fig. 22.4 where the increase in the money supply from M_S^2 to M_S^3 leaves the interest rate unchanged at $0i_2$. In this extreme case, the velocity of circulation falls as all increases in the money supply are added to 'idle' balances, and monetary policy is powerless to drive down interest rates and, therefore, is unable to give any stimulus to investment or consumption.

In retrospect, it might be argued that the significance of the liquidity trap was over-emphasised. Modern econometric work has found no conclusive evidence for the existence of a liquidity trap. However, the major weakness of the Keynesian theory of the demand for money is that it is couched in terms of a choice simply between money and bonds. More recent work has attempted to allow for the fact that holders of money balances may switch into a whole spectrum of assets, such as equities, trade bills and certificates of deposit.

The modern quantity theory

Milton Friedman restated the quantity theory of money in 1956 as a theory of the demand for money, and this 'modern quantity theory' has become the basis of views put forward by monetarists. In this theory, money is seen as just one of a number of ways in which wealth can be held, along with all kinds of financial assets, consumer durables, property and 'human wealth'. According to Friedman, money has a convenience yield in the sense that its holding saves time and effort in carrying out transactions.

Friedman sees the real demand for money (M_D/P) as depending on total wealth (W), the expected rates of return on the various forms of wealth (r), the ratio of human wealth to non-human wealth (w) and society's tastes and preferences (T). Using functional notation, we can write:

$$\frac{M_D}{P} = f(W, r, w, T)$$

Consider each of the independent variables in turn.

Total wealth The demand for money will be directly related to total wealth (which is the sum of human and non-human wealth) so long as money is regarded as a 'normal good' by wealth holders. Thus, as total wealth increases, the desire to hold money (one of the components of total wealth) will also increase.

Expected rates of return on wealth Since the rates of return on bonds and equities represent the opportunity cost of holding money, we can expect an inverse relationship between these expected rates of return and the demand for money. Notice that, in addition to the various market rates of interest, the expected rate of inflation should also be taken into account here. The higher is the rate of inflation, the greater is the negative return from holding money and the more attractive are the alternative interest-bearing assets. Thus, there is also an inverse relationship between the rate of inflation and the real demand for money.

The ratio of human wealth to non-human wealth Friedman includes this variable because human wealth is so illiquid. It cannot be sold (in the absence of slavery) and individuals have only a limited ability to transfer non-human wealth into human wealth (though individuals can, of course, invest in themselves through education or by undertaking training courses). The higher the *w* ratio, the greater will be the demand for money in order to compensate for the limited marketability of human wealth.

Tastes and preferences Friedman argues that the demand for money also depends on a number of factors which are likely to influence wealth holders' tastes and preferences for money.

The main problem with this demand for money function is that of finding a method of measuring total wealth. Friedman suggested that *permanent income* (Y_p) may provide an acceptable proxy variable. Recall from Ch. 20 that this is a long-run measure of income which can be thought of as the present value of the expected flow of income from the stock of human and non-human wealth over a long period of time. It can be estimated as an average of past, present and expected future incomes. Incorporating this into the function, and assuming that *w* and *T* are constant in the short-run, we can write:

$$\frac{M_D}{P} = f(Y_p, r)$$

This formulation is not dissimilar in appearance from the Keynesian liquidity-preference function, $L = f(Y, i)$. There are, however, two crucial differences. First, the Keynesian function includes *current* national income, whereas Friedman is using permanent income as a proxy for total wealth. Secondly, in the Keynesian function (where money is a close substitute for bonds), the demand for money is interest-elastic because if the rate of interest earned from holding bonds changes, wealth holders are assumed to react only by changing their money holdings; but in Friedman's function (where money is a substitute for *all* other assets, both financial and real), the demand for money is believed to exhibit low interest-elasticity.

Effects of a change in the money supply

Now suppose that the central bank increases the money supply – for example, by purchasing government securities on the open market. Assuming that the money market is in equilibrium initially, the policy will raise the supply of money above the demand for money, and wealth holders will find themselves holding more money than they desire in their portfolios. They will attempt to adjust their portfolios by spending their excess money balances on a wide range of assets, financial and real.

This brings us to the key difference between the Keynesian and monetarist models. In the Keynesian model, wealth holders attempt to spend their excess money balances on bonds, thereby forcing down interest rates. In the monetarist case, wealth holders attempt to spend their excess money balances on all types of assets, including physical goods. Thus, there is an effect on interest rates downwards (as in the Keynesian model), *but also a direct effect upwards on the output or prices of goods and services*. This is illustrated in Fig. 22.5 where the increase in the money supply is shown by the shift from M_S^1 to M_S^2. *If the demand for money curve remained unchanged, the interest rate would fall to* Oi_2. The increased demand for goods and services, however, leads to an increase in the output or prices of these goods and services, so that the nominal demand for money increases at every interest rate. The

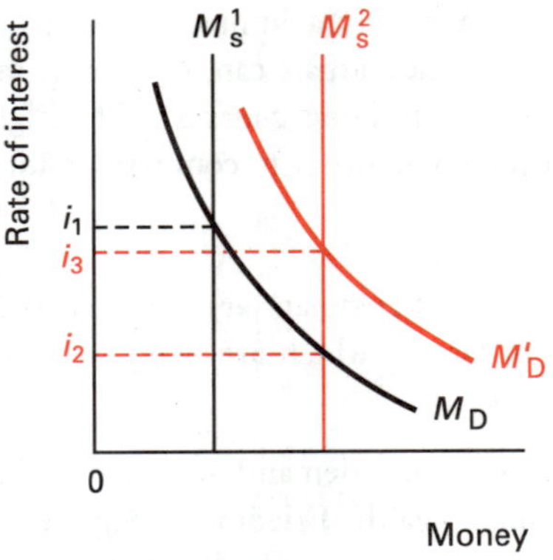

Fig. 22.5. Effect of an increase in the money supply. In a monetarist model, an increase in the money supply has a direct effect on spending. This causes the demand for money curve to shift to the right.

demand for money curve shifts from M_D to M'_D, and the interest rate $0i_3$ and a higher level of money national income result.

Notice that in Fig. 22.5, the demand for money curves are drawn fairly steeply. This reflects the monetarist view that the demand for money is interest-inelastic. A summary of the main tenets of monetarism and the monetarist policy recommendations are summarised in the next chapter.

Transmission mechanisms

Transmission mechanism *The ways in which changes in one economic variable affect other economic variables*

The term transmission mechanism refers to the channels through which the effects of changes in one economic variable are transmitted to other variables. In this section, we are concerned with the channels through which the effects of an increase in the money supply are transmitted to real expenditure decisions (and hence to money national income). The traditional Keynesian and monetarist transmission mechanisms are summarised in Fig. 22.6.

The Keynesian transmission mechanism We have seen that in the Keynesian model, changes in the money supply only affect spending indirectly. As shown in Fig. 22.6, an *increase in the money supply* will reduce the rate of interest and hence the cost of borrowing. As the interest rate falls, investment spending may rise, though (as we indicated in Ch. 20) empirical evidence suggests that investment may be interest-inelastic. If the fall in the rate of interest is accompanied by a fall in the mortgage rate, it is possible that the demand for home loans will increase and this may stimulate the demand for housing construction. At the same time, the lower cost of borrowing may encourage additional consumption spending. Thus, there are a number of ways in which a fall in the rate of interest may lead to an increase in spending, but in general Keynesians have remained sceptical about the overall effectiveness of interest rate changes on real expenditure.

For an open economy, it is important to mention a further possible indirect effect of a change in the money supply on spending. In an open economy, an increase in the money supply which depresses the rate of interest will lead to an outflow of short-term capital seeking higher rates of return overseas. As indicated in Fig. 22.6, the effect of this on the domestic economy will depend on whether the country operates a fixed or flexible exchange rate regime.

Fig. 22.6. ***Keynesian and monetarist transmission mechanisms.*** Alternative theories of the effects of an increase in the money supply in an open economy.

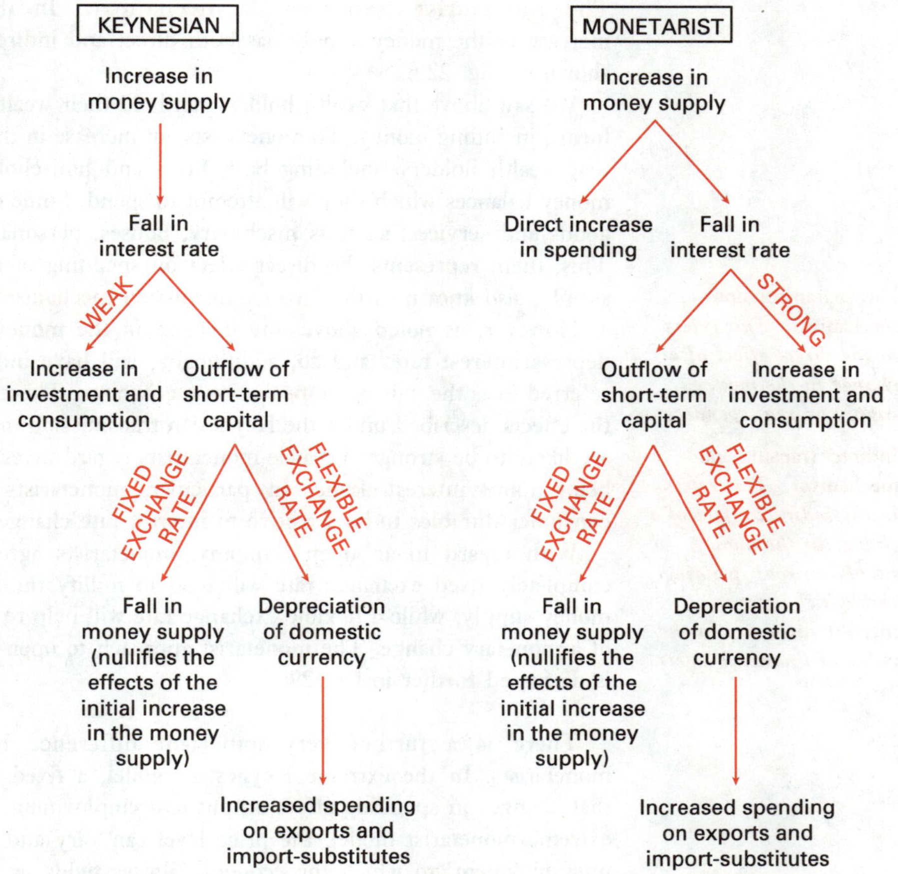

Fixed exchange rate *One in which the value of one currency in terms of another is held constant by government intervention on the foreign exchange market*

Flexible exchange rate *One in which the value of one currency in terms of another is determined by the forces of supply and demand in the foreign exchange market*

With a completely fixed exchange rate, the outflow of short-term capital will cause the domestic money supply to fall (unless the central bank offsets this effect with a further expansionary monetary policy). Assuming no central bank intervention, the initial increase in the money supply will then be completely reversed and there will be no overall effect on the economy. We can say that fixed exchange rates insulate the domestic economy from the effects of domestic monetary changes.

With a flexible exchange rate, the outflow of short-term capital will lead to a depreciation of the domestic currency which, in turn, will cause a rise in the demand for the country's exports and a fall in the demand for imports. This extra spending will add to any increases in investment or consumption induced by the lower domestic interest rate. Thus, with a flexible exchange rate, there are two main channels through which an increase in the money supply can be transmitted to spending: (a) through the effect of the fall in the interest rate on investment and consumption; and (b) through the effect of the fall in the exchange rate on the demand for exports and import-substitutes.

The mechanism operating in an open economy is discussed more fully in the introduction to open-economy macroeconomics in the final section of Ch. 29.

The monetarist transmission mechanism In the monetarist model, an increase in the money supply has both direct and indirect effects on spending, as shown in Fig. 22.6.

We saw above that wealth holders can hold their wealth in a number of different forms, including money. To monetarists, an increase in the money supply will mean that wealth holders (including both firms and households) will be holding *excess* money balances which they will attempt to spend. Some of this spending will be on goods and services, such as machinery, houses, personal computers and holidays. This, then, represents the direct effect on spending of the increase in the money supply, also known as the direct transmission mechanism.

Direct transmission mechanism *This refers to the direct effect of a change in the money supply on real spending*

Indirect transmission mechanism *This refers to the indirect effect of a change in the money supply on real spending through changes in interest rates and in the value of financial assets*

However, as noted above, the increase in the money supply will also tend to depress interest rates and so, additionally, will have indirect effects on spending, referred to as the indirect transmission mechanism. These are essentially the same as the effects described under the Keynesian transmission mechanism, except that they are likely to be stronger because monetarists regard investment and consumption as being more interest-elastic. In particular, monetarists believe the demand for consumer durables to be sensitive to interest rate changes.

With regard to an open economy, monetarists agree that the adoption of a completely fixed exchange rate will tend to nullify the effects of a change in the money supply, while a flexible exchange rate will help to reinforce the effectiveness of a monetary change. The monetarist approach to open-economy macroeconomics is discussed further in Ch. 29.

There is a further very important difference between Keynesians and monetarists. In the extreme Keynesian model, a fixed price level is assumed so that changes in spending affect output and employment, rather than prices. In the extreme monetarist model, the price level can vary and there is a 'natural rate of unemployment' to which the economy always tends in the long-run. This means that changes in spending only affect output and employment in the short-run: in the long-run, only the price level is affected. This aspect of the debate between Keynesians and monetarists is discussed further in the next chapter.

Summary

1. Both the Fisher and Cambridge versions of the quantity theory of money state that an increase in the money supply will lead directly to an increase in spending and, with full employment, the general price level will be proportional to the quantity of money in circulation.
2. Keynes divided the demand for money into three types: the transactions, precautionary and speculative demands for money. Transactions demand is the demand by firms and households for money to finance day-to-day transactions. Precautionary demand arises out of the need to provide for unexpected and unplanned expenditures. Speculative demand is a demand for money as part of a wealth portfolio.

3. The transactions and precautionary demands for money are assumed to be positively related to money national income. The speculative demand for money is assumed to be inversely related to the rate of interest. In the Keynesian liquidity-preference theory, interaction of the demand for and supply of money determines the equilibrium rate of interest.
4. In the modern quantity theory, it is emphasised that money is just one of a number of ways in which wealth can be held. The real demand for money is assumed to depend on a number of factors, including total wealth and the expected rates of return on the various forms of wealth.
5. One of the main differences between monetarists and Keynesians concerns their analysis of the effect of an increase in the money supply. In the Keynesian model, wealth holders attempt to spend excess money balances on bonds, and so force down interest rates. In the monetarist model, wealth holders attempt to spend their excess balances on all types of assets, including goods: this causes both a fall in interest rates *and* an increase in either the output or prices of goods and services.

Exercises

1. Review your understanding of the following terms:

Fisher's 'equation of exchange'	liquidity-preference
transactions velocity of circulation	liquidity trap
income velocity of circulation	interest-elasticity of demand for money
Cambridge cash-balance approach	modern quantity theory
transactions demand for money	direct transmission mechanism
precautionary demand for money	indirect transmission mechanism
speculative demand for money	

2. A worker's average earnings are £100 per week, all of which is spent at an even rate throughout each period. What are the worker's average money holdings if wages are paid: (a) weekly; (b) monthly? Suppose the worker's income increases by 25 per cent. How are the answers to (a) and (b) affected?

3. Consider the following information about a hypothetical economy:
Stock of money = £50 million.
Each pound changes hands on average 3 times per year.
The number of transactions is 30 million per year.

   (a) Find the average price level.
   (b) Suppose the stock of money increases to £60 million, but that the velocity of circulation and number of transactions remain constant. What is the new average price level?
   (c) Now suppose the velocity of circulation rises to 5 and the number of transactions increases to 40 million. What is the new average price level?
   (d) Suggest possible reasons for the increase in the velocity of circulation.

4. Assuming an initial equilibrium in the money market, describe the effects of an increase in the money supply: (a) in the context of a Keynesian model; (b) in the context of the 'modern quantity theory'.

5. Explain why there is an inverse relationship between the speculative demand for money and the rate of interest in the Keynesian liquidity-preference theory. Under what circumstances might the demand for money be perfectly interest-elastic?

6. Discuss the qualitative effect on the demand for money of the following changes:

   (a) an increase in the use of credit cards;
   (b) an increase in the rate of return from holding bonds;
   (c) a fall in the general price level;
   (d) a decrease in the proportion of human wealth to non-human wealth.

23 MONEY AND NATIONAL INCOME

Learning objectives

After reading this chapter, you should be able to:

- define and understand the IS curve and the LM curve and show how a general equilibrium is achieved in the IS–LM model
- use the IS–LM model for comparative static equilibrium analysis and appreciate the limitations of the model
- define and understand the AD curve and the AS curve and show how an equilibrium is achieved in the AD–AS model
- use the AD–AS model to illustrate the key differences between Keynesian and monetarist economics
- understand the basis of the differing policy views of Keynesians and monetarists

Introduction

Real sector *That part of the economy in which goods and services are bought and sold*

Monetary sector *That part of the economy concerned with financial assets, institutions and markets (including the supply of and demand for money)*

In Chs 19–22, we examined the real and monetary sectors of the economy. Our objective in the first part of this chapter is to combine these pieces of analysis and derive a fairly general model (developed originally by J. R. Hicks in 1937) in which the equilibrium level of income and the equilibrium rate of interest are determined simultaneously. This model is expressed graphically using IS and LM curves, so part of our task is to derive and explain these curves.

One of the main assumptions of the simple Keynesian model which we constructed in Ch. 19, and of the IS–LM model which we construct in the first part of this chapter, is that *wages and prices are fixed*. This assumption means that these models are unable to deal adequately with the policy issue of inflation. Once the assumption of fixed wages and prices is relaxed, it becomes necessary to analyse the effects of changes in the general price level on aggregate demand and aggregate supply and, of course, to distinguish carefully between real and monetary variables. A useful way of analysing an economy with flexible prices is by means of aggregate demand (AD) and aggregate supply (AS) curves. The AD–AS model is therefore developed and explained in the second part of the chapter.

The AD–AS model also proves to be a useful way of distinguishing between Keynesian and monetarist economics. The main differences between these two schools of thought, therefore, are summarised at the end of the chapter.

Finally, it must be emphasised that both the IS–LM model and the AD–AS model, as outlined in this chapter, still have one serious limitation for open economies. Although both models include imports and exports as variables, neither explicitly considers the balance of payments or takes account of the effect on the domestic money supply of an external disequilibrium. This limitation is remedied in the final part of Ch. 29 where we present an introduction to open-economy macroeconomics.

The IS–LM model

The IS curve

IS curve *An IS curve joins together combinations of the rate of interest and the level of income at which the real sector is in equilibrium*

In Ch. 19, we showed that the equilibrium level of national income is determined at the point where *total withdrawals* from the flow of income $(S + T + M)$ are just equal to *total injections* into that flow $(I + G + X)$. Suppose now that we introduce the rate of interest into the analysis and thus provide a link between the real and monetary sectors of the economy. The variable most likely to be influenced by changes in interest rates is investment. Assume that a rise in interest rates causes a fall in investment and vice versa. With a given level of government spending and exports, it follows that total injections will also be inversely related to the rate of interest. An IS curve joins together all those combinations of the rate of interest and the level of income at which the real sector of the economy is in equilibrium – that is, at which total injections equal total withdrawals.

An IS curve is derived in Fig. 23.1 which shows four interconnected graphs for a hypothetical economy. Graph (a) shows the inverse relationship between total injections (J) and the rate of interest (i). Graph (b) represents the equilibrium condition that total injections should equal total withdrawals (W). Since J is measured along the horizonal axis and W along the vertical axis, the only points on the graph at which $J = W$ must lie along the 45° line from the origin (assuming, of course, that both axes are in the same scale). Graph (c) illustrates the direct relationship between total withdrawals and national income (Y).

Notice from graph (a) that at an interest rate of 5 per cent, total injections amount to £20 million. Graph (b) tells us that, for equilibrium, total withdrawals must also be equal to £20 million. It is clear from graph (c), however, that there is only one level of national income at which $W =$ £20 million. This is an income level of £100 million. It follows that an interest rate of 5 per cent and an income level of £100 million is one combination of interest and income at which the real sector is in equilibrium. This combination must be one point on the IS curve and is plotted as point A in graph (d).

Now consider an interest rate of 10 per cent. At this higher interest rate, total injections amount to only £10 million. This means that, for equilibrium, total withdrawals must also be £10 million and therefore that income must be £40 million. This gives us a second combination of interest and income (10% and £40m.) which must also be on the IS curve. It is plotted as point B in graph (d).

Choosing other interest rates and finding the level of income required for equilibrium in each case will yield a series of combinations, all of which will lie along the downward-sloping IS curve shown in graph (d). It should be clear that for total injections and total withdrawals to remain equal requires that a rising interest rate be accompanied by a falling level of income, and vice versa.

You should be able to confirm that if investment were completely interest-inelastic so that the injections line in graph (a) were vertical, the IS curve would also be vertical. Given a stable withdrawals line, the steepness of the IS curve depends on the interest-elasticity of investment.

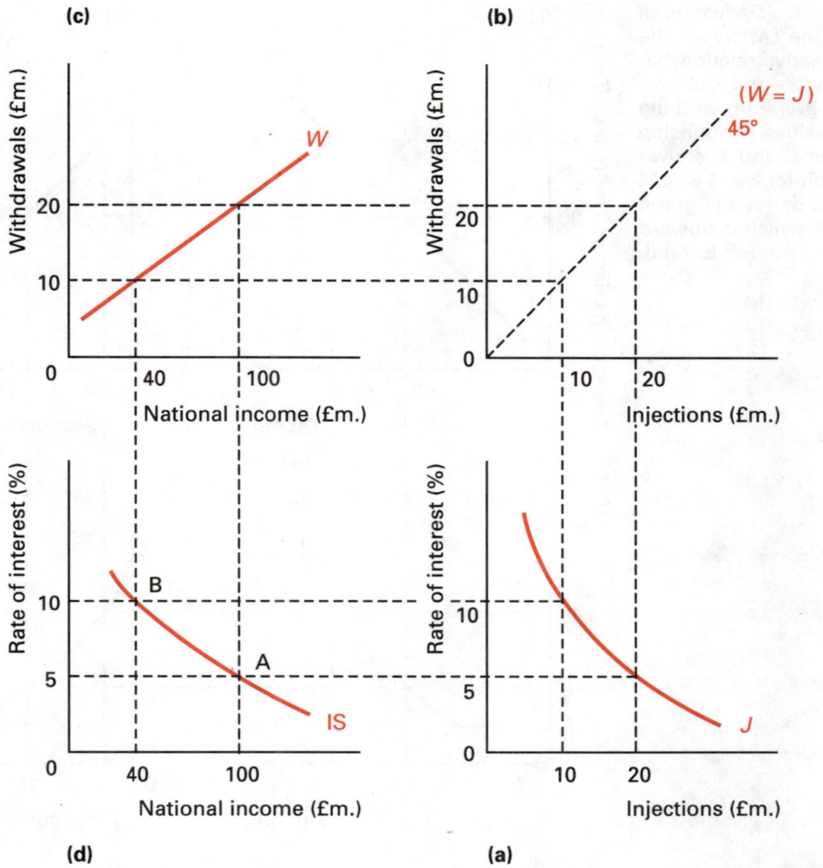

Fig. 23.1. ***Derivation of the IS curve.*** The negative relationship between injections and the rate of interest, shown in graph (a), and the positive relationship between withdrawals and National income, shown in graph (c), mean that the IS curve, derived in graph (d), slopes downwards from left to right.

The LM curve

LM curve *An LM curve joins together combinations of the rate of interest and the level of income at which the monetary sector is in equilibrium.*

Now consider the monetary sector of the economy. We saw in the previous chapter that equilibrium is achieved in the money market when the total demand for money (which depends on the interest rate and the level of income) is equal to the money supply (which is assumed to be autonomous). An LM curve joins together all those combinations of the rate of interest and the level of income at which the monetary sector of the economy is in equilibrium – that is, at which the demand for money equals the supply of money.

An LM curve is derived in Fig. 23.2 using the same procedure as above. Graph (a) shows the Keynesian speculative demand for money (L_s) on the assumption that it is inversely related to the rate of interest between the interest rates $0i_0$ and $0i_1$: above $0i_1$, the speculative demand is assumed to be zero and below $0i_0$, it is assumed to be perfectly elastic. Graph (b) represents the equilibrium condition that the sum of the speculative and transactions demands for money should equal the given money supply. The line MM shows how a money supply of £50 million can be divided between transactions and speculative holdings. Graph (c) shows the direct relationship between the transactions demand for money (L_t) and national income.

Fig. 23.2. ***Derivation of the LM curve.*** The negative relationship between L_S and i, shown in graph (a), and the positive relationship between L_t and Y, shown in graph (c), yield an LM curve, derived in graph (d), which is upward sloping from left to right.

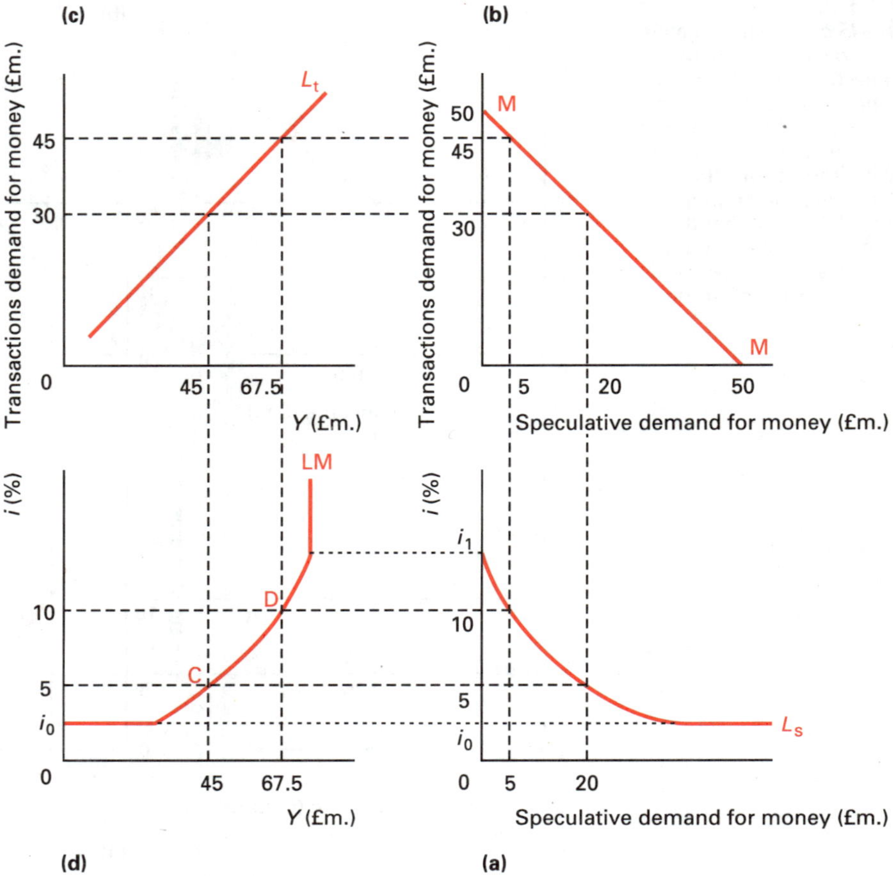

Notice from graph (a) that at an interest rate of 5 per cent, the speculative demand for money is £20 million. Inspection of graph (b) shows that with a given money supply of £50 million, equilibrium is achieved when the transactions demand is equal to £30 million. From graph (c), however, we see that the transactions demand will only be equal to £30 million when national income is £45 million. This gives us one combination which must be on the LM curve: it is plotted as point C in graph (d).

Now consider the higher interest rate of 10 per cent. The speculative demand for money is very low at this interest rate and equal to only £5 million. For equilibrium, transactions demand must be equal to £45 million and, from graph (c), we see that income has to be £67.5 million. The combination of a 10 per cent rate of interest with a £67.5 million level of income represents a second point on the LM curve, plotted as point D in graph (d).

Choosing other interest rates (between $0i_0$ and $0i_1$) and finding the level of income required for equilibrium in each case will yield a series of combinations, all of which lie along the upward-sloping LM curve shown in graph (d). It should be clear that, in this range of interest rates, for the demand for and supply of money to remain equal, a rising interest rate must be accompanied by a rising level of income, and vice versa.

In Fig. 23.2, you should be able to confirm that for interest rates above $0i_1$, where the speculative demand for money is zero, the LM curve becomes vertical. At interest rate $0i_0$, where the speculative demand is perfectly elastic, the LM curve becomes horizontal.

General equilibrium

General equilibrium
General equilibrium in the IS–LM model is achieved when both the real and monetary sectors are in equilibrium

An IS curve and an LM curve are drawn together in Fig. 23.3. The point of intersection determines the rate of interest and the level of income at which both the real and monetary sectors of the economy are in equilibrium. The only combination of interest and income at which both markets are in equilibrium is interest rate $0i_1$ and income level $0Y_1$. This is called the point of general equilibrium. The equations of the IS and LM curves are derived algebraically in the Appendix.

Stability of the general equilibrium Recall from Ch. 6 that an equilibrium is said to be a stable one when economic forces tend to push the market towards it. Figure 23.4 illustrates that the general equilibrium we have just derived is indeed a

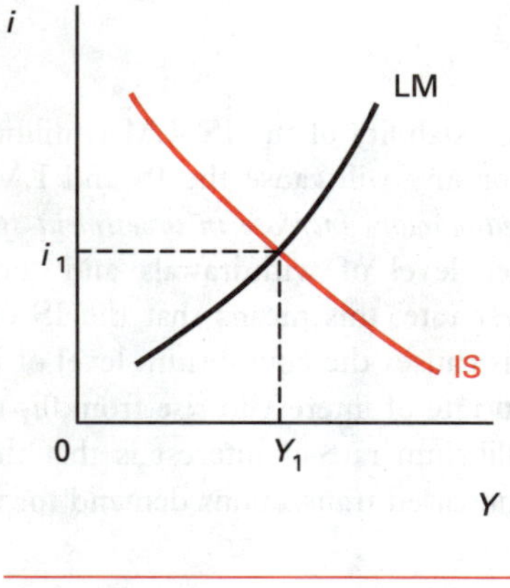

Fig. 23.3. The point of general equilibrium. The intersection of the IS curve and the LM curve determines the equilibrium interest rate, $0i_1$, and the equilibrium level of national income, $0Y_1$

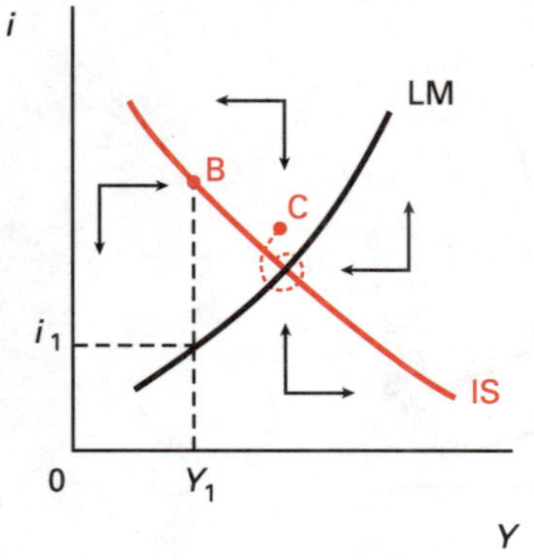

Fig. 23.4. The stability of the general equilibrium. At any point other than the point of general equilibrium, economic forces are generated to push the economy towards the intersection of the IS and LM curves.

stable one. To show this, consider all the points to the left of the IS curve, like point A: at this point, with the given interest rate $0i_1$, the level of income is too low for equilibrium to be achieved in the real sector. This means that injections exceed withdrawals and the total value of output is less than the economy's aggregate demand. In this situation, firms find their inventories being run down involuntarily and so act to increase output. This is the economic force which pushes up national income. For all points to the left of the IS curve, then, there is pressure on income to rise. Similarly, for all points to the right of the IS curve, there is pressure on income to fall.

Now consider points above the LM curve, like point B: at this point, with the given level of income $0Y_1$, the interest rate is too high for equilibrium to be achieved in the monetary sector. This means that the supply of money exceeds the demand for money and so downward pressure is exerted on the rate of interest. This is true for all points above the LM curve and it similarly follows that upward pressure will be exerted on interest rates at all points below the LM curve.

The directions of the pressures being exerted on income and the interest rate in the four quadrants of the graph are indicated by the arrows in Fig. 23.4. It follows that at any disequilibrium point, such as point C, economic forces will be pushing the market towards the general equilibrium position. The actual path to equilibrium may be a spiral (as illustrated) rather than a direct route, but eventually, given sufficient time with other variables remaining unchanged, the equilibrium should be reached.

Shifting the IS and LM curves

Having demonstrated the stability of the IS–LM equilibrium, we can now consider what changes in the economy will cause the IS and LM curves to shift. Consider first the effects of an *autonomous increase in investment spending*. For equilibrium to be maintained, a higher level of withdrawals and therefore national income is required at every interest rate; this means that the IS curve shifts to the right, as shown in Fig. 23.5. This causes the equilibrium level of income to rise from $0Y_1$ to $0Y_2$ and the equilibrium rate of interest to rise from $0i_1$ to $0i_2$. Note that the reason for the rise in the equilibrium rate of interest is that the higher income level will have brought forth an increased transactions demand for money. The rise in the rate

Fig. 23.5. A shift in the IS curve. When the IS curve shifts to the right, caused for example by an increase in autonomous investment, both the equilibrium interest rate and the equilibrium level of national income will rise.

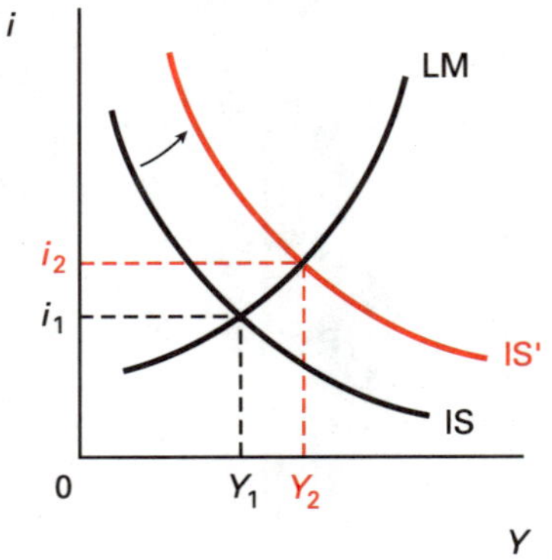

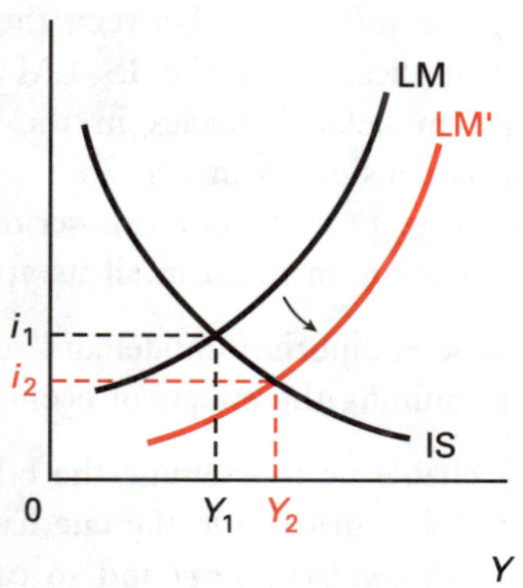

Fig. 23.6. *A shift in the LM curve.* When the LM curve shifts to the right, caused for example by an increase in the money supply, the equilibrium interest rate falls and the equilibrium level of national income rises.

Table 23.1 Summary of the causes and direction of shifts in the IS and LM curves.

Increase in investment	IS shifts right
Decrease in investment	IS shifts left
Increase in consumption	IS shifts right
Increase in savings	IS shifts left
Increase in government expenditure	IS shifts right
Increase in taxation	IS shifts left
Increase in money supply	LM shifts right
Decrease in money supply	LM shifts left
Increase in the demand for money	LM shifts left
Decrease in the demand for money	LM shifts right

of interest chokes off some of the initial demand increase, hence making the multiplier effect smaller.

Secondly, consider the effect of an *autonomous increase in the money supply*. This will cause the LM curve to shift to the right, as shown in Fig. 23.6. The reason for this is that every income level (which determines the transactions demand for money) must now be associated with a lower interest rate and therefore a higher speculative demand for money if equality between the total demand for and supply of money is to be maintained. Notice that the new equilibrium is characterised by a lower rate of interest, $0i_2$, and a higher level of income, $0Y_2$. In this case, the increased money supply has reduced the interest rate which, in turn, has caused a rise in investment spending; it is this rise in investment which causes the increase in the level of income.

Table 23.1 summarises the changes in the economy which cause either the IS curve or the LM curve to shift. All the changes are autonomous in the sense that they are not themselves caused by changes in income or interest rates. The reader should be able to confirm the direction of the shifts either graphically or by reasoned argument.

Uses and limitations of the IS–LM model

It must be emphasised that the IS–LM model is a theoretical construction based on many assumptions. Since the assumptions we have made are the same as those in the simple Keynesian model and the Keynesian theory of money, the IS–LM model derived above is sometimes called the general Keynesian model. It can, however, be modified to take account of different assumptions and this means that it is a useful

General Keynesian model *This analyses both the real and monetary sectors of the economy, and takes account of the interaction between these sectors*

framework for illustrating the differences between the various schools of thought. For example, one major application of the IS–LM model is in comparing the effectiveness of fiscal and monetary policies in the Keynesian and neo-classical theories. This application is considered in Ch. 26.

It is important at this stage to point out two serious limitations of the IS–LM model and these should be borne in mind in all its applications.

(a) It is a comparative static equilibrium model and so ignores the time-lags which are so important in examining the effects of economic policy changes.

(b) The model does not enable us to examine the effects of changes in aggregate demand on *both* output and prices. On the one hand, the Keynesian version of the model assumes a *constant price level* and so cannot analyse the problem of inflation. On the other hand, in the neo-classical version of the model, which applies when full employment is reached, the price level is determined by the nominal money supply and output is assumed to be determined exogenously. A more general model which shows more clearly how the equilibrium level of real national income (or real output) *and* the price level are determined is the aggregate demand-aggregate supply (AD–AS) model. This is considered next.

Aggregate demand and supply analysis

Aggregate demand

Aggregate demand *The total quantity of all final goods and services demanded over a period of time*

Aggregate demand is the total quantity of all final goods and services demanded over a period of time and consists of the sum of the demands of consumers, firms, central and local governments and foreigners. Like all aggregates, aggregate demand has to be measured in value terms and this means that it is necessary to ensure that the measure is adjusted for price changes and so expressed in real terms. Another way of defining aggregate demand, therefore, is as *the total value of real national product demanded over time*.

The value of aggregate demand in any particular year will depend on decisions taken by households, firms, governments and overseas buyers. One important factor that will influence these decisions, but which we have so far assumed constant in our macroeconomic analysis, is the average level of prices. We saw in Ch. 3 that the market demand for a normal good and the good's price are inversely related, giving a negatively sloped market demand curve. It is similarly true that the *aggregate* demand for the national product will be inversely related to the price level, giving a negatively sloped aggregate demand curve (or AD curve) as shown in Fig. 23.7. As

Fig. 23.7. *The AD curve.* As the price level falls from $0P_0$ to $0P_1$, aggregate demand rises from $0Y_0$ to $0Y_1$.

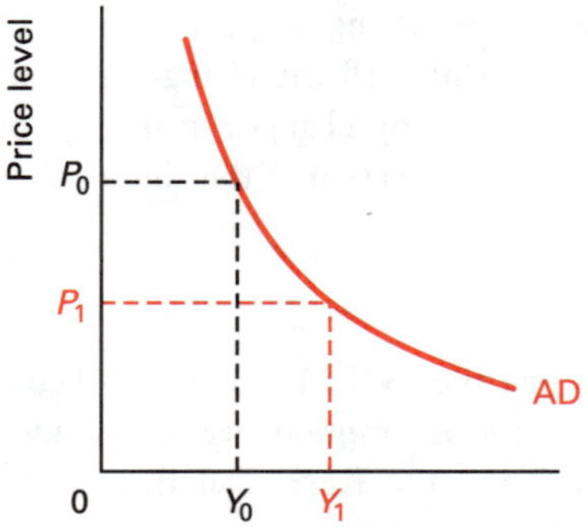

the price level falls from $0P_0$ to $0P_1$, the quantity of real output demanded rises from $0Y_0$ to $0Y_1$. Similarly, a rise in the price level causes a fall in the quantity of real output demanded.

There are three main reasons why the AD curve slopes downwards from left to right: the money supply effect, the real balance effect and the macroeconomic substitution effect. Consider these in turn.

(a) *The money supply effect.* With the nominal money supply remaining unchanged, a rise in the price level will reduce the *real* value of the money supply and shift the LM curve to the left. We saw in Ch. 22 that a contractionary monetary change of this kind will in most circumstances reduce total spending and therefore cause a fall in aggregate demand. Similarly, a fall in the price level will increase the real value of the money supply and lead to a rise in aggregate demand.

Real balance effect *This results from the influence of a change in the price level on the real value of financial assets. An increase in the price level, for example, reduces the real value of financial assets and so may depress spending on goods and services*

(b) *Real balance effect.* The real balance effect is related to the change in the real value of the money supply, described above. We saw in Ch. 20 that, although the main determinant of consumer spending is household income, one of the other factors affecting consumption is *consumers' wealth*. Wealth can be held in many forms. Some of these are assets such as cash holdings and savings accounts, the real value of which falls as prices rise and *vice versa*. As an example, consider an individual who holds a building society share account. If the general price level should rise during the course of a year, the real value (or purchasing power) of the account will fall. It is probable that this will have the effect of curbing to some extent the individual's spending during the year. Similarly, a fall in the price level which raises the purchasing power of an individual's savings will probably lead to an increase in spending. For many consumers, the effects of changes in the price level on their spending may be very small. But for the economy as a whole, the effect could be quite significant. We can therefore expect a rise in the price level to reduce aggregate demand, and a fall in the price level to increase aggregate demand.

(c) *Macroeconomic substitution effect.* As the price level falls, consumers may decide to buy goods now which they were planning to buy in the future. If the price level rises, they may decide to postpone purchases which were originally planned for the present. This effect, which probably depends strongly on expectations of future inflation rates, is called an *intertemporal* substitution effect.

In addition to this effect, there may be an *international* substitution effect as domestic buyers decide to buy more home-produced goods and fewer imports as the domestic price level falls, and more imports and fewer home-produced goods as the price level rises.

These substitution effects will tend, therefore, to cause aggregate demand to decrease following a rise in the price level, and increase following a fall in the price level.

Derivation of the AD curve

To derive an AD curve, we assume that the nominal money supply, interest rates, government expenditure and tax rates all remain unchanged, and we examine the effect on the equilibrium level of real income (or aggregate demand) of a change in the price level. When the price level falls, the LM curve will shift to the right because of the increase in the real value of the money supply described above. In

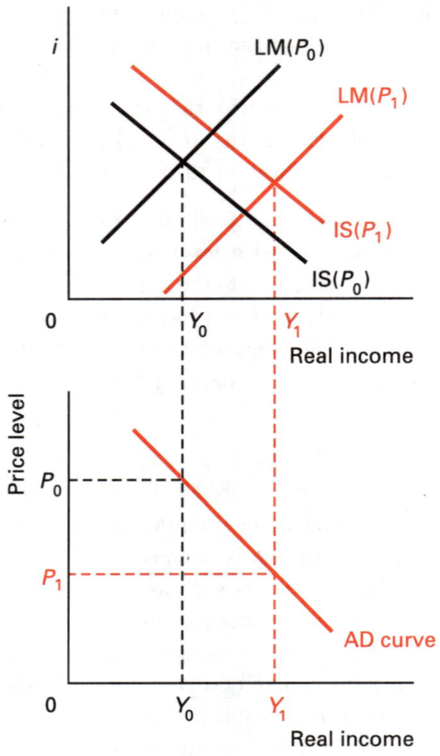

Fig. 23.8. Derivation of the AD curve. The AD curve can be derived from the IS–LM model by tracing out the effect on real output of a change in the price level.

addition, the IS curve will shift to the right because of the real balance effect and the macroeconomic substitution effects. These shifts are shown in the upper graph of Fig. 23.8 where the price level falls from $0P_0$ to $0P_1$. LM(P_0) and IS(P_0) are the LM and IS curves before the fall in the price level, and LM(P_1) and IS(P_1) are the curves after the fall in the price level. Equilibrium real output rises from $0Y_0$ to $0Y_1$. The combinations (P_0, Y_0) and (P_1, Y_1) are shown as two points on the AD curve in the lower graph of Fig. 23.8. Other points along the downward-sloping AD curve can easily be derived in a similar manner. Since every combination of real output and the price level along the AD curve is associated with a point of intersection between the IS and LM curves, we can say that the AD curve joins together all those combinations of the price level and real output at which both the real sector and the monetary sector of the economy are in equilibrium.

Shifts in the AD curve

It should be clear that an expansionary change in the economy (which shifts either the IS or LM curve to the right) will also shift the AD curve to the right. Similarly, a contractionary change will shift the AD curve to the left. The main causes of shifts in the AD curve are summarised below:

(a) *A change in government spending.* Since government demand is a component of aggregate demand, it follows that an increase in government spending, *ceteris paribus*, will cause the AD curve to shift to the right. Similarly, a decrease in government spending will cause the AD curve to shift to the left.

(b) *A change in taxation.* An increase in taxation, *ceteris paribus*, will reduce consumption and, therefore, aggregate demand. This will cause the AD curve to shift to the left. Similarly, a decrease in taxation will cause the AD curve to shift to the right.

(c) *A change in the nominal money supply.* An increase in the nominal money supply will lead to an increase in spending (either directly or as a result of a reduction in interest rates), and so will cause the AD curve to shift to the right. Similarly, a decrease in the nominal money supply will cause the AD curve to shift to the left.

Aggregate supply

Aggregate supply ***The total quantity of all goods and services that firms wish to supply over a period of time***

Aggregate supply is the total quantity of all goods and services that firms wish to supply over a given time period. We saw in Ch. 5 that the quantity of a good produced by profit-maximising firms depends on the price of the good, as well as on certain other factors such as the prices of related goods, the prices of factors of production and the state of technology. We then drew an upward-sloping supply curve to depict the relationship between the quantity of a good supplied and the good's price on the assumption that all the other determinants of supply remained unchanged (i.e. *ceteris paribus*). We can similarly depict the relationship between the aggregate supply of all goods and services and the average price level, *ceteris paribus*, by means of an aggregate supply curve (or AS curve).

The shape of the AS curve is a matter of great controversy. In what follows, we shall see that different shapes of the AS curve can be used to distinguish between Keynesian and monetarist economics.

The AS curve

A typical AS curve, sloping upwards from left to right, is shown in Fig. 23.9. As the price level rises from $0P_0$ to $0P_1$, the quantity of goods and services produced rises from $0Y_0$ to $0Y_1$, *ceteris paribus*. We showed in Chs 9 and 10 that a profit-maximising firm expands production of a good in response to an increase in price because the higher price makes the production of additional units profitable. With respect to the macro-economy, it is true that not all firms have profit maximisation as their main objective; also, a rise in the average price level does not necessarily mean that all product prices will rise. Furthermore, some firms whose products do rise in price may at the same time experience similar rises in their costs of production. We would not expect these firms to increase their outputs.

Fig. 23.9. The AS curve. As the price level rises from $0P_0$ to $0P_1$, the quantity of real output supplied rises from $0Y_0$ to $0Y_1$. With excess capacity in the economy, the AS curve will be fairly flat (as in the range A to B), but as full employment is approached, the AS curve will become steep (as in the range B to C).

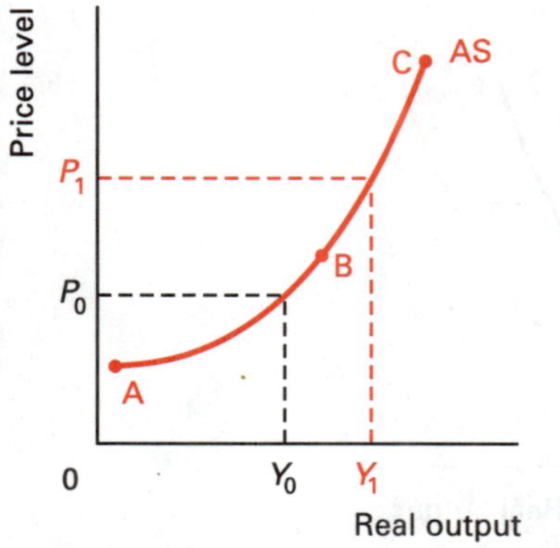

Nevertheless, there will be many firms whose product prices will rise without an accompanying increase in production costs. This is because a large number of firms enter into contracts (implicit or explicit) to increase wages and salaries just once a year and to buy their raw materials at pre-arranged fixed prices. These contracts help to keep firms' costs constant, at least in the short-run, while product prices are rising, and it is for this reason that we expect a rising average price level to lead to a rise in aggregate supply. The more excess capacity there is in the economy, the flatter will be the AS curve, as in the range A to B in Fig. 23.9. As full employment is approached and many firms find themselves operating at or close to full capacity, the AS curve will become steeper, as in the range B to C.

Shifts in the AS curve

There are a number of important factors which determine the position of the AS curve. Changes in any of these factors will cause the AS curve to shift. The main ones are summarised as follows:

(a) *The level of money wages.* Labour cost is the largest component of the total cost of production for most firms. An increase in money wage rates, *ceteris paribus*, will raise firms' costs and so make the production of marginal units less profitable. Firms will react to this by reducing output and the AS curve will therefore shift to the left. Similarly, a reduction in money wage rates, *ceteris paribus*, will cause the AS curve to shift to the right.

(b) *Other input prices.* As in the case of money wages, a change in the price of any other input will also cause the AS curve to shift. In general, an increase in an input price, *ceteris paribus*, will cause the AS curve to shift to the left, while a decrease will cause the AS curve to shift to the right.

(c) *The available supply of inputs and the state of technology.* Growth in the available supplies of inputs in the economy and/or an improvement in the state of technology (which raises the productivity of one or more inputs) will shift the AS curve to the right.

Figure 23.10 illustrates an AS curve which has shifted to the right from AS_1 to AS_2. This shift may have been caused by a fall in input prices, an increase in the supply of inputs or by technological improvements.

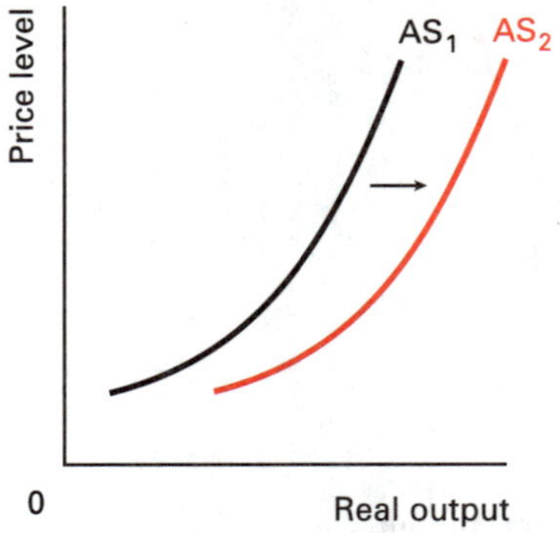

Fig. 23.10. *A shift in the AS curve.* A fall in input prices, an increase in the supply of inputs or technological progress would all cause the AS curve to shift to the right, as shown.

Fig. 23.11. ***Macroeconomic equilibrium.*** The equilibrium price level and the equilibrium level of real output are determined (at point E) by the intersection of the AD and AS curves.

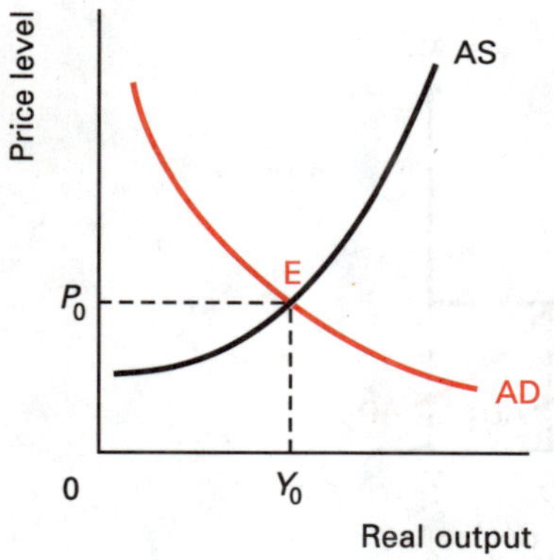

Fig. 23.12. ***The effects of an increase in aggregate demand.*** As the AD curve shifts to the right from AD_1 to AD_2, the equilibrium price level rises from $0P_0$ to $0P_1$ and the equilibrium quantity of real output rises from $0Y_0$ to $0Y_1$.

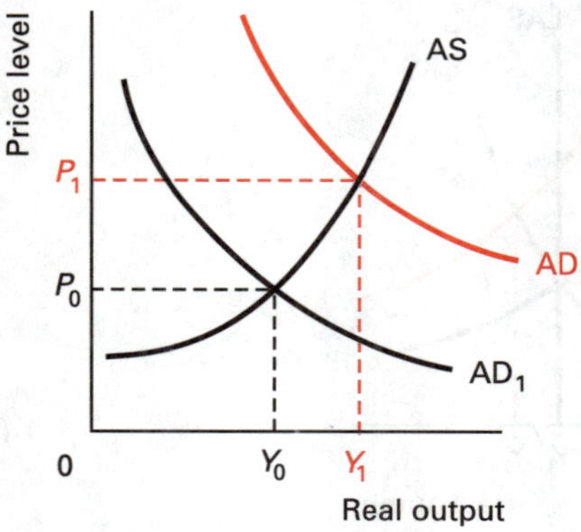

Macroeconomic equilibrium

In Fig. 23.11, the AD and AS curves intersect at point E where the equilibrium level of real output is $0Y_0$ and the equilibrium price level is $0P_0$.

Point E represents the level of real output and the price level towards which the economy will tend. The AD–AS model depicted in Fig. 23.11 is particularly useful because it enables predictions of the effects on real output (and, therefore, employment) and the price level of various economic changes to be made. For example, we have seen that an increase in real government expenditure, or a decrease in the level of taxation, will shift the AD curve to the right, as shown in Fig. 23.12. We can predict that real output will rise from $0Y_0$ to $0Y_1$ and the equilibrium price level will increase from $0P_0$ to $0P_1$, the sizes of the changes depending on the slopes of the two curves. The slope of the AS curve, in fact, is particularly contentious and is at the heart of the debate between Keynesian and monetarist economists.

An extreme Keynesian view of the AD–AS model For extreme Keynesians, the AS curve is horizontal up to the point at which full employment is reached, so that in this range the price level is constant. Once full employment is reached, however, real output becomes impossible to increase further (at least in the short-run) and the AS curve becomes vertical. This version of the AD–AS model, with an inverted L-shaped AS curve is shown in Fig. 23.13 where $0Y_F$ is the full employment

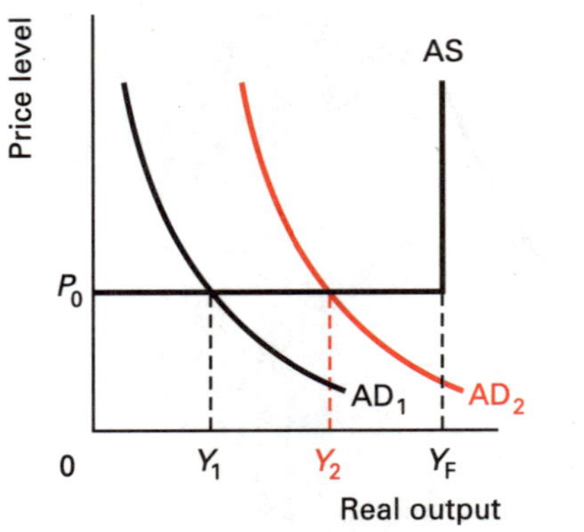

Fig. 23.13. *An extreme Keynesian view.* The inverted L-shaped AS curve illustrates an extreme Keynesian view. As aggregate demand increases from AD_1 to AD_2, real output increases from $0Y_1$ to $0Y_2$, but the price level remains unchanged at $0P_0$.

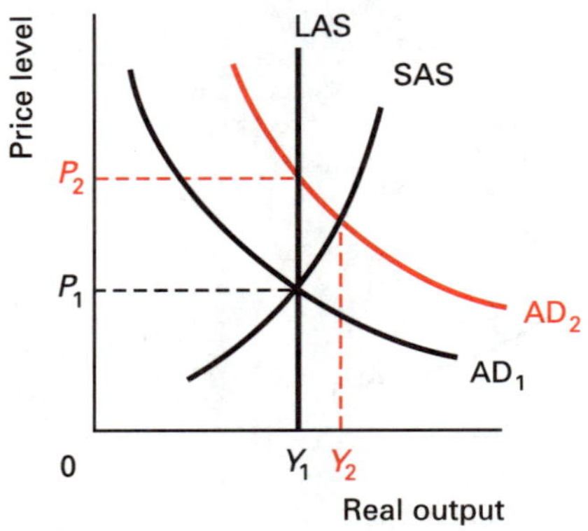

Fig. 23.14. *An extreme monetarist view.* The vertical LAS curve illustrates the extreme monetarist view that real output always returns to the level ($0Y_1$ in the diagram) associated with the natural rate of unemployment in the long-run. The increase in aggregate demand from AD_1 to AD_2 causes the price level to rise from $0P_1$ to $0P_2$, but leaves real output unchanged.

level of real output. A shift in the AD curve from AD_1 to AD_2 (caused, for example, by an increase in investment spending) will raise real output from $0Y_1$ to $0Y_2$, but leave the price level unchanged. This is a similar prediction to the one we made using the IS–LM model (see Fig. 23.5).

An extreme monetarist view of the AD–AS model For extreme monetarists, the *long-run* AS curve is vertical, so that in the long-run any increase in aggregate demand will raise the equilibrium price level, but leave real output unchanged. This is illustrated in Fig. 23.14 where an increase in aggregate demand which shifts the AD curve from AD_1 to AD_2 at first raises real output from $0Y_1$ to $0Y_2$ along the short-run aggregate supply curve, SAS. This is only a short-run effect, however, because in the longer term the economy returns to the long-run aggregate supply curve, LAS. The price level rises from $0P_1$ to $0P_2$, and real output returns to $0Y_1$. This view depends on the existence of a 'natural' rate of unemployment towards which the economy always tends in the long-run. (The 'natural' rate of unemployment is defined and discussed more fully in Chs 27 and 28.)

With regard to government macroeconomic policy, attempts to raise real output and employment by increasing the money supply or by increasing government spending or reducing taxation are, according to monetarists, doomed to failure. Increasing demand may increase output and reduce unemployment below its 'natural' rate in the short-run as information failures lead to movements along the short-run aggregate supply curve, but in the longer term, the economy will return to the 'natural' rate of unemployment so that the only lasting effect of the policy will be on the price level. This is why monetarists have advised the use of supply-side policies (discussed in detail in Ch. 27), designed to shift the long-run AS curve to the right, as ways of increasing real output and employment in the long-term.

The Keynesian-monetarist debate

Figures 23.13 and 23.14 depict extreme versions of the Keynesian and monetarist views of the determination of real output and the price level. Less extreme advocates of the two schools would admit that increases in aggregate demand are likely to have some effect on both output *and* prices. Indeed, one way of illustrating the difference between Keynesian and monetarist economics is to draw a fairly flat AS curve to show the Keynesian case and a fairly steep AS curve to show the monetarist case, as shown in Fig. 23.15. In these cases, Keynesians would emphasise the output effect of an increase in aggregate demand, while monetarists would argue that the greater effect would ultimately be on the price level. In graph (a), which shows the Keynesian case, an increase in aggregate demand from AD_1 to AD_2 causes a relatively large increase in real output (from $0Y_1$ to $0Y_2$), but only a very small increase in the price level (from $0P_1$ to $0P_2$). In graph (b), which shows the monetarist case, the increase in aggregate demand causes only a small increase in real output (from $0Y_3$ to $0Y_4$), but a substantial increase in the price level (from $0P_3$ to $0P_4$).

We conclude this chapter by attempting to summarise the main differences between Keynesian and monetarist economics under two headings: the velocity of circulation; and the role of demand-management policies.

(a) *The velocity of circulation.* One of the most important assertions of monetarists is that the velocity of circulation of money, although not constant, is predictable, independent of the money supply and stably related to a limited number of variables. This assertion leads directly to the proposition that money national income and the nominal money supply must be positively correlated with each other. To show this,

Fig. 23.15. More moderate Keynesian and monetarist views. In graph (a), the fairly flat AS curve illustrates the moderate Keynesian view that a change in aggregate demand will affect mainly real output. In graph (b), the steep AS curve illustrates the moderate monetarist view that changes in aggregate demand affect mainly the price level.

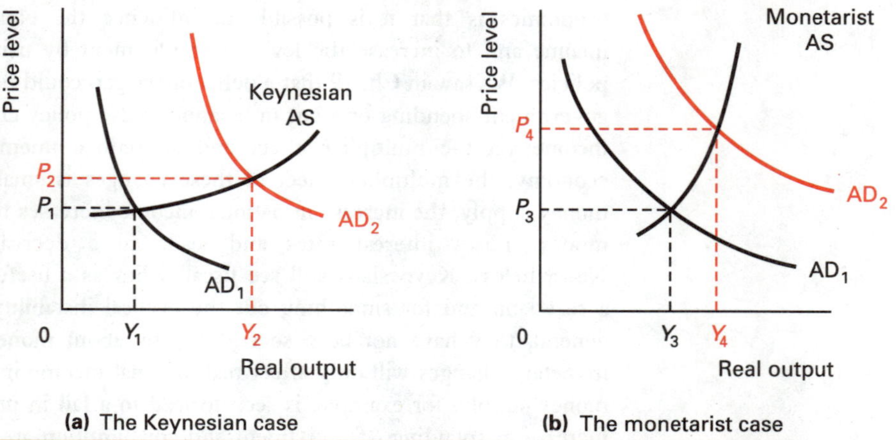

consider the following version of the quantity theory of money:

$$MV = PY$$

where M is the nominal money supply, V is the *income* velocity of circulation and PY is the money value of national income. Given V, all changes in M must be associated with changes in PY in the same direction. Milton Friedman has written that 'there is a consistent though not precise relation between the rate of growth of the quantity of money and the rate of growth of nominal income'. We saw in Ch. 22 that an increase in M which raised the supply of money above the demand for money would mean that wealth-holders would have more money than they desired in their wealth portfolios. According to monetarists, they would adjust their portfolios by increasing their spending on both financial and real assets, thereby affecting money national income directly and keeping the velocity of circulation more or less unchanged. According to Keynesians, the wealth-holders would attempt to spend their excess money balances on financial assets only: this would force down interest rates, and then only if the lower interest rates induced extra investment or consumption spending would the change in the money supply affect money national income.

In 1963, Friedman and Anna Schwartz undertook extensive empirical work on the correlation between the growth of the money supply and the growth of money national income in their book *A Monetary History of the United States, 1867–1960.* The results they obtained suggested that there was a close relationship between long-run changes in the United States' money supply and changes in money national income. Correlation, of course, does not necessarily mean causation. Friedman and Schwartz claimed, however, that it was changes in the nominal money supply which *caused* changes in money national income and, once again, they appealed to empirical evidence to support their case. For example, they looked in detail at each major recession and argued from their observations that the money supply declined for reasons other than the recession itself and that the fall in money national income generally followed the fall in the money supply. Keynesians, however, remain unconvinced. Lord Kaldor, for example, has argued that the money supply is passively adjusted to the level required to accommodate the current level of economic activity.

(b) *The role of demand-management policies.* One conclusion of Keynesian economics is that it is possible to influence the equilibrium level of national income and to increase the level of employment by using fiscal and/or monetary policies. We saw in Ch. 19 that a deflationary gap could be reduced by an increase in government spending or a cut in taxation: these policy changes would raise national income via the multiplier effect and so reduce unemployment. In a monetary economy, the multiplier effect of these changes is smaller (because, with a fixed money supply, the increase in national income increases the transactions demand for money, raises interest rates and leads to a decrease in private spending). Nevertheless, Keynesians still see fiscal policy as a useful weapon for dealing with a recession and for smoothing out the cyclical instability of market economies. In general, they have not been so enthusiastic about monetary policy, believing that monetary changes will only affect real national income indirectly: an increase in the money supply, for example, is seen to lead to a fall in interest rates and then to an increase in spending (if investment and consumption are responsive to interest rate changes). The possible interest-inelasticity of investment and consumption is one of the main reasons why Keynesians have favoured fiscal policy over monetary policy. The factors which determine the relative effectiveness of fiscal and monetary policies in the IS–LM model are discussed further in Ch. 26.

Monetarists disagree with the Keynesian predilection for fiscal policy as a means of managing the macro-economy. Indeed, they are almost entirely against the use of short-run demand management policy. Instead, they recommend a steady, annual expansion of the money supply at a rate determined by the predictable steady growth in the velocity of circulation and the predicted growth in the country's potential output. No attempt should be made to use monetary policy to offset any disturbances that may occur from time to time. Any such attempts would most likely fail and possibly make matters worse because of the difficulties of predicting short-run changes and because of the variability of the time-lags with which changes in the money supply affect nominal national income.

Similarly, fiscal policy, according to monetarists, has no role to play in demand-management. Any increase in government spending will increase the demand for money and so *crowd out* private spending through rising interest rates. This is the case illustrated in Ch. 26, in Fig. 26.3, where the LM curve is vertical. If the expansionary fiscal policy were accompanied by an increase in the money supply to counter the crowding-out effect, the long-term result would be little more than a higher rate of inflation as the economy automatically tended towards its 'natural rate of unemployment'.

In general terms, we can conclude that the monetarists' major policy recommendation is: maintain a steady constant growth in the money supply, otherwise leave things well alone. They tend to subscribe to the libertarian belief that individual freedom and the operation of the free market can be relied upon to tackle economic problems efficiently without the need for government intervention. They argue that, in the absence of government intervention, the economy will not be subject to any inherent instability. Indeed, they suggest that instability in the past has been caused, rather than smoothed out, by governments' attempts at demand-management policies.

Further discussion of the Keynesian-monetarist controversies can be found in Chs 26–29.

Summary

1. The IS–LM model represents a synthesis of the real and monetary sectors of an economy.
2. The IS curve links together combinations of the rate of interest and national income at which the real sector is in equilibrium. The LM curve links together combinations of the rate of interest and national income at which the monetary sector is in equilibrium. The point of intersection between the two curves represents a general equilibrium towards which the economy will tend. The model is a comparative static equilibrium model which may be used to predict the effects of economic changes on the equilibrium level of national income and

the rate of interest. The Keynesian version of the model, however, is restricted by its assumption of fixed wages and prices.

3. The AD–AS model is a more general model in which the general price level is assumed to be flexible. The AD curve depicts the relationship between aggregate demand and the price level, while the AS curve depicts the relationship between aggregate supply and the price level. The equilibrium price level and the equilibrium level of real output are jointly determined by the intersection of the AD and AS curves.
4. The shape of the AS curve is a matter of controversy and helps to illustrate the difference between Keynesian and monetarist economists. To Keynesians, the AS curve will be fairly flat until full employment is reached when it will become vertical. This means that changes in aggregate demand when the economy has unused resources available will have a large effect on output and little or no effect on prices. To monetarists, the AS curve is steep and in the long-run will be vertical at the output level associated with the natural rate of unemployment. This means that changes in aggregate demand will affect mainly the price level and will have little or no effect on output.
5. Keynesians and monetarists disagree about the variability of the velocity of circulation, with monetarists arguing that it is predictable and unrelated to the money supply. They also disagree about the role of demand-management policies. Keynesians see fiscal, and to a lesser extent, monetary policies as useful weapons for managing the macroeconomy, while to monetarists the ineffectiveness of fiscal policy and the inflationary effect of a monetary expansion (after uncertain time lags) make demand-management policies futile.

Exercises

1. Review your understanding of the following terms:

real sector	aggregate demand
monetary sector	aggregate supply
IS curve	AD curve
LM curve	AS curve
general equilibrium	fiscal policy
real money supply	monetary policy
nominal money supply	monetarism
wage and price flexibility	income velocity of circulation
real balance effect	crowding out

2. Consider a simple closed economy with no government and no inflation. The following equations represent the investment and saving functions respectively:

$I = 20 - 2i$
$S = 0.5Y$

where i is the rate of interest and Y is the level of national income. Find the equation of the IS curve and plot it on a graph. If the equation of the LM curve is $Y = 4 + 2i$,

(a) find the equilibrium level of national income and the equilibrium rate of interest;
(b) calculate the effect on the level of income and the rate of interest of an autonomous fall in investment of 10;
(c) explain why the fall in income is less than that predicted by the simple multiplier derived in Ch. 19.

3. 'The IS–LM model is based on comparative static analysis and ignores the dynamic processes of a modern economy.' Discuss.

4. In the context of (a) the IS–LM model and (b) the AD–AS model, illustrate the effects on the equilibrium level of income and the rate of interest of an increase in the demand for money.

5. Discuss the view that completely flexible wages and prices would ensure the automatic attainment of full employment in an economy.

6. Use AD–AS analysis to discuss the effects of the following policies on real output and the price level, first, under Keynesian assumptions, and secondly, under monetarist assumptions:

(a) A reduction in the rate of income taxation;
(b) A reduction in the level of government expenditure;
(c) Additional open-market purchases of government securities by the Bank of England.

Appendix

Algebraic derivation of the IS and LM curves

The IS–LM model may be expressed in algebraic form using the following set of equations:

Real sector

Equilibrium condition, $Y = C + I + \bar{G} + \bar{X} - M$ (1)

Consumption function, $C = a + b(Y - \bar{T})$ (2)

Import function, $M = c + dY$ (3)

Investment function, $I = e - fi$ (4)

Monetary sector

Equilibrium condition, $\bar{M}_S = L_t + L_S$ (5)

Transactions demand for money, $L_t = kY$ (6)

Speculative demand for money, $L_S = g - hi$ (7)

where Y is national income, C is planned consumption, I is planned investment, $\bar{G}$ is planned government spending, $\bar{T}$ is lump-sum taxation, $\bar{X}$ is planned exports, M is planned imports, i is the rate of interest, $\bar{M}_S$ is the money supply, L_t is the transactions demand for money and L_S is the speculative demand for money. Of the eleven variables, Y, C, I, M, i, L_t and L_S are endogenous: this means that their values are determined by forces operating *within* the model. The remaining four variables, $\bar{G}$, $\bar{T}$, $\bar{X}$ and $\bar{M}_S$, are exogenous (indicated by the 'bars'): this means that their values are determined by forces operating *outside* the model. Thus, there are seven equations in the model and seven endogenous variables.

The equation of the IS curve can be found by substituting equations (2) to (4) into the equilibrium condition for the real sector (1). This gives

$$Y = a + b(Y - \bar{T}) + e - fi + \bar{G} + \bar{X} - c - dY$$

Solving this for Y in terms of i gives

$$Y = \frac{a - b\bar{T} + e + \bar{G} + \bar{X} - c}{1 - b + d} - \frac{f}{1 - b + d}\,i \qquad (8)$$

This is the equation of the IS curve.

The equation of the LM curve can be found by substituting equations (6) and (7) into the equilibrium condition for the monetary sector (5). This gives

$$\bar{M}_S = kY + g - hi$$

Solving this for Y in terms of i gives

$$Y = \frac{\bar{M}_S - g}{k} + \frac{h}{k}\,i \qquad (9)$$

This is the equation of the LM curve. Expressions for the equilibrium level of national income and the equilibrium rate of interest can now be found by solving equations (8) and (9) simultaneously.

THE ECONOMICS OF CYCLES AND GROWTH

CYCLICAL FLUCTUATIONS

ECONOMIC GROWTH AND DEVELOPMENT

24 CYCLICAL FLUCTUATIONS

Learning objectives

After reading this chapter, you should be able to:

- describe the four main phases of a trade cycle: slump, recovery, boom and deflation
- show how interaction between the multiplier and the accelerator can result in cumulative movements in national income and possibly also account for turning points in national income movements
- work through a numerical example showing under what conditions the multiplier-accelerator interaction may lead to cyclical variations in national income
- discuss the importance of ceilings, floors, random disturbances and monetary influences on the trade cycle

Introduction

Cyclical fluctuations in the level of economic activity in an economy can be observed by examining *annual* changes in real national income (or real output) over a long period of years; these changes are inversely related to variations in the rate of unemployment. Figure 24.1 shows the fluctuations in the rate of unemployment in the United Kingdom from 1878 to 1992. Notice that the fluctuations up to 1920 were fairly regular with an average of about eight or nine years from peak to peak and trough to trough. After the Great Depression of the 1920s and 1930s, however, the fluctuations were much reduced, possibly a result of the adoption of Keynesian demand-management policies by successive governments in the 1950s and 1960s. None the less, even in this period, the economy was subjected to fairly regular cycles of minor expansions and recessions. In the 1970s, the trade cycle was masked by world recession, due in part to the energy crisis, which resulted in an upward trend in the rate of unemployment. The downturn in economic activity in the early 1980s pushed the unemployment rate over 10 per cent. The recovery of the late 1980s was followed by a further downturn which caused unemployment to rise yet again in the early 1990s.

Trade cycle *A trade cycle depicts fluctuations in the level of economic activity over a period of time*

The phases of the trade cycle (sometimes called the business cycle) – slump, recovery, boom and deflation – are illustrated in Fig. 24.2. An economy in a slump or depression is generally characterised by high demand-deficient unemployment of both labour and capital. A low level of both consumption and investment demand leads firms to cut back on their production, lay off workers and leave capital equipment lying idle. Although money may be available for firms to borrow and

Slump *The phase of a trade cycle in which aggregate demand is low relative to full employment output*

Fig. 24.1. *The rate of unemployment in the United Kingdom, 1878–1992.* Notice the fairly regular cycles from 1878 to 1920, the high unemployment of the Great Depression, and the marked upward trend of unemployment since about 1970.

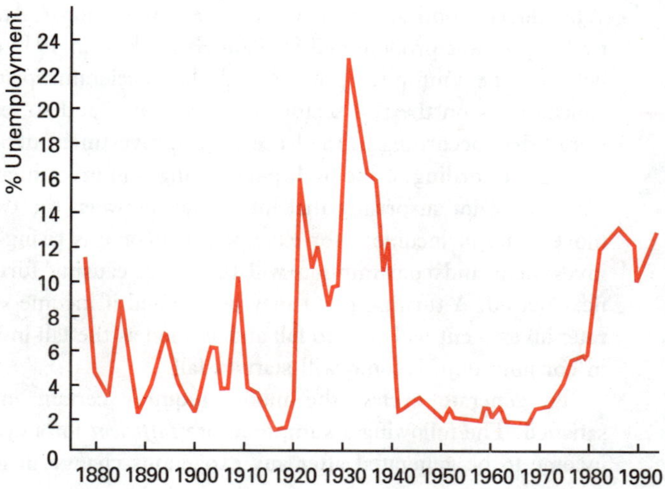

Fig. 24.2. *The phases of a trade cycle.* There are four main phases to a typical trade cycle: slump, recovery, boom and deflation.

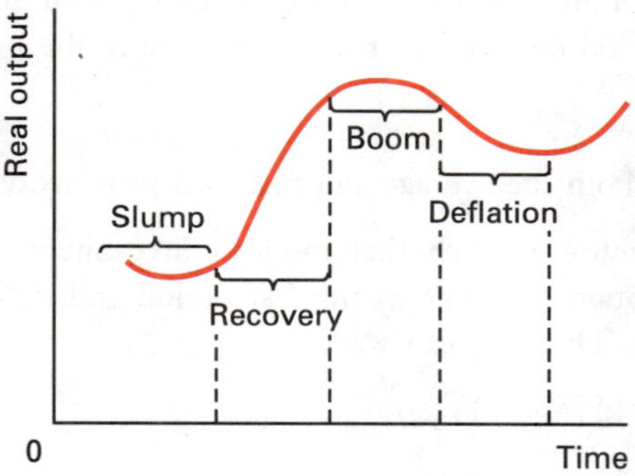

interest rates may be low, investment will not be increased because of pessimistic expectations.

Recovery *In this phase, aggregate demand is increasing and business expectations are improving*

In the recovery phase, however, the level of aggregate demand is rising and consequently businesses become more optimistic. Generally, this is a period of rising consumer demand, rising investment demand, expanding output levels and a falling rate of unemployment. Eventually, the economy reaches the peak of the cycle – the so-called boom period. This is a time of low unemployment, a high level of demand, firms working at full capacity earning high profits, an increasing rate of inflation and probably rising interest rates as investors compete with each other for limited loanable funds.

Boom *The phase in which aggregate demand is close to full employment output. With firms working at full capacity, inflation may increase*

Finally, in the deflation or recession phase, the demands of both firms and households start to fall, firms' profits dwindle and output and employment levels are reduced. Businesses, once again, become pessimistic about the future level of demand for their products and so become extremely reluctant to invest in new capital, even for replacement purposes. Eventually, this contracting economy reaches the slump again and the whole process restarts.

Deflation *The phase in which aggregate demand starts to decline and business confidence to sag. The level of unemployment increases*

The objective of this chapter is to consider the possible causes of this cyclical movement in economic activity. We concentrate on the famous multiplier–accelerator theory, so this is a good point at which to review your understanding of the multiplier process (Ch. 19) and the accelerator principle (Ch. 20).

Multiplier–accelerator interaction

Why do economies experience cyclical fluctuations? An interesting theory of the trade cycle was propounded by Paul Samuelson in 1939 and is based on interaction between the multiplier process and the accelerator principle. This simple model concentrates on the real sector of the economy and so excludes monetary variables. Recall that, according to the 'accelerator', investment depends on *changes* in income, and that according to the multiplier, changes in investment cause changes in income. Thus, it is not surprising that interaction between the two can result in cumulative movements in income – for example, if income is rising at an increasing rate, both investment and consumption will be rising, causing further rises in income in the next period. A turning point may be reached if income starts to rise at a decreasing rate; investment will start to fall and as soon as the fall in investment exceeds the rise in consumption, income will start to fall.

To generate cycles, the model requires certain important conditions to be satisfied. The following assumptions are *sufficient* for a cyclical movement in national income to be generated after any exogenous change in investment or consumption spending:

(a) The consumption function is lagged one period so that consumption in the current period depends on national income in the previous period. That is,

$$C_t = cY_{t-1}$$

where c is both the average and marginal propensity to consume.

(b) The accelerator is such that induced investment depends on the difference between national income in the last period and national income in the period before that. Thus, we can write:

$$I_t = I_0 + v(Y_{t-1} - Y_{t-2})$$

where I_0 is exogenous investment and v is the accelerator coefficient.

Damped cycle *A cycle in which the fluctuations in real output become smaller and smaller over time*

(c) The values of c and v must both lie below the curve shown in Fig. 24.3. For example, if the values of c and v lie in the area ABC (say, $c = 0.5$ and $v = 0.5$ as at point E) then any exogenous change in consumption or investment will generate a damped cycle like that illustrated in Fig. 24.4; it is said to be damped because the fluctuations in real output become smaller and smaller over time. But

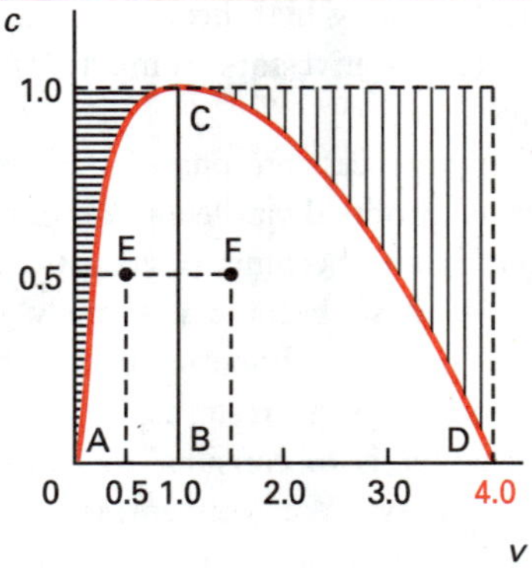

Fig. 24.3. ***Different values of c and v to generate cycles.*** Values of *c* and *v* in the area ABC generate damped cycles. Values in the area BCD generate explosive cycles. Values above the curve do not generate cycles.

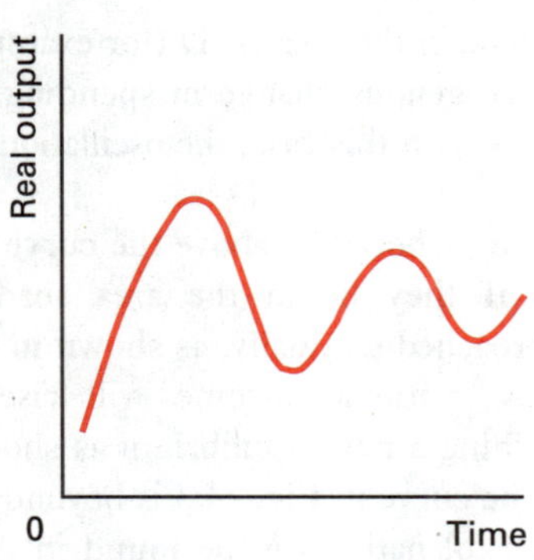

Fig. 24.4. ***A damped cycle.*** The fluctuations become smaller and smaller over time.

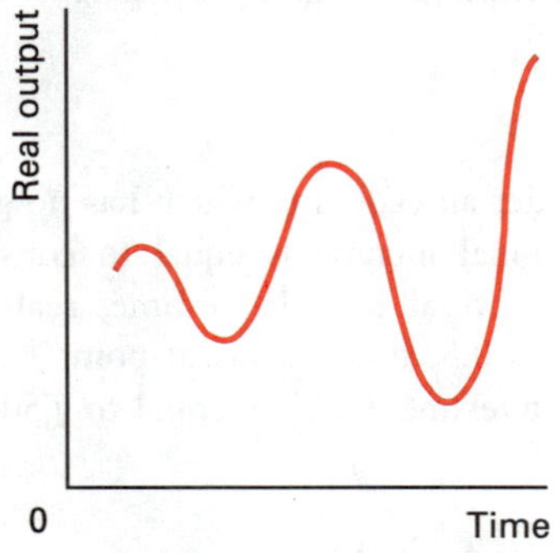

Fig. 24.5. ***An explosive cycle.*** The fluctuations become larger and larger over time.

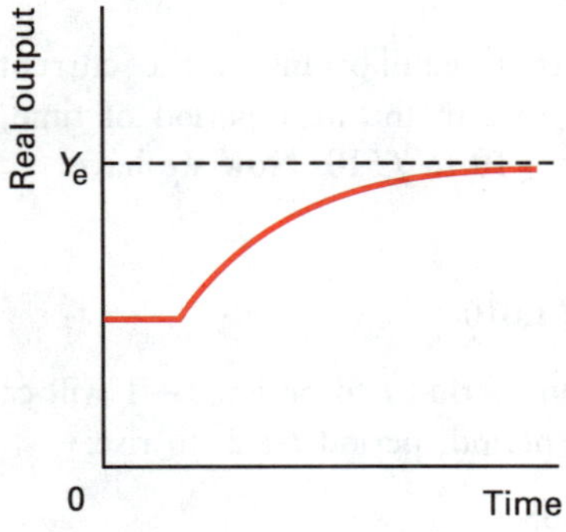

Fig. 24.6. ***No cycle, but damped.*** The value of real output gradually approaches the new equilibrium value, Y_e.

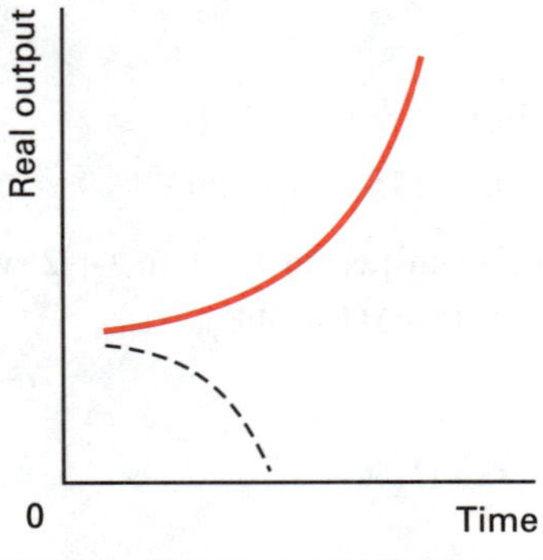

Fig. 24.7. ***No cycle, but explosive.*** The value of real output rises (or falls) indefinitely.

Explosive cycle *A cycle in which the fluctuations in real output become larger and larger over time*

if the values of c and v lie in the area BCD (for example, $c = 0.5$ and $v = 1.5$ as at point F) then any exogenous change in spending will generate an explosive cycle like that in Fig. 24.5; in this case, the oscillations get larger and larger over time.

If the values of c and v should lie above the curve in Fig. 24.3, no cycles will be generated at all. If they lie in the area shaded horizontally, the new equilibrium Y_e is approached gradually, as shown in Fig. 24.6. If they lie in the area shaded vertically, national income will rise or fall explosively and indefinitely never reaching a new equilibrium as shown in Fig. 24.7.

The derivation of the curve in Fig. 24.3 is beyond the scope of this textbook. A full derivation and explanation can be found in A. C. Chiang, *Fundamental Methods in Mathematical Economies*, McGraw-Hill, 1984 (Ch. 17). However, we can partially demonstrate its validity by means by two simple numerical examples.

Example I: a damped cycle

To simplify matters, consider an economy which has no government activity and no foreign trade, so that national income is equal to consumption plus investment. Suppose that for the last several periods of time, real national income has been constant at £1,000. Let $c = 0.5$, $v = 0.5$ (as at point E in Fig. 24.3) and suppose that initially autonomous investment (I_0) is equal to £500. We have

$$C_t = 0.5Y_{t-1} = £500$$

$$I_t = 500 + 0.5(Y_{t-1} - Y_{t-2}) = £500$$

$$Y_t = C_t + I_t = £1,000$$

This economy, then, is in equilibrium in the current period (called period t). Suppose now, though, that in the next period of time, period $t+1$, autonomous investment (I_0) rises by £10 to £510. Now we have

$$Y_{t+1} = C_{t+1} + I_{t+1}$$

$$= 500 + 510 = £1,010$$

This rise in income from period t to period $t+1$ will cause both consumption and investment in the next period, period $t+2$, to rise:

$$C_{t+2} = 0.5Y_{t+1} = £505$$

$$I_{t+2} = 510 + 0.5(Y_{t+1} - Y_t)$$

$$= 510 + 5 = £515$$

This means that $Y_{t+2} = C_{t+2} + I_{t+2}$

$$= 505 + 515 = £1,020$$

This further rise in income from period $t+1$ to $t+2$ will cause consumption and investment in period $t+3$ to rise yet again:

$$C_{t+3} = 0.5Y_{t+2} = £510$$

$$I_{t+3} = 510 + 0.5(Y_{t+2} - Y_{t+1})$$

$$= 510 + 5 = £515$$

Therefore, $Y_{t+3} = 510 + 515 = £1{,}025$

Notice that this rise in income is smaller than the previous rises. Consumption will rise in period $t+4$:

$$C_{t+4} = 0.5Y_{t+3} = £512.50$$

But investment will start to fall because, according to the accelerator, the *level* of investment depends on the *change* in income (which has now begun to decrease):

$$I_{t+4} = 510 + 0.5(Y_{t+3} - Y_{t+2})$$
$$= 510 + 2.5 = £512.50$$

Therefore, $Y_{t+4} = 512.5 + 512.5 = £1{,}025$

So, after rising from periods t to $t+3$, income has now stayed the same from period $t+3$ to $t+4$. Consumption in period $t+5$ will therefore be unchanged:

$$C_{t+5} = 0.5\ Y_{t+4} = £512.50$$

But investment will fall again:

$$I_{t+5} = 510 + 0.5(Y_{t+4} - Y_{t+3})$$
$$= £510$$

Since investment falls and consumption stays the same, income in period $t+5$ will be lower than in period $t+4$:

$$Y_{t+5} = 512.5 + 510 = £1{,}022.50$$

So far in the analysis, the single increase in autonomous investment of £10 has caused income to rise from £1,000 to £1,025 in the first four time periods and then to start to fall in the fifth. Taking the time-path to period $t+12$, we obtain a clearly *damped*, cyclical variation in real national income. This is summarised in Table 24.1 and graphed in Fig. 24.8.

Table 24.1 Cyclical variations in consumption, investment and national income following an increase in autonomous investment – damped case.

Time period	Consumption $C_t = 0.5Y_{t-1}$	Investment $I_t = I_0 + 0.5 (Y_{t-1} - Y_{t-2})$	National $Y_t = C_t + I_t$
t	500	500	1,000
$t+1$	500	510	1,010
$t+2$	505	515	1,020
$t+3$	510	515	1,025
$t+4$	512.5	512.5	1,025
$t+5$	512.5	510	1,022.5
$t+6$	511.25	508.75	1,020
$t+7$	510	508.75	1,018.75
$t+8$	509.375	509.375	1,018.75
$t+9$	509.375	510	1,019.375
$t+10$	509.6875	510.3125	1,020
$t+11$	510	510.3125	1,020.3125
$t+12$	510.15625	510.15625	1,020.3125
⋮	⋮	⋮	⋮

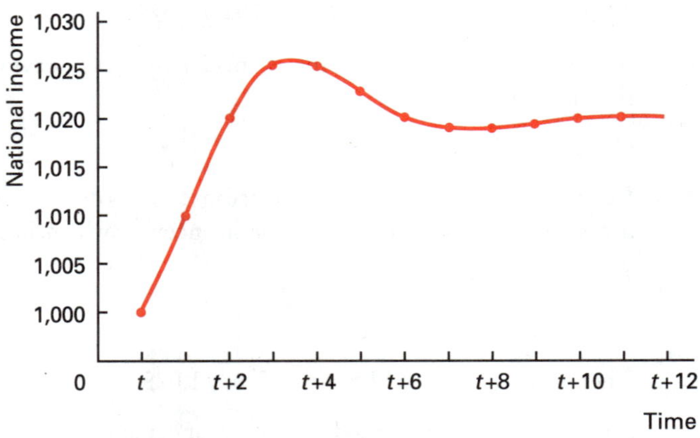

Fig. 24.8. Damped cyclical variation in national income. National income gradually approaches the new equilibrium value.

Notice that eventually the cycle will converge on the new equilibrium level of income of £1,020 (that is, an increase of £20 since the multiplier is 2 in this example). Only when income settles at £1,020 can we say that the full multiplier effect has taken place. However, no new equilibrium position is reached in the case of an explosive cycle, as is shown in the next example.

Example II: explosive cycle

In the same closed economy with no government, suppose now that $c = 0.5$ and $v = 1.5$ (as at point F in Fig. 24.3). Assume as before that national income has been constant for several time periods at £1,000, and that autonomous investment is

Table 24.2 Cyclical variations in consumption, investment and national income following an increase in autonomous investment – explosive case.

Time period	Consumption $C_t = 0.5Y_{t-1}$	Investment $I_t = I_0 + 1.5(Y_{t-1} - Y_{t-2})$	National $Y_t = C_t + I_t$
t	500	500	1,000
$t + 1$	500	510	1,010
$t + 2$	505	525	1,030
$t + 3$	515	540	1,055
$t + 4$	527.5	547.5	1,075
$t + 5$	537.5	540	1,077.5
$t + 6$	538.75	513.75	1,052.5
$t + 7$	526.75	472.5	999.25
$t + 8$	499.63	430.12	929.75
$t + 9$	464.88	405.75	870.63
$t + 10$	435.31	421.31	856.62
$t + 11$	428.31	489	917.31
$t + 12$	458.66	601.03	1,059.69
$t + 13$	529.84	652.38	1,182.22
$t + 14$	591.11	693.8	1,284.91
$t + 15$	642.45	664.03	1,306.48
$t + 16$	653.24	542.37	1,195.61
$t + 17$	597.80	343.69	941.49
$t + 18$	470.75	255.9	726.65
⋮	⋮	⋮	⋮

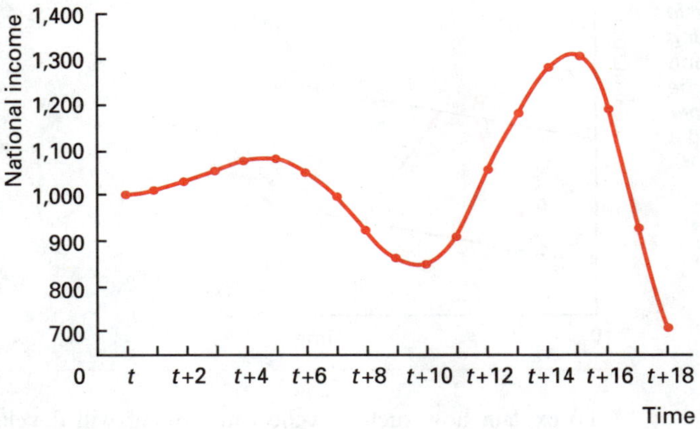

Fig. 24.9. Explosive cyclical variation in national income. The fluctuations in national income become larger and larger over time in this case.

initially equal to £500. This means that the economy is in equilibrium in period t. Now suppose, as before, that autonomous investment rises to £510 in period $t+1$. This rise in spending will raise national income to £1,010 in period $t+1$ and this will cause both consumption and investment to increase in the next period, period $t+2$:

$$C_{t+2} = 0.5Y_{t+1} = £505$$

$$I_{t+2} = 510 + 1.5(Y_{t+1} - Y_t)$$

$$= 510 + 15 = £525$$

This means that $Y_{t+2} = 505 + 525 = £1{,}030$

Notice that both investment and national income have already risen above the levels reached in the previous example. The time-path to period $t+18$ is summarised in Table 24.2 and graphed in Fig. 24.9. An *explosive* cyclical variation in national income results. Although the arithmetic becomes quite laborious, it is a worthwhile exercise for the reader to work through the table carefully and confirm the results. Some further exercises, which include non-cyclical time-paths, are set at the end of the chapter.

Ceilings and floors

We have seen that the multiplier–accelerator model outlined above is capable under certain circumstances of generating cycles automatically following any change in autonomous spending. Depending on the values assigned to c and v, the cycle may be damped or explosive. A re-examination of Fig. 24.1 shows that cycles in practice display no obvious tendency either to diminish or increase in amplitude over time – indeed, particularly in the nineteenth century, the amplitude of the cycles was remarkably constant. A possible explanation for this is that the cycle is inherently explosive, as in our Example II, but is constrained within a band determined by an upper limit above which real output cannot rise, called a *ceiling*, and a lower limit below which real output will not fall, called a *floor*. The cycle thus generated will tend to have a constant amplitude determined by the distance between the ceiling and floor. Such a cyclical movement in real output is illustrated in Fig. 24.10.

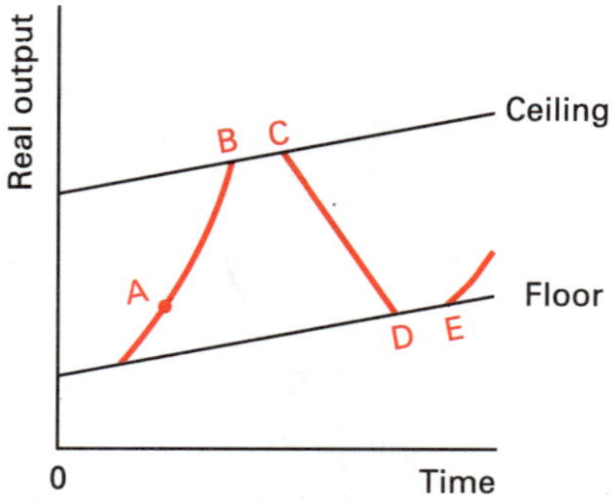

Fig. 24.10. ***A cycle constrained by a ceiling and floor.*** The rises and falls in real output may be constrained by an upper limit (a ceiling) and a lower limit (a floor).

To explain how such a cyclical movement will develop, start at point A on the graph in Fig. 24.10. This is in the recovery phase: consequently demand is increasing, output is expanding and unemployment is falling. In terms of the multiplier–accelerator interaction, rising investment is causing national income to rise via the multiplier effect and the rising level of national income induces more investment to occur, after a lag, via the accelerator. Soon, though, full employment will be reached (point B on the graph); this determines the so-called ceiling because now real output can only rise as new net investment comes into operation. Firms may want to produce more at point B but are unable to do so because of insufficient resources. This check to the growth of output and income will soon affect firms' investment plants via the accelerator. In fact, since the increase in income has slowed down, induced investment will actually fall and it will not be long before this causes income itself to fall via the multipier. The existence of the ceiling, then, brings about a turning-point and after point C, real output starts to fall.

Real output will continue to fall with the multiplier and accelerator interacting with each other until the floor is reached. What determines the position of the floor? Well, clearly income cannot fall below zero, so in a sense that represents an 'absolute' floor; in practice, however, although investment demand can fall to zero when firms are so pessimistic that they have no demand for either new or replacement capital, consumption demand must always be positive, if only to sustain life. This consumption spending must represent the floor below which the level of income cannot realistically be expected to fall. Furthermore it is likely that some investment will be occurring somewhere in the economy so that aggregate investment is never likely actually to disappear completely. Once point D has been reached, output will have stopped falling and eventually, as existing machines wear out or become obsolete, some replacement investment will become unavoidable. This will set the multiplier–accelerator interaction into operation again.

The existence of the floor, then, brings about yet another turning-point so that after point E on the graph, real output is rising. This brings us back to the recovery phase and the whole process starts over again. Notice that each successive peak and trough is likely to be above all preceding ones because of underlying growth in the economy's productive capacity.

Random disturbances

The existence of ceilings and floors can help to explain the regularity of cycles when c and v are such that, without these constraints, cycles would be explosive. But suppose that c and v took on values consistent with damped cycles, how then could

Fig. 24.11. ***A cycle caused by random disturbances.*** Within a ceiling and floor, changes in real output may be caused by a variety of random disturbances.

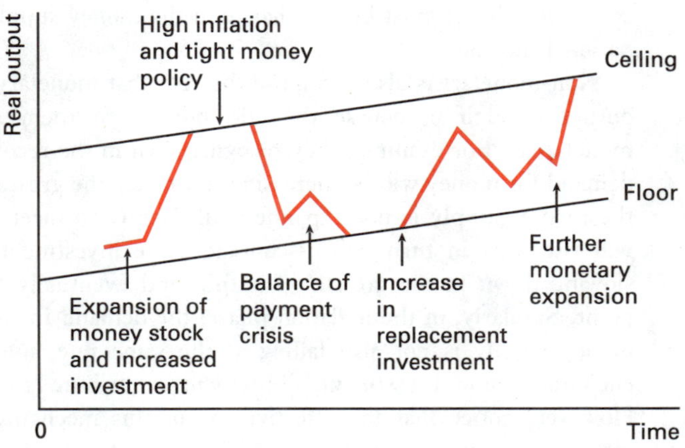

we explain the observed regularity of cyclical fluctuations? (In fact, this is an important question because empirical studies suggest that both c and v are less than 1, so damped rather than explosive cycles are likely.)

One possible answer has been suggested by the economist R. Frisch. He argues that, even though fluctuations around a country's equilibrium growth path are likely to be damped, random disturbances will be continually occurring to stop the equilibrium path from being achieved and to maintain the cyclical variations in a fairly regular pattern. No sooner has one cycle started to diminish in amplitude than another disturbance to the economy occurs, starting off a new cycle. The types of disturbances which could do this are *sudden changes in investment, balance of payments crises, changes in the money supply, rapid inflation and the policies designed to curb it, population movements, industrial disputes*, or even *wars*.

Of course, it is possible for more than one disturbance to occur at the same time so that the cyclical variations generated, although inherently damped, may be quite large. This means that the 'ceiling' and 'floor' analysis may become relevant here as well as in the explosive cycles case. Consider the hypothetical random disturbances shown in Fig. 24.11 which give rise to fairly realistic variations in real output.

In this kind of model, real output is volatile, occasionally reaching the ceiling or floor, with each successive random disturbance pushing real income upwards or downwards and with the underlying stabilising influences of the multiplier and accelerator.

Monetary influences

One of the random disturbances mentioned in the previous section was a change in the money supply. Consider now to what extent changes in a country's monetary variables may be responsible for cyclical variations in real output.

Recall from Ch. 23 that monetarists put a great deal of faith in the observed correlation between changes in the money supply and changes in national income. In particular, the study by Friedman and Schwartz emphasises the observation that all major recessions have been preceded by a fall in the money supply and all major inflations by an increase in the money supply. By attempting to show that the monetary changes were not caused by the changes in national income, they concluded that it must be the change in the money supply that causes the change in national income.

Non-monetarists also recognise the role that monetary changes may have on real output, though of course they do not assign them such a major role as the monetarists. For example, they recognise that in the recovery phase of the cycle, the demand for money will be increasing to finance the greater volume of transactions. If the money supply is not expanded sufficiently to meet this demand, interest rates will rise, this in turn will discourage some investment and so contribute to the slowing down in the growth of output and eventually lead to the upper turning-point. Similarly, in the deflation phase, the demand for money will be falling. If the money supply is not also falling at the same rate, interest rates will fall and so encourage new investment. This will contribute to the lower turning-point. However, notice that the effectiveness of this mechanism clearly depends on the interest-elasticity of investment which, as pointed out in Ch. 20, is likely to be very low in the boom and slump periods of a trade cycle.

Summary

1. The four phases of the trade cycle (or business cycle) are slump, recovery, boom and deflation. In a slump (or depression), there is generally high unemployment, low spending and low business confidence. In the recovery, aggregate demand starts to increase leading to an expanding level of output and a falling rate of unemployment. The boom is typically a period of high employment, output growth and an increasing rate of inflation. Finally, in the deflation (or recession) phase, aggregate demand starts to fall and business confidence is diminished.
2. The purpose of trade cycle theory is to explain the cumulative movements in national income and the upper and lower turning points which characterise cyclical movements in economic activity.
3. Interaction between the multiplier process and the accelerator principle can generate cyclical movements in national income, given certain values for the marginal propensity to consume and the 'accelerator coefficient'. A damped cycle gradually approaches the new equilibrium level of income. An explosive cycle has fluctuations which become larger and larger over time.
4. A possible explanation for the relatively constant amplitude of trade cycles may lie in the existence of ceilings and floors. A ceiling is an upper limit above which real output cannot rise (for example, the full employment level of real output), while a floor is a lower limit below which real output cannot fall (possibly determined by some minimum level of consumption).
5. Changes in real output may also be caused by various types of random disturbances. Given the existence of a ceiling and floor, random

disturbances may be responsible for inducing the upward or downward movement of the cycle.

6. Monetarists stress the role of changes in the money supply in the determination of trade cycles, arguing that many major recessions have been preceded by falls in the money supply, and many major inflations have been preceded by excessive increases in the money supply.

Exercises

1. Review your understanding of the following terms:

trade cycle	damped cycle
slump	explosive cycle
recovery	ceiling
boom	floor
recession	turning-point
deflation	random disturbance

2. Using the multiplier–accelerator model developed in this chapter, trace out the time-path for national income over 10 years when

   (a) $c = 0.8$ and $v = 0.1$;
   (b) $c = 0.5$ and $v = 4$.

   Comment on your results.

3. Obtain data on gross domestic fixed capital formation, real national income and the number of unfilled job vacancies for the United Kingdom from 1970 onwards. Plot the data on a graph and comment on any cyclical variations.

4. Discuss the extent to which the cyclical fluctuations observed in question (3) may be a result of : (a) monetary variables; (b) random disturbances.

5. 'An essential characteristic of cyclical behaviour is not only that expansion and contraction follow each other, but that each phase of the cycle contains within it the seeds to generate the succeeding phase' (R. Levacic, *Macroeconomics*). How can this aspect of the trade cycle be explained?

25 ECONOMIC GROWTH AND DEVELOPMENT

Learning objectives

After reading this chapter, you should be able to:

- identify the main factors influencing the economic growth of a country
- outline the major benefits and costs that result from economic growth
- describe the key indicators of developing countries
- explain the main theories of economic development
- appreciate the role of population in economic development
- assess the contribution that international trade, investment and aid can make to economic development.

Introduction

Economic growth *A sustained increase in a country's productive capacity*

Less developed country *A country with low real national income per capita, a large agricultural sector, high population growth, a low capital-labour ratio and poor infrastructure*

Developed country *A country in which real national income per capita is relatively high and which enjoys a relatively high standard of living*

Economic growth may be defined as an increase in a country's productive capacity, identifiable by a sustained rise in real national income over a period of years. A country's annual rate of economic growth, then, can best be measured by taking the average percentage increase in national income over a long period of time, say five or ten years. The figure obtained will be an estimate of the average annual rate of growth in the country's productive capacity, assuming that the rate of unemployment is roughly the same at the beginning and end of the period.

Economic growth and economic *development* are obviously closely related; for the purposes of this chapter, however, we draw an important distinction between them. A country is enjoying economic development when it is experiencing economic growth, as defined above, and at the same time is undergoing major structural changes in its economy, like a shift from agriculture to manufacturing. With this distinction in mind, we deal with economic growth in the context of an industrialised economy, such as the United Kingdom or the United States, and economic development in the context of a less developed country, such as India or Nigeria. In general, less developed countries can be identified by their relative poverty. They do have other characteristics which distinguish them from the developed countries, but low national income per head is their major distinguishing feature.

In the first section of this chapter, we examine the main determinants of economic growth and their policy implications. In the second section, we consider some of the main problems of less developed countries and the possible ways of alleviating them.

Main determinants of economic growth

There are three main determinants of a country's rate of economic growth which we consider: the growth of its labour force; the growth of its capital stock; technical progress.

Growth of the labour force

A growing labour supply may enable a community to produce bigger combinations of goods and services and so bring about an outward shift in its production possibility frontier. This, in turn, can lead to an increase in output per head and hence a potential improvement in social welfare. The growth of the labour force itself will depend on the following main factors: (a) the 'natural' increase in the population; (b) international migration; (c) the participation rate. Consider these in turn.

(a) *The natural increase in population* is determined by the excess of the birth rate over the death rate. If a country's population is below its 'optimum' size (see below), then a natural increase in population will eventually lead to a rise in output of goods and services *per head*. The population growth rate, though, is influenced by complex social factors such as customs, attitudes and beliefs about marriages and family size. Death rates and birth rates are also influenced by such factors as the availability of medical facilities, old peoples' homes and ante-natal care, including help and advice on contraception.

In general, a fast growing population means that younger people form an increasing proportion of the labour force. A younger work-force may be presumed to be more energetic and diligent with a potential for greater geographical and occupational mobility than an older work-force. A slow-growing population, on the other hand, tends to lead to a rising proportion of older people in the economically active sector and a rising dependency ratio of the old and retired to the total population.

Finally, note that since population growth causes an increase in the number of consumers as well as an expansion of the labour force, the rate of economic growth caused by population growth must exceed the rate of population growth if output *per head* (and therefore potential social welfare) is to increase. If we denote the rate of economic growth by g and natural population growth by n, then, other things being equal, for an increase in potential social welfare, we require that $g>n$.

(b) *International migration* is the flow of people between countries and is largely determined by the degree of international labour mobility. Net immigration will tend to add to a country's labour force while net emigration will tend to reduce it. Such labour mobility, though, is influenced by differences in languages, customs and traditions between countries, job opportunities and promotion prospects, and perhaps more important, laws governing immigration.

(c) *The participation rate* is the proportion of the economically active population to the total population. A rise in this rate would amount to an increase in the size of the labour force. The participation rate is determined by the extent to which the different age groups and the sexes in the population are able by law, customs, tradition and trade union regulations and attitudes to participate in labour market activity. For instance, the equal pay legislation in the United Kingdom should tend to raise the participation rate of the female labour force (see Ch. 16). On the other hand, raising the school-leaving age and lowering the retirement age have the effect of reducing the participation rate.

Growth of the capital stock

An expansion of a country's capital stock through net investment, just like an expansion of its labour force, increases the country's stock of productive resources and so represents another possible source of economic growth. We have noted before that investment (which enables more consumer goods to be produced in the future) requires refraining from some current consumption so that resources can be channelled into the production of the various forms of capital. In other words, savings are required in order that investment can take place.

In our analysis of the simple Keynesian model in Ch. 19, we highlighted *one* role of investment in the economy: that it is a component of aggregate demand. Since that model is short-term only, we were able to ignore the fact that when net investment takes place, an addition to the country's stock of capital occurs (recall that by net investment we mean that over and above the investment required to replace worn out or obsolete equipment). In a long-term model, however, we must take into account the two roles of investment: that it is *a component of aggregate demand* and that it is *an addition to the stock of productive resources*. This is the objective of the Harrod–Domar model of economic growth – one of the simplest growth theories which extends the simple short-run Keynesian model into the long-run.

The Harrod–Domar growth model This model is named after its originators, the English economist, Sir Roy Harrod and the American, E. Domar. Since it is a simple model, we must start by setting out its major assumptions:

(a) We assume that the economy is closed and that there is no government economic activity. This means that there are no imports, exports, government expenditures or taxes in the model and the condition for equilibrium is that planned investment should equal planned saving.

(b) There are only two factors of production, labour (L) and capital (K), and in our simple version of the model, there is no technical progress.

(c) Labour is homogeneous, measured in its own units and grows at the constant natural rate of growth, n.

(d) There are constant returns to scale. This means that if both labour and capital are increased by a given proportion, output will also increase by that proportion.

(e) Saving (S) is a fixed proportion of income (Y). That is, $S = sY$ where s is both the average and marginal propensity to save. Investment (I) is autonomous and there is no depreciation.

Fixed proportions production function *A production function in which the factor inputs are employed in fixed proportions*

(f) The potential level of national income (Y_p) is proportional to the quantity of capital and to the quantity of labour. Thus, we can write $K = vY_p$ and $L = uY_p$, where v is a constant capital–output ratio and u is a constant labour–output ratio. This type of production function is called a fixed proportions production function. The isoquants illustrating such a function are L-shaped as shown in Fig. 25.1. Both labour and capital have to be employed in fixed

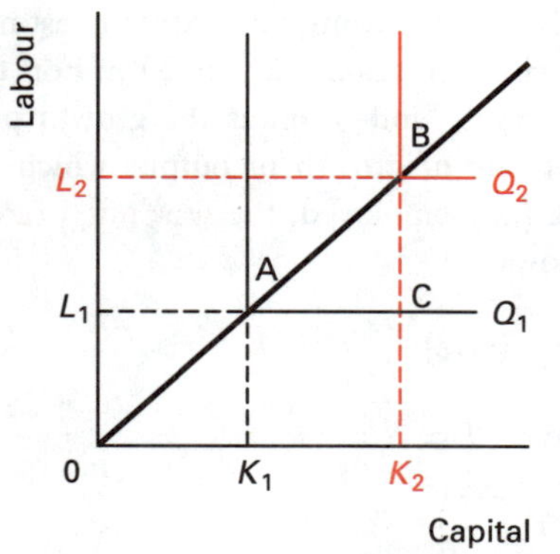

Fig. 25.1. Isoquant map illustrating a fixed proportions production function. Cost-minimising producers employ labour and capital in fixed proportions along the ray 0AB.

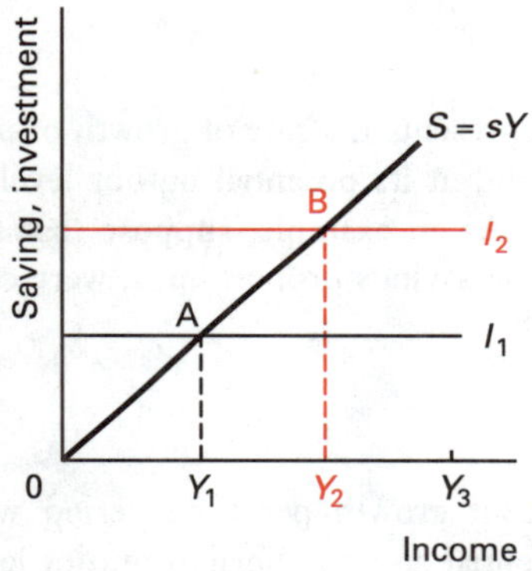

Fig. 25.2. Determination of the equilibrium level of income with a growing capital stock. An increase in investment leads to an increase in the equilibrium level of income, but also raises potential output. This requires a further increase in investment in order to maintain the equilibrium level of income at the potential output level.

combinations: in the graph, increasing labour and capital from $0L_1$ and $0K_1$ to $0L_2$ and $0K_2$ increases output from Q_1 to Q_2 (that is, from point A to B). Increasing only one of the factors, though, say capital from $0K_1$ to $0K_2$, keeping labour unchanged, leaves output unchanged at Q_1 (that is, from point A to C).

Now consider Fig 25.2, starting at the equilibrium point A. The initial level of investment is I_1 which equals saving at the income level $0Y_1$. Over time, however, the investment adds to the capital stock and so increases the economy's level of potential output, say to $0Y_2$. The following analysis shows what the increase in potential output (ΔY_p) will be:

$K = vY_p$ (from assumption (f))

Therefore, $\Delta K = v\Delta Y_p$

But $\Delta K = I_1$, so we have

$$\Delta Y_p = \frac{I_1}{v} \qquad [1]$$

The new level of income, $0Y_2$, will only be an equilibrium level of income if aggregate demand increases. Assuming that the consumption and saving functions are stable, this increase in demand must come from an increase in investment. In fact, investment must rise to I_2 as shown in Fig. 25.2. Now I_2 intersects the saving line at point B where $0Y_2$ is the equilibrium level of income.

As soon as the new capital from this extra investment comes into operation, potential output will rise yet again, say to $0Y_3$. For this to be an equilibrium, investment must rise again – and so on as the growth process take place.

Warranted rate of growth *The rate of growth which keeps the capital stock fully employed*

Harrod named that rate of growth of output which maintains equilibrium and keeps the capital stock fully employed, the warranted rate of growth (g_w). This rate can be derived as follows.

$$\Delta Y = \frac{I}{v} \qquad \text{(from [1] above)}$$

In equilibrium, we have $I = S = sY$

By substitution, $$\Delta Y = \frac{sY}{v}$$

Rearranging, $$\frac{\Delta Y}{Y} = \frac{s}{v} = g_w$$

The expression $\Delta Y/Y$ represents the rate of growth of output required to keep the economy in equilibrium and at its potential output level. It is, therefore, Harrod's warranted rate of growth. As an example, suppose that the capital–output ratio, v, were equal to 4 and that the savings proportion, s, were equal to 0.2. The warranted rate of growth would be:

$$g_w = \frac{0.2}{4} = 5 \text{ per cent}$$

This means that 5 per cent growth per time period would be necessary in this economy to keep the potential and equilibrium output levels equal. Notice that the warranted rate of growth can be increased by policies designed to increase the propensity to save or to reduce the capital–output ratio by increasing the productivity of capital.

Natural rate of growth *The rate at which the labour force is growing*

Of course, given the fixed proportions production function in this model, output can only grow at the warranted rate, s/v, if sufficient labour is made available. The labour force, however, is assumed to be growing at the constant natural rate of growth n: if this exceeds s/v, the warranted rate can be achieved but will lead to an increasing rate of labour unemployment; if n is less than s/v, the actual rate of growth will fall short of the warranted rate and unemployed capital will be created. Thus, for an equilibrium growth path which maintains full employment of both labour and capital, the following condition must be satisfied:

$$\frac{s}{v} = n$$

That is, the warranted rate of growth must be equal to the natural rate of growth.

Unfortunately, s, v and n are all constants in the Harrod–Domar model and unrelated to one another. It would, therefore, be a 'fluke' if the ratio of s to v should just be equal to n. We can conclude that the equilibrium rate of growth in the Harrod–Domar model is highly unlikely to be achieved automatically. Furthermore, when s/v is not equal to n, the economy will either experience increasing labour unemployment (when $s/v<n$) or increasing under-utilisation of capital (when $s/v>n$). When such disequilibria occur, there are no forces generated to restore the equilibrium growth path. In other words, the equilibrium in the Harrod–Domar model is an unstable, or 'knife-edge', equilibrium.

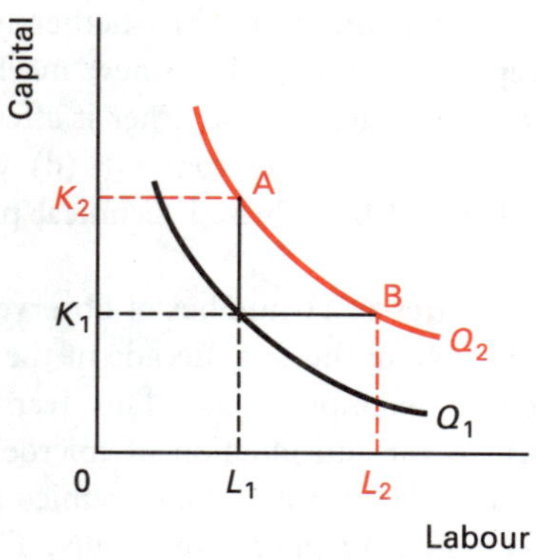

Fig. 25.3. Isoquant map illustrating a neo-classical production function. With this production function, it is possible to increase output from Q_1 to Q_2 by increasing the capital stock from $0K_1$ to $0K_2$ keeping the labour force unchanged, or by increasing the labour force from $0L_1$ to $0L_2$ keeping the capital stock unchanged.

Main drawback of the Harrod–Domar model The model's major drawback is its dependence on an inflexible production function where no substitution whatever is possible between labour and capital. For example, with a fixed proportions production function (illustrated by the L-shaped isoquants in Fig. 25.1), it is not possible to expand output by increasing the supply of one factor of production only – if more machines are acquired but the labour force is unchanged, output cannot expand; similarly, output cannot be kept unchanged by cutting back on the labour force and increasing the capital stock.

It is clearly more realistic to assume that there is some (though not perfect) substitutability between labour and capital. If there is some factor substitution, the isoquant map will have the more familiar shape shown in Fig. 25.3. It is now possible to increase output from Q_1 to Q_2 by increasing the capital stock from $0K_1$ to $0K_2$ keeping the labour force unchanged, or by increasing the labour force from $0L_1$ to $0L_2$, keeping the capital stock unchanged.

With a production function of this kind, the capital–output ratio (v) can vary: for example, v is higher at point A than at point B in Fig. 25.3. Suppose now that the warranted and natural rates of growth are not equal. As an example, let $s/v>n$; this means that the capital stock is growing faster than the labour force and also faster than output. Consequently, the capital–output ratio will rise and as it does so, s/v will fall. This tendency will continue until $s/v = n$ again.

This view, that any discrepancy between the warranted and natural rates of growth will be corrected by a change in v, is the basis of the so-called *neo-classical growth model.*

Technical progress

Technical progress which, as pointed out in Ch. 17, can either be neutral or non-neutral, is another possible source of economic growth. It can take the form of improved techniques of production, improved machinery, inventions or improvements in education; in other words, it is anything which improves the *quality* of the capital stock or labour force. The effect of technical progress is to raise the productivity of the stock of capital and labour. If it is neutral and so raises the productivity of capital and labour by the same proportion, then (given constant returns to scale) output will also rise by that proportion.

Note that the effect of technical progress on a country's equilibrium growth path depends on: (a) whether it raises in the same proportion the productivity of *all* capital and *all* labour, both old and new; (b) whether it raises the productivity of only new labour and capital, including those new machines which are created to replace those which have depreciated; (c) whether it affects only the productivity of capital (that is, capital-biased technical progress); (d) whether it affects only the productivity of labour (that is, labour-biased technical progress).

Technological unemployment *The loss of jobs caused by technological change, such as the introduction of machinery that makes some labour skills obsolete*

Technological unemployment A number of observers have expressed the view that rapid technological change in the final decade of the twentieth century will lead to widespread technological unemployment. This fear has been most frequently illustrated with reference to the introduction of microelectronic technology. As is well known, the real cost of manufacturing semiconductor integrated circuits (employing silicon chips) has been falling dramatically. This development means that it is possible to introduce computer-controlled equipment in a wide range of applications. In warehousing and distribution, products can be transported into stores and even loaded semi-automatically. In manufacturing, computer-controlled machinery can be used for paint-spraying and welding. In fact, the new technology has widespread applications in many fields, from computer typesetting in newspaper production to word processing in offices.

Because the most obvious effect of the introduction of microelectronic technology is the reduction in labour required to perform a given task, the fears of widespread technological unemployment have been expressed. A Department of Employment report argued, however, that the introduction of microelectronic technology would not in itself cause unemployment. Indeed, the report claimed that a bigger threat of unemployment would result from a failure by the United Kingdom to introduce the technology as this would make British industry uncompetitive in international markets.

To the extent that the introduction of new technology increases productivity and reduces costs, demand for products will increase and new jobs can be created. This happened, for example, in the case of banking where, despite the introduction of computers, the level of employment was maintained through diversification and the provision of extra services to customers. The introduction of new machinery also creates new jobs in their design and maintenance.

Growth policies

Assuming that a government's objective is to raise the growth rate, we can conclude that the appropriate policies must be those which influence the growth of the labour force, the growth of the capital stock and the quality of the country's labour and capital.

Fiscal and monetary policies could be used to try and shift resources from the production of consumer goods into the production of investment goods. As far as monetary policy is concerned, low interest rates and increased availability of credit may encourage firms to invest more and so increase the capital stock. Unfortunately, this policy tends not to reduce consumption spending – indeed, it is more likely to increase such spending and so possibly lead to the building up of inflationary pressures. We see later that a high rate of inflation can actually discourage investment.

Fiscal policy may have more chance of success. Assuming that the economy already has full employment and reasonably stable prices, the government may be able to keep aggregate demand unchanged by increasing taxes and directing the revenue raised into capital-creating expenditures. Such a policy should cut aggregate consumption (because disposable income is reduced) and increase aggregate investment and so lead to a higher rate of growth. Increased expenditures on retraining schemes, road-building, financial aid to firms setting up in depressed regions, education, health and research and development are the ones most likely to increase the economy's productive capacity. Unfortunately, policy conflicts still cannot be completely ruled out: raising taxes may lead to higher wage claims which, together with the increased government spending, may have a net inflationary effect on the economy.

In general, governments have given greater priority to the objectives of full employment and stable prices than the growth objective. Consequently, fiscal and monetary policies have been used mostly for the purposes of short-run demand-management and not for the longer-run objective of economic growth.

Indicative planning
A process by which a government sets targets for the growth of output of different sectors. The government may give positive encouragement, such as financial incentives, to producers to achieve these targets

Indicative planning In planned economies (such as China), it is possible for the government to direct resources out of consumer goods industries and into capital goods industries as part of a long-term plan to achieve a higher rate of economic growth. In mixed economies (such as the United Kingdom), however, such direction of resources is not possible. One thing that governments in mixed economies can do is to *indicate* target levels of output for the various industrial sectors and for the economy as a whole. So in the United Kingdom, for example, the government could publish target growth rates for different industries and for national income over the next five years and set out a list of policies designed to assist the growth plan. If firms have confidence in the government's estimates, the figures should provide producers with information which would enable them to harmonise their production decisions more efficiently with those of related firms. Such planning is called 'indicative' planning and was practised successfully in France after the Second World War. It was attempted in the 1960s in the United Kingdom with the setting up of the National Economic Development Council in 1962, the Department of Economic Affairs in 1964 and with the publishing of the National Plan in 1965. There was no coercion and no sanctions were imposed against firms which failed to achieve the stated targets; the aim was simply to indicate the growth path which the government regarded as desirable and thereby guide firms along it.

Indicative planning has both its proponents and opponents. On the one hand, proponents say that it creates growth by giving firms an expectation of increased future demand for their products and, perhaps more important, by helping to harmonise different firms' production decisions. On the other hand, opponents say that such planning represents nothing more than a waste of resources to produce inaccurate statistics. Confidence in the scheme will soon be lost, they say, when firms realise that the government's targets generally fail to be achieved.

Benefits and costs of economic growth

Benefits of economic growth Consider the following reasons why most governments have a high rate of economic growth as a major objective:

(a) *It leads to an increased standard of living.* So long as economic growth results in a rising real income *per head*, then this should mean that a greater quantity or better quality (or both) of goods and services is made available for each person to consume. Recall from Ch. 18, however, that this may not result in an actual improvement in economic welfare – it may only be a potential or pseudo-improvement.

(b) *It can eliminate poverty.* The view that economic growth enables economies to eliminate poverty is debatable and depends upon whether poverty is a relative or absolute term. If it is a relative term, then it will always exist (given a constant distribution of income and wealth) whether economic growth occurs or not. For example, if everyone enjoys a 10 per cent rise in income, the poor remain in exactly the same relative position as before and so are still poor. It should be noted that the poor (who are often pensioners and the unemployed) depend for their incomes on what the government gives them and so are the least likely members of society to benefit directly from economic growth.

(c) *It can redistribute income without making anyone worse off.* It must be emphasised that economic growth itself does not necessarily improve the distribution of income. However, it is possible, when economic growth is taking place, to change the distribution of income in an attempt to achieve greater equity without having to make anyone worse off in absolute terms.

Costs of economic growth Economic growth also imposes some costs on society which has made some economists doubtful as to its continued desirability. Consider the following:

(a) *Growth involves change which benefits many but may harm some.* For example, technological progress may create many new jobs but at the same time may make current jobs obsolete and therefore lead to some redundancies. The need to move to another area or to retrain in order to take up a new job imposes significant costs on those affected.

(b) *Growth has an opportunity cost.* Where economic growth is created by investment of resources in capital goods, the opportunity cost of growth is the current consumption which could otherwise have been enjoyed. The more resources a country devotes to the production of investment goods, the faster the rate of economic growth it can expect to attain and the greater the quantity of consumer goods it can expect to enjoy in the future. So, in effect, current consumption is being sacrificed in order to achieve a higher rate of consumption in the future. Whether or not the sacrifice is worthwhile depends on the amount of extra consumer goods produced in the future and how long it takes to make up for the sacrificed goods.

(c) *Continued growth may not be possible for much longer.* Resources on the Earth are finite and largely irreplaceable. It is argued that at some critical date in the future, economic growth must cease. No matter what new discoveries are made, resources must eventually run out and so the greater the rate of economic growth today, the sooner that critical date will be reached. It is possible, therefore, to argue in favour of a reduced rate of economic growth because this will reduce the rate at which our resources are being used up.

(d) *Growth causes negative externalities.* A rising real national income may impose costs on society in the form of pollution, noise and increased congestion. Besides,

Table 25.1 Average annual growth of GNP per capita, 1965–90: selected countries

Country	Average rate of growth (%)
Japan	4.1
Ireland	3.0
Italy	3.0
Portugal	3.0
Greece	2.8
Belgium	2.6
France	2.4
Spain	2.4
West Germany	2.4
Denmark	2.1
United Kingdom	2.0
Sweden	1.9
Netherlands	1.8
United States	1.7

Source: World Bank, *World Development Report,* 1992.

the losses arising from the exhaustion of non-renewable resources have been underestimated. If these costs could be properly evaluated and included in the estimates of real national income, present estimates would be shown to overstate the benefits of economic growth.

Most governments aim for a high rate of economic growth because of the higher standard of living which they expect it to create in their countries and possibly also because of their desire for national prestige. Economists, however, must bear in mind that growth can impose costs as well as benefits on society and these must be taken into consideration in evaluating the desirability of growth. An added complication arises because many of these costs and benefits have significant inter-generational implications. Table 25.1 shows the average annual growth rates of GNP per capita for the period 1965–90 for the member states of the EC and other selected countries.

Economic development

Economic development
A process in which an economy not only experiences an increase in its real output per head, but also undergoes major structural changes, such as infrastructure development and a reallocation of resources between the agricultural, industrial and service sectors

About one hundred less developed countries (LDCs) in Asia, Africa and Latin America are engaged in a struggle to escape from poverty. Within LDCs, there are often extreme inequalities of income and wealth with pockets of extreme poverty and high levels of unemployment. In the world as a whole, the low- and middle-income countries have about 78 per cent of the total population but only 16 per cent of total income. The disparities of income between the poor and rich nations of the world are illustrated for selected countries in Table 25.2. Notice that per capita income in the United States is one-hundred and eighty-one times that in Ethiopia and more than sixty times that in India.

In spite of some remarkable rates of growth in per capita incomes in recent decades, studies have shown that income inequalities have been widening in a number of LDCs. Perhaps more important, these countries' growth policies have failed to create employment opportunities to match the rates of growth in the labour force and unemployment rates are much higher than the rates of unemployment experienced by the developed countries.

Table 25.2 Per capita incomes for selected countries in 1990.

Country	Per capita income ($)
Developed countries	
Sweden	23,660
West Germany	22,320
Denmark	22,080
United States	21,790
France	19,490
Italy	16,830
United Kingdom	16,100
Less developed countries	
Brazil	2,680
Mexico	2,490
Philippines	730
Egypt	600
Zambia	420
India	350
Nigeria	290
Bangladesh	210
Ethiopia	120
Tanzania	110
Mozambique	80

Source: The World Bank, *World Development Report,* 1992.

Indicators of a developing country

Developing countries are normally characterised by a number of key indicators. These include:

- low GNP per capita
- large agricultural sector
- high population growth rate
- low capital–labour ratio
- poor infrastructure and social services

Consider these in turn.

Low GNP per capita As noted above and illustrated in Table 25.2, developing countries have low GNP per capita figures. The World Bank uses estimates of GNP per capita to classify countries into income groups. In its *World Development Report 1992*, the World Bank defined:

- *low-income economies* as those with a GNP per capita of $610 or less in 1990;
- *middle income economies* as those with a GNP per capita of more than $610 but less than $7,620 in 1990;
- *high-income economies* as those with a GNP per capita of $7,620 or more in 1990.

The low-income and middle-income economies are sometimes referred to as developing economies. As an example, consider India which had a GNP per capita in 1990 of $350. The very low levels of income for much of the Indian population are widely acknowledged with television pictures showing many destitute people living and sleeping on the streets of large cities such as Bombay and Calcutta. On the other hand, of course, there are some groups within the Indian population of about 850 million with relatively high incomes.

Large agricultural sector Developing economies typically have a relatively large proportion of the labour force engaged in agriculture. In most cases, a significant part of the rural population will be engaged in subsistence agriculture. The food and other agricultural outputs are normally consumed within the family and are not marketed.

Subsistence agriculture *Agricultural activity where the outputs are consumed within the family and are not marketed*

World Bank estimates indicate that in 1990, for example, both Mozambique and Somalia derived 65 per cent of their GDP from agriculture. As the economies of low-income countries develop, the share of agriculture in total output and employment declines, and the shares of industry and services increase. Between 1965 and 1990, the contribution of agriculture to India's GDP, for instance, fell from 44 per cent to 31 per cent.

High population growth rate Poor countries often display high rates of population growth. This may be partly due to traditional attitudes towards large families (for example, as a source of help in carrying out tasks or as a source of prestige). Contrast the average annual population growth rate between 1980 and 1990 of a developing country such as Kenya at 3.8 per cent with that of the United Kingdom at only 0.2 per cent: such rapid population growth in a low-income country like Kenya imposes severe strains on limited social facilities, such as education, health and housing.

Low capital–labour ratio A developing country is generally characterised by a low capital–labour ratio. The lack of capital limits the country's ability to employ modern production techniques. A farmer in a developing country might employ a large number of workers with simple tools and equipment, rather than the combine-harvester that would be used in most high-income countries, such as Canada and the United States.

Poor infrastructure and social services Developing countries often suffer from the lack of an adequate infrastructure, such as roads, drinking water and sewerage systems and electricity distribution systems. The World Bank, for example, estimates that some 1.7 billion people in developing countries lack access to sanitation, and about 1 billion do not have access to clean drinking water. In many cases, the absence of electricity and other fuels results in the use of indoor fires for cooking which can lead to serious indoor air pollution.

In addition, rapid population growth and poverty have contributed to severe strains in the provision of social services, such as education and basic health facilities. In general, the inhabitants of low-income countries have a lower life expectancy than those in high-income countries. Contrast, for example, the life expectancy in Mozambique of about 47 years in 1990 with that in high-income countries (about 77 years).

Similar contrasts might be made between levels of literacy in low-income and high-income countries. Despite recent economic progress, it was estimated in 1990 that only 35 per cent of the population in Pakistan was literate. This contrasts with estimates of only 4 per cent illiteracy for high-income countries.

Clearly, the problem of development is not merely that of increasing the national incomes of the LDCs. It is also the problem of finding ways to remove the related evils of poverty, inequality and unemployment. To devise appropriate policies, we must first examine the main causes of economic development.

Theories of economic development

The most frequently asked question in the study of development economics is: what initiates the process of economic development? Unfortunately, there is no single theory which fully explains the causes of development, nor can one draw general conclusions from the economic history of the rich industrial nations whose experiences have been unique. One lesson that can be learned from the industrialised countries is that growth and development are exceedingly complex processes – they combine changes in social and political institutions, the countries' sense of values and belief systems with changes in the methods of production and in the means of exploiting productive resources.

It is now being increasingly recognised that there are no 'laws' of economic development. No *single* theory can be used to explain the ways in which full employment might be achieved in LDCs which have diverse social, geographic and economic characteristics. The following summaries of development theories, therefore, should be treated with care. They merely highlight a few of the main factors which can contribute to industrialisation and economic development.

Classical theory of development This theory asserts that the major cause of economic development is the *rate of investment* which, in turn, depends on the share of profits in the national income. The higher the rate of profits, the faster will be the rate of investment and the rate of economic development.

Early classical writers, like Adam Smith, David Ricardo and J.S. Mill, made contributions to this theory. They maintained that the growth of capital would make more division of labour and specialisation possible and so lead to increased labour productivity and higher wages. As development proceeded, both profits and wages would be high. But high wages would encourage earlier marriages and a higher birth rate, leading to rapid population growth. In the course of time, as capital accumulated and population grew, with a fixed area of land, diminishing returns would set in, wages would gradually return to the subsistence level and profits would decline. Investment would then cease and the development process would come to an end. At this point, the economy was said to have reached a *stationary state*.

The fact that the economy reaches a stationary state in this theory is a direct result of the classical economists' belief in the law of diminishing returns and the Malthusian theory of population. They made little or no allowance for the effect of technological change on the process of development. The theory fails to provide any guidance to development planners as to the ways of generating increased employment opportunities and reducing poverty and inequality.

Marxian theory of development Karl Marx's theory strives to combine economics and sociology and views economic development as a continuous change in the social, cultural and political life of a society. Such a change is brought about by changes in the methods of production and in property rights by a class of people in society seeking economic power and prestige. According to this theory, the major

Labour surplus value *The difference between the value of output and the amount paid in wages. This surplus value accrues to the owners of capital*

factor in economic development is the rate of accumulation of labour surplus value – that is, the rate of profit appropriated by capitalists from workers. Such surplus value arises in every society irrespective of its stage of development because labour, the sole producer of value, is capable of producing more than is necessary for payment of subsistence wages. Labour surplus value, then, is the difference between the value of what is produced and the amount paid in wages.

It follows that the nearer wages are to the subsistence level, the larger will be the surplus for investment. However, a fall in the rate of profit becomes inevitable when a capitalist society reaches an advanced stage of industrialisation. In an effort to arrest the decline in profits, capitalists resort to labour-saving technology and so add to the 'reserve army' of unemployed workers. This intensifies the struggle between capitalists and workers until capitalism is replaced by a new social order. Clearly, this Marxist prediction has not been fulfilled. Instead, in recent years, we have witnessed the break-up of the USSR and a dramatic shift away from communism towards capitalism in Eastern Europe.

Neo-Marxists have extended the scope of Marxist theory to encompass the international dimension of the role of capital in economic development. They maintain that the international capitalist system, which has led to great inequalities between the rich and poor countries, has increased the dependence of the LDCs on the industrial capitalist countries for their basic economic and development needs. Perversely, this has resulted in a large transfer of capital and other resources from the poor to the rich countries. Thus, this phenomenon of 'international dependence' is the major cause of worsening inequalities and the resulting poverty, hunger and disease in many LDCs. In order to alleviate these problems confronting the LDCs, it is necessary, in the view of neo-Marxists, to restructure the world capitalist system on a major scale. This restructuring would transform the relationship between the rich and poor countries and would help promote an independent and self-reliant development effort based upon the LDCs' own resource endowments, markets and technology.

Rostow's 'stage' theory of development This theory, developed by W.W. Rostow, asserts that the transition of an economy from being less developed to being developed is possible through a series of steps or stages. The most important of these is the so-called take-off stage when resistance to change in traditional values and in the social, political and economic institutions of a less developed country is finally overcome and modern industries begin to expand.

Take-off stage *A stage of development where an economy is able to achieve a high rate of economic growth due to the existence of favourable conditions, such as an increased capital stock or expanding markets*

The theory can be criticised for viewing development as simply a matter of higher savings and investment ratios. Many LDCs did, in fact, achieve remarkable growth rates (5 to 6 per cent) in the 1950s and 1960s, yet poverty, unemployment and income inequalities worsened.

Harrod–Domar growth theory This theory, as outlined earlier in this chapter, has a special analytical appeal to development planners. The planners have to make appropriate assumptions about capital–output and labour–output ratios, the sources of savings and the rate of population growth when formulating their development plans.

The modern view of economic development This approach views economic development in terms of reducing poverty, income inequalities and high unemployment through a carefully selected strategy of development projects. The per capita income criterion of economic development is relegated to secondary place of importance.

Structural rigidities
Factors, such as the lack of skills and the lack of a modern infrastructure, that hinder the process of economic development

In order that such strategies succeed in realising the goals of development, emphasis is placed on removing the structural rigidities in an LDC through such measures as land reforms, better farm practices and the improvement of access of farmers, craftsmen and traders to the marketing and credit facilities of the modern sector. In addition, a great deal of emphasis is placed on changes in attitudes and the belief systems of individuals and social groups so that these groups are able to evolve and enjoy their own sense of values, self-esteem and freedom from the degradation of poverty, unemployment and starvation.

The modern view of development perceives the problems of poverty and income inequality in an international setting – that is to say, between the rich and poor nations of the world. It focuses attention, therefore, on the need for reforming the United Nations' agencies, such as the World Bank, the International Development Association and other regional bodies such as the EC. The aim is to improve the access of the LDCs to the commodity and capital markets of the industrialised economies so as to effect a large-scale transfer of technology as well as real and financial resources from the rich to the poor nations of the world.

Population aspects of economic development

Students of economic development show considerable interest in the study of population. This is because a growing population, and hence a growing labour force, not only poses problems for full employment policies in the LDCs, it also has a direct effect on living standards and society's welfare. We have already noted that classical economists paid attention to the problem of population growth which they considered to be the major limitation on the process of development. T.R. Malthus, one of the famous classical economists, published his *Essay on the Principles of Population* in 1798, a time when England's population was growing rapidly. The essay won immediate acclaim and became the major focus of controversy in the decades which followed.

Malthusian theory of population

Malthus's basic proposition was that there was a direct relationship between population growth and the supply of food. A given increase in food supplies and hence living standards would tend to cause an increase in the country's population. Malthus judged society's welfare by the strict criterion of the amount of food available to the people of the country.

Malthus employed the law of diminishing returns to support his view that food production grew *more slowly* than population. Indeed, he proposed that: (a) population tended to grow in a geometric progression, while (b) food production tended to increase in an arithmetic progression. These two propositions are illustrated in Table 25.3 for a hypothetical country with an initial population of 10 million in 1970. As can be seen from the table, the population doubles itself every thirty years – that is, it increases in the geometric ratios 1, 2, 4, 8, etc. On the other hand, food supplies only grow in the arithmetic ratios 1, 2, 3, 4, etc. It follows that

Table 25.3 Population growth and food supplies for a hypothetical economy, in which population grows in a geometric progression and food supply grows in an arithmetic progression.

Year	Population (millions)	Food supply (millions of tonnes)	Food supply per head (tonnes)
1970	10	10	1.0
2000	20	20	1.0
2030	40	30	0.75
2060	80	40	0.5

Table 25.4 Comparison of population growth rates for selected areas.

Area	Average annual % increase in population, 1989–2000 (projected)
High-income economies	0.5
Middle-income economies	1.9
Low-income economies	1.8
South Asia	1.8
Sub-Saharan Africa	3.0

Source: World Bank, *World Development Report*, 1992.

Population explosion *A situation in which the population grows at a rapid rate relative to the growth of the food supply*

food supplies per head must fall as population increases. This imbalance between the growth of population and foodstuffs illustrates what might be called a population explosion. Malthus painted a dark and depressing picture of future human societies.

The decline in food supplies per head could not continue indefinitely, however. Malthus argued that food shortages would eventually act as a check on population growth. In fact, he identified two types of checks: first, *positive* checks (like famine, disease, epidemics and wars) which increase death rates; and secondly, *preventive* checks (like late marriages, celibacy and voluntary restraint) which slow down birth rates. Being the son of a clergyman, Malthus was a strong advocate of preventive checks. He warned that if people failed to control the birth rate, Nature would apply the more unpleasant positive checks to reduce population.

Can the Malthusian theory be applied to the LDCs? Because of rapid rises in their populations, countries like India, Bangladesh and Indonesia are heavily dependent on imports of food. Unfortunately, the greater the quantity of food imports, the smaller is the amount of foreign exchange available for importing machinery, equipment and technical know-how for economic development. In other words, the large food imports necessitated by the rapidly growing populations in the LDCs tend to slow down their rate of development.

As illustrated in Table 25.4, the low-income economies as a group are projected to have more than three times the rate of population growth of the high-income countries. In contrast, the domestic production of foodstuffs in the LDCs has scarcely kept pace with population growth and, as a result, their dependence on imports from the developed countries has increased. Supporters of the Malthusian theory, therefore, have argued in favour of population controls. They point out that modern medical facilities have reduced death rates in the LDCs, but that it has often proved difficult to popularise modern techniques of birth control.

Criticisms of Malthusian theory The following criticisms may be levelled against the Malthusian theory when applied to LDCs:

(a) It underestimates the impact on economic development in general and food production in particular of (i) technological advances, and (ii) international trade. These two factors enable a country to increase the production of food and other goods and so support a growing population and labour force. Historically, European countries experienced rapid population growth in their early stages of development, but they escaped the Malthusian catastrophe through increased food imports from the newer areas of North America, Australia and New Zealand.

(b) The well publicised instances of mass starvation in several countries of sub-Saharan Africa, such as the Sudan and Somalia, in recent years, have been the result of drought and civil wars rather than the result of the law of diminishing returns which underlies the Malthusian theory.

(c) Malthus argued that population would not grow without growth in food supplies or a rise in living standards above the subsistence level. The populations of the LDCs, however, have grown without significant rises in food production or incomes per head.

The theory of optimum population

Optimum population
The optimum population of a country is that size of population at which income per head is maximised

A country's optimum population can be defined as that size of population at which, given the volume of all capital and land resources and the state of technology, income per head is maximised. This is illustrated by the curve 0A in Fig. 25.4, which shows income per head for different population sizes. Income per head is maximised at population 0*P* and this, therefore, is the optimum population. If the country has a population below 0*P*, it can be described as *underpopulated*: this means that the country does not have sufficient labour resources to exploit all the other resources to the full and an increase in population will give rise to an increase in income per head. If the country has a population above 0*P*, it can be described as *overpopulated*: in this case, the law of diminishing returns is operating and a decrease in population would increase income per head.

Note that for a developing country, the optimum size of population is not rigidly fixed, but will itself be increasing as economic development proceeds. As the state of

Fig. 25.4. The optimum population. The size of population at which income per head is maximised, given the resources of the country and technology.

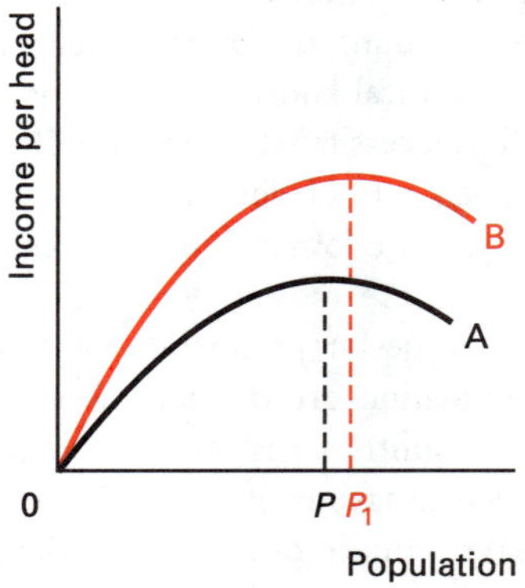

technological knowledge improves and the volume of resources increases, so the optimum population shifts upwards. This is illustrated in Fig. 25.4 for a country in which the capital stock increases and technology improves. The new relationship between the size of population and income per head is depicted by the relationship 0B. As indicated on the graph, the optimum population has increased to $0P_1$.

One major difficulty, however, that confronts the development planner is that of estimating the optimum population. Apart from the actual calculation problems, economic development involves continual changes in the data. This means that no sooner are the estimates calculated than they become out of date. Furthermore, the concept of the optimum population is based on a narrow economic viewpoint and fails to take into account social and political factors.

The roles of international trade and aid in the process of development

It has been argued that a major limitation on the speed of economic development is the volume of foreign exchange available to the LDCs. Foreign exchange is needed to fill several 'gaps' which characterise many LDCs; examples include the 'technological gap', the 'managerial and entrepreneurial gap' and the gap between domestic savings and the target level of investment. Foreign exchange is also needed to be channelled into those investment projects which benefit the poorer sections of the population and so reduce relative poverty. However, these needs have persistently exceeded the sources of foreign exchange earnings during the past two decades when effective international and regional action to augment the foreign exchange earnings of many LDCs has been lacking. Broadly, foreign exchange earnings arise from three sources: (a) export earnings from international trade; (b) foreign private investment; (c) development aid. Consider these in turn.

International trade

International trade is by far the largest earner of foreign exchange: it enables the LDCs to use their export receipts to pay for imports of food, capital goods and technical information. However, in the 1980s, Third World debt and its servicing costs rose faster than the growth of exports to pay for them. The International Monetary Fund and other independent bodies have estimated that for the fifteen most highly indebted countries (including Brazil, Nigeria and the Philippines), external debt rose from $17.5 billion in 1970 to about $500 billion in 1989. As a result, the debt service ratios of low-income countries accounted for over 30 per cent of their export receipts in 1986. The obligation to service their external debt in addition to their import requirements, means that the LDCs are faced with an ever increasing need for export receipts.

Debt service ratio *The ratio of repayments of interest and capital to total export earnings during a given time period*

Most LDCs export primary commodities, raw materials and some finished manufactures. The export earnings of the very low income countries declined in real terms in the 1970s and 1980s. The prices of many imports, however, rose rapidly during the same period. According to World Bank estimates, for example, the oil import bill of the developing countries rose from only $4 billion in 1972 to about $42 billion in 1980. Consequently, the trade deficits of many LDCs increased enormously with a mounting level of international indebtedness and a worsening of poverty and unemployment.

Several factors have contributed to the decline in export earnings. Consider the following:

(a) Quotas, tariffs and non-tariff regulations by the developed countries on imports from the LDCs.

(b) The development of substitutes by the rich countries for the exports of LDCs. One example is the increased use of synthetic rubber in place of natural rubber.

(c) Financial incentives, such as subsidies and tax rebates, to export industries in developed countries so that the exports of LDCs have been subject to intense competition from the exports of developed countries in world markets. The EC's Common Agricultural Policy, for example, has led to greatly increased exports of agricultural products from member countries at the expense of producers in LDCs who face depressed commodity prices in world markets.

(d) In some markets, the share of LDCs has fallen because of the low income elasticities of demand for primary products.

Many observers have urged that in order to augment the export earnings of LDCs, the rich nations of the 'North' must reduce the trade restrictions on imports from the poor countries of the 'South'. The Independent Commission on International Development Issues (or Brandt Commission) in a report called *North–South: A Programme for Survival*, published in 1980, placed a major emphasis on the need for expanding world trade between North and South as a means of overcoming the growing payments deficits of the LDCs and of averting the dangers of world-wide recession, poverty and starvation. The Commission took the view that increased North–South trade was also in the interests of the North and argued that economic growth in the South would provide new markets for exports from the North in the future. This partly explains the Commission's recommendations for a 'comprehensive trade institution combining the functions of UNCTAD and GATT'. Such an institution would be concerned with reducing trade barriers and implementing the rules of free trade.

In its second report in 1983, the Brandt Commission gave a much stronger expression of the views put forward in its first report. It was concerned about the deflationary economic policies of the developed countries which were worsening the trade deficits of many LDCs and so contributing to the growing debt crisis.

Foreign private investment

Foreign private investment in LDCs is undertaken largely by multinational corporations (MNCs) mainly in extractive and manufacturing industries. In the 1960s and 1970s, it appears that investment by MNCs became less welcome to some countries. There has been some criticism, for example, that in many cases the net contribution to foreign exchange earnings and to the economic development of the host country has been relatively small. The capital inflows, including the transfer of technology, resulting from the activities of multinationals have often failed to create the anticipated employment opportunities for the local population. The machinery and equipment imported into the host country is typically capital-intensive, creating relatively few jobs. Secondly, repatriated profits and interest on loans impose strains on the host country's weak balance of payments position. Thirdly, host governments have been less able to influence the investment decisions of large MNCs with head

Transfer of technology *The movement of technical knowledge, advanced capital equipment and skills from one country to another* offices in the developed countries. At the same time, some corporations, fearful of potential nationalisation and confiscation of their assets, have been reluctant to invest large sums of money in LDCs. Thus, the conflict of interests between the host countries and MNCs has been a major element in the decline in the rate of growth of the inflows of foreign exchange into the LDCs from foreign private investment.

Changing attitudes Since the mid-1980s, there has been a marked shift in the attitudes of many LDCs towards foreign private investment. Such investment is frequently viewed in a much more favourable light. Governments of LDCs place more emphasis on the *benefits* that can accrue as a result of foreign investment. These countries find it difficult to generate adequate levels of domestic savings to finance investment. Multinational companies can provide finance for investment. Other benefits that may accrue to the host countries from foreign investment include the transfer of technology, employment opportunities and associated training, export revenues and contribution to infrastructure development. As an example, consider the case of India. Until 1991, the Indian government maintained a 40 per cent limit on foreign ownership of companies operating in India. But in the 1990s, it has become more favourably disposed towards inward investment by MNCs, approving joint ventures, for example, between Indian companies and a number of MNCs (including Coca Cola and Pepsico from the United States, and Peugeot, the French car producer).

The Brandt Commission recommended the creation of a well-defined legal framework for reconciling the potentially conflicting interests of host countries and MNCs. It called for well-defined arrangements concerning transfer pricing, tax incentives and the avoidance of restrictive practices, for example. Given the right environment, the Commission saw an important role for MNCs in bringing about a large-scale transfer of technology from North to South, as well as participating in a significant change in the pattern of world trade, mutually beneficial to North and South.

Development aid

Petro-funds *The foreign exchange earnings of oil-exploring countries. These may be placed on deposit with international (mainly Western) banks*

Development aid (or assistance) comes directly from individual national governments of developed countries, largely in the form of concessionary loans and grants or technical assistance. Developed countries also provide aid indirectly through international agencies, such as the World Bank, the International Development Association and the Commonwealth Development Corporation. The emergence of surplus petro-funds of the OPEC countries since 1974 opened up new sources of aid to the poorer countries of the Third World. Countries such as Saudi Arabia, Abu Dhabi and Kuwait consequently set up special development assistance funds to provide aid, especially to the poor Muslim countries. Because of the decline in real terms in foreign exchange earnings from international trade and foreign private investment, development aid is of critical importance to the economic development of the LDCs. Such assistance supplements meagre domestic savings and helps to relieve pressures on the balance of payments.

In the 1980s and 1990s, advances in communication technology have made possible an extensive media coverage of famine, poverty and disease in Africa and the development problems of other poor countries. There is evidence that television and other media coverage of famine, drought and disease in sub-Saharan Africa and other LDCs has helped to increase public awareness of the problems of development. Consequently, there has been considerable public interest in development aid. Indeed, there has been an unprecedented public response to the fund-raising activities of charities.

Tied aid *Official development assistance given on condition that the funds are spent in the donor country*

Major criticisms of aid, however, are that it is often 'tied' to the exports of donor countries and often results in a substantial debt repayment burden. Tied aid limits the freedom of the recipient countries to obtain capital goods and technical know-how at competitive prices in world markets. The World Bank set a target for developed countries to give an equivalent of 0.7 per cent of GNP in the form of aid. World Bank statistics show that in 1965, official development assistance represented 0.47 per cent of the total GNP of the OECD countries. But this figure had fallen to 0.34 per cent by 1970 and remained fairly constant up to 1990, in which year OECD countries gave 0.36 per cent of GNP in official development assistance. In 1990, Sweden, Denmark, the Netherlands and Norway each gave more than 0.9 per cent of GNP as official development assistance. At the other end of the scale, the United States and United Kingdom gave only 0.21 and 0.27 per cent of GNP respectively.

The Brandt Commission, conscious of the decline in development assistance, recommended that industrialised countries meet the 0.7 per cent of GNP target by 1985. The Commission also recommended that industrialised countries meet a target of 1 per cent of GNP by the end of the century. In the final analysis, though, the amount and nature of assistance will depend upon the willingness and determination of donor countries to reduce inequalities of income and wealth between the rich and poor nations of the world.

Third World debt

Before the onset of the Third World debt crisis in 1982, most LDCs had benefited from a flow of funds from the rich industrialised countries to supplement their export earnings and receipts from foreign direct investment. This additional flow of funds was partly in the form of lending, principally by international commercial banks at market interest rates, and partly in the form of aid. Several factors contributed to the growth of Third World debt prior to 1982:

(a) *Oil price shocks.* The rises in oil prices during the 1970s led many oil exporting countries to deposit their surplus revenues with commercial banks, and these in turn recycled a large proportion of the funds to the oil importing countries in the Third World. In fact, the rapid rise in Third World debt during the 1970s was not primarily intended to help LDCs in their development efforts. Profit-seeking banks were encouraged by western governments to lend to LDCs to avoid the effects of recession in their own economies following the oil price rises. The resulting competition among banks encouraged lending without regard to criteria for credit-worthiness and in particular to the debt and interest payment capacity of the borrowing countries. There was held in some quarters the naïve view that lending to sovereign governments was default-free. The LDCs, attracted by easy access to bank loans with no strings attached, borrowed continuously on a substantial scale both for essential and non-essential purposes.

(b) *International economic recession.* At the end of the 1970s, governments in countries such as the United Kingdom and the United States decided to use monetary policy, including high interest rates, to combat inflation. Partly as a consequence of these deflationary policies, several industrialised countries experienced major recessions at the start of the 1980s so that their imports from

LDCs did not grow as fast as expected. The resultant decline in the LDCs' export earnings further stimulated demand for international borrowing.

(c) *Rise in interest rates.* A significant proportion of debt was borrowed at variable interest rates. Thus, the increase in world interest rates in the early 1980s led to a significant rise in the debt-service burden for debtor countries.

With the onset of recession, a number of LDCs and middle-income countries declared their inability to meet the interest and principal payments from their export revenues following Mexico's debt default in August 1982. For many LDCs, the debt burden rose faster than the growth of exports so that living standards fell and unemployment and poverty became intensified. In 1983, thirty countries, including almost half of the major twenty-five debtors, were engaged in debt-rescheduling arrangements aimed at extending loan periods.

Some efforts have been made to tackle the Third World debt problem by governments, international financial agencies and commercial banks. The development of loan trading markets by creditor banks in the last few years is one short-term measure whereby banks, anxious to reduce their exposure to debt default, offer to sell loans, often at large discounts. In other cases, banks have accepted equity stakes in industries in debtor countries in exchange for debt. In 1989, there was discussion at both the World Bank and the International Monetary Fund (IMF) on a plan, proposed by Nicholas Brady, the United States Treasury Secretary, for debt reduction partly on a voluntary basis by commercial banks and partly as a result of financial aid from World Bank and IMF resources. The debt problem is of such enormity, however, that it is likely to persist as a major international issue for the foreseeable future.

Summary

1. Economic growth refers to an increase in a country's productive capacity. Growth may be stimulated by an increase in the quantity or quality of the factors of production, such as labour and capital.

2. According to the Harrod–Domar model, a full employment equilibrium growth path requires that the warranted rate of growth (s/v) should equal the natural rate of growth (n). This is a 'knife-edge' equilibrium growth path.

3. Some economists have contended that indicative planning may result in a higher growth rate in a mixed economy. Indicative planning is based on the belief that growth will be stimulated by the government setting targets for the growth of output in individual sectors within the economy.

4. Economic growth results in a number of benefits, such as an increased standard of living and a reduction in poverty levels. On the other hand, growth may lead to costs, such as technological unemployment, rapid depletion of non-renewable resources and negative externalities.

5. Economic development involves major structural changes in the economy, as well as a rapid growth in real output per head. Developing countries normally exhibit characteristics such as a low GNP per capita, large agricultural sectors, high population growth rates and poor infrastructures.
6. The Malthusian theory of population contends that there is a relationship between population growth and food supply. In this theory, the relatively slow rate of growth of food production acts as a check on the growth of population.
7. Access to world markets through international trade can give an important impetus to a country's economic development effort. Similarly, foreign direct investment may result in significant benefits, including increased employment opportunities, higher foreign exchange earnings and access to new technology. Finally, financial assistance to poor countries from rich countries can also support and stimulate the process of economic development in the recipient countries.

Exercises

1. Review your understanding of the following terms:

economic growth
economic development
natural rate of growth
warranted rate of growth
fixed proportions production function
neo-classical production function
technical progress
indicative planning
less developed country
stationary state
labour surplus value
subsistence wage
positive checks to population growth
preventive checks to population growth
optimum population
foreign aid

2. Consider Table 25.5 which shows comparative rates of growth of GDP for selected developed countries for the period 1980–90.

Table 25.5 Comparative GDP growth rates of selected countries, 1980–90.

Country	Average annual growth of GDP, 1980–90
Japan	6.4
Canada	4.8
Spain	4.6
Italy	4.3
France	4.0
Germany	3.3
United States	2.7
United Kingdom	2.3

Source: The World Bank, *World Development Report*, 1992.

Comment on the figures and account for the low relative rate of growth in the United Kingdom during this period.

3. Discuss the extent to which increased expenditure on education in the United Kingdom might contribute to a faster rate of economic growth.

4. Outline the arguments for and against the use of indicative planning in a mixed economy.

5. Describe the major economic problems facing a less developed country of your choice. How might a study of the theories of development help the policy-makers to solve these problems?

6. Consider the view that foreign aid hinders rather than helps the economic development of a less developed country.

MACROECONOMIC POLICY ISSUES

MACROECONOMIC POLICIES

UNEMPLOYMENT

INFLATION

THE BALANCE OF PAYMENTS AND EXCHANGE RATES

INTERNATIONAL TRADE AND POLICY

THE EUROPEAN COMMUNITY

ECONOMIC INEQUALITY

26 MACROECONOMIC POLICIES

Learning objectives

After reading this chapter, you should be able to:

- explain the distinction between active and passive policies, and between 'rules' and 'discretion' in macroeconomic policy-making
- define and understand monetary policy and fiscal policy
- use the IS–LM model and the AD–AS model to analyse the effectiveness of fiscal and monetary policies under different assumptions
- use the AD–AS model to illustrate supply-side policies
- describe the main features of, and discuss the effectiveness of, supply-side policies, prices and incomes policy and regional policy, with examples from the United Kingdom and the EC

Introduction

The major macroeconomic policy objectives which most western governments strive to achieve are: a high level of employment, stable prices, a high growth rate, external equilibrium and an equitable distribution of income and wealth. Having discussed the growth objective in Ch. 25, we turn in this final part of the book (Chs 26–32) to a more detailed consideration of the problems of unemployment (Ch. 27), inflation (Ch. 28), external balance (Chs 29 and 30) and economic inequality (Ch. 32). In this introductory chapter, we start by discussing the role of macroeconomic policy-making; we then outline the major policy instruments in turn – fiscal and monetary policies and their effectiveness; supply side policies; prices and income policy; and regional policy.

A most important point to make at this stage is that the policy recommendations made by economists are based on economic theories. This is why we have spent so much time setting out the current theories of employment, money and growth. Unfortunately, as we have seen, different schools of thought subscribe to different theories and this means that they also often disagree about which policies should be used. Probably the most marked disagreements exist between monetarists and Keynesians. In this and the remaining chapters, one of our aims is to give the reader a flavour of the important debate between these two groups.

The role of macroeconomic policy-making

Active policy-making *That in which the government tries to stabilise the economy by formulating and implementing policy actions in response to changing economic events and forecasts*

Passive policy-making *That in which the government aims to facilitate the working of the economy in the long-run, but refrains from using short-term stabilisation policies*

Policy rules *Announced monetary or fiscal targets which a government sets and tries to achieve*

Discretionary policy-making *Policy-making is based on discretion if the government remains free to choose whatever policy action it believes to be appropriate for the set of circumstances which prevail at the time*

An important distinction may be drawn between active and passive policy-making. A government is said to be an active policy-maker when it makes regular adjustments to its policy actions in response to changing macroeconomic circumstances or in response to revised economic forecasts. A government which adheres to a predetermined policy in the attempt to facilitate the achievement of long-run stability, regardless of any short-run fluctuations in economic activity, is said to be a passive policy-maker.

Macroeconomic policy-making may additionally be based on *rules* or *discretion*. Policy rules are usually stated targets for policy variables (such as the money supply or the PSBR) which a government will try to achieve in the medium- or long-term. Discretionary policy-making, on the other hand, leaves the government free to select whatever policy actions it believes to be appropriate for the current set of economic circumstances.

Discretionary policy-making is clearly active, rather than passive because it involves selecting stabilisation policies in response to changing economic circumstances. Policy rules, however, can be either active or passive. An example of an *active policy rule* is a monetary target which specifies that the growth of the money supply for the coming year will be, say, '3 per cent, plus 1 per cent for every percentage point the unemployment rate exceeds 8 per cent'. With this rule, monetary growth would be adjusted upwards whenever the unemployment rate rose above 8 per cent. This rule may be regarded as an active policy rule, therefore, because the policy responds to changing economic conditions.

An example of a *passive policy rule* is a monetary target which specifies that the growth of the money supply for the coming year will be fixed at, say, 2 per cent, regardless of any changes in economic conditions.

Keynesian and monetarist views of macroeconomic policy-making As we saw in Ch. 23, an important difference between Keynesians and monetarists concerns their views of the role to be played by macroeconomic policy-makers. Keynesians tend to believe that the economy is inherently unstable and that it is the job of policy-makers to design and implement policies which will stabilise (or *fine tune*) the economy by smoothing out excessive fluctuations in economic activity. Thus, Keynesians tend to support *active*, rather than passive, policy-making. Keynesian short-run demand-management was applied in the United Kingdom throughout the post-war period until 1976 with mixed success: for example, although unemployment was much lower than it has been in the 1980s and 1990s, the policies were unable to prevent the rate of inflation from rising above 20 per cent in the mid-1970s.

Monetarists tend to believe that the economy is inherently stable in the long-run, and that attempts to smooth out short-run fluctuations are likely to be unsuccessful and may themselves be destabilising. This view leads monetarists to support the application of *passive* policy-making. In the United Kingdom, a monetarist approach to macroeconomic policy-making was adopted in 1980 with the introduction of the 'medium-term financial strategy'. The strategy set target ranges for the annual growth of the money supply and targets for the PSBR as a percentage of GDP. Although many of the targets were not actually achieved, the policy survived into the 1990s. In 1993, the policy of monetary targets was superseded by a policy of 'inflation targets' and money supply monitoring.

It may at first seem strange that monetarists, who recognise that economies are prone to shocks of various kinds and therefore periodic fluctuations in economic activity, nevertheless reject the application of short-term stabilisation policies. The reason for their rejection of active policy-making lies in the potentially serious problems associated with short-term macroeconomic policy actions. While Keynesians regard these problems as surmountable, monetarists see them as potential sources of further instability. The main problems are as follows:

(a) *Lagged responses.* A serious practical difficulty associated with short-run demand-management is that changes in policy variables do not affect other economic variables immediately. Instead, there are *time lags*, some of which may be long and difficult to predict. To explain the lags involved, suppose that the economy suffers a shock which causes a rise in the rate of unemployment, and that the government wishes to respond to this shock by implementing an appropriate stabilisation policy. There are two lags which are relevant here:

Inside lag *The time interval between the recognition of an economic problem or shock and the implementation of appropriate policy measures*

(i) *Inside lag.* The inside lag is the time interval between the occurrence of the shock to the economy and the implementation of the policy response. This is the time it takes to recognise that the shock has taken place and then to formulate and implement an appropriate policy action. In general, fiscal policy is thought to have a longer inside lag than monetary policy. Changes in tax rates or in the level of government expenditure usually only occur after a lengthy period of discussion and are normally announced during the annual budget statement: this clearly delays their implementation. Changes designed to affect the money supply or interest rates, on the other hand, can be undertaken by the central bank much more rapidly.

Outside lag *The time interval between the implementation of policy measures and the resultant effects on the intended targets*

(ii) *Outside lag.* The outside lag is the time interval between the implementation of a policy action and the policy's effect on the targeted economic variables. This lag depends on the dynamic relationship between policy instruments and policy targets. In general, monetary policy is thought to have a longer outside lag than fiscal policy. Tax and spending changes affect aggregate demand directly via the multiplier, though the effect on employment is likely to be felt later. Monetary changes, however, work partly through interest rates, changes in which affect investment and consumption, and the full effect on aggregate demand may take up to a year to be completed; there will then be a further interval before employment is affected.

Automatic stabiliser *An economic policy variable that responds automatically to changes in the level of economic activity. An example is a progressive tax system whereby the amount of tax paid falls as real output falls*

One possible way of shortening these time lags is by designing tax systems and monetary rules which act as automatic stabilisers. For example, with a progressive income tax system and a monetary target according to which the money supply grows faster when real output falls and more slowly when real output rises, policy actions will automatically respond to economic shocks. As real output falls and unemployment rises, for example, taxpayers will pay progressively less tax and the money supply will grow faster. Automatic stabilisers reduce the inside lag, but may still leave lengthy and unpredictable outside lags.

(b) *Inaccurate forecasting.* Decisions about stabilisation policies have to be based on economic forecasts: if the forecasts are inaccurate, the policies adopted may be inappropriate and so lead to further destabilisation. In reacting to a shock to the economy, policy-makers need to be able to forecast both the likely effect of the shock on the economy *and* the likely effects of alternative policy actions. In both cases, forecasts may prove to be inaccurate either because the forecasting model is deficient in some way or because of unforeseeable events which occur subsequently. In either case, inaccurate forecasting may lead to unsatisfactory policy decisions.

We turn now to a more detailed discussion of fiscal and monetary policies and, in particular, we analyse the relative effectiveness of these policies in the context of the IS–LM and AD–AS models. In this analysis, it is important to bear in mind the above problems associated with short-term stabilisation policies.

Fiscal and monetary policies in the IS–LM model

Fiscal policy

Fiscal policy is the government's attempt to influence aggregate demand in the economy by regulating the amount of public expenditure and the rates of taxation. This policy is made more flexible by the fact that governments do not need to keep 'balanced budgets' – they can run a *budget surplus* by spending less than they raise in taxes or they can run a *budget deficit* by spending more than they raise in taxes. In this latter case, as we showed in Ch. 14, the excess spending can be financed either by borrowing or by 'printing money'. This is not to deny that an excessively large budget deficit may be harmful – in particular, a large deficit financed by expanding the money supply is likely to be inflationary.

In Ch. 19, we saw in the context of the simple Keynesian model how such policies could be used to affect the equilibrium level of income via the multiplier. An increase in government spending or a cut in taxes increased the equilibrium level of income, while a decrease in government spending or a rise in taxes reduced the equilibrium level of income. This can also be illustrated in the context of the IS–LM model. An expansionary fiscal policy (that is, an increase in government spending or a cut in taxes) will shift the IS curve to the *right*, while a contractionary fiscal policy will shift it to the *left*. This is illustrated in Fig. 26.1 where the IS and LM curves have their normal shapes and the original equilibrium is at $0Y_1$ and $0i_1$. As drawn, fiscal policy is seen to be reasonably effective – it causes a significant change in the

Fig. 26.1. *Fiscal policy in the IS–LM model.* An increase in government spending shifts the IS curve to the right to IS′. This causes an increase in national income and an increase in the rate of interest.

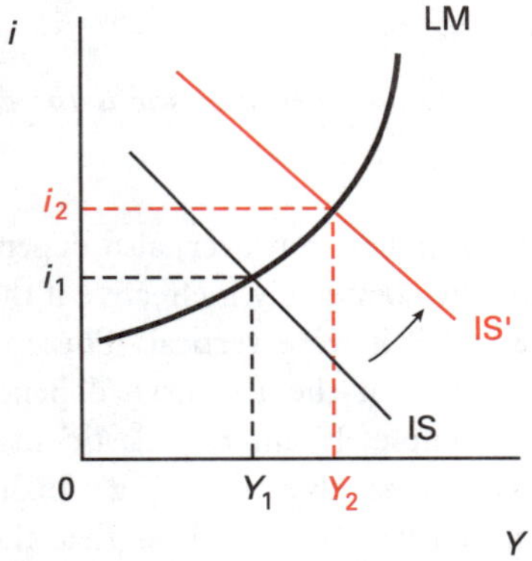

Fig. 26.2. The shape of the LM curve and the effectiveness of fiscal policy. (a) With a vertical LM curve, fiscal policy has no effect on national income. (b) With a horizontal LM curve, fiscal policy affects national income, but leaves the interest rate unchanged.

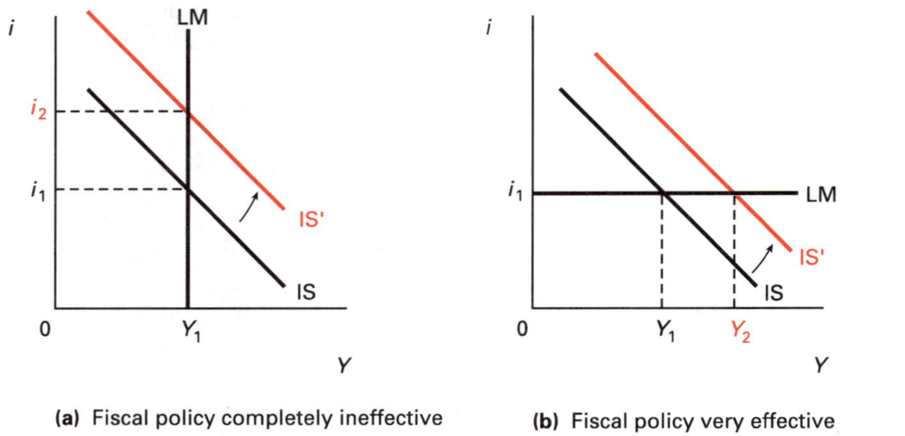

equilibrium level of national income. Notice, however, that a change in government spending does not have a full multiplier effect on income as predicted by the formulas derived in Ch. 19. In this 'general equilibrium' model, a rise in government spending causes income to rise and this, in turn, causes the transactions demand for money to increase: with a constant money stock, less is now available for speculative purposes, so that interest rates are pushed upwards and this causes private investment to be cut back, so offsetting to some extent the effect of the increase in government spending on income. The new equilibrium position is at the higher income level $0Y_2$ and at the higher interest rate $0i_2$. Taking both the real and monetary sectors of the economy into account, fiscal policy is not necessarily so effective as it appeared in the simple Keynesian model.

Indeed, it is possible for fiscal policy to be *completely ineffective* so far as its influence over the equilibrium level of income is concerned. Recall from Ch. 23 that if the total demand for money were perfectly interest-inelastic, the LM curve would be vertical and there would only be one level of income consistent with equilibrium in the money market. In this case, as shown in Fig. 26.2(a), the level of income remains unchanged whichever way the IS curve shifts. At the other extreme, fiscal policy will be very effective if the demand for money is perfectly interest-elastic. In the liquidity trap, where the LM curve is horizontal, interest rates are unaffected by fiscal policy, but income rises by the full multiplier effect. This is illustrated in Fig. 26.2(b).

Result: Ceteris paribus, *the more interest-elastic is the demand for money, the more effective is fiscal policy.*

The effectiveness of fiscal policy, however, also depends on the steepness of the IS curve. The policy would be completely ineffective if the IS curve were horizontal, but would have its full effect if it were vertical. These cases are illustrated in Fig. 26.3(a) and (b). The steepness of the IS curve depends largely on the interest-elasticity of investment. Completely interest-elastic investment (highly unlikely) yields a horizontal IS curve, as shown in Fig. 26.3(a); increased government expenditure leaves the IS curve unchanged so that the policy has no effect on income. Perfectly interest-inelastic investment would yield a vertical IS curve, as

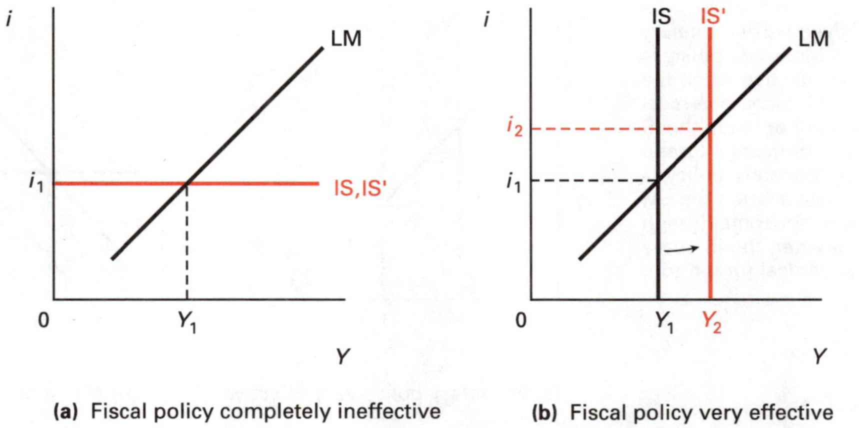

Fig. 26.3. The shape of the IS curve and the effectiveness of fiscal policy. (a) With a horizontal IS curve, fiscal policy has no effect on either national income or the rate of interest. (b) With a vertical IS curve, fiscal policy affects both national income and the rate of interest.

shown in Fig. 26.3(b) and, in this case, an increase in government expenditure would have a full multiplier effect.

Result: Ceteris paribus, *the more interest-inelastic is investment, the more effective is fiscal policy*.

Monetary policy

Monetary policy is the government's attempt to influence aggregate demand in the economy by regulating the cost and availability of credit. We saw in Chs 21 and 22 that in the United Kingdom, the government can influence both the cost and availability of credit by following measures designed to affect the country's supply of money – these include open market operations, special deposits and various forms of requests and direct controls over lending by banks and other financial institutions.

If we now analyse monetary policy in the context of the IS–LM model, this should enable us to compare its effectiveness with that of fiscal policy. Recall that an expansionary monetary policy will shift the LM curve to the right, while a contractionary monetary policy will shift it to the left. This is illustrated in Fig. 26.4 where the original equilibrium is at $0Y_1$ and $0i_1$. As was explained in Ch. 23, the

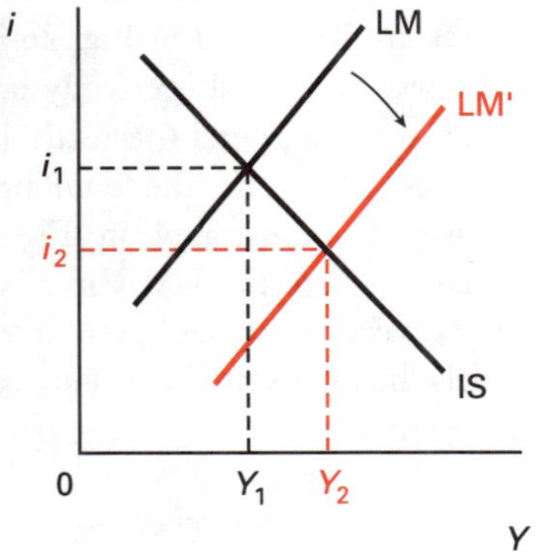

Fig. 26.4. Monetary policy in the IS–LM model. An increase in the money supply shifts the LM curve to the right to LM′. This causes an increase in national income and a fall in the rate of interest.

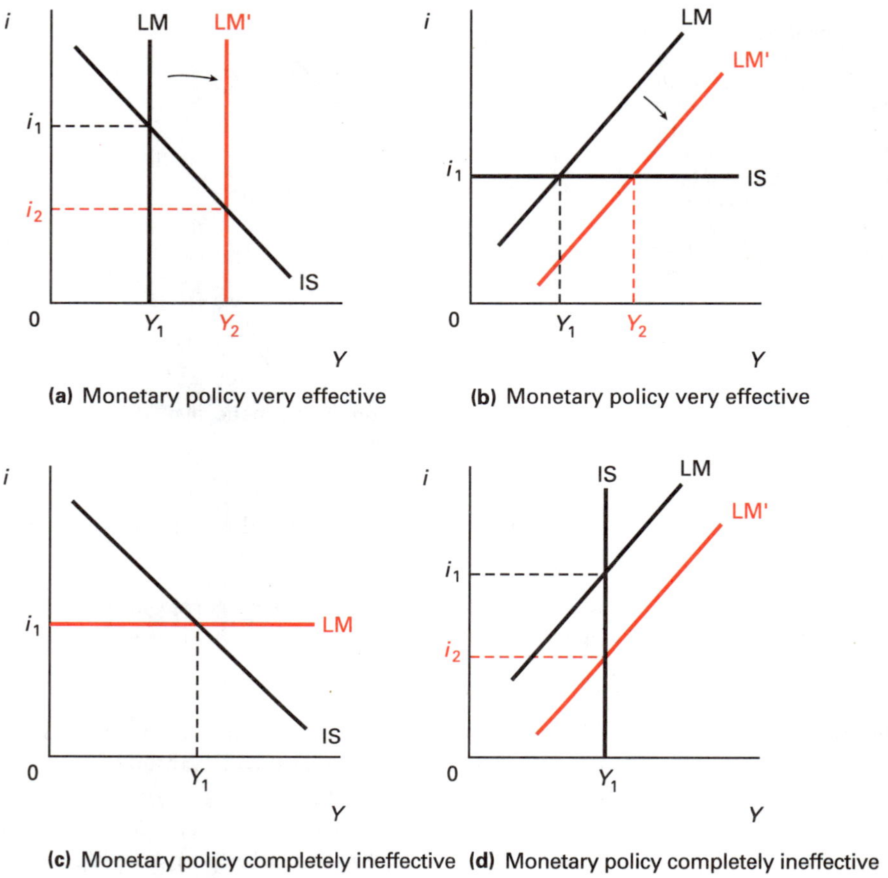

Fig. 26.5. The effectiveness of monetary policy. Monetary policy is most effective when the LM curve is vertical (graph (a)) or when the IS curve is horizontal (graph (b)). Monetary policy is ineffective when the LM curve is horizontal (graph (c)) or when the IS curve is vertical (graph (d)).

increase in the money supply causes the interest rate to fall (assuming that the economy is not in the liquidity trap); this lower interest rate in turn gives rise to increased investment spending (assuming that investment is not completely interest-inelastic) and this increased spending raises national income. In Fig. 26.4, the new equilibrium position is at the higher level of income $0Y_2$ and the lower interest rate $0i_2$.

As with fiscal policy, the effectiveness of monetary policy depends on the interest-elasticity of the demand for money and on the interest-elasticity of investment. The possible cases are illustrated in Fig. 26.5(a), (b), (c) and (d). It can be seen that where the LM curve is vertical (perfectly interest-inelastic demand for money) and where the IS curve is horizontal (perfectly interest-elastic investment), monetary policy has its biggest effect on the equilibrium level of income and employment. These two cases are illustrated in Fig. 26.5(a) and Fig. 26.5(b) respectively. On the other hand, where the LM curve is horizontal (liquidity trap) and where the IS curve is vertical (completely interest-inelastic investment), monetary policy is completely ineffective. These two cases are illustrated in Fig. 26.5(c) and Fig. 26.5(d) respectively.

Results: Ceteris paribus, *the more interest-inelastic is the demand for money, the more effective is monetary policy.*

Ceteris paribus, *the more interest-elastic is investment, the more effective is monetary policy*.

Notice that these results concerning monetary policy are the opposite of the results concerning fiscal policy. We can conclude that fiscal policy is likely to be more effective than monetary policy, the more interest-elastic is the demand for money and the more interest-inelastic is investment.

With reference to the different schools of thought, Keynesians generally believe the demand for money to be fairly elastic and tend to cast doubt on the responsiveness of investment to interest rate changes. Consequently, Keynesians have tended to regard fiscal policy as a more effective and useful means of influencing aggregate demand than monetary policy. Monetarists, on the other hand, claim that the demand for money is fairly interest-inelastic and that changes in the money supply have a more *direct* effect on aggregate demand than is envisaged by Keynesians. This leads monetarists to conclude that fiscal policy will be relatively ineffective in its influence on aggregate demand, and that monetary policy will be very effective. *However, as we see below, monetarists argue that monetary changes which influence the level of aggregate demand will mainly affect the price level rather than real income and employment.*

Fiscal and monetary policies in the AD–AS model

From the foregoing analysis, we can conclude that as long as the IS curve is not horizontal and the LM curve is not vertical, an expansionary fiscal policy will increase the level of aggregate demand. Similarly, as long as the IS curve is not vertical and the LM curve is not horizontal, an expansionary monetary policy will also increase the level of aggregate demand. The sizes of these increases in aggregate demand will depend on factors like the interest-elasticity of investment and the interest-elasticity of the demand for money. In the IS–LM model, where a *fixed price level* is assumed, an increase in the level of aggregate demand will cause an increase in the equilibrium level of *real* income and so lead to a higher level of employment in the economy.

This result cannot be guaranteed, however, once we allow the price level to vary. In the more general AD–AS model, the effect of an increase in aggregate demand on real income depends on the shape of the AS curve. Putting it simply: only if the AS curve is horizontal will the effect be entirely on real income; if the AS curve is upward-sloping but fairly flat, the effect will be mainly on real income, with just a small rise in the price level; if the AS curve is steep, the effect will be mainly on the price level, with just a small rise in real income; if the AS curve is vertical, the effect will be entirely on the price level.

The Keynesian case

In Ch. 23, we saw that in the extreme Keynesian case, the AS curve is horizontal up to the point at which full employment is reached, and then becomes vertical. In this case, assuming that the economy does not reach full employment, an increase in aggregate demand will increase real income and employment and leave the price level unchanged. This is shown in Fig. 26.6(a) where an expansionary fiscal policy is assumed to shift the AD curve from AD_1 to AD_2. Real income rises from $0Y_1$ to $0Y_2$ with no change in the price level.

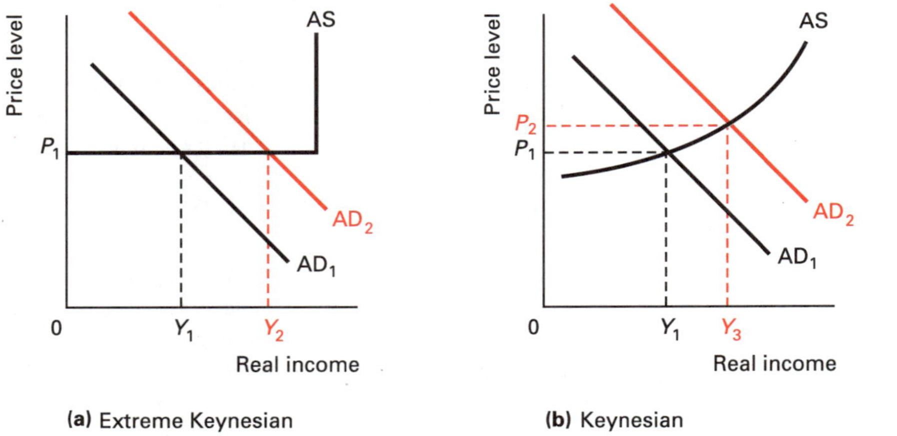

Fig. 26.6. The effect of an expansionary fiscal policy. (a) In an extreme Keynesian model, fiscal policy affects real income and employment, but has no effect on the price level. (b) In a less extreme Keynesian model, the main effect of fiscal policy is on real income, but there is also a small rise in the price level.

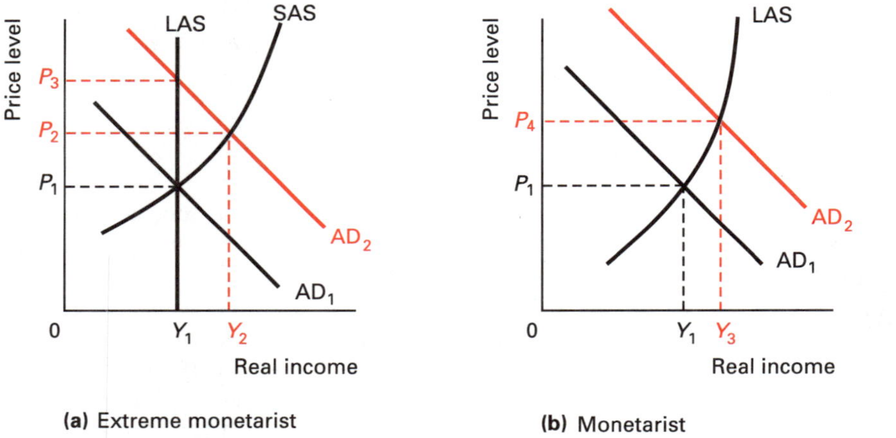

Fig. 26.7. The effect of an expansionary monetary policy in a monetarist model. (a) In an extreme monetarist model, the long-run effect is entirely on the price level, with no lasting effect on real income. (b) In a less extreme monetarist model, the long-run effect is mainly on the price level, but there is a small increase in real income.

A less extreme Keynesian would probably draw a fairly flat upward-sloping AS curve (at least until full employment is approached) similar to the one shown in Fig. 26.6(b). In this case, the expansionary fiscal policy which shifts the AD curve from AD_1 to AD_2 causes real income to rise from $0Y_1$ to $0Y_3$. At the same time, there is a small rise in the price level from $0P_1$ to $0P_2$.

The monetarist case

In the extreme monetarist version of the model, the long-run AS curve is vertical so that any increase in real income and employment will only be temporary. This is shown in Fig. 26.7(a) where LAS is the long-run AS curve and SAS is a short-run AS curve. An expansionary monetary policy is assumed to shift the AD curve from AD_1 to AD_2. Monetary policy is chosen here because in a monetarist model, fiscal policy would be unlikely even to shift the AD curve. In the short term, real income will rise from $0Y_1$ to $0Y_2$ and the price level will rise from $0P_1$ to $0P_2$ as we move along SAS. But this reduces unemployment below its 'natural rate'. In the longer term, the economy will return to the 'natural rate' of unemployment, real income will return to $0Y_1$ and the price level will rise to $0P_3$. This means that in the long-run, the monetary expansion has led to a movement along LAS, causing a rise in the price level, but having no lasting effect on output and employment. The 'natural rate' hypothesis and the role of inflationary expectations in explaining the above mechanism are discussed more fully in Ch. 28.

A less extreme monetarist might draw a steep (but not vertical) long-run AS curve, similar to the one shown in Fig. 26.7(b). In this case, an expansionary monetary policy would affect mainly the price level (raising it from $0P_1$ to $0P_4$) and lead to only a small increase in real income (from $0Y_1$ to $0Y_3$).

Supply-side policies

Supply-side policies *Policies designed to influence aggregate supply by improving the productivity of the free market economy*

We saw in Ch. 24 and above that in extreme monetarist models, the long-run AS curve is vertical at the level of national income associated with the 'natural rate' of unemployment. Figure 26.8 illustrates a long-run equilibrium position in a monetarist model using AD and AS curves. The equilibrium price level is $0P_0$ and the equilibrium level of real income is $0Y_0$, the level associated with the 'natural rate' of unemployment. This suggests that demand-side (fiscal and monetary) policies are ineffective if higher employment is the government's objective. Indeed, as we shall see in Ch. 28, monetarists argue that attempts to raise employment by demand-management policies will be inflationary and will have no long-run effect on the level of employment.

Instead of demand-management policies, therefore, monetarists recommend supply-side policies. These are policies which are intended to improve the efficiency of the free market economy and so contribute to economic growth. In recent years, we have seen many of these policies in action in the United Kingdom. The main ones are outlined below:

(a) *Deregulation.* This involves the removal of government regulations which hinder competition by restricting the actions of consumers and producers in one way or another. Examples include the 1980 Transport Act which deregulated long-distance coach travel and the 1986 'Big Bang' which heralded the removal of many Stock Exchange restrictions. In 1993 the wages councils that set minimum wage rates in some labour markets were abolished. Monetarists favour deregulation as a means of opening up previously protected markets to competitive forces.

Fig. 26.8. *The effect of supply-side policies on the equilibrium level of income.* Successful supply-side policies will shift the AS curve to the right to AS′. This reduces the price level and increases real income.

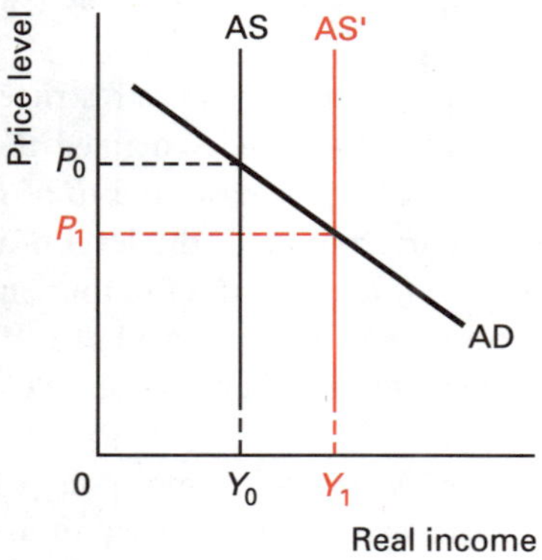

(b) *Privatisation.* This policy is discussed in greater detail in Ch. 15. Monetarists see it as a way of reducing government 'interference' in a market economy and, when accompanied by appropriate deregulation, as a means of promoting competition. We saw in Ch. 15 that, in recent years in the United Kingdom, a large number of industries have been privatised, including the steel industry, the gas and electricity utilities and the water industry.

(c) *Tax changes intended to reduce disincentive effects.* The argument that direct taxes act as a disincentive to work and take business risks, has led to calls for cuts in these taxes and, where possible, their replacement by indirect taxes.

(d) *Labour market policies.* In general, monetarists support policies to reduce the power of trade unions, to reduce labour costs and to increase the geographical and occupational mobility of labour. Some specific labour market policies are outlined in Ch. 27. Labour market policies include improvements in the dissemination of information; the provision of retraining schemes; assistance with family relocation; special employment assistance for teenagers; and subsidies to firms which reduce working hours rather than the size of the work-force. These policies are discussed more fully in Ch. 27.

If supply-side policies are successful in increasing the economy's productive capacity (through the creation of a more efficient and smooth-running market system with greater incentives), the AS curve depicted in Fig. 26.8 will shift to the right, say to AS′. This raises the equilibrium level of national income to $0Y_1$ and reduces the price level to $0P_1$.

Critics of supply-side economics insist that the economy does not have the long-term inherent stability assumed by monetarists and that government intervention is necessary to prevent long periods of high unemployment and to ensure an equitable distribution of income and wealth.

Prices and incomes policy

Prices and incomes policy *A policy designed to reduce price and wage inflation by requesting voluntary restraint or by imposing statutory controls*

A prices and incomes policy takes the form of exhortation or legislation in the attempt to reduce rates of price and wage inflation below what they would otherwise be. When a government requests (or exhorts) producers and trade unions to keep down the rate of increase of prices and wage rates, this can be described as a *voluntary* policy. When, on the other hand, a government introduces legislation that limits the rate of increase of prices and wage rates by law, this can be described as a *statutory* policy.

In the United Kingdom, price increases were restricted by the operation of Price Codes from 1972 to 1979. The Price Codes defined the permitted price increases with references to increases in allowable costs and to profit margins. Critics of price controls argue that if profits are restricted, the level of investment will be reduced resulting in an adverse effect on the growth of output and the level of employment. The imposition of price controls is, in part, symbolic. If they were not introduced, the task of gaining acceptance for a policy of restraint of incomes would be made more difficult.

We now turn to the rationale for an incomes policy, confining the discussion to controls on incomes from employment (as opposed to incomes from rent or shares). It is widely accepted that if a government introduces deflationary fiscal and monetary policies to combat inflation, this will result (at least in the short-run) in increased unemployment. An incomes policy can be seen as a way of attempting to reduce the rate of inflation without the undesirable side-effect of creating unemployment. In terms of the Phillips curve (see Ch. 28), incomes policy is seen as a method of shifting the Phillips curve nearer to the origin, thus easing the conflict between the objectives of full employment and stable prices. An incomes policy might be appropriate if inflation results from cost-push factors, particularly from powerful trade unions exercising their monopoly power to force wage increases irrespective of the level of excess demand for or supply of labour.

If inflation is due to generalised excess demand, however, an incomes policy is likely to result in disguised increases in earnings, as employers who wish to hire extra labour will attempt to find loop-holes or other ways round the policy. Even so, there is a logical argument for the introduction of an incomes policy in a situation of excess demand as a means of reducing inflationary expectations. As outlined below in more detail in Ch. 28, monetarists argue that inflation develops initially if the money supply is expanded faster than the economy's long-run growth of productive capacity. But once inflation is under way, it develops a momentum of its own because people expect further inflation and incorporate these expectations in their price fixing and wage demands. The duration and amount of unemployment above the 'natural' rate that is required to reduce the rate of inflation depends on the length of time that it takes for inflationary expectations to be reduced. Thus, if an incomes policy succeeds in reducing inflationary expectations, it will enable a government to reduce inflation with less unemployment than would otherwise be necessary.

There is, however, evidence from surveys that the imposition of an incomes policy does not in fact reduce inflationary expectations. This may be because the policy merely transfers money wage increases from the initial period of the policy to later years when the policy is beginning to crumble or when it is finally abandoned.

Problems of implementing incomes policies

Consider the following problems associated with the implementation of incomes policies:

(a) It is widely recognised that the operation of an incomes policy imposes costs on an economy. If, for example, a limitation on wage increases results in almost all workers receiving a similar wage rise, the allocation of labour through changes in relative wage rates is impeded. Companies that wish to expand may be penalised as they will find it more difficult to attract extra labour. An incentive will exist for such employers to evade the policy through relatively inefficient methods of remuneration (such as grants for children's education and cheap mortgage loans).

(b) If the government recommends a 'norm' or a target average pay rise for the whole work-force, trade union leaders and workers may regard the 'norm' as the minimum target that can be accepted. Thus, because of 'wage drift' (resulting from increased overtime, incremental payments and so on) average earnings will increase by more than the 'norm'.

(c) A flat rate increase represents a bigger percentage increase for low-paid workers than for high-paid workers. This may result in the high-paid workers calling for further wage increases to restore their differentials.

(d) Workers in the public sector often claim that an incomes policy discriminates against them because the policy is typically pursued rigidly in the public sector. It is further claimed that in the private sector an incomes policy can often be avoided through the payment of fringe benefits or by other means.

(e) A government may be put in a dilemma as to whether it should introduce a voluntary or statutory policy. The problem with a voluntary policy is that powerful groups may break it, perhaps leading to a widespread sense of injustice and pressure from other groups to break through the policy. If the government introduces a statutory policy, the danger of confrontation exists.

Are incomes policies effective?

There have been several periods in the United Kingdom when an incomes policy has been in operation. In the 1970s, for example, a form of incomes policy operated from 1972 to 1974 and from 1975 to 1979. The accumulated experience appears to indicate that the policy has the effect of reducing the rate of wage increase in its initial year or two of operation. After the policy has been in operation for a substantial period, unrest and pressure for greater flexibility develop. The United Kingdom policies have all been abandoned after a few years and typically been followed by a 'wage explosion'. Econometric evidence indicates that in the long-run incomes policies in the United Kingdom have had no significant influence on the increase in wage rates or the level of prices.

Perhaps one problem with the use of incomes policies in the United Kingdom is that they have been introduced as a possible solution to a crisis when the balance of payments deteriorates or the rate of inflation accelerates. Some politicians have argued that in order to achieve long-term success in controlling inflation, a 'permanent' incomes policy is desirable and have remarked on the apparent success of such policies in countries such as Sweden and Austria.

Regional policy

Regional policy refers to those measures introduced by a government in order to discriminate in favour of less prosperous regions with a view to reducing certain economic disparities with the more prosperous regions. In the United Kingdom, several regions (for example, north-east England, Wales and Scotland) have at times experienced higher unemployment rates, lower activity rates, lower incomes per capita and higher emigration rates than the average.

Regional policy
A policy designed to help the less prosperous regions in a country

A regional policy can be justified on several grounds. It might aim to reduce the economic disparities between regions by increasing the level of economic activity in the relatively depressed regions. Apart from criteria of social justice, reducing the levels of unemployment in depressed areas will, *ceteris paribus*, increase the level of national income and the rate of economic growth.

Alternatively, a successful regional policy may enable the government to operate the economy at any given level of unemployment with a lower rate of inflation than would otherwise be possible. Consider an economy in which there exist initially widespread disparities in unemployment rates between regions. If the government attempts to achieve a high level of employment by introducing expansionary fiscal and monetary policies, full employment will be attained in the more prosperous regions while substantial unemployment still exists in the less prosperous regions. If the government persists in its attempts to reduce unemployment in the less prosperous regions, excess demand will develop in the more prosperous regions leading to inflation. If, however, a successful regional policy eliminates the disparities in regional unemployment rates, these excess demands are less likely to develop and the government will be able to achieve any given level of unemployment with a lower inflation rate than would otherwise be possible.

Finally, a regional policy might aim to prevent the decline of local communities in order to maintain a geographically balanced population and prevent possible underutilisation of social capital, such as schools and hospitals. Net outward migration tends to lead to congestion costs and severe pressure on social capital in the prosperous regions that gain population. This point has been made in relation to the south-east of England which has tended to gain population at the expense of other areas in the United Kingdom.

Policy instruments

In many cases, a regional problem exists because regions have adapted inadequately to changing economic conditions, such as the decline of old industries (like shipbuilding and coal-mining in the north-east of England and other regions in the United Kingdom). Typically, this results in an excess supply of labour in the problem region. Conceivably, a government might seek to promote a wages policy that led to a relative reduction in wage rates in this area in order to clear the regional labour market. In a country like the United Kingdom, however, there are severe limitations on this approach because of the prevalence of national wage agreements and trade union opposition. Nevertheless, the United Kingdom government has introduced a number of supply-side policies in the 1980s and 1990s with the intention of allowing labour markets to operate more flexibly. Examples include trade union reform and the abolition of the wages councils. A government has two main alternative policy approaches: first, it can attempt to increase the demand for labour in the problem regions, perhaps by encouraging firms to move there or by increasing public expenditure in these regions; secondly, it could attempt to reduce the supply of labour by promoting labour mobility from these regions.

Policy measures in the United Kingdom In fact, the United Kingdom policy has been basically one of the former approach – that is, taking work to the workers. Some areas of the country are designated as 'assisted areas' which are eligible for assistance.

The government changed the emphasis of regional policy in the mid-1980s. Overall, it planned to spend substantially less in real terms on regional aid, reflecting its belief in the 'natural adjustment of labour markets'. The government argued that previous regional policy had concentrated too much on manufacturing industry. The intention was, therefore, to reduce the bias towards manufacturing and to widen the scope of regional aid to cover some service industries. It was also argued that the automatic cash grants available for expenditure on buildings, plant and equipment were not tied directly to job creation. Capital expenditure on a highly automated oil refinery, for example, might result in the transfer of large sums of taxpayers' money to help finance a project that would have been undertaken in any case and which results in the creation of relatively few jobs.

In measures introduced in 1984, the intention was to tie regional aid more closely to job creation. The category of 'special development area' was abolished, thereby leaving only two tiers of assisted areas: *development areas* and *intermediate areas*. Development areas include the most depressed areas, such as the Central Lowlands of Scotland and Merseyside, and cover about 15 per cent of the working population in Great Britain.

In 1988, the government announced the end of automatic regional grants. The policy is to focus on selective assistance which will only be granted if the applicants are able to produce evidence to show that the project would not go ahead without the assistance. The government also introduced small investment grants of 15 per cent of the cost of fixed assets for small firms (with less than 25 employees) in development areas. These firms can also apply for innovation grants for up to 50 per cent of the cost of product and process development.

The policy also provides financial assistance for small and medium-sized businesses in the assisted areas, and those in inner-city areas in the Urban Programme, to use consultants to improve the marketing and design of their products.

The government has made extensive use of selective assistance in recent years to induce multinational companies to locate their new production facilities in the United Kingdom. Examples include assistance to Nissan for a new car assembly plant near Sunderland, and to Ford for a new engine plant in Wales.

The assistance provided to firms in the development and intermediate areas represents a *positive* inducement for firms to move to these areas. From 1947 to 1981, there was also a negative measure. Firms that wished to engage in significant expansion outside an assisted area had to obtain an industrial development certificate from the government. If a certificate was refused, the hope was that the project would take place in an assisted area. In announcing the abolition of the scheme in 1981, the government pointed out that only 28 out of 7,000 applications for certificates had been refused in the period 1975–81. The scheme was judged to have outlived its usefulness.

Faced with the decline in inner cities, the government introduced the so-called *enterprise zones* in 1981. These zones, which are not strictly part of regional policy, offer a number of financial incentives to firms located in them. The incentives to both new and existing firms are available for a ten-year period from the date of designation and include exemption from rates, minimal planning restrictions and 100 per cent allowances against corporation and income tax for capital expenditure on industrial and commercial buildings. Twenty-seven zones were designated between 1981 and 1989: examples include those in steel closure areas such as Workington and Scunthorpe, and those in areas of industrial decline, such as Dudley and the Isle of Dogs.

An important criticism of enterprise zones is that they have made it financially attractive for existing firms outside the zones to relocate inside the zones. One study reported that 85 per cent of companies commencing operations in enterprise zones had transferred from within the same economic region. Thus it may be argued that the major effect is to transfer existing jobs rather than to create new jobs.

In comparison, the help given by the United Kingdom government to promote labour mobility and migration away from the assisted areas has been of minor significance. This may be because of a feeling that migration from an already depressed region compounds its problems by further reducing demand and by draining the region of its young, well-qualified workers.

EC regional policy A European dimension was added to regional policy with the formation of the EC Regional Development Fund (ERDF) in 1975. In principle, expenditure by the ERDF should be in addition to the planned expenditure on regional aid by the national governments, but there was some discussion between the EC and the United Kingdom government over the extent to which that criterion was met.

Firms in both development areas and intermediate areas are eligible for support from the ERDF. Examples of projects that have received assistance from the ERDF have included the Ford Motor Company plants at Halewood on Merseyside and at Bridgend in Wales. A wide range of infrastructure developments in the assisted regions, such as road construction and port developments, have also received aid. In this context, it should also be noted that the European Social Fund which concentrates on job training, particularly of young people, places a high proportion of its expenditure in assisted areas.

The effectiveness of regional policy in the United Kingdom After more than fifty years of regional policy in the United Kingdom, significant disparities in economic indicators, such as unemployment rates, persist between regions. This does not necessarily imply that regional policy has been completely without success. As with assessing the effectiveness of any economic policy, there is the problem of estimating what would have happened in the absence of the policy. Defenders of regional policy might claim that the regional unemployment problem would have been more severe had the policy not been in operation.

Moore, Rhodes and Taylor have estimated that, during the period 1960–81, regional policy created a total of 604,000 manufacturing jobs in the development areas. They further estimated, however, that about 154,000 of these jobs were lost before 1981. Thus, the estimated net increase in manufacturing jobs from regional policy is 450,000. The cost to government funds of creating each new job on average was estimated to be about £40,000 in 1982 prices.

Summary

1. Active policy-making requires the government to adjust its policies in response to changing economic circumstances, while passive policy making requires the government to stick to predetermined policy decisions regardless of short-term fluctuations in economic activity. Policy rules are announced targets which a government tries to achieve, while discretionary policy-making allows the government to choose the most appropriate policy action for the set of circumstances which prevail at the time.
2. Fiscal policy is the attempt to influence aggregate demand, and therefore income and employment, by regulating public expenditure and rates of taxation. Monetary policy is the attempt to influence aggregate demand by regulating the cost and availability of credit.

3. In the IS–LM model, the relative effectiveness of fiscal and monetary policies depends on the interest-elasticity of investment and the interest-elasticity of the demand for money. In general, the more interest-elastic is investment, the more effective is monetary policy and the less effective is fiscal policy; similarly, the more interest-elastic is the demand for money, the more effective is fiscal policy and the less effective is monetary policy.
4. In the AD–AS model, the effectiveness of demand-management depends on the shape of the AS curve. If the AS curve is horizontal, an increase in aggregate demand will raise real income and leave the price level unchanged. If the AS curve is vertical (as in the long-run in a monetarist model), an increase in aggregate demand will raise the price level and leave real income unchanged.
5. Supply-side policies are designed to improve the productivity of the market economy and so shift the aggregate supply curve to the right. These policies include deregulation, privatisation and various measures designed to improve the efficiency of the labour market.
6. Prices and incomes policy is a direct control on price and wage inflation through exhortation or legislation or both. Prices and incomes policy has been out of favour in the United Kingdom since 1979.
7. Regional policy is intended to reduce economic disparities between a country's regions. The policy in the United Kingdom has been mainly concerned with 'taking work to the workers', i.e. providing assistance to regions with high unemployment.

Exercises

1. Review your understanding of the following terms:

active policy making	pay 'norm'
passive policy-making	voluntary policy
policy rules	discretionary policy-making
fiscal policy	statutory policy
monetary policy	regional policy
prices policy	assisted area
incomes policy	industrial development certificate
supply-side policies	enterprise zones

2. Using the IS–LM model, illustrate an economy in the liquidity trap. Show graphically and explain carefully the effects of: (a) an increase in government spending; (b) an increase in the money supply.

3. Consider an economy with three policy targets: 3 per cent unemployment, 5 per cent rate of inflation and balance of payments equilibrium. Discuss what policy instruments are available to a government to achieve these targets.

4. Consider the view that since the economy is dynamic, neither the IS–LM model nor the AD–AS model (both comparative static equilibrium models) can assist in the formulation of policies designed to achieve full employment equilibrium.
5. Discuss the costs and problems that result from the introduction of an incomes policy which specifies a maximum annual rise in wages for all workers.
6. Discuss the view that both regional policy and a prices policy create a misallocation of resources by impeding the operation of the price mechanism.
7. Assess the effectiveness of the supply-side policies used in the United Kingdom in the 1980s and 1990s.

27 UNEMPLOYMENT

Learning objectives

After reading this chapter, you should be able to:

- explain the meaning of unemployment and appreciate the difficulties of measuring the number of people unemployed
- assess the costs of unemployment in terms of the harmful effects it can have on individuals and on society
- show that there are different types of unemployment and alternative explanations of what causes unemployment
- recognise that there are alternative policy measures which may be used in the attempt to reduce the rate of unemployment

Introduction

In the early 1980s and the early 1990s, unemployment was one of the most serious economic problems in the United Kingdom, as well as in many other countries of the western world. The purpose of this chapter is to discuss the nature of the problem, to analyse its causes and to examine the main policy alternatives. We start with an explanation of the meaning and measurement of the rate of unemployment and we consider whether the official unemployment figures in the United Kingdom overstate or understate the 'true' unemployment problem. Secondly, we outline the main costs imposed on a society by high unemployment. Thirdly, we discuss three main types of unemployment: *natural* unemployment, *demand-deficient* unemployment and *excessive real wage* unemployment. The chapter ends with a discussion of the available policy measures.

The meaning and measurement of unemployment

It is important to remember that unemployment cannot simply be defined as the number of people without jobs. Such a wide definition would include children who are too young to work, pensioners who are retired and housewives and others who choose not to take up paid employment. Since these groups pose no serious economic problems, it is correct that they should be omitted from the unemployment figures. Unemployment in a country refers to all those people who are willing and able to work, but are unable to find work.

In the United Kingdom, the number of people unemployed is measured for official purposes as *the number of people claiming benefit (that is, unemployment benefit, income support or national insurance credits) at Unemployment Benefit Offices on the day*

Table 27.1 The number unemployed and the unemployment percentage in the United Kingdom, 1973–92.

Year	Number employed (000s) (annual averages)	Unemployment percentage (%)
1973	517.1	2.0
1974	520.4	2.0
1975	798.2	3.1
1976	1,093.3	4.2
1977	1,162.7	4.4
1978	1,145.7	4.3
1979	1,075.8	4.0
1980	1,365.7	5.1
1981	2,173.6	8.1
1982	2,546.7	9.5
1983	2,790.5	10.5
1984	2,920.6	10.7
1985	3,035.7	10.9
1986	3,107.2	11.1
1987	2,822.3	10.0
1988	2,294.5	8.0
1989	1,784.4	6.3
1990	1,661.7	5.8
1991	2,289.1	8.1
1992	2,778.6	9.8

Note: The above series is consistent with current coverage.
Source: Employment Gazette, various issues.

Unemployment *The number unemployed consists of all those people in a country who are willing and able to work, but are unable to find jobs*

of the monthly count, who on that day were unemployed and willing and able to do any suitable work. This is the official definition used by the Department of Employment. The statistics used in the unemployment count are available in the form of computerised records. The official definition of the unemployment rate in the United Kingdom is *the number of unemployed claimants expressed as a percentage of the estimated total work-force (which comprises all employees in employment, the self-employed, HM Forces, participants in work-related government training programmes and the unemployed claimants).* Thus the following formula is used to calculate the unemployment rate (U) in the United Kingdom:

$$U = \frac{\text{Number of unemployed claimants}}{\text{Work-force}} \times 100 \text{ per cent}$$

The numbers unemployed and the unemployment rate for the United Kingdom for the period 1973–92 are shown in Table 27.1. It is clear that the trend of unemployment from 1973 to 1986 was steadily and ominously upwards, with the period 1980–83 seeing the most rapid rise in unemployment ever recorded in the United Kingdom. Having fallen to 5.8 per cent in 1990, the rate increased again in the early 1990s, reaching 9.8 per cent in 1992.

A further measure of unemployment in the United Kingdom is provided by the annual Labour Force Survey, conducted by the Office of Population Censuses and Surveys. This measures unemployment according to the internationally agreed definition recommended by the International Labour Organisation. The definition of unemployment used refers to people without a job in the week before the survey

Table 27.2 Comparative unemployment rates, latest month available, 1993: selected countries.

Country	Unemployment rate
Belgium	12.1
Denmark	11.3
Germany	7.5
Greece	4.6
Spain	15.3
France	10.5
Ireland	17.8
Italy	11.1
Netherlands	4.3
United Kingdom	10.6
United States	7.1
Sweden	5.6
Japan	2.2

Source: Employment Gazette, March 1993.

who were available to start work within the next two weeks, and who had either looked for work in the four weeks before the survey or were waiting to start a job. This 'survey method' of estimating unemployment is the main method used in some countries, including the United States, Canada, Australia and Japan. The survey method has the advantage that no one who could reasonably be said to be unemployed is excluded and no one who is clearly *not* unemployed is included. However, the estimates are of course subject to sampling error.

Comparative unemployment rates for ten of the member countries of the EC and other selected countries are shown for the latest months available in 1993 in Table 27.2. It can be seen from this table that the United Kingdom rate exceeded 10 per cent in the early part of 1993.

Interpreting the unemployment figures

There are reasons for believing that the official United Kingdom unemployment figures, measured as the number of people claiming benefits, may *understate* the actual number of people unemployed. This is because there are undoubtedly some people who are out of work and seeking jobs, but are not claiming any form of social security benefit: such people are not counted in the official statistics. On the other hand, it is arguable that the official United Kingdom figures *overstate* the 'true' unemployment problem by including people who are not seriously unemployed. In this section, we consider these two possibilities.

Only those people who are eligible to claim benefits are counted. The group of 'uncounted unemployed' is likely to consist largely of women and school-leavers who have not worked before and so are not eligible for unemployment benefit. There is no reason to suppose, however, that unemployment among this group creates so few problems that we can ignore it. It is true that the cost to the Exchequer is below average because no benefits are paid (though there is still a loss of potential taxation), but the unemployed may suffer from lack of income, boredom and depression in just the same way as the counted unemployed; furthermore, since they are capable and available for work, they represent a loss of potential output.

In addition to those unemployed who are not claiming benefits, another form of 'hidden' unemployment exists among those people who are in paid employment, but whose services and skills are being underutilised. This may be because they are not working full-time or are not doing jobs which make full use of their abilities. The size of this type of unemployment is obviously extremely difficult to estimate, but it may be quite substantial, particularly in those industries with powerful trade unions where employers are reluctant to lay off workers for fear of initiating an industrial dispute.

Given the existence of the uncounted unemployed and the underutilised labour force, we might reasonably conclude that the official statistics seriously underestimate actual unemployment.

However, it has to be recognised both in collecting unemployment data and in interpreting the unemployment figures that the unemployment pool is constantly turning over. As some people join others leave, so that even though the total number of unemployed may have remained unchanged from one month to the next, the composition of that unemployment may have changed considerably. This means that it is important in analysing unemployment to take account of the average duration of unemployment spells, as well as the total number unemployed. Unemployment is clearly a more serious problem *the greater is the number of unemployed and the longer is the average duration of unemployment spells.*

Consideration of the duration of unemployment leads us to the possibility that a significant proportion of the unemployed could be short-term – perhaps less than four weeks in duration. Should such short-term unemployment be counted in the official unemployment figures? It still represents a cost to the Exchequer and a loss of potential output, but it can be argued that it is not particularly distressing to the people concerned and, for the economy as a whole, it may actually result in a more efficient use of labour: this is because high short-run unemployment may be a reflection of greater mobility of labour between jobs and areas and consequently may result in the labour force being more suitably and productively employed. Some economists have argued that short-term unemployment should be excluded from the official figures in order that the statistics be made more useful to policy-makers.

It goes without saying that it would also be desirable to exclude from the unemployment figures those who are employed but are making fraudulent claims for unemployment benefit or supplementary benefits. Since such fraudulent claimants are not actually unemployed, it is wrong that they should be counted with the unemployed. Unfortunately, it is very difficult to estimate the number of fraudulent claims (for obvious reasons). Estimates suggest that the number is relatively small, probably no more than 3 per cent of the total unemployed.

The costs of unemployment

Unemployment is harmful because it imposes costs on society. The cost of unemployment to a nation can be categorised under three headings: the social cost; the cost to the Exchequer; the economic cost. We briefly consider these in turn.

The social cost of unemployment

The social cost of involuntary unemployment is incalculable. For an individual, the demoralising effect that it can have clearly depends upon whether the period of unemployment is short-term or long-term. Short-term unemployment may have no serious effect on an individual; long-term unemployment can be devastating.

In 1991, according to the Labour Force Survey, just over 51 per cent of people unemployed for more than a year were over 35 years of age. Many of these people believe that they are failing to find jobs because they are too old and a large number of older people have become reconciled to the prospect of never working again. A major problem, of course, is that as job-searchers become more and more pessimistic about their chances of finding work, so their motivation is reduced and their chances of succeeding in finding jobs become even more remote.

According to a survey carried out by the Manpower Services Commission, many of the longer-term unemployed become bored, idle, lose their friends and suffer from depression. One respondent to the survey stated: 'It's not just the money. Work gives you something to do. I'm just wasting away.' There is also evidence of increased family tensions leading in some cases to violence, divorce and family break-ups. Unemployment can also lead to homelessness, as in some circumstances building societies may foreclose on a mortgage if the repayments are not kept up. One can only speculate on the effect of long-term unemployment on vandalism, football hooliganism and the crime rate in general.

In countries without adequate welfare provisions for the poor, unemployment may be very much more severe in its effects. It may lead to a considerable degree of social deprivation and a miserable existence for the families involved. In extreme cases (for example, where unemployment means no income at all), it can lead to starvation.

The cost to the Exchequer

Voluntary unemployment *A situation in which workers refuse to accept a cut in real wages, so that the prevailing real wage is above the market-clearing level*

Involuntary unemployment *A situation in which a worker is unable to find a job at the going wage rate*

The cost of both voluntary and involuntary unemployment to the Exchequer is more readily quantifiable than the social cost. It consists of the following three components:

(a) Benefits which have to be paid to the unemployed: these include unemployment benefit, supplementary benefit, housing benefit, government contributions to redundancy payments and payments to those men aged between 60 and 65 who no longer register as unemployed.

(b) The loss of tax revenues which would otherwise have been received: this consists mostly of lost income tax, but also includes lost indirect taxes because of the reduction in spending.

(c) The loss of national insurance contributions which would otherwise have been received.

At the time of writing, estimates of the average annual cost of unemployment to the Exchequer in the United Kingdom range from £8,000 to £9,000 per unemployed worker. With 3 million unemployed people, this represents a total annual cost of between £24 billion and £27 billion.

The economic cost

So far as the economic cost is concerned, unemployment represents a waste of resources and means that the economy is producing a lower rate of output than it could do if there were full employment. Figure 27.1 shows a time-series of actual gross domestic product in the United Kingdom measured at 1975 prices since 1960. The trend line drawn through the peaks of the time-series can be regarded as providing a rough estimate of the economy's potential output during the period.

Fig. 27.1. *The output gap in the UK, 1960–92.* The shaded area represents the gap between estimated potential output and actual output. It represents a crude measure of the economic cost of unemployment.

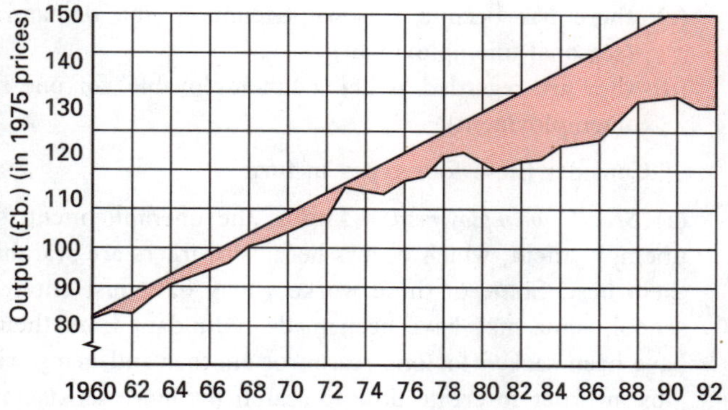

Potential output is that rate of gross domestic product which would result if all resources were fully employed.

The shaded area between the actual time-series and the trend line in Fig. 27.1 is called the output gap and is a reflection of the output of goods and services which has been lost as a result of the unemployment. It is clear from Fig. 27.1 that the output gap has been steadily increasing in size since 1960, apart from a period of full employment in 1973–74. This means that society is increasingly experiencing a lower standard of living than would be possible without rising levels of unemployment.

Output gap *The loss of the output of goods and services as a result of unemployment*

The loss of potential output resulting from involuntary unemployment is clearly a serious matter for an economy. Resources which are willing and able to work in order to raise the rate of output and to boost living standards are failing to be employed. This is a true waste of resources. It is not so clear, however, whether the loss of potential output through voluntary unemployment is so serious. It may simply be that more people are taking advantage of higher social security benefits to spend more time searching for suitable jobs. It may be argued that the longer people search for jobs, the more satisfied they will be with their eventual choices. They may consequently be more content in their work and more productive.

Causes of unemployment

It is convenient to discuss the causes of unemployment under three main headings: 'natural' unemployment, demand-deficient unemployment and excessive real wage unemployment.

Natural unemployment

The level of natural unemployment can be defined as the number of persons who are unemployed even when the labour market is in long-run equilibrium; that is, when the total demand for labour is equal to the supply of labour at the prevailing level of real wage rates. In this situation, people may be unemployed because:

Natural unemployment *The level of unemployment in an economy when the labour market is in long-run equilibrium*

(a) they are between jobs and are taking time to search for the most appropriate job with the highest wage (search unemployment);
(b) the industry in which they have traditionally worked has experienced a structural decline or has been influenced by technological advances (structural unemployment);

(c) there has been a seasonal decline in the demand for their labour services (seasonal unemployment);
(d) they are regarded as being 'unemployable' for one reason or another (residual unemployment).

Consider these four types in turn.

Search unemployment *This refers to people who are temporarily between jobs. It persists because of imperfect information in the labour market*

Discouraged worker *A worker who withdraws from the labour market because of poor job prospects*

(a) *Search unemployment.* This is the unemployment, sometimes called frictional unemployment, which occurs because workers are searching for the jobs which suit them best. Some of these workers may have just entered the labour market from school, some may have been made redundant from their previous jobs, some may have been sacked for one reason or another and many will have quit their previous jobs in order to create time to search for more satisfactory ones.

All unemployed workers are, of course, searching for new jobs (apart, that is, from those discouraged workers who regard themselves as having withdrawn from the labour market). This does not mean, however, that all unemployment is of the 'search' type. Search unemployment can be seen as part of the annual turnover of the job market – firms rid themselves of workers who have proved to be unproductive or unsatisfactory in some way, and workers quit jobs which have failed to meet their expectations or which were intended only as stop-gaps in the first place.

There are two main reasons why these unemployed workers do not find jobs immediately. First, there is imperfect knowledge and the collection of information is time-consuming. Second, most workers believe that the more time they spend searching for a job, the more likely it is that they will obtain one which meets their requirements, particularly so far as the wage rate and working conditions are concerned. Thus, the search for jobs is *not* a period of inactivity – it involves finding out what jobs are available, sending off application forms, going to interviews and perhaps attending courses, all of which make job-searching a very busy time.

Reservation wage *The lowest wage at which an individual is willing to accept a job offer*

As we saw in Ch. 16, the economic theory of job-search has grown into an important aspect of labour economics in recent years. This theory sees the unemployed person as continuing the job-search (that is, remaining unemployed) so long as wage offers are less than a certain reservation wage. The reservation wage is the *minimum wage* the individual is prepared to accept. It will depend to some extent on the net costs of searching – the lower the search costs, the higher the reservation wage is likely to be and, therefore, the longer the spell of unemployment. This is illustrated in Fig. 27.2, where it is assumed that wage offers increase over time as the individual searches. The initial reservation wage is RW_1 and the expected length of the unemployment spell is $0t_1$. Higher net search costs (caused, for example, by a reduction in unemployment benefit) reduce the reservation wage to RW_2 and so reduce the expected duration of unemployment to $0t_2$. Other things being equal, the higher is the average for the length of time a person is unemployed, the greater will be the number unemployed at any moment in time.

Structural unemployment *This refers to people who have lost their jobs because of changes in the structure of demand or technological developments, such as automation*

It should be mentioned that many economists regard search unemployment as inevitable and, at least in one sense, desirable. They see it as an indication that workers are moving out of jobs where they are no longer very efficient to areas where they are more productive. This improved allocation of resources should raise real output in the economy as a whole.

(b) *Structural unemployment.* This is a more serious type of natural unemployment and is caused by changes in the structure of demand for goods and services in an

Fig. 27.2. Search unemployment. An unemployed person will remain unemployed as long as wage offers are less than the individual's reservation wage.

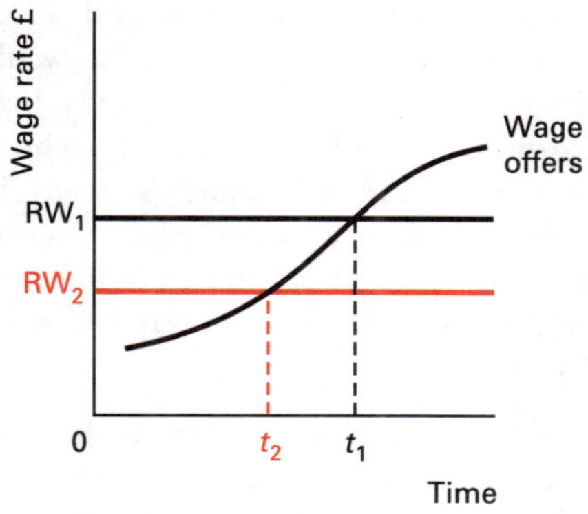

economy and by technological changes, both of which affect the composition of the demand for labour. To illustrate more clearly what is meant by structural unemployment, consider a region within a country which has traditionally specialised in shipbuilding. Suppose, as has in fact happened, that the world demand for ships decreases and shifts to more efficient producers overseas. Although the demand for *other* goods and services may increase at the same time, this does not immediately help the obsolete shipbuilders. As they become unemployed, they find that there are few jobs available in their local area and no jobs at all which require their specialised skills. They face the prospect of having to accept unskilled jobs at lower wages, or of retraining; in either event, they may have to move to another part of the country. The fact that certain regions in the United Kingdom have come to depend on declining industries explains in part the regional disparities of unemployment.

Structural unemployment persists mostly because of the geographical and occupational immobility of labour. The major causes of *geographical immobility* include social ties and a reluctance to move away from family and friends; indeed, the problems and costs of moving to a new location may be prohibitive for many people. The major cause of *occupational immobility* is the fact that many skills are not easily transferable from one occupation to another. The occupational mobility of labour can often be overcome by a period of retraining, but this takes time and may be costly for the unemployed worker. Also, workers may be reluctant to retrain until they are convinced that their present skills are not sufficient to enable them to find work. *Lack of information* is another reason for the persistence of structural unemployment, being itself one of the causes of geographical and occupational immobility. Often the unemployed are not aware of the opportunities available in other parts of the country or in other occupations.

In recent years, a great deal of emphasis has been placed on *technological progress* as a cause of structural unemployment. Advances in automation, the development of word processors and the many other applications of information technology have all been blamed for rising unemployment. It is true that these developments are likely to reduce the labour–capital ratios in a wide range of industries. This implies that the number of jobs associated with any *given* level of output in the economy will be smaller than it would have been without the technological advances. However, the increased productivity of labour may help many firms to cut costs, enabling them to reduce prices and to *expand* their levels of output, thereby increasing their demands for all factor inputs, including labour. The final effect on the overall level of unemployment is uncertain. For this reason, it would not be appropriate to discourage technological progress on the grounds that it is likely to increase structural unemployment. Indeed, discouraging technological progress within a particular country would make the country's goods less competitive in world markets and this might lead to an even greater increase in unemployment. An extensive retraining scheme for those who enter the unemployment pool with the 'wrong' skills would be a more efficient way of reducing this type of natural unemployment.

Seasonal unemployment *This refers to people who lose their jobs because of a fall in the demand for labour at certain times of the year*

(c) *Seasonal unemployment.* At any given time of the year, there are always likely to be some workers who are temporarily laid off because of a seasonal fall in demand for their services. In the winter months, for example, many building workers find themselves without work because of bad weather and many workers in the tourism industry are also laid off. Similarly, in the summer months, workers associated with the winter sports industry and with the rush to produce and sell goods and services during the lead-up to Christmas find that their services are no longer required.

This type of unemployment can undoubtedly cause hardship to the workers involved; also, it represents a waste of resources and is a drain on the Exchequer. It should, therefore, be some cause for concern. On the other hand, seasonal employment is thought by many to be a convenient source of casual work which enables extra income to be earned without the ties of a more permanent job.

(d) *Residual unemployment.* This is the label given to that group of unemployed workers who suffer from mental and/or physical disabilities which may limit the number of job opportunities available to them.

Hysterisis *A phenomenon that comes into effect when an economy in long-run equilibrium experiences a disturbance such as a recession. The result of the recession is such that when the disturbance has finally disappeared, the economy is unable to attain the initial long-run equilibrium level of output and employment*

The sum of frictional, structural, seasonal and residual unemployment equals the total amount of natural unemployment in an economy. Some economists claim that the natural rate of unemployment is roughly constant over time, possibly about 5 per cent of the labour force in the United Kingdom. Others believe that the natural rate can vary considerably over time and will depend on such factors as the size of any structural changes taking place, and on the application of supply-side policies.

In addition, some economists argue that the reductions in aggregate demand which occur during a recession may have a long-term effect on the natural rate of unemployment. For example, a recession which lasts several years may cause some workers to lose their job skills and/or become discouraged from finding jobs in the future, so increasing frictional unemployment. This long-term effect of changes in aggregate demand on unemployment is referred to as hysteresis.

Demand-deficient unemployment

Demand-deficient unemployment *Unemployment caused by a general deficiency of aggregate demand.*

As its name implies, demand-deficient unemployment occurs when there is a general deficiency of the demand for labour in the economy such that it is impossible for all those who are seeking work to be employed. It was emphasised in Ch. 16 that the demand for labour is a derived demand – it is derived from the demand for goods and services. Thus, when we say that unemployment is caused by a general deficiency of the demand for *labour*, this is equivalent to saying that unemployment is caused by a general deficiency of the demand for goods and services. As we have seen, the importance of demand-deficient unemployment was emphasised by

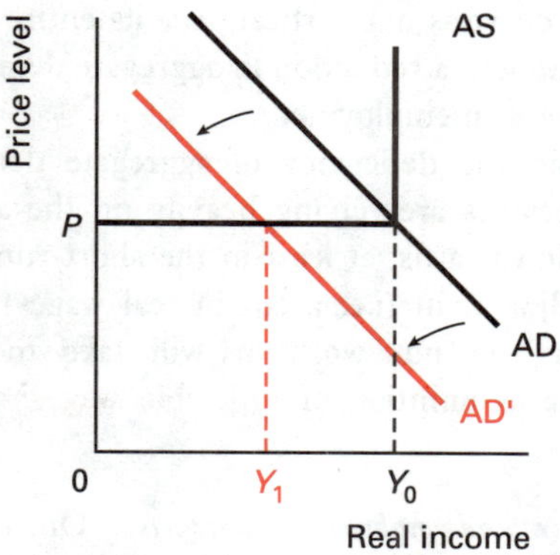

Fig. 27.3. ***Demand-deficient (Keynesian) unemployment.*** With an extreme Keynesian inverted-L shaped AS curve, any change in the economy which shifts the AD curve to the left will reduce the equilibrium level of real income and create demand-deficient unemployment.

Keynes. It is because of this that demand-deficient unemployment is sometimes referred to as Keynesian unemployment.

We can illustrate demand-deficient unemployment using the AD and AS curves derived in Ch. 23. To do this, we assume that it is possible to identify a zero demand-deficient unemployment level of national income ($0Y_0$). As its name implies, this is the level of national income at which there is no deficiency of aggregate demand and so at which unemployment is at its 'natural' level. In Fig. 27.3, which shows an extreme Keynesian AS curve, the initial equilibrium level of national income is equal to $0Y_0$ and we can say, therefore, that there is no demand-deficient unemployment.

Demand-deficient unemployment will arise if the AD curve should shift to the left, thereby reducing the equilibrium level of national income below $0Y_0$. To investigate the possible causes of demand-deficient unemployment, therefore, we need to examine the possible causes of a decrease in aggregate demand. Consider the following possibilities:

(a) *A decrease in I or G or X.* If domestic firms decide to invest less at all interest rates (perhaps because they are less confident about future economic prospects), or if the government decides to cut its expenditure, or if there is a loss of export markets, then the AD curve will shift to the left. The effect of this is illustrated in Fig. 27.3 where the new equilibrium level of income, $0Y_1$ is below $0Y_0$, indicating that some demand-deficient unemployment has been created.

(b) *An increase in S or T or M.* Other things being equal, any increase in the desire to save by households, or in the amount of taxation taken by the government, or in the amount households spend on imports, will also shift the AD curve to the left. Since this also has the effect of reducing the equilibrium level of income below $0Y_0$, increases in *S*, *T* or *M* may also be regarded as potential causes of demand-deficient unemployment.

(c) *A decrease in the money supply.* If the monetary authorities should decide to reduce the nominal money supply, the effect will be to shift the AD curve to the left. Once again, the equilibrium level of income falls below $0Y_0$.

(d) *An increase in the demand for money.* With a given money supply, an increase in the demand for money will also shift the AD curve to the left.

As long as the AS curve is not vertical over its entire length (as it would be in a long-run monetarist model), a reduction in aggregate demand will reduce the level of real income and increase unemployment.

In concentrating on the deficiency of aggregate demand as a determinant of unemployment, Keynesians are relying heavily on the assumption that wages and prices are inflexible downwards, at least in the short-run. This assumption ensures that labour market adjustment (i.e. a cut in real wages) as a means of eliminating unemployment either will not work or will take too long. How do modern Keynesians justify the assumption of inflexible wages? A number of explanations have been proposed:

Inflexible wages *A situation in which money wage rates do not respond to the conditions of supply and demand in the labour market*

Implicit contract *Terms and conditions of employment that are not expressly (or explicitly) stated in the contract*

Explicit contract *Terms and conditions of employment that are expressly (or explicitly) stated in the contract*

Efficiency wage *A wage above the market equilibrium rate paid with a view to encourage effort and to achieve efficient production*

Insiders *Members of the labour force who are able to influence wage negotiations by virtue of their current employment*

Outsiders *Members of the labour force who are not able to influence wage negotiations by virtue of being unemployed*

(a) *Trade union pressure and employment contracts.* One of the main reasons for wage rigidity stems from imperfect competition in the labour market. In Ch. 17, we emphasised that labour is not a homogeneous factor of production, and that the markets for different types of labour are not perfectly competitive. Instead, some firms have some degree of monopsonistic power in their demand for certain types of labour (as well as monopoly power in the product markets) and, at the same time, trade unions have some degree of monopoly control over the supply of certain types of labour. Consequently, in practice, many wage rates are determined annually by the process of collective bargaining in which union representatives push for wage increases for their members and strongly resist any proposals to reduce wage rates. The outcome of the bargaining process will be *contracts* (implicit or explicit) between employers and employees stating the wage rates for the coming year or years. Thus, in many cases, wage rates are downwardly rigid and contractually fixed for one or more years. Under these circumstances, it is not surprising that the labour market may be in disequilibrium for long periods of time.

(b) *Efficiency wages.* Some firms may prefer to pay wage rates above the market equilibrium rates as they believe that this will improve the performance and loyalty of their employees and help to discourage 'shirking'; it may also reduce labour turnover which is costly to firms; and it will enable firms to be more selective in hiring their workers. The intention is to achieve greater efficiency in the use of labour.

(c) *Insiders and outsiders.* One possible reason why high unemployment may not immediately exert downward pressure on wage rates is the existence of insiders and outsiders in the labour market. Insiders are the employed who are able to take part in negotiations with employers to determine wage rates and working conditions. Outsiders are the unemployed who may be large in number but, by virtue of the fact that they are outside the labour market, have no real influence on the level of wages. Although outsiders may be prepared to accept lower wages than insiders, the costs of firing, hiring and training may make it impractical for most firms to switch to lower-paid workers.

Excessive real wage unemployment

Monetarists deny the existence of demand-deficient unemployment and instead subscribe to the view that unemployment above the natural rate is caused by real wages being too high as a result of restrictive practices in the labour market

Fig. 27.4. *Excessive real wage unemployment.* At the real wage $(W/P)_1$, there is an excess supply of labour. This unemployment could be eliminated by a fall in the real wage to $(W/P)_0$.

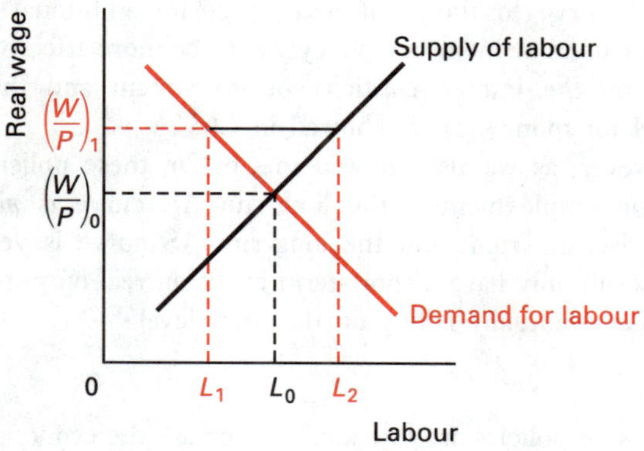

Excessive real wage unemployment
Unemployment that results from the real wage being above the market clearing level because of restrictive practices in the labour market

(primarily the monopoly power of trade unions). This is illustrated in Fig. 27.4 where $(W/P)_1$ is the prevailing real wage: it is clear that there is an *excess* supply of labour equal to L_1L_2 at this real wage. This means that the total level of unemployment *exceeds* the natural level – i.e. the level of unemployment which would still have existed even if the real wage had been $(W/P)_0$ which cleared the labour market. According to this approach, the solution to unemployment is a cut in the real wage, achievable either by cutting the money wage or by allowing the price level to rise more rapidly than money wages. Monetarists believe that this real wage adjustment will eventually occur in the long-run, and will occur more quickly if the labour market can be made more competitive.

An interesting debate between Keynesian and neo-classical economists concerned the question of whether unemployment above the natural rate would necessarily be eliminated *if wages and prices were perfectly flexible*. Neo-classical economists stated that it would be eliminated, arguing their case along the following lines. An excess supply of labour will cause money wages to fall. As real wages fall, employment and output will start to rise: this will create an excess supply of goods and services and so exert downward pressure on the price level. The result will be a general deflation of both money wages and prices which will: (i) increase the real value of the country's money supply; and (ii) raise the real value of people's money holdings (the *real balance effect*). Neo-classical economists have stressed that it is the increase in the real money supply and the real balance effect which will lead to an expansion of aggregate demand and so eliminate excessive real wage unemployment. Keynesians have remained very sceptical of this mechanism, arguing that neither the increase in the real money supply nor the real balance effect will have a significant effect on aggregate demand and so cannot be relied upon to reduce unemployment.

Alternative policy measures

Fiscal and monetary policies

Fiscal and monetary policies, sometimes called *demand-management* or *demand-side* policies, are intended to increase aggregate demand and, therefore, the equilibrium level of national income. The principal policy instruments are government expenditure, taxation and the stock of money in circulation. If unemployment is caused by a general deficiency of aggregate demand, as illustrated in Fig. 27.3, then it may be appropriate to increase aggregate demand (for example, by increasing government expenditure, cutting taxation or expanding the money supply) to shift the AD curve to the right and so create additional income and employment. Whether fiscal or monetary policy would be more effective for this purpose depends largely on the interest-elasticity of investment and the interest-elasticity of the demand for money, as we showed in Ch. 26.

However, as we also showed in Ch. 26, these policies can only have a lasting effect on employment if the long-run AS curve is *not vertical.* If the extreme monetarists are right and the long-run AS curve is vertical, fiscal and monetary policies will only have a short-term effect on real output and employment, with the full effect eventually falling on the price level.

Supply-side policies

Supply-side policies are intended to increase the economy's potential rate of output by increasing the supply of factor inputs, such as labour inputs and capital inputs, and by increasing productivity. Labour market policies specifically designed to reduce natural unemployment might include the following:

(a) *Improvements in information dissemination.* A lack of information is a likely cause of natural unemployment for two main reasons. First, unemployed workers may take a long time to find suitable jobs if they are not made aware of all the available opportunities. In these days of information technology, job search periods could be reduced if all employment offices had access to a fully computerised data processing system capable of identifying all the possible matches between the available vacancies and the unemployed at any moment in time. Secondly, many employers may themselves be guilty in many instances of failing to provide sufficient information about the nature of the jobs they offer and the working conditions. In this case, it is not surprising that workers who accept jobs soon drop them again when they turn out unexpectedly to be unsuitable. The government may be able to improve the quality of information by financing an upgrading of the services provided by employment offices and job centres, and by adopting a campaign to encourage and persuade employers to provide detailed and truthful job descriptions for all job applicants.

(b) *Provision of retraining schemes.* We have seen that the occupational immobility of labour is one of the major determinants of structural unemployment. One way of tackling this problem is for the government to finance retraining schemes for those unemployed workers who wish to acquire new skills. It is, of course, important to ensure that the new skills are those for which there is greatest demand in the labour market.

(c) *Assistance with family relocation.* We have also seen that geographical immobility is a determinant of structural unemployment. To tackle this problem, the provision of information concerning recreational facilities, schools and the quality of life in general in other parts of the country may be helpful, but perhaps more important would be the provision of financial help to cover moving costs and to assist with home purchase.

(d) *Special employment assistance for teenagers.* One of the most worrying aspects of the high unemployment percentages in recent years has been the increase in youth unemployment. Many teenagers leave school without having studied work-related subjects and with little or no work experience. This makes it difficult for them to find jobs; those who do become employed may soon find that the work is not at all what they expected and so quit in order to search for more suitable posts. The strengthening of vocational counselling, the expansion of work-related studies (such as business practice, catering and information technology) and the payment of subsidies to those firms who take on young people for short periods of work experience may all help to alleviate youth unemployment. Work-related training schemes for school-leavers may also be useful in this respect.

(e) *Subsidies to firms which reduce working hours rather than the size of the work-force.* This proposal may help to reduce that structural unemployment caused by the displacement of workers by new technology. We have seen that it would be counter-productive to discourage firms from adopting new technology. The government could, however, encourage firms and trade unions to work towards a reduction in average weekly working hours rather than a reduction in the size of the work-force. This might be achieved by paying a subsidy to those firms which adopt new technological equipment and at the same time negotiate successfully with the relevant trade unions to reduce working hours rather than lay off workers.

Minimum wage laws

In recent years, there have been calls from some quarters for the establishment of a legal minimum wage in the United Kingdom as a means of bringing certain groups of workers (especially unskilled workers) up to a reasonable standard of living. A possible problem with this proposal, however, is that if the minimum wage is above the equilibrium wage for a certain group of workers, its implementation will have the effect of reducing the quantity of labour being demanded in that market and increasing unemployment amongst those workers. This is illustrated in Fig 27.5 where $0W_m$ is the minimum wage and $0W_0$ is the equilibrium wage in a competitive market for a particular type of labour. The minimum wage reduces actual employment from $0L_0$ to $0L_1$ and creates unemployment in the market equal to L_1L_2.

One group likely to be affected by the implementation of a legal minimum wage is teenage trainees and apprentices who earn very low wages. A minimum wage will

Fig. 27.5. The effects of minimum wage legislation. In a competitive labour market, a minimum wage set above the equilibrium wage creates unemployment in the market equal to L_1L_2.

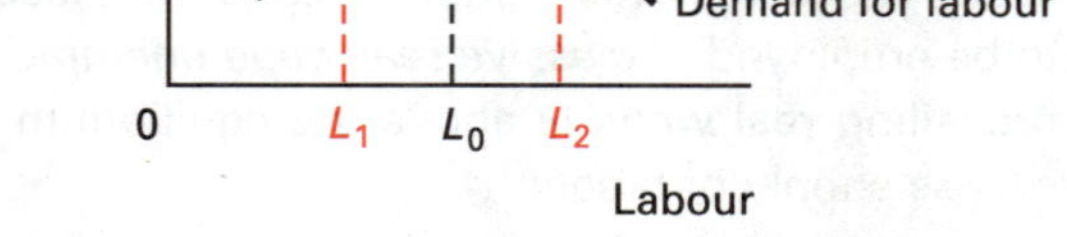

raise their incomes but may also increase teenage unemployment. Since these workers are receiving compensation in the form of training as well as wages from their employers, some economists have argued that they should be exempt from any minimum wage laws.

As long as the minimum wage is set at a low level, it will have little or no effect on most labour markets, and its effect on total unemployment is likely to be slight. Also, it is important to point out that Fig. 27.5 illustrates a *competitive* labour market and assumes that firms attempt to maximise profits. In markets where groups of unskilled workers are being paid very low wages by firms which possess some degree of monopoly power (and monopoly profits), minimum wage legislation might be a successful way of redistributing incomes from profit-earners to the working poor without causing additional unemployment.

Summary

1. Unemployment is defined as the number of people in a country who are willing and able to work but are unable to find jobs, measured in the United Kingdom as the number of benefit claimants. The rate of unemployment is measured as the number of unemployed claimants expressed as a percentage of the total workforce.
2. This measurement of unemployment may underestimate the actual number of people unemployed because there are undoubtedly some people who are unemployed but who do not claim benefits. On the other hand, some benefit claimants may simply be between jobs for a short period and so may not be seriously unemployed. Factors such as these should be taken into consideration in interpreting unemployment statistics.
3. Unemployment is harmful because it imposes three types of costs on a country: first, there is a *social cost* in terms of the psychological effect it can have on individuals and the social problems it can cause; secondly, there is a *cost to the Exchequer* in terms of the benefits that have to be paid and loss of taxation and national insurance contributions; thirdly, there is an *economic cost* in terms of the loss of output that could have been produced under conditions of full employment.
4. The causes of unemployment may be discussed under three main headings. *Natural unemployment* can be defined as the amount of unemployment which exists when the labour market is in equilibrium; it includes search, structural, seasonal and residual unemployment. *Demand-deficient unemployment*, or Keynesian unemployment, occurs when there is a general deficiency of aggregate demand in the economy such that it is impossible for all those who are seeking work to be employed. *Excessive real wage unemployment* occurs when the prevailing real wage is above the equilibrium real wage, creating an excess supply of labour.

5. Demand-side policies, such as fiscal and monetary policies, can be used to increase the level of aggregate demand and so may be appropriate means of reducing demand-deficient unemployment.
6. Supply-side policies are intended to improve the efficiency and productivity of factor inputs. Examples include improvements in information dissemination about job opportunities and retraining schemes.
7. The establishment of a legal minimum wage is one possible way of raising the standard of living of the working poor. A possible problem is that a minimum wage may reduce the quantity of labour being demanded in low-wage markets and so raise unemployment.

Exercises

1. Review your understanding of the following terms:

unemployment rate	seasonal unemployment
output gap	residual unemployment
natural unemployment	demand-deficient unemployment
search unemployment	excessive real wage unemployment
reservation wage	demand-side policies
structural unemployment	supply-side policies
implicit contract	explicit contract
efficiency wages	insiders
outsiders	hysteresis

Table 27.3 GDP at factor cost and retail prices in the United Kingdom, 1975–91.

Year	Gross domestic product at factor cost (£b.)	Retail Price Index (1985 = 100)
1975	95.6	36.1
1976	112.6	42.1
1977	129.6	48.8
1978	149.5	52.8
1979	173.2	59.9
1980	201.0	70.7
1981	218.8	79.1
1982	238.2	85.9
1983	261.1	89.8
1984	280.8	94.3
1985	307.9	100.0
1986	328.1	103.4
1987	360.6	107.7
1988	401.1	113.0
1989	441.1	121.8
1990	479.5	133.3
1991	497.0	141.4

Source: Economic Trends Annual Supplement, 1992.

2. Using the figures from Tables 27.1 and 27.3: (a) calculate GDP at factor cost in 1985 prices; (b) compare time-series graphs for unemployment and real GDP for the period 1975–91.

3. 'Full employment is achieved when the number of people unemployed is equal to the number of job vacancies.' Discuss.

4.** Explain what is meant by 'natural' unemployment. What policies might be used to reduce this type of unemployment?

5. Discuss the adverse effects on a society of a high rate of unemployment. To what extent can fiscal and monetary policies be used to alleviate the problem?

6. Discuss the view that excessive wage increases cause unemployment.

7. Discuss the view that the introduction of a minimum wage in the United Kingdom would increase unemployment among teenagers.

28 INFLATION

Learning objectives

After reading this chapter, you should be able to:

- explain the meaning of inflation and show how it is measured in the United Kingdom
- recognise the redistributive, administrative and international effects of inflation
- appreciate that there has been a long-standing debate about the main causes of inflation and understand the terms 'demand-pull inflation', 'cost-push inflation' and the Phillips curve
- explain the role played by expectations in generating and sustaining inflation
- recognise that there are alternative policy measures which may be used in the attempt to reduce the rate of inflation

Introduction

Inflation *A persistent tendency for the general price level to rise*

Inflation is a phenomenon which affects everybody in one way or another. It can be argued that mild inflation (say, no more than 5 per cent per annum) may have beneficial effects on an economy; for example, it may be consistent with a low level of unemployment and, if prices tend to be inflexible downwards, it may enable the price mechanism to work more effectively. However, inflation can have adverse effects on the economy, and it may give rise to the fear of a hyperinflation – a very rapidly accelerating inflation which usually leads to the breakdown of the country's monetary system. Germany experienced a hyperinflation in 1923 when the price level increased by more than ten billion fold in just over one year! The existing currency had to be withdrawn and replaced by a new one whose supply was subjected to greater control.

But what is inflation and how is the rate of inflation measured? Inflation has to be carefully defined. It is not simply 'rising prices' for as the prices of some goods rise, others may fall, leaving the general level of prices unchanged. Nor should inflation be defined simply as 'an increase in the general price level' for an increase one month may be offset by a decrease the next. For inflation to be taking place, it is necessary that the general price level be rising continuously over a fairly long period of time (for example, several months or a year).

The next question is: which measure of the general price level should be used to calculate the rate of inflation? The general price level can be estimated in different ways: in the United Kingdom, for example, there are producer price indices and a Retail Price Index. The Retail Price Index is undoubtedly the most commonly quoted and in this book we define the *rate* of inflation as *the percentage increase in the Retail Price Index over a period of one year.*

Retail price index *An index which aims to measure the change in the average price of a basket of goods and services that represents the consumption pattern of a typical household*

Consider now how the United Kingdom Retail Price Index is calculated. The index is a measure of the changes in the average price of a basket of those goods and services on which most households spend their income. The actual goods and services included in the basket and the weights given to each item are determined by the Family Expenditure Survey in which approximately 7,000 households a year provide a record of their spending over a fortnightly period. Having determined the composition of the basket, civil servants collect monthly price quotations from retail outlets all around the country and a *weighted* average of these is calculated, the weights reflecting the relative importance of the items in the basket. For example, the average household spends more on food than it does on tobacco: it is correct, therefore, that the average price of food should have more weight than tobacco in calculating the overall average price level. Table 28.1 shows the actual weights which were attached to the major expenditure groups included in the index in 1992. As can be seen from the table, food, motoring expenditure and housing have the biggest weights. Finally, the average is expressed, not in pounds and pence, but as an index showing the percentage changes in prices from a selected reference base (which at present is 1985). The price of the basket is set equal to 100 in the base period and the current index (say, 140) indicates the change in prices since that period (that is, 40 per cent). The index can also be used to estimate the percentage change in prices between any two months.

Table 28.2 shows the United Kingdom Index of Retail Prices and the annual rates of inflation from 1972 to 1992. In the 1960s, the rate of inflation did not exceed 6 per cent. In the 1970s, the rate of inflation increased rapidly to rates never before experienced in the United Kingdom. The rate has been in single figures since 1982.

Table 28.1 Weights used in compiling the Retail Price Index, 1992.

Item	1992 weights
Food	152
Alcoholic drink	80
Catering	47
Tobacco	36
Housing	172
Fuel and light	47
Household goods	77
Household services	48
Clothing and footwear	59
Personal goods and services	40
Motoring expenditure	143
Fares and other travel	20
Leisure goods	47
Leisure services	32
	1,000

Source: Employment Gazette, March 1993.

Table 28.2 Prices and inflation statistics for the United Kingdom, 1972–92.

Year	Retail Price Index (1985 = 100)	Annual rate of inflation (%)
1972	23.0	7.1
1973	25.1	9.1
1974	29.1	15.9
1975	36.1	24.1
1976	42.1	16.6
1977	48.8	15.9
1978	52.8	8.2
1979	59.9	13.4
1980	70.7	18.0
1981	79.1	11.9
1982	85.9	8.6
1983	89.8	4.6
1984	94.3	5.0
1985	100.0	6.1
1986	103.4	3.4
1987	107.7	4.2
1988	113.0	4.9
1989	121.8	7.8
1990	133.3	9.4
1991	141.1	5.9
1992	149.2	5.7

Source: Economic Trends, Annual Supplement, 1993.

Table 28.3 Comparative inflation rates, 1991: selected countries.

Country	Inflation rate
Belgium	3.2
Denmark	2.4
Germany	3.5
Greece	19.5
Spain	6.0
France	3.0
Ireland	3.1
Italy	6.4
Netherlands	3.9
United Kingdom	5.9
United States	4.2
Sweden	9.4
Japan	3.3

Source: Employment Gazette, March 1993.

Comparative inflation rates are shown for ten of the member states of the EC and other selected countries for 1991 in Table 28.3.

In the remainder of this chapter, we first describe some of the main effects of inflation on both the economy as a whole and the groups and individuals within it. Secondly, we consider the conflicting explanations of inflation, together with an examination of the view that there is a trade-off between inflation and unemployment (the Phillips curve). Thirdly, we consider the monetarist theory of inflation and the role of rising costs. Finally, we consider the pros and cons of alternative policy measures: fiscal and monetary policies, prices and incomes policy, and indexation.

Effects of inflation

Anticipated inflation *Inflation that all groups and individuals in the economy are able to predict. They are able, therefore, to protect themselves against it*

Unanticipated inflation *Inflation that groups and individuals in the economy are not able to predict. They are not able, therefore, to protect themselves against it*

Inflation can either be anticipated or unanticipated. If it is fully anticipated, then all groups and individuals in the economy expect it and are able to gain full compensation for it. In this case, the inflation will have no appreciable effect on the distribution of income and wealth in the economy. Inflation, however, may be unanticipated for three possible reasons: (a) if there is a general failure on the part of the economy as a whole to predict the inflation correctly so that the actual rate of inflation exceeds the expected rate; (b) if certain groups or individuals in the economy fail to predict the inflation correctly so that they seek lower money wage increases than are actually necessary to maintain real wages; (c) if certain groups or individuals, even though they may correctly predict the inflation, are unable to gain full compensation for it (for example, if they have weak unions or if they earn contractually fixed incomes).

Where the inflation is unanticipated (either by the economy as a whole or by groups or individuals within it), there will be a *redistribution effect*: that is to say, some people will be made better off while others are made worse off. Whether the redistribution effect of inflation increases or decreases the economy's total welfare is an equity consideration and therefore a question of normative economics.

The following are some of the possible redistribution effects of unanticipated inflation.

From fixed-income earners and weakly unionised workers to strongly unionised workers Anyone earning a fixed income (for example, some rental income) or anyone relying on the return from fixed-interest investments will find the real value of his or her income being eroded by inflation. Furthermore, weakly unionised workers who cannot gain full compensation for price rises will lose at the expense of strongly unionised workers who can do so.

From lenders to borrowers Lenders will lose and borrowers will gain because when debts are repaid, their real value will be less than that prevailing when the loans were made. Even where interest is payable, borrowers will still gain if the nominal rate of interest is less than the rate of inflation – a situation where the *real* rate of interest is negative. For example, if the nominal rate of interest is 10 per cent per annum but the rate of inflation is unexpectedly high at 15 per cent, then the real rate of interest is approximately *minus* 5 per cent.

From taxpayers to the government As money incomes rise, earners with the same real income move into higher tax bands (unless these are adjusted) and so pay a bigger proportion of their income in tax. This is known as *fiscal drag*. This applies, of course, only to a country with a progressive income tax system. Since the government may redistribute the extra revenue back to consumers in some way, the final redistribution effect is uncertain.

From public sector employees to private sector employees If the government is trying to control inflation by means of a prices and incomes policy, it may set an example by resisting the wage claims of public employees. If private employers are more willing to concede wage increases, there will be a redistribution from public sector employees to private sector employees. This does depend, though, on the relative strengths of the public and private sector unions and on the ability of the private sector to provide wage increases.

From profit earners to wage earners If wage demands are met by squeezing profit margins, then the share of profits in the national income will fall and the share of wages will rise.

Some effects of inflation exist whether it is fully anticipated or not. These are the *administrative costs of adjustment* and the *international effects*. Both of these effects can reasonably be described as *costs* of inflation since they are both adverse effects as far as the country with the inflation is concerned. Remember that this cannot be said of the redistribution effects which may be costs or benefits depending on the form of social welfare function employed.

Administrative costs of adjustment arise because, with inflation, both households and firms incur costs of adjusting to the new sets of prices. Households have to intensify their search for the most favourably priced goods, while firms have to incur the costs of determining the new prices and disseminating the information (for example, new labelling, advertising, new price lists and so on). In addition, there are obvious costs to the economy when unions decide to take some form of industrial action in order to gain the wage increases which compensate their members for inflation. Strikes, go-slows and working-to-rule all have the effect of reducing the economy's total output.

The international effects of inflation depend on whether the country has a fixed or flexible exchange rate. With a *fixed* exchange rate, a country with a faster rate of inflation than its major trading partners is likely to develop a deficit on its balance of payments (because the domestic inflation makes its exports less competitive and its imports relatively more competitive). The deficit will tend to deplete the country's reserves; it may eventually require deflationary policies which will conflict with the domestic goal of full employment; and it may lead to speculative pressure against the country's currency on the foreign exchange market. With a *flexible* exchange rate, the country with the faster inflation is likely to experience a depreciating currency. Although many economists believe that the international costs of inflation are minimised by the adoption of flexible rates, there are two dangers which should not be overlooked:

(a) The currency depreciation itself may create some further inflationary pressure on the domestic economy. After all, the depreciation has the effect of increasing the price of the country's imports so that, unless there is a fall in some domestic goods' prices, the general price index will rise. This higher rate of inflation will, of course, put even greater downward pressure on the exchange rate, so that there is a danger that the situation will become unstable.

(b) Speculators, seeing the depreciation, may increase their sales of that currency in anticipation of further depreciation. This speculative activity is likely to cause the exchange rate to fall by more than would otherwise have been necessary.

These costs, together with the fear of the extremely destructive phenomenon of hyperinflation, have made the control of inflation one of the major policy objectives of governments. Before we can consider some of the possible means of reducing inflation, we must first examine the (sometimes conflicting) views about what causes it.

Demand-pull, cost-push and the Phillips curve

Demand-pull inflation
Inflation caused by excess aggregate demand when the economy is at, or close to, full employment

Demand-pull inflation exists when aggregate demand exceeds aggregate output at (or close to) full employment. Demand-pull theorists argue that it is excess demand which initiates inflationary pressure. The inflation may then give rise to wage claims which increase firms' costs, but the inflation is actually caused by excess demand. The excess demand itself can originate in either the real or monetary sectors of the economy – that is, it can be caused by autonomous increases in government spending, investment, consumption or exports in the real sector; or by an autonomous rise in the money supply or fall in the demand for money in the monetary sector. These possibilities are illustrated in the AD–AS graph of Fig. 28.1. An increase in aggregate demand shifts the AD curve to the right. This increases the equilibrium level of real income from $0Y_1$ to $0Y_2$ (thereby reducing the rate of unemployment) and raises the equilibrium price level from $0P_1$ to $0P_2$. Clearly, the closer the economy is to full employment and the steeper is the AS curve, the greater will be the effect of an increase in aggregate demand on the price level.

It can be argued that the government is a likely source of demand-pull inflation: through policy measures, the government has some control over the money supply and can finance its own spending by raising taxes, borrowing or by printing money. Households and firms can only increase their spending by using their savings or by borrowing – they are not in the position of being able to raise taxes or print money for themselves.

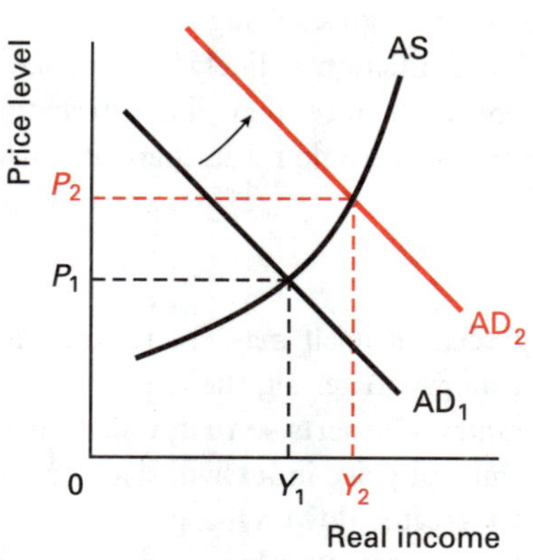

Fig. 28.1. Demand-pull inflation. An increase in aggregate demand shifts the AD curve to the right. At the original price level $0P_1$, there is excess demand which pulls the price level up to $0P_2$.

Fig. 28.2. ***Cost-push inflation.*** Rising production costs shift the AS curve to the left from AS_1 to AS_2. With an unchanged AD curve, the price level is pushed up from $0P_1$ to $0P_2$.

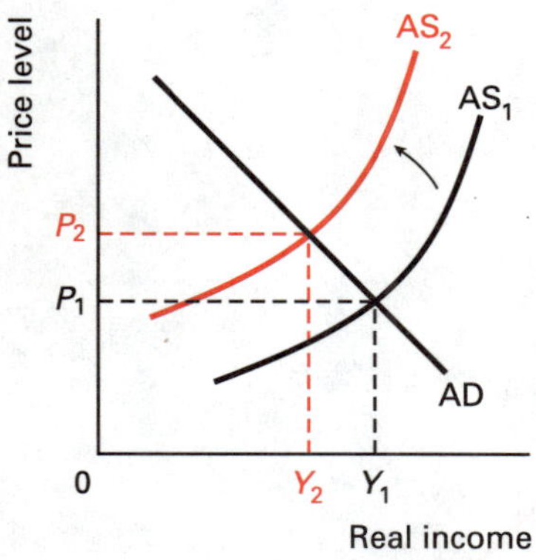

Cost-push inflation *Inflation caused by rising production costs*

Cost-push inflation exists when rising money wages or other production costs (for example, the costs of imported raw materials) are passed on to the consumer in the form of higher prices. As prices rise, so *real* wages fall and this gives rise to another round of wage claims so that an inflationary spiral develops. Most cost-push theories are based on the existence of imperfect competition in the labour market, particularly the existence of strong trade unions who make use of their monopoly power in the control of the supply of labour to push for wage increases in excess of those required to offset rising prices. Rising costs shift the AS curve upwards, as shown in Fig. 28.2. This reduces the equilibrium level of real income from $0Y_1$ to $0Y_2$ (thereby creating some unemployment) and raises the price level from $0P_1$ to $0P_2$.

Although cost-push inflation can exist when there is less than full employment, it is reasonable to suppose that wage claims are more likely to be successful when the economy is at (or close to) full employment because then employers will be competing with each other for the existing work-force.

Both the demand-pull and cost-push theories outlined above are consistent with the following result: *that the closer the economy is to full employment, the greater the inflationary pressure; the greater the rate of unemployment, the less the inflationary pressure*. Keynes argued that with unemployed resources, money wages would be more or less constant, but at low levels of unemployment, money wages would start to rise as bottlenecks occurred in the labour market. As full employment was reached, money wages would rise rapidly as employers competed vigorously with each other for the existing workers. All this suggests that there may be a trade-off (or inverse relationship) between the rate of unemployment (U) and the rate of money wage inflation ($\dot{W}$).

Trade-off *The rate at which the attainment of one objective must be given up in order to achieve an alternative objective*

Phillips curve *A curve which depicts the inverse relationship between the unemployment rate and the rate of money wage inflation*

This relationship was analysed statistically by A.W. Phillips in 1958. Using United Kingdom data, he examined annual figures for U and $\dot{W}$ first for the fifty-two year period 1861–1913, and then for the periods 1913–48 and 1948–57. Phillips best-fitting curve through the scatter of observed combinations of U and $\dot{W}$ is reproduced in Fig. 28.3: this curve has become known as the Phillips curve.

The Phillips curve appears to have been a remarkably stable relationship for almost a hundred years and, indeed, the continued existence of such a stable relationship would have extremely important policy implications for a government. It would mean that the control of inflation and the maintenance of full employment

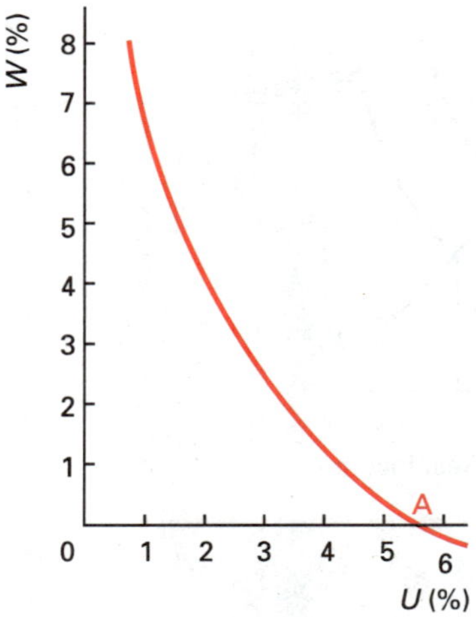

Fig. 28.3. The original Phillips curve. The statistical relationship known as the Phillips curve depicts an inverse relationship between the unemployment rate and the rate of money wage inflation.

were conflicting objectives, but (perhaps more important) that the attainable combinations were known. For example, from Fig. 28.3, it is clear that zero wage inflation could only be achieved at a cost of a 5.5 per cent rate of unemployment; similarly, a 1 per cent rate of unemployment could only be achieved at a cost of about 7.5 per cent rate of wage inflation. There is little doubt that this trade-off relationship between unemployment and inflation influenced policy-making in the United Kingdom during the 1960s.

One of the main critics of the original Phillips curve was Friedman who argued that the vertical axis of the Phillips curve graph should be labelled the rate of change of *real* (rather than money) wages. Theoretically, point A on the Phillips curve in Fig. 28.3 is achieved when the total demand for labour is equal to the total supply of labour, so that the existing unemployment 0A is 'natural'. At this point, Friedman argues, it is the real wage that will be in equilibrium and therefore constant, not the

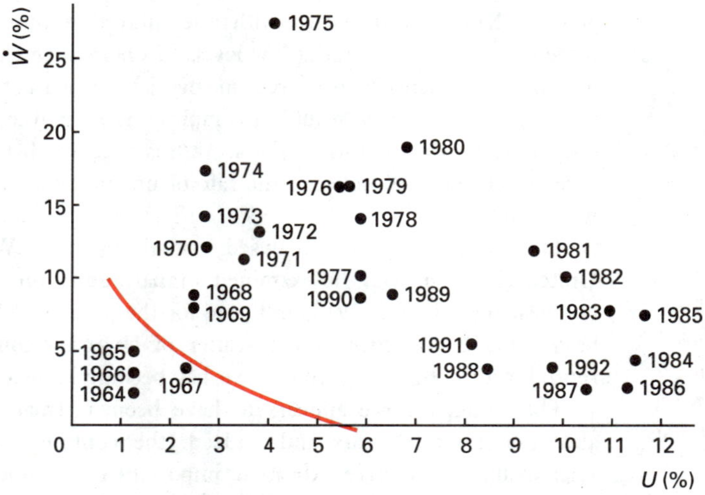

Fig. 28.4. The empirical breakdown of the Phillips curve after 1966. Most of the observed combinations of *U* and *Ẇ* after 1966 lie well away from the original Phillips curve.

money wage. When the real wage is constant, the money wage need not be constant: in fact, it can be rising at any rate *so long as the price level is rising at the same rate.*

Despite Friedman's theoretical assault, many economists throughout the 1960s continued to regard the Phillips curve as a stable relation, useful for policy purposes. After 1966, however, some strange things began to happen as both high rates of inflation and high rates of unemployment were experienced at the same time. Figure 28.4 shows the original Phillips curve together with points on the graph representing the combinations of U and $\dot{W}$ in the United Kingdom for the period 1964–92. The points after 1966 lie nowhere near the original Phillips curve and it is safe to say that the empirical evidence shows the original Phillips curve relationship to have broken down after 1966. Furthermore, the breakdown of this historical relationship between U and $\dot{W}$ was repeated in other industrial countries.

The main problem after the breakdown of the original Phillips curve, was to modify inflation theories in an attempt to find an explanation for the coexistence of high rates of inflation with high rates of unemployment.

The monetarist theory of inflation

Monetarists argue that sustained and severe inflation can be produced only by excessive increases in the money supply. Indeed, Friedman has said that 'inflation is always and everywhere a monetary phenomenon'. As discussed in Ch. 23 this view is backed up by an impressive amount of empirical evidence showing a correlation between increases in the money supply and consequent increases in the price level. Less extreme forms of the view that excess demand is the main cause of inflation tend to place more emphasis on fiscal, rather than monetary, factors as the source of the excess demand – that is, government overspending, however financed, is seen as the main cause of inflationary pressure by some economists.

How do these views account for the apparent breakdown of the original Phillips curve relationship after 1966? They do it by introducing expectations into the analysis, in the expectations-augmented Phillips curve. This was originally developed separately by Friedman and E. Phelps and in what follows we examine the proposal put forward by Friedman.

Expectations-augmented Phillips curve *A short-run Phillips curve whose position is determined by the expected rate of inflation*

Friedman argues that an inverse relationship may exist between the rate of wage inflation and the rate of unemployment in the short-run, but that there is no such relationship in the long-run. Instead, the long-run Phillips curve is vertical at the 'natural' rate of unemployment. (Recall that the 'natural' rate of unemployment is that rate established by market forces.) He claims that there must be a different short-run curve for every different expected rate of inflation: the higher the expected rate of inflation, the further up and to the right will be the relevant short-run Phillips curve. This is illustrated in Fig. 28.5 where curve A is relevant when the expected rate of inflation ($\dot{P}_e$) is zero, and curve B is relevant when $\dot{P}_e$ is 4 per cent.

Starting at point U_n on the graph, the natural rate of unemployment prevails and there is zero wage and price inflation. The expected rate of inflation is also zero so that expectations are being realised and there is no pressure being exerted to change either prices or the level of employment. Suppose now, that the government tries to reduce unemployment by following some expansionary policy (for example, by increasing government spending financed by printing money). As aggregate demand increases, firms will attempt to increase output, and to attract the required labour,

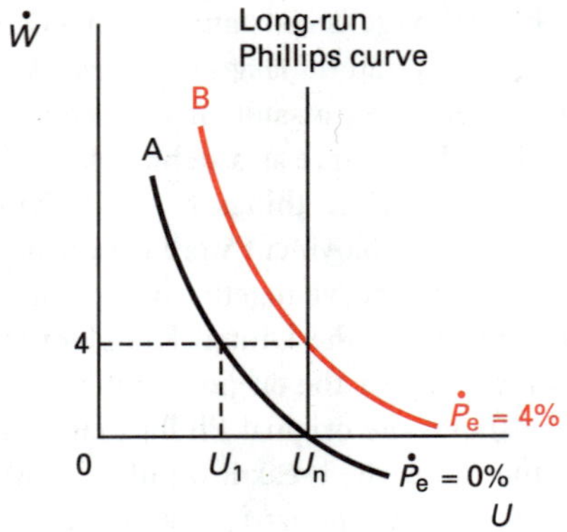

Fig. 28.5. The expectations-augmented Phillips curve. With a vertical long-run Phillips curve, the economy always returns to the natural rate of unemployment. Thus, in the long-run, changes in aggregate demand affect only $\dot{W}$ and there is no long-run effect on U.

Money illusion *This occurs when workers interpret a money wage rise as a corresponding rise in the real wage, without taking account of inflation*

money wages will rise, say by 4 per cent. Although this rise in money wages will soon be followed by a rise in prices, workers will at first interpret the rise in money wages as a 4 per cent rise in *real* wages – that is to say, in the short-run, the workers suffer from money illusion. The existing unemployed workers respond to this apparent increase in real wages by reducing their search periods (see Ch. 16) and total unemployment falls, say to U_1 in Fig. 28.5.

This, then, is the short-run trade-off: 4 per cent inflation is the penalty being paid for the reduction in unemployment. Friedman argued, however, that in the long-run, all money illusion will disappear as the workers come to realise that price inflation is depriving them of their increased real income. Search periods will be lengthened again and some workers will withdraw their labour. At the same time, employers who initially demanded more labour in response to the increased prices (which led them to believe that real wages were falling) eventually come to realise that real wages have not fallen at all and so revise their employment plans downwards. As some workers withdraw their labour and employers reduce their demand for labour, unemployment rises back to the natural rate. But now there is an actual and expected rate of inflation of 4 per cent. If the government should again attempt to reduce the rate of unemployment below U_n, the economy would this time move along the short-run Phillips curve, B, which is relevant when the expected rate of inflation ($\dot{P}_e$) is 4 per cent.

It is the complete absence of money illusion in the long-run which ensures that any trade-off between unemployment and inflation can only be temporary so that the long-run Phillips curve is vertical at the natural rate of unemployment. This means, of course, that any rate of inflation is possible at the natural rate of unemployment. The vertical Phillips curve is of little use to policy-makers except as a warning that continued attempts to reduce unemployment below its natural rate can only lead to increasing inflation.

It is not difficult to see that the view that the long-run Phillips curve is vertical is essentially the same as the monetarist view that the long-run AS curve is vertical. A vertical long-run AS curve (LAS) is shown in Fig. 28.6, together with two upward-sloping short-run AS curves (SAS_1 and SAS_2). $0Y_n$ is the level of real national income associated with the natural rate of unemployment. Suppose that initially the macro-economy is in equilibrium at point A where the AD curve, AD_1, intersects the short-run AS curve, SAS_1. The equilibrium price level is $0P_0$ and the

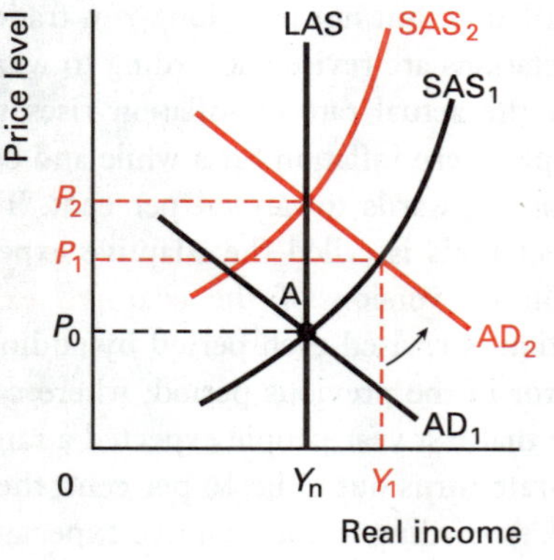

Fig. 28.6. ***The short- and long-run effects of an increase in aggregate demand in a monetarist model.*** **An increase in aggregate demand shifts the AD curve from AD_1 to AD_2. In the short-run, this causes an increase in both real income and the price level. But because the long-run aggregate supply curve (LAS) is vertical, the long-run effect is entirely on the price level.**

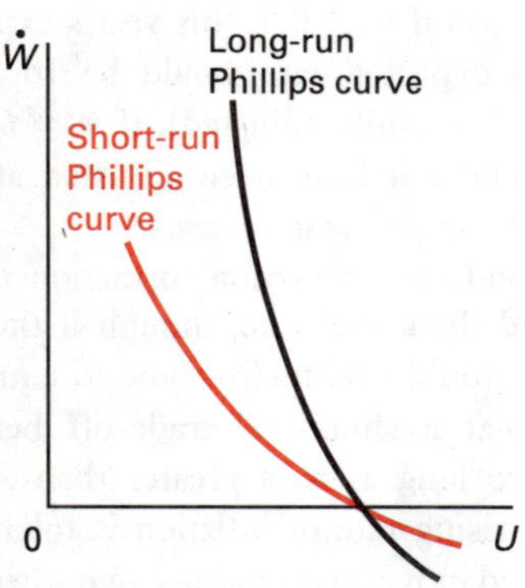

Fig. 28.7. ***A non-vertical long-run Phillips curve.*** **If the long-run Phillips curve has a negative slope, it is possible to reduce unemployment at the expense of a higher inflation rate.**

equilibrium level of real income is $0Y_n$. Now let an increase in aggregate demand shift the AD curve to the right to AD_2. *In the short-run*, this causes real income to rise to $0Y_1$ (so that unemployment falls below its natural rate) and the price level to rise to $0P_1$. *In the long-run*, however, the rise in the actual price level leads to a rise in the *expected* price level and so causes the short-run AS curve to shift upwards to SAS_2. Real income returns to $0Y_n$ and the price level rises even further to $0P_2$.

Thus, with a vertical long-run AS curve we obtain the same result as we obtained with a vertical long-run Phillips curve: *an increase in aggregate demand causes only a short-run increase in output and employment; in the long-run, the effect is entirely on the price level.*

Less extreme views of the expectations-augmented Phillips curve allow for some long-run money illusion, and in this case, the long-run Phillips curve does slope downwards from left to right, but is steeper than the short-run curve. Since a trade-off does exist in this case, it becomes possible for a government to reduce the rate of unemployment so long as the economy is prepared to accept a high rate of inflation. This is illustrated in Fig. 28.7. This is essentially the same as saying that the long-run AS curve slopes upwards from left to right, but is steeper than the short-run AS curve.

Adaptive expectations The above description of the expectations-augmented Phillips curve allows for the existence of a short-run trade-off between unemployment and inflation, but not for a long-run trade-off. The reason for this is that inflationary expectations are revised according to what has happened to inflation in the past. So when the actual rate of inflation rises to 4 per cent in Fig. 28.5, people continue to expect zero inflation for a while and only in the long-run do they revise their expectations upwards towards 4 per cent. This assumption concerning the formation of expectations is called the adaptive expectations hypothesis.

Adaptive expectations hypothesis *This states that the expected rate of inflation is determined from observations of past rates of inflation*

According to a simple version of the adaptive expectations hypothesis, the expected rate of inflation is revised each period by adding on some proportion (say, w) of the observed error in the previous period, where w lies between zero and one. For example, suppose that last year people expected a rate of inflation this year of 10 per cent; if the actual rate turns out to be 16 per cent, the expectation will have been in error by 6 per cent. According to the adaptive expectations hypothesis, this year's expectation will be equal to last year's expectation (10 per cent) plus some proportion (w) of the error. So if $w = 0.5$, this year's expected rate would be 13 per cent; if $w = 1$, this year's expected rate would be 16 per cent (in this case, the expectation is said to have been fully adjusted); if $w = 0$, the expectation would be 10 per cent (that is, it would not have been adjusted at all). The proportion w is sometimes referred to as the *adjustment parameter*.

One result of this method of expectation formation is that the expected rate of inflation always lags behind the actual rate, though if the actual rate should remain constant the expected rate would eventually come to equal it. It is this result which enables us to conclude that a short-run trade-off between unemployment and inflation exists, but that (so long as w is greater than zero) no long-run trade-off exists unless a continually rising rate of inflation is tolerated.

One problem with the adaptive expectations hypothesis is that it presumes that people do not learn from their past mistakes. To show this, consider an individual for whom w is 0.5 and suppose that the individual's expected rate of inflation for this year was 8 per cent, but that the actual rate is 16 per cent. This year's expectation for next year will be 12 per cent. Now suppose that the actual rate increases by 8 percentage points every year for the next three years as a result of annual increases in the nominal stock of money. The actual and expected rates are shown in Table 28.4.

It is clear that the individual is not acting rationally in this example: the expectation error is increasing every year and the individual is failing to predict inflation even though it is rising by a constant amount every year and is caused by the same factor (monetary growth) every year. It was this criticism of the adaptive expectations hypothesis that led to the development of the rational expectations hypothesis.

Rational expectations hypothesis *This states that individuals take into account all available information in determining the expected rate of inflation*

Rational expectations According to the rational expectations hypothesis, individuals (and all other economic agents) take all the information available to

Table 28.4 Expected and actual rates of inflation.

Time period	Expected rate	Actual rate	Error
This year (t)	8	16	8
Next year ($t + 1$)	12	24	12
Year $t + 2$	18	32	14
Year $t + 3$	25	40	15

them into consideration in forming their inflationary expectations, not just past inflation rates. In other words, they take into account such information as what is happening to the money supply (assuming that they believe money supply growth to be a cause of inflation) and what is happening to such factors as world oil prices, trade union militancy and the exchange rate (depending on which of these are perceived as major determinants of inflation). Thus, they are viewed as having in mind an analytical model which they believe explains how the economy works. In some macroeconometric models, inflationary expectations are based on the models' own predictions of the future inflation rate. The theory implies that, as long as people believe that policy-makers are committed to reducing inflation, then changes in economic policy variables (if announced beforehand) will be anticipated by adjustments in inflationary expectations, which will then cause a shift in the short-run Phillips curve.

With rational expectations formation there will be no systematic prediction errors and the inflation rate is likely to be predicted more accurately and more quickly. This implies that a trade-off between unemployment and inflation may exist only in the very short term. Indeed, some New Classical economists (who subscribe to the rational expectations hypothesis) claim that even the short-run Phillips curve may be vertical.

The New Classical version of the theory implies that a change in an economic policy variable which is believed to affect inflation (or simply the *announcement* of a change in such a variable) will be anticipated *immediately* by an adjustment of inflationary expectations. To show this, suppose that unemployment is initially at the 'natural rate' and that both the actual and expected rates of inflation are zero. Now let the government announce that it intends to increase the money supply by 5 per cent over the coming year. Economic agents will take this information into consideration and immediately adjust the expected rate of inflation to 5 per cent. This suggests that both the short- and long-run Phillips curves, are vertical at the natural rate of unemployment. It also means that the anticipated monetary policy will be totally ineffective in influencing output and employment, in either the short-run or the long-run.

Rational expectations theory has been criticised for assuming that economic agents are able to form expectations as if they knew the 'correct' model of the economy. This is clearly an unreasonable assumption, but supporters of the theory have defended it with two main arguments:

(a) These days, individuals are able to obtain a tremendous amount of information about the economy at low cost. Newspapers, television and radio are constantly providing information about the state of the economy and offering informed opinions about what is likely to happen to inflation, unemployment, output growth and other economic variables in the coming months. The main advantage of the rational expectations theory lies in its recognition of the fact that economic agents use all this information to help them form expectations.

(b) The theory does not require all individuals to form the same expectations, nor does it require that people's expectations should always be correct. All that is required is that expected values be distributed around the true value, so that they are correct *on average* and so will not exhibit the systematic prediction error of adaptive expectations formation.

Rising costs as a cause of inflation

Emphasis has been placed on rising wage costs as a possible cause of inflation. There are a number of different versions of this view. One version is that trade unions put in for wage increases in an attempt to gain a bigger share of the national income for members, and that in doing so they take little or no account of the possible effects of their actions on the economy as a whole. In this approach, unions may be seen to be in conflict with capitalists as both groups strive to achieve bigger shares of the national income. Alternatively, each union may be seen as competing with other unions for bigger wage increases regardless of whether more inflation or more unemployment result.

Advocates of this view argue that the rate of wage inflation depends on the degree of *militancy* exerted by trade unions and a number of attempts have been made to test this hypothesis empirically. The main problem, of course, is that of measuring trade union militancy. In a study by A.G. Hines in 1964, militancy was proxied by 'the rate of change of the labour force unionised', the argument being that rapidly rising union membership would tend to make union leaders more militant, would strengthen the union's bargaining position and would generally raise the morale of the workers. Hines obtained good results for this hypothesis for the period 1949–61, but Hines' approach was later criticised by Purdy and Zis who carried out further tests and obtained far less favourable results. A second possibility is to use strike activity as a proxy for trade union militancy. In studies by Taylor and Godfrey, 'the number of stoppages at work due to industrial disputes' was used as a measure of strike activity, but no conclusive results were obtained.

In addition to rising wage costs, a number of other cost increases may be sources of inflationary pressure. In the United Kingdom, it has been claimed that *rising import prices* have raised the cost of many fuels, raw materials and semi-finished products to industry and also led to wage claims because of the rising prices of imported food and consumer goods. Import prices may rise for two main reasons:

(a) *Rising world prices.* If world prices are rising, there is little a single country can do to isolate itself from inflationary pressure. In the 1970s, for example, the shortage and rapidly rising price of oil in the world exerted inflationary pressure on the United Kingdom and many other countries.

(b) *Currency depreciation.* A country with a flexible exchange rate and a persistent deficit on its balance of payments will tend to experience a depreciating currency. This will have the effect of raising the domestic price of all imported goods (thereby creating some cost-push inflationary pressure) and, at the same time, will increase the demand for exports and import-substitutes (which may create excess demand inflation if the country is at or close to full employment).

Monetarist view of cost-push inflation

Monetarists argue that rising costs can only be inflationary in the long-run if the money supply is increased to enable the greater value of transactions to be financed. Thus, although a rise in the price level may have its origin in cost increases, it can only be sustained if it is accompanied by growth in the money supply. Once again, the monetarist view can be illustrated with reference to the vertical long-run AS curve.

Consider Fig. 28.8 which shows an initial equilibrium at point A, where the AD curve, AD_1, intersects the short-run AS curve, SAS_1: the equilibrium price level is $0P_0$ and the equilibrium level of real income is $0Y_n$ (assumed to be the level of real

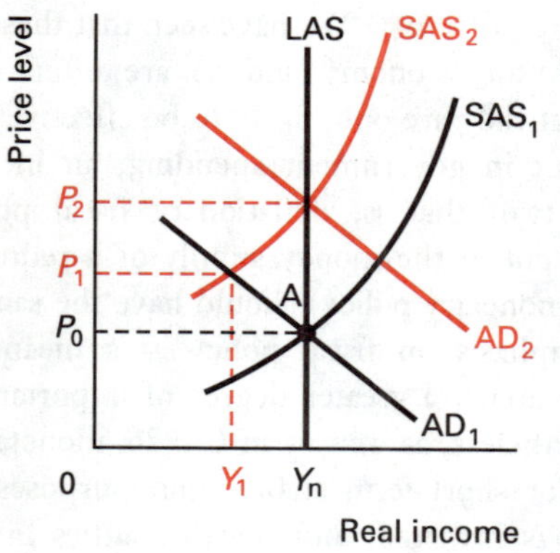

Fig. 28.8. **Cost-push inflation in a monetarist model.** An increase in production costs shifts the short-run aggregate supply curve to the left from SAS_1 to SAS_2. In the short-run, this reduces real income to $0Y_1$ and raises the price level to $0P_1$. In the long-run, real income returns to $0Y_n$: the price level will return to $0P_0$ if there is no increase in the money supply, and will rise to $0P_2$ if there is an increase in the money supply.

income associated with the 'natural' rate of unemployment). Now suppose that some large trade unions force up wage rates in a number of key industries. This rise in costs shifts the short-run AS curve upwards to SAS_2, causing the price level to rise to $0P_1$ and real income to fall to $0Y_1$ (so that unemployment rises above the 'natural' rate).

If the money supply is kept unchanged, this position can only be temporary. The higher unemployment will eventually lead to a fall in wages and so cause the short-run AS curve to shift back to SAS_1. In this case, the trade union activity will have no lasting effect on either employment or the price level.

However, suppose now that the government reacts to the increased costs by *increasing the money supply* in an attempt to prevent the rise in unemployment. This will cause the AD curve to shift to the right to AD_2. In this case, there will be no fall in real income and no change in the level of employment, but there will be a rise in the price level to $0P_2$.

Multi-causal inflation

We have seen that there are a number of conflicting views about what causes inflation. Some blame excessive increases in the money supply; some blame excessive government spending or overspending by other groups in society; some place the blame squarely on rising costs. It could be, of course, that there is some truth in all of these views – that is to say, inflationary pressure may stem from a number of causes all acting simultaneously. If this is so, then it is only by further analysis and empirical testing that the main cause will be determined.

With *multi-causal* inflation, no single policy measure will be sufficient to control it. For example, if the recent United Kingdom inflation has been caused by government overspending financed by excessive increases in the money supply, at a time when unions have been pushing for large wage increases, a single policy measure (such as a cut in the money supply, or a cut in government spending, or an incomes policy) is unlikely to be very successful. What is needed is some combination of policies.

We turn now to an examination of the various policy alternatives, including the suggestion that a policy of indexation might alleviate some of the adverse effects of inflation.

Alternative policy measures

Fiscal and monetary policies We have seen that these policies affect the level of aggregate demand in the economy and so are often called *demand-management* policies. It follows that they are only likely to be effective against inflation caused by excess demand. A cut in government spending, an increase in taxation or some combination of the two (that is, deflationary fiscal policy) will directly reduce aggregate demand; a cut in the money supply or a reduction in its rate of growth (that is, deflationary monetary policy) should have the same effect. As we have seen, Keynesians place emphasis on fiscal policy as a means of controlling aggregate demand. Monetarists attach a greater degree of importance to the influence of the money supply. Nevertheless, as we saw in Ch. 26, monetarists do not favour the use of monetary policy for short-term stabilisation purposes because of the uncertain length of the time-lags involved, and the difficulties involved in making accurate forecasts.

If Friedman is right and the long-run Phillips curve is vertical, so that a high rate of inflation can exist at the natural rate of unemployment sustained by inflationary expectations, then the appropriate action to bring down the rate of inflation will be to keep a tight rein on the growth of the money supply. This will increase the rate of unemployment above its natural rate and reduce the *actual* rate of inflation below the *expected* rate. Expectations will then be revised downwards and eventually the natural rate of unemployment can be restored at a lower rate of inflation. As we explained in Ch. 26, the monetarists then favour a passive policy rule according to which the long-run growth of the money supply is kept at a constant annual rate, preferably announced in advance by the monetary authorities.

If, on the other hand, inflation is caused by the actions of trade unions, fiscal and monetary policies are both inappropriate. Deflationary policies will not necessarily reduce the militancy of unions and may create unacceptable unemployment.

Prices and incomes policy This is the main recommendation of those who support the view that inflation is caused by rising wages costs. As we explained in Ch. 26, such a policy involves the direct intervention of the government in an attempt to moderate union demands for wage increases and to prevent unjustified price increases. This type of policy action can take a number of forms which can be summarised as follows:

(a) Government exhortation to firms to avoid unjustified price rises and to unions to avoid unjustified wage claims.

(b) The setting up of a prices and incomes board to examine proposed price increases and to contribute to collective bargaining between employers and unions.

(c) The bringing together of employers' and unions' organisations (the Confederation of British Industries and the Trades Union Congress in the United Kingdom) in an attempt to obtain some voluntary agreement from both parties to keep prices and incomes down; this may also involve the setting up of a 'norm' for wage and price increases.

(d) The imposition of legislation to regulate or even freeze wages and prices.

It should be pointed out that, even if inflation is caused by union militancy, a prices and incomes policy may still not work. Some groups inevitably find ways of evading it and some unions may become so frustrated with the policy that they take industrial action against it: this is particularly likely when wages are controlled more strictly than prices. If inflation is caused mainly by excess demand, prices and incomes policy is inappropriate – during the course of the policy, the excess demand will build up so that when the policy is relaxed, prices and wages may increase faster than ever.

Indexation *A process whereby the value of an economic variable, such as a pension or wage, is adjusted in line with changes in a price index*

Indexation This policy, sometimes called index-linking, works by linking economic variables (such as wages, salaries and interest payments) to an index of price inflation, like the Retail Price Index in the United Kingdom. This means that if the price index rises by $5\frac{1}{2}$ per cent, then all wages, salaries and interest payments should rise automatically by $5\frac{1}{2}$ per cent. It is a method of removing the main redistributive effects of inflation so that a society can live with inflation in such a way that no individuals or groups suffer disproportionately.

There are, however, two main objections to indexation:

(a) It may itself be inflationary. Indexation cannot be a direct cause of inflation since it only comes into operation after prices have risen. But it could be an indirect cause: since unions no longer have to negotiate for money wage rises to compensate their members for price inflation, they are free to use their full bargaining strength to push for real wage increases. Thus, total wage increases may be greater than they would have been without indexation.

(b) Indexation does nothing to reduce the other costs of inflation. The administrative costs of adjustment and the international costs of inflation are not likely to be much affected by a policy of indexation.

In spite of these possible disadvantages, and given that inflation appears to be very much part of the way of life of many economies, any policy which makes it less uncomfortable to live with may have much to commend it.

Summary

1. Inflation may be defined as a persistent tendency for the general price level to rise. In the United Kingdom, the rate of inflation is normally measured as the annual percentage increase in the Retail Price Index.

2. Inflation can affect the distribution of income. It is likely to redistribute income from fixed-income earners and weakly unionised workers to strongly unionised workers; from lenders to borrowers; from taxpayers to the government; from public sector employees to private sector employees; and from profit earners to wage earners. Inflation also imposes administrative costs of adjustment, and can affect the balance of payments and the exchange rate.

3. Demand-pull inflation is caused by an increase in aggregate demand. Cost-push inflation is caused by rising costs of production. According

to the Phillips curve, there is (at least in the short-run) an inverse relationship between the rate of inflation and the rate of unemployment. A relatively stable Phillips curve was observed from 1861 until the 1960s. After 1966, the original relationship observed by Phillips broke down.

4. According to the monetarist theory of inflation, sustained inflation can only be produced by increases in the money supply. Monetarists believe that the original Phillips curve represented only a short-run trade-off between unemployment and inflation. In the long-run, the Phillips curve (like the long-run AS curve) is believed to be vertical at the 'natural' rate of unemployment, and there are different short-run curves for different *expected* rates of inflation. The two main theories of expectations formation are the 'adaptive expectations' and the 'rational expectations' theories.
5. Theories which suggest that rising costs are the main cause of inflation have placed emphasis on rising *wage* costs resulting from trade union activity. Monetarists argue that rising costs can only lead to sustained inflation if the money supply is increased to prevent a rise in unemployment.
6. Fiscal and monetary policies, prices and incomes policy and indexation have all been suggested as measures which might be used to reduce the rate of inflation. Monetarists favour the application of a passive monetary rule.

Exercises

1. Review your understanding of the following terms:

price inflation	expectations-augmented Phillips curve
wage inflation	adaptive expectations
anticipated inflation	rational expectations
unanticipated inflation	natural rate of unemployment
demand-pull inflation	money illusion
cost-push inflation	trade union militancy
Phillips curve	multi-causal inflation
trade-off	indexation

2. Examine the statistics shown in Table 28.2. Discuss the main causes of the rapid rise in the rate of inflation during the 1970s in the United Kingdom. Can you account for the simultaneous increase in the rate of unemployment?
3. Discuss the redistribution effects of a rapid rise in oil prices (a) between countries; and (b) within a country.
4. 'Inflation is always and everywhere a monetary phenomenon.' (Milton Friedman). Discuss.

5. According to the monetarist theory, what will be the effect on the rate of inflation if the government attempts to reduce unemployment below its 'natural rate'?
6. Suggest ways in which trade union militancy may be measured in order to test the cost-push theory of inflation.
7.** Compare Keynesian and monetarist views of the alternative methods available for controlling inflation.

29 THE BALANCE OF PAYMENTS AND EXCHANGE RATES

Learning objectives

After reading this chapter, you should be able to:

- define the balance of payments and outline the main components of the current and capital accounts
- explain the meaning of a deficit and a surplus on the balance of payments and explain why these may be regarded as policy problems
- describe the activities of the main transactors in the foreign exchange market (hedging, speculation and arbitrage) and show how the forces of demand and supply determine the equilibrium rate of exchange in a simple model
- explain the *elasticities* and the *absorption* approaches to the analysis of the effects of a change in the exchange rate on a trade balance
- assess the efficiency of alternative exchange rate systems in terms of three desirable characteristics (adjustment, confidence and liquidity) and discuss the advantages and disadvantages of fixed and flexible exchange rates
- examine the effects on an open economy of changes in the money supply and changes in government spending, first, in the context of the Keynesian IS–LM–EE model, and secondly, in the context of a monetarist model

Introduction

In this chapter, we are concerned with problems, like balance of payments disequilibria and unstable exchange rates, which are largely monetary in nature and arise because countries use different currencies.

In the first part of the chapter, we set out and explain the United Kingdom balance of payments accounts for 1991 and discuss the implications of a deficit and a surplus. Secondly, we outline the main functions of the foreign exchange market and discuss the determination of the equilibrium rate of exchange. Thirdly, the effects of a change in the exchange rate on the balance of payments and on the level of income and employment are considered. Fourthly, the advantages and disadvantages of different exchange rate systems – the gold standard, a common currency area, a completely flexible exchange rate system, the IMF system and various forms of 'managed flexibility' – are set out. Finally, to complete the macroeconomic model-building that we began in Ch. 23, we develop and apply open-economy versions of the IS–LM model and the AD–AS model.

It is of crucial importance to recognise that international policy objectives cannot be considered in isolation from the internal objectives of full employment and stable prices. Indeed, policy conflicts can and often do arise and these should always be borne in mind when proposing policies designed to correct a payments deficit or to stabilise the international value of the pound.

The United Kingdom balance of payments

The balance of payments is a set of accounts which shows all the economic transactions which take place between the residents of one country and the residents of all other countries during a given time period, usually one year. The items included in the balance of payments are normally denominated in the home country's currency: for example, all the items in the United Kingdom balance of payments accounts are measured in sterling. In general terms, a country's balance of payments can be described under two main headings: the current account and the capital account.

The balance of payments *A set of accounts which shows all the economic transactions which take place between the residents of one country and the residents of all other countries during a given time period*

Current account *A part of the balance of payments that records transactions in both visible and invisible trade*

Visible items *Imports and exports of physical merchandise of all kinds*

Invisible items *Imports and exports of services, transfers and interest, profits and dividends*

Capital account *A part of the balance of payments which records long-term and short-term capital movements between countries*

The current account This account includes both 'visible' and 'invisible' items. The visible imports and exports consist of physical merchandise of all kinds, whereas the invisible imports and exports are mainly services and come under the following major headings: net income from services rendered by residents to non-residents (this includes tourism, shipping and various financial services like insurance and banking); the balance of gifts and the transfer of migrants' funds; net grants by the government to other countries; interest, profits and dividends. All inflows of money, which result from 'visible' and 'invisible' *exports*, are recorded as *credit* items in the accounts. All outflows of money, which result from 'visible' and 'invisible' *imports*, are recorded as *debit* items in the accounts. It follows that an excess of imports over exports will give rise to a current account *deficit* and an excess of exports over imports will give rise to a current account *surplus*.

The capital account This account includes both long-term and short-term capital movements between the home country and all other countries. The long-term capital movements include *direct investments* (which involve the actual setting up and controlling of an enterprise in a foreign country), *portfolio investments* (which involve the purchasing of the securities of a foreign company or government) and *intergovernmental loans*. The short-term capital movements include all forms of short-term private lending and short-term investments, many of which are designed to exploit international interest rate differentials.

The capital account also includes those transactions which are necessary to cover any overall deficit or surplus in the rest of the accounts. These transactions include changes in the official reserves and foreign currency lending and borrowing. The inclusion of these transactions ensures that the balance of payments will always balance in an accounting sense. However, this does not mean that the balance of payments is always in equilibrium. If we define those transactions which exist only because of a deficit or surplus in the rest of the accounts as *accommodating* and those which occur independently of all other items as *autonomous*, we can define a deficit as occurring when the value of autonomous debits exceeds the value of autonomous

Table 29.1 Summary figures for the United Kingdom balance of payments, 1991.

	£ million
Current account	
Visible trade: exports	103,413
imports	−113,703
Visible balance	−10,290
Invisible trade: exports	116,164
imports	−112,195
Invisible balance	3,969
Current balance	−6,321
Transactions in UK assets and liabilities	
UK external assets	−20,780
UK external liabilities	26,029
Net transactions	5,249
Balancing item	1,072
Balance of transactions in assets and liabilities	6,321

Source: United Kingdom Balance of Payments, 1992.

A deficit *A deficit exists when the value of autonomous debit items exceeds the value of autonomous credit items*

A surplus *A surplus exists when the value of autonomous credit items exceeds the value of autonomous debit items*

credits. Similarly, we can define a surplus as occurring when the value of autonomous credits exceeds the value of autonomous debits.

Now consider Table 29.1 which shows the summary balance of payments for the United Kingdom in 1991. There is a current account deficit of over £6 billion. The capital account (which is called Transactions in UK External Assets and Liabilities) covers inward and outward investment; overseas transactions by banks in the United Kingdom; borrowing and lending overseas by other United Kingdom residents; drawings on and additions to the official reserves; and other capital transactions. Unfortunately, it is not possible to distinguish easily between the accommodating and autonomous financial transactions in the accounts, and this has led many commentators to concentrate on the current account balance (or even the visible trade balance) when interpreting the accounts. This can, however, give a misleading picture of the state of a country's international indebtedness because it is the overall balance of payments position (preferably measured over a period of years) which is important.

Suppose now that a country does have a persistent deficit or surplus on its balance of payments. Such an imbalance will have two major implications:

(a) In the case of a deficit, a country with a fixed exchange rate will be losing its reserves of foreign currency and getting more and more into debt with overseas monetary authorities. Clearly, this cannot go on indefinitely as both reserves and sources of borrowing are limited. In the case of a surplus, the country will be accumulating reserves (though only at the expense of other deficit countries) and may be experiencing inflationary pressure as the net currency inflow boosts the domestic money supply.

(b) In the case of a deficit, there will be downward pressure exerted on the country's exchange rate; in the case of a surplus, upward pressure will be exerted. Whether or not the monetary authorities allow the exchange rate to change depends (as we see shortly) on the exchange rate system.

Now consider briefly what actions can be taken by a country with a persistent payments imbalance. There are three main possibilities.

It could adopt demand-management policies In the case of a deficit, a contractionary fiscal or monetary policy would be appropriate – it would reduce aggregate demand, including the demand for imports, and may at the same time reduce inflationary pressure and so make exports more competitive in world markets. It follows that an expansionary policy would be appropriate in the case of a surplus. Unfortunately, such policies may conflict with the domestic objectives of full employment, stable prices and economic growth. In particular, if a country has both a deficit and high unemployment, a demand-reducing policy designed to correct the balance of payments will tend to worsen the rate of unemployment.

It could impose import controls The advantages and disadvantages of import controls together with other trade restrictions are considered in Ch. 30.

It could allow the exchange rate to change Normally, a currency depreciation is appropriate to correct a deficit and an appreciation is appropriate to correct a surplus. However, before we can analyse this in any detail, we must first of all examine the foreign exchange market and the meaning and determination of the equilibrium rate of exchange.

The foreign exchange market and the rate of exchange

Since different countries use different currencies, there is an obvious need for the conversion of domestic currency into foreign currencies and vice versa so that international transactions can take place. The *foreign exchange market* permits the conversion of currencies in an efficient way and can be thought of as the market in which rates of exchange are determined.

Rate of exchange *The price of one currency in terms of another*

A rate of exchange, as its name implies, is the rate at which one currency can be exchanged for another and can be regarded as the price of one currency in terms of another. We should at this point mention the distinction between the spot rate of exchange and the forward rate. The spot rate is the rate at which one currency can *currently* be exchanged for another, while the forward rate is an agreed rate at which one currency can be exchanged for another at some prearranged date in the future (usually 90 days). The existence of the 'forward' exchange market (and the similar markets for currency 'futures' and 'options') enables traders to *hedge* against the foreign exchange risk and it gives rise to certain types of *speculative activity, foreign exchange arbitrage* and *interest arbitrage*. Consider briefly these four activities in turn.

Spot exchange rate *The exchange rate at which one currency can be exchanged for another and where the transaction is settled within two days*

Hedging *The elimination of foreign exchange risk by matching foreign currency assets and liabilities*

Hedging An importer may incur a debt which has to be paid at some date in the future. The 'foreign exchange risk' is the risk that the exchange rate will change in the meantime involving the importer in a possible loss. The trader can hedge against this risk by buying 'forward' foreign exchange. This means that the trader enters into a contract with a bank to purchase an amount of foreign exchange at the appropriate future date at a rate of exchange agreed upon now (the 'forward' rate). Banks levy a small charge for this service.

Speculation *The acceptance of foreign exchange risk to make a profit by taking up a position in which foreign currency assets and liabilities are not matched*

Speculation Some speculators attempt to take advantage of the difference between the 'forward' rate for some given time period and the 'spot' rate which they expect to prevail at the end of that time period. As an example, consider an American speculator and suppose that the 90-day forward rate is £1 = \$2 and that the speculator believes that the spot rate at the end of 90 days will be £1 = \$2.20. The speculator would take up a *long* position by buying, say, £1,000 forward-sterling for \$2,000. In 90 days, he or she would receive £1,000 and (provided the spot rate had risen to £1 = \$2.20 as expected) this amount could be sold for \$2,200, yielding a profit of \$200.

Arbitrage *The exploitation of price differences in order to make a risk-free profit*

Foreign exchange arbitrage Foreign exchange arbitrage is the exploitation of exchange rate differentials or inconsistencies to make a riskless profit. An important characteristic of arbitrage is that it has the effect of *eliminating the differentials which give rise to profit opportunities.* As an example of foreign exchange arbitrage, suppose that the sterling exchange rate quoted in London is £1 = \$2, while the rate quoted in New York is £1 = \$1.95. Assuming no transactions costs, it would be profitable to sell sterling in London and simultaneously buy sterling in New York. A sale of £1,000 in London, for example, would yield \$2,000. These dollars could then be exchanged for £2,000/1.95 = £1,025.64 in New York, making a riskless profit for an arbitrageur of £25.64. Such purchases and sales, however, will lead to an appreciation of sterling in New York and a depreciation of sterling in London until the two quotations are identical.

Interest arbitrage The objective of interest arbitrage is to allocate funds between financial centres in response to interest rate differentials and so realise the highest possible rate of return. If, for example, 90-day interest rates are higher in New York than in London, it may be worthwhile for investors to transfer short-term funds from London to New York. To do so, they will have to convert pounds into dollars at the spot rate and at the same time they can avoid the 'foreign exchange risk' by arranging to convert the proceeds of the investment back into pounds at the forward rate. It follows that whether or not this transaction is worthwhile depends on the interest rate differential between the two financial centres and the difference between the 90-day forward rate and the spot rate. Once again, however, if a riskless profit opportunity does occur, the activities of arbitrageurs will soon have the effect of eliminating the differentials which cause the profit opportunity. Of course, in reality, small differences in interest rates and exchange rate quotations can persist because of transactions costs.

Determination of the rate of exchange

Since we can regard the rate of exchange as the price of one currency in terms of another, its equilibrium level must be determined in a free market by the forces of demand and supply. The demand for and supply of a currency in international markets are in turn determined by the activities of traders, speculators and arbitrageurs. To simplify our analysis and yet to give some insight into the determination of rates of exchange, we make two important assumptions in this section:

(a) We consider trade between two countries only, say the United Kingdom and the United States. This means that there are only two currencies, pounds and

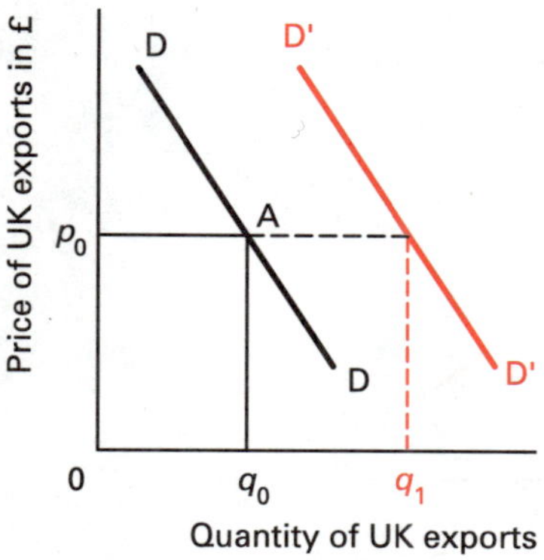

Fig. 29.1. The effect of a depreciation of the pound on the US demand for UK exports. DD represents the original demand for UK exports prior to a depreciation. The sterling depreciation reduces the dollar price of UK exports. The effect is to shift the demand curve when plotted against the sterling price to the right. Consequently, the value of exports rises.

dollars, and we define the rate of exchange as the price of a pound in terms of dollars.

(b) We ignore the activities of investors, speculators and arbitrageurs. This means that the demand for pounds depends only on the US demand for UK exports (because UK exporters require payment in pounds) and the supply of pounds depends only on the UK demand for imports from the United States (because pounds are supplied in exchange for dollars to pay for US goods and services).

Consider first the *demand for pounds*. This arises because US importers wish to buy UK exports. We should start, therefore, by examining the US demand for UK exports. This is illustrated in Fig. 29.1 where DD represents the US demand curve for UK exports. The price of UK exports is measured in pounds on the vertical axis and the quantity of UK exports is measured on the horizontal axis. Suppose that the initial position is at point A so that the total demand for pounds (equal to the total value of UK exports) is p_0q_0. Now suppose that the exchange rate depreciates, say from £1 = \$2 to £1 = \$1.50. This reduces the dollar price of UK exports and so makes them cheaper to US buyers. This should lead to an increase in US demand for UK goods at every pound price – in other words, the US demand curve will shift to the right, to D′D′ in Fig. 29.1. As can be seen from the graph, the sterling value of UK exports increases to $p_0 q_1$. It follows that a fall in the exchange rate causes an increase in the demand for pounds; this means that the demand curve for pounds must be downward-sloping from left to right, as shown in Fig. 29.2.

Next, consider the *supply of pounds*. This arises because UK importers wish to buy US goods. In this case, then, we should examine the UK demand for imports which is shown in Fig. 29.3, where DD represents the UK demand curve for US goods. The initial position is at point B so that the total supply of pounds (equal to the total value of UK imports) is P_0Q_0. Now suppose, as before, that sterling depreciates from \$2 to \$1.50. This has the effect of raising the sterling price of US goods, making them more expensive to UK importers. The UK demand for imports will fall and this is shown as a movement along the demand curve in Fig. 29.3 from point B to point C. The new supply of pounds is P_1Q_1.

We now have to determine whether the supply of pounds has increased or decreased following the depreciation – in other words, we have to determine which is bigger, P_1Q_1 or P_0Q_0. The answer depends on the elasticity of the UK demand for imports. If it is *elastic*, the quantity of imports will have fallen by a bigger proportion than their price will have risen, so the total value of imports and the total supply of

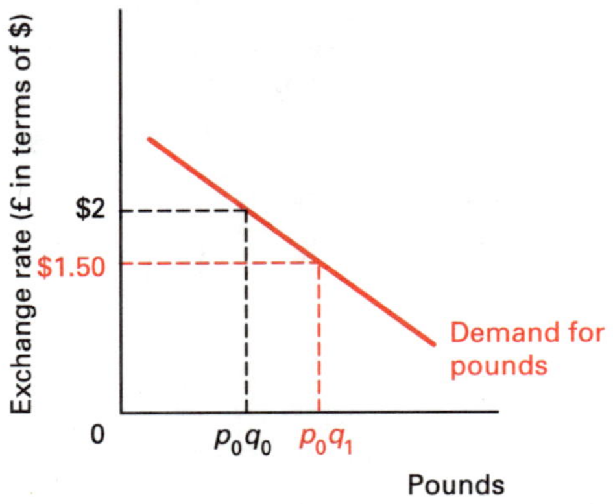

Fig. 29.2. The demand for pounds. A fall in sterling's exchange rate from $2 to $1.50, results in an increase in the demand for sterling.

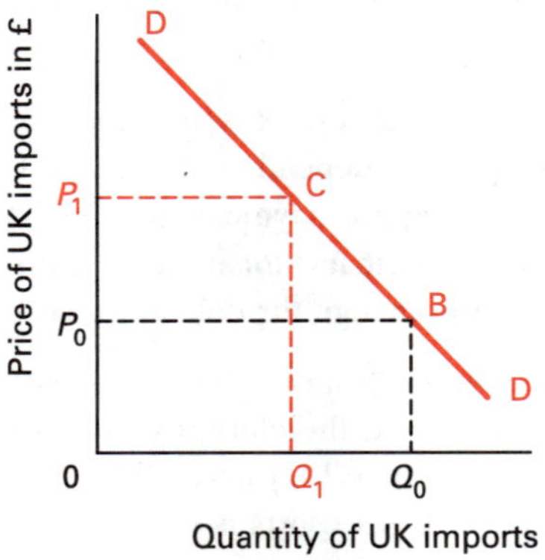

Fig. 29.3. The effect of a depreciation of the pound on the UK demand for imports. A sterling depreciation raises the sterling price of UK imports. This causes a movement along the demand curve from B to C and changes the total value of imports from P_0Q_0 to P_1Q_1.

pounds will have fallen. In this case, the supply curve of pounds will slope upwards from left to right as shown in Fig. 29.4(a). If it is *inelastic*, the quantity of imports will have fallen by a smaller proportion than their price will have risen, so that the total supply of pounds will have risen. In this case, the supply curve will be abnormal and slope downwards from left to right as shown in Fig. 29.4(b). If the demand curve had *unitary elasticity*, the supply of pounds would remain unchanged and the supply curve of pounds would be vertical.

Stable and unstable equilibria The equilibrium rate of exchange is determined where the demand for pounds is equal to the supply of pounds. This is at $0r_1$ in Fig. 29.5(a). All other rates of exchange are disequilibrium rates. For example, at $0r_2$, the quantity of pounds demanded on the foreign exchange market exceeds the quantity supplied. Given free competitive forces, the exchange rate will be pushed upwards and so back towards $0r_1$. At $0r_3$, the quantity of pounds supplied exceeds the quantity demanded and the exchange rate will fall back towards $0r_1$. Clearly, as drawn in Fig. 29.5(a), the equilibrium is a *stable* one.

Now consider Fig. 29.5(b) where the supply curve of pounds slopes downwards from left to right and is less steep than the demand curve. The exchange rate, $0r_4$, is an equilibrium rate, but this time is *unstable*. At the disequilibrium rates, $0r_5$ and $0r_6$, competitive forces act to push the exchange rate further away from the equilibrium position.

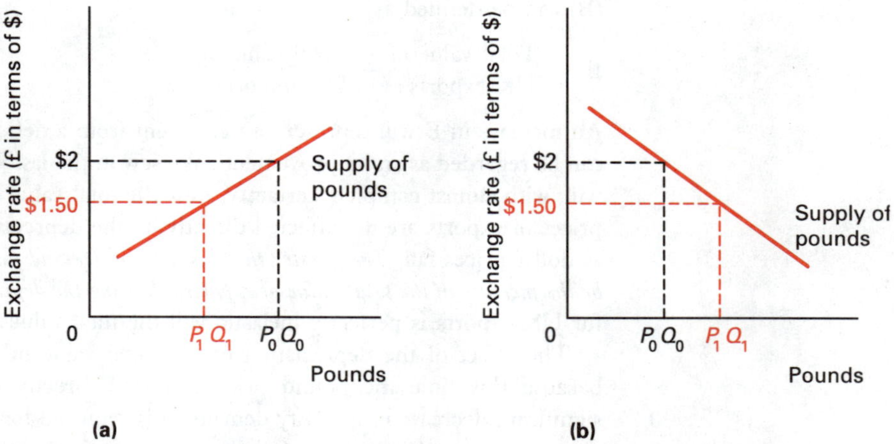

Fig. 29.4. The supply of pounds. (a) If the UK demand for imports is *elastic*, a sterling depreciation will cause a fall in the supply of pounds. (b) If the UK demand for imports is *inelastic*, a sterling depreciation will cause a rise in the supply of pounds.

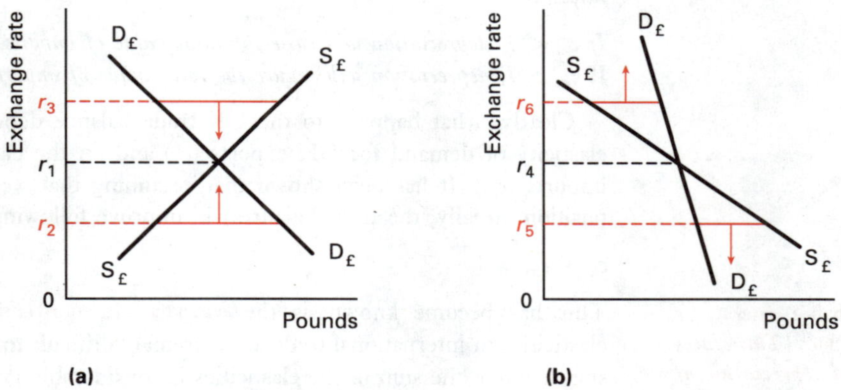

Fig. 29.5. Equilibrium in the foreign exchange market. (a) In this case, any divergence from the equilibrium generates forces which restore the equilibrium at $0r_1$. (b) In this case, any divergence from the equilibrium pushes the exchange rate further away from the equilibrium at $0r_4$.

As we shall see, the stability or instability of the equilibrium in the foreign exchange market has very important implications for exchange rate policy.

The effects of a change in the exchange rate

In this section, we examine the effects on the United Kingdom economy of a *fall* in the exchange rate – that is, a depreciation of the pound. As in the previous section, we keep the analysis fairly simple by considering two-country trade only, so we continue to refer to the United States as if it represented the 'rest of the world'.

A depreciation of the pound will immediately affect the relative prices of traded goods: the dollar price of UK exports will fall and the pound price of UK imports will rise. These price changes will in turn cause a rise in the demand for UK exports and a fall in the demand for UK imports – so long as these demand changes can be realised, they will affect the UK balance of payments. The price effects of the depreciation, however, do not tell the complete story because it is likely that UK national income will also be affected: changes in income will cause changes in the demand for imports and this will exert a further influence on the trade balance.

Consider first the *price effects* of the depreciation under the following two assumptions: (a) that supply elasticities are very large so that increases in demand can easily be met, and (b) that for now we ignore income changes. The UK trade balance

(B) can be defined as:

$$B = \text{Total value of UK exports} - \text{Total value of UK imports}$$

An increase in B will represent a movement from a deficit towards a surplus and so can be regarded as an 'improvement'. We saw in the last section that the depreciation will, with almost complete certainty, *raise* the total value of UK exports – the pound prices of exports are not affected directly by the depreciation, but demand increases as dollar prices fall. *The greater the elasticity of demand for UK exports, the bigger will be the increase in the total value of exports following the depreciation.* Only if the demand for UK exports is perfectly inelastic will the total value remain unchanged.

The effect of the depreciation on the total value of UK imports is less certain because this time the pound price is raised directly by the depreciation and a significant decrease in quantity demanded is required for their total value to fall. We can summarise the result as follows, where e_m is the elasticity of demand for UK imports:

If $e_m < 1$, *depreciation will raise the total value of imports.*
If $e_m > 1$, *depreciation will reduce the total value of imports.*

Clearly, what happens to the UK trade balance depends crucially on both the elasticity of demand for UK exports (e_x) and on the elasticity of demand for UK imports (e_m). It has been shown that, assuming that we start from an equilibrium position initially, the trade balance will improve following a depreciation if:

$$e_x + e_m > 1$$

Marshall–Lerner condition *This states that a depreciation of a currency will result in an improvement in the balance of trade if the sum of the elasticities of demand for exports and for imports exceeds unity*

This has become known as the **Marshall–Lerner condition**. Although demand elasticities in international trade are extremely difficult to estimate, existing evidence suggests that the sum of the elasticities is considerably greater than one in the long-term. It is possible, though, that the condition may not be satisfied in the short-term. For one thing, it may take time for the country's importers to find alternative supplies in response to the increase in import prices. It may also take time for American buyers to increase their purchases of UK exports following the fall in prices. So a depreciation may at first cause the trade balance to deteriorate. Eventually, perhaps after a year, importers and exporters should respond to the changed prices and the trade balance should improve. This delayed improvement in the trade balance following a depreciation is often referred to as the **J-curve effect**. This is illustrated in Fig. 29.6 where the curve BB shows the trade balance over time following a depreciation at time t_0. The trade balance worsens at first and then improves, so that the curve traces out the shape of a J.

J-curve effect *This results when low elasticities of demand for exports and imports in the short-term give rise to an initial worsening of the trade balance*

The income effect in the simple Keynesian model Now consider the *income effect* of the depreciation. This is important because an increase in the value of UK exports will induce, via the multiplier, an increase in national income which in turn will raise the demand for imports. This mechanism should be taken into account, therefore, in examining the effects of a depreciation. This analysis is sometimes called the **absorption approach**.

Absorption approach *This takes into account the impact that a change in the level of national income, following a depreciation, has on the balance of trade*

Consider this problem in the context of a simple Keynesian model. Ignoring government spending and taxation, and using the familiar *injections = withdrawals*

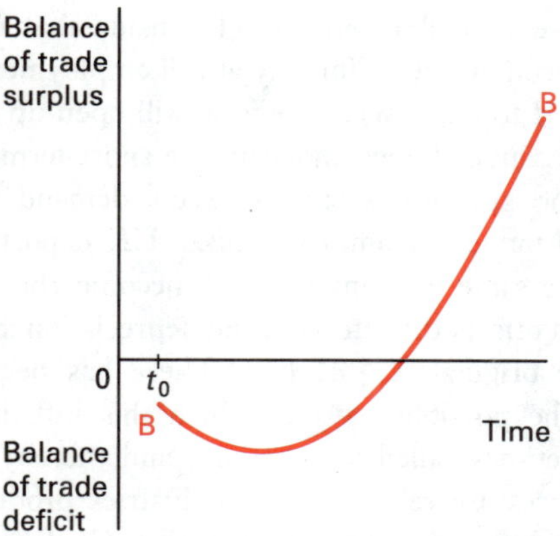

Fig 29.6. The J-curve. A sterling depreciation occurs at time t_0. Initially, the trade deficit worsens due to low short-run elasticities of demand for exports and imports.

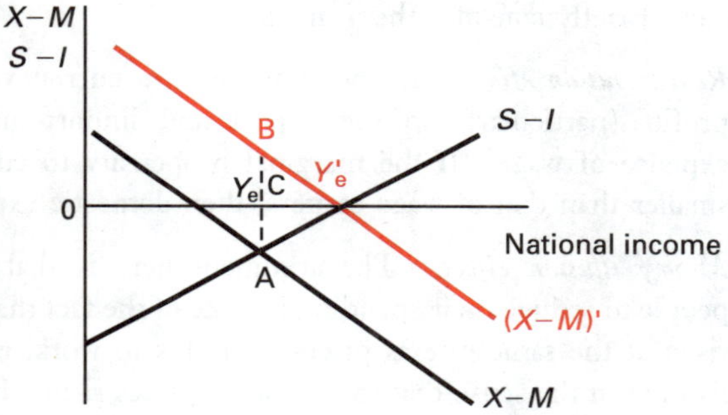

Fig 29.7. Effects of a depreciation on the trade balance and the level of national income. A sterling depreciation shifts the *X–M* line to the right. This raises national income and reduces the deficit. But if there is full employment initially, the sterling depreciation will open up an inflationary gap.

condition for the equilibrium level of income, we can write:

In equilibrium, $\mathcal{J} = W$

$$I + X = S + M$$

or $$X - M = S - I$$

In other words, the equilibrium level of income is achieved when the planned value of exports minus imports $(X - M)$ is equal to the planned value of saving minus investment $(S - I)$. The determination of this equilibrium is illustrated in Fig. 29.7, where savings and imports are, as usual, directly related to income and investment and exports are autonomous of income. The initial position, then, is at $0Y_e$ and there is a small trade deficit equal to AC. Given that the Marshall–Lerner condition is satisfied and that there are some unemployed resources in the economy, a currency depreciation will have the effect of shifting the $X - M$ line upwards to the right to $(X - M)'$ raising the equilibrium level of income to $0Y'_e$, removing some of the unemployment and at the same time eliminating the deficit. This is one case where the two policy problems of unemployment and a trade deficit may be tackled by the one policy action of currency depreciation. Notice that the improvement in the trade deficit is less than that suggested by our analysis of the price effects alone: with the income change ignored, the trade balance improvement would be AB in Fig. 29.7, but with the increase in income taken into account, the improvement is only AC.

In fact, the rise in real income is of considerable importance. To show this, suppose that the economy were initially at full employment. A currency depreciation which shifts $X - M$ to $(X - M)'$, as before, will open up an *inflationary gap* equal to BA. Since output cannot be expanded in the short-term, the increased demand for exports and import-substitutes creates excess demand inflation. This inflation of money prices and money incomes will make UK exports less competitive in world markets and at the same time imports will become cheaper to domestic buyers. In short, the inflation offsets the effects of the depreciation and the $(X - M)'$ line moves back towards the original $X - M$ line. There has been much discussion in the literature about the possible ways in which this inflation might reduce domestic expenditure (sometimes called 'absorption') and thereby allow the trade balance to improve as resources are released from industries producing for the home market into industries producing for the export market. Of these, the income redistribution effect, the money illusion effect and the real balance effect have received most attention. Briefly consider them in turn.

(a) *Redistribution effect.* In the short-term, a currency depreciation may increase profits (particularly in the export and import-substitute industries) at the expense of wages. If the marginal propensity to consume of profit earners is smaller than that of wage earners, then domestic expenditure will fall.

(b) *Money illusion effect.* The argument here is that higher prices will induce people to reduce their spending in spite of the fact that, on average, incomes have risen at the same rate as prices. For this to work, people have to have a price fixation in the sense that they observe prices rising, but fail to observe that their wages are rising at the same rate.

(c) *Real balance effect.* According to this effect, with a constant nominal money stock, people will see that rising prices are reducing the real value of their money balances: they will attempt to restore this real value by reducing their spending and increasing their savings.

If we can rely on one or more of the above effects to reduce absorption, then it is possible for a depreciation of the pound to improve the UK trade balance, even if there is full employment or near full employment initially. Too much reliance cannot be placed on these effects, however, and it may, therefore, be necessary to accompany a currency depreciation with expenditure-reducing fiscal and monetary policies. If, in addition, it is felt that rising import prices will exert some cost-push inflationary pressure on the economy, a government may find it necessary to impose some direct controls on domestic factor costs (for example, by means of an incomes policy) at the same time as the currency depreciates.

Expenditure-reducing policy *A policy that is intended to reduce the level of aggregate demand. Such a policy may accompany a devaluation in order to free resources for exports*

It has to be emphasised that the above analysis is based on a simple Keynesian model. A more general analysis of open-economy macroeconomics is presented in the final part of the chapter.

Exchange rate systems

One of the most important international decisions that governments have to make is what kind of exchange rate system to adopt. In other words, they have to determine how their own currency should be related to other currencies in the world. If they choose to fix the value of their currency in terms of other currencies, how is that to be accomplished and what balance of payments adjustment mechanism will exist? If, instead, they choose to allow the value of their currency to fluctuate against other currencies, how much flexibility should be permitted and how can a reasonable degree of certainty and stability be safeguarded?

We attempt to answer these questions in this section by outlining some of the possible ways in which exchange rate systems can be arranged. Some of these have been tried and tested in the past, others are in current use, while others are still only proposals. We start by considering a completely fixed exchange rate system; secondly we look at the advantages and disadvantages of a completely flexible exchange rate system; thirdly, we examine the International Monetary Fund's adjustable-peg system which was set up at Bretton Woods in 1944 and existed until 1972; finally, we consider some of the proposed variations of 'managed flexibility'.

The efficiency of any exchange rate system can in part be judged by the extent to which it achieves three desirable characteristics, adjustment, confidence and liquidity:

Adjustment *The process by which a disequilibrium situation in the balance of payments is corrected*

Confidence *The level of certainty that importers and exporters hold in relation to the stability of future exchange rates*

Liquidity *The quantity of reserve assets available to stabilise exchange rates*

(a) *Adjustment.* The system should enable countries to correct payments disequilibria without placing too much strain on their domestic economies.

(b) *Confidence.* The system should be such that traders have confidence that international payments can be made efficiently and safely without the danger of large losses.

(c) *Liquidity.* If the adopted system requires central banks to intervene in the foreign exchange market to stabilise exchange rates, there should be a sufficient quantity of reserve assets to enable this to be done efficiently.

These three characteristics should be borne in mind in considering the efficiency of different international monetary arrangements.

Completely fixed exchange rate system

Fixed exchange rate system *A system in which the value of a country's currency is held constant in terms of other currencies through central bank intervention*

The main characteristic of this system is that each country's currency is fixed in terms of all other currencies. One notable example of this was the *gold standard* system which was employed in one form or another until 1931 in the United Kingdom. A more extreme example of fixed exchange rates is a *common currency area*. Consider these two in turn.

The gold standard Under the *gold standard*, the value of each currency is fixed in terms of gold and this necessarily means that the value of any particular currency must be fixed in terms of any other currency. For example, if £1 is worth so many grains of gold in the United Kingdom and the same quantity of gold is worth $2 in the United States, it follows that £1 must exchange for $2 – if not, any individual could buy £1 worth of gold in London, ship it to New York and sell it for $2. (Note that the exchange rate £1 = $2 is then called the 'mint parity'). In practice, the exchange rate can vary within a narrow band around the mint parity because of the transport and insurance costs involved in shipping gold from one country to another. The permitted variation is so small, however, that exchange rates can be regarded to all intents and purposes as fixed.

In its most extreme form, the system requires: (a) that gold be used as the only international means of payment; (b) that there be a rigid relationship between a country's gold reserves and its supply of money; (c) that there be flexible wages and prices and the operation of the 'quantity theory of money'. The *adjustment* of imbalances should then occur by means of David Hume's 'price-specie-flow' mechanism:

Deficit countries lose gold; their money supplies fall; wages and prices fall making exports more competitive – the trade balance improves. Surplus countries accumulate gold; their money supplies rise; wages and prices rise making their exports less competitive – the trade balance returns to equilibrium.

The main problem with this adjustment mechanism stems from its dependence on the flexibility of wages and prices and the quantity theory of money. It is possible that the fall in the money supply experienced by deficit countries will create unemployment rather than falling prices.

Assuming that the exchange rate is kept permanently fixed under the gold standard, traders should have *confidence* in the system. They will know with certainty what exchange rates are now and what they will be in the future. A problem of *liquidity* could arise, however, because the world supplies of gold are finite and a point may be reached where it becomes impossible to increase supplies further: this could lead to problems if the total value of trade continued to rise. Finally, a major disadvantage of using gold so extensively is that it is so much more costly to produce than paper forms of currency – after all, gold has to be mined and manufactured into ingots or some other form before it is suitable for use as an international currency. On the other hand, some economists have seen a virtue in the limited supply of gold as a check to any temptation on governments to expand the money supply excessively.

Common currency area *A type of exchange rate system in which different countries adopt the same currency*

Common currency area Turning now to a *common currency area*, this is a very extreme form of fixed exchange rate system where different countries simply adopt identical currencies which, of course, can be exchanged for each other on a one-to-one basis. Such a system is highly unlikely ever to be established on a world-wide basis, but it is possible for a group of countries to use the same form of money whose supply would then have to be controlled by a centralised monetary authority. Indeed, it is proposed that the EC countries should eventually adopt a common currency and have both a centralised monetary and fiscal policy. Economically, the countries of such an area would become indistinguishable from regions within a country.

With reference to our three desirable characteristics, a common currency area would have no need for reserves to cover internal balance of payments deficits and traders would have no worries about possible exchange rate changes (at least, within the area), so that the criteria of *liquidity* and *confidence* should be satisfied. However, as in the case of the gold standard, the main problem arises in the *adjustment* mechanism. To show this, consider an imbalance which can arise between the regions of a single country. Suppose, for example, that there is a shift in demand from one region (say, region A) to the rest of the country – with wages and prices inflexible downwards, the result will be an increase in unemployment in region A. In a sense, we can say that region A is likely to develop a deficit with the rest of the country as it will probably find itself consuming more than its income. Such overspending will be financed, not by using reserves, but by borrowing from financial institutions and by receipts of government transfers in the form of unemployment benefits and social security payments. At the same time, of course, the amount of tax paid by the region will decrease.

The problem with a common currency area is that adjustment to imbalances cannot take place through exchange rate changes (because exchange rates are permanently fixed) or through monetary changes (because a country's money supply cannot be separated from the area's money supply). In fact, if the price level is inflexible as well, then none of the traditional adjustment mechanisms exists. The only way in which adjustment can take place is through factor mobility – the unemployed resources must move into alternative activities either within the home country or in other countries of the area. With this in mind, an optimum currency area has been defined as an area of countries which can employ a common currency efficiently without serious regional problems arising. Such an area should have a reasonable degree of labour and capital mobility and integrated monetary and fiscal arrangements so that the adverse effects of any imbalance may be reduced by borrowing and transfer payments. The pros and cons of adopting a single currency in the EC are considered in greater detail in Ch. 31.

Optimum currency area *The geographical area in which a single currency can circulate efficiently without causing significant regional problems*

Completely flexible exchange rate system

Flexible exchange rate system *A system in which the value of a country's currency is permitted to fluctuate in response to market forces without central bank intervention*

In this system, exchange rates would not be stabilised by monetary authorities in any way, but would be allowed to fluctuate in response to market forces. This means that a United Kingdom deficit (which gives rise to an excess supply of pounds on the foreign exchange market) would put downward pressure on the exchange rate, and a surplus (which gives rise to excess demand) would put upward pressure on the exchange rate. As we have seen, these are *usually* the appropriate movements in the rate to correct the imbalances.

It has been claimed by some economists that this automatic adjustment mechanism is the great virtue of a flexible exchange rate system. Indeed, many proponents of flexible rates have claimed that governments could concentrate their policies on the domestic problems of inflation and unemployment, leaving automatic exchange rate changes to deal with any external imbalances. Another advantage claimed for flexible rates is that governments would no longer need to hold large quantities of international reserves – after all, if monetary authorities were not intervening in the foreign exchange market to stabilise rates, reserves would be unnecessary. According to these claims, it would seem that a completely flexible system should satisfy our criteria of *adjustment* and *liquidity*. Such a system, however, may also suffer from a number of disadvantages, some of which could make it unworkable. Consider the following.

The Marshall–Lerner condition may not be satisfied If the elasticities condition (that $e_x + e_m > 1$) were not satisfied, a flexible exchange rate system would run into difficulties. To show this, consider what would happen if a deficit developed. The excess supply of the country's currency would cause an automatic depreciation which would make the deficit bigger. Similarly, with a surplus, the excess demand for the currency would cause an appreciation which would lead to an even bigger surplus. We commented earlier that the elasticities are likely to be quite large in the long-term, but may be small in the short-term. If this is the case, a completely flexible exchange rate system may be subject to extreme fluctuations in the rates in the short-term. Such instability would cast doubts on the efficiency of the *adjustment* mechanism.

Uncertainty Since the adjustment mechanism depends on automatic exchange rate changes, it can be argued that importers and exporters may be discouraged from trading because of the 'exchange rate risk'. They can 'hedge' against this risk by

Fig. 29.8. ***Destabilising speculation.*** The effect of speculation in this case is to increase the amplitude of the oscillations of the time path of the exchange rate.

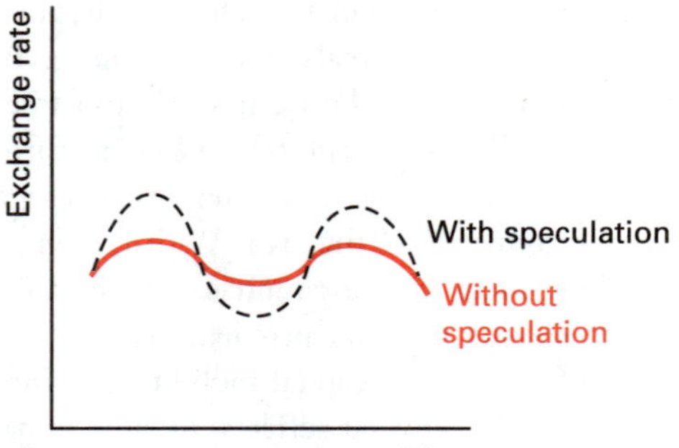

Fig. 29.9. ***Stabilising speculation.*** In this case the effect of speculation is to reduce the amplitude of the oscillations of the time path of the exchange rate.

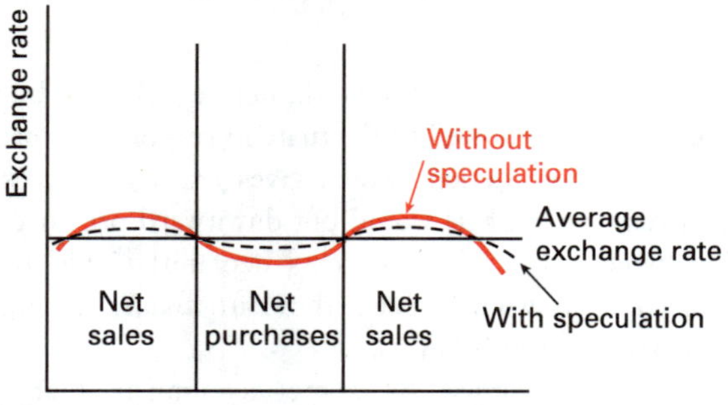

operating on the 'forward' market, but this may involve them in costs which would not exist if rates were fixed. The uncertainty introduced by flexible rates may cause traders to lose some of their *confidence* in the system.

Destabilising speculation
Speculative purchases or sales which result in an exchange rate fluctuating more than it would have done in the absence of speculation

Stabilising speculation
Speculative purchases or sales which result in the exchange rate fluctuating less than it would have done in the absence of speculation

Destabilising speculation A further reason for doubt to be cast on the *adjustment* and *confidence* aspects of the system is the possibility of large fluctuations in the rates caused by the activities of speculators. There has been much debate in the literature about whether speculation has a stabilising influence or a destabilising influence on flexible exchange rates. Consider the following two cases, the first of which suggests that speculation is destabilising and the second of which suggests that it is stabilising.

(i) Suppose that when speculators see the pound depreciating, they expect it to continue depreciating. They will sell pounds and buy stronger currencies so as to make a capital gain later. This activity will tend to put even greater pressure on the pound to depreciate. Similarly, when they observe the pound appreciating, they will increase their purchases of pounds and so put even greater upward pressure on it. In this case, we should expect speculative activity to cause faster and bigger exchange rate changes than would have occurred without speculation. This is illustrated in Fig. 29.8 which shows the hypothetical time-paths of the exchange rate with and without speculative activity.

(ii) It can be argued that in order to make profits speculators in general must buy a currency when its exchange rate is below its average level and sell when its exchange rate is higher than its average level. Since purchases push the rate upwards and sales push it downwards, this activity should tend to stabilise the rate. Friedman has argued that since speculators tend to be well-informed and make profits, their activities must be stabilising. Stabilising speculative activity is illustrated in Fig. 29.9.

It may be inflationary for deficit countries A country with a persistent deficit will experience a depreciating currency. As we have seen, such a depreciation will raise the price of imports and, at the same time, increase the demand for the country's exports and import-substitutes. It may, therefore, exert both cost-push and demand-pull inflationary pressure on the domestic economy. Strong trade unions may, for example, resist any fall in real wages by pressing for compensating money wage increases. This may be particularly severe if the country is close to full employment.

The IMF adjustable-peg system

The IMF system was set up at Bretton Woods in 1944 in an attempt to avoid the disadvantages of the gold standard and the 'instability' and 'uncertainty' of completely flexible exchange rates. The main objectives of the system were to achieve stability of exchange rates and 'to lessen the duration and reduce the degree of disequilibrium in members' balances of payments'.

The principal rules of the system were as follows:

(a) Members were required to establish the parity of their currencies in terms of gold or the dollar and then to maintain the values of their currencies within 1 per cent of parity. So, in the case of the United Kingdom, if parity were set at £1 = $2, the pound should not be allowed to exceed $2.02 or fall below $1.98.

(b) No members were allowed to alter their parities without notifying the IMF, but the IMF could not object if the change was to be less than 10 per cent. If the proposed change was to be greater than 10 per cent, the Fund's permission was required – the member countries made their decision by means of a majority vote.

(c) Before changing the parity of its exchange rate (that is, devaluing or revaluing), a country should be faced with what the IMF called a 'fundamental disequilibrium' in its balance of payments.

The system was clearly something of a compromise. Normally, exchange rates should be kept within the 1 per cent band, but if a persistent imbalance occurred, they could be adjusted once and for all by means of a policy devaluation or revaluation. An exchange rate change, however, was seen by most countries as a last resort policy. Consequently, short-term imbalances were sustained through intervention by the member countries' stabilisation funds (the Exchange Equalisation Account in the United Kingdom), buying or selling currencies on the foreign exchange market. In the case of a UK deficit, for example, the exchange rate would fall to its lower limit, but would not be allowed to depreciate further. The Exchange Equalisation Account would be used to buy up the excess supply of pounds. Similarly, in the case of a surplus, pounds would be supplied to the foreign exchange market to meet the excess demand which would otherwise push the rate above its upper limit.

If a deficit persisted, countries could not continue to sustain it indefinitely. Eventually, reserves would reach uncomfortably low levels and further loans from overseas would become difficult to negotiate. Countries would then typically follow domestic policies to try and correct the deficit. The appropriate policies would be deflationary fiscal and monetary policies designed to reduce the domestic rate of inflation and to cut the demand for imports. Only if these policies failed and the deficit still persisted, would a country consider a devaluation of its currency.

We can identify three main drawbacks to the IMF system.

(a) It was not easy for a government to decide *when* and *by how much* to devalue. Most countries tended to put off devaluation until the last minute by which time some international monetary crisis may have arisen. Consequently, when the devaluation came, it was often quite large and so represented a severe shock to traders, particularly those in the devaluing country.

(b) Policy conflicts arose, particularly for deficit countries with high rates of unemployment. The deflationary policies required to correct the deficit tended to worsen the unemployment.

(c) Speculation may have been destabilising. Speculators, predicting a devaluation, could lose very little by selling the weak currency and purchasing stronger currencies, thereby adding even greater downward pressure on the weak currency. It can be argued that such activity may have brought about a devaluation which may otherwise have been unnecessary or may have brought about a bigger devaluation than was actually necessary to restore equilibrium.

It was partly for these reasons that the IMF system was abandoned in 1972 and more flexibility was introduced into the international monetary system.

Managed floating

Managed floating
An exchange rate system in which exchange rates are determined mainly by the forces of supply and demand, but with some intervention by central banks to influence exchange rate movements

By the term managed floating, we refer to an exchange rate system in which the rates are determined in the main by the conditions of demand and supply, but in which monetary authorities intervene at times to stabilise the rates or influence them in some way. With 'managed floating', the fluctuations in a country's exchange rate are smoothed out whenever the country's monetary authority regards the upward or downward movements as becoming excessive. Thus, in the case of the United Kingdom, if the pound were depreciating rapidly, the authorities would sell part of the reserves of foreign currencies and buy pounds – this should help to reduce the rate of decline. Similarly, if the pound were thought to be appreciating too rapidly, the authorities would sell pounds on the foreign exchange market to smooth out the rise.

In 'managed floating', the decision when to intervene and by how much is an arbitrary one. The main objective is to have reasonable stability in exchange rates and so maintain *confidence* in the system. Since the system does have some degree of flexibility, it is also hoped that the *adjustment* mechanism will work with reasonable efficiency, though it is possible that central bank intervention may lead exchange rates away from rather than towards their equilibrium values. Unlike countries with completely flexible rates, those whose monetary authorities intervene in the foreign exchange market will still have a need for international reserves – this means that 'managed floating' will not necessarily overcome problems of *liquidity*.

Exchange rate bands

This is a system in which central bank intervention is determined more rigidly than in 'managed floating'. In this system, a country will allow its exchange rate to

Fig. 29.10. A band proposal. A government decision to maintain the exchange rate within a band (for example, ±5 per cent) either side of an initial central rate.

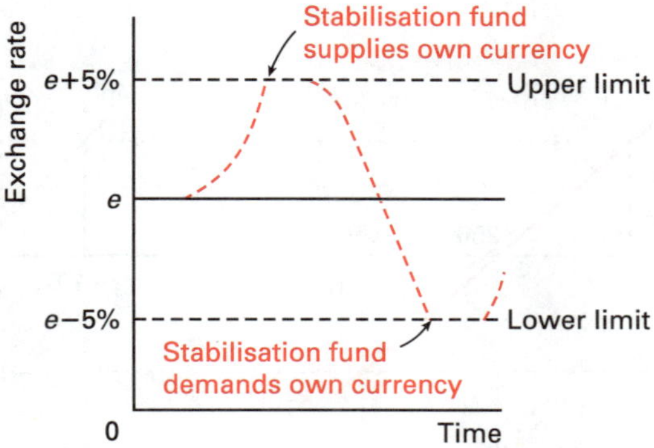

fluctuate against some other currency (like the dollar) or against some 'average' of other currencies within a pre-arranged band. This would, therefore, be similar to the IMF system, but in most proposals the band is wider. One possibility would be for a country to allow its currency to fluctuate in value against some average 'basket' of other currencies by plus or minus 5 per cent around some initial central value. Such a system is illustrated in Fig. 29.10. The country's stabilisation fund would intervene only when the exchange rate reached the upper or lower limit of the band.

Band proposals, then, represent a compromise between fixed and flexible rates. One problem is that once a currency reaches the upper or lower limit, the position is very similar to that of a disequilibrium in the IMF system and the same disadvantages apply.

Another possibility is for a group of currencies to be pegged to each other in some way and then to float freely (or within a band) against outside currencies. The European Monetary System is an example of this kind of exchange rate system. It is described more fully in Ch. 31.

Introduction to open-economy macroeconomics

Recall that in Ch. 23, we developed two macroeconomic models, the IS–LM model and the AD–AS model. The IS–LM model explicitly takes into account both the real and monetary sectors of the economy, but the Keynesian version of the model is limited by its assumption that the price level is fixed. The AD–AS model is the more general of the models we have so far considered: it assigns an important role to both real and monetary variables in the economy and allows the price level to vary. However, although we included the value of imports and the value of exports as variables in both models, in the interests of simplicity we did not take any account of the country's balance of payments position, nor did we attempt to analyse the effects of a balance of payments disequilibrium on the other variables in the models.

In this section, we propose to remedy this deficiency, first, by developing and applying the IS–LM–EE model (which is an open-economy general Keynesian model, developed by R. Mundell and R. Fleming in the 1960s), and secondly, by applying the AD–AS model to illustrate a simple version of the monetarist theory of the balance of payments.

The IS–LM–EE model

We saw in the first part of Ch. 23 that the general Keynesian model can be illustrated using IS and LM curves. The point at which the two curves intersect indicates the rate of interest and the level of national income at which both the real and monetary

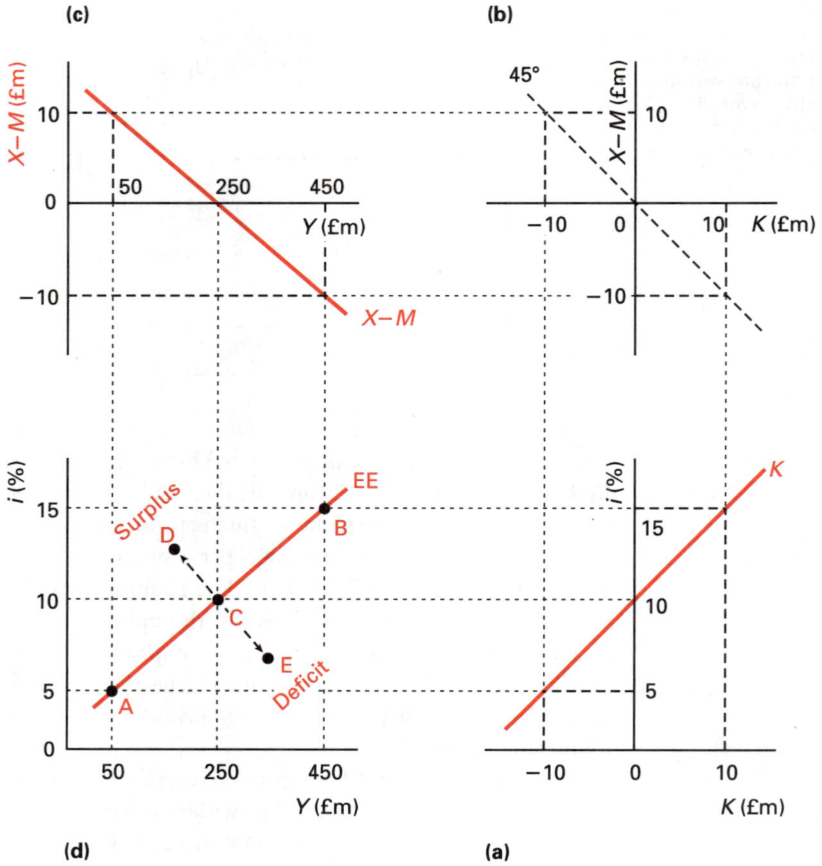

Fig. 29.11. Derivation of the EE curve. The positive relationship between *K* and *i*, shown in graph (a), and the negative relationship between (*X–M*) and *Y*, shown in graph (c), mean that the EE curve, derived in graph (d), slopes upwards from left to right.

The EE curve *This joins together all those combinations of the rate of interest and the level of income at which the balance of payments is in equilibrium*

sectors of the economy are in equilibrium. In an open-economy version of the model, it is useful also to know whether the home country's balance of payments is in equilibrium or disequilibrium. It is with this aim in mind that we now derive a third curve, the 'external equilibrium' or EE curve, which traces out combinations of the rate of interest and the level of income which are compatible with balance of payments equilibrium.

To derive the EE curve, we start by defining the balance of payments. The overall balance of payments is assumed to be divided into two sections: the current account and the capital account.

The *current account* is said to be in equilibrium when the total value of exports (X) is equal to the total value of imports (M). Thus, the condition for current account equilibrium may be written as:

$$X - M = 0$$

where X is assumed to be independent of both national income and the rate of interest, while M is assumed to be positively related to national income. Thus, other things being equal, a rise in national income will lead to a decrease in $X - M$ and a fall in national income will lead to a rise in $X - M$. This negative relationship between national income (Y) and the current account balance ($X - M$) is illustrated in graph (c) of Fig. 29.11.

The *capital account* position is measured by net autonomous capital inflows (K) which are assumed to be positively related to the domestic rate of interest. This means that a rise in the domestic rate of interest (i), given the rate of interest in the rest of the world, will lead to an increase in K (and will, for example, push the capital account from deficit towards surplus), while a fall in the domestic rate of interest will lead to a decrease in K. This relationship is illustrated diagrammatically in graph (a) of Fig. 29.11.

For the overall balance of payments to be in equilibrium, we require that:

$$X - M + K = 0$$

or

$$X - M = -K$$

This balance of payments equilibrium condition is satisfied at every point along the negatively sloping 45° line shown in graph (b) of Fig. 29.11.

An EE curve is derived in Fig. 29.11 using the same procedure as that used in Ch. 23 to derive the IS and LM curves. Notice from graph (a) that at an interest rate of 5 per cent, there is a capital account deficit equal to £10 million. Graph (b) tells us that, for overall balance of payments equilibrium, there must be a current account surplus of £10 million. It is clear from graph (c), however, that there is only one level of national income at which $X - M = £10$ million. This is an income level of £50 million. It follows that an interest rate of 5 per cent and an income level of £50 million is one combination of interest and income at which the balance of payments is in equilibrium. This combination must be one point on the EE curve and it is plotted as point A in graph (d).

Now consider an interest rate of 15 per cent. At this higher interest rate, there is a capital account surplus equal to £10 million. This means that for overall balance of payments equilibrium, there must be a current account deficit of £10 million. It can be seen from graph (c) that this only occurs at an income level of £450 million. This gives us a second combination of interest and income (15 per cent and £450 million) which must also be on the EE curve. It is plotted as point B in graph (d).

Choosing other interest rates and finding the level of income required for equilibrium in each case will yield a series of combinations, all of which will lie along the upward-sloping EE curve shown in graph (d). For example, at an interest rate of 10 per cent and a national income of £250 million, both the current and capital accounts are balanced. Thus, this represents another point on the EE curve, plotted as point C in graph (d). It should be clear by now that for the overall balance of payments to remain in equilibrium requires that a rising interest rate be accompanied by a rising level of income, and vise versa.

As shown in graph (d) of Fig. 29.11, combinations of the interest rate and the level of income *above and to the left* of the EE curve will create an overall balance of payments surplus. Moving from point C to point D, for example, simultaneously raises the rate of interest and lowers the level of income: both of these changes help to push the balance of payments into surplus. Similarly, combinations *below and to the right* of the EE curve will create an overall balance of payments deficit. Moving from point C to point E, for example, lowers the rate of interest and raises the level of income: both of these changes help to push the balance of payments into deficit.

The slope of the EE curve is influenced by the degree of international capital mobility. When capital is perfectly immobile internationally, so that a rise or fall in

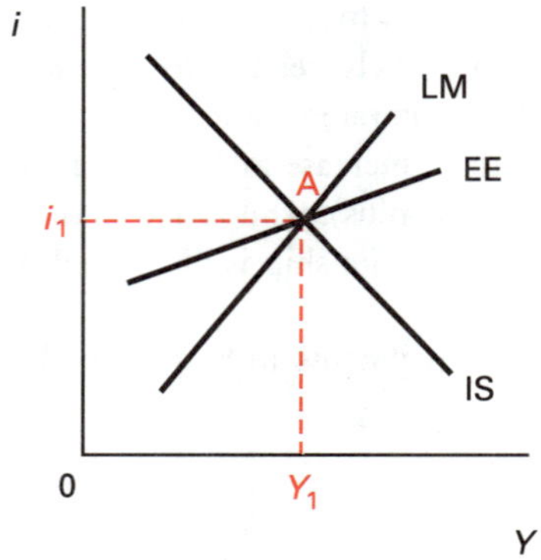

Fig. 29.12. The point of general equilibrium. The intersection of the IS and LM curves at point A determines the equilibrium interest rate, $0i_1$, and the equilibrium level of national income, $0Y_1$. As point A is also on the EE curve the balance of payments is also in equilibrium.

the domestic interest rate above or below the world level has no effect on capital inflows, the EE curve is vertical. When capital is perfectly mobile, the EE curve is horizontal. In general, the more internationally mobile capital is, the flatter is the EE curve. As there is a high degree of international capital mobility in the modern world, we shall draw the EE curve fairly flat. Although it cannot easily be determined whether the LM curve is steeper or flatter than the EE curve, in what follows we shall assume that the EE curve is flatter than the LM curve. [This assumption does affect some of our results and you are invited in Exercise 9 to re-work our examples on the assumption (a) that the EE curve is steeper than the LM curve, and (b) that there is a perfect degree of international capital mobility.]

The IS–LM–EE initial equilibrium An initial equilibrium position is illustrated in Fig. 29.12 where the IS, LM and EE curves all intersect at point A. The equilibrium rate of interest is $0i_1$, the equilibrium level of national income is $0Y_1$ (assumed to be less than the full employment level of income) and the balance of payments is in equilibrium. To show how the model may be applied, we shall examine the effects of a change in the domestic money supply and the effects of a change in government spending, first, on the assumption that the exchange rate is fixed, and secondly, on the assumption that the exchange rate is floating. *Throughout this section, we assume that there are unemployed resources available in the economy and that the price level remains fixed.*

An increase in the money supply with a fixed exchange rate (IS–LM–EE model) Suppose that there is an increase in the domestic money supply which shifts the LM curve from LM_1 to LM_2, as shown in Fig. 29.13. At first, the economy will move from point A to point B, where the IS curve intersects the new LM curve. The equilibrium rate of interest falls from $0i_1$ to $0i_2$, and the equilibrium level of income rises from $0Y_1$ to $0Y_2$ (which will also raise the level of employment). Note that this is equivalent to the case illustrated in Fig. 23.6. However, in an open economy it is not the end of the story, because point B lies below the EE line. This means that an overall balance of payments deficit will occur which, with the exchange rate fixed, will cause a net outflow of currency. Unless this is countered (or sterilised) by a central bank expansionary open market operation, the domestic money supply will contract and the LM curve will shift back to its original position. The rate of

Sterilisation *Offsetting action by the central bank, such as an open-market operation, to prevent a change in the money supply as a result of a balance of payments disequilibrium*

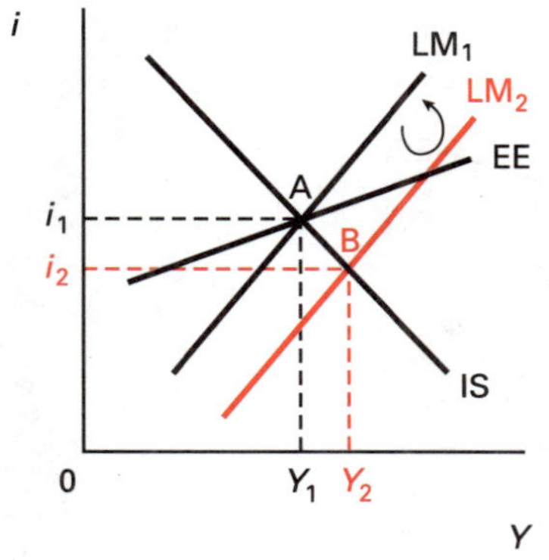

Fig 29.13. An increase in the money supply with a fixed exchange rate. An increase in the money supply shifts the LM curve to the right. This reduces the rate of interest and increases the level of income. However, it also has the effect of creating a deficit on the balance of payments. Unless sterilised, this will reduce the domestic money supply and shift the LM curve back to LM$_1$.

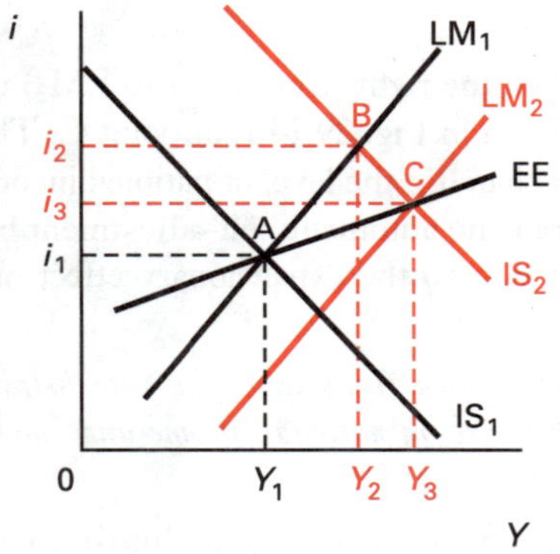

Fig 29.14. An increase in domestic spending with a fixed exchange rate. An increase in domestic spending shifts the IS curve to the right. This creates a surplus on the balance of payments which, unless sterilised, will increase the domestic money supply and shift the LM curve to the right. This leads to a further increase in income.

interest will rise back to $0i_1$, the level of income will fall back to $0Y_1$ and external equilibrium will be restored.

In this case, then, the increase in the domestic money supply has no lasting effect on national income and employment. Only if the central bank continued to expand the domestic money supply to offset the contractionary effect of the external deficit would the economy remain at point B.

Result: *With no sterilisation, a fixed exchange rate will help to insulate the economy from domestic monetary changes.*

An increase in government spending with a fixed exchange rate (IS–LM–EE model) Suppose now that there is an increase in autonomous spending caused by a rise in the level of government expenditure. This causes the IS curve to shift to the right from IS$_1$ to IS$_2$, as shown in Fig. 29.14. At first, the economy will move from point A to point B, where the original LM curve intersects the new IS curve. The equilibrium rate of interest rises to $0i_2$ and the equilibrium level of income rises to $0Y_2$. Note that this is identical to the case illustrated in Fig. 23.5. Once again, however, this is not the end of the story, because point B lies above the EE line. This means that an overall balance of payments *surplus* will occur which, with the exchange rate remaining fixed, will cause a net inflow of currency. Unless sterilised by a contractionary open-market operation, the domestic money supply will expand and

Fig. 29.15. An increase in the money supply with a floating exchange rate. An increase in the money supply shifts the LM curve to the right. This creates a temporary deficit on the balance of payments so that the exchange rate depreciates. This causes the IS curve and the EE curve to shift to the right, leading to a further rise in national income.

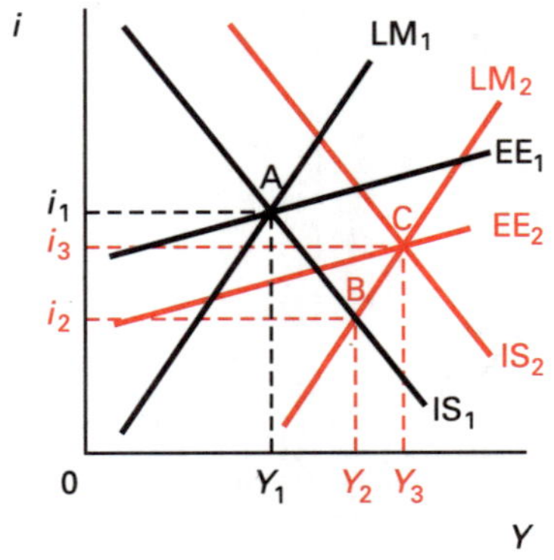

the LM curve will shift to the right (from LM_1 to LM_2) until external equilibrium is restored. The final position in Fig. 29.14 is at point C. The rate of interest has fallen to $0i_3$, but is still higher than $0i_1$; the level of national income has risen further to $0Y_3$. Thus, in this case, there is no automatic self-adjustment back to point A: instead, the external disequilibrium *adds* to the expansionary effect on national income.

Result: *With no sterilisation, a fixed exchange rate helps to reinforce the effect of a change in domestic expenditure on national income and employment.*

An increase in the money supply with a floating exchange rate (IS–LM–EE model) In a country with a floating exchange rate, an increase in the domestic money supply which shifts the LM curve to the right will create a *temporary* deficit on the overall balance of payments. This is shown in Fig. 29.15: as in Fig. 29.13, the rise in the money supply shifts the LM curve from LM_1 to LM_2 and the economy moves from point A to point B. The deficit on the balance of payments, however, cannot be sustained as the excess supply of domestic currency will cause the exchange rate to depreciate. The currency depreciation will cause an increased demand for exports and a reduced demand for imports, and so cause both the EE curve *and* the IS curve to shift to the right until external equilibrium is restored. The EE curve shifts from EE_1 to EE_2, and the IS curve shifts from IS_1 to IS_2. The final position in Fig. 29.15 is at point C, where the rate of interest has risen to $0i_3$ (still lower than $0i_1$) and the level of national income has increased further to $0Y_3$.

Result: *A floating exchange rate helps to reinforce the effect of a monetary change on national income and employment.*

An increase in government spending with a floating exchange rate (IS–LM–EE model) With a floating exchange rate, an increase in government spending which shifts the IS curve to the right will create a *temporary* surplus on the overall balance of payments. This is shown in Fig. 29.16: as in Fig. 29.14, the rise in government spending shifts the IS curve from IS_1 to IS_2 and the economy moves from point A to point B. The surplus on the balance of payments, however, cannot be sustained as the excess demand for domestic currency will cause the exchange rate

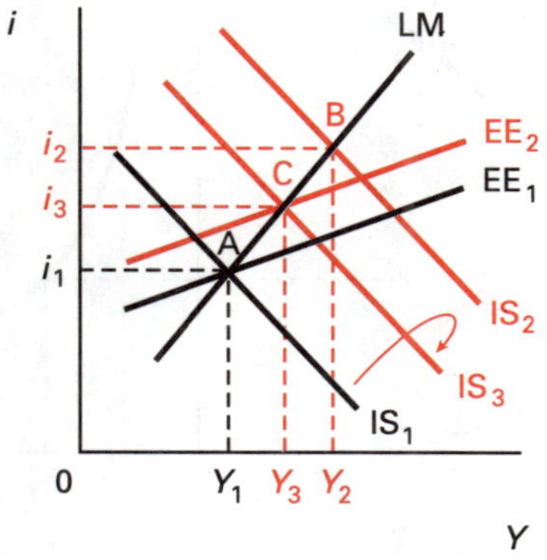

Fig. 29.16. An increase in domestic spending with a floating exchange rate. An increase in domestic spending shifts the IS curve to the right. This creates a temporary surplus on the balance of payments so that the exchange rate appreciates. This causes the IS curve and the EE curve to shift to the left and so offsets to some extent the effect of the increase in spending on national income.

to appreciate. The currency appreciation will cause a reduced demand for exports and an increased demand for imports, and so cause both the EE curve *and* the IS curve to shift to the left until external equilibrium is restored. The EE curve shifts from EE_1 to EE_2 and the IS curve shifts back from IS_2 to IS_3. The final position in Fig. 29.16 is at point C where the rate of interest has fallen to $0i_3$ (but is still higher than $0i_1$) and the level of national income has fallen back to $0Y_3$ (but is still higher than $0Y_1$). Thus, in this case, the induced change in the exchange rate tends to offset the effect of the increase in spending on national income and employment.

Result: *A floating exchange rate helps to offset the effect of a change in domestic expenditure on national income and employment.*

A limitation of the IS–LM–EE model Perhaps the main limitation of the IS–LM–EE model, as applied above, is the assumption of a fixed price level. If we relax this assumption, the analysis becomes rather unwieldy, to say the least. To show this, suppose that the initial equilibrium level of national income is close to the full employment level of income. This means that any increase in the money supply or rise in spending is likely to lead to an increase in both output *and* the price level. This cannot easily be analysed using the IS–LM–EE diagram because it is unable to tell us what the separate effects on output and prices will be.

Also, it is likely that a rise in the price level will cause all three curves to shift: the LM curve will shift to the left because of the fall in the real value of the money supply; the IS and EE curves will shift to the left because the higher price level will reduce the demand for exports; and the IS curve may shift further to the left because of the real balance effect. Thus, the analysis becomes quite complicated.

It is for this reason that in the next section, where we examine a simple version of the monetarist approach to open-economy macroeconomics, we leave the IS-LM–EE model and employ instead the AD–AS model. The AD–AS model proves to be a more appropriate framework for analysing an open economy with flexible prices.

The monetarist approach

Monetarists argue that balance of payments problems are 'fundamentally monetary in nature' and they emphasise the role played by a country's money market in

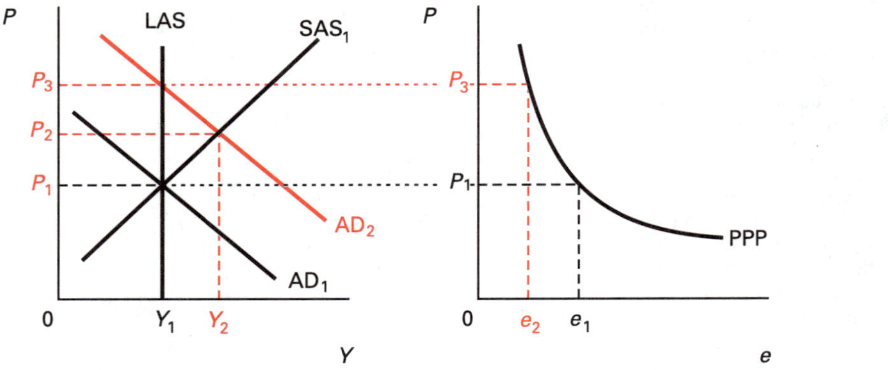

Fig. 29.17. ***An increase in the money supply in a monetarist model.*** An increase in the money supply shifts the AD curve to the right. This raises the price level and creates a deficit on the balance of payments. With a fixed exchange rate, the money supply will fall back to its original level and the AD curve will shift back to the left. The price level will then return to $0P_1$. With a flexible exchange rate, the deficit will cause a currency depreciation, (from $0e_1$ to $0e_2$) which will restore purchasing power parity and eliminate the deficit. In this case, the new equilibrium price level will be $0P_3$.

determining its balance of payments position and exchange rate. The theory assumes that the total demand for money is a stable function of money national income and rates of interest, based on a version of the quantity theory of money, as described in Ch. 22. For simplicity, in what follows, we shall concentrate on the extreme monetarist view that the long-run AS curve is vertical at the level of real income associated with the 'natural' rate of unemployment (as explained in Ch. 23).

A further assumption of the monetarist open-economy model is that *purchasing power parity* is achieved: this means that the exchange rate and/or the price level always adjust(s) to ensure that the domestic and foreign price levels are equal when they are both measured in the same currency. That is,

$$P = P^*/e$$

where P is the domestic price level, P^* is the foreign price level in foreign currency and e is the exchange rate (defined as the number of units of foreign currency per unit of domestic currency). Thus, if an average basket of goods costs £100 in the United Kingdom, while exactly the same basket of goods costs 500DM in Germany, purchasing power parity requires that the sterling-mark exchange rate should be £1 = 5DM.

An initial long-run equilibrium position is shown in Fig. 29.17, where the left-hand diagram shows the familiar AD–AS graph: the equilibrium price level is $0P_1$ and the equilibrium level of real income is $0Y_1$. The purchasing power parity (PPP) curve in the right-hand diagram shows the combinations of the domestic price level and the exchange rate at which purchasing power parity is achieved. The curve is a rectangular hyperbola, obtained by plotting the relationship, $P = P^*(1/e)$. At points to the right of the curve, the domestic currency is said to be overvalued. At points to the left of the curve, the domestic currency is said to be undervalued. With a given foreign price level and a domestic price level equal to $0P_1$, the exchange rate which ensures purchasing power parity is $0e_1$.

The monetarist approach places emphasis on the fact that a change in a country's monetary base (ΔMB) can be caused either by a change (through open market operations) in the quantity of domestic bonds held by the monetary authorities (denoted by ΔD) or by any net inflows or outflows from abroad arising from a balance of payments disequilibrium (denoted by ΔR, or change in reserves). Using symbols, we can write:

$$\Delta MB = \Delta D + \Delta R$$

It follows that, with a fixed exchange rate, a balance of payments deficit, which reduces the quantity of foreign exchange reserves being held by the central bank, will lead to a fall in the domestic money supply (unless this effect is sterilised by a domestic open market operation). Similarly, a balance of payments surplus will, unless sterilised, lead to a rise in the domestic money supply. These monetary changes (which are the same as those we employed in the IS–LM–EE model) will tend to correct the balance of payments disequilibria which cause them.

According to monetarists, a rise in domestic spending (for example, a rise in government spending) will 'crowd out' other spending in the economy and so will have little or no effect on real income, employment, the price level or the balance of payments. Consequently, to illustrate the monetarist approach, we shall consider the effects on the economy of an increase in the domestic money supply, first, assuming a fixed exchange rate, and secondly, a floating exchange rate.

An increase in the money supply with a fixed exchange rate (monetarist model) An increase in the nominal money supply will lead to an increase in aggregate demand. This is shown in Fig. 29.17, where the AD curve shifts from AD_1 to AD_2. In the short-run, this causes a movement along the short-run AS curve, SAS_1, so that real income rises to $0Y_2$ and the price level rises to $0P_2$. In the long-run, if nothing else happened, the full effect would be on the price level which would rise to $0P_3$. The price level may not actually reach $0P_3$, however, because as domestic prices rise, purchasing power parity is spoiled and the country's exports become less competitive in world markets. This creates a deficit on the balance of payments. To prevent the exchange rate from depreciating, the monetary authorities have to purchase domestic currency and reduce their holdings of foreign exchange reserves. This will have the effect of reducing the domestic money supply back to its original level. As it does so, the AD curve will shift back towards AD_1 and the price level will eventually fall back to $0P_1$. The balance of payments will then be back in equilibrium and purchasing power parity will be restored.

Thus an important implication of the monetarist approach is that, with a fixed exchange rate, a government of an open economy does not have independent control over its domestic money supply. Attempts to raise the money supply by means of a domestic open market operation will cause a balance of payments deficit which, unless sterilised, will have the effect of reducing the money supply again.

Result: *Fixed exchange rates mean that governments have no independent control over their domestic money supplies.*

An increase in the money supply with a floating exchange rate (monetarist model) With a floating exchange rate, an increase in the nominal money supply will raise aggregate demand and create a *temporary* deficit on the balance of payments as the domestic price level rises. The deficit will cause a depreciation of the domestic currency which will restore purchasing power parity and eliminate the deficit. Although there will be a short-run effect on real income and employment, the effect in the long-run will be a lower exchange rate and a higher price level. This is also shown in Fig. 29.17, where the final equilibrium exchange rate will be $0e_2$ and the final equilibrium price level will be $0P_3$. A conclusion that we can draw from this is that floating exchange rates enable countries to pursue independent monetary policies.

Result: *Floating exchange rates mean that governments have independent control over their domestic money supplies.*

This brief examination of the monetarist theory of the balance of payments concludes our introduction to open-economy macroeconomics. In recent years, this has developed into a major branch of economics with important implications for the stability of the international monetary system. Our discussion of the international economy is, however, continued in the next two chapters where we consider international trade and policy (in Ch. 30) and the economics of the European Community (in Ch. 31).

Summary

1. A country's balance of payments accounts record all the economic transactions which take place between the residents of that country and residents of all other countries during some time period. A persistent disequilibrium on a country's balance of payments may pose a serious policy problem.
2. The equilibrium spot and forward rates of exchange for a currency are determined by the forces of demand and supply in the foreign exchange markets. In turn, the demand for and supply of currencies are influenced by the activities of traders and investors engaging in hedging, speculation and arbitrage.
3. The Marshall–Lerner condition states that a country's balance of trade can only improve following a depreciation if the sum of the elasticities of demand for imports and exports is greater than one.
4. The depreciation of a country's currency is likely to induce an increase in the country's national income which in turn will raise the demand for imports and so tend to offset any initial improvement in the trade balance.
5. Exchange rate systems may in part be judged by the extent to which they achieve three desirable characteristics: adjustment, confidence and liquidity. Fixed exchange rate systems include the gold standard, common currency areas and the adjustable peg system. Managed floating is a system in which exchange rates are determined in the main by the forces of demand and supply, but in which the monetary authorities stand by to intervene to stabilise exchange rates.
6. The IS–LM–EE model is an open-economy general Keynesian model which can be used to analyse the effects of changes in real and monetary variables on the rate of interest and the level of national

income and employment. The model is limited by its assumption of a fixed price level.

7. The AD–AS model, which assumes a variable price level, can be used to illustrate the monetarist theory of an open economy. Monetarists argue that balance of payments problems are fundamentally monetary in nature and they emphasise the role played by a country's money market in determining its balance of payments position and rate of exchange.

Exercises

1. Review your understanding of the following terms:

foreign exchange market	absorption
'spot' rate of exchange	adjustment, confidence, liquidity
'forward' rate of exchange	gold standard
foreign exchange risk	common currency area
hedging	optimum currency area
foreign exchange arbitrage	flexible exchange rates
interest arbitrage	destabilising speculation
demand for pounds	IMF adjustable-peg system
supply of pounds	joint floating
Marshall–Lerner condition	sterilisation

2. Consider the following data for a hypothetical country with a floating exchange rate in 1993:

   Effective exchange rate (1985 = 100): 1st January 1993: 80.0
   31st December 1993: 75.0

   Rate of inflation during 1993: 3.0 per cent
   Current account surplus in 1993: £1 billion, equivalent to 2 per cent of GDP.
   Net increase in official reserves: £1.3 billion.
   Discuss reasons for the fall in this country's effective exchange rate in 1993 when there was a low rate of inflation and a current account surplus.

3. Outline the monetarist approach to the balance of payments. Critically evaluate this approach.

4.** Explain what is meant by a devaluation of a currency and discuss the likely internal and external effects of a devaluation.

5. Discuss the view that currency depreciation may be inflationary and therefore ineffective as a means of correcting a balance of payments deficit.

6. What considerations are relevant in identifying the boundaries of an optimum currency area? Discuss the implications for the United Kingdom of an EC decision to adopt a common currency.

7. Under a regime of flexible exchange rates, do speculators have a stabilising or destabilising effect?

8. What are the objectives of the IMF and how does it seek to achieve them?

9. In the IS–LM–EE model, consider the effects on an economy with a fixed exchange rate of:

   (a) a decrease in the money supply, and
   (b) a decrease in government expenditure,
   assuming, first, that the EE curve is steeper than the LM curve, and secondly, that the EE curve is a horizontal line.

   Repeat the exercise for an economy with a floating exchange rate.

30 INTERNATIONAL TRADE AND POLICY

Learning objectives

After reading this chapter, you should be able to:

- explain the theory of comparative advantage and demonstrate that trade is potentially beneficial to participating countries
- appreciate that there are alternative theories of why trade takes place
- describe the various forms of protection: tariffs, quotas, exchange controls, subsidies and so on
- use partial equilibrium analysis to examine the effects of imposing a tariff on a single good
- discuss the microeconomic and macroeconomic arguments for protection
- appreciate of the role of the General Agreement on Tariffs and Trade

Introduction

In Ch. 7, we considered resource allocation within a simple general equilibrium model of a closed economy with only two goods (cloth and food). The preferences of the community were reflected in the community indifference map (shown in Fig. 7.1) and we saw that the optimum output combination was at the point on the production possibility frontier where the community was on its highest attainable indifference curve. In a closed economy, of course, the community can only consume goods and services produced within the country – that is to say, it can consume at points on or inside the production possibility frontier. In this chapter, we show that in an open economy, mutually advantageous trade between countries may enable the participating countries to consume combinations of goods to the 'north-east' of their production possibility frontiers.

In the first section of this chapter, we consider how a freely operating price system can give rise to international trade and thus influence the pattern of the allocation of resources within the countries. We also demonstrate that such trade will be beneficial to those who take part in it. We then consider the adverse effects of a tariff, including that of resource misallocation, at the microeconomic level. Finally, we discuss the microeconomic arguments in favour of a tariff and consider the case for import controls at the macroeconomic level.

The theory of comparative advantage

Clearly, much trade takes place because one country is better able to produce particular products than its trading partners. A tropical country, for example, is better suited to growing fruits that require a lot of sunshine than a temperate country; similarly, some natural resources are only found in plentiful supplies in certain locations. Japan, for example, has to import oil from Indonesia, the Middle East and other oil-rich areas. A large amount of trade in the world, however, is in goods that could conceivably be produced in either the importing or the exporting country; many countries, in fact, choose to specialise in producing particular products. The case where country A is more efficient than country B at producing, say, cloth and country B is more efficient than country A at producing, say, food is known as absolute advantage. It is fairly obvious that if A specialises in cloth production and B in food production, the total production of both goods will increase, giving rise to the possibility of mutually beneficial trade.

Absolute advantage *A country is said to have an absolute advantage in the production of a commodity if it can produce that commodity more efficiently. This means that production in this country yields more output for a given level of inputs*

However, what if country A is more efficient than B at producing all products? David Ricardo in the early nineteenth century developed the theory of comparative advantage which showed that it was relative efficiency that was relevant when considering the possibility of gains from trade. So long as the relative costs of production in countries A and B differ, increased specialisation and exchange can potentially benefit both countries. Ricardo's original theory was based on the *labour theory of value*, but was refined in the 1930s by an approach based on opportunity costs developed by Haberler. Consider now an illustration of the theory based on opportunity costs.

Comparative advantage *The theory of comparative (or relative) advantage shows that relative costs are important in determining which products are imported and exported. A country will export a product for which it has relatively low production costs, and will import a product for which it has relatively high production costs*

The theory of comparative advantage demonstrates that trade is potentially beneficial to the welfare of a country if it specialises in the production of those commodities in which it has a comparative advantage. To illustrate the theory by means of a numerical example, consider two countries of equal size, A and B, both of which produce and consume two goods, food and cloth. Suppose that when both countries use all their resources efficiently to produce food, the corresponding outputs are as follows:

Country A – 100 tonnes
Country B – 200 tonnes

Similarly, suppose that when they use all their resources efficiently to produce cloth, the corresponding outputs are:

Country A – 100 metres
Country B – 100 metres

Assume that both countries face constant opportunity costs of production and have full employment at all times. Assume further that factors of production are perfectly mobile between the cloth and food industries within each country, but immobile between the countries. The *perfect conditions* we had earlier in considering the operation of the price mechanism in a closed economy are assumed to prevail in both countries.

Country B is more efficient than A in the production of food and equally efficient in the production of cloth. Why should B wish to trade with A?

Given the assumption of constant opportunity costs, the two countries' production possibility frontiers will be straight lines. Country A's frontier is shown as line ab in Fig. 30.1(a) and country B's frontier is line cd in Fig. 30.1(b). To discover whether or not it would pay the countries to specialise in production and to

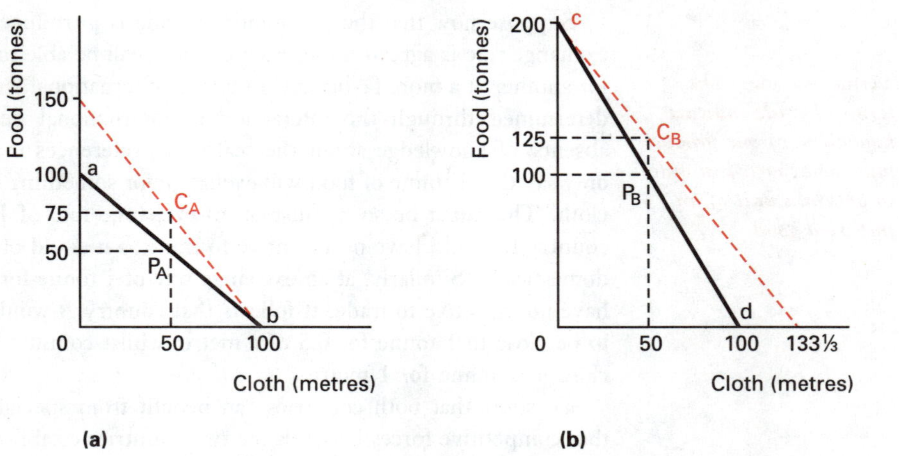

Fig. 30.1. The gains resulting from trade between two countries. The introduction of trade enables both countries to consume a larger bundle of goods compared with the pre-trade situation.

trade with each other, we have to consider each country's opportunity costs of production. Country A can produce either 100 tonnes of food or 100 metres of cloth: the opportunity cost of producing one extra tonne of food is one metre of cloth. Country B can produce either 200 tonnes of food or 100 metres of cloth: in this case, the opportunity cost of producing one extra tonne of food is 0.5 metre of cloth.

We see then that country B can produce food at a lower real cost (that is, in terms of cloth) than country A. *Country B, therefore, is said to have a comparative advantage in food production. Country A, on the other hand, has a comparative advantage in cloth production*: this is so because the opportunity cost of an additional metre of cloth in country A is 1 tonne of food, whilst in country B the opportunity cost of a metre of cloth is 2 tonnes of food. Under *perfect conditions*, 1 metre of cloth will exchange for 1 tonne of food in country A and for 2 tonnes of food in country B. These exchange ratios represent the pre-trade relative prices of the two goods in the two countries. Both countries can potentially gain if they specialise along the lines of their respective comparative advantages and then trade with each other.

To illustrate this, suppose that before any trade takes place, both countries divide their resources equally between food and cloth production. The resulting outputs are as follows:

	Pre-trade output and consumption	
	Food (tonnes)	Cloth (metres)
Country A	50	50
Country B	100	50
World total	150	100

In the pre-trade situation, of course, each country's consumption coincides with its production. If each country exists in isolation, the rate at which it can substitute one product for another is fixed by technology and is represented by the slope of its production possibility frontier.

Terms of trade *The terms of trade indicate how much of one product must be exported in order to obtain a unit of an imported good*

Suppose now that the possibility of trade is introduced. If a mutually acceptable exchange rate is agreed upon, each country will be able to substitute one commodity for another at a more favourable rate. The international terms of trade will, in fact, be determined through the interaction of international demand and supply. In the absence of knowledge about the scales of preferences in the two countries, we can only say that 1 tonne of food will exchange for something between 0.5 and 1 metre of cloth. This must be so because at an exchange rate of 1 tonne for 0.5 of a metre, country B would have no incentive to trade as it could obtain extra cloth at this rate domestically. Similarly, at an exchange rate of 1 tonne for 1 metre, country A would have no incentive to trade. It follows that country A would prefer the terms of trade to be close to 1 tonne for 0.5 of a metre, whilst country B would prefer them to be close to 1 tonne for 1 metre.

To show that both countries can benefit from specialisation and trade, suppose that competitive forces between the two countries establish the international terms of trade at 1 tonne of food for $\frac{2}{3}$ of a metre of cloth. If both countries specialise completely in the production of the good in which they have a comparative advantage, their outputs will be as follows:

	Production after specialisation	
	Food (tonnes)	Cloth (metres)
Country A	0	100
Country B	200	0
World total	200	100

Notice that the total world production of food has increased with cloth production remaining unchanged. One possible post-trade position might involve country A in exporting 50 metres of cloth in return for imports of 75 tonnes of food. The post-trade consumption pattern will be as follows:

	Post-trade consumption	
	Food (tonnes)	Cloth (metres)
Country A	75	50
Country B	125	50
World total	200	100

Compared with their pre-trade consumption, both countries are consuming 25 extra tonnes of food and no less cloth. *Specialisation and exchange have unambiguously benefited both countries.*

In terms of Fig. 30.1, before trade, country A is consuming at point P_A and country B is consuming at point P_B, both points being on the production possibility frontiers. After trade, country A is able to reach point C_A and country B is able to reach point C_B – notice that both of these points are outside the countries' respective production possibility frontiers. If we were, in addition, to draw the two countries' community indifference maps on the graphs, it would be clear that international trade can enable both countries to reach indifference curves which without trade would be unattainable. International trade can, therefore, increase social welfare.

The theory of comparative advantage developed by Ricardo took as its starting-point the assumption that different countries had different production costs for the same good. It is logical now to ask what lies behind these cost differences.

The *Heckscher–Ohlin theorem* (named after the Swedish economists, Eli Heckscher and Bertil Ohlin) attributes these cost differences to differences in factor endowments between countries. A country with an abundance of natural resources and agricultural land can be described as land-abundant and may be expected to have a comparative cost advantage in the production of commodities which are land-intensive. Conversely, a country with an abundant labour force may be expected to have a comparative cost advantage in goods whose production uses labour intensively. Thus, the theorem predicts that a country will tend to export those goods which are intensive in the country's relatively abundant factor and import those goods which are intensive in the country's relatively scarce factor.

Trade resulting from technological change

In recent years, increasing attention has been paid to the importance of technological progress in the generation of international trade. A country which makes a technological breakthrough and develops a new product will have a temporary monopoly in its production. If a demand for the new product exists (or is developed) in other countries, trade is likely to result. This trade is sometimes described as technological gap trade, referring to the time-lag or gap before other countries start to produce the new good with equal efficiency. Some empirical evidence does indicate that those American industries with a high level of 'research and development' effort (such as aerospace and electronics) do have an export performance significantly above average.

Technological gap *The time-interval over which a particular country has a temporary monopoly in the production of a good as a result of its innovation*

In addition, R. Vernon has developed a 'product-cycle' model which describes the development of, in particular, labour-saving products which meet demands in countries with high *per capita* incomes. He argues that initially production of the new product will take place in the country for whose market it is intended. When the product is being developed, producers require continuous feedback from consumers and need good communications with numerous suppliers. Later, when the product becomes standardised, other countries may offer comparative cost advantages so that gradually production shifts to these countries. It is possible that exports back to the country which originally developed the product will then occur.

Trade policy

We have seen that free trade and consequent specialisation along the lines of comparative advantage potentially maximises world welfare in a world of perfectly mobile factors of production and of no externalities. Nevertheless, much attention has been devoted to the important question of whether protection can increase the welfare of a single country. By 'protection', we refer to barriers to free trade which tend to 'protect' the domestic industries against foreign competition.

Tariff *A tax that is levied on imported products*

Quota *A limit imposed on the quantity of goods that may be imported during a given time period*

Protection can take several forms. Much of the technical discussion has concerned the effects of an imposition of a tariff – that is, a tax on imported goods. A quota is the establishment by a government of a physical limit on the quantity of a good that can be imported over a given period; a quota may be expressed in physical, value or market share terms, but all imply that when a given quantity has already been imported, no more of that good will be allowed into the country. An exchange control system requires residents to obtain central bank permission to buy foreign currency for certain purposes, and perhaps multiple exchange rates with adverse exchange rates for luxury goods or unapproved uses.

Exchange control system *A set of regulations that restricts domestic residents' access to foreign exchange*

Subsidies to domestic industries and *export subsidies* both have the effect of protecting domestic industries against foreign competition. An import deposits scheme requires importers to lodge some money with the central bank for a given time period. The effect is to increase the cost of importing and to tighten up on credit conditions. In recent years, new types of non-tariff barriers have been given increasing attention. Non-tariff barriers include *special regulations* that have to be met and the official form-filling necessary for goods to be imported into a particular country. Many regulations are imposed by governments on the grounds of consumer protection or public safety, but the effects may be to protect domestic production. There has been suspicion that some countries have imposed safety and other regulations as a means of discriminating against imports. In addition, a public procurement policy which requires some proportion of public expenditure to be spent domestically is a form of protection. Some countries, which officially adhere to free trade principles and are signatories of liberal international trade agreements, have become concerned at the levels of imports of particular products (for example, car imports into the United Kingdom and other EC countries from Japan) and have negotiated voluntary agreements with the overseas producers, which are designed to limit imports. We see from this brief discussion that protection can take many forms.

Import deposits scheme *A requirement that obliges importers to deposit a sum of money with the central bank. The sum deposited is normally related to the value of goods imported*

Public procurement policy *A preference by public sector agencies for the purchase of domestically produced goods*

Voluntary agreement *An agreement whereby a country voluntarily undertakes to restrict exports*

In the following discussion, we concentrate on the arguments for and against tariffs, but much of the discussion applies to the concept of protection as a whole.

Adverse effects of tariffs

Consider the imposition of a tariff on a particular good X. For simplicity, we assume that the world supply is infinitely elastic, that the good imposes no externalities, that the marginal utility of income is constant and that perfect competition prevails in both commodity and factor markets. In Fig. 30.2, S_W is the world supply curve of good X which is infinitely elastic at price $0w_1$. D_dD_d and S_dS_d are the domestic demand and supply curves respectively.

Prior to the imposition of the tariff, consumers buy the quantity $0q_4$, of which domestic producers supply quantity $0q_1$. Thus, quantity q_1q_4 is imported initially. Now assume that a tariff equal to w_1p_1 is imposed on each unit of X imported, so that the effective world supply curve to this country shifts up to S_w + tariff. At the new domestic price $0p_1$, consumers buy a smaller quantity $0q_3$, of which a larger quantity, $0q_2$, is produced domestically. Imports fall to the quantity q_2q_3.

The imposition of the tariff imposes a cost on society in the form of *resource misallocation*. Consumer surplus, which was equal to the area ABw_1 prior to the imposition of the tariff, is reduced to the area ACp_1. Part of the reduction in consumer surplus accrues to producers as an increase in producers' surplus – that is, area w_1p_1RQ. Another part of the reduction in consumer surplus, rectangle RSTC, is collected by the government as tariff revenue. The resource misallocation costs of the tariff are represented by the areas of triangle QRS and triangle CTB. These areas are called *deadweight loss* of the tariff.

The consumption loss *The loss of welfare imposed on consumers as a result of their inability to purchase a product at the world price following the imposition of a tariff*

The consumption loss represented by triangle CTB arises because consumers are prevented by the tariff from buying X at the world price $0w_1$. At the new price $0p_1$,

Fig. 30.2. **The resource allocation effects of the imposition of a tariff.** The tariff causes the domestic price to rise from the world price $0w_1$ to $0p_1$. The consumption loss is represented by the area CTB and the production loss by the area QRS.

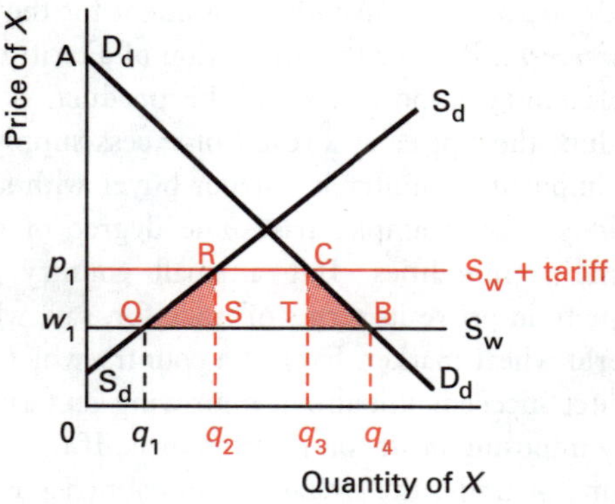

consumers reduce the quantity bought by amount q_3q_4. Consumers value these units more highly than the world price, and thus the tariff imposes a loss on them. The production loss represented by triangle QRS arises because the quantity q_1q_2 is produced domestically after the imposition of the tariff. Under competitive conditions, the domestic supply curve S_dS_d represents the marginal cost of producing extra units. Thus, the total cost of producing quantity q_1q_2 domestically is represented by the area q_1QRq_2. Prior to the imposition of the tariff, the country imported this quantity at a cost represented by the area q_1QSq_2. Thus, triangle QRS represents the extra cost of domestic production.

Production loss *The loss of welfare sustained by society as a result of increased domestic production at a higher cost relative to the world price*

Enforcement of the tariff will require resources to be diverted to this task, such as extra customs officials and civil servants. Thus, part of the tariff revenue accruing to government will probably be spent on enforcement. If so, this socially unproductive use of resources increases the deadweight loss of the tariff.

Another argument against a tariff kept in force over a long period is that it may enable inefficient firms to survive, which would otherwise have gone out of business. As a result, resources may be prevented from transferring to other industries in which the country has developed a comparative advantage. Similarly, a tariff may result in the creation of a domestic monopoly if foreign competitors are excluded, with the dangers that the monopoly may exploit the consumer and allow costs to rise unnecessarily.

Microeconomic arguments for protection

It appears that there are formidable microeconomic arguments against the imposition of a tariff, but now consider some microeconomic arguments in favour of a tariff.

Strategic industry argument The strategic industry argument is basically non-economic; it is that certain industries are of strategic importance in times of crises or armed conflict. Thus, a government might wish to expand or maintain the capacity of domestic production of a strategic industry through protection. It can be argued that industries such as agriculture, aerospace, armaments, shipbuilding and fuel industries are strategic. A decision to protect an industry on strategic grounds is clearly political. The economist can only point out that protection of an industry with a comparative disadvantage has an economic cost, and attempt to quantify that cost.

Strategic industry *An industry that a government considers is vital to the interests of the country*

Terms of trade argument Another argument for the imposition of a tariff is the *terms of trade argument*. If, after the imposition of a tariff on a particular product, the tariff-imposing country imports less of the product, it may be able to force the suppliers to reduce their price as a result of excess supply. Clearly, this will only be effective if the importing country is a major buyer with some monopsonistic power. The United States, for example, has some degree of monopsonistic power with respect to some commodities. But a small country, like Belgium, could not realistically hope to improve its terms of trade for, say, wheat, as Belgium is a price-taker in the world wheat market. Even if a country which is an important buyer of a particular product succeeds initially in improving its terms of trade, other countries may retaliate by imposing tariffs on their imports. If this happens, with a consequent fall in the volume of trade, the welfare of all countries is likely to be reduced.

Infant industry *An industry that needs temporary protection against well-established foreign competitors in the early stages of its life*

Infant industry argument Perhaps the oldest and most widely accepted argument for protection is the *infant industry argument*. This argument is often applied to new industries in developing countries. When the industry is first established, the argument runs, it will be unable to compete effectively with the already well-established industries in other countries. The infant industry is likely to be producing on a small scale, and thus will not benefit from economies of scale. It is also likely to have a relatively inexperienced and less productive work-force. If, however, the industry is given some temporary protection, it will be able to develop a comparative advantage, and will ultimately be able to survive without protection. Thus, this argument incorporates a dynamic element, as the industry is held to develop a comparative advantage over time.

This argument appears valid and many economists have endorsed it, including Alexander Hamilton in 1791 and Friedrich List in 1841. But in recent times, some economists have put the infant industry argument under close scrutiny. If the infant industry will make temporary losses, but will ultimately be profitable, then surely entrepreneurs should be willing to withstand those initial losses in return for the prospect of future profits. If this does not in fact happen, it could be due to an imperfection or distortion in the capital market. In fact, many of the cases when protection has been called for an infant industry are examples of imperfections or distortions in the economy. Perhaps the capital market is inefficient in raising funds, or perhaps entrepreneurs are poorly informed about the future prospects of the industry. Alternatively, the development of the infant industry might result in external economies for other sectors of the economy. It might, for example, train a skilled work-force, some of whom will eventually transfer into other sectors of the economy. However, the entrepreneurs in the infant industry may not provide sufficient training from the viewpoint of society, as they recognise that some of the benefits will accrue to other industries.

Recent analysis has argued that if a *distortion, imperfection* or *externality* exists, then protection is an indirect and relatively inefficient method of dealing with the problem. Although protection can help the infant industry, it results in resource misallocation. The government should aim to remedy the imperfection, distortion or externality problem more directly. In the case of an imperfect capital market, for example, the government could provide loans, perhaps on preferential terms, to the entrepreneurs in the infant industry. If the entrepreneurs are poorly informed about the future prospects for the industry, the government can improve the flow of information through publications and counselling services.

Where entrepreneurs are not willing to provide the socially optimal amount of job-training, the government can give specific subsidies for training, or can set up government training centres. In the case where a government wishes to encourage production of a good domestically, because of external economies, national prestige or whatever, a production subsidy will be more efficient than protection of the industry. Such a subsidy stimulates production without introducing a distortion on the consumption side, as would a tariff.

Thus, when the infant industry argument is subjected to closer scrutiny the case for protection does not appear very strong. The argument is further weakened because of the danger that a protected infant industry may never grow up. It may never be able to discard its protection and compete effectively. A subsidy for training or to encourage domestic production is also more visible in the government's budget than a tariff, and is more likely to intensify public pressure for the industry to stand on its own feet. The United Kingdom government gave assistance to the microelectronics industry for the development and application of silicon chip technology. An argument for this support is that a successful microelectronics industry in the United Kingdom will generate many benefits, some of which will not be appropriated by the industry itself – for example, increased employment, a faster rate of economic growth and increased exports.

Dumping *This occurs when a firm sells a product in an overseas market at a price below that prevailing in its home market*

Anti-dumping argument Another microeconomic argument for protection is as a counter-measure against dumping. Dumping occurs when a firm sells a product in an overseas market at a price below the price in the country of origin, after making appropriate allowances for differences in taxation, transport and insurance costs and tariffs. A firm acting as a discriminating monopolist, for example, may sell a product at a lower price in an overseas market. Recall from Ch. 10 that a discriminating monopolist can increase profit by selling a product at different prices in separate markets which have different demand elasticities.

Another motive for dumping is the intention by a firm to increase its market by driving its competitors out of business; this is sometimes known as 'predatory dumping'. The dumping firm may be able to sell temporarily at a loss-making low price in a particular market through cross-subsidisation from other markets. It is generally accepted that protection against predatory dumping is justifiable. In theory, persistent dumping benefits the consumer and no good case for protection against this form of dumping can be made. In practice, it is virtually impossible to distinguish the motives for dumping or to predict how long it will continue.

Dubious arguments

Some arguments advanced for protection do not stand up to careful inspection and have little validity. *Special interest groups,* such as producers and workers in a particular industry can, of course, benefit from protection of this industry. But the special interest groups will gain at the expense of consumers who are forced to pay higher prices and the community as a whole, as resources are diverted away from their areas of comparative advantage. It is common for producers and trade unions to call for protection against 'unfair competition' from lower paid foreign labour. If this argument were pursued to its logical implication, the United States and most of western Europe would refuse to trade with the United Kingdom, as wages in the United Kingdom are below those in these countries. As we note above, differences in comparative costs lie at the heart of the reasons for trade. If all countries had the same costs of production, there would be no gains from trade.

Pleas for protection often arise when an old established industry finds itself losing its comparative advantage and moving into a period of decline. In these circumstances, the resources freed from the declining industry should move to new expanding industries. But often this transfer is slow and painful and structural unemployment results. Permanent protection would mean supporting an inefficient industry. One could, however, put forward a case for some *temporary* protection with a strict time limit and specific measures laid down to encourage adjustment. The appropriate policies for the government are to subsidise the retraining of the workforce and to encourage the development of new industries. It can be argued that the burden of adjustment should be borne by the whole community rather than only by those directly involved.

Macroeconomic arguments for protection

We now turn from the effects of protecting a single industry to a consideration of the wider macroeconomic arguments for protection. We consider the effects of widespread protection – if not on all imports, at least on a significant proportion of imports, such as manufactured goods. It will be convenient to consider the case for and against import controls as each point arises. In the 1970s, a significant body of opinion in the United Kingdom, for example, supported the view that a system of import controls would improve the economy's performance. Proponents of this view included the Cambridge Economic Policy Group (CEPG) and the Trades Union Congress.

The CEPG argued that in a situation of full employment, the United Kingdom has a propensity towards a balance of payments deficit, which conventionally in the recent past has forced the government to impose deflationary policies. Even when deflation cured the balance of payments problems, it was at the expense of increased unemployment. It was claimed that the introduction of import controls would enable the growth in imports to be restricted to the level that could be financed from export earnings and full employment to be achieved through fiscal policy. Thus, the major advantages claimed were increased output and employment. In the longer run, the growth of effective demand would stimulate confidence in industry and investment, which would improve the United Kingdom's competitiveness and rate of economic growth.

Such protectionist views have been challenged on several grounds. In an era when there are already strong undercurrents of protectionist sentiments in various parts of the world, it is argued that by imposing import controls the United Kingdom might spark off a generalised trade war. Other countries might retaliate by imposing controls on their imports from the United Kingdom. Eventually, the whole liberalised trading structure of the western world might be undermined. If there were a large fall in world trade, the existing high living standards based on international specialisation would decline.

Trade war *A situation in which trading countries resort to a series of protectionist measures aimed at reducing imports from rival countries*

When the possibility of foreign retaliation is considered, it is not certain that the imposition of import controls by the United Kingdom will lead to a net improvement in the balance of payments and level of employment. There are several other factors that throw serious doubt on the ability of import controls to effect a lasting improvement in the balance of payments.

Consider the following:

(a) When the United Kingdom imports less from other countries after the imposition of import controls, this will lead to a fall in the national incomes of these countries, *ceteris paribus*. As a result, their imports will fall which means that United Kingdom exports also decline.

(b) There is also the likelihood that some United Kingdom exports will be diverted to domestic consumption to make up for the fall in imports. Similarly, foreign goods now excluded from the United Kingdom market may be diverted to third country markets, where they may displace United Kingdom exports to some extent.

(c) If imports of particular finished goods are restricted, expenditure may increase on 'home-produced' goods that in fact contain a high proportion of imported materials. While imports of finished goods fall, imports of raw materials are likely to increase.

(d) Finally, if the import controls succeed in increasing the incomes of United Kingdom producers and their workers, part of the increased incomes will be spent on imports and on goods that would otherwise have been exported. Imports will increase and exports are likely to fall at every stage in the multiplier process, as the initial increase in incomes spreads through the economy.

GATT

Both selective and generalised import controls have distinct disadvantages. Although a case for protection of specific industries may be made (for example, a strategic industry or against dumping), it is by no means clear that generalised import controls will increase the level of employment or improve the balance of payments when the long-term implications are considered. Indeed, there is the risk that a trade war might result in lower living standards and it is no doubt largely due to this danger and to recognition of the benefits of trade that western governments have resisted some of the more extreme calls for the introduction of widespread protectionism.

The General Agreement on Tariffs and Trade (GATT) is an international treaty that commits participating countries to abide by specified rules concerning international trade, with the overall aim of encouraging trade and raising living standards. The original GATT was signed by 23 countries in October 1947 in Geneva, and was intended to avoid a repetition of the destructive beggar my neighbour types of trade policies that were introduced in the inter-war period. The GATT encourages *fair trade* rather than completely free trade. For example, it allows free trade areas and customs unions (such as the EC) which are designed to encourage trade liberalisation among the member countries. Critics argue that such agreements discriminate against outside countries against which trade barriers are still imposed. Special preferences for developing countries are also permitted by the GATT.

Beggar my neighbour policy *A policy that attempts to gain an unfair competitive advantage for a country's exports at the expense of other trading countries*

The significance of the GATT has grown substantially in recent years. By 1992, 108 countries were members or *contracting parties* to the GATT. Most signatories to the GATT adhere to its various codes and agreements. The code on anti-dumping, for example, specifies international rules under which anti-dumping action may be introduced.

An important feature of the GATT is the 'most favoured nation' clause which requires that any tariff reduction (or other benefit) made available to one GATT member must also be made available to all other members. A number of 'rounds' of tariff reductions have been negotiated by the GATT countries. The most significant have been the Kennedy Round (1954–67) and the Tokyo Round (1973–79) which brought the average level of tariffs for the EC, United States and Japan to less than 5 per cent. A further round of tariff reductions (the Uruguay Round) was launched in 1986.

Intellectual property
The ownership of property rights relating to printed and recorded material and patented discoveries and inventions

The negotiations on the Uruguay Round were also intended to extend the GATT to cover services, intellectual property and agricultural products. These negotiations proved to be long and tortuous and at the time of writing were still incomplete. The major area of contention was the level of subsidies to agricultural products. The United States and the Cairns group of cereal-exporting countries aimed at achieving major reductions in agricultural subsidies, but came up against some opposition, particularly from France.

Summary

1. International trade is of crucial significance for the maintenance and improvement of living standards in the world economy.
2. Trade may occur because one country is endowed with particular natural resources, such as oil or minerals. The theory of comparative advantage demonstrates that countries can benefit from specialisation and trade even when one country is more efficient than another at producing all goods and services.
3. The introduction of barriers to trade may result in *resource misallocation*. There are, however, a number of arguments that can be used to justify such trade barriers. Examples at the microeconomic level include the infant industry argument and the terms of trade argument.
4. At the macroeconomic level, it is sometimes argued that protection can result in an improvement in a country's balance of payments and a reduction in unemployment. The biggest danger of protection is probably that of retaliation and the possibility of a generalised trade war.
5. The GATT was set up in 1947 in order to promote *fair trade*, to reduce tariff levels and to avoid the introduction of generalised protectionist measures.

Exercises

1. Review your understanding of the following terms:

theory of comparative advantage	quota
terms of trade	exchange control
factor endowments	export subsidy
factor intensity	import deposits scheme
Heckscher–Ohlin theorem	'deadweight' loss
product cycle	strategic industry
technological gap	infant industry
tariff	dumping
GATT	

2. Superimpose community indifference curves on the graphs in Fig. 30.1(a) and (b) to show that trade has increased social welfare in both countries.

3. Consider two countries, A and B, which produce and consume two goods, *X* and *Y*. Assume that both countries face constant opportunity costs and operate under the perfect conditions described in this chapter. Suppose that when both countries use all their resources efficiently to produce *X*, the resulting outputs are:

   Country A: 1,000 units
   Country B: 1,000 units.

   When they use all their resources to produce *Y*, the resulting outputs are:

   Country A: 600 units
   Country B: 200 units.

   (a) Draw the countries' production possibility frontiers.

   (b) Explain which country has a comparative advantage in *X* and which has a comparative advantage in *Y*.

   (c) Choose plausible international terms of trade and use your diagrams to show how specialisation and trade between the two countries can be mutually beneficial.

4. The following information shows the domestic demand and supply conditions for good *X*:

Price (£)	5	10	15	20	25	30
Domestic quantity demanded	100	90	80	70	60	50
Domestic quantity supplied	10	30	50	70	90	110

The world supply curve of good *X* is perfectly elastic at the price of £10 per unit.

(a) Using a graph, find the equilibrium total domestic consumption, domestic quantity supplied and the quantity imported.

(b) Now suppose a tariff of £5 per unit is imposed on the import of *X*. Calculate: (i) the reduction in total consumption; (ii) the fall in imports; (iii) the total tariff revenue and (iv) the deadweight loss of the tariff.

5. Consider the case for and against protection by tariffs and quotas of the United Kingdom microelectronics industry. Contrast this case with the arguments for and against financial support of the industry by the United Kingdom government.

6. Discuss the relative advantages and disadvantages of tariffs, quotas, voluntary agreements and an import deposits scheme as means of restricting imports.

31 THE EUROPEAN COMMUNITY

Learning objectives

After reading this chapter, you should be able to:

- describe the historical development of the European Community from the formation of the European Coal and Steel Community in 1952 to the present day
- differentiate between a free trade area, a customs union, a common market and an economic union
- use demand and suppply analysis to analyse the production and consumption effects of the formation of a customs union, differentiating between trade creation and trade diversion
- assess the benefits and costs to the United Kingdom of membership of the European Community
- explain the working and assess the importance of the Common Agricultural Policy of the European Community
- outline the main aims of the Single European Act and assess the benefits to be gained from completing the single market
- explain the working of the European Monetary System, including the European currency unit, the exchange rate mechanism and the European Monetary Co-operation Fund
- outline the proposals for monetary union and assess the advantages and disadvantages of adopting a single currency in the EC

Introduction

The EC comprises twelve nations with a total geographical area in excess of 2.37 million square kilometres and a combined population of over 345 million people. It is, therefore, a trading bloc which is able to match the United States in terms of size and influence. Although each individual member state values its sovereignty and, to a large extent, follows policies designed to further its own interests, there is an increasing degree of economic and political co-operation which gives the EC a powerful voice in international economic and political affairs.

We have already referred to the EC's industrial policy in Ch. 15 and regional policy in Ch. 26. In this chapter, we first describe briefly the historical development of the EC from 1952 to the present day. Secondly, we outline the main forms of economic integration and consider the main features of the EC's commercial policy. This leads to a discussion of the theory of customs union and the benefits and costs of the United Kingdom's membership. The working of the Common Agricultural Policy (CAP) is then discussed. We then turn to a brief assessment of the changes designed to 'complete the internal market'. The chapter ends with a description of the working of the European Monetary System and a discussion of the propopsals for monetary union contained in the Maastricht Treaty.

Historical development of the EC

The origins of the movement for a united western Europe go back to the tragedies of the two World Wars which brought so much devastation to Europe and the rest of the world. The 'founding fathers' of modern Europe argued that integration of the economies, particularly France and West Germany, would make war between these countries less likely. It was also believed that the world in the second half of the twentieth century would be dominated by two 'super-powers' – the United States and the Soviet Union, but that a united Europe would be able to make its voice heard more strongly.

The European Coal and Steel Community (ECSC) was formed by Belgium, France, Italy, Luxembourg, the Netherlands and West Germany in 1952. The integration of these strategically important industries was symbolic of the desire to make it impossible for these countries to go to war against one another again. The ECSC plan provided for a High Authority, a supra-national body that has some direct control over the coal, iron and steel industries in the member countries. The United Kingdom was invited to join the ECSC but refused. The success of the ECSC led to pressure for more economic integration and the Treaty of Rome setting up the European Economic Community was signed on 25 March 1957 by the six member countries of the ECSC. The EEC (now known as the European Community or EC), came into operation on 1 January 1958. The long-term aim of the EC is to achieve an economic union – that is, to achieve a high degree of integration between the economic policies of the member countries and a measure of political unity.

The United Kingdom was involved in the early discussions on the proposal for some degree of integration, but it favoured the creation of a free trade area and withdrew from the discussions in November 1955. Various reasons have been suggested to explain the United Kingdom's reluctance to join the EC as a founder member; in the mid-1950s the United Kingdom was still heavily involved in administering and developing the Empire into the Commonwealth; at that time its trade was weighted towards trade with the Commonwealth and colonies; the government also laid stress on its 'special relationship' with the United States. Thus, for these and other reasons, the United Kingdom did not join the EC at its inception.

Perhaps partly because the United Kingdom government later realised that it had missed an opportunity by not joining the EC, it initiated talks leading towards the formation of a free trade area in Europe. The Stockholm Convention which formed the European Free Trade Association (EFTA) was signed in 1960; its members were Austria, Denmark, Norway, Portugal, Sweden, Switzerland and the United Kingdom; Finland joined as an associate member in 1961. The EFTA agreement provided for free trade in industrial goods and, apart from a few exceptions, did not cover agricultural products.

The British government applied for membership of the EC in 1961, and negotiations began. They were, however, broken off in January 1963 following a veto by the French President, General de Gaulle. The Labour government again applied for membership in May 1967, but once again General de Gaulle effectively vetoed the application and negotiations were not opened. Following M Pompidou's accession to the French Presidency, the original six members of the EC indicated in 1969 that they were now favourably disposed to consider the application for United Kingdom membership. Negotiations were opened on 30 June 1970, following the general election in that month, which returned a Conservative government. The negotiations on the major questions concerning the United Kingdom's entry were completed by July 1971 and the terms of entry obtained were accepted in principle by the House of Commons on 28 October 1971. The Treaty of Accession of the United Kingdom (and Denmark, Eire and Norway) was signed in Brussels on 22 January 1972. The people of Norway subsequently voted against entry in a referendum, but the United Kingdom, Denmark and Eire acceded to the EC on 1 January 1973.

When the Labour government returned to power in 1974, it made clear that it was not happy with the terms of entry obtained by the previous administration and would renegotiate the terms. After further discussions it obtained minor concessions on the maximum contribution to the budget and on the access of New Zealand butter and Commonwealth sugar to the EC market. The government recommended the electorate to vote in favour of continued membership of the EC in the referendum held in July 1975. A two-thirds majority voted in favour of continued membership.

In recent years, the trend towards European economic integration has continued. Greece became a member of the EC in 1981 and Spain and Portugal became members in 1986. There are now twelve full members: Belgium, Denmark, Germany, Greece, France, Ireland, Italy, Luxembourg, the Netherlands, the United Kingdom, Spain and Portugal. At the time of writing, talks were being held with Austria, Sweden, Norway and Finland with a view to future membership.

The member states of the EC negotiated the Maastricht Treaty in December 1991. In addition to its monetary provision, considered below, the treaty extended the political dimension of the EC. It introduced the concept of the European Union (EU) with all citizens of all EC countries also being recognised as citizens of the EU, an acronym increasingly adopted in place of EC.

The EC and economic integration

Free trade area *An area in which there are no barriers to trade among the member countries, but each country maintains its own restrictions on trade with non-members*

There are varying degrees of economic integration among the groupings formed between countries with a view to encourage trade. In a free trade area, barriers to trade between the members are eliminated, but each member country maintains its own kind of restrictions and tariffs on trade with countries that are not members of the free trade area. With a customs union, tariff-free trade between member countries is created and, in addition, a common external tariff on imports from third countries is levied. In a common market, there is in addition to free trade and a common external tariff, free movement of labour and capital between member countries. The highest degree of integration is that of an economic union where the aim is to achieve a high degree of integration between the economic policies of the member countries.

Customs union *A free trade area in which members levy a common external tariff on non-members*

Common market *A customs union with free movement of labour and capital*

Economic union *A common market with a high degree of integration between members' economic policies*

The EC is intended to be a trading entity of twelve nations, with free trade within the community and a common external tariff imposed on imports from outside. Although there are still some regulatory and administration restrictions on trade, serious attempts have been made to remove these and so 'complete the internal market'. We can say, therefore, that the EC just about satisfies the conditions required for a customs union. In addition, many of the barriers to the free movement of labour and capital have been removed (although many language and cultural barriers remain), and the member states co-operate in many aspects of economic policy. For example, most member states have been full participants of the EMS and all abide by the rules of the CAP. So the EC has taken a number of steps towards full economic union. The remaining steps, which would require, for example, a common central bank and monetary policy and complete fiscal harmonisation, represent too great a loss of sovereignty to be acceptable to many of the states at the present time.

Before examining the benefits and costs to the United Kingdom of membership of the EC, it is useful to consider the basic theory of customs unions.

The theory of customs unions

Trade creation *This refers to a shift of production from a high-cost to a low-cost source within the customs union*

Trade diversion *This refers to a shift in production from a low-cost source outside the customs union (which is now subject to a tariff) to high-cost source within the union*

The traditional analysis of the formation of a customs union argued that the removal of tariffs was a move towards free trade and would, therefore, increase welfare. Jacob Viner showed that in fact the formation of a customs union might or might not increase welfare. Viner introduced the concepts of trade creation and trade diversion. Trade creation occurs when, after the formation of the union, production is shifted away from a higher-cost source towards a low-cost source within the union. Trade diversion occurs when production is shifted away from a low-cost source of production outside the union to a high-cost source of production within the union.

The effects of the formation of a customs union We can illustrate the concepts of trade creation and trade diversion after the formation of a customs union with analysis that is the mirror-image of our analysis of the resource-misallocation effect of the imposition of a tariff. Consider the following two cases:

(a) *An example with trade creation only* Consider two countries A and B. Prior to the formation of the customs union, A imposes a tariff on imports of product X. In Fig. 31.1, D_dD_d and S_dS_d represent A's domestic demand and supply curves respectively. Note that for simplicity we assume that the supply of X from B is

Fig. 31.1. Trade creation after the formation of a customs union When A and B form a customs union and so eliminate the tariff on good X, there is a net addition to welfare equal to the sum of the areas JCD and EFG.

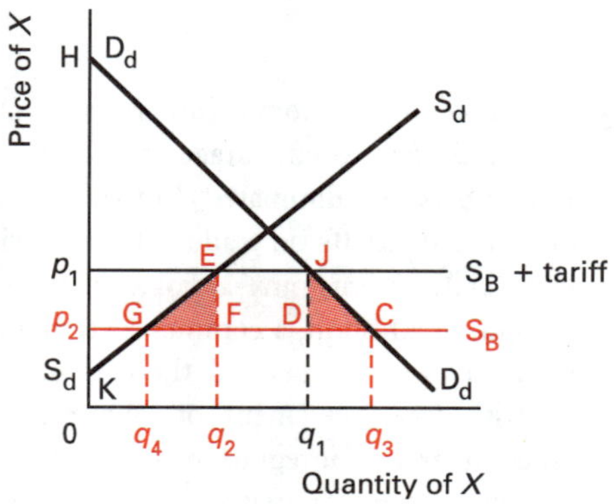

Fig. 31.2. Trade creation and trade diversion after the formation of a customs union. The trade diversion cost is represented by the area ECGH, while the trade creation benefit is represented by the sum of the areas KLC and DEF.

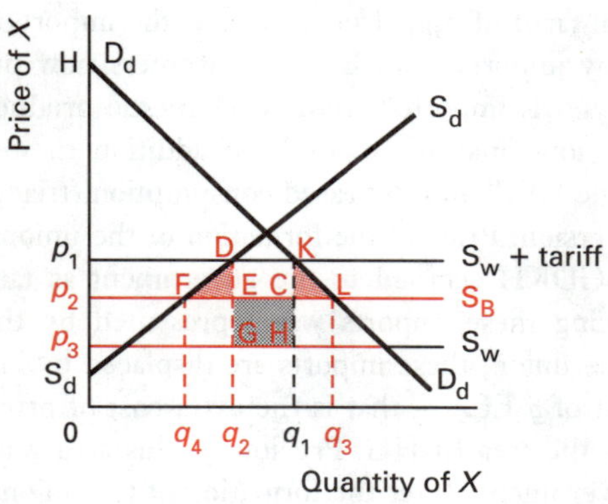

perfectly elastic. We assume that there is no other source of supply apart from B. Suppose that A is imposing a tariff of p_2p_1 on each unit of X imported so that the effective supply curve of X from B is S_B + tariff. Initially, A's consumers purchase $0q_1$ of X, of which $0q_2$ is provided by domestic suppliers and q_2q_1 is imported. Consumer surplus is represented by the area of triangle HJp_1. Producer surplus is represented by the area of the triangle p_1EK.

When A forms a customs union with B, it removes tariffs on imports of X from B. Consumers in A can now purchase X from B at price $0p_2$. They purchase a total of $0q_3$; domestic A production falls to $0q_4$, and imports from B increase to q_4q_3. This represents trade creation as production is shifted to lower cost supplies from B. Consumer surplus is now represented by the area of triangle HCp_2; thus, consumer surplus has increased by the area p_1 JCp_2 as a result of the formation of the customs union. But not all of the increase in consumer surplus represents an addition to welfare. Producer surplus is now given by the area p_2GK. Thus, the area p_1EGp_2 is simply transferred from the producer surplus of domestic A suppliers of product X. The rectangle EJDF previously represented tariff revenue to the government. These areas then merely represent transfers to consumers from producers and the government respectively.

The net additions to welfare are represented by triangle JCD and triangle EFG. Triangle JCD represents a consumption gain since consumers in A are now able to purchase the extra quantity q_1q_3 at the lower price of $0p_2$. Triangle EFG represents a gain in production efficiency as the quantity q_4q_2 is imported at a lower cost than when produced domestically. In this example, *the formation of the customs union unambiguously increases A's welfare.* But now consider a case in which opposing effects on welfare occur.

(b) *An example with both trade creation and diversion* In Fig. 31.2, D_dD_d and S_dS_d again represent country A's domestic demand and supply curves for product X. S_B is the perfectly elastic supply curve of country B and S_w is the perfectly elastic supply curve of the rest of the world. Prior to the formation of the customs union A is imposing a tariff of p_3p_1 on imports of good X. Consequently B's production is excluded from A's market, and the effective supply curve from the rest of the world becomes S_w + tariff which is perfectly elastic at the price $0p_1$. Consumers in A buy quantity $0q_1$ of which $0q_2$ is produced domestically and q_2q_1 is imported.

Suppose now that A and B form a customs union so that imports from B now enter the A market without any tariff, while imports from the rest of the world still pay the original tariff of p_3p_1. Consequently, the imports from the rest of the world are displaced by imports from B. A's consumers now purchase a total quantity of $0q_3$, of which q_4q_3 is imported from B. Domestic production in A falls to quantity $0q_4$. As in previous analysis, there is an addition to welfare resulting from trade creation (triangle DEF) and increased consumption (triangle KLC). But there is also some trade diversion. Prior to the formation of the union, A imported quantity q_2q_1 and rectangle GDKH accrued to the government as tariff revenue. The resource cost of producing these imports was represented by the area q_2GHq_1. After the formation of the union, these imports are displaced by imports from B produced at the greater cost of q_2ECq_1 – that is the extra cost of producing this amount in B is represented by the area ECHG. Previously, this area was part of the tariff revenue accruing to government. After the formation of the union, it represents the resource miscallocation cost of the trade diversion.

In this example, the formation of the customs union leads to trade creation which increases welfare (by triangles DEF and KLC), and to trade diversion which reduces welfare (by ECHG). The customs union only results in a net addition to welfare for A if the sum of the areas DEF and KLC is greater than the area ECHG. We have thus demonstrated that *if the formation of a customs union results in trade diversion, it may or may not lead to an increase in welfare.*

Benefits and costs of United Kingdom membership

When discussing the economic benefits and costs of EC membership it must not be forgotten that major political advantages are claimed to result. Mention has already been made of the hope that integration would lessen the danger of war between European countries and that the United Kingdom would be able to make its voice heard more clearly as a member of an important economic bloc. Even prior to Britain's membership, its trade with the EC was becoming increasingly important and was growing faster than its trade with the Commonwealth. The growing importance of trade with other EC members in recent years is shown in Table 31.1.

Trade creation is a major potential advantage of joining a customs union. But empirical studies carried out prior to entry indicated that likely welfare gains to the United Kingdom from trade creation and losses from trade diversion were not likely to be large as a proportion of national income. The overall net welfare loss taking into account trade creation, trade diversion and the balance of payments effects of the Common Agricultural Policy (CAP) was typically estimated at about 1 per cent of national income.

Table 31.1 Area composition of UK visible trade, 1968 and 1991.

	Exports (%)		Imports (%)	
	1968	1991	1968	1991
EC	26.7	56.7	27.6	52.1
Other western Europe	15.0	8.3	14.0	12.1
North America	17.4	12.6	20.0	13.4
Other developed countries	12.5	3.8	10.7	6.7
Oil exporting countries	5.7	5.6	7.8	2.3
Rest of world	22.6	13.0	19.8	13.4

Source: Calculated from data in *United Kingdom Balance of Payments*, various issues.
Note: Some totals do not sum to 100 because of rounding.

Dynamic effects *Effects which occur over a period of time, and typically interact and reinforce one another*

Prior to entry, British governments and economists placed greater emphasis on the dynamic effects of EC membership; producers would have a much expanded 'home' market, which would enable many firms to benefit from greater economies of scale. The increased competition from EC producers would, it was hoped, stimulate firms to greater efficiency and also lead them to invest more. With increased research and development expenditure, a higher rate of technological innovation was likely. It was argued that these dynamic effects would enable the economy to grow faster than it otherwise would. Because of the uncertainties regarding the outcome and future economic developments, no reliable estimates of the likely beneficial dynamic effects were possible.

Prior to entry, it was also recognised that there would be significant balance of payments costs for the United Kingdom. The budgetary agreements and the CAP which were formulated prior to British membership did not work to Britain's advantage. It was recognised that these two factors would have an adverse effect on the United Kingdom's balance of payments.

The EC budget is financed by members handing over 90 per cent of the receipts from levies on agricultural imports and on customs duties, by a contribution from the VAT receipts of each country and by a contribution of up to 1.2 per cent of a member's GNP. The maximum VAT contribution is equivalent to a 1.4 per cent rate of VAT. It is argued that this budgetary arrangement works against the United Kingdom because it imports a relatively high proportion of agricultural products, raw materials and other products from outside the EC. But not only does the United Kingdom make a disproportionately high contribution to the EC budget, it also receives relatively low payments. This is because the CAP accounts for over 50 per cent of expenditure from the EC budget and Britain has a smaller proportion of its work-force in agriculture than any other EC country. We now turn to a more detailed discussion of the CAP.

The Common Agricultural Policy

Common Agricultural Policy (CAP) *A set of arrangements that aims to stabilise farm prices, support farmers' incomes and ensure security of supply of food within the EC*

We saw in Ch. 6 that agricultural markets tend to be characterised by fluctuating prices and incomes from season to season. In a free market, good harvests lead to price falls and poor harvests lead to price rises, *ceteris paribus*, and the effects of these price changes on farmers' revenues depend on the elasticities of demand for the products concerned. As the demand for foodstuffs is typically price-inelastic, we can say that, in general, underproduction raises farm revenues and overproduction reduces farm revenues. The problem is exacerbated by time-lags. Farmers have to take decisions now about the output they plan to produce in the coming season and these decisions will be based on prices (and other factors) now. By the time the product comes on to the market, conditions may have changed.

The governments of most countries intervene in agricultural markets in an attempt to stabilise prices and incomes. Some use physical controls on output and prices; others aim to influence the market by actually buying and selling agricultural products themselves. The CAP is the latter type. Its main objectives are:

(a) To expand the EC's agricultural production by promoting technical progress and encouraging an optimum allocation of resources.
(b) To ensure a 'fair' standard of living for farmers.
(c) To stabilise markets, at the same time guaranteeing the availability of supplies and reasonable consumer prices.

Price-support system
A set of measures designed to raise the prices of agricultural products above the free market price through intervention

In seeking to achieve these objectives, the EC has established a price-support system alongside internal free trade. The cost of operating the system (which is managed by the European Agricultural Guidance and Guarantee Fund) takes over 50 per cent of the EC's total budget and there has been much discussion of the burden of this cost on the EC's citizens.

Furthermore, there have been problems with the operation of the CAP which have led to calls for its reform.

How the price-support system works

The system works by establishing a *target price* for each agricultural product, based on the price which producers would need to cover their costs (including profit) in the highest cost area of the EC. An *intervention price* is then set about 7–10 per cent below the target price. The intervention price is intended to be the theoretical minimum price for the product, so if the market price should fall to this level, intervention boards purchase the product and so prevent the price from falling further. Another possibility is the payment of subsidies to traders to enable them to export excess supplies to outside markets. Separate target and intervention prices are set in each area of the EC, depending on costs.

In effect, the intervention price is a *price floor* below which the market price is not allowed to fall. This is illustrated in Fig. 31.3. The market demand for the product is shown by the curve DAD and the market supply is shown by the curve SS. The interaction of demand and supply in a free market would give an equilibrium price of $0P$, below the intervention price. The intervention demand curve, however, is DAd and Community purchases of the product equal to q_1q_2 are required to keep the price at the intervention level, $0P^*$.

To ensure the smooth working of the intervention system, tariffs are imposed on agricultural imports to protect EC farmers from competition from outside countries.

Green (exchange) rates
A set of artificial exchange rates used in intra-EC agricultural trade

One problem with the system is posed by the flexibility of exchange rates. EC food prices are set in terms of 'units of account'. If these prices were simply converted to the member states' currencies at the current 'spot' exchange rates, it would be possible for exchange rate adjustments to cause food prices to rise in one country and fall in others. To prevent this and so maintain stable agricultural prices, the EC introduced a system of green rates, fixed administratively. The problem with this system is that when the spot exchange rates are adjusted so that they diverge from the green rates, opportunities arise for profitable speculation between

Fig. 31.3. *The EC's price support system.* The equilibrium price and quantity are given by $0P$ and $0q$ respectively. Since the equilibrium price is below $0P^*$, the intervention agency must purchase q_1q_2 to keep the price at the intervention level.

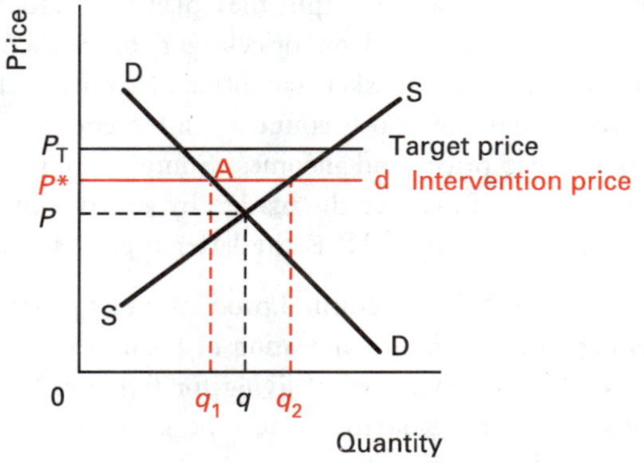

agricultural products and currencies. To stop this, it was necessary to impose a set of border taxes and subsidies on agricultural trade between member states, the total amount of subsidy being referred to as 'monetary compensation amounts'.

It is intended eventually that the EMS will stabilise exchange rates within the EC and so make the green rates obsolete.

Problems with the CAP

The main problem is that the system of price-support encourages overproduction. The resulting surpluses eventually have to be disposed of in ways which do not destabilise agricultural prices in the EC. The usual way has been to 'dump' the surplus products on non-member states. Unfortunately, this may have the effect of destabilising world markets and open up the EC to the charge of unfair competition. Other commentators have pointed out that, by encouraging increased production, the price-support system has contributed to the loss of hedges and their associated wildlife, and has encouraged the use of chemical fertilisers with possible adverse effects on health.

In an attempt to tackle the problem of overproduction, the EC has resorted to the imposition of quotas on certain products. For example, in 1984 milk quotas were introduced. This had the effect of reducing the production of milk, but only at the expense of many dairy farmers who found themselves unable to continue in business.

Perhaps the major problem is the extremely high cost of operating the CAP. It is estimated that in 1993, agricultural expenditure in the EC will represent about 50 per cent of the total EC budget of £56 billion. Added to this is the amount spent by the member states on research, infrastructure and advisory services. As important as these financial costs to the taxpayer are the costs to consumers who have to pay higher prices than they would without the price-support scheme. OECD estimates show that the total cost of agricultural support in the EC totalled £88 billion in 1992. This amount of support was equivalent to more than £10,000 for every full-time farmer in the EC, and corresponds to £634 for every hectare of farmland, nearly four times the OECD average.

Reforms to the CAP were negotiated in 1992. These reforms include price cuts, for which farmers will be compensated by direct grants based on the area of land cultivated, provided that they leave 15 per cent of their arable land fallow each year (known as the 'set aside' scheme). It is estimated that prices should fall over three years by 29 per cent for grain, 15 per cent for beef and 5 per cent for butter. Officials have estimated that the overall reduction in food prices at the end of the three year period will be about 2 per cent.

The Common Fisheries Policy

In addition to the CAP, the EC has a common fisheries policy. This developed as a result of overfishing which led to the serious depletion of certain fish stocks. The current EC policy has a number of objectives, the principal one of which is to conserve the supply of fish. This is achieved by means of quotas and various controls over the methods of fishing (such as the imposition of minimum net sizes). The aim is to reduce the quantity of fish caught to the 'optimum sustainable yield'. The policy also aims to reduce the level of 'overmanning' in the industry, preserve employment (particularly among the inshore fishing fleets) and avoid unfair competition. The policy has not been over-costly and appears to have been reasonably successful in curbing the depletion of fish stocks.

Completing the internal market

In the Single European Act 1986, the EC agreed to take further steps along the road to economic union. It was agreed, among other things, that there should be a greater degree of co-operation among member states with respect to economic policy, and that an attempt should be made to formulate a European foreign policy. Also, it was agreed that the 'completion of the internal market' should be achieved by 1992.

The EC internal market *The notion that there should be free movement of goods and services and factors of production within the EC*

The completion of the internal market involves the removal of all remaining regulatory and administrative barriers to trade and to the free movement of labour and capital. It is hoped that this will increase competition and so give consumers greater choice and lower prices. It is also possible that the expanded markets within which many firms will find themselves will enable firms to benefit from economies of scale.

The proposals are wide-ranging: they include (a) the removal of physical barriers, (b) the removal of technical barriers and (c) the removal of fiscal barriers. Consider these in turn.

Physical barriers *Border checks carried out on the flow of goods and the movement of people between countries*

(a) *The removal of physical barriers.* The main physical barriers are the checks that are made at border posts between countries. These are intended to check that all indirect taxes have been properly paid and to protect a country's citizens from terrorists and from imports of drugs. However, border controls are very costly and can hold up lorries and other vehicles for several hours. The proposals are designed to make the movement of goods between member states easier and quicker.

Technical barriers *The different rules and regulations imposed by countries on goods for reasons such as safety, health and environmental protection*

(b) *The removal of technical barriers.* The existence of *different* technical standards (of health and safety, for example) in different member states represents important technical barriers to trade which the Commission aims to remove. This objective has been supported by a series of judgements in the European Court which have taken the view that the mutual acceptance of one country's goods by other countries is required.

In the area of financial services, the Commission's aim is to achieve complete freedom of capital movements and, for any financial institution, freedom to establish in any EC country and to offer cross-border financial services. This has been achieved by harmonising some of the rules and regulations and then applying the concepts of 'mutual recognition' (so that each country recognises the prudential regulations of the others) and 'home country control' (according to which the primary task of supervision falls on the authorities in the institution's country of origin with the host country having a minor complementary role).

Fiscal barriers *The different tax rates applied to goods and services in member countries. One result of a high indirect tax is to discourage consumption, including imports, of the taxed product*

(c) *The removal of fiscal barriers.* The Commission aims to remove all fiscal barriers and to harmonise the structure and rates of indirect taxation. This will reduce the need for border controls and remove the price distortions which adversely affect resource allocation. The Commission has suggested that some divergence between member states' VAT rates could remain but should not exceed 5 per cent.

Commission research suggested that gains from the completion of the internal market would, over a period of 6–8 years, represent an increase in EC output roughly equivalent to between 4.3 and 6.4 per cent of GDP. The sources of these gains are summarised in Table 31.2.

Table 31.2 EC gains from completing the internal market.

	% of GDP
Removal of barriers affecting trade	0.2–0.3
Removal of barriers affecting overall production	2.0–2.4
Economies of scale and increased competition	2.1–3.7
Total gains	4.3–6.4

Source: European Commission, 1988.

Reports produced by the Commission suggested that the internal market would result in downward pressure on costs and prices. The induced increase in demand would increase output and employment over the medium-term. There may, however, be an initial increase in unemployment as less efficient production units close down in the face of increased competition.

Increasingly, firms regard the whole of the EC as a home market and often produce goods and services that are marketed throughout the EC and beyond. As noted in Ch. 10, the United Kingdom, for example, is host to a considerable number of subsidiaries of Japanese and American multinationals. These subsidiaries typically export a high proportion of their output. Multinationals often produce components in a number of countries, as is the case with motor vehicle assemblers, such as Ford and General Motors. The actual location of the final assembly plant is relatively unimportant. For example, a Vauxhall Cavalier assembled by a subsidiary of General Motors in Luton, England, might have an engine from Germany, and a gearbox from Austria.

In banking, the Second Banking Co-ordination Directive allows banks authorised in one member state to operate in any other member state without further authorisation. Essentially, authorisation in one country acts as a passport that enables a bank to carry on business throughout the EC.

There are, however, still some obstacles that may impede progress towards the achievement of a single market. Remaining barriers might include consumer loyalty to domestic producers, language and cultural barriers, differences in legal systems between countries and lack of knowledge on the part of consumers and producers.

The EC Social Chapter The Social Chapter is designed to deal with the social aspects of the EC single market. It seeks to harmonise a range of employment and social provisions, such as rights relating to membership of trade unions, equal opportunities for men and women, freedom of movement between countries for employees, and maximum hours of work. It is claimed that this harmonisation of employment and social provisions should facilitate the movement of workers to jobs in other EC countries, thereby improving EC labour market efficiency. A further provision concerns the establishment of minimum wage laws. As we discussed in Ch. 27, the introduction of minimum wage rates may have the effect of increasing unemployment. It was this fear which accounted for the United Kingdom government's decision to insist on an opt-out clause from the Social Chapter at the Maastricht Summit in December 1991.

The European Monetary System

The European Monetary System (EMS) was established in 1979 with the main objective of creating greater monetary stability in the EC. Described simply, it is a system in which EC currencies are pegged to each other within a narrow band and are then allowed to float freely against outside currencies. Thus, the EMS is a compromise between fixed and flexible exchange rates. Proponents of the system claim that the greater stability of exchange rates within the EC will lead to increased certainty for traders. At the same time adjustment will be facilitated by the limited flexibility of exchange rates within the bands, the free floating against outside currencies and the possibility of realignments within the system. As we see below, however, the system has been subjected to severe strains in recent years.

The EMS has three principal features:

European Currency Unit (ECU) *An artificial currency that has no physical existence. It represents a combination or basket of all the EC currencies, and may be used as a medium of exchange for trading or investment purposes*

(a) *The European Currency Unit (ECU).* The ECU is a unit of account which is valued in terms of a combination, or 'basket', of the EC currencies. Each currency is allocated a different weight in the composition of the ECU, determined primarily by the size of the country and the importance of the currency in foreign exchange markets. The ECU may therefore be regarded as a *weighted average* of the EC currencies. As a weighted average, its value is more stable than any single currency. The ECU is an important unit of currency which acts as a 'numéraire' in the exchange rate system and for operations in both the intervention and credit systems. It is also acceptable as a means of settlement between the EC's monetary authorities.

Exchange rate mechanism (ERM) *An arrangement that seeks to maintain stable exchange rates between the currencies of the EC countries*

(b) *The exchange rate mechanism (ERM).* The ERM operates by establishing a grid of central rates between every pair of currencies included in the mechanism. Each member country's exchange rate is then pegged within a band which establishes the maximum divergence from the central rate allowed between any two currencies. Until August 1993, the band was set at ±2.25 per cent for most of the participating currencies. Exceptions included sterling, which participated from 1990 to 1992, and the peseta, both of which were allowed ±6 per cent bands.

Whilst the currencies remain within the ERM bands, monetary authorities may intervene to influence the exchange rates if they wish, but no compulsory intervention is called for until an upper or lower limit is reached. Whenever the divergence between two currencies approaches the limit, both countries' central banks are required to intervene. In this way, the burden of adjustment is shared between the countries with weak and strong currencies. A central bank is advised to begin intervening whenever its currency reaches 75 per cent of its maximum allowed divergence from the ECU. This is called the *divergence indicator*. However, intervention only becomes compulsory when the maximum divergence is reached.

A realignment of the central rates is permitted by mutual agreement of the participating countries. In the early years, there were several realignments, but for the five years from 1987, a remarkable degree of stability of EC exchange rates was achieved. This stability undoubtedly contributed to the decision, after much debate, to bring sterling into the mechanism in 1990. However, in 1992, turbulence returned to the EC foreign exchanges, the United Kingdom withdrew from the ERM after sustained speculative sales of sterling, and a number of other currencies (primarily the Spanish peseta, French franc and the Irish punt) had to be defended against speculative pressures.

The ERM received a further severe shock in August 1993 when heavy speculative sales of the Belgian and French francs, the escudo, peseta and Danish krona put the system under immense strain. The pressure was so great that the narrow bands had to be abandoned for all but two of the currencies (the mark and the Dutch guilder). At the time of writing, a ±15 per cent band applies to all other participating currencies, a band so wide that the ERM may be said to have been effectively abandoned for the time being.

Some economists have argued that the main cause of the ERM's problems has been the failure of the EC countries to achieve sufficient convergence of inflation rates and co-ordination of economic policies. Under these circumstances, a greater willingness to re-align the participating currencies might have enabled the system to operate more successfully. Others argue that the removal of exchange controls made it inevitable that speculators would eventually find potentially profitable opportunities which would destabilise the system.

(c) *The European Monetary Co-operation Fund.* This fund receives 20 per cent of each member's gold and foreign currency reserves (on a 3 months' renegotiable basis), and the members receive ECUs in return. The fund can then provide assistance to member states via a range of short- to medium-term financing arrangements.

It is eventually intended to establish a common currency area in the EC together with a European central bank. We turn now, therefore, to a discussion of the proposal for establishing a monetary union in the EC.

Monetary Union in the EC

A monetary union may be interpreted in a number of different ways. It may simply mean fixed exchange rates and liberalised capital movements within the EC. In such a scheme, national currencies would be retained and, even though the member states may intend to keep their exchange rates fixed, future exchange rate changes could not be completely ruled out. Alternatively, monetary union may mean the establishment of a parallel currency (such as the ECU) to circulate alongside national currencies. However, once again, although the member states may initially intend to keep the exchange rates between the parallel currency and the national currencies fixed, future realignments could not be ruled out.

The only scheme in which future exchange rate changes among the member states could be truly ruled out is the scheme envisaged in the Delors Report and included in the Maastricht Treaty, signed in 1992 – a currency union in which the member states adopt a single currency controlled by a single central bank. Some important steps have already been taken along the road to full monetary union, but of all the countries concerned, the United Kingdom appears to be the least enthusiastic about the formation of a currency union. Indeed, the United Kingdom (together with Denmark) has retained the right within the Maastricht Treaty to opt out of the single currency.

Currency union *An arrangement whereby member countries decide to adopt a single currency controlled by a single central bank*

Our intention in the next two sections is to discuss the economic consequences of establishing a currency union in the EC.

Benefits of monetary union

The supporters of monetary union have been quick to claim that it is only by establishing a single currency that the full benefits of the European single market can be realised. These commentators see the need for currency conversion as yet another barrier to trade which must be swept away if the single market is to be established. The main benefits claimed for a single currency may be discussed under three main headings:

(a) *The removal of exchange rate risk.* By removing the risk of exchange rate changes between union members, it is argued that a single currency will lead to an expansion of intra-union trade and consequent gains in welfare for the participating countries. This is based on the view that exchange rate risk and instability discourage trade, and is probably an acceptable argument when comparing a single currency with a system of floating exchange rates. In the context of the relatively fixed exchange rate regime of the EMS, however, it is an argument which loses much of its potency. After all, within the EMS, exchange rates have been reasonably stable over long periods and the remaining risk of realignments can be effectively and cheaply avoided by hedging. Also, the effects of exchange rate variability on international trade are not well-understood and depend on whether companies are risk-averters or risk-takers. There is some evidence that many large companies are prepared to take speculative risks.

(b) *Reduction of transaction costs.* This is certainly a strong advantage of a currency union and some have argued that the savings may be substantial. For example, the European Commission has estimated that overall transactions costs resulting from currency conversions and exchange rate variability within the EC amount to approximately one-half of one per cent of Gross Domestic Product for the EC as a whole, and may be as high as one per cent of Gross Domestic Product for some of the smaller member states which have very open economies and minor currencies.

Set against this is the view that for each company engaged in foreign trade, the cost saving will be relatively small. Even so, the savings would undoubtedly be welcomed by most United Kingdom companies. In general, small and medium-sized firms bear a heavier burden of transactions costs than larger firms and so stand to benefit proportionately more from the elimination of such costs.

These transactions cost savings are often overstated by proponents of monetary union by using the interesting, but misleading, result that if a person started with £100 in London and then travelled around Europe changing it into the local currency of every country of the EC, one after the other, and finally back into sterling, there would only be about £28 left at the end of the journey. This may be true, but it is not an exercise that companies engage in and the apparent 72 per cent transaction cost is a gross exaggeration. Also, it has to be remembered that, although a single currency will reduce costs for companies and travellers, it will also reduce the revenues of the financial institutions which supply foreign exchange services.

(c) *Greater price stability.* The adoption of a single currency will lead to a convergence of the member states' inflation rates. At the same time, the establishment of an *independent* central bank charged with the responsibility for maintaining price stability should, it is argued, ensure that the European inflation rate is kept low. This is based on the belief that an independent central bank will not be influenced (in the same way that national central banks might be) by political factors, such as the desire to attract votes at a forthcoming election, and so will not engage in injudicious monetary policies.

A disadvantage of monetary union

Probably the main drawback of a single currency in the EC is that each member state will lose the use of exchange rate and monetary policies as means of achieving domestic policy objectives. How serious is this loss?

To answer this question, consider the effect of a reduction in the foreign demand for United Kingdom exports (an asymmetric demand shock) which forces the current account into deficit and threatens to raise the rate of unemployment. In this case, a fall in the nominal sterling exchange rate (that is a sterling devaluation) should, as we saw in Ch. 29, improve the current account and cushion the effect of the demand shock on unemployment. But if exchange rates are irreversibly fixed within a currency union, this adjustment mechanism would no longer be available. What would happen then?

Monetarists argue that an exchange rate change is actually not necessary because the decrease in the demand for labour in the United Kingdom would eventually reduce real wages which would restore employment and improve the country's international competitiveness. Sceptics of this view, however, point out that rigidities in the labour market mean that real wages are sluggish in the downward direction so that this adjustment mechanism is at best unreliable. Monetarists agree that the adjustment of real wages may take several years to achieve. A devaluation would make it possible, at least for a few years, to avoid a serious increase in unemployment, though it may also lead to a higher inflation rate.

This analysis has established that there are strong economic arguments for and against monetary union in the EC. Indeed, the contemporary debate has stirred strong sentiments in many countries. This is because some groups in each sovereign state have shown great reluctance to accept the loss of sovereignty implied in giving up control over their own economic policies.

Summary

1. The Treaty of Rome, which established the European Economic Community, was signed in 1957 by Belgium, France, Italy, Luxembourg, the Netherlands and West Germany. The United Kingdom, along with Denmark and Eire, joined in 1973. Greece became a member in 1981 and Spain and Portugal joined in 1986, making twelve member states in all.

2. In a customs union, there is tariff-free trade among the members and a common external tariff is imposed on imports from outside countries. The EC may be regarded as a customs union which is moving towards economic and monetary union.

3. The formation of a customs union may cause trade creation or trade diversion. Trade creation occurs when production is shifted from a high-cost to a low-cost source. Trade diversion occurs when production is shifted from a low-cost to a high-cost source. The 'dynamic' effects of a customs union include an expanded market which would enable some firms to benefit from economies of scale, and increased competition which may lead to greater efficiency.

4. The common agricultural policy is essentially a price-support system for agricultural products intended to stabilise farm prices and farmers' incomes. It has been criticised for encouraging overproduction. The common fisheries policy aims to conserve fish supplies by means of quotas and various controls over fishing methods.

5. The Single European Act aims to complete the single market in the EC by removing physical, technical and fiscal barriers to trade. It is claimed that the removal of these barriers will reduce prices and so benefit consumers.

6. The European Monetary System aims to create exchange rate stability within the EC. The system operates by fixing each member's exchange rate within a band that limits the maximum allowed divergence between any two currencies. The ECU acts as a base currency within the exchange rate mechanism.

7. One of the aims of the Maastricht Treaty is to achieve a single currency throughout the EC. The main advantages of adopting a single currency include less exchange rate risk, reduced transactions costs and greater price stability. A disadvantage is that each member state loses the use of exchange rate and monetary policies as means of achieving domestic policy objectives.

Exercises

1. Review your understanding of the following terms:

free trade area	Common Agricultural Policy
customs union	price-support system
common market	intervention price
economic union	green rate
trade creation	Common Fisheries Policy
trade diversion	home country control
European Monetary System	exchange rate mechanism
European currency unit	currency union

2. Reconsider the domestic demand and supply conditions for good X shown in Exercise 4 at the end of Ch. 30. Let the home country be country A. Suppose that the supply of good X from country B is perfectly elastic at a price of £15 and that the supply from the rest of the world is perfectly elastic at a price of £10. If A imposes a tariff of £7 per unit on imports of good X:

   (a) Find the amount of the good being domestically produced and imported from the rest of the world prior to the formation of any customs union. What is the tariff revenue?

   (b) Find the amount of the good being domestically produced and imported from country B after the formation of a customs union between A and B. (Assume that the common external tariff is £7 per unit.)

(c) Calculate the trade creation and trade diversion resulting from this customs union.

3. 'A customs union may or may not increase the welfare of its member countries.' Discuss with reference to the theory of second best.

4. How can the EC solve the problem of surplus agricultural production?

5. Discuss the likely gainers and losers following the removal of all barriers to trade in the EC in the areas of:

   (a) manufacturing and
   (b) financial services.

6. Consider the extent to which the CAP affects (a) the welfare of different sections within a member country; and (b) the welfare of different member countries.

7. Identify the problems associated with attempts to maintain exchange rates within the ±2.25 per cent bands that were generally applied in the European Monetary System from 1979 to 1993.

32 ECONOMIC INEQUALITY

Learning objectives

After reading this chapter, you should be able to:

- outline the main components of total personal income and show how they measure the pattern and trends in income distribution
- state and explain the significance of Pareto's Law
- recognise that there are different methods of measuring the distribution of income and wealth, and interpret the Lorenz curve and the Gini coefficient
- assess the effects of taxation and social services benefits on the distribution of income
- define poverty in both the absolute sense and the relative sense, and make international comparisons of poverty levels and income distribution
- discuss the main causes of economic inequality

Introduction

This final chapter attempts to investigate the phenomenon of the inequality of incomes in human societies. The analysis of inequality is essentially the study of the distribution of personal incomes – that is, how the total income of a country is shared out among individuals and families. Inequality can be observed between different income groups, between different regions of the same country and, of course, between different countries – particularly, as we saw in Ch. 25, between the industrially advanced and the less developed countries of the world.

Economists are interested in both the pattern and trends of income distribution because they have a direct bearing on social welfare. As Ch. 8 showed, social welfare is a function of, among other things, the size of national income and the pattern of its distribution. This means that before any conclusions can be drawn about social welfare, both changes in the size of national income and changes in its distribution must be taken into account. This is equivalent to saying that both efficiency and equity criteria must be considered. As we emphasised in Ch. 8, the equity question as to what degree of inequality a society is prepared to tolerate is a value judgement and so part of normative economics.

In mixed economies, like the United Kingdom, the public sector plays a key role in implementing society's views about the desirable income distribution. We showed in Ch. 11 that one of the functions of the public sector is the redistribution of income and wealth through taxation and expenditure policies. Ch. 14 indicated some of the taxation measures which have been directed towards the goal of reducing inequality. In this chapter, we reflect on the degree of success achieved by these redistribution policies in the United Kingdom. We consider the following aspects of inequality: the components of total personal income and the methods of measuring the distribution of income; the distribution of personal incomes before and after tax; the incidence of taxes and the benefits of social services; the meaning and measurement of poverty; international comparisons of income distributions and inequality; and the major causes of inequality.

Components of total personal income

In any study of inequality, we need to know the composition of total personal income as this enables us to assess the pattern and trends in income distribution. As shown in Table 32.1, total personal income in the United Kingdom has three main components: earned income, investment income and transfer income.

Earned income is by far the largest of these components, making a contribution of almost 75 per cent to the total personal income of about £519 billion in 1991. This suggests that the distribution of earned income plays a key role in determining the pattern of income distribution over all income groups in the United Kingdom. However, although investment income only accounts for 11 per cent of the total, it is far more unequally distributed than other forms of income: in fact, in the United Kingdom, more than 60 per cent of all investment income accrues to the top 10 per cent of all tax-paying units.

Table 32.1 Major components of total personal income, 1991.

	£ million	% share
1. *Earned income*		
Income from employment	329,808	63.5
Income from self-employment	57,507	11.1
2. *Investment income*		
(rent, dividends and net interest)	56,874	11.0
3. *Transfer income*	73,955	14.3
4. *Imputed charge for capital consumption of private non-profit-making bodies*	600	0.1
Total personal income	518,744	100.0

Source: UK National Accounts, 1992.

Data on personal incomes in the United Kingdom can be obtained from the Family Expenditure Survey (FES). This is conducted by the Office of Population Censuses and Surveys on behalf of the Central Statistical Office. Each person aged 16 and over in co-operating households keeps a full record of payments made during 14 consecutive days and answers questions about hire purchase and other payments. Participants also give information on their incomes, cash benefits and income tax payments.

In any study of income inequality, the question of what is and what is not income is of great importance. Only the adoption of a wide definition of income, including incomes from all conceivable sources, will yield an accurate representation of the distribution of income and hence inequality. A narrow definition will have the effect of distorting the picture of income inequality.

In what follows, it is very important to bear in mind the limitations of the data presented.

Pareto's Law

The Italian economist, Vilfredo Pareto, carried out a detailed study of the income tax data of several European countries, including Britain, towards the end of the nineteenth century. He discovered that there was some statistical regularity between a given income and the number of persons earning at least that income. This fixed relationship became known as Pareto's Law which stated that the number of income recipients earning at least a given level of income would tend to fall by a fixed percentage as that given level of income rose by a fixed percentage.

A most important implication of this law is that inequality is inescapable and so policy measures designed to reduce inequality are likely to be fruitless. It may, however, be argued that Pareto's Law is true only of high incomes and so does not throw much light on distribution between high and low income groups: the law is derived from income tax data, and as we know, income tax in the last century had a very narrow base, being levied mainly on property (or investment) incomes.

Pareto's work did, however, stimulate great interest in empirical research into personal income distribution in the years that followed. In the postwar years, F.W. Paish in 1957 and H.F. Lydall in 1959 studied the changes in the distribution of personal incomes in the United Kingdom. Using estimates from the National Income and Expenditure Blue Book, they compared personal incomes before and after tax between 1938 and 1955 (in the case of Paish) and between 1938 and 1957 (in the case of Lydall). Their conclusions were that there was a substantial reduction in inequality in the postwar years.

These conclusions, though, were criticised by R.M. Titmuss who stressed the inadequacies of the data. He pointed to the many rapid demographic and social changes following the Second World War which affected the pattern of distribution in the postwar years. These included changes in the age of marriage, changes in the proportion of the total married population and changes in the number of women going out to work – all of these would tend to affect the distribution of personal incomes regardless of the public sector's redistribution policies. R.J. Nicolson in 1967 suggested that the trend towards greater equality in the United Kingdom may have come to a halt after the 1950s because of the onset of rapid inflation and the attendant counter-inflation policies.

Methods of measuring the distribution of personal incomes

A common way of measuring income inequality is to arrange all individuals in descending (or ascending) order of personal income and then to divide the total population into distinct groups. For example, the population can be divided into successive fifths (called quintiles) or tenths (called deciles). From this arrangement, the proportion of total income received by each group can be determined. Table 32.2 illustrates this statistical method for incomes before tax, but including cash benefits, in the United Kingdom in 1984–85 and 1991. The tax-paying units (or income recipients) are broken down into quintiles in this example. The table shows that the income share of the top 20 per cent of the population fell from 46.3 per cent in 1984–85 to 44 per cent in 1991, while there was a rise in the bottom 20 per cent's share from 5.8 per cent in 1984–85 to 6.7 per cent in 1991.

This suggests that during this period there was a decrease in the inequality of personal incomes before tax in the United Kingdom. The ratio of the share of income received by the bottom 20 per cent of income recipients to the share received by the top 20 per cent provides a crude numerical measure of inequality: this ratio is shown in Table 32.2 for 1984–85 and 1991 and is seen to have risen from 0.13 to 0.15. The larger this ratio is, the more equal is the distribution of income. A value equal to 1 would imply complete equality, but it must be remembered that the measure is based on extreme values only and ignores all those income recipients between the twentieth and eightieth percentiles.

The statistical distribution of personal incomes, as shown in Table 32.2, tells us nothing about the locational and occupational sources of incomes. In other words, the incomes of doctors, solicitors, engineers, teachers and factory workers are all merged into relevant income brackets.

Table 32.3 illustrates the effect of direct taxes on the distribution of income in the United Kingdom in 1991. It can be seen that direct taxes have the effect of reducing the degree of inequality. It should be emphasised, though, that taxation and public expenditure policies are capable of influencing the distribution of both gross and net incomes. For instance, personal income tax, including national insurance contributions, may influence gross earnings by affecting the willingness to work and the number of hours of work offered per week. Government benefits in cash and in kind may similarly affect gross earnings.

Table 32.2 The distribution of personal incomes before tax, 1984–85 and 1991.

Income recipients (quintiles) (%)	% share in 1984–85	% share in 1991
Top 20	46.3	44.0
21–40	23.3	23.0
41–60	14.8	16.0
61–80	9.8	10.0
81–100	5.8	6.7
Measure of inequality (Ratio of bottom 20% to top 20%)	5.8/46.3 = 0.13	6.7/44.0 = 0.15

Source: Economic Trends, November 1987 and May 1993.

Table 32.3 The distribution of personal incomes after direct tax, 1984–85 and 1991.

Income recipients (quintiles) (%)	% share in 1984–85	% share in 1991
Top 20	43.1	42.0
21–40	23.4	23.0
41–60	15.7	16.0
61–80	10.9	11.0
81–100	6.9	7.2
Measure of inequality (Ratio of bottom 20% to top 20%)	6.9/43.1 = 0.16	7.2/42.0 = 0.17

Source: Economic Trends, May 1993.

The Lorenz curve

Lorenz curve *A curve which shows the relationship between total income and the recipients of that income on a cumulative basis. It is used to measure inequality of income and to make comparisons over time and between countries*

Another way of illustrating inequality is to present the data of Tables 32.2 and 32.3 graphically. Such a graphical representation of the distribution of personal incomes is called a Lorenz curve, named after the American statistician, M.O. Lorenz. Figure 32.1 shows the Lorenz curves for the distributions of personal incomes in Tables 32.2 and 32.3. The curves are constructed in the following way:

(a) The percentage frequency distributions are converted to *cumulative* percentage frequency distributions. As shown in Table 32.4, this is done by finding the percentage of income earned by the 'bottom 10 per cent', then the 'bottom 20 per cent', then the 'bottom 30 per cent' and so on – the final class interval is the

Fig. 32.1. *Lorenz curves for the United Kingdom.* Curves a and b show the distribution of income before and after direct taxes respectively in 1991.

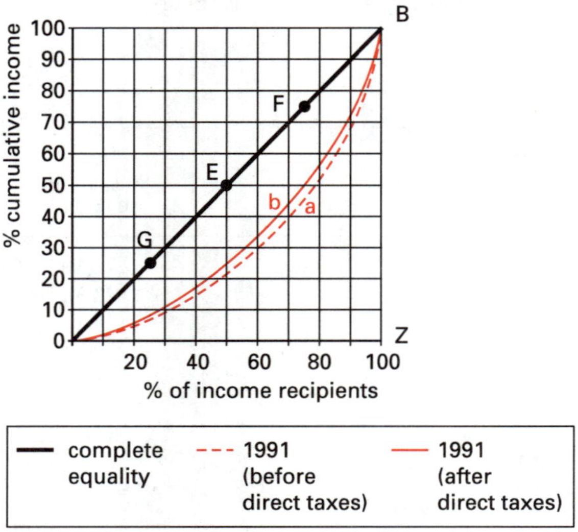

Table 32.4 The cumulative distributions of personal incomes, 1991.

Income recipients (%)	1991 (before tax)	1991 (after direct taxes)	1991 (after direct and indirect taxes)
Bottom 20	6.7	7.2	6.6
40	16.7	18.2	17.6
60	32.7	34.2	33.6
80	55.7	57.2	56.6
100	100.0	100.0	100.0

Source: Economic Trends, May 1993.

'bottom 100 per cent' which, of course, includes *all* income recipients who must therefore earn 100 per cent of total personal income.

(b) These figures are then plotted on a graph with 'percentage cumulative income' on the vertical axis and 'percentage of income recipients' on the horizontal axis. The resulting curve is called the Lorenz curve.

The 45° line, OB, drawn from the origin in Fig. 32.1 is called the *line of complete equality*. At every point on this line, the percentage of income received is exactly equal to the percentage of income recipients. Consider, for example, point E which is half-way along the length of OB. At this point, 50 per cent of total personal income is earned by 50 per cent of all income recipients. At point F, 75 per cent of income recipients receive 75 per cent of total income; at point G, 25 per cent earn 25 per cent of total income; and so on.

The curves a and b are the Lorenz curves for 1991 (before tax) and 1991 (after direct taxes) respectively. The further away a Lorenz curve is from the line of complete equality, the greater is the degree of inequality. Notice that the after-tax Lorenz curve, b, is nearer to OB, suggesting that the direct taxation policies of the United Kingdom do tend to reduce income inequality. It can also be noted from Table 32.4 that if indirect taxes were also included, the Lorenz curve would shift back towards curve a.

A commonly used measure of the overall degree of inequality in the distribution of income is found by calculating the ratio of the area between the Lorenz curve and the line of complete equality and the total area 0BZ (in Fig. 32.1). This ratio is known as the Gini concentration ratio or more simply, the 'Gini coefficient', named after the Italian statistician, C. Gini. It can be expressed as a percentage so that the closer the coefficient is to 100 per cent, the greater is the degree of inequality; similarly, the closer it is to zero, the smaller is the degree of inequality. For the United Kingdom in 1991, the Gini coefficient for before-tax income was 37 per cent and for after-tax income 35 per cent.

Gini concentration ratio
A measure of the degree of inequality in a given income distribution. The coefficient can be presented as a percentage, with 100 per cent representing perfect inequality and a value of zero representing perfect equality

It should be emphasised, however, that the Gini coefficient is not an ideal measure of income inequality. Figure 32.2 illustrates two Lorenz curves, A and B, which represent different distributions of personal income, but which have the same Gini coefficient. The problem with the Gini coefficient is that all the percentile information is collapsed into a single figure. Valid comparisons between two Gini coefficients cannot be made if the associated Lorenz curves intersect, as in Fig. 32.2.

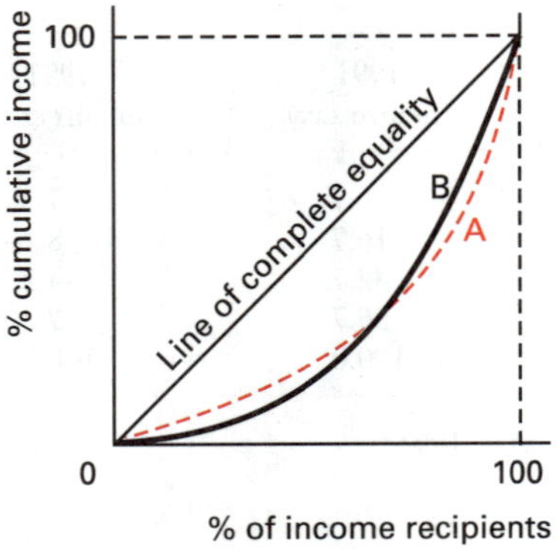

Fig. 32.2. Two intersecting Lorenz curves with identical Gini coefficients. It is possible for two intersecting Lorenz curves, such as A and B, which represent different distributions of income, to have the same Gini coefficient.

The incidence of taxes and social services benefits

The question of who pays taxes and who benefits from public expenditure is an exercise in the study of the redistribution policies of the public sector. In the United Kingdom, this study is undertaken by the Central Statistical Office which publishes its estimates from the Family Expenditure Survey annually in *Economic Trends*.

We have shown in this chapter and in Ch. 14 that the public sector can attempt to reduce inequality: (a) through progressive taxes which directly reduce spending power; (b) through influencing the pattern of demand for finished goods by indirect taxes (like VAT and customs and excise duties); and (c) through influencing the allocation pattern of resources between private and public goods through its own expenditures.

Some parts of government expenditure and revenue cannot be easily allocated to particular households. The CSO study allocates about two-thirds of government revenue and half of government expenditure to households.

Original income
Household income before the deduction of taxes or the addition of social security benefits

Gross income
Household original income together with income from social security benefits

Disposable income
Gross income minus direct taxes

Table 32.5 summarises the redistributive stages used by the CSO in its analysis of the redistributive effects of taxes and benefits. The starting point of the CSO's analysis is original income which is the annual cash income of all members of the household before the deduction of taxes or the addition of any state benefits. The next stage is to add cash benefits to original income to obtain gross income. Cash benefits include both contributory benefits, such as retirement pensions, and non-contributory benefits, such as income support and child benefit.

Next, direct taxes are deducted from gross income to obtain disposable income. The direct taxes that are deducted are income tax, local taxes and national insurance contributions. Note that taxes on capital, such as capital gains tax and inheritance

Table 32.5 Income: redistributive stages used in the CSO study of the effects of taxes and benefits on household income.

Stage	
1.	Original income + cash benefits = gross income
2.	Gross income − direct taxes = disposable income
3.	Disposable income − indirect taxes = post-tax income
4.	Post-tax income + benefits in kind = final income

Table 32.6 Percentage shares of total household income and Gini coefficients, 1991.

	Percentage shares of total income for households ranked by disposable income			
	Original income	Gross income	Disposable income	Post-tax income
Quintile group				
Bottom	2.0	6.7	7.2	6.6
2nd	7.0	10.0	11.0	11.0
3rd	16.0	16.0	16.0	16.0
4th	26.0	23.0	23.0	23.0
Top	50.0	44.0	42.0	44.0
All households	100	100	100	100
Decile group				
Bottom	0.7	2.8	3.0	2.5
Top	32.0	27.0	26.0	28.0
Gini coefficient (per cent)	51	37	35	39

Source: Economic Trends, May 1993.

tax, are not deducted because the data is not available from the FES and because there is no clear conceptual basis for doing so.

Post-tax income *Disposable income minus indirect taxes*

The next stage is to deduct indirect taxes from disposable income to obtain post-tax income. The indirect taxes on final consumer goods and services include VAT and excise duties. It is assumed that the incidence of indirect taxes is borne by consumers. Indirect taxes are also levied on intermediate goods and services purchased by industry. Examples include employers' contributions to national insurance and motor vehicle duties paid by businesses. The CSO assumes that these indirect taxes on intermediate goods and services are shifted fully to the consumer.

Final income *Post-tax income plus the estimated value of benefits in kind*

Finally, benefits in kind are added to post-tax income to obtain final income. Examples of allocated benefits in kind include state education, the National Health Service and housing subsidies.

Table 32.6, which reproduces some of the figures from Tables 32.2 and 32.3, depicts the CSO estimates of the effects of taxes and benefits on the distribution of household income in 1991. Consider the bottom quintile group which comprises the 20 per cent of households with the lowest incomes. It can be seen that cash benefits raise this group's share of total household income from 2.0 per cent of original income to 6.7 per cent of gross income. The effect of direct taxes is to increase this group's share further to 7.2 per cent of disposable income. Thus, for the bottom quintile group, *direct* taxes are progressive. But the effect of *indirect* taxes on this group is regressive as it reduces the share of total post-tax income to 6.6 per cent.

The bottom line of Table 32.6 depicts the Gini coefficients for the different types of income corresponding to the various stages of redistribution. It can be noted that the effect of both cash benefits and direct taxes is to reduce the Gini coefficient, indicating a reduction of inequality in the distribution of household income. The effect of indirect taxes, however, is to increase inequality somewhat. Nevertheless, the overall conclusion of the study is that the effect of taxes and cash benefits is to make an important contribution towards reducing inequality.

International comparisons of income distribution

One way of judging the inequalities between societies is to compare the distributions of incomes of different countries. As we pointed out in Ch. 18, such inter-country comparisons are exceedingly difficult. Different countries collect data for different purposes; they tend to adopt different definitions of income and income units; and they employ different cost-of-living indices. Furthermore, exchange rates reflect only to a very limited extent the domestic purchasing power of different currencies and so are not necessarily the most appropriate way of converting from one currency to another. As might be expected, the difficulties of comparing income distributions are much more severe between the developed and less developed countries than between developed countries.

Table 32.7 illustrates the pattern of distribution of pre-tax total personal incomes for a selection of industrially advanced countries, subject to the limitations of the data mentioned above. We can see from Table 32.7 that the top 20 per cent of income recipients in developed countries typically earn about 40 per cent of total personal income, while the bottom 20 per cent earn between 4 and 6 per cent of total personal income.

Inequality tends to be more marked in the less developed countries. It might be emphasised, however, that considerable difficulties arise in studying the distribution of incomes in less developed countries. To start with, there is the difficulty of obtaining comprehensive data on family expenditures because households rarely keep records of their spending. Higher income groups often receive part of their incomes in kind and lower income groups (who comprise self-employed workers, tenants, farm workers and artisans) live mainly in rural areas and consume the bulk of their subsistence production themselves. This consumption of non-marketed goods by low income groups poses serious problems for statisticians seeking monetary valuations. The problem is accentuated by the fact that a high proportion of the population in less developed countries lives in rural areas where price levels differ widely for the same assortment of goods in urban areas. For instance, the costs of fuel, lighting and housing figure more prominently in urban living than in rural life. In the latter, the estimation of rent-free accommodation and virtually free fuel and lighting is an immensely difficult task. Rural communal life also provides for a collective funding of ceremonial functions. This means that the conventional

Table 32.7 The distributions of pre-tax personal incomes in selected countries.

Country and year	Top 20%	21–40%	41–60%	61–80%	81–100%
Australia (1985)	42.2	24.8	17.5	11.1	4.4
Canada (1987)	40.2	24.6	17.7	11.8	5.7
Germany (1984)	38.7	24.1	17.8	12.7	6.8
UK (1984)	46.3	23.3	14.8	9.8	5.8
USA (1985)	41.9	25.0	17.4	11.0	4.7

Sources: World Bank *World Development Report*, 1992 and *Economic Trends*, November 1987.

concepts of 'wage incomes' and 'capital incomes' are less relevant to the 'true' income distribution, though statisticians still attempt to apply such concepts.

Defining poverty

Poverty may be defined in two different ways: poverty in the *absolute* sense, and poverty in the *relative* sense.

Poverty in the absolute sense This approach defines poverty in terms of a minimum income that is necessary for subsistence. Rowntree used a definition of poverty in the absolute sense in his study of York in 1899, defining poor families as those with 'an income insufficient to obtain the minimum necessaries for the maintenance of merely physical efficiency'. In his study, Rowntree utilised estimates of minimum nutritional requirements, and requirements of clothing, fuel and other household necessities.

Defining poverty in an absolute sense involves some arbitrary assumptions. It is difficult to make precise definitions of minimum nutritional requirements as each individual's needs differ, depending on factors such as physiology and level of physical activity. Nevertheless, agencies concerned with famine relief, such as the Red Cross and Oxfam, may employ this concept of poverty in planning their emergency relief efforts.

Poverty in the relative sense In this approach, a household is defined as being in poverty if its income is insufficient to enable its members to participate in the normal life of the society. Clearly, to make this definition operational would require the application of value judgments. What constitutes 'normal life' will differ greatly from country to country and may even differ between social strata within a country.

In a modern developed economy, such as the United Kingdom, members of a household might expect to own a range of domestic appliances, such as a washing machine and telephone, participate in social events and to take an annual holiday. Such facilities, regarded as part of normal life in a developed country, would be beyond the expectations of a poor family in a developing country, such as Bangladesh.

International dimensions of poverty The World Bank defines poverty as 'the inability to attain a minimal standard of living'. The Bank employs a consumption-based poverty line that includes two elements:

- the expenditure necessary to purchase a minimum nutritional standard and other household necessities
- an amount necessary to enable participation in the every day life of society.

Thus, this definition seeks to take account of poverty in both the absolute and relative senses. The Bank defines the *extremely poor* as those with an income of up to $275 per capita per year in 1985 purchasing power parity (PPP) dollars. The World Bank figures reflect exchange rates that seek to measure each currency's domestic purchasing power, rather than market exchange rates. As shown in Table 32.8, an application of this poverty line yields an estimate of 633 million extremely poor people in 1985.

Table 32.8 The world's poor in 1985.

Region	Extremely poor (millions)	Poor (including extremely poor) (millions)
Sub-Saharan Africa	120	180
East Asia	120	280
of which China	*80*	*210*
South Asia	300	520
of which India	*250*	*420*
Eastern Europe	3	6
Middle East and North Africa	40	60
Latin America and the Caribbean	50	70
All developing countries	633	1,116

Note: The poverty line in 1985 PPP dollars is $275 per capita per year for the extremely poor, and $370 per capita a year for the poor.
Source: World Bank, *World Development Report,* 1990.

The World Bank defines the *poor* as those with an income of up to $370 per capita per year in 1985 PPP dollars. The estimates shown in Table 32.8 indicate that there were 1,116 million poor people (including the extremely poor) in developing countries in 1985. Nearly half of the developing countries' poor live in South Asia, mainly India. Other regions with a large number of poor people include East Asia and sub-Saharan Africa.

Causes of economic inequality

There are complex sociological, cultural, historical, political and religious factors which conspire to bring about economic inequality. A number of specific causes of inequality, however, can be identified. Consider the following.

Differences in wealth ownership Perhaps one major cause of inequality in the distribution of income is the unequal distribution of wealth. The holding of wealth represents not only direct command over goods and services (in that it can yield a cash income), it also confers status, security and potential spending power in the future. Life-time saving is one important source of wealth, but it may also be accumulated from gifts, inheritances, capital gains, and collections of rare stamps, coins and paintings. In developed societies, wealth may be held in the form of *physical assets*, like land, buildings and household goods, or *financial assets*, like cash, stocks and shares, building society accounts and life policies.

The actual measurement of the wealth held by individuals and families is by no means a simple task. This is because wealth holders in many countries are not obliged by law to keep records of their wealth, nor are they required to disclose the value of their wealth if they do not wish to do so. Another difficulty is that of putting monetary valuations on certain types of wealth, particularly those like pension rights,

Table 32.9 The distribution of marketable wealth in the United Kingdom.

	Percentages and £ billion	
	1986	1990
Marketable wealth		
Percentage of wealth owned by:		
Most wealthy 1%	18	18
Most wealthy 5%	36	37
Most wealthy 10%	50	51
Most wealthy 25%	73	72
Most wealthy 50%	90	93
Total marketable wealth (£ billion)	955	1,689

Source: Social Trends, 1993.

historic buildings and private estates, where there are no readily available markets for disposal.

In most countries, then, only crude measures of personal wealth are available. In the United Kingdom, estimates are made by the Inland Revenue from estates notified for probate – though there are some other independent estimates too.

Marketable wealth
Those assets that can be sold and, therefore, converted into cash. Pension rights and human capital cannot be sold and are referred to as non-marketable wealth

Table 32.9 illustrates the distribution of marketable wealth, excluding non-marketable rights in pension schemes, derived from Inland Revenue estimates. It can be seen that in 1990 the wealthiest 1 per cent and 10 per cent of the adult population owned 18 per cent and 51 per cent of the marketable wealth respectively. Comparing these figures with those of Table 32.6, it is apparent that wealth is more unevenly distributed than personal income in the United Kingdom.

The value of the absolute amount of wealth held by the personal sector rose from around £1,485 billion in 1986 to about £2,352 billion in 1989. In 1989 over a third of all this wealth was in dwellings so that the sharp increases in house prices in the early 1970s and the mid-1980s had a noticeable effect on the growth of the sector's wealth. In addition, the increase in home ownership has had a significant effect on the distribution of wealth in the United Kingdom.

In the 1980s, stocks and shares became a more popular form of holding wealth for individuals. The proportion of wealth invested in stocks and shares had fallen from about 20 per cent in 1971 to only 5.5 per cent in 1981. However, in recent years the privatisation of state-owned companies, accompanied by incentives for employee share-ownership and schemes, such as Personal Equity Plans, have led to the growth of this form of wealth-holding which accounted for about 8 per cent of all the personal sector's wealth in 1989.

Operation of factor markets Inequalities may result from the way in which factor markets operate. For instance, if the supply of a factor is scarce relative to its demand, it would command a high price and hence an economic rent. In markets where trade union monopolies and employers' monopsonies and oligopsonies prevail, such imperfections affect the shares of wages and profits in the national income. For instance, in labour markets, trade union rules may affect rates of pay, the standard working week, apprenticeship periods, redundancy and lay-off pay and the age of retirement. Studies indicate that workers in unionised sectors generally earn more for similar jobs than workers in non-unionised sectors. Clearly there are also inequalities between the incomes of the economically active and inactive. The Royal Commission on the Distribution of Income and Wealth showed, however, that in the United Kingdom, the degree of inequality in the economically active population is less than in the inactive population (which includes the unemployed, the aged, the sick and disabled).

Differences in natural abilities, education, training and opportunities These differences all contribute to inequalities in earnings and wealth. In Ch. 16 we outlined in greater detail the reasons for wage differentials between different occupations and industries within the same country. Inequalities between countries may in addition be due to differences in factor endowments which, as we showed above, also affect the pattern of resource allocation.

Economic growth policies The postwar policies aiming for economic growth, both in the industrially advanced and the less developed countries, have lacked explicit redistribution objectives. Furthermore, it is possible that the growth of national income weights the income changes of individuals and families in proportion to their existing share of the national income. This would mean that economic growth would tend to benefit the higher-income groups more than the lower-income groups in absolute terms.

Summary

1. The three main components of total personal income are earned income (which is the biggest component), investment income (which is the most unequally distributed component) and transfer income. Knowledge of the composition of total personal income in a country helps policy makers to assess the pattern and trends in income distribution.
2. Pareto's Law states that the number of income recipients earning at least a given level of income tends to fall by a fixed percentage as the given level of income rises by a fixed percentage. This implies that income inequality is inescapable and that policy measures designed to reduce inequality are likely to be fruitless. The 'law' has stimulated a great deal of empirical research into personal income distribution.
3. Income distribution may be measured in tabular form by ranking all income recipients and then dividing them into distinct groups, such as quintiles or deciles. The Lorenz curve is a graphical method of illustrating the distribution of income (or wealth).
4. The extent to which the income tax system reduces inequality can be assessed by comparing 'before tax' and 'after tax' Lorenz curves. An examination of the distribution of the income tax burden among

different income groups also highlights the role played by taxation in determining the distribution of income.

5. Poverty can be defined in the absolute sense and in the relative sense. The World Bank defines poverty in terms of the amount required to obtain a minimum nutritional standard and other household necessities, together with the amount necessary to enable participation in the everyday life of society.

6. Income inequality may be caused by a number of possible factors: differences in wealth ownership; the operation of the markets for factors of production; differences in natural abilities, education, training and opportunities; and economic growth policies which lack redistributive objectives.

Exercises

1. Review your understanding of the following terms:

personal income	poverty
earned income	original income
investment income	gross income
transfer income	disposable income
Pareto's Law	post-tax income
Lorenz curve	final income
Gini coefficient	marketable wealth
line of complete equality	non-marketable wealth

2. Consider the data on the distributions of wealth in France and West Germany shown in Table 32.10. Draw the Lorenz curves for the two countries and estimate the Gini coefficients. Comment on your results.

Table 32.10 The distributions of wealth in France and West Germany.

Top	5%	10%	20%	40%	60%	80%	100%
% share of wealth in France, 1975	36.2	51.7	71.0	91.8	98.3	99.6	100.0
% share of wealth in West Germany, 1973	18.7	45.3	57.4	73.4	84.5	92.9	100.0

Source: Royal Commission on the Distribution of Income and Wealth: Background Paper to *Report No. 7.*

3. Discuss the limitations of the official statistics on the distribution of personal incomes as a measure of economic inequality. Pay particular attention to the extent to which fringe benefits distort the pattern of inequality.

4. Account for the increasing tax burden on the lower-income groups in the United Kingdom since 1979.

5. Explain why the distribution of income tends to be more unequal in less developed countries than in industrially advanced countries.
6. 'The British tax system fails to tackle adequately the problem of inequality in the distribution of personal wealth.' Discuss.
7. How would you define poverty? Discuss the problems of applying your definition to such different societies as those in the United Kingdom and India.

SELECTED ECONOMISTS

Contributions to mainstream economic theory

Mainstream economic theory, which this textbook seeks to explain, has evolved over several centuries. Every generation of economists has sought to explain the problems faced by different societies and to suggest solutions. They have had to develop theories, propositions and techniques of analysis to explain the problems and related issues confronting societies at different times. Thus, Adam Smith, whose name is associated with what is now called 'modern economics', developed the doctrine of *laissez-faire* (that is, minimum state intervention) as a reaction to the ideas of the mercantilist writers of the seventeenth and eighteenth centuries, who advocated comprehensive restrictions and state regulation of national economies. Keynes' *General Theory* was developed in response to the problem of mass unemployment in the 1930s. The development of *monetarism* was a response to the perplexing phenomenon of stagflation in the 1960s and 1970s.

Clearly, a detailed account of the life and work of all the major contributors to the development of economic thought is outside the scope of this textbook. We can only sample the contributions of a selected few great economists. Our sample contains Smith, Ricardo, Marshall, Keynes and Friedman.

Adam Smith

Adam Smith (1723–90) was born in Kirkcaldy, Scotland, and was educated at Glasgow and Oxford Universities. After completing his formal education, he returned to Scotland to lecture at Glasgow University where he became professor of logic and moral philosophy. The publication of his work in 1776 entitled *An Enquiry into the Nature and Causes of the Wealth of Nations* was the first comprehensive study of economics as a separate and independent subject, then known as political economy.

The Wealth of Nations develops a theory of prices and distribution. The price of a commodity, according to Smith, is made up of three elements: wages, rents and profits which 'are the three original sources of all revenues as well as exchangeable value'. Thus, the total national product is distributed amongst the owners of labour, land and capital. Smith also discusses the idea of the embodied labour theory of value. He states that 'it was not by gold or by silver, but by labour that all the wealth of the world was originally purchased'. He also declares that 'the annual labour of every nation is the fund which originally supplies it with all the necessaries and conveniences of life which it annually consumes, and which consist always, either in the immediate produce of that labour, or in what is purchased with that produce from other nations'. It can be noted that Ricardo and Marx capitalised on Smith's ideas in developing the labour theory of value.

In his theory of the determination of prices, Smith distinguishes between *natural* and *market* prices which correspond to the Marshallian long-run and short-run equilibrium prices respectively. The long-run equilibrium price of a commodity is equal to its natural price which is sufficient to pay wages, rent and profit.

Production

In the field of production Smith's most important contribution is his notion of *specialisation* and *division of labour*, the benefits of which he illustrates with his well-known visits to pin and nail factories. Note that he was writing at a time when the full potential of the Industrial Revolution in terms of specialisation and industrial processes had yet to be realised. He declared that 'the division of labour is limited by the extent of the market', by which he meant that total production can be expanded through specialisation of tasks, provided a market exists to absorb the larger volumes of production. We saw in Ch. 9 that increasing returns and falling average costs are associated with the division of labour and specialisation.

The invisible hand

Probably Adam Smith's most original contribution is the concept of the *invisible hand* and the philosophy of *laissez-faire*. The concept of the invisible hand enables Smith to argue that the market mechanism is a self-regulating natural order and therefore, the state should not intervene through rules and regulation in the price system. He maintains that the motive of every individual in society is self-interest. Every individual 'intends to promote his own gain, and he is in this, as in many other cases, led by an invisible hand to promote an end which was no part of his intention'. Thus, according to Smith, there is a harmony of individual and social interests. Social interest is simply the sum of the interests of the individuals comprising society.

With the *laissez-faire* philosophy, Smith championed the cause of free international trade. It does not pay an individual to produce himself, he argued, what he can buy more cheaply from someone else, and what is 'prudence in the conduct of every private family can scarce be folly in that of a great kingdom'. However, we showed in Chs 7 and 11 that private and social interests are not always compatible. The price mechanism is far more complex than visualised by Smith and modern governments play a much more supportive role in market economies. However, Smith's laissez-faire ideology and free trade philosophy find support in our own time with the creation of the GATT and other bodies that seek to reduce barriers to trade.

Notice that Smith's invisible hand is an important concept that may be used to promote benefits of competition. Indeed, competition and *laissez-faire* are the major vehicles in his argument in favour of private enterprise. This explains why he is so critical of the many laws that conferred special benefits on the business classes of his time and hindered competition and labour mobility. Smith warns of the consequences of anti-competitive trade practices, and states that 'people of the same trade seldom meet together, even for merriment and diversion, but the conversation ends in a conspiracy against the public, or in some contrivance to raise prices'.

Public finance

Smith enunciated the four famous principles or canons of taxation, amongst which the *ability to pay* principle has become an important element in economics textbooks on taxation (see Ch. 14). Given his strong belief in the *laissez-faire* ideology, Smith is sceptical about high public expenditure financed with large amounts of taxes and public debt. He views such an approach to government revenues and spending as the diversion of labour from 'productive' to 'non-productive' activities. Thus he proposes limiting the state's functions to defence, the administration of justice, and public works, such as roads, bridges and education.

David Ricardo

David Ricardo (1772–1823) was born in London into a Jewish family of Dutch origin. At the age of fourteen, he joined his father's stockbroking business and, in the course of time, became a successful stockbroker in his own right. After making large fortunes on the stock market, he retired from business at the age of forty-two and concentrated mainly on reading and writing. He noted several inadequacies in the treatment of the economic policy issues of the time in books like *The Wealth of Nations*. Unlike Adam Smith, Ricardo was a self-taught man and never went to a college or university.

Thomas Malthus was a contemporary of Ricardo, and Malthus' writing on such matters as population growth and the law of diminishing returns had a major influence on Ricardo's work. The most famous of Ricardo's work is the *Principles of Political Economy and Taxation* (1817) in which the main lasting contributions are the theory of rent (and the associated theory of distribution) and the principle of comparative costs. The strong influence of Smith and Malthus can be noted in many parts of this publication.

The theory of distribution

Ricardo's theory of rent which has withstood the test of time is outlined and discussed in Ch. 17. As we also mention in Ch. 17, Ricardo, like Smith, identified three classes (or owners of the three factors of production): workers, land-owners and capitalists, who receive rewards in the form of wages, rents and profits respectively. But because of his belief in the law of diminishing returns, and in the Malthusian theory of population, Ricardo visualised the economy eventually (in the decades to come) reaching a *stationary state*.

In a stationary state, natural resources are exhausted and economic stagnation sets in, and there is the possibility of conflict amongst the three classes as one class attempts to improve its relative share in the total national product at the expense of others. This vision of class conflict paved the way for Marxist economics in subsequent years. In the event, technological advances have so far prevented diminishing returns and the arrival of a stationary state, as predicted by Ricardo.

Theory of international trade

As we noted in Ch. 30, Ricardo developed the theory of comparative cost advantage. For this, he applied Smith's ideas of the division of labour and specialisation to trade between countries. This theory was a response to the food problem which England faced at the time. The theory suggested as a solution that England should exchange its manufactured goods for cheap food from abroad.

Ricardo was concerned at the apparent inability of England to feed its growing population from its domestic supply of food, a problem which was worsened by the Corn Laws prohibiting the import of cheap grains from Europe. Ricardo campaigned for the gradual reduction of import duties on grains and for free international trade. He was aware of the fact that this would mean a fall in rent through falling food prices for landlords, but he argued that this loss would be more than offset by the gains to other classes.

Ricardo may be credited as being the first economist to engage in rigorous theoretical analysis. He reduced complex problems to simple abstractions and assumptions with a view to drawing policy conclusions, a method of approach just as valid today. Mark Blaug in his *Economic Theory in Retrospect* writes that 'if the problem of economics is growth and development, as is sometimes said, there is ... more in Smith than in Ricardo. But if economics is essentially an engine of analysis, a method of thinking rather than a body of substantive results, Ricardo literally invented the technique of economics'.

Alfred Marshall

Alfred Marshall (1842–1924) was born in London. His father was a cashier at the Bank of England and wanted Marshall to go into ecclesiastical service. However, Marshall went to Cambridge University where he studied mathematics. Later he studied economics, logic and moral philosophy. Marshall was elected to a fellowship and gave lectures in logic and economics to students of the Moral Science Tripos at Cambridge. But he left Cambridge in 1867 and took academic posts in Bristol and Oxford before returning to Cambridge as a Professor of Political Economy in 1885. He then set up the Cambridge School with a Tripos in Economics and Politics. Marshall's most famous work is the *Principles of Economics*, first published in 1890.

Marshallian economics is an important link between the *classical economics* of Adam Smith and Ricardo and the modern economic theory of demand, supply and welfare. In the chapter entitled *On wants and their satisfaction* he declares that: 'Until recently, the subject of demand or consumption has been somewhat neglected ... For although he [Ricardo] and his chief followers were aware that the conditions of demand played as important a part as those of supply in determining value, yet they did not express their meaning with sufficient clearness; and they have been misunderstood by all but the most careful readers'.

Supply, demand and equilibrium

Marshall's important contribution to economics is one of synthesis, linking the supply conditions of the classical economists (based on costs of production) with utility and demand. Our discussion in Chs 3–6 reflects in large part Marshall's contribution to economics. Marshall tends to view the forces of demand and supply in the context of time. He makes the point in the *Principles* that: 'We might as reasonably dispute whether it is the upper or under blade of a pair of scissors that cuts a piece of paper, as whether value is governed by utility or cost of production ... as a general rule, the shorter the period which we are considering, the greater must be the share of our attention which is given to the influence of demand on value; and the longer the period, the more important will be the influence of cost of product on value'.

Recall that Ch. 5 in this book discusses supply in the context of time. Chs 3 and 5 utilise the *ceteris paribus* assumption in the analysis of demand and supply which Marshall introduced into economics in order to derive a *partial equilibrium*. As we have seen, a partial equilibrium approach to the analysis of a market for a single commodity, a firm or industry has the merit of highlighting important policy issues.

The discussion of types of costs and of internal and external economies in Ch. 9 also owes a great deal to Marshallian economics.

Marshall as a precursor of modern welfare economics

Marshall may be considered to have laid a firm basis in his *Principles* for modern welfare economics which seeks to judge a given economic situation by both efficiency and equity criteria. Thus, the Hicks–Kaldor compensation test utilises Marshall's concept of consumer surplus developed in Ch. 4.

Note that Marshall was writing at a time when industrialisation was causing increased inequality of income and wealth, and was producing poverty and slums in Victorian England. Thus he wrote that: 'Political Economy or Economics is a study of mankind in the ordinary business of life; it examines that part of individual and social action which is most closely connected with the attainment and with the use of the material requisites of wellbeing. Thus it is on the one side a study of wealth; and on the other, and more important side, a part of the study of man ... broadly speaking, the destruction of the poor is their poverty and the study of the causes of poverty is the study of the causes of the degradation of a large part of mankind'.

Unlike his predecessors, Smith and Ricardo, Marshall seems less enchanted with the *laissez-faire* ideology. Marshall appears to favour government intervention in a market economy in order to reduce the worst consequences of inequality and poverty.

John Maynard Keynes

Keynes was born in Cambridge, England in 1883 and died in 1946. Educated at Eton and Cambridge, Keynes entered the Civil Service in 1907. He worked at the India Office before joining the Treasury during the First World War, where he worked on methods of financing the war effort.

Keynes argued against the onerous terms imposed on Germany by the Treaty of Versailles. After the peace conference, he wrote *The Economic Consequences of the Peace* (1919) in which he contended that the heavy reparations imposed on Germany would create instability. In the *Treatise on Money* (1930), Keynes developed his ideas on the demand for money and analysed the alternative motives for holding money.

In the 1930s Keynes developed his analysis in an attempt to account for the persistence of large-scale unemployment. At that time, conventional economic thought maintained that full employment was the normal state of affairs. Keynes labelled supporters of Say's Law as *classical* economists. Recall from Ch. 19 that Say's Law contends that any increase in national output will automatically create sufficient demand to purchase that output, so that full employment will be maintained.

In his analysis, developed in *The General Theory of Employment, Interest and Money* (1936), Keynes demonstrated the possibility of an equilibrium level of national income that could persist below the full employment level. In Ch. 19 above, this condition is described as a *deflationary gap*. Such a gap develops because the market fails to coordinate the decisions of households to save and of businesses to invest. In these circumstances, he maintained, government intervention may be necessary to achieve full employment. For this purpose, Keynes argued in favour of a programme of public works, such as building roads and bridges, demonstrating that such expenditure would have a multiplier effect on national income.

Keynesian analysis also demonstrated its relevance during the Second World War when there was an excess demand for resources. Keynes wrote a pamphlet *How to*

Pay for the War (1940) in which he called for measures such as high taxes on households, to reduce consumers' demand on resources. This was necessary in order to control possible inflationary pressures.

Keynesian analysis based on *The General Theory* dominated both macroeconomic theory and policy-making until the late 1960s. In the macroeconomic sections of this book, we deal in detail with the Keynesian theory of national income determination and the multiplier (Ch. 19), the Keynesian consumption function (Ch. 20), the Keynesian theory of money and interest rate determination (Ch. 22), the general Keynesian model in the shape of the IS–LM and IS–LM–EE models (Chs 23 and 29) and Keynesian approaches to unemployment and inflation (Chs 27 and 28).

In addition to being a scholar and author, Keynes represented the United Kingdom at the Bretton Woods conference in 1944 which led to the establishment of the International Monetary Fund (and its associated exchange rate system) and the World Bank. It is hard to over-estimate the influence that Keynes has had on the development of macroeconomics.

Milton Friedman

Milton Friedman was born in New York in 1912. He studied economics at Rutgers University in New Jersey, and later undertook post-graduate studies at the University of Chicago and then at Columbia University where he was awarded a PhD in 1946. Since that time, Friedman has enjoyed an illustrious career spent mainly at the University of Chicago where he became a leading contributor to the *Chicago school* of economics. He is well-known for his work on the methodology of economics (see, for example, his article 'The methodology of positive economics' in his book, *Essays in Positive Economics*, 1953) and the theory of consumption (see *A Theory of the Consumption Function*, 1957). But his greatest contributions, which have given him world-wide recognition, have been his advocacy of a free market economy (see *Free to Choose* written by Milton and Rose Friedman in 1979) and the development of monetarism (see, for example, the classic article 'Quantity Theory of Money: A Restatement' in *Studies in the Quantity Theory*, edited by Friedman himself in 1957, and *A Monetary History of the United States 1867–1960* written jointly with Anna Schwartz in 1963). He was awarded the Nobel Prize for economics in 1976.

Friedman's 'permanent income' hypothesis of consumption is outlined in Ch. 20, and his approach to the demand for money and the role of money in the economy are discussed in Chs 22, 23, 26, 27 and 28. Indeed, Friedman's work has been of such importance to the development of modern macroeconomic theory and policy that it has been a recurring theme throughout the macroeconomic sections of this book.

Friedman's work has, however, also been highly controversial. In reviving the quantity theory of money and developing the modern tenets of monetarism, he challenged the Keynesian theory and policy prescriptions which had occupied a secure place in mainstream economics for over two decades. Keynesians have retorted that monetarists have tended to overemphasise the importance of the money supply in the economy and ignore other important variables on the demand side. The view that inflation and balance of payments problems are essentially monetary in nature has been criticised for being too simplistic and for leading to policy rules which have had adverse effects on the real economy. Similarly, Friedman's view that unemployment always returns to its 'natural rate' in the long-run so that demand-side policies to reduce unemployment are ineffective has also been severely criticised by Keynesians. Indeed, most Keynesians blame the high unemployment experienced in the 1980s and 1990s in the United Kingdom and many other industrialised countries on the influence of monetarism which led to a general failure to employ appropriate demand-management strategies.

Friedman's view that market economies are inherently stable and work most efficiently in the absence of government intervention is also very controversial. Friedman is a supporter of *libertarianism*, a set of beliefs that go way beyond economics. Libertarians are on the political right wing and believe in the overriding importance of individual freedom, opposing all but the most basic forms of government regulation. It will come as no surprise that, in economic affairs, Friedman is a strong supporter of *laissez-faire*, believing that the free competitive market is the most efficient method of resource allocation. This is of course consistent with his hands-off approach to macroeconomic policy-making: that is the view that, left to itself, the economy will achieve long-run stability and growth, and that attempts to stabilise short-run fluctuations will fail and may even create greater instability. Modern Keynesians reject these ideas, arguing that unregulated free market economies will create severe problems in the form of inequalities, exploitation, externalities and periodic recessions, and that government intervention is necessary to correct these problems.

There is no doubt that Milton Friedman has been one of the most influential economists of the 20th century, and one of the major sources of heated debate in the economics profession over the last forty years.

QUESTIONS AND ANSWERS

The following twelve essay questions are fairly typical of questions set in first-year economics examinations. After each question we give a brief suggested answer. This should not be regarded as a 'model answer', but simply as one possible way of tackling the question. Constructing your own outline answers first and then working through and discussing our suggested answers critically will help you in your preparations for examinations.

1. *Discuss the meaning of the concept of opportunity cost. Illustrate the concept with practical examples.*

The opportunity cost of a good or service may be defined as the next best forgone alternative. A decision to produce more of a commodity with a given set of resources necessarily means having to give up some units of another commodity. For example, in order to increase the output of vans, a vehicle assembler may have to reduce the output of cars. The economic problem of choice arises from the scarcity of resources in relation to the limitless calls made upon these resources. In economics, resources are generally categorised under the headings of the *factors of production*: land, labour, capital, and enterprise (see Ch. 2).

The concept of opportunity cost is relevant to consumers when allocating their limited incomes among alternative goods and services. For example, a student's decision to purchase one good (say, a compact disc) may mean giving up the purchase of an alternative good (say, a textbook).

Thus the concept of opportunity cost emphasises the economic problem of choice by measuring the *real* rather than money cost of obtaining an extra unit of a commodity. The production possibility frontier (see Fig. 1.2 and the associated text) can be used to illustrate this economic problem.

Governments, like firms and consumers, also operate with limited resources and have to take account of the forgone alternatives of their expenditure decisions. A decision to build a new school, for example, may mean the cancellation of the planned building of a new hospital. Government budgets face competing claims from many sources, including health, social security, education and defence.

Finally, it can be noted that there may be an element of subjectivity associated with the measurement of opportunity cost. This may arise because different decision-makers may place different valuations on forgone alternatives. The oportunity cost of a new road, for example, includes the environmental damage (such as the loss of beautiful countryside) that may ensue. Different groups or policy-makers often place different values on these intangible elements of cost. Thus conflicting views may be held as to whether the new road is desirable or not.

2. *Explain the various measures of elasticity of demand and consider their practical uses.*

Consider the main measures of elasticity of demand in turn.

Price elasticity of demand Define price elasticity and state the formula for its calculation. Demonstrate that price elasticity typically varies along the demand curve (see Fig. 3.9). Show that the effect on sales revenue of a change in a good's price depends on price elasticity (see Table 3.4). Discuss the influence of price elasticity on the tax revenue raised by a sales tax (see Ch. 6). Also, consider the importance of price elasticity in estimating the likely effects on the trade balance of a currency devaluation (see Ch. 29).

Income elasticity of demand Define income elasticity and state the formula for its calculation. Distinguish between normal and inferior goods (see Ch. 3). A brief account of upward- and downward-sloping Engel curves could also be included (see Fig. 3.6). To discuss its practical uses, show how estimates of income elasticity enable economists and businesses to derive estimates of the growth in demand for different goods and services from estimates of income growth. For example, food tends to have a relatively low income elasticity in developed countries, thereby restricting the likely growth in demand, while many services (such as foreign travel) have relatively high income elasticities.

Cross elasticity of demand Define cross elasticity and state the formula for its calculation. Give examples of a pair of substitutes and a pair of complements. Use the concept of cross elasticity to distinguish between the effect on the demand for a good of (a) an increase in the price of a substitute, and (b) an increase in the price of a complement. Show that knowledge of cross elasticities can assist companies to maintain their market shares by identifying close substitutes and adopting policies to counter competitors' market strategies.

3. *Discuss the economic effects of (a) a maximum price, and (b) a minimum price in the potato market.*

(a) *Maximum price* A maximum price (or price ceiling) involves an outside agency setting a price above which it is not permitted to sell a given product. Generally, this is done when the agency fears a shortage of the product, which would otherwise push up the price. The intention of the price control is, therefore, to avoid a situation in which the high price of the product puts it beyond the reach of low-income consumers. In times of war when food is scarce, for example, price ceilings may be imposed on basic foodstuffs, such as bread, milk and potatoes. The intention would be to try to ensure that everyone, including the poor, can afford to buy such essential foodstuffs.

Consider the imposition of a maximum price in the potato market. To be effective, the maximum price has to be set below the equilibrium price of potatoes. If the maximum price were set *above* the equilibrium price, the regulation would have no effect because sellers would still be free to sell potatoes at the lower equilibrium price. A numerical example would help illustrate this point.

The consequences of an effective maximum price should now be discussed with reference to Fig. 6.12(a). As illustrated by the diagram, excess demand for potatoes results. To deal with the problem, an alternative allocation system is likely to develop.

This may take the form of (a) allocation by sellers' preferences; (b) allocation on the basis of 'first come first served' or (c) rationing. A brief explanation or comment on each alternative system of allocation would be appropriate.

In such a situation of excess demand for potatoes the emergence of a 'black market' is likely. Some consumers will be willing to pay more than the maximum price and may deal illegally on the black market.

(b) *Minimum price* A minimum price (or price floor) involves an outside agency setting a price below which it is not permitted to sell a given product. The agency may impose the price floor to increase or to stabilise the incomes of producers.

Consider the imposition of a minimum price in the potato market. To be effective the minimum price has to be above the equilibrium price of potatoes. If the minimum price were set *below* the equilibrium price, the regulation would have no effect because sellers would still be free to sell potatoes at the higher equilibrium price.

The consequences of an effective minimum price should now be discussed with reference to Fig. 6.12(b). As illustrated by the diagram, an excess supply or glut of potatoes develops. To maintain the artificially high price, the excess supply will have to be withheld from the market. This is likely to involve the potato producers or outside agency in storing the excess supply of potatoes. As long as the price floor is maintained, the glut will persist, resulting in rising storage costs for the surplus potatoes. The producers or agency will not be able to off-load the surplus in this market as this would depress the price. The surplus might be sold in other markets or even destroyed.

4. *'The price mechanism is an efficient method of allocating resources'. Discuss.*

The price mechanism operates in a market economy to allocate scarce resources to alternative uses. Prices act as signals to consumers and producers in their consumption and production decisions. Consumers buy their preferred baskets of goods and services in the market, subject to their incomes and tastes. It is as if there is a general election every day with consumers casting their 'money votes' in favour of their preferred commodities.

Profit-seeking producers allocate resources to the production of commodities which attract consumers' money votes. Thus the economic problems of *what*, *how* and *for whom* to produce are resolved through the free forces of supply and demand (see Ch. 7). You could draw Fig. 7.2 which illustrates the interaction between the markets for substitute goods.

Economic analysis demonstrates that when all markets operate under *perfect* conditions, the resulting allocation of resources will satisfy the conditions necessary for a Pareto optimal allocation of resources. In such circumstances the working of the price system will result in the fulfilment of the three requirements for Pareto efficiency: efficiency in production; efficiency in exchange; and an efficient output mix (see Ch. 8). Economic efficiency in the Pareto sense exists when it is not possible to change the allocation of resources to make any individual better off without making someone else worse off.

However, an important criticism of resource allocation through the price mechanism is that in real market economies, resources are allocated under ***imperfect*** conditions. (List some examples of imperfections and give a brief explanation of each one.) These imperfect conditions prevent a market economy from attaining Pareto efficiency and therefore from reaching a social welfare maximisation point, such as Z in Fig. 7.1.

5. *Why are some groups of workers paid more than others?*

All workers would receive the same wages only if the following conditions were satisfied: all workers would have to be homogeneous; all jobs would have to display identical non-monetary advantages and disadvantages; there would have to be perfect knowledge and perfect mobility of labour.

It is because these conditions are not satisfied in practice that some groups of workers are paid more than others. The equilibrium wage rate of a particular group of workers is the outcome of interaction between the demand for and supply of the specific type of labour. The demand for labour is *derived* from the demand for the products which the labour helps to make. Firms demand labour because of the value of the workers' output. Thus, a profit-maximising firm will hire workers up to the point at which the marginal revenue product of the last worker employed equals the marginal cost of employing that worker (see Ch. 16).

Skilled workers, such as doctors and plumbers, tend to earn high wage rates as the derived demand for their services is high. The demand for skilled workers will be high because of their high levels of productivity and ability. On the other hand, the supply of skilled workers is relatively inelastic because of the need for training and the specific abilities required to perform the jobs. In some occupations, it is necessary to obtain advanced qualifications (or licences) to practice. In contrast, unskilled workers, such as labourers, tend to earn low wage rates because the demand for their services is limited, while the supply is relatively high and elastic. The graphs below illustrate these points. In graph (a), the high demand for and low supply of a certain group of skilled workers combine to produce a relatively high equilibrium wage of $0W_1$. In graph (b), on the other hand, the low demand for and high supply of a particular group of unskilled workers result in a relatively low equilibrium wage of $0W_2$.

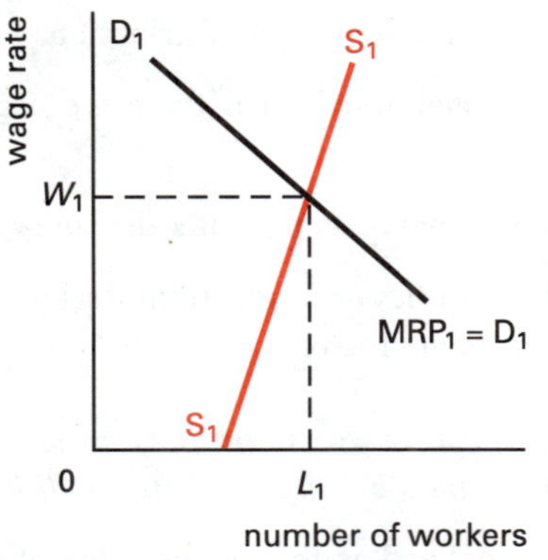

(a) Market for skilled workers

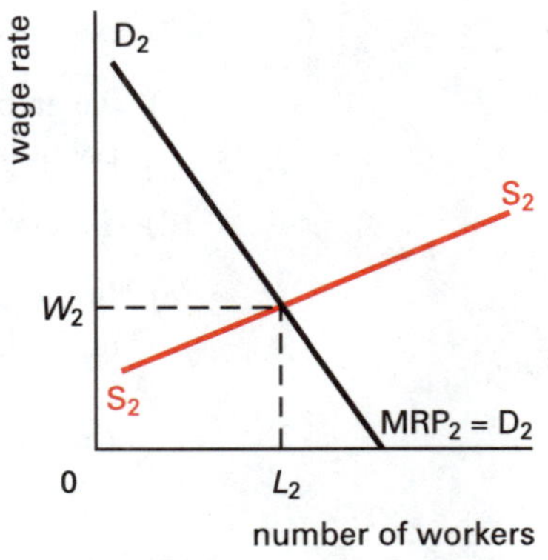

(b) Market for unskilled workers

Thus the differences in wages paid to different groups of workers are essentially the outcome of the forces of demand and supply. However, it is also important to mention the following points: different jobs do not offer identical non-monetary advantages and disadvantages; employers and employees do not have perfect knowledge about the wage rates and conditions of service in all available occupations; and labour tends to be geographically and occupationally immobile. All of these factors contribute to wage differentials.

6. *Distinguish between the various kinds of taxes imposed by governments and explain why governments impose taxes.*

Define taxes as compulsory transfers of money from tax-paying units to the government. In this answer, it is important to distinguish between direct and indirect taxes, progressive and regressive taxes, and specific and *ad valorem* taxes.

In the case of direct taxes, the payment of the tax brings the taxpayer directly into contact with the tax collector. Examples include taxes on income, taxes on capital and the council tax. In the case of indirect taxes, payment does not bring the taxpayer directly into contact with the tax collector. Instead, the tax is paid indirectly through an intermediary who acts as a tax gatherer for the authorities. Examples include taxes on spending, such as value added tax and customs and excise duties.

Direct taxes can easily be made progressive. Indirect taxes, on the other hand, often tend to be regressive. See Ch. 14 for definitions of proportional, progressive and regressive taxes. When considering indirect taxes, a distinction may also be drawn between specific and *ad valorem* taxes. A specific tax is levied at a fixed sum per unit sold, while an *ad valorem* tax is levied as a percentage of the value sold.

Governments impose taxes for a number of reasons. The following could be discussed in the answer:

(a) To raise revenue to pay for the goods and services which the government provides for the community. These include public goods such as defence, law and order, and roads.

(b) To influence the distribution of income and wealth. Progressive taxes may be designed to achieve a more equitable distribution.

(c) To improve resource allocation when there are negative externalities, such as pollution.

(d) To curb inflationary pressure as part of a demand-management package.

(e) In the case of customs duties or tariffs, to protect an infant or strategic industry, or for balance of payments reasons.

7. *Discuss the use of national income statistics as an indicator of living standards and economic well-being within a country and between different countries.*

National income may be defined as the money value of all final goods and services produced in a country during a year. There are three ways of estimating the value of a country's output: the income, expenditure, and output approaches. (See Ch. 18 for a full description of these approaches.) If the price level is rising, the national income must be deflated by an appropriate price index to convert it to 'real' terms.

Living standards refer to the basket of goods and services available to individuals. Thus in order to draw conclusions about living standards in a country it is necessary to divide real national income by the number of people in the population. The result is referred to as 'real national income per capita'.

Real national income per capita is, of course, an average figure and tells us nothing about the distribution of income. If the distribution of income in a country is unequal, the real national income per capita figure may give a misleading picture of the living standards of the average inhabitant.

National income figures do not take account of economic activity in the 'black economy' where transactions are not recorded. Nor do the figures reflect the value of activity that is not marketed (such as subsistence farming and do-it-yourself work).

An increase in living standards does not necessarily mean an increase in economic well-being (or welfare) if there is an increase in the extent of negative externalities such as noise, pollution and crime. This is because the national income statistics do not reflect divergences between private and social costs. (See the distinction between actual, potential and pseudo-improvements in welfare discussed in Ch. 18).

When making comparisons between different countries, account must be taken of the different social and geographical conditions. An inhabitant of Canada, for example, will need to spend a lot on heating, while an inhabitant of Jamaica will have no such need.

In addition, such comparisons necessitate the conversion of each country's national income into a common unit, such as the United States dollar. The use of a market exchange rate may be unsatisfactory if it does not accurately reflect the respective internal purchasing power of the currencies concerned. It is preferable to use a purchasing power parity exchange rate when making such comparisons.

The composition of a country's output is also relevant. Two countries may have the same national incomes but if one devotes a higher proportion of its resources to defence, then its living standard is likely to be lower.

National income may be regarded as a useful indicator of living standards and economic well-being, but it is not a completely satisfactory measure of these concepts.

8. *Discuss the likely economic consequences of a large increase in government expenditure.*

A large increase in government expenditure may mean higher spending on goods and services and/or higher spending on transfer payments. This answer concentrates on the likely effects of higher spending on goods and services. Such spending is an injection into the circular flow of income (see Ch. 19).

With some unemployed resources, increased government expenditure will have a multiplier effect on the level of national income. This effect may be illustrated by means of the Keynesian cross diagram (see Ch. 19) or by using appropriate versions of the IS–LM or AD–AS diagrams (see Ch. 23).

The matter of how the increased government expenditure is financed must be considered. If it is tax-financed, the additional taxation will lead to a fall in consumer spending (see the 'balanced budget' multiplier in Ch. 19). If it is financed by selling gilt-edged stock, interest rates may increase as a result of which some private sector expenditure (such as investment) may be crowded out. The crowding-out effect may be illustrated with the IS–LM diagram developed in Ch. 23.

The type of exchange rate regime is also important. With a *fixed exchange rate*, the crowding-out effect will be limited as the authorities cannot allow domestic interest rates to rise relative to interest rates in other countries. With a *floating exchange rate*, the crowding-out effect is strengthened. This is because the increase in domestic interest rates will lead to additional capital inflows from other countries and so cause an appreciation of the home country's currency. The appreciation will tend to cause a fall in the value of exports and a rise in the value of imports. Such a fall in net exports will help to offset the multiplier effects of the increase in government expenditure (see Ch. 29).

With no excess capacity, the increase in government expenditure may result in demand-pull inflation. The extreme monetarist view is that equilibrium real output is determined by supply-side factors, with a vertical AS curve. In this case, the effect of higher government expenditure (financed by an increase in the money supply) will be to increase the price level and leave real output unchanged.

It is clearly possible to hold different views on the effects of higher government expenditure. These range from the extreme Keynesian case where the effect is wholly on real output through to the extreme monetarist (and New Classical) case where, assuming that the money supply is increased to accommodate the extra government spending, the effect is wholly on the price level. Intermediate positions between these extremes can of course also be held.

9. *Describe the methods available to a central bank to control the supply of money. What are the limitations on these methods of controlling the money supply?*

In developed financial systems, a range of financial assets are used as money, such as cash in circulation, sight deposits and time deposits. Thus, before a central bank is able to control the money supply, it has to define the money supply which it is seeking to control.

A central bank may seek to control a narrow monetary aggregate, such as M2 in the United Kingdom, which includes notes and coins and sterling retail deposits with banks and building societies. Alternatively, the central bank may attempt to control a broad monetary aggregate, such as M4, which includes notes and coins and all sterling deposits with banks and building societies (see Ch. 21 for a description of the United Kingdom monetary aggregates).

A central bank has a number of monetary control techniques at its disposal. Consider first the use of open-market operations. These involve the purchase or sale of government securities by the central bank on the open market. The effect of a sale of securities is to reduce the cash reserves of commercial banks which have to maintain a prudent ratio of cash holdings to total deposits. So a fall in cash reserves forces banks to reduce their lending and so reduces the money supply. But if the commercial banks hold excess cash reserves, the open market sale may simply result in a fall in these reserves with little or no effect on the money supply.

Interest rate policy is another important means by which a central bank can dictate a desired interest rate to the money market. Indeed, open market operations may be used to create a deliberate cash shortage which will force commercial banks to borrow from the central bank (as lender of last resort) at its own chosen interest rate. In this way, the central bank can influence the general level of interest rates.

It is important to note that a multiple contraction of credit and a fall in the money supply may not occur in response to central bank policy if banks have excess reserves; or if they are able to replenish reserves by borrowing from abroad; or if they can persuade the public to lower its ratio of cash holdings to bank deposits.

A central bank could also change the commercial banks' required cash ratio. An increase in reserve requirements lowers the *credit multiplier* and, hence, the money supply. However, if banks are not fully loaned up, the increase in the cash ratio may not be effective in reducing the money supply.

A central bank could also call for *special deposits* to be lodged by commercial banks in an account which is inaccessible. In this way, the central bank is able to reduce the commercial banks' cash holdings and hence reduce their ability to create credit.

Other methods available to a central bank include lending ceilings and direct requests. A lending ceiling is a quantitative limit on the growth of commercial bank lending. The existence of unused overdraft facilities may make it difficult to implement such a ceiling. Also, ceilings may be by-passed, in the absence of exchange controls, by borrowing from overseas financial institutions. Direct requests are simply attempts by the central bank to persuade commercial banks to exercise voluntary restraint in their lending.

Given the uncertainties and limitations associated with these monetary control techniques, a central bank may decide to employ a combination of techniques in its attempts to control the money supply.

10. *Explain what is meant by 'natural' unemployment. What policies might be used to reduce this type of unemployment?*

Natural unemployment may be defined as that unemployment which exists when the aggregate labour market is in long-run equilibrium. It would be useful in this first part of the answer to distinguish between natural unemployment, demand-deficient unemployment and excessive real wage unemployment (see Ch. 27). The different types of natural unemployment include *search*, *structural* and *seasonal unemployment*. These should be described and their main causes highlighted.

Search unemployment arises because at any one time some workers will be searching for the jobs which suit them best. They do not accept job offers immediately because there is imperfect knowledge in the labour market and the collection of information is both time-consuming and costly. Also, most workers believe that the more time they spend searching for a job, the more likely it is that they will find one which meets their requirements. Structural unemployment is caused by changes in the structure of demand and by technological advances. It tends to persist because of the geographical and occupational immobility of labour, and because of a lack of information about the opportunities available in other parts of the country and in other occupations. Seasonal unemployment arises because of seasonal variations in the demand for certain types of labour.

Having defined natural unemployment and discussed its main causes, it would be useful to explain briefly the role played by the 'natural rate' of unemployment in the expectations-augmented Phillips curve analysis (see Ch. 28). In this context, the 'natural rate' may be defined as that unemployment rate towards which the economy tends in the long-run, and at which the actual inflation rate equals the *expected* inflation rate (see Fig. 28.5 and the associated text).

Supply-side policies specifically intended to reduce natural unemployment might include the following: improvements in information dissemination; the provision of retraining schemes; assistance with family relocation; special employment assistance for teenagers looking for jobs; subsidies to firms which reduce working hours rather than lay off workers. Each of these should be briefly discussed (see Ch. 27).

Finally, it should be noted that while some economists claim that the natural rate of unemployment is roughly constant over time, others believe that it can vary considerably, depending on the size and nature of structural changes to which the economy is subjected, and on the success of supply-side policies. Indeed, some have argued that a long-lasting recession will cause many workers to lose job skills or become 'discouraged workers', so increasing natural unemployment. This effect is a form of *hysteresis*.

11. *Compare Keynesian and monetarist views on the alternative methods available for controlling inflation.*

Inflation may be defined as a persistent tendency for the general price level to rise. It may cause unfairness, inhibit economic growth and investment, and hinder international trade. Economists agree on these undesirable effects of inflation. But there is wide disagreement about the methods of controlling inflation.

Keynesians see excess demand and rising costs as the main causes of inflation and are in favour of discretionary interventionist policies to stabilise the economy. Many Keynesians maintain that fiscal policy, supported by selective monetary controls, is an effective method of reducing aggregate demand. To them, inflation arises when the economy is close to full employment with excess demand, as shown by the AD–AS graph in Fig. 28.1. The purpose of fiscal policy (that is, a cut in government spending and/or an increase in taxation) is to shift the AD curve to the left and so reduce the inflationary pressure. In addition, some Keynesians stress the role of rising wage costs in generating inflation and so tend to support some form of prices and incomes policy as a means of controlling prices and wages directly.

As we saw in Ch. 28, monetarists argue that inflation is caused by excessive monetary growth and sustained by inflationary expectations. The rate of inflation can be brought down, therefore, by reducing the growth of the money supply. In general, as we saw in Ch. 26, monetarists support a 'passive monetary rule', according to which the money supply is allowed to grow by a certain percentage each year. Short-term stabilisation policies are rejected because of their uncertain time-lags and the problems caused by inaccurate forecasting.

To monetarists, rising costs can only be inflationary in the long-run if the money supply is increased to allow the greater value of transactions to be financed. Prices and incomes policy is, therefore, unnecessary and may be harmful because it interferes with the free operation of the market mechanism.

Finally, it might be noted that the use of the labels 'Keynesian' and 'monetarist' to categorise alternative schools of thought has been criticised in some quarters. This is because in fact there are many different groups of economists with varying views on issues like inflation.

12. *Explain what is meant by a devaluation of a currency and discuss the likely internal and external effects of a devaluation.*

A devaluation is a deliberate government decision to reduce the value of its currency in terms of other currencies, normally in the context of a fixed exchange rate system (see Ch. 29). A government might decide to devalue its currency if its economy is experiencing a current account deficit. This will make its exports cheaper in terms of foreign currencies, and its imports more expensive in terms of domestic currency. To show this, suppose that the sterling–dollar exchange rate is initially £1 = $1.50. A British shirt producer who sells shirts at £20 each will charge $30 per shirt in the

United States. If sterling is now devalued to £1 = \$1, the shirt producer will be able to reduce the dollar price of a shirt to \$20 and still achieve the target sterling price of £20. Now consider a United States vineyard which sells wine at \$6 per bottle and so initially (with an exchange rate of £1 = \$1.50) charges £4 per bottle in Britain. After the sterling devaluation to £1 = \$1, the wine producer will need to charge £6 per bottle in order to achieve the target price.

The intention of the policy-makers is to increase the total value of exports and reduce the total value of imports, thereby eliminating the current account deficit. However, a devaluation does not necessarily result in an improvement in the current account. The elasticities of the demand for exports and imports must be considered. The Marshall–Lerner condition (admittedly based on restrictive assumptions) suggests that the sum of the elasticities of demand for exports and imports should exceed one for a devaluation to improve the balance of trade.

While it is likely (on most empirical estimates) that long-run elasticities will satisfy the Marshall–Lerner condition, short-run elasticities may be low. As a result, the initial effect of the devaluation is likely to worsen the trade balance. This is the so-called J-curve effect (see Ch. 29). It takes time for domestic consumers to react to the new relative prices, and for domestic resources to be transferred into export- and import-replacement industries.

The effect of the devaluation may be offset if other countries retaliate, either by devaluing their own currencies or imposing import controls, as they strive to protect their own industries. Retaliation is likely if other countries interpret the devaluation as a 'beggar my neighbour' policy. If the devaluation is successful in increasing net exports, this represents an increase in injections into the circular flow of income. This will lead to a rise in national income which will be strengthened through the multiplier effect. A possible threat to the success of the devaluation is then posed by the induced increase in imports resulting from the rise in national income. To counter this threat and to ensure that resources are free to move into export- and import-replacement industries, the government may employ deflationary (or expenditure-reducing) policies to accompany the devaluation.

Deflationary measures would be essential if the devaluation occurred under conditions of full employment. A successful devaluation at full employment would spark off demand-pull inflation. This may have both adverse and beneficial effects. An adverse effect is that it will erode the competitive advantage gained for the country's exporters by the devaluation. On the other hand, the inflation may have the effect of reducing domestic spending (or absorption) through the redistribution, money illusion and real balance effects (see Ch. 29).

The effects of a devaluation in response to an economic change which creates an overall balance of payments deficit can be analysed using the IS–LM–EE model developed in Ch. 29. For example, starting with the initial equilibrium position illustrated in Fig. 29.12, an exogenous fall in demand for the country's exports would shift both the IS and EE curves to the left, creating an overall balance of payments deficit. A devaluation would shift both curves back to the right, raising national income and the interest rate and restoring external equilibrium. The effectiveness of devaluation as a means of offsetting other shocks to the economy might also be discussed.

We can conclude that devaluation may be an appropriate policy for a country faced with a balance of payments deficit, but the possibility of induced domestic inflation should not be overlooked if the economy is close to full employment.

INDEX